Introducing Philosophy Through Pop Culture

T0369683

Introducing Philosophy Through Pop Culture

From Socrates to *Star Wars* and Beyond

Edited by William Irwin and
David Kyle Johnson

Second Edition

WILEY Blackwell

This edition first published 2022
© 2022 John Wiley & Sons Ltd

Edition History
Blackwell Publishing Ltd (1e 2010)

The rights of William Irwin and David Kyle Johnson to be identified as the authors of editorial material in this work have been asserted in accordance with law.

Registered Offices
John Wiley & Sons, Inc., 111 River Street, Hoboken, NJ 07030, USA
John Wiley & Sons Ltd, The Atrium, Southern Gate, Chichester, West Sussex, PO19 8SQ, UK

Editorial Office
111 River Street, Hoboken, NJ 07030, USA

For details of our global editorial offices, customer services, and more information about Wiley products visit us at www.wiley.com.

Wiley also publishes its books in a variety of electronic formats and by print-on-demand. Some content that appears in standard print versions of this book may not be available in other formats.

Library of Congress Cataloging-in-Publication Data applied for
ISBN 9781119757177 (Paperback)

Cover Design: Wiley
Cover Image: © fredmantel/Getty Images

Set in 10/12pt Minion by Straive, Pondicherry, India

10 9 8 7 6 5 4 3 2 1

Contents

Notes on Contributors   xi
Acknowledgments   xvii
Sources   xix

Introduction   1

Part I: What is Philosophy?   3

Socrates and the Spirit of Philosophy
1   Flatulence and Philosophy: A Lot of Hot Air, or the Corruption
     of Youth?   5
     William W. Young, III

Logic and Fallacies
2   The Chewbacca Defense: *A South Park* Logic Lesson   14
     Robert Arp

Relativism and Truth
3   Wikiality, Truthiness, and Gut Thinking: Doing Philosophy
     Colbert Style   23
     David Kyle Johnson

Part II: Epistemology   35

Introduction   35

The Ethics of Belief
4   You Know, I Learned Something Today: Stan Marsh
     and the Ethics of Belief   37
     Henry Jacoby

Skepticism
5 Tumbling Down the Rabbit Hole: Knowledge, Reality, and the Pit of Skepticism 44
Matt Lawrence

Definition of Knowledge
6 Adama's True Lie: Earth and the Problem of Knowledge 54
Eric J. Silverman

7 Wakandan Resources: The Epistemological Reality of *Black Panther*'s Fiction 62
Ruby Komic

Part III: Metaphysics 71

Introduction 71

The Nature of Reality
8 Life on a Holodeck: What *Star Trek* Can Teach Us About the True Nature of Reality 73
Dara Fogel

Mind and Body
9 Astral Bodies and Cartesian Souls: Mind–Body Dualism in *Doctor Strange* 82
Dean A. Kowalski

10 Mind and Body in Zion 90
Matt Lawrence

Personal Identity
11 Amnesia, Personal Identity, and the Many Lives of Wolverine 101
Jason Southworth

Freedom and Determinism
12 The Consolation of Bilbo: Providence and Free Will in Middle-Earth 107
Grant Sterling

13 Inception and Free Will: Are They Compatible? 115
John R. Fitzpatrick and David Kyle Johnson

Consciousness and Artificial Intelligence
14 Turing's Dream and Searle's Nightmare in *Westworld* 123
Lucia Carrillo González

15 What is it Like to Be a Host? 128
Bradley Richards

Time Travel
16 The Time Travel in *Avengers: Endgame* 136
David Kyle Johnson

Part IV: Philosophy of Religion   145

    Introduction   145

    The Problem of Evil
17 South Park, Cartmanland, and the Problem of Evil   147
    David Kyle Johnson

    The Existence of God
18 Hidden Mickeys and the Hiddenness of God   156
    Robert K. Garcia and Timothy Pickavance

    Faith
19 The Jedi Knights of Faith: Anakin, Luke, and Søren (Kierkegaard) 164
    William A. Lindenmuth

Part V: Ethics   173

    Introduction   173

    Utilitarianism and Deontology
20 Why Doesn't Batman Kill the Joker?   175
    Mark D. White

21 Means, Ends, and the Critique of Pure Superheroes   183
    J. Robert Loftis

    Virtue Ethics
22 Can Eleanor Really Become a Better Person? (*The Good Place*)   191
    Eric J. Silverman and Zachary Swanson

    Friendship
23 "You're a Sucky, Sucky Friend": Seeking Aristotelian Friendship
    in *The Big Bang Theory*   198
    Dean A. Kowalski

    Stoicism
24 "You Are Asking Me to Be Rational": Stoic Philosophy and the Jedi Order 207
    Matt Hummel

Part VI: Challenges to Traditional Ethics   215

    Introduction   215

    Nietzschean Critique
25 Rediscovering Nietzsche's Übermensch in Superman as a Heroic Ideal 217
    Arno Bogaerts

    Existentialist Ethics
26 Knowing Who You Are: Existence Precedes Essence in *Moana*   228
    William J. Devlin

Feminist Critique

27 Becoming a (Wonder) Woman: Feminism, Nationalism,
    and the Ambiguity of Female Identity   236
    J. Lenore Wright

28 The Silence of Our Mother: Eywa as the Voice of Feminine
    Care Ethics (*Avatar*)   245
    George A. Dunn and Nicolas Michaud

Environmental Ethics

29 "Everything Is Backwards Now": *Avatar,* Anthropocentrism,
    and Relational Reason   253
    Jeremy David Bendik-Keymer

Part VII: Social and Political Philosophy   263

    Introduction   263

Social Contract Theory

30 Maester Hobbes Goes to King's Landing (*Game of Thrones*)   265
    Greg Littmann

31 *Lost*'s State of Nature   273
    Richard Davies

Marxism

32 Federation Trekonomics: Marx, the Federation, and the Shift
    from Necessity to Freedom   284
    Jeff Ewing

Rawls

33 Superman and Justice   292
    Christopher Robichaud

Libertarianism

34 Cartman Shrugged: *South Park* and Libertarian Philosophy   299
    Paul A. Cantor

Race

35 Ninjas, Kobe Bryant, and Yellow Plastic: The LEGO
    Minifigure and Race   311
    Roy T. Cook

36 When Tech Meets Tradition: How Wakandan Technology
    Transcends Anti-Blackness   321
    Timothy E. Brown

Political Manipulation

37 *Black Mirror* and Political Manipulation: How Are We
    Tricked into Dehumanizing Others?   329
    Bertha Alvarez Manninen

Contents ix

The #MeToo Movement
38 *Black Mirror* and #DeathTo: What Are the Consequences
of Trial by Twitter? 338
Aline Maya

Part VIII: Eastern Views 349

Introduction 349

39 The Brick, the Plate, and the Uncarved Block: LEGO as
an Expression of the *Dao* 351
Steve Bein

40 LEGO, Impermanence, and Buddhism 359
David Kahn

41 Zen and the Art of Imagineering: Disney's Escapism
Versus Buddhism's Liberation 367
Steve Bein

Part IX: The Afterlife and Meaning 375

Introduction 375

An Afterlife Gives Meaning
42 Beyond Godric's Hollow: Life After Death and the Search
for Meaning (*Harry Potter*) 377
Jonathan L. Walls and Jerry L. Walls

An Afterlife Wouldn't Give Meaning
43 Why it Wouldn't be Rational to Believe You're in The
Good Place (and Why You Wouldn't Want to Be Anyway) 384
David Kyle Johnson

Index 393

Notes on Contributors

Robert Arp works for the US Army at Fort Leavenworth and teaches philosophy courses at several schools online. He has edited and co-edited nearly two dozen books, as well as authored and co-authored some three dozen chapters, in the pop culture and philosophy realm.

Steve Bein is Associate Professor of Philosophy at the University of Dayton, where he is a specialist in Asian philosophies. He is a regular contributor to volumes on philosophy and pop culture, including chapters on *Star Trek*, *Wonder Woman*, LEGO, *Blade Runner*, Disney, Mr. Rogers, *Batman*, and the forthcoming *Black Panther and Philosophy*. He's also a novelist, and his sci-fi short stories have been used in philosophy and science fiction courses across the US. His philosophy books include *Purifying Zen* and *Compassion and Moral Guidance*.

Jeremy David Bendik-Keymer holds the Beamer-Schneider Professorship in Ethics in the Department of Philosophy at Case Western Reserve University in Cleveland, Ohio, where the land is occupied only through violated indigenous treaties from the late eighteenth century. His books include *The Ecological Life: Discovering Citizenship and a Sense of Humanity* and *The Wind ~ An Unruly Living*, and *Involving Anthroponomy in the Anthropocene: On Decoloniality*.

Arno Bogaerts finished his studies in philosophy and ethics at the Vrije Universiteit Brussel in Belgium, where he wrote several essays focusing on the superhero genre. He is a writer and editor for the Belgian comic book website Brainfreeze and has contributed chapters to *The Avengers and Philosophy* and *Superman and Philosophy*. Currently, Bogaerts owns and manages a rock bar and is thinking about getting yet another Superman tattoo.

Timothy E. Brown is Assistant Professor of Bioethics and Humanities at the University of Washington. Dr. Brown is a founding member of and long-term contributor to the Neuroethics Thrust within the Center for Neurotechnology at UW. He also leads diversity, equity, and inclusion efforts with the International Neuroethics Society. Dr. Brown works at the intersection of biomedical ethics, philosophy of technology, (black/latinx/queer) feminist thought, and esthetics. His research explores the potential impact of neurotechnologies – systems that record and stimulate the nervous system – on end users' sense of agency and embodiment. His work also interrogates neurotechnologies for their potential to exacerbate or create social inequities, in order to establish best practices for the design of future devices and techniques.

Paul A. Cantor is Clifton Waller Barrett Professor of English at the University of Virginia. He has also taught at Harvard University in both the English and the Government departments. He has published widely on popular culture, including his books *Gilligan Unbound: Pop Culture in the Age of Globalization, The Invisible Hand in Popular Culture: Liberty vs. Authority in American Film and TV*, and *Pop Culture and the Dark Side of the American Dream: Con Men, Gangsters, Drug Lords, and Zombies*.

Roy T. Cook is Professor of Philosophy at the University of Minnesota – Twin Cities. He works primarily on the philosophy of mathematics, logic, and the aesthetics of popular culture. He is the author of *The Dictionary of Philosophical Logic, Key Concepts in Philosophy: Paradoxes, The Yablo Paradox: An Essay on Circularity*; and editor or co-editor of *The Arche Papers on the Mathematics of Abstraction, The Art of Comics: A Philosophical Approach* (with Aaron Meskin), *The Routledge Companion to Comics* (with Frank Bramlett and Aaron Meskin), *LEGO and Philosophy: Constructing Reality Brick-by-Brick* (with Sondra Bacharach), and *Hilary Putnam on Logic and Mathematics* (with Geoffrey Hellman).

Richard Davies studied and taught Philosophy at Trinity College, Cambridge (Ph.D. 1992). He now lives in Italy, where he is a professor of Theoretical Philosophy at the University of Bergamo. He has written books and articles on a range of topics, most recently on women in Plato's *Republic*, on the interpretation of logical symbolism and on the notion of a fallacy.

William J. Devlin is Professor of Philosophy at Bridgewater State University, offering classes in existentialism, nineteenth-century philosophy, philosophy of science, and philosophy of film. His publications in philosophy and popular culture include chapters in *Westworld and Philosophy, Game of Thrones and Philosophy, Lost and Philosophy*, and *South Park and Philosophy*.

George A. Dunn has taught philosophy in both the United States and China. He is currently a special research fellow with the Institute for Globalizing Civilization in Hangzhou China. He has edited or co-edited several volumes in the Philosophy and Pop Culture series. His latest book is *A New Politics for Philosophy: Essays on Plato, Nietzsche, and Strauss*.

Jeff Ewing is a film and culture analyst whose work has appeared in *Forbes, Looper*, and numerous other periodicals. In addition to publishing various chapters exploring the philosophical underpinnings of popular culture, he has co-edited *Alien and Philosophy* and *Stranger Things and Philosophy*. Beyond print, Jeff hosts a podcast dedicated to exploring the deeper ideas behind our favorite monsters and monster movies, *Humanoids from the Deep Dive*.

John R. Fitzpatrick was a lecturer in philosophy at the University of Tennessee at Chattanooga and the author of *John Stuart Mill's Political Philosophy* and *Starting With Mill*.

Dara Fogel is a philosopher, author, and educator. She holds a doctorate in Philosophy from the University of Oklahoma and has taught philosophy, religious studies, and humanities at several universities and colleges in the Southwest. She has published four books, including her bestselling steampunk conspiracy series, the GrailChase Chronicles, and one non-fiction. A confirmed geek, she bridges the gaps between popular culture, cutting edge sciences, mysticism, philosophy and dramaturgy, to bring a deeper perspective of self-knowledge and ancient wisdom to new audiences.

Robert K. Garcia is an Associate Professor of Philosophy at Baylor University, where he works in analytic metaphysics and philosophy of religion. He is the co-editor of *Is Goodness without God Good Enough?* and is writing a book on C. S. Lewis's views about the uniqueness of persons.

Lucia Carrillo González is a philosophy secondary teacher in Andalucia, Spain and is very passionate about the role of philosophy in the education system. Her main area of research is metaphysics, specifically truth-making and possibilities.

Matt Hummel works as a paralegal for the Public Defender Agency in Evansville, IN. He is also an adjunct instructor of Legal Studies, Legal Ethics, and Criminal Justice Ethics at Ivy Tech Community College. He has published two chapters in the Blackwell *Pop Culture and Philosophy* series as well as a blog entry for *Black Mirror and Philosophy*.

William Irwin is Herve A. LeBlanc Distinguished Service Professor in the Philosophy Department at King's College (PA) and the General Editor of The Blackwell Philosophy and Pop Culture Series. Irwin originated the popular culture and philosophy genre of books in 1999 with *Seinfeld and Philosophy*. He co-edited *The Simpsons and Philosophy* and edited *The Matrix and Philosophy, Metallica and Philosophy*, and *Black Sabbath and Philosophy*. Irwin is the author of *The Free Market Existentialist: Capitalism without Consumerism* and has published two novels.

Henry Jacoby taught philosophy for nearly 40 years, most of them at East Carolina University in Greenville, North Carolina, before his retirement in 2020. He is the editor of *House and Philosophy*, and *Game of Thrones and Philosophy*, and the author of *Why Philosophy Matters*. He now spends his time practicing kung fu, playing guitar, and writing horror novels. He lives in Goldsboro, North Carolina with his wife Kathryn, their dog Benjen, and their two cats, Kameko and Grynx.

David Kyle Johnson is a professor of philosophy at King's College (PA), and he also produces lecture series for The Teaching Company's *The Great Courses* (such as *Sci-Phi: Science Fiction as Philosophy, The Big Questions of Philosophy*, and *Exploring Metaphysics*). Kyle is the editor-in-chief of The *Palgrave Handbook of Popular Culture as Philosophy* and also regularly edits volumes for the Blackwell-Wiley Philosophy and Pop Culture series. Most recently this includes *Black Mirror and Philosophy: Dark Reflections*. He also maintains two blogs for *Psychology Today*: *Plato on Pop* (with William Irwin) and *A Logical Take*.

David Kahn is the author of *Case, Spandex, Briefcase: Leadership Lessons from Superheroes*. As a Human Resource Executive, executive coach, and speaker, David concentrates on incorporating the principles of positive culture, leadership, and organizational development to improve business strategies and, ultimately, performance.

Ruby Komic is a pop-culture-overthinker from Melbourne, Australia. In 2021, she completed her Master of Arts in Philosophy, at the University of Melbourne. Her thesis and writing centers around social epistemology, justice issues, and the imagination. Her future work will aim to break down the barriers of accessibility between academic philosophy and mainstream culture.

Dean A. Kowalski is a professor of philosophy and chair of the Arts & Humanities department in the College of General Studies at the University of Wisconsin-Milwaukee. He is the author of *Joss Whedon as Philosopher, Classic Questions and Contemporary Film*, 2nd edition, and *Moral Theory at the Movies*. He is the editor of *The Big Bang Theory and Philosophy, The Philosophy of* The X-Files, revised edition, and *Steven Spielberg and Philosophy*; he is the coeditor of *The Philosophy of Joss Whedon*.

Matt Lawrence teaches philosophy at Long Beach City College in California. He has authored two Wiley-Blackwell titles: *Like a Splinter in Your Mind: The Philosophy Behind the Matrix Trilogy* and *Philosophy on Tap: Pint-Sized Puzzles for the Pub Philosopher*.

William A. Lindenmuth is Associate Professor of Philosophy at Shoreline College. Specializing in moral psychology through the mediums of literature and film, William argues that our stories show us both who we are and who we'd like to be. He's contributed to a number of books on the intersections of philosophy and popular culture, including *The Ultimate Star Trek and Philosophy, Alien and Philosophy*, and the upcoming *Ethics and Science Fiction*.

Greg Littmann is Associate Professor of Philosophy at Southern Illinois University Edwardsville, where he teaches metaphysics, epistemology, and philosophy of art. He publishes in metaphysics, philosophy of logic, philosophy of professional philosophy, and philosophy of art, and has written numerous chapters for volumes relating philosophy to popular culture.

J. Robert Loftis is Professor of Philosophy at Lorain County Community College, where he teaches ethics and critical thinking. In addition to writing on *Watchmen*, he has published articles on philosophy and *Battlestar Galactica* and *Buffy the Vampire Slayer*. When not writing about philosophy and popular culture, he works on medical and environmental ethics.

Bertha Alvarez Manninen is Professor of Philosophy at Arizona State University. Her main areas of teaching and research are normative ethics, applied ethics, bioethics, philosophy and film, social/political philosophy, and philosophy of religion.

Aline Maya is an associate university teacher in Mexico City, a comic-book writer, and an entrepreneur specializing in augmented reality technologies. She is interested in philosophy of mind and philosophy of psychiatry, and she combines these interests with questions about the impact of new technologies. Her blog features opinions on classic literature, comic books, philosophy, and movies. Twitter: @AlineMayaP

Nicolas Michaud is an adjunct philosophy instructor at Florida State College Jacksonville and is the coeditor of *The Hunger Games and Philosophy*.

Timothy Pickavance is Associate Professor of Philosophy and Chair of the Talbot Department of Philosophy at Biola University. His philosophical interests are all over the map. But his published work is mostly in metaphysics, and include *Metaphysics: The*

Fundamentals and *The Atlas of Reality: A Comprehensive Guide to Metaphysics* (both co-authored with Robert Koons).

Christopher Robichaud is Senior Lecturer in Ethics and Public Policy at the Harvard Kennedy School of Government. He has published many articles in the Philosophy and Pop Culture series, including contributions to *Batman and Philosophy*, *Watchmen and Philosophy*, *Spider-Man and Philosophy*, *Avengers and Philosophy*, and *X-Men and Philosophy*. He also edited the volumes *The Walking Dead and Philosophy* and *Dungeons & Dragons and Philosophy*. Christopher designed an online course for the Smithsonian, *Power and Responsibility: Doing Philosophy with Superheroes*, and he is currently writing a book on superheroes and democracy for Harvard University Press.

Bradley Richards is a philosophy lecturer at Ryerson University. His research concerns consciousness, attention, and aesthetics. He also enjoys working in cognitive science and film.

Eric J. Silverman is Associate Professor of Philosophy at Christopher Newport University in the US. He has more than 20 publications on topics in ethics, philosophy of religion, and medieval philosophy. His publications include two monographs, *The Prudence of Love: How Possessing the Virtue of Love Benefits the Lover* and *The Supremacy of Love: An Agape-Centered Vision of Aristotelian Virtue Ethics,* as well as two edited collections, *Paradise Understood: New Philosophical Essays about Heaven* and *Sexual Ethics in a Secular Age: Is There Still a Virtue of Chastity?*

Jason Southworth is an adjunct philosopher who refuses to give the schools he teaches for free advertising in his bios as long as they refuse to pay their workers a living wage or offer them health insurance. He is the co-editor of *Saturday Night Live and Philosophy: Deep Thoughts Through the Decades* with Ruth Tallman, and has recently completed work on the 4th edition of *Critical Reasoning: A User's Manual* with Chris Swoyer, a free open resource textbook.

Grant Sterling is Professor of Philosophy and General Education Coordinator at Eastern Illinois University. He teaches courses in ethics, law, religion, and the history of philosophy. Sterling has twice served as President of the Illinois Philosophical Association, and is the author of *Ethical Intuitionism and Its Critics*, as well as several articles and chapters.

Zachary Swanson is a graduate student at The University of Tennessee at Chattanooga, where he studies moral psychology, and other topics such as religion, meaning, well-being, and aging. He has co-authored a chapter for one other volume in the Blackwell Philosophy and Pop Culture Series, and is working on several publications for academic journals in psychology and philosophy.

Jerry L. Walls is Professor of Philosophy and Scholar in Residence at Houston Baptist University. He has authored or edited a number of books and articles, both academic and popular. Among his books is a trilogy on the afterlife, dealing with heaven, hell, and purgatory.

Jonathan L. Walls is a filmmaker residing in Los Angeles. To date, he has written and directed three feature films. He is the Editor of *The Legend of Zelda and Theology*, and co-Editor of *Tarantino of Theology*.

Mark D. White is chair of the Department of Philosophy at the College of Staten Island/CUNY, where he teaches courses in philosophy, economics, and law. He has edited or co-edited eight volumes in the Blackwell Philosophy and Pop Culture Series, contributed chapters to many more, and authored books on Batman, Captain America, and Marvel Comics' *Civil War*.

J. Lenore Wright is the Director of the Academy for Teaching and Learning (ATL) and Associate Professor of Interdisciplinary Studies & Philosophy at Baylor University. Wright serves as an expert reviewer for the *International Journal of Feminist Approaches to Bioethics* and a regular reviewer for *Feminist Philosophy Quarterly*. She received Baylor's Outstanding Professor Award in 2008–2009 for distinctive teaching.

William W. Young III is professor of religion and philosophy at Endicott College in Beverly, Massachusetts. He has published essays on baseball, poker, and *The Shawshank Redemption*. His most recent book is *Listening, Religion, and Democracy in Contemporary Boston: God's Ears*.

Acknowledgments

We would like to thank our friends, colleagues, and students who offered feedback and advice in assembling this volume. Courtney Zabresky provided excellent secretarial support. Thanks are also due to our editor Marissa Koors and the reviewers who helped us shape this new edition. The contributing authors were consummate professionals who literally made this book possible. We especially appreciate all the instructors who assigned the first edition and whose continued support has made this second edition a reality. Kyle wishes to thank his wife Lori for supporting him throughout his many projects and Sabrina Traver for her peerless proofreading and formatting skills. Bill wishes to thank his wife Megan and his children Daniel and Kate for making home so happy and philosophy friendly.

Sources

The editors and publisher gratefully acknowledge permission to reprint the copyright material in this book.

1   William W. Young III, "Flatulence and Philosophy: A Lot of Hot Air or the Corruption of the Youth?" from Robert Arp (ed.) *South Park and Philosophy: You Know, I Learned Something Today* (Oxford: Wiley-Blackwell, 2006), pp. 5–16. Reprinted by permission of Blackwell Publishing Ltd.

2   Robert Arp, "The Chewbacca Defense: A South Park Logic Lesson," from Robert Arp (ed.) *South Park and Philosophy: You Know, I Learned Something Today* (Oxford: Wiley-Blackwell, 2006), pp. 40–53. Reprinted by permission of Blackwell Publishing Ltd.

3   David Kyle Johnson, "Wikiality, Truthiness, and Gut Thinking: Doing Philosophy Colbert-Style." No permission required. Written for the first edition.

4   Henry Jacoby, "You Know, I Learned Something Today: Stan Marsh and the Ethics of Belief" from Robert Arp (ed.) *South Park and Philosophy: You Know, I Learned Something Today* (Oxford: Wiley-Blackwell, 2006), pp. 57–65. Reprinted by permission of Blackwell Publishing Ltd.

5   Matt Lawrence "Tumbling Down the Rabbit Hole: Knowledge, Reality, and the Pit of Skepticism," from Matt Lawrence, *Like a Splinter in Your Mind: The Philosophy Behind the Matrix Trilogy* (Oxford: Wiley-Blackwell, 2004), pp. 20–31. Reprinted by permission of Blackwell Publishing Ltd.

6   Eric J. Silverman, "Adama's True Lie: Earth and the Problem of Knowledge," from Jason T. Eberl (ed.) *Battlestar Galactica and Philosophy: Knowledge Here Begins Out There* (Oxford: Wiley-Blackwell, 2008), pp. 192–202. Reprinted by permission of Blackwell Publishing Ltd.

7   Ruby Komic, "Wakandan Resources: The Epistemological Reality of *Black Panther's* Fiction," from Edwardo Perez and Timothy E. Brown (eds.) *Black Panther and Philosophy* (Hoboken: Wiley-Blackwell, forthcoming 2022). Reprinted by permission of John Wiley & Sons, Inc.

8   Dara Fogel, "Life on a Holodeck: What Star Trek Can Teach Us about the True Nature of Reality," from Kevin S. Decker and Jason T. Eberl (eds.) *The Ultimate Star Trek and Philosophy: The Search for Socrates* (Oxford: Wiley-Blackwell, 2016), pp. 275–287. Reprinted by permission of John Wiley & Sons, Inc.

9   Dean A. Kowalski, "Astral Bodies and Cartesian Souls: Mind–Body Dualism in Doctor Strange," from Mark D. White (ed.) *Doctor Strange and Philosophy: The Other Book of Forbidden Knowledge* (Hoboken: Wiley-Blackwell, 2018), pp. 101–110. Reprinted by permission of John Wiley & Sons, Inc.

10   Matt Lawrence, "Mind and Body in Zion," from Matt Lawrence, *Like a Splinter in Your Mind: The Philosophy Behind the Matrix Trilogy* (Oxford: Wiley-Blackwell, 2004), pp. 32–46. Reprinted by permission of Blackwell Publishing Ltd.

11   Jason Southworth, "Amnesia, Personal Identity, and the Many Lives of Wolverine," from Rebecca Housel and Jeremy J. Wisnewski (eds.) *X-Men and Philosophy: Astonishing Insight and Uncanny Argument in the Mutant X-Verse* (Hoboken: Wiley, 2009), pp. 17–26. Reprinted by permission of John Wiley & Sons, Inc.

12   Grant Sterling, "The Consolation of Bilbo: Providence and Free Will in Middle-Earth" from Gregory Bassham and Eric Bronson (eds.) *The Hobbit and Philosophy: For When You've Lost Your Dwarves, Your Wizard, and Your Way* (Hoboken: Wiley, 2012), pp. 206–217. Reprinted by permission of John Wiley & Sons, Inc.

13   John R. Fitzpatrick and David Kyle Johnson, "Inception and Free Will: Are they Compatible?" from David Kyle Johnson (ed.) *Inception and Philosophy: Because It's Never Just a Dream* (Hoboken: Wiley, 2012), pp. 152–165. Reprinted by permission of John Wiley & Sons, Inc.

14   Lucia Carrillo González, "Turing's Dream and Searle's Nightmare in Westworld" from James B. South and Kimberly S. Engels (eds.) *Westworld and Philosophy: If You Go Looking for the Truth, Get the Whole Thing* (Hoboken: Wiley-Blackwell, 2018), pp. 73–78. Reprinted by permission of John Wiley & Sons, Inc.

15   Bradley Richards, "What Is It Like to Be a Host?" from James B. South and Kimberly S. Engels (eds.) *Westworld and Philosophy: If You Go Looking for the Truth, Get the Whole Thing* (Hoboken: Wiley-Blackwell, 2018), pp. 79–89. Reprinted by permission of John Wiley & Sons, Inc.

16   David Kyle Johnson, "Time Travel in The Avengers." Reprinted by permission of http://Psychologytoday.com

17   David Kyle Johnson, "Cartmanland and the Problem of Evil," from Robert Arp (ed.) *South Park and Philosophy: You Know, I Learned Something Today* (Oxford: Wiley-Blackwell, 2006), pp. 213–223. Reprinted by permission of Blackwell Publishing Ltd.

18   Robert K. Garcia and Timothy Pickavance, "Hidden Mickeys and the Hiddenness of God," from Richard B. Davis (ed.) *Disney and Philosophy: Truth, Trust, and a Little Bit of Pixie Dust* (Hoboken: Wiley-Blackwell, 2020), pp. 35–44. Reprinted by permission of John Wiley & Sons, Inc.

19   William A. Lindenmuth, "Jedi Knights of Faith: Anakin, Luke, and Søren (Kierkegaard)" from Jason T. Eberl and Kevin S. Decker (eds.) *The Ultimate Star Wars and Philosophy: You Must Unlearn What You Have Learned* (Oxford:

Wiley-Blackwell, 2016), pp. 31–41. Reprinted by permission of John Wiley & Sons, Inc.

20 Mark D. White, "Why Doesn't Batman Kill the Joker?" from Mark D. White and Robert Arp (eds.) *Batman and Philosophy: The Dark Knight of the Soul* (Hoboken: Wiley, 2008), pp. 5–16. Reprinted by permission of John Wiley & Sons, Inc.

21 J. Robert Loftis, "Means, Ends, and the Critique of Pure Superheroes," Mark D. White (ed.) *Watchmen and Philosophy: A Rorschach Test* (Hoboken: Wiley, 2009), pp. 63–77. Reprinted by permission of John Wiley & Sons, Inc.

22 Eric J. Silverman and Zachary Swanson, "Can Eleanor Really Become a Better Person? (The Good Place)" from Kimberly S. Engels (ed.) *The Good Place and Philosophy Everything Is Forking Fine* (Hoboken: Wiley, 2021), pp. 37–46. Reprinted by permission of John Wiley & Sons, Inc.

23 Dean A. Kowalski, "You're a Sucky, Sucky Friend": Seeking Aristotelian Friendship in The Big Bang Theory," from Dean A. Kowalski (ed.) *The Big Bang Theory and Philosophy: Rock, Paper, Scissors, Aristotle, Locke* (Hoboken: Wiley, 2012), pp. 21–34. Reprinted by permission of John Wiley & Sons, Inc.

24 Matt Hummel, "You Are Asking Me to Be Rational": Stoic Philosophy and the Jedi Order," from Jason T. Eberl and Kevin S. Decker (eds.) *The Ultimate Star Wars and Philosophy: You Must Unlearn What You Have Learned* (Oxford: Wiley-Blackwell, 2016), pp. 20–30. Reprinted by permission of John Wiley & Sons, Inc.

25 Arno Bogaerts, "Rediscovering Nietzsche's Übermensch in Superman as a Heroic Ideal," from Mark D. White (ed.) *Superman and Philosophy: What Would the Man of Steel Do?* (Oxford: Wiley-Blackwell, 2013), pp. 85–100. Reprinted by permission of John Wiley & Sons, Inc.

26 William J. Devlin, "Knowing Who You Are: Existence Precedes Essence in Moana," from Richard B. Davis (ed.) *Disney and Philosophy: Truth, Trust, and a Little Bit of Pixie Dust* (Hoboken: Wiley-Blackwell, 2020), pp. 107–117. Reprinted by permission of John Wiley & Sons, Inc.

27 J. Lenore Wright, "Becoming a (Wonder) Woman: Feminism, Nationalism, and the Ambiguity of Female Identity," from Jacob M. Held (ed.) *Wonder Woman and Philosophy: The Amazonian Mystique* (Hoboken: Wiley-Blackwell, 2017), pp. 5–18. Reprinted by permission of John Wiley & Sons, Inc.

28 George A. Dunn and Nicolas Michaud, "The Silence of Our Mother: Eywa as the Voice of Feminine Care Ethics (Avatar)," from George A. Dunn (ed.) *Avatar and Philosophy: Learning to See* (Hoboken: Wiley-Blackwell, 2014), pp. 7–18. Reprinted by permission of John Wiley & Sons, Inc.

29 Jeremy David Bendik-Keymer, "Everything is Backwards Now": Avatar, Anthropocentrism, and Relational Reason," from George A. Dunn (ed.) *Avatar and Philosophy: Learning to See* (Hoboken: Wiley-Blackwell, 2014), pp. 115–124. Reprinted by permission of John Wiley & Sons, Inc.

30 Greg Littmann, "Maester Hobbes Goes to King's Landing (Game of Thrones)," from Henry Jacoby (ed.) *Game of Thrones and Philosophy: Logic Cuts Deeper Than Swords* (Hoboken: Wiley, 2012), pp. 5–18. Reprinted by permission of John Wiley & Sons, Inc.

31 Richard Davies, "Lost's State of Nature," from Sharon Kaye (ed.) *Lost and Philosophy: The Island Has Its Reasons* (Oxford: Wiley-Blackwell, 2007), pp. 177–190. Reprinted by permission of Blackwell Publishing Ltd.

32 Jeff Ewing, "Federation Trekonomics: Marx, the Federation, and the Shift from Necessity to Freedom," from Kevin S. Decker and Jason T. Eberl (eds.) *The Ultimate Star Trek and Philosophy: The Search for Socrates* (Oxford: Wiley-Blackwell, 2016), pp. 115–126. Reprinted by permission of John Wiley & Sons, Inc.

33 Christopher Robichaud, "Superman and Justice," from Mark D. White (ed.) *Superman and Philosophy: What Would the Man of Steel Do?* (Oxford: Wiley-Blackwell, 2013), pp. 61–70. Reprinted by permission of John Wiley & Sons, Inc.

34 Paul A. Cantor, "Cartman Shrugged: South Park and Libertarian Philosophy," from Robert Arp and Kevin S. Decker (eds.) *The Ultimate South Park and Philosophy: Respect My Philosophah!* (Oxford: Wiley-Blackwell, 2013), pp. 177–193. Reprinted by permission of John Wiley & Sons, Inc.

35 Roy T. Cook, "Ninjas, Kobe Bryant, and Yellow Plastic: The LEGO Minifigure and Race," from Roy T. Cook and Sondra Bacharach (eds.), *Lego and Philosophy: Constructing Reality Brick By Brick* (Hoboken: Wiley-Blackwell, 2017), pp. 91–101. Reprinted by permission of John Wiley & Sons, Inc.

36 Timothy E. Brown "When Tech Meets Tradition: How Wakandan Technology Transcends Anti-Blackness," from Edwardo Perez and Timothy E. Brown (eds.) *Black Panther and Philosophy* (Hoboken: Wiley-Blackwell, forthcoming 2022). Reprinted by permission of John Wiley & Sons, Inc.

37 Bertha Alvarez Manninen, "Black Mirror and Political Manipulation: How Are We Tricked into Dehumanizing Others?" from David Kyle Johnson (ed.) *Black Mirror and Philosophy: Dark Reflections* (Hoboken: Wiley-Blackwell, 2020), pp. 118–127. Reprinted by permission of John Wiley & Sons, Inc.

38 Aline Maya, "Black Mirror and #DeathTo: What are the Consequences of Trial by Twitter?" from David Kyle Johnson (ed.) *Black Mirror and Philosophy: Dark Reflections* (Hoboken: Wiley-Blackwell, 2020), pp. 128–140. Reprinted by permission of John Wiley & Sons, Inc.

39 Steve Bein, "The Brick, the Plate, and the Uncarved Block: LEGO as an Expression of the Dao," from Roy T. Cook and Sondra Bacharach (eds.), *Lego and Philosophy: Constructing Reality Brick By Brick* (Hoboken: Wiley-Blackwell, 2017), pp. 175–184. Reprinted by permission of John Wiley & Sons, Inc.

40 David Kahn, "LEGO, Impermanence, and Buddhism," from Roy T. Cook and Sondra Bacharach (eds.), *Lego and Philosophy: Constructing Reality Brick By Brick* (Hoboken: Wiley-Blackwell, 2017), pp. 185–195. Reprinted by permission of John Wiley & Sons, Inc.

41 Steve Bein, "Zen and the Art of Imagineering: Disney's Escapism Versus Buddhism's Liberation," from Richard B. Davis (ed.) *Disney and Philosophy: Truth, Trust, and a Little Bit of Pixie Dust* (Hoboken: Wiley-Blackwell, 2020), pp. 25–34. Reprinted by permission of John Wiley & Sons, Inc.

42 Jonathan L. Walls and Jerry L. Walls, "Beyond Godric's Hollow: Life after Death and the Search for Meaning (Harry Potter)," from Gregory Bassham (ed.) *The Ultimate Harry Potter and Philosophy: Hogwarts for Muggles* (Hoboken: Wiley, 2010), pp. 246–257. Reprinted by permission of John Wiley & Sons, Inc.

43 David Kyle Johnson, "Why It Wouldn't Be Rational to Believe You're in The Good Place (and Why You Wouldn't Want to Be Anyway)," from Kimberly S. Engels (ed.) *The Good Place and Philosophy Everything Is Forking Fine* (Hoboken: Wiley, 2021), pp. 270–282. Reprinted by permission of John Wiley & Sons, Inc.

Introduction

Philosophy has a public relations problem. Just the sound of the word "philosophy" scares a lot of people, conjuring images of long-dead Greeks and crusty old professors. But the stereotypes of philosophy are just that – stereotypes. They are mistaken exaggerations and overgeneralizations. Some philosophy professors may be egg-headed, ivory-tower intellectuals, but most are not. In fact, many philosophy professors like the same things you like: television, movies, music, and video games. We see connections between these elements of pop culture and philosophy. So this book, written by philosophy professors, takes you from pop culture to philosophy; we wade into the water before swimming out deep. Each chapter in this new edition focuses on a piece of pop culture, like *Harry Potter*, *Star Wars*, or *Wonder Woman*, and teaches you about a particular issue in philosophy. We think you'll agree that, to paraphrase a classic Disney truism, a spoonful of pop culture helps the philosophy go down.

The idea of using examples to facilitate learning is not new to philosophy. Famously, Plato (428–348 BCE) used the story of the ring of Gyges, and Descartes (1596–1650) imagined a deceitful demon. However, most examples in philosophy are rather dry – finding people with bland names like Jones and Brown in difficult to describe circumstances, such as those in which we are potentially justified in believing that "Jones owns a Ford, or Brown is in Barcelona." Thankfully, Hollywood writers do a much better job of creating engaging, imaginative scenarios than philosophers do. So why not use their creations to add spice to philosophy? As you'll discover in this book, *The Matrix* provides a vivid way of picturing Descartes's concerns about deception and knowledge, and *South Park* hilariously dramatizes the problem of evil by asking why good things (like inheriting a million dollars) happen to bad people (like Cartman). Indeed, many other insightful philosophical illustrations from pop culture await your reading.

Now, of course, you may be concerned that you're in trouble because in addition to being clueless about philosophy you're also clueless about *The Matrix* and *South Park*.

Introducing Philosophy Through Pop Culture: From Socrates to Star Wars *and Beyond*, Second Edition.
Edited by William Irwin and David Kyle Johnson.

There's no need to worry. You don't have to be an expert on Marvel movies or to have seen every episode of *The Good Place* to benefit from this book. Even a passing acquaintance with the pop culture icon discussed in any given chapter will be enough for you to learn the philosophy to which it is connected. You can get that easily enough on the internet. In fact, you can visit the website for this book at https://introducingphilosophy throughpopculture.com for all kinds of helpful up-to-date links.

In sum, this book is intended to make initial connections between pop culture and philosophy that will pique your interest in the latter and lead you to study and appreciate the subject more deeply. Maybe you'll even decide to tell your friends that philosophy has gotten a bad rap. Certainly, we believe you'll find that philosophy is relevant, fun, and exciting.[1]

Note

1   For pop culture resources and philosophical resources related to all chapters please visit the website for this book: https://introducingphilosophythroughpopculture.com.

Part I

What is Philosophy?

Introduction

The word "philosophy" is often confused with the words "opinion," "theory," or "approach"–as in, "What is your philosophy of life?" or "Our philosophy is never to be undersold!" As a result, some students have mistaken ideas about what a philosophy class is. "Can you even give a wrong answer in a philosophy class? Isn't it just whatever you think?" Well, yes you can, and no it's not.

The word "philosophy" comes from the Greek language and means "love of wisdom." Philosophers seek truth and wisdom above all else. The questions for which true answers are most important, but most elusive, form the core of philosophy. What is the nature of reality? What is knowledge, and how can one attain it? Is there a God? What is the nature of good and evil? How can I live a good life? How should we govern ourselves? What is the meaning of life? So how do philosophers seek answers to these questions? Are there really answers? Or is whatever anyone thinks just "true for them" because they have a "right to their opinion?" What role does philosophy play in society? And what attitude does philosophy require?

In Chapter 1, William Young argues that philosophy and the TV show *South Park* share some common aims. Like the philosopher Socrates (469-399 BCE), *South Park* is charged with corrupting the youth, inappropriately challenging moral norms, and being a social nuisance. But the accusations are unfounded for both Socrates and *South Park*. The accusers are actually the corruptors; for example, parents corrupt the youth when they leave their kids to be raised by television without educating them about what they are seeing. Thankfully *South Park*, like Socrates, teaches us to draw our own conclusions–not merely accept the consensus of the crowd–and to reach those conclusions by considering the perspectives of others. Clearly, Young argues, *South Park* is not mindless and harmful; the show, like philosophy, is a gadfly, "an annoying pest that goes around 'stinging people'

Introducing Philosophy Through Pop Culture: From Socrates to Star Wars *and Beyond*, Second Edition.
Edited by William Irwin and David Kyle Johnson.
© 2022 John Wiley & Sons Ltd. Published 2022 by John Wiley & Sons Ltd.

with. . .challenging questions and critical reflections so as to keep them intellectually awake and on their toes."

Philosophers' appetite for truth is insatiable, but they do not always agree. To solve their disputes they use logic. In Chapter 2, Robert Arp takes examples from *South Park* to teach some of the basics of logic including the structure of arguments, the differences between good and bad arguments, and the distinction between inductive and deductive arguments. The lesson concludes with common logical fallacies, illustrated by *South Park* for comedic effect. In one classic episode, for example, the cartoon version of Johnnie Cochran commits the red-herring fallacy by suggesting that Chef must not have written the Alanis Morissette song "Stinky Britches" because Chewbacca spent most of his time on Endor: "If Chewbacca lives on Endor, you must acquit."

South Park is not the only show that plays philosopher. Late night talk show hosts can be gadflies as too. In Chapter 3, David Kyle Johnson uses Stephen Colbert to teach us about the philosophical attitude. Relativism (what Colbert calls "wikiality") and intuitionism (What Colbert calls "truthiness") are contrary to the endeavor of philosophy. More importantly, Johnson enlists Colbert to dispel a myth that holds back almost every philosophy course–the myth that everyone has a right to their opinion on every subject. Attempts to end philosophical discussion with appeals to "a right to my opinion" only reveal a disregard for truth and a desire to protect entrenched beliefs. Real philosophers must be willing to give up disproven beliefs and embrace the truth.

1

Flatulence and Philosophy

A Lot of Hot Air, or the Corruption of Youth?

William W. Young, III

Summary

Though Trey Parker and Matt Stone haven't been killed for it (they did receive death threats after their 200th episode) the creators of *South Park* have faced accusations much like those that led to Socrates's execution: the corruption of youth and the teaching of vulgar, irreligious behavior. A closer examination, however, reveals that *South Park* is very much within the Platonic tradition, as Kyle and Stan engage in questioning and dialogue in order to "learn something today." Moreover, the mob mentality of the parents, along with the malicious yet mimetic evil of Cartman, demonstrates how evil emerges from thoughtlessness: a failure to ask if one can live with oneself, and a failure to out oneself in the place of others. Through its different characters, and even its apparently mindless vulgarity, *South Park* shows the need for engaging in dialogue and thinking from others' perspectives, in order to pursue wisdom, examine life, and make it worth living.

The "Danger" of *South Park*

In the episode "Death" Kyle's mother leads a boycott of the boys' favorite cartoon show – *Terrance and Phillip* – because of its continuous farting, name-calling, and general "potty humor." While the parents are up in arms over this "moral" issue, the boys wrestle with the problem of euthanasia for Stan's grandfather, something none of the parents will discuss with them. "Death" brings together many of the central issues that have made *South Park* successful and controversial – vulgarity, the misplaced moral concerns of American culture, the discussion of controversial moral topics, and the criticism that *South Park* itself is a "disgusting" show. Since "Death" the criticism of the show has only grown – getting even bigger than Cartman's fat ass – drawing fire for its obscene language, criticisms of religion, and emphasis upon freedom of speech.[1]

Like the parents protesting *Terrance and Philip*, critics of *South Park* make claims that are strikingly similar to those that have been leveled against Western philosophy since its

Introducing Philosophy Through Pop Culture: From Socrates to Star Wars *and Beyond*, Second Edition.
Edited by William Irwin and David Kyle Johnson.

beginnings. It mocks religious beliefs, leads younger folks to question accepted authority and values, and corrupts our children and culture. The "it" in the previous sentence refers to *South Park*, but in fact, the same criticisms formed the basis for Socrates's (470–399 BCE) trial and execution in Athens, Greece in 399 BCE.[2] So, in this chapter we'll explore the heretical possibility that people perceive *South Park* as dangerous precisely because it is a form of philosophy. The "danger" that *South Park* poses has to do with its depiction of dialogue and free thinking. In the end we will have learned something: Like Socrates, *South Park* harms no one. Philosophy and *South Park* actually instruct people and provide them with the intellectual tools they need to become wise, free, and good.

Oh My God! They Killed Socrates! You Bastards!

In Plato's (428–348 BCE) *Apology*, Socrates defends himself against two charges: (i) impiety (false teachings about the gods, possibly that they don't exist) and (ii) corrupting the youth of Athens. In reality, Socrates probably had as much chance of winning his case as Chef did against Johnny Cochran's "Chewbacca" defense! What is most important about Socrates's defense, however, is not so much what he says as *how* he says it. He defends himself by questioning his accuser, Meletus, leading him through a process of reasoning. For example, Socrates refutes the charge of corrupting the youth as follows:

> *Socrates:* You say you have discovered the one who corrupts them, namely me, and you bring me here and accuse me to the jury. . .All the Athenians, it seems, make the young into fine good men, except me, and I alone corrupt them. Is that what you mean? *Meletus:* That is most definitely what I mean. *Socrates:* You condemn me to a great misfortune. Tell me: does this also apply to horses do you think? That all men improve them and one individual corrupts them? Or is quite the contrary true, one individual is able to improve them, or very few, namely the horse breeders, whereas the majority, if they have horses and use them, corrupt them? Is that not the case, Meletus, both with horses and all other animals? . . . It would be a happy state of affairs if only one person corrupted our youth, while the others improved them. You have made it sufficiently obvious, Meletus, that you have never had any concern for our youth; you show your indifference clearly; that you have given no thought to the subjects about which you bring me to trial.[3]

Through the analogy with horse training, Socrates shows how illogical the accusations against him really are. Just as a majority of people would injure horses by training them, and only a few good trainers improve them, so too it is likely that a few teachers improve the virtue of the youth, while many others corrupt them. Socrates argues, further, that he is in fact the one who is teaching Athens' youth what virtue involves, while many others – including the idiots sitting before him – corrupt them. (As you can imagine, this did not go over well with the jury.)

While showing that the accusations are groundless, this "apology" – a word that also can mean *defense* – demonstrates why Socrates got a death sentence of hemlock. Socrates is famous for saying "I know that I don't know" and, actually, this is a wise insight. For Socrates, philosophy was the love and pursuit of wisdom, and this required questioning others to find out what they do or don't know. Unfortunately, people often believe they are wiser than they are. By questioning them, Socrates would show them that they don't know what they believe they know: "I go around seeking out anyone, citizen or stranger, whom I think wise. Then if I do not think he is, I come to the assistance of the god and show him that he is not wise."[4] What makes Socrates wise is his recognition of his own ignorance, through continuous questioning of himself and others. Many powerful people in Athens saw him as dangerous because his questioning and debate would undermine their bases for power.

In the town of South Park, people in positions of power believe they are teaching the children wisdom and virtue. However, as in Athens, the many people of South Park seem to make the children worse, not better. For example, Mr. Garrison "teaches" the children creationism before switching to an absolutist Darwinism, Mrs. Broflovski always goes to crazy extremes with her "moral" outrage, Uncle Jim and Ned teach the boys to kill harmless bunnies and squirrels in "self-defense," and the mayor panders shamelessly to voters. None of the townsfolk really *talk* to the children, except Chef (R.I.P.), who taught the art of making sweet, sweet love to a woman. Blindly following the crowd, from protesting *Terrance and Philip* to boycotting Harbucks, to – yes – burying their heads in the sand to avoid watching *Family Guy*, the parents of South Park corrupt the children far more than a television show ever could. As in "Something Wal-Mart This Way Comes," their mindless consumption leads to an unrestrained cycle of economic and mob destruction. Like the Athenians, the adults don't know as much as they believe they know. Ultimately, if television does corrupt the children, it does so because they are left to it by their parents, with no one to educate them about what they are seeing. Of course, there are also cases where parents and people in powerful positions *do* try to discuss issues and ideas with the children. These discussions, though, support the same point, as the adult usually sounds like a bumbling idiot.

Cartman Gets a Banal Probe

One of the most significant philosophical reflections on evil in the twentieth century is Hannah Arendt's *Eichmann in Jerusalem: A Report on the Banality of Evil*, a study of the trial of Adolf Eichmann for his role in the deportations of millions of European Jews to concentration camps during the Jewish Holocaust. Eichmann just followed the law of the land, whatever it happened to be, and when Hitler was making the laws, Eichmann simply carried them out.[5] In the words of Arendt, Eichmann was an unreflective person, unable to think for himself and *definitely* unable "to think from the standpoint of somebody else."[6] What was really monstrous about Eichmann was not his vicious cruelty, but rather the way that he was not that different from so many Germans who, under Hitler, accepted and supported laws that were obviously evil and believed that they were doing what was right. Eichmann's banality – the fact that there is nothing distinctive or exceptional about him – is *precisely* what makes him evil. He was one of the "crowd" who *didn't* walk to the beat of a different drummer and *didn't* rock the boat. He embodied complicit citizenship under a dictatorship, which speaks *for* its subjects and, thus, cuts off their reflective and critical thought.

Thoughtlessness leads to evil, as Arendt says, because it doesn't let us see things from others' perspectives. By blindly following orders, Eichmann didn't think about what his actions were doing to others, or even what they were doing to himself. By saying he was "following the law" and "doing his duty," he ignored how his actions sent millions to their deaths and, despite his protests, made him a murderer. Thinking, according to Arendt, requires taking another's standpoint, reflecting on how you might be harming others, and asking if you can live with what you are doing.

While the adults in *South Park* blindly follow the latest fad, or what they are told, it is the children who bring out the absurdity and potential harm that lurks in such thoughtlessness. To be more accurate, it's usually Kyle and Stan who are the reflective ones, while Cartman's mind is as empty as the *Cheesy Poofs* he devours daily. He is often sadistic, cruel, and evil. Like Eichmann, Cartman is probably evil because, when it comes to "authoritah," he lacks reflection and critical analysis. (And like Eichmann, he has a Nazi uniform that he has sported on occasion). Cartman sings the *Cheesy Poofs* song so well because all he can do is imitate what he hears on television. His evil is an imitation of the evil characters of our culture, as prepackaged as his afternoon snacks. Cartman consumes evil and imitates it as blindly and thoughtlessly as Eichmann – even when feeding Scott Tenorman his own parents (like Medea), trying to kill Kyle and Stan on a lake (like Fredo), or torturing Muslims with his farts (like Jack Bauer) to find the "snuke." Most importantly, because of this thoughtlessness, Cartman is unable to see things from anyone else's viewpoint (as illustrated most clearly in his manipulation of his mother). As Arendt says, such thoughtlessness is precisely what allows evil to emerge in modern society, and Cartman's mindless consumption is as thoughtless as it gets.

Friendship Kicks Ass! The Dialogues of Kyle and Stan

Part of what makes *South Park* philosophically interesting is the contrast between Cartman's evil stupidity and the nonconformist, reflective virtue of Kyle and Stan. Philosophers like Plato and Aristotle (384–322 BCE) have noted the importance of how critical reflection leads to harmony or balance and helps us to avoid extremes. After all, the "extremes" of thinking and acting often lead to mistaken beliefs and harmful behavior. In fact, following Plato's lead, Aristotle put forward the idea that *virtue* is concerned with striking a balance or hitting the mark between two extreme viewpoints, ideas, beliefs, emotions, or actions.[7] *South Park* addresses moral issues through a discussion and criticism of established "moral" positions, both conservative and liberal, which are found to be inadequate. Kyle and Stan come to a virtuous position, in part, by negotiating and listening to these views before reaching their own conclusion through questioning and reason. Frequently, their conclusion recognizes that there is some truth to each position, but that its limited perspective is still dangerous. For example, it's true that hybrid cars are more environmentally responsible than gas-guzzling SUVs. But when an air of moral superiority clouds one's judgment, this "smug cloud" creates hostility and pollutes society in other ways.

How Stan and Kyle reach their conclusions is more significant than the conclusions themselves. Think of how they discuss whether it's wrong to kill Stan's grandpa, who he wants to die. They, like Socrates, question those around them, seeking to know if the people are as wise as they believe. Their parents, Mr. Garrison, and Jesus won't discuss or touch this issue "with a 60-foot pole." What Kyle and Stan ultimately realize – with the help of Stan's great-great-grandfather's ghost – is that they shouldn't kill his grandfather, because the action would change and harm them. As it turns out, Stan's grandfather is wrong in asking them to do this vicious action. Note that the boys reach this conclusion through living with each other, recognizing their differences, and engaging in debate. Stan and Kyle – unlike Eichmann and Cartman – learn to see things from others' perspectives, through their ongoing conversation.

In the *Apology* Socrates makes the claim that a good person cannot be harmed by the actions of others. This seems false. After all, aside from being a cartoon character, what could prevent Cartman from punching out the Dalai Lama? But what Socrates means by "good" is something different than we often realize. Goodness means reflectively thinking about one's actions and *being able to live with what one has done*. Despite any *physical* harm – torture, imprisonment, exile, or death – that may come that person's way, no one could "hurt" a virtuous person by making them *do* something bad. Cartman, for example, couldn't make the Dalai Lama punch *him*. Socrates, for his part, refused to execute an innocent person, or to try generals for "crimes" beyond the laws of the city. And, significantly, Socrates would rather die than give up the thinking and questioning that he sees as central to philosophy:

> Perhaps someone might say: But Socrates, if you leave us will you not be able to live quietly, without talking? Now this is the most difficult point on which to convince some of you. If I say that it is impossible for me to keep quiet because that means disobeying the god, you will not believe me . . . On the other hand, if I say that it is the greatest good for a man to discuss virtue every day and those other things about which you hear me conversing and testing myself and others, for the unexamined live is not worth living for man, you will believe me even less.[8]

Arendt has a similar conception of goodness. Ethics, for those (unlike Eichmann) who resisted the Nazis, was being able to look back on one's life without shame, rather than adhering to a set of rules. Her description deserves quoting:

> Their criterion [for goodness], I think, was a different one; they asked themselves to what extent they would still be able to live in peace with themselves after having committed certain deeds; and they decided that it would be better to do nothing, not because the world would then be changed for the better, but simply because only on this condition could they go on living with themselves at all. Hence, they also chose to die when they were forced to participate. To put it crudely, they refused to murder . . . because they were unwilling to live together with a murderer – themselves. The precondition for this kind of judging is not a highly developed intelligence or sophistication in moral matters, but rather the disposition to live together explicitly with oneself, to have intercourse with oneself, that is, to be engaged in that silent dialogue between me and myself which, since Socrates and Plato, we usually call thinking.[9]

Thinking, for Arendt, is a twofold process: it involves seeing things through another's eyes, in dialogue and reflection, as well as asking what you can live with for yourself. It is, then, both an internal and an external dialogue, and it is only through this dialogue that critical reflection and goodness become possible. Whereas Eichmann and Cartman do not critically reflect upon the consequences of actions, nor put themselves in another's shoes, thoughtful dialogue makes us attentive to others around us, lets us live with them, and helps us attend to our own goodness. Such dialogue allows us to live with ourselves – even when, like Socrates or those who resisted the Nazis, this means we must die.

Of course, in the town of South Park there is no Socrates to teach philosophy or help us engage in dialogue. Surrounded by ignorance and violence, the boys are on their own. While the four are friends, *South Park* makes a compelling point about philosophy and ethics through the particulars of the friendship of Kyle and Stan. For instance, in "Spooky Fish," where the "evil" Cartman (who is good) arrives from a parallel universe, an evil

Kyle and Stan arrive *together*. Their friendship – thinking from one another's perspective – is what helps them to be good, both for themselves and for others. In Arendt's words, to live well is to "be plural," so that the good life is never simply one's own.[10] This is probably why Plato wrote about important philosophical issues in a dialogue format, so that it becomes clear that debate and discussion of ideas is essential to any intellectual and moral growth.

For all their faults, Kyle and Stan still debate and discuss whether certain actions are wrong. On his own, Stan sometimes just goes along with the crowd, though his early refusal to kill a deer grows into a general refusal to do harm over the show's history.[11] After the boys toilet paper the art teacher's house, Kyle cannot live with what he has done. Through their conversations they learn goodness and engage in the "thinking" Arendt describes. Friendship, then, helps us to examine our lives. In the episode "Prehistoric Ice Man" Larry says that "living is about sharing our ups and downs with our friends," and when we fail to do this we aren't really living at all. If thinking and goodness only arise through real dialogue with others – through critically questioning and examining *our own* views – then we need more friendships like the one Kyle and Stan share.

An Apology for *South Park*: Getting in Touch with Your Inner Cartman

If friendships help us to critically examine the lives that we lead, then perhaps it's no accident that the critical voice of *South Park* has been created by two friends – Trey Parker and Matt Stone. In the *Apology* Socrates likens himself to a *gadfly*, an annoying pest that goes around "stinging" people with his challenging questions and critical reflections so as to keep them intellectually awake and on their toes. *South Park*, too, serves as a gadfly, trying to wake American culture from its thoughtlessness and ignorance. The show generates discussion and debate and leads many people into discussions of ethical issues that would otherwise be passed over in silence. For a show that supposedly corrupts, it has far more of a focus on religion, ethics, and democracy than its critics would like to admit. But of course we could still ask if the *way* that *South Park* presents these issues is really necessary. For example, is it philosophically wise and necessary to use the word *shit* 163 times in one show? Or have so much, farting, vomiting, and violence? What philosophical goal can such vulgarity serve?

The vulgarity and crudeness of *South Park* are often defended on the grounds of free speech. However, a different issue is also in play. *South Park* often says what is not socially or morally acceptable to say – what, in Freudian terms, must be repressed. According to Freud, our thoughts and actions are shaped by what he calls "drives," examples of which include emotions, desires, and energy that can be aggressive, hostile, and consumptive. (Freud would have a field day with Cartman's twisted little mind, on this score.) These drives are part of our embodied being, yet, since they are dangerous and often violent, we try to control or even silence them. This control is a form of repression, but it can often have unintended consequences. Repression of a drive can lead to other sorts of unconscious, violent behavior, and such suppressed wishes form the content of dreams, our "unconscious" life.[12] Repression, as a form of internal censorship, redirects but does not diminish our aggression. In spite of our intentions, this unconscious aggression often shapes who we are, how we think, and what we do.

What Freud discovered with psychoanalysis was that talking out and interpreting our dreams may serve as a way to address this repression and its associated violence. When we talk these ideas and feelings out, the repression is broken and, through the realization, we can come to terms with the desire and shape it through thinking. Representing desires lets them be *expressed*, and this helps us to integrate them into the structure of our lives.[13] By bringing to light what had been unconscious, dream interpretation lets us think through these aspects of ourselves.

Freud thought that jokes work much like dreams. When one person tells a joke, its spontaneous and unexpected word form breaks through another person's repression. Laughter is a "release of energy" that has been blocked because we have tried to repress the wish or drive; this is why many jokes have a vulgar or obscene dimension. As Freud points out, the one who supplies it has to deny it – jokes only really work when the person telling them doesn't laugh, so that the surprise can make others laugh.[14] There is pleasure in laughing at the joke, and in telling it, as well as pleasure in freeing others from their repression.

Through its vulgarity, *South Park* verbalizes the drives and desires that we often repress; and it allows us to laugh so as to reveal these inhibitions. This is what makes the show's crudeness essential. By showing us "Token" or the conjoined fetus nurse, or saying *shit* over and over, it brings out the aggression and desire that we feel we cannot express. And, for things that really *shouldn't* be said, Kenny says them in a muffled way, and the other boys comment on it. By verbalizing these drives, the show lets us begin to think these through – it makes it possible to analyze them, and thereby distance ourselves from them. For instance, many episodes address how outsiders are berated and subjected to racist or xenophobic slander. However, by working through these statements, the show argues that in many cases, such slander is used among friends as well – and that such verbal sparring, when so understood, need not lead to violence or exclusion. It doesn't justify such speech, but it does create a space in which the hostility can be interpreted and analyzed.

Likewise, one can analyze all of the farting on *Terrance and Philip*. At least two interpretations of this show-within-the-show are possible. First, there is the issue of why the boys love such a stupid show so much. It's not that they wish they could fart all the time. Rather, when they fart, Terrance and Philip do what is forbidden: they transgress the parents' social prohibition. This appeals to the boys, because they wish they too could be free from parental control and regulation.

Second, regular viewers (mostly my students) have noted that *Terrance and Philip* is self-referential, a way for *South Park* to comment on itself. The opening of *South Park* tells us that, like *Terrance and Philip*, the show has no redeeming value and should be watched by no one. The stupidity and vulgarity of the cartoon is better understood, however, if we look beyond *South Park*. Is *Terrance and Philip* really more vapid, crude, and pointless than *Jerry Springer* or *Wife Swap*? Is it more mindless than *Fox News*, *The 700 Club*, or *Law and Order*? Some would say no. When we see Kyle, Cartman, Kenny, and Stan watching *Terrance and Philip*, it shows us that television fulfills our wish for mindlessness. What offends the parents in South Park, and the critics of *South Park*, is not that the show is vulgar and pointless, but that it highlights the mindlessness of television in general.

What both of these interpretations show is that there are multiple levels of censorship that need to be questioned. On the one hand, there is the censorship that simply looks at vulgarity, and decides what can and cannot be seen, based upon social norms. *South*

Park clearly questions this sort of censorship, saying so often what cannot be said and challenging social forms of repression. But, if part of *South Park*'s message is the need for thinking, then it also questions how television, by fulfilling our wish for mindlessness, supposedly represses thinking. Of course, such mindlessness can't simply be blamed on one's parents, or television corporations, or two doofuses from Colorado who can't draw straight. Like the mindless Athenians who were to blame for their own ignorance, or Eichmann's responsibility when he thought he was just obeying the law, if we really hold a mirror up to ourselves, as political philosophers say, we will find that our own mindlessness is the heart of Wal-Mart. Like Socrates, perhaps *South Park* – and Kyle and Stan more specifically – presents us with a way to reflect on what *we think* we really know, and through reflection move beyond our mindlessness.

The Talking Cure for Our Culture

By ceaselessly testing the limits of our culture's tolerance, *South Park* asks us to examine the things we think we know, why certain words and actions are prohibited, what we desire, and what we are teaching our children. Through its provocation, it asks us to think about what is truly harmful and what issues we really should be outraged about. Breaking the silence of our culture's repressions could be the starting point for a Socratic dialogue that helps us to think, analyze our desires and aggression, and become good. If we take the opportunity to discuss the show, why it is funny, and what it tells us about our culture and our own desires, then the show need not be mindless, vulgar, or corrupting, but rather a path to thinking that helps us to live with one another, and with ourselves.[15]

Notes

1   For pop culture resources and philosophical resources related to this chapter please visit the website for this book: https://introducingphilosophythroughpopculture.com.
2   Plato (1981). *Apology*. In: *Five Dialogues: Euthyphro, Apology, Crito, Meno, Phaedo* (trans. G.M.A. Grube). Indianapolis, IN: Hackett Publishing. Also see Xenophon (1965). *Recollections of Socrates, and Socrates' Defense before the Jury* (trans. A. Benjamin). Indianapolis: Bobbs-Merrill.
3   *Apology*, 30.
4   *Apology*, 28–29.
5   H. Arendt (2003). Personal responsibility under dictatorship. In: *Responsibility and Judgment*, 40–41. New York: Schocken.
6   Arendt, 49.
7   See Plato (1991). *The Republic of Plato* (trans. D. Bloom). New York: Basic Books; Aristotle (1999). *Nicomachean Ethics*, (trans. T. Irwin). Indianapolis, IN: Hackett Publishing.
8   *Apology*, 41.
9   Arendt, H. (1964). *Eichmann in Jerusalem: A Report on the Banality of Evil*, 135–150. New York: Viking Press.
10 Arendt, Some questions of moral philosophy. In: *Responsibility and Judgment*, 96–7.
11 I owe this insight to Kyle Giroux.
12 See Freud, S. (1965). *The Interpretation of Dreams*, 156–166. New York: Avon Books.
13 For more on this issue, see Lear, J. (1990). *Love and Its Place in Nature: A Philosophical Interpretation of Freudian Psychoanalysis*. New York: Farrar, Strauss, and Giroux.
14 Freud (1993). *Wit and Its Relation to the Unconscious* (trans. A.A. Brill), 261–73. New York: Dover.

15 My thanks to Kyle Giroux for his work as a "*South Park* consultant" and his suggestions for ways to update this version. Additional thanks to Keith Wilde and Nicole Merola for their comments and suggestions on this essay, and to numerous students from Endicott College for their discussions of an earlier version of the essay. Errors remain my own.

2

The Chewbacca Defense

A South Park *Logic Lesson*

Robert Arp

Summary

The creators of *South Park* are aware of logical principles and purposely violate them to show the absurdities associated with certain beliefs, opinions, ideas, and arguments. In fact, much of *South Park*'s humor concerns logical violations and the contradictions and problems that result. Logic is the study of the principles of correct reasoning associated with the formation and analysis of arguments. Using examples from *South Park*, this chapter offers a short logic lesson as an introduction to what philosophers do when they put forward and critique arguments. Topics covered include the parts of an argument (premise and conclusion), premise- and conclusion-indicating words, deductive versus inductive arguments, good versus bad arguments, and a few common fallacies such as the famous Chewbacca defense utilized by the cartoon Johnny Cochran in the episode "Chef Aid."

The Goth kids on *South Park* crack me up because they remind me of the Goths at the high school where I taught in the early 1990s, sitting around all looking like the bastard children of Robert Smith from *The Cure* and an 80s-ish Tori Amos. In fact, my first reaction to seeing a group of kids dressed like that at a mall is automatically to think, "They're *all* saturnine, shady, surly, and, of course, suspect." Alliteration aside, that conclusion is unfair, isn't it? It's an example of the *fallacy of hasty generalization*, actually. A *fallacy* occurs when we inappropriately or incorrectly draw a conclusion from reasons that do not support the conclusion, and *hasty generalization* is a common fallacy often lampooned on *South Park*. In a hasty generalization, a person fallaciously draws a conclusion about characteristics of a whole group based upon premises concerning characteristics of a small sample of the group. Most times, when we think to ourselves "they're all like that" in talking about anything – cars, movies, Goths – based upon a small sample of the group we're talking about, we commit a hasty generalization. There is usually no way *definitely* to conclude something about the characteristics of an entire group since we have no knowledge of the entire group. The next member of the group

Introducing Philosophy Through Pop Culture: From Socrates to Star Wars and Beyond, Second Edition.
Edited by William Irwin and David Kyle Johnson.
© 2022 John Wiley & Sons Ltd. Published 2022 by John Wiley & Sons Ltd.

we encounter may turn out to have different characteristics from members of the group we know thus far. In fact, many of those little Goths at the high school where I taught were not at all saturnine, shady, or surly once you chatted with them, and I was reasoning fallaciously by immediately jumping to that conclusion.

Any form of prejudice and stereotyping, by definition, constitutes a hasty generalization.

Consider the way Kyle's Jewish cousin, Kyle 2, is stereotyped in "The Entity," or how Mexicans are type-cast as lazy, gay people are *all* flamboyant like Big Gay Al or Mr. Slave, and African Americans are reverse type-cast as "richers" in "Here Comes the Neighborhood." Even Officer Barbrady commits the fallacy of hasty generalization in "Chickenlover" when, after reading a copy of Ayn Rand's *Atlas Shrugged*, he concludes that all books must be this bad, and reading "totally sucks ass." The creators of *South Park* play on people's hasty generalizations to make their points in episode after episode, probably because not only is prejudice something that *morally* harms people, but it also *logically* "harms" people's thinking as well.

This chapter offers a short logic lesson as an introduction to what philosophers and other critical thinkers do when they put forward and critique arguments. Logic is the study of the principles of correct reasoning associated with the formation and analysis of arguments.[1] The creators of *South Park*, for the most part, are aware of these logical principles, and purposely violate them to show the absurdities associated with certain beliefs, opinions, ideas, and arguments. In fact, much of *South Park*'s humor concerns logical violations and the absurdities, contradictions, and problems that result. The way people reason correctly, or incorrectly, has real consequences. It affects the policies they adhere to, the laws they make, the beliefs they are willing to die for, and the general way in which they live their lives.

For example, in the episode "Death" because of Mrs. Broflovski and the town's belief that the *Terrance and Phillip Show* promotes immorality, the entire community not only boycotts the show, but also sacrifices members of the community to get the producers of the show to take it off the air. This fictional morality tale parallels parts of reality, and raises questions as to whether TV promotes immorality, as well as what people are willing to do based upon their perceived connection between TV and immorality. Can we draw the general conclusion that a show like *South Park*, even if viewed by children, is bad for *all* children, from evidence that supports the fact that it is bad for *some* children? Further, even if it does promote immorality, is that the kind of thing we are willing to die for? This may seem like a silly question, but the actions of the South Park townspeople get us to think about what kinds of things people are willing to believe or do based upon their faulty reasoning.

Consider a somewhat parallel case. Are all Americans immoral? And even if so, should we sacrifice people so as to make our point about them being immoral by flying planes into a skyscraper? Again, how we live our lives, as well as how we affect others' lives, depends upon whether we reason correctly or incorrectly. (You, the reader, may even find what I have said in this paragraph to be logically questionable). In what follows, we'll consider some basics of logic and, using examples from *South Park* episodes, show some differences between correct and incorrect reasoning.

If You Do Drugs, Then You're a Hippie

Logic is the study of the principles of correct reasoning associated with the formation and analysis of arguments. An *argument* consists of two or more claims, one of which is called the *conclusion*. The conclusion is the claim in the argument that is supposed to be supported by, shown to be the case by, demonstrated by, justified by, warranted by, or proved to be the case by the premise or premises. A *premise* is a claim in the argument that is supposed to support, show, demonstrate, justify, warrant, or prove the conclusion. The fundamental purpose of an argument is to persuade or convince someone of the truth of one's concluding claim. In other words, when we put forward an argument, we want others to be persuaded or convinced of the conclusion we arrived at and believe to be true, and we use another claim, or other claims, as supposed support for the truth of that conclusion.

My fallacious argument about Goths can be rephrased, simply, like this: "Because every Goth I've ever met and know of has been saturnine, shady, surly, and, of course, suspect (the premise of my argument), therefore all Goths I meet will in fact be saturnine, shady, surly, and, of course, suspect (the conclusion of my argument)." A complete argument has at least one premise and only one conclusion, but arguments usually have two or more premises. So, for example, I was watching a *South Park* rerun one night called "Ike's Wee," and Cartman put forward an argument for why we should be convinced drugs are bad that could be paraphrased like this: "If you do drugs, then you're a hippie; if you're a hippie, then you suck; if you suck, then that's bad (all premises); so, if you do drugs, then that's bad (conclusion)."

Arguments are composed of claims, a concluding claim (the conclusion) and at least one supporting claim (the premise). A *claim* is a statement, proposition, judgment, declarative sentence, or part of a declarative sentence, resulting from a person's beliefs or opinions, which communicates that something is or is not the case about the self, the world, states of affairs, or reality in general. Claims are either true or false, and again, are the results of beliefs or opinions that people have concerning any part of what they perceive to be reality. We make our beliefs and opinions known through claims. For example, the claims "I am typing this chapter on a laptop" and "Chewbacca is a Wookie" are true, whereas the claims "I was the 40th president of the United States" and "The Sun revolves around the Earth" are false. A claim is shown to be true or false as a result of *evidence*, which can take the forms of either direct or indirect testimony of your senses, explanations, the testimony of others, appeal to well-established theories, appeal to appropriate authority, appeal to definitions, and good arguments, among others. So, that I am typing on a laptop is shown to be true by the direct testimony of my own senses, that Chewbacca is a Wookie is true by definition of "Chewbacca," that I was president of the United States is false because of the testimony of the senses of others and authorities, and that the Sun revolves around the Earth is false because of indirect sensory evidence as well as the well-established heliocentric theory. Some claims are difficult, or impossible, to show true or false with evidence. Claims like "God exists," "Abortion is always immoral," and "I have an immortal soul" would fall into this ambiguous category. That is probably why ideas, issues, and arguments surrounding these claims are considered to be "philosophical."

As rational, adult critical thinkers, we have beliefs or opinions that we think are true about reality as we perceive it, and we express those beliefs or opinions in written or spoken claims. But we can't stop there. We must convince or persuade others as to why we hold these beliefs, and when we do so, we must give a reason or set of reasons (the premises of our argument) for why we hold to a particular belief (the conclusion of our argument). So, for example, in "The Passion of the Jew" Kyle believes strongly that the

Jewish community in his hometown should apologize for Jesus's death. If asked why the Jewish community in his hometown, or anyone, should be convinced or persuaded to apologize, Kyle's argument might look like the following:

Premise 1: Since Jews are known to have been partly responsible for the death of Jesus
Premise 2: And, since an action like this requires that one should apologize
Premise 3: And, since the Jews in South Park are part of the Jewish community
Conclusion: Therefore, the Jews in South Park should apologize for Jesus' death

Let's note a few things about this argument. First, it has been placed into standard form. Putting an argument in standard form means placing the premises of the argument first, the conclusion last, and clearly dividing the premise(s) and conclusion with a horizontal line. This is a handy tool because it helps make the logical form and parts of the argument clear. And, as we will see later, standard form makes the argument easier to analyze in terms of whether the conclusion follows from the premises as well as whether all the premises are true.

Notice the word *since* at the beginning of the premises and the word *therefore* at the beginning of the conclusion. The word *since* is an example of a premise-indicating word, along with words like *because, for, for the reason that*, and *as*, among others. The word *therefore* is an example of a conclusion-indicating word, along with words like *hence, so, thus, this shows us that, we can conclude that*, and *we can reason/deduce/infer that*, among others. Premise-indicating and conclusion-indicating words are important because they usually let us know that premises and a conclusion are coming in an argument. At times, it can be incredibly difficult to tell if someone is putting forward an argument, so you can look for these indicating words to see if there is an argument in front of you and, further, you can identify what the conclusion and the premise(s) of the argument are. Unfortunately, these indicating words are not always present, and people sometimes place the conclusion anywhere in their argument (sometimes it will be the first claim, sometimes the second, sometimes the last). In such cases you must supply these words to make the structure and parts of the argument apparent.

Deductions and Inductions

Broadly speaking, there are two kinds of arguments, *deductive arguments* and *inductive arguments*. In deductive arguments, the speaker intends the conclusion to follow from the premises with absolute certainty such that, if all of the premises are true, then the conclusion must be true without any doubt whatsoever. To say that a conclusion *follows* from a premise means that we are justified in having reasoned appropriately from one claim (the premise) to another claim (the conclusion). Cartman puts forward a deductive argument in "The Tooth Fairy Tats 2000" episode that goes something like this:

Premise 1: If the boys combine their lost teeth, then they'll get money from the Tooth Fairy
Premise 2: If they get money from the Tooth Fairy, then they can buy a Sega Dreamcast
Conclusion: Hence, if the boys combine their lost teeth, then they can buy a Sega
   Dreamcast

We can see that, provided that the two premises are true, the conclusion absolutely must be true. We can also see that there is no other conclusion that could correctly be drawn from these premises. In fact, from looking at the premises alone you know the conclusion before even seeing it. The previous argument about Jews apologizing for Jesus's death is also a deductive argument. Just like with the Tooth Fairy argument, if all the premises are true then the conclusion must be true, there is no other conclusion that possibly could be drawn from the premises, and you know exactly what the conclusion is without even seeing it.

In inductive arguments, the speaker intends the conclusion to follow from the premises with a degree of probability or likelihood such that, if all of the premises are true, then the conclusion probably or likely is true, but it is still possible that the conclusion is false. In the "Towelie" episode, the boys notice that when they speak about anything having to do with towels, Towelie shows up, and so they reason like this:

Premise 1: Because in the past, when we mentioned towel-related things, Towelie showed up
Premise 2: And because we will mention something towel-related now
Conclusion: We can conclude that Towelie will show up

We can see that, provided the premises are true, the conclusion is probably or likely true, but not definitely true. It makes sense to conclude that Towelie will show up, given past experience. But the truth of Towelie showing up in the past does not guarantee that, with absolute certainty or without a doubt, Towelie *will* show up. It is still possible that Towelie will not show up, so the conclusion is merely probable or likely. In the episode, Towelie does show up, but he need not necessarily have shown up.

Consider Stan's reasoning at the end of the episode "Scott Tenorman Must Die" after it has been revealed that Cartman orchestrated the death of Scott's parents, the subsequent addition of their bodies to the chili, and Radiohead's witnessing the entire event so as to make fun of Scott for being a woosie.

Premise 1: Since Cartman does horrible things to people for minor offenses (like being cheated out of $16.12)
Premise 2: And since we (the boys) commit, at least, minor offenses against Cartman frequently, and he may retaliate like he did with Scott
Conclusion: Therefore, we had better not piss Cartman off in the future, for fear of retaliation

Again, even if both of the premises are true, it does not follow with absolute certainty that the boys had better not piss off Cartman in the future. In fact, as it turns out, the boys piss off Cartman numerous times without receiving the kind of retaliation given poor Scott Tenorman. So, the conclusion is false.

The Good, the Bad, and . . . Well, That's it Really

Our goal is not just to form arguments. We need to form *good arguments*, and we need to evaluate the arguments of others. There are good arguments and there are bad arguments in both the deductive and inductive realms. A good argument, in either realm, is one in which the conclusion logically follows from the premises and all of the premises are true. If either one of these conditions is absent, then the argument is bad and should be rejected.

In the deductive realm, that a conclusion follows from premises means that the argument is *valid* (or *invalid* if the conclusion does not follow). When an argument is valid and all the premises are true, the argument is said to be a good, *sound argument*. The conclusion absolutely, positively, without a doubt, is true, and this is a good thing! In the inductive realm, that a conclusion likely will follow from premises means that the argument is *strong* (or *weak* if the conclusion likely does not follow). When an argument is strong and all the premises are true, the argument is said to be a good, *cogent argument*. The conclusion is most likely or probably true, and this is a good thing too!

So, as rational, adult critical thinkers we must always go through this two-step procedure of checking our own arguments and the arguments of others to see if (A) the conclusion follows from the premises (is the argument deductively valid or inductively strong?) and (B) all of the premises are true. If the argument fails to meet either (A) or (B) or both, then we should reject it, thereby rejecting the person's conclusion as either absolutely false or probably false. For example, Cartman's argument for pooling together the boys' teeth is probably a bad one because Premise 2 seems false, given the information. It is not true that if they get money from the Tooth Fairy then they will be able to buy a Sega Dreamcast, because the Tooth Fairy only gave Cartman $2.00. The sum of $2.00 × 4 boys is $8.00 and, provided we are talking about a new one from the store, that is not enough to buy a Sega Dreamcast. So in the case of this particular deductive argument, the conclusion "If the boys combine their teeth, then they can get a Sega Dreamcast" is false. On the other hand, the Towelie argument was a good one. It was true that the few times they mentioned towel-related things, Towelie showed up. And given this fact, they had a strong case for drawing the conclusion that he would show up again asking, of course, "Wanna get high?"

"If Chewbacca Lives on Endor, You Must Acquit"

At times, checking to see if conclusions follow from premises and if premises are true can be very difficult. Some words have multilevel meanings. And some people will try to convince us of the truth of claims in order to deceive us, or sell us something, or get us to vote for them, or become part of their group, or share their ideology. Often, people will try to convince us that a conclusion follows from a premise or premises when, in fact, it does not, kind of like what the cartoon Cochran does with the Chewbacca defense in the episode, "Chef Aid," a satire of Cochran's actual closing arguments in the O.J. Simpson case.

In the episode, Alanis Morissette comes out with a hit song "Stinky Britches," which, it turns out, Chef had written some 20 years ago. Chef produces a tape of himself performing the song, and takes the record company to court, asking only that he be credited for writing the hit. The record company executives then hire Cochran. In his defense of the record company, Cochran shows the jury a picture of Chewbacca and claims that, because Chewbacca is from Kashyyyk and lives on Endor with the Ewoks, "It does not make sense." Cochran continues: "Why would a Wookie, an eight-foot-tall Wookie, want to live on Endor with a bunch of two-foot-tall Ewoks? That does not make sense . . . If Chewbacca lives on Endor, you must acquit! The defense rests." The jury is so convinced by Cochran's "argument," that not only do they apparently deny Chef's request for credit recognition but they also find Chef guilty of harassing a major record label, fining him $2 million to be paid within 24 hours. Friends of Chef then organize "Chef Aid" to pay his fine.

We laugh at Cochran's defense because it has absolutely nothing to do with the actual case. We laugh all the more at the absurdity when the Chewbacca defense is also used to find Chef guilty of harassing the very record company that had produced a stolen song. The issue of Chewbacca living on Endor has absolutely nothing to do with, and is in no way logically related to, the issues of whether Chef should receive credit for the song, or whether he has harassed the record company. As rational thinkers, we recognize this, laugh at the absurdities, and wonder why anyone in their right mind would be convinced that the Chewbacca defense and the other issues are related.

As we have seen in Section 2.1, logicians have a special term for these bad arguments in which the conclusion does not follow from a premise. They call it a *fallacy*, and a fallacy occurs when we inappropriately or incorrectly draw a conclusion from reasons that do not support the conclusion. Fallacies are so common that logicians have names for different types of fallacies.

The Chewbacca defense is an example of a *red herring* fallacy, which gets its name from a police dog exercise in which police officers, while trying to discern the best trail hunters, use strong-smelling red herring fishes in an attempt to throw dogs off the trail of a scent. In a red-herring fallacy, someone uses claims and arguments that have nothing to do with the issue at hand in order to get someone to draw a conclusion that they believe to be true. So, the claims and arguments are the "red herrings" they use to throw you off the "trail" of reasoning that would lead to another, probably more appropriate, conclusion altogether. In the episode "Weight Gain 4000," Wendy seems to have a legitimate complaint that Cartman cheated to win the essay contest, but people refuse to draw that conclusion given that they are diverted by the idea of Kathy Lee Gifford coming to town. Even after Wendy produces the evidence that Cartman had really handed in a copy of *Walden* as his essay, they simply do not care about drawing the conclusion that Cartman had cheated. In a lot of *South Park* episodes, people are thrown off the track of issues or arguments by other circumstances or events that capture their attention. This is a humorous way for Trey and Matt to make their points about people's faulty and crazy reasoning.

Slippery Slopes

The *slippery slope* is another fallacy often lampooned on *South Park*. This fallacy occurs when one inappropriately concludes that some further chain of events, ideas, or beliefs will follow from some initial event, idea, or belief and thus we should reject the initial event, idea, or belief. It is as if there is an unavoidable "slippery" slope that one is on, and there is no way to avoid sliding down it. Mrs. Broflovski's reasoning about the *Terrance and Phillip Show* being taken off the air might go something like this: "If we allow a show like the *Terence and Phillip Show* on the air, then it will corrupt my kid, then it will corrupt your kid, then it will corrupt all of our kids, then shows like this one will crop up all over the TV, then more and more kids will be corrupted, then all of TV will be corrupted, then the corrupt TV producers will corrupt other areas of our life, etc., etc., etc. So, we must take the *Terrance and Phillip Show* off the air; otherwise, it will lead to all of these other corruptions!" If I have accurately characterized Mrs. Broflovski's reasoning here, then we can see the slippery slope. It does not follow that the corrupt TV producers will corrupt other areas of our life. All of a sudden we're at the bottom of the slope! What just happened!

In "Clubhouses," Mrs. Marsh uses a kind of slippery-slope fallacy in combination with a hasty generalization in response to Stan's grabbing a cookie. Here, we can see the obvious humor involved, as she is going through a rough separation time with her husband: "You men are all alike. First you get a cookie and then you criticize the way I dress, and then it's the way I cook! Next you'll be telling me that you need your space, and that I'm sabotaging your creativity! Go ahead Stanley, get your damn cookie!" Her conclusion is obviously that Stan should not grab a cookie because, otherwise, all of these other things will happen. Further, the "you men are all alike" comment is the result of a hasty generalization.

A *false dilemma* is the fallacy of concluding something based upon premises that include only *two* options, when, in fact, there are three or more options. People are inclined to an "all-or-nothing" approach to matters, and this usually is reflective of a false dilemma in their thinking. In some situation, could it be that we have a little bit of both, so that we get a both-and, rather than an either-or as our conclusion? In "Mr. Hankey, The Christmas Poo," the people of *South Park* have an all-or-nothing kind of thinking when they conclude that the only way not to offend anyone is to rid the Christmas show of any and all Christmas references. This kind of logic has disastrous consequences, as the show is ruined and people wind up fighting over it. Could they have *included* a few other religious traditions, instead of *excluding* all of them? Now the both-and strategy, which can avoid a false dilemma, might not always have the best consequences. Consider "Chef Goes Nanners," where, in the end, even though a both-and solution is reached and supposed "ethnic diversity" is added to the South Park flag, it is obviously questionable whether such an addition is good, let alone right, for the townsfolk.

An *argument from inappropriate authority* is a fallacy that sounds like what it is, incorrectly drawing a conclusion from premises based upon a non-credible, non-qualified, or illegitimate authority figure. The best way to avoid this fallacy altogether is to become an authority concerning some matter yourself by getting all of the relevant facts, understanding issues, doing research, checking and double-checking your sources, dialoguing with people, having your ideas challenged, defending your position, being open to revise your position, and the like. However, since we can't become authorities on everything, we need to rely upon others. In "Do the Handicapped Go to Hell?" Fr. Maxi claims that Kyle (who is Jewish) and Timmy (who is limited in his verbal communication) will both go to hell if they don't confess their sins and, apparently, accept Christ as their savior. At first glance, the boys' conclusion that Kyle and Timmy will go to hell if they don't confess and convert seems not to be a case of the fallacy of appeal to inappropriate authority. After all, Fr. Maxi is an authority of the Church. However, if one investigates Church doctrine, one can see that no human being – pope, priest, or layperson – can make pronouncements about who will go to hell or who won't go to hell.

In an *ad hominem* fallacy someone concludes that a person's claims or arguments are false or not worth listening to because of premises that concern an attack on the actions, personality, or ideology of the person putting forward the claim or argument. In other words, instead of focusing on the person's issue, claims, or argument, one attacks the person (*ad hominem* is Latin for *to the man*). This strategy of discrediting a person's argument by discrediting the person is common. But notice, the person and the person's arguments are two distinct things, and they are not logically related to one another. For example, in "Butt Out" a cartoon Rob Reiner puts forward an argument for why kids in South Park should not smoke, and he goes on a campaign to get a law enacted to ban smoking in the town. However, not only is he portrayed as having a junk food vice but he also wants to deceptively use the boys to get the law passed. Now, even if Reiner does have a junk food problem, and even if he does something immoral in trying to get the boys to help him, what does this have to do with the arguments concerning whether kids should smoke or whether laws against smoking should be passed in South Park? The answer is, absolutely nothing! Yet, we could be led to the conclusion that no law should be set up in South Park against smoking based upon premises that portray Reiner's apparent hypocrisy and deviance. Again, Reiner's hypocrisy and deviance have nothing to do with the arguments for or against smoking.

"The Defense Rests"

At least part of the appeal of *South Park* has to do with pointing out the flaws in our thinking, and no one is free from blame. We all occasionally forget to check if all of our premises are true, or believe that a conclusion follows from premises when it doesn't. But the biggest logical problem we have has to do with our staunchly held emotional beliefs, the ones that we just can't let go of no matter what evidence and arguments are presented to us. Often times, this logical problem turns into a factual problem, and people suffer as a result. Some people are almost phobic in their fear of letting go of some belief.

In "All About the Mormons," Stan yells at the Mormons for believing in their religion without any proof, and they smile and explain that it is a matter of faith. Without insulting the Mormons, or any religion for that matter, in that moment Stan is hinting at part of what a rational, adult critical thinker should constantly do. As you read the chapters in this book, I ask you to be mindful of claims, arguments, deductive arguments versus inductive arguments, good versus bad arguments, and fallacies that are spoken about by the authors. And, hopefully, the authors have avoided fallacies and bad arguments in putting forward their own positions! With this logic lesson in mind, you can be the judge of that.

For pop culture resources and philosophical resources related to this chapter please visit the website for this book: https://introducingphilosophythroughpopculture.com.

Note

1 For more extensive discussions of logic, see Watson, J.C. and Arp, R. (2015). *Critical Thinking: An Introduction to Reasoning Well*, 2e. London: Bloomsbury; Bassham, G., Irwin, W., Nardone, H., and Wallace, J.M. (2018). *Critical Thinking: A Student's Introduction*, 6e. New York: McGraw-Hill; Hurley, P.J. and Watson, L. (2017). *A Concise Introduction to Logic*, 13e. New York: Cengage.

3

Wikiality, Truthiness, and Gut Thinking
Doing Philosophy Colbert Style

David Kyle Johnson

Summary

When Stephen Colbert hosted *The Colbert Report* on Comedy Central, everyone thought he was playing a character. He even admitted as much when he began hosting *The Late Show* on CBS. But how can we know for sure? After all, when Jordan Klepper started hosting *The Opposition*, everyone thought he was playing a conservative "Alex Jones" type character, but then Jordan said that he wasn't. Instead it was his liberal persona on *The Daily Show* that was the character. Indeed, Alex Jones's lawyers have argued, in court, that he's playing a character on his show. So who can tell? It turns out, the philosopher can. By using philosophy, and a little something called the principle of charity, we can examine what Stephen Colbert said on *The Colbert Report* and determine that he must have been playing a character. The ideas he espoused – like relativism, truthiness, gut thinking, and an unrestricted right to one's opinion – are so clearly absurd, he must be kidding. And in revealing this, we will be learning how to do philosophy.

Every night on my show, The Colbert Report, I speak straight from the gut . . . I give people the truth, unfiltered by rational argument.

> – Stephen Colbert
> White House Correspondents Dinner
> April 29, 2006

Stephen Colbert became the host of CBS's *The Late Show* in 2015, but his previous gig (2005–2014) was hosting *The Colbert Report* on Comedy Central. (Pronounce that "Cole-bear Re-pore," so that both "t"s are silent.) He was kind of a hard nut to crack in those days. Colbert is an Irish Catholic born in Washington D.C. and raised as the

Introducing Philosophy Through Pop Culture: From Socrates to Star Wars *and Beyond*, Second Edition.
Edited by William Irwin and David Kyle Johnson.
© 2022 John Wiley & Sons Ltd. Published 2022 by John Wiley & Sons Ltd.

youngest of 11 children in South Carolina. On *The Colbert Report* he (supposedly) played a character – an Irish Catholic born in Washington D.C. and raised as the youngest of 11 children in South Carolina. You read that right. The descriptions are exactly the same.

Now you might think this means that he wasn't really playing a character, but there is one major difference between the Colbert that hosts *The Late Show*, and the Colbert that hosted *The Colbert Report*: their political views. For example, while Late-Show-Colbert spent most of his monologues during the Trump presidency trashing Trump and the Republicans, Report-Colbert endlessly spouted right-wing talking points and defended politically conservative ideologies. For example, in an interview about global warming, Colbert asked CNN News Anchor Anderson Cooper "What's wrong with the ice melting . . . maybe now Greenland will actually turn green."[1] And in doing so, he was not repeating but actually anticipating something that would eventually be said by right-wing radio talk show host Rush Limbaugh.[2]

Now, again, conventional wisdom holds that Report-Colbert was a character, and that when he began hosting *The Late Show*, he revealed his true self. Indeed, Report-Colbert occasionally appears as a character on *The Late Show*. *The Colbert Report* was satire, the theory goes – a satire of conservative "talking head" shows that you could find on FOX News at the time, like Bill O'Reilly's *The O'Reilly Factor*. But Colbert delivered his lines in such a "dead-pan style" that it was difficult for those unfamiliar with Colbert to realize he was joking. Studies – real, honest to God, studies – showed that most conservatives seeing Colbert for the first time thought that he was completely serious and defending the conservative positions he was stating.

Of course, those same studies also showed that liberals seeing Colbert for the first time were apt to think that he agreed with them and was mocking conservatives. So they really just reveal the human propensity to see what we want.[3] But that raises an interesting question. If there is a human propensity to just see what we want in Colbert, how can anyone know that they are reading Colbert correctly? Was Report-Colbert really kidding? Or could he have been serious? Maybe it's Late-Show-Colbert that is the character.

"But," you might argue, "Colbert said that he was just playing a character on *The Colbert Report*, once he started hosting *The Late Show*."[4] Indeed he did.[5] But that's exactly what Jordan Klepper said when he started hosting *The Opposition* (one of the many shows that tried to replace *The Colbert Report* on Comedy Central). Klepper said he was only playing a character on *The Daily Show*. "This is the real me," he said on the first episode of *The Opposition*.[6] And yet, everyone knew he was playing a character![7] Indeed, *The Opposition* was an admitted satire of Alex Jones's *Info Wars*.[8] And to make matters worse, not only did Alex Jones's lawyer argue, in court, that Jones is just playing a character on *Info Wars*,[9] but few who listen to *Info Wars* think that he is playing a character – and those that do, only think so because they think that *all news* pundits are playing a character.[10] As Klepper put it (even *before* Jones's lawyer said Jones was playing a character):

> If you see me in an interview, or a deposition, say that I'm playing a character, that's because in that moment, I'm simply playing a character who, to throw them off the scent, would say that he's playing a character. Because, the truth is, "I'm not playing a character, except when I am."[11]

How the hell can *anyone* tell who's playing a character and who's not?

Well, this is where philosophy, and a little thing called "the principle of charity," comes in handy. According to this principle, when it is unclear what someone means, we should always choose the most charitable interpretation – for example, the one that makes them look least dimwitted. Such interpretations are usually right because, usually, people aren't that stupid. So what I would like to do this chapter is use this principle to argue that Report-Colbert had to have been a character. *The Colbert Report* was satire. Colbert had to be kidding. Why? Because if he really meant most of the things he said on that show, Stephen Colbert would be idiotic beyond all comprehension. "Wrong!" Colbert said after scientists unveiled a 47-million-year-old "missing link" fossil.[12] "The Earth is 6000 years old. Always has been, always will be."[13] He cannot be serious because, not only is the idea that the Earth is 6000 years old contrary to all relevant modern scientific findings, but the idea that the Earth does not age – that it has *always* been 6000 years old – is absurd.

Now to those who, like me, have watched Colbert for years, this might seem like a waste of time. We all know that *The Colbert Report* was satire (and thus that Late-Show-Colbert is the real McCoy). "It's obvious." But the argument I am about to lay out, which exposes just how ludicrous Report-Colbert was, will teach some of the most fundamental and important lessons about how to do philosophy.

My Truth (Individual Relativism)

[My book is] not just some collection of reasoned arguments supported by facts. That is the coward's way out. This book is Truth. My Truth.

– Stephen Colbert
From the introduction to *I Am America (And So Can You!)*[14]

His use of the phrase "My Truth" was the first clue that Colbert was kidding. He was suggesting that, somehow, truth belongs to him and can be solely determined by him. In doing so, Colbert was espousing a naive "individual relativism." In general, relativism says that there are no truths in a universal sense; truth is relative. More specifically, individual relativism says that truth is relative to individuals. But to understand what this means, and why the real Colbert cannot possibly be an individual relativist, some questions need answering.

If truth is relative, what is truth? Truth is a property of beliefs and propositions. ("Proposition" is a term the wordinistas came up with because "sentence" wasn't good enough.) A belief or proposition is true if it corresponds to the way the world is; it is false if it does not. Philosophers call this "the correspondence theory of truth." The part of the world that a true belief or proposition corresponds to is called that proposition's "truthmaker" – it is the part of the world that makes that proposition or belief true.

What does it mean for a truth to be relative? This is a question best answered by example. "You should drive on the right side of the road." This truth is relative to culture; it is true in the United States but false in the United Kingdom. There is no universal truth about what side of the road you should drive on – it's a matter of convention. The truth of "Baconnaise tastes great" is relative to individuals. One person thinks it's true, and another thinks it's false, but neither one is right or wrong because there is no universal fact of the matter about it. Or consider whether Colbert's *The Late Show* is funny. You think he's hilarious; your mother does not get it: but neither of you is wrong or right (but, between you and me, your mom is wrong).[15]

The individual relativist thinks all truths are like this, but obviously this cannot be the case. For example, whether or not you exist is not a matter of convention or taste. If someone believes that you do not exist, it is not "true for them." Your existence is a matter of fact. They might believe you do not exist, sure, but their belief is false. In addition, individual relativism in this form is self-contradictory. It says there are no universal truths. But is not the individual relativist trying to establish that individual relativism is universally true? How can it be universally true that there are no universal truths? And, since something is true if it corresponds to the way the world is, if there were no universal truths there would be no world. The only way *everything* can be relative is if nothing exists to make any proposition universally true. And that's crazy!

Some individual relativists do not think everything is relative, just some things. For example, some people think only moral truths are relative to individuals. Is abortion immoral? The individual relativist would say that, for people who believe abortion is wrong, it *is wrong* – "wrong for them." But for people who do not think abortion is wrong, it *is right* – "right for them." Because moral questions, like the abortion question, are often very hard to answer, this is a very tempting line to take. Whatever each person thinks is the right answer, is the right answer for that person.

But individual relativism has harrowing consequences if true. If individual relativism was true, being racist or white supremist would be the morally acceptable attitude for a neo-Nazi, Proud Boy, or Oath Keeper to take. Killing people and eating them would be morally acceptable for Jeffery Dahmer. That such things are morally acceptable would be "true for them." I think it safe to assume, not very many people are going to agree. Disagreements from racists and the cannibals cannot make racism and murderous cannibalism right.

So Report-Colbert cannot have really believed that his book, *I Am America (And So Can You!)*, was "his Truth." It might be a collection of opinions he thought were true, but that does not make those opinions "Truth."

Wikiality (Cultural Relativism)

I love Wikipedia. Any site that's got a longer entry on Truthiness than on Lutherans has its priorities straight . . . any user can change any entry, and if enough other users agree with him it becomes true . . . If only the entire body of human knowledge worked this way. And it can, thanks to tonight's word: wikiality . . . We should apply these principles to all information. All we need to do is convince a majority of people that some factoid is true . . . what we're doing is bringing democracy to knowledge.

– Stephen Colbert
The Colbert Report, July 31, 2006

Wikipedia no longer operates like it did in 2006. Not everyone can edit it, those who do are vetted, and additions and changes are carefully sourced and fact-checked. As online encyclopedias go, it's fairly reliable and useful–especially as a starting point for research. But in 2006, not so much; that's why Colbert coined the term to describe the "reality" created by majority consensus. Report-Colbert told us that if someone writes something on Wikipedia and enough people believe it, it "becomes true." With *Wikiality*, Colbert espoused a naive "cultural relativism." The cultural relativist, like the individual relativist, says that truth is relative. However, the cultural relativist says truth is relative to whole cultures, rather than to individuals. In the moral realm, the cultural relativist says that the majority consensus on morality in a culture defines morality for that culture. For example, if the majority of the people in a culture agree that abortion is moral, then abortion is moral *for the members of that culture.*

Cultural relativism is tempting because it appears to resolve cultural conflicts. In America, most people marry for love. However, for most of human history, marriage was socially motivated and arranged by family. Until recently, for example, nearly all Hindu marriages were arranged by the parents of the couple. As Colbert himself said, "They [don't] fall in love, they [learn] to love. It's a wonderful system."[16] Unlike Colbert, most Americans would think it morally wrong for Indian parents to determine their child's marriage partner. But the cultural moral relativist would say that it is "true for them" that arranged marriage is morally right since it is the custom of the majority in their culture. And this seems to have some intuitive appeal, because there does not seem to be a universal "right answer" to the question, "What is the correct motivation for marriage?"[17] It also would seem to promote tolerance between cultures.

Indeed, it seems that the morality of some things *is* relative to culture. For example, in many places in Europe, men and women share the same public toilet facilities. And (transgender issues aside) it would be morally wrong of a European, who was used to this practice, to use the opposites sex's bathroom in America (as long as s/he was aware of the American custom.) But it cannot be that the answers to all moral questions are relative to culture. Consider female circumcision – where the clitoris of a nine-year-old girl is cut off without anesthetic and her vagina is sewn shut. Since this practice is culturally accepted in many parts of Africa, cultural relativism would say it's morally acceptable in those parts of Africa. But clearly most people will disagree and appeal to moral facts that transcend culture to insist that female circumcision is always wrong, regardless of what culture it occurs in.

Contrary to its aims, cultural moral relativism can actually promote intolerance between cultures. For example, during the Third Reich in Germany, the oppression of Jews was accepted as moral by the majority. Thus, according to cultural moral relativism, the intolerance of the Nazi party was morally justified. Of course, you probably do not agree . . . despite what Colbert's "child-safe Nazi" video might have made some think,[18] and the fact that *Valkyrie* taught us that there were "some good Nazis."[19] Thus, cultural moral relativism is hard to swallow.[20]

The follies of cultural moral relativism do not stop there, however. Consider the United States when it was founded. Slavery was a culturally accepted practice. According to cultural relativists, that means that (at that time), in the United States, slavery was not morally wrong. And they are not just saying that it was not *seen* as morally wrong; that's obvious, since the majority accepted it. More dramatically, the cultural relativist would say that slavery actually *was* morally acceptable. Not only is this contrary to intuition – slavery was wrong even before we figured out it was wrong – but it means that the abolition of slavery was not a real step forward in moral progress for the nation. To progress morally, one must stop doing something wrong and start doing something right. According to the cultural moral relativist, however, when America abolished slavery it went from doing something right (majority approved slavery) to something else right (majority approved abolition). It did not progress morally; it just changed its definition of what was moral. *Obviously* most will think this absurd because *obviously* most think slavery was wrong and that we *obviously* made moral progress as a nation by abolishing it. If we had not, Colbert would not have sung Honest Abe – our greatest non-Reagan president – "Happy Birthday" on his 200th.[21]

So, the principle of charity demands we conclude that Colbert is not a cultural relativist. He does not really think that the entire body of human knowledge works like Wikipedia used to. He does not really think that "[t]ogether we can create a reality that we can all agree on – the reality we just agreed on."[22] Wikialty is just one of his "WØRDs."[23]

Truthiness (Intuitionism)

like our Founding Fathers, I hold my Truths to be self-evident, which is why I did absolutely no research. I didn't need to. The only research I needed was a long hard look in the mirror.

– Stephen Colbert
From the introduction of *I Am America (And So Can You!)*

[They] cannot be mistaken in what they feel. [This is how] they support themselves and are sure reason hath nothing to do with what they see and feel in themselves: what they have a sensible experience of admits no doubt, needs no probation . . . It is its own proof and can have no other.

– John Locke
An Essay Concerning Human Understanding[24]

Speaking of WØRDs, on his very first show, Colbert coined a new word in his segment "THE WØRD." That word, of course, was "Truthiness."[25] Thanks to our humble correspondent, "truthiness" is now an official English word; in fact it was Merriam-Webster's Word of the Year in 2006.[26] Something has truthiness if your gut tells you it's true. To *think with the gut* is to accept something's truthiness as evidence that, in fact, it is true. On his show, Colbert constantly professed to be a gut thinker. But we know he cannot have been serious because gut thinking is ridiculous.

Locke (1632–1704) called gut thinkers, "enthusiastic." The problem with gut thinking is that it provides insufficient evidence. People's intuitions vary widely and no one has reason to think their gut gets things right more often than anyone else's. Locke points out that gut thinkers are essentially arguing in a circle. "This is the way of talking of these men: they are sure because they are sure, and their persuasions are right only because they are strong in them."[27] In other words, they trust what comes from their gut because they think it gives them the truth, but they think it is true because it comes from their gut. This is like pulling yourself up by your own bootstraps – it does not work.

Locke argues that, if something is really true, it can stand up to rational inquiry and should be subjected to it. So one's gut should be tested. If it happens to get things right, it will be proven and then can be justifiably believed. If it gets things wrong, it should be abandoned. Locke points out that even the prophets of the Old Testament knew this, for when they received a revelation from God, they did not merely trust their gut instinct that it was God, but asked for signs to verify the revelation's source. For example, Gideon in *Judges 6* asks a voice to prevent a fleece from getting wet in the morning dew to verify that it is God's voice. God sometimes even provided the sign without asking, like with Moses and the burning bush. You may not be like Report-Colbert, who thought science should aim to make the world more like the Old Testament (by strapping rockets onto the Sun to make it orbit the Earth)[28] – but the lesson remains the same; gut feeling is not good enough to justify beliefs on its own.

Thinking from the gut should not be confused with "appealing to intuition." Philosophers will sometimes use their own intuition as a litmus test; if an argument or position is contrary to their intuition, then the argument or position is thought to be faulty. But the intuitions in these cases are almost universally accepted and thus are thought to point to facts. For example, a philosopher might argue, "Jimmy's (Colbert's director's) ethical theory can't be right because if it is, that would mean that it can be acceptable to torture babies just for fun – and that can't be right."

If the intuition is not as universally accepted as "baby torture = wrong," the philosopher will not think the theory is refuted, but merely point out the theory's cost. "Esteban Colberto's (Colbert's Cuban alter ego's) ethical theory implies that discrimination can be okay; so if you accept that theory you will have to abandon your intuition that discrimination is always wrong." (This might be said in a debate about affirmative action – which, of course, Colbert would never have taken part in since he said he was colorblind and literally unable to tell the difference between the colors black and white – although he did still discriminate against bears.) Philosophers will sometimes defend gut feelings with an argument. But good philosophers will never let their gut be the last word. If their argument fails and their gut is disproven, they reject what it says in favor of the truth.

In his bestseller *Blink*, Malcolm Gladwell argued that when it comes to recognizing danger and "reading people," our gut is actually more trustworthy than our intellect.[29] However, *Blink*'s thesis has been largely discredited,[30] and Colbert was suggesting that gut thinking can justify beliefs about issues as cerebral as politics and philosophy. So, Gladwell cannot be used to defend Colbert's suggestion.

I was surprised to discover, though, that some philosophers think that gut thinking can be acceptable, even in politics and philosophy. In "Truth, Truthiness, and Bullshit for the American Voter,"[31] Matthew Peirlott argues that, even when it comes to important political and philosophical issues, one can be allowed to think with one's gut to draw a conclusion. Regarding major political matters, there is a large amount of information one has to process and verify before one comes to a truly informed decision. Peirlott argues, because so many different people are giving us this information, and it's hard to determine "which facts are facts,"[32] we are allowed to choose who to listen to with our gut.

> It's not that we ignore facts; it's that we select which "facts" presented to us we will accept as facts . . . we follow our guts and trust the people whose hearts we think we know . . . When there are too many "facts" to be accessed, and the situation is too complicated for an individual to understand fully without dedicating his whole waking life to that issue, truthiness seems to be the only thing we have to go on.[33]

He does have a point about conflicting "facts" and the difficulty of determining the truth, but I do not think "I'll just trust my gut to tell me who to believe" is the correct response to this difficulty. If it was, the guy who only relies on *Fox and Friends* for his "facts" because he likes what his gut says about them would be justified in believing all the stories they report, including that beer pong causes herpes – a hoax news story they reported as genuine without checking it.[34] Instead, one should try to determine which facts to believe despite the difficulty. It may take a little time, but if the issue is important the time is worth it.

But what if one simply does not have the time to do the proper research, as Peirlott suggests? Regardless of why one has not done the research, if one has not done it, one should not pretend one has. Instead, one should admit that one does not know what facts to accept. A better response to the difficulty is agnosticism – the suspension of belief and admission of ignorance.[35] If you do not know, admit it.

By admitting our ignorance we emulate Socrates (469–399 BCE). The Oracle at Delphi said "no one is wiser" than Socrates, but not because he knew everything – it was because he was the only one to admit he knew nothing. Socrates spent his entire life trying to find someone who had knowledge – because he knew he lacked it – but only found supposed "experts" who professed to have knowledge, but in fact had none. Not only does Socrates give us a good belief-forming model, but he also gives us good reason not to trust who we would like to think are "experts" simply because our gut tells us to. Very often, those who claim to be experts aren't, and they do not know what they think they know.

Indeed, their expertise in one thing can make them think they are qualified to talk about something else, when it does not. Take Linus Pauling, for example, the famous Nobel Prize-winning chemist, who fathered the idea that Vitamin C can boosts your immune system. This idea is still around today, but its utterly false.[36] Pauling fooled even himself because he thought his knowledge of chemistry qualified him to draw a conclusion about the immune system. But chemistry is not immunology.

So, again, the principle of charity dictates that Report-Colbert cannot have been serious – the real Colbert cannot really be a gut thinker. But that is not the only way that Report-Colbert defended his positions.

A Right to Your Opinion

Now Folks, I'm no fan of reality [It Has a Liberal Bias] and I am no fan of encyclopedias [Just Fat-Ass Dictionaries]. I've said it before: "Who is Britannica to tell me George Washington had slaves?" If I want to say he didn't, that's my right.
                                                                        – Stephen Colbert
                                                          The Colbert Report, July 31, 2006

Suppose you are arguing with Report-Colbert about whether George Washington owned slaves. You present historical evidence and arguments that he did, but Colbert simply says, "Doesn't it feel like he wouldn't own slaves?" When you point out to Colbert that he is thinking with his gut, and explain why gut thinking is wrong, he will respond, "Well, I have a right to my opinion." This is a common thing for people to say, so maybe the real Colbert believes it. But do people really have a right to their opinion? Before answering, we need to figure out what people like Report-Colbert mean when they claim this alleged right.

Colbert might mean he has a legal right to his opinion. If this is what he means, he is correct. No one can haul him away for just thinking or speaking his opinion. But I doubt this is what he had in mind. Was he actually thinking you were about to call the cops to haul him off? No. Instead, Colbert might mean that he has an epistemic right to his opinion. "Epistemic" comes from "Epistemology," which is the study of knowledge and how knowledge is justified (obviously Colbert missed that day of philosophy class). A belief to which one has an epistemic right is a belief that is justified by rational defense and argument. But, given that we have already established he is just thinking with his gut, it's obvious that he has no rational defense or argument. Thus, he is mistaken if he thinks he has an epistemic right to his opinion.

What Colbert probably means is that he has a moral right to his opinion. Moral rights create moral duties in others.[37] For example, people's moral right to freedom gave Colbert the moral duty to free the Jews living under his desk on Birkat Hachama.[38] So, if Colbert has a moral right to his opinion, then you have a corresponding moral duty to treat that opinion in a certain way. What way? In *Crimes Against Logic*,[39] Jamie Whyte makes three suggestions.

Maybe Colbert thinks you have a moral duty to agree with his opinion. But if he has a right to his opinion, you have a right to yours, and that would mean that he is obligated to agree with you. Not only would Report-Colbert never agree with anyone but himself, but given that the two of you disagree, that does not make any sense.

So maybe he thinks you have a duty to listen to his opinion. He may want that, but that cannot be right either. Everyone has a right to his/her opinion if Colbert does, so we would be obligated to listen to everyone's opinion, and that is impossible. There is just not enough time. And we cannot be obligated to do the impossible. (Besides, Colbert would also have that duty and to "hear" everyone's opinion would require a lot of reading – and Report-Colbert was certainly no fan of reading.)

Given that Colbert is trying to end the discussion without changing his mind, what he probably means is that you have a duty to let him keep his opinion – you should stop arguing with him and looking stuff up in books and just let him think what he wants to think. He thinks he has a right to believe whatever he wants, and thus you have a duty to let him. But your possession of such a duty is far from obvious. Suppose Colbert is about to cross the street in Baghdad, to go to Saddam's Water Palace to do a week of shows in Iraq.[40] He believes there are no insurgents around, poised to shoot him, but his escort corrects him, points out the insurgence, and tells him to wait until they are dealt with. Does his escort violate Colbert's right by curing Colbert of his ignorance? Of course not. And Colbert would agree; he would rather not be shot. "If someone is interested in believing the truth, then she will not take the presentation of contrary evidence and argument as some kind of injury."[41]

This reveals what is at the heart of Report-Colbert's claim that he has a right to his opinion. He does not care about believing what is true, but only believing what he wants to believe. Your presentation of arguments and evidence is keeping him from doing this, and so he sees it as an injury and thinks you have a moral duty to stop.

But, even though Colbert does not care about truth and even though you are "injuring him" by keeping him from believing what is most comfortable, you still do not have a duty to let him keep his belief. If there is a duty to let people believe what is most comfortable, then the factanistas in the media violate our rights every time they tell us something we do not want to hear – like when they reported the NSA wiretapping and our secret European prisons. As Colbert pointed out at the White House Correspondents Dinner in 2006:

> Those things are secret for a very important reason: they're super-depressing. And if that's your goal, well, misery accomplished. Over the last five years you people were so good – over tax cuts, WMD intelligence, the effect of global warming. We Americans didn't want to know and you had the courtesy not to try to find out. Those were good times – as far as we knew.[42]

If we each had the duty to let everyone believe what they wanted and what was comforting, then educators – and particularly philosophers – would have the most immoral jobs on the planet. As Report-Colbert pointed out in his book, nothing endangers cherished beliefs like education and philosophy, and nothing hurts more than learning new ideas.

> Let me ask you this: Why were you happier when you were a kid? Because you didn't know anything. The more you know, the sadder you get. ***Don't believe me?*** By the time you finish reading this chapter, over a hundred dogs and cats in animal shelters around the nation will be euthanized. Bet you wish you could erase that knowledge. But it's too late. You learned a <u>New Idea</u>, and it made you sad . . . Look at the story of Adam and Eve. Their lives were pretty great – until they ate from the Tree of Knowledge . . . **God's point**: Ignorance isn't just bliss, it's paradise.[43]

We clearly do not have a right to opinions we cannot defend, especially if they are so clearly contrary to fact. Thus, the real Colbert cannot really think he has a right to believe, contrary to fact, that George Washington did not have slaves – or, for that matter, that the Panama Canal was finished in 1941 (instead of 1914).[44]

How to do Philosophy

If a tree falls in the forest and no one hears it, I hope it lands on a philosophy professor.
– Stephen Colbert
I Am America (And So Can You!)[45]

We've considered many examples of Report-Colbert saying things so profoundly stupid that we have to conclude that he was only kidding. But wait, is not he mocking conservative pundits, like Rush Limbaugh and Bill O'Reilly, by imitating them? We know Rush and Bill were not offering up satire (sadly, both were deadly serious about the moronic things they said). Neither was Sarah Palin when she said she had foreign policy experience because of Russia's proximity to her home state of Alaska, or Donald Trump when he said that climate change was a Chinese hoax, or used the phrase "for the 1/100th time" (when he meant *for the hundredth time*) when talking about Coronavirus testing. How do we know that Colbert is not doing the same thing?

Part of it is context – he was on Comedy Central after all. But another big reason is that Report-Colbert always took it just a bit further than Bill and those like him. Although Bill could benefit from taking one of my critical thinking classes, he would not endorse things as noticeably false as relativism and that the Earth never ages. And while we cannot be sure that Colbert wasn't lying when he "broke character" and said that was just playing a character, he really did seem to give away the game when he spoke out in an interview against the things I have condemned in this chapter: relativism, truthiness, right to opinion, and gut thinking.

> Truthiness is tearing apart our country . . . it does not seem to matter what facts are. It used to be, everyone was entitled to their own opinion, but not their own facts. But that's not the case anymore. Facts matter not at all. Perception is everything. It's certainty. People love . . . president [Bush] because he's certain of his choices as a leader, even if the facts that back him up do not seem to exist. It's the fact that he's certain that is very appealing to a certain section of the country. I really feel a dichotomy in the American populace. What is important? What you want to be true, or what *is* true?[46]

So, it seems, the real Stephen Colbert agrees. We do not want to be relativists, thinking that groups or individuals can determine what is true. We also do not want to be gut thinkers, believing our intuition can be enough justification for controversial beliefs. We should defend our positions against argument, and when we cannot defend them we should give them up. We want to have a concern for truth and try our best to find out what it true. And, when we realize that we do not have enough evidence to draw an informed conclusion about something, we should be agnostic – we should admit, like Socrates, that we simply do not know the answer – instead of hiding behind a call for "a right to our opinion."

All of these mistakes are tempting when doing philosophy because philosophical questions are so hard to answer. It's easy to give up, think there is no answer, and just appeal to the majority, your gut, or your right to believe whatever you want. But the fact that an answer is hard to find does not entail that the answer is not there. Philosophy does make progress – it just takes a while. By engaging in the philosophical endeavor, you are taking part in a very large and long process that answers the most important questions a person can ask. They will not all be answered in your lifetime, but you should be able to discover answers that you can at least defend with rational argument.

For pop culture resources and philosophical resources related to this chapter please visit the website for this book: https://introducingphilosophythroughpopculture.com.

Notes

1 *The Colbert Report*, October 18, 2007.
2 *The Rush Limbaugh Show*, www.rushlimbaugh.com.
3 LaMarre, H.L., Landreville, K.D., and Beam, M.A. (2009). The irony of satire: political ideology and the motivation to see what you want to see in *The Colbert Report*. *The International Journal of Press/Politics* 14: 212.
4 Wilstein, M. (2019). Stephen Colbert: I Could Never Play Right-Wing "Colbert Report" Character Under Trump. *Daily Beast*. https://www.thedailybeast.com/stephen-colbert-i-could-never-play-colbert-report-character-under-trump (November 8, 2019).
5 See Kurtz, H.. (2005). Tv's Newest Anchor: A Smirk in Progress. *Washington Post*. http://www.washingtonpost.com/wp-dyn/content/article/2005/10/09/AR2005100901551.html (October 10, 2005). See also Bierly, M.. (2006). Show Off. *Entertainment Weekly*. http://www.ew.com/ew/article/0,,677356,00.html. (July 22, 2006).
6 "*The Daily Show* . . . unwittingly paid 'Jordan Klepper' to be a mole against them. They had no idea I was playing them this whole time . . . I played them so hard. I learned their liberal ways, I donated to their liberal causes, I voted for their liberal candidates . . . 'This [pointing to a picture of himself in the same clothes] is not a character. This is the real me.'" *The Opposition*, September 25, 2017.
7 Bradley, L. (2017). Your First Look at Jordan Klepper's Alex Jones-Inspired Late-Night Show. *Vanity Fair*. https://www.vanityfair.com/hollywood/2017/08/jordan-klepper-comedy-central-show-trailer-the-opposition (August 23, 2017).
8 Bradley, "Your First Look at Jordan Klepper's Alex Jones-Inspired Late-Night Show."
9 Wilstein, M. (2019). Jordan Klepper Loved Watching Alex Jones Admit That He's 'Playing a Character. *Daily Beast*. https://www.thedailybeast.com/jordan-klepper-loved-watching-alex-jones-admit-that-hes-playing-a-character (May 29, 2019).
10 Tarrant, D. (2018). Why Do People Listen to Infowars' Alex Jones At All? We Asked Them. *The Dallas Morning News*. https://www.dallasnews.com/news/texas/2018/08/10/why-do-people-listen-to-infowars-alex-jones-at-all-we-asked-them (August 10, 2018).
11 *The Opposition*, September 25, 2017.
12 Strong, S. and Schapiro, R. (2009). Missing Link Found? Scientists Unveil Fossil of 47-Million-Year-Old Primate, Darwinius Masillae. *New York Daily News*. http://www.nydailynews.com/news/us_

world/2009/05/19/2009-05-19_missing_link_found_fossil_of_47_millionyearold_primate_sheds_light_on_.html (May 19, 2009).

13   *The Colbert Report*, May 21, 2009.
14   Colbert, S. (2007). *I Am America (And So Can You!)*. New York: Grand Central Publishing.
15   Of course, you can find philosophers who disagree about whether there are facts about the taste of Baconnaise and whether Colbert is funny. If they are right, my point is all the stronger – for even these things are not relative.
16   *The Colbert Report*, October 26, 2005.
17   In case you think there is a universal truth in this matter, keep in mind that "love marriages" end in divorce more often than "arranged marriages." Of course, this might be due to social pressures instead of marital bliss – such things are hard to tell. But that one kind of marriage is more moral than another is far from clear.
18   *The Colbert Report*, April 27, 2009.
19   *The Colbert Report*, May 27, 2008.
20   My examples here are all applying American moral intuitions to practices outside of its boarders. That is because I am writing to Americans. I do not mean to imply that American moral values are somehow superior to the rest of the world. We do plenty of things wrong. For example, my guess is, in the near future, the American banning of gay marriage will be used as an example of something that was clearly morally wrong despite the majority consensus.
21   *The Colbert Report*, February 12, 2009.
22   *The Colbert Report*, July 31, 2006.
23   To be fair, there are non-naive versions of relativism out there defended by very smart people – Gilbert Harman of Princeton, for one. For example, see Harman, G. (1975). Moral relativism defended. *The Philosophical Review* 84: 3–22.
24   Locke, J. (1978). *An Essay Concerning Human Understanding*, 291. New York: Dutton.
25   *The Colbert Report*, October 17, 2005.
26   CBS News. (2006). The Word of the Year: Truthiness. https://www.cbsnews.com/news/the-word-of-the-year-truthiness (December 6, 2006).
27   Locke, 291.
28   *The Colbert Report*, March 20, 2007.
29   Gladwell, M. (2005). *Blink*. New York: Little, Brown and Company.
30   See Abbott, A. (2015). Unconscious Thought Not So Smart After All. *Scientific American*. https://www.scientificamerican.com/article/unconscious-thought-not-so-smart-after-all1 (January 28, 2015). See also Clancy, K. and Kreig, P. (2007). *Your Gut is Still Not Smarter Than Your Head: How Disciplined, Fact-Based Marketing Can Drive Extraordinary Growth and Profits*. Hoboken: Wiley.
31   Peirlott, M. (2009). Truth, truthiness, and bullshit for the American voter. In: *Stephen Colbert and Philosophy* (ed. A. Schiller), 77–94. Chicago: Open Court.
32   Peirlott, 83.
33   Peirlott, 91.
34   Colbert called them out on this, *The Colbert Report*, March 3, 2009.
35   This is Ethan Mills' conclusion in (2009). Truthiness and the appearances. In: *Stephen Colbert and Philosophy* (ed. A. Schiller), 95–114. Open Court.
36   For a readable debunking of this myth, see Lanese, N. (2020). Why vitamin C won't "boost" your immune system against the coronavirus. *Live Science*. https://www.livescience.com/coronavirus-vitamin-c-myth.html (March 10, 2020).
37   Do moral rights always create moral duties? There are those who contest the issue. See Feinberg, J. (1973). *Social Philosophy*, 61–64. Englewood Cliffs, NJ: Prentice-Hall, Inc..
38   *The Colbert Report*, April 8, 2009.
39   Whyte, J. (2004). *Crimes Against Logic*, 1 10. New York: McGraw-Hill.
40   Which he did in *The Colbert Report*, June 8–11, 2009.
41   Whyte, 9.
42   Colbert, S. (2006). White House Correspondents Dinner. (29 April 2006).
43   Colbert (2007), 120, 122.
44   *The Colbert Report*, October 17, 2005.
45   Colbert (2007), 126.
46   Rabin, N. (2006). [An Interview with] Stephen Colbert. *A.V. Club*. http://www.avclub.com/articles/stephen-colbert,13970 (January 25, 2006).

Part II

Epistemology

Introduction

Epistemology is the study of knowledge. Is it even possible to acquire knowledge? If so, how does one acquire it? How should one acquire it? If knowledge really is justified, true belief – which has been contested – what is truth anyway? These are the questions an epistemologist asks.

In Chapter 4, Henry Jacoby takes us to *South Park* to teach us about the ethics of belief. Blaise Pascal (1623–1662) suggests that belief in God can be rational because, even though it lacks evidence, it is the better bet. In contrast, William Clifford (1845–1879) argues that it is always morally wrong to believe without evidence. Stan Marsh of South Park, Colorado agrees with William Clifford. Stan is critical of belief without (and contrary to) evidence, like Kyle's mom's beliefs in holistic healing, the Mormon belief that the first man and woman lived in Missouri, and John Edward's claims that he can communicate with the dead. Examples from *South Park* demonstrate the dangers of belief without evidence, such as blindly following David Blaine into a mass suicide, and a mental laziness that, Stan tells John Edward, is "slowing down the progress of all mankind."

In *The Matrix Trilogy*, it is revealed that the everyday world humans experience is actually a computer simulation designed to keep humans under control while an artificially intelligent civilization harvests our energy. In Chapter 5, Matt Lawrence uses the predicament in which humanity finds itself in *The Matrix* to explain what philosophers call "The Skeptical Problem" and Descartes's (1959–1650) solution to it. How can we be sure we're not being deceived on a grand scale like the prisoners of the Matrix?

In *Battlestar Galactica*, the 12 colonies are destroyed and humanity finds itself looking for a new home. Commander Adama claims he knows the location of the 13th colony – called Earth – when, in fact, he knows nothing of the kind. He simply told a lie to give

Introducing Philosophy Through Pop Culture: From Socrates to Star Wars *and Beyond*, Second Edition.
Edited by William Irwin and David Kyle Johnson.
© 2022 John Wiley & Sons Ltd. Published 2022 by John Wiley & Sons Ltd.

people hope. It turns out, however, that there actually is an Earth and humanity eventually finds its way there. In Chapter 6, Eric Silverman uses Adama's lie to explore the classic definition of knowledge and the contemporary philosopher Edmund Gettier's conclusion that mere justified, true belief is insufficient for knowledge. The chapter concludes with a discussion of what William Clifford (1845–1879) and William James (1842–1910) have to say about whether holding non-justified beliefs can be ethical.

In Chapter 7, Ruby Komic examines epistemic resources, the resources held by a community that an individual must draw upon to gain knowledge. Challenging racist stereotypes, *Black Panther* provides the viewer with epistemic resources in the form of conceptual tools to understand and communicate about Black, and particularly African American, culture and experience.

4

You Know, I Learned Something Today

Stan Marsh and the Ethics of Belief

Henry Jacoby

Summary

The nineteenth-century English mathematician and philosopher W.K. Clifford famously argued that it is always wrong to believe anything upon insufficient evidence, even if such beliefs provide comfort and hope. Such beliefs weaken the mind while preventing the search for truth and understanding. This chapter explores Clifford's view through *South Park*'s resident voice of reason, Stan Marsh, as he takes on the crazy and the credulous.

A wise man, therefore, proportions his belief to the evidence.

– David Hume

People believe all sorts of things for all sorts of reasons; sadly, few people pay attention to reasons based on logic, rules of argumentation, theory, or evidence. And the inhabitants of South Park are no different. But why should we think critically and rationally? Why does it matter? What harm is there in believing something if it makes you feel good, provides you with comfort, or gives you hope? If evidence is lacking, so what?

In his essay "The Ethics of Belief," William Kingdom Clifford (1845–1879), an English mathematician and philosopher, explained the potential harm of believing just anything. "Every time we let ourselves believe for unworthy reasons, we weaken our powers of self-control, of doubting, of judicially and fairly weighing evidence," he wrote, concluding that it's "wrong always, everywhere, and for anyone, to believe anything upon insufficient evidence."[1]

Amid the exaggerated craziness and illogic of the citizens of South Park, we're sometimes treated to flashes of insight and well-thought-out ideas that surprise us. Stan shows off his critical thinking skills as he takes on TV psychics, various cults, and unsupported religious beliefs in a way that would've made Clifford proud. In this chapter, we'll examine how Stan exposes the frauds and the harm they bring to people, while defending scientific thinking and a healthy skepticism.

Introducing Philosophy Through Pop Culture: From Socrates to Star Wars *and Beyond*, Second Edition.
Edited by William Irwin and David Kyle Johnson.
© 2022 John Wiley & Sons Ltd. Published 2022 by John Wiley & Sons Ltd.

Belief and Evidence

We acquire our beliefs in various ways. Some come from observation of the physical world, and this is usually our best evidence. The kids believe that Mr. Hankey exists because they see him, but what we see isn't always trustworthy. Cartman, after all, sees pink Christina Aguilera creatures floating around, but they aren't real. Often, our beliefs come on the authority or the testimony of others. The parents believe the children have ADD because that's the conclusion reached by school psychologists. Such a belief may sometimes be a reliable one, but not when it comes from the South Park testers, who are fools. Further, we must be careful when relying on authority figures. Maybe Scientologists believe that there were once frozen alien bodies put in the volcanoes in Hawaii because their leaders say so. But this is nonsense that should be rejected by any sane person.

We see, then, that rational belief requires evidence. The more outrageous the belief, the more evidence is required. As Stan told the Mormon family in "All About Mormons," "If you're going to say things that have been proven wrong, like the first man and woman lived in Missouri and Native Americans came from Jerusalem, then you better have something to back it up!" Stan is pointing out here that Mormon beliefs should be rejected unless they can be defended, since they're implausible in the face of accepted facts. The Mormons have *the burden of proof*, that is, the obligation is on them to provide the evidence to back up their claims.

Sadly, for most of the crazy claims made in *South Park*, that obligation is never met. But there are exceptions. In "Pandemic" one of the imprisoned members of a Peruvian flute band makes the seemingly preposterous assertion that their music (annoying though it may be) is the only thing keeping away "the furry death." We later learn that he is correct, as giant guinea pigs wreak havoc in the band's absence. Sometimes what seems absurd can be defended after all! But extraordinary evidence is required. So if you're going to suggest that an alien wizard is causing sexual addiction in some kids ("Sexual Healing"), or that the first pope was really a rabbit ("Fantastic Easter Special"), you'd better have compelling reasons.

Returning to "All About Mormons," two villagers are talking about Joseph Smith. One of them says, "He claims he spoke with God and Jesus." The other one asks, "Well how do you know he didn't?" Is this a fair question? Should unproven claims be accepted when it appears that they can't be disproved? No. A request to disprove something isn't a request that needs to be answered. This is because the burden of proof always lies with the person making the additional claim, not with those who doubt its truth. If this were not the case, then we would be required to entertain *any* belief, no matter how absurd. I can't disprove the existence of alien souls inhabiting our bodies, but that doesn't mean I should consider this Scientological claim to be likely. Or to take another example, when Cartman suggests ("Jewpacabra") that the Jewpacabra is real and coming for them, the leaders of Sooper Foods reluctantly cancel the Easter egg hunt since they can't prove that no such creature exists. Kyle has it right here, as he tells Cartman, "There's no reference of it anywhere on the known species webpage," and anyone who says otherwise "is either lying or stupid." We shouldn't fall into the "disproof" trap. If our beliefs can't be supported, then they should be rejected, or at least put aside until further evidence comes about.

But believing things without sufficient evidence hardly seems like a good way to lead a successful life. It's difficult to understand how making decisions without evaluating the available evidence would work in the long run. Imagine picking a college, a career, a place to live, a mechanic, a doctor, or anything, for that matter, without reasoning and examining the facts involved. Imagine going through your life merely guessing whenever a decision is to be made, or going by how you feel at the moment, or basing decisions on what's said by someone who may not be reliable.

Take as an illustration the time when Kyle became very ill and needed a kidney transplant ("Cherokee Hair Tampons"). Instead, his mother took him to the new "Holistic Healer" in town, Miss Information. At her shop, the townspeople lined up to buy all sorts of useless products. Her employees, introduced as Native Americans, must surely know all about healing! Fortunately for Kyle, these "Native Americans" (who turned out to be Cheech and Chong) were honest enough to convince Mrs. Broflovski that Kyle was really sick and should be taken to a real doctor. Stan, who realized from the start that the "healers" were frauds and their methods unscientific, had been urging this all along. He later tricks Cartman into giving up a kidney, so everything works out well for Kyle in the end. Often though, when we start with beliefs that have been uncritically accepted, the outcome isn't so fortunate. When the *South Park* version of the company BP (the one who caused the oil spill in the Gulf of Mexico), continued drilling without carefully examining the potential risks, they proceeded to create an even worse disaster by ripping a dimensional hole in space allowing the evil Cthulhu to cause great devastation ("Coon2: Hindsight").

What's at stake is not just having correct beliefs. As we've seen, having incorrect beliefs can have dire consequences. Notice too, how closely beliefs are tied to action. In "Trapped in The Closet," Stan tells Tom Cruise that he's not as good of an actor as Leonardo DiCaprio, Gene Hackman, or "the guy who played Napoleon Dynamite." This causes poor Tom to become depressed, and he locks himself in the closet. Now, why should a famous actor care what a little boy thinks of his acting skills? Well, he *would* care if he was a Scientologist and believed that that little boy is the reincarnation of Scientology founder L. Ron Hubbard. And Mr. Cruise believes *this*, because the current Scientology leaders told him. So his illogical actions are motivated by a ridiculous belief that's held, not on the basis of any testable evidence (well, they did test Stan's "body thetans" with their "E-Meters"—more unsupported nonsense), but solely on the basis of authority. And the "authority" here is hardly reliable or objective; in fact, later Cruise admits to Stan that it's all made up and he's doing it for the money.

Faith, Self-Interest, and Evidence

Many people say their beliefs – especially their religious beliefs – are based on faith. What does this mean? And is this connection a good idea? First, let's be clear what is meant by *faith* in this context. Sometimes faith means a kind of confidence. In "Scott Tenorman Must Die" Cartman was confident that his friends would betray him, and they did. This allowed his plan for revenge on Scott to work perfectly. Cartman, we might say, had faith that his plan would work.

Now this kind of faith isn't opposed to reason and evidence. Cartman reasoned that he could accurately predict what his friends would do based on their past actions. This is perfectly reasonable. If, on the other hand, Mr. Garrison had faith that his students would all work hard on their homework assignments, his confidence would be misplaced. He has no good reason to think so. So faith in the sense of being confident may be reasonable or not, depending on one's evidence.

Talking about religious faith, however, we don't mean confidence based on reason. This kind of faith is in fact *opposed* to reason; quite simply, it is belief without good evidence. After hearing the story of Joseph Smith, a story that Stan points out is unsupported and contrary to known facts, Stan says, "Wait: Mormons actually know this story, and they still believe Joseph Smith was a prophet?" The reply, of course, is "Stan, it's all a matter of faith." So, faith appears to be a kind of fallback position we can take when we can't support our views. But this shouldn't be encouraged, for it would render any belief whatsoever acceptable.

Does a belief have to be supported by evidence in order for it to be a rational belief? Can there be *reasons* that justify believing something besides just evidence? Let's make a distinction between *prudential* reasons and *evidential* reasons. The difference between them is easy to illustrate with an example. Suppose that I tell you that John Edward – the self-proclaimed psychic whom Stan puts in his place – really can communicate with the dead. Since you watch *South Park*, you know that John Edward is the "biggest douche in the universe," so you don't believe my claim for a second and you demand proof. Suppose I tell you that if you do believe it, I'll give you lots of money (I show you the full briefcase); but if you don't believe it, you get nothing. Now you have a reason to believe that John Edward is not a fraud, and it's a *good reason*. But you still don't have a shred of evidence. Your reason, instead, is prudential: it's in your best interest to believe.

Blaise Pascal (1623–1662), a French mathematician and philosopher, attempted to justify religious belief in exactly the same way. His argument has come to be known as "Pascal's Wager."[2] Pascal urges us to think of belief in God as a bet. If you wager on God existing (if you believe in Him) and God exists, you win. God rewards believers with eternal joy and happiness. But if you don't believe and God exists, then you lose. God punishes nonbelievers with eternal suffering and pain. What if God doesn't exist? Well, in that case the nonbeliever has the truth and the believer doesn't; but whatever positive or negative results emerge are negligible in comparison to what happens if there is a God. The point is, if you have *any chance at all* to achieve eternal peace and avoid eternal damnation, you're a fool not to go for it. Prudential reasons reign: it's in your best interest to believe in God.

Notice a few things about Pascal's Wager. First, he's not trying to prove that God exists. If we could prove that there is a God, then the Wager would be pointless (the same would be true if we could prove that there is no God). Pascal starts by assuming that we don't know either way. Second, Pascal isn't arguing that we should simply go on faith alone. He's instead arguing that religious belief is *reasonable* because it's prudential. Of course, there have also been many criticisms of the wager that show that it's not a very good argument for religious belief. Let's look at two of these, as they are nicely illustrated in *South Park*.

First, you might wonder why God would choose to torture someone for all eternity simply because they don't believe in Him. Isn't God supposed to be perfectly good? Why would a good being wish pain and suffering for anyone? In the episode "Cartmanland," Kyle wonders the same thing. Cartman inherits a million dollars and buys an amusement park, while Kyle suffers from hemorrhoid pain. Kyle begins to lose his faith as well as his will to live. If there were a God, he reasons, He wouldn't reward someone like Cartman (who's evil) while allowing Kyle (who's good) to suffer. Kyle says: "Cartman is the biggest asshole in the world. How is it that God gives him a million dollars? Why? How can you do this? There are people starving in Alabama, and you give Cartman a million dollars? If someone like Cartman can get his own theme park, then there is no God. There's no God, dude."

Kyle's parents, in an attempt to restore his faith, tell him that God sometimes causes us to suffer, perhaps to test our faith, and they read him the story of Job. (Incidentally, the idea of God testing us makes little sense. If he is all-knowing, he would already know what we would do, rendering any test pointless.) But the story horrifies Kyle: "That's the most horrible story I've ever heard. Why would God do such horrible things to a good person just to prove a point to Satan?" Kyle reasons here that if there really were a God, there would be justice in the world. God wouldn't reward someone like Cartman and neither would he allow people like Job and Kyle to suffer.

We can see how all of this applies to Pascal's Wager. Imagine someone who's a really good person – loving, honest, helpful, kind – yet she doesn't believe in God. She thinks she ought to be moral to make the world a better place, let's say, not because God says so or to get some personal reward. Does it really make sense to think that God (who is supposed to be supremely good, remember) would allow such a person to be tormented for all eternity?

A second – and much worse problem for Pascal's argument – is that he assumes that we *know* the possible outcomes of our wager. Pascal says that God rewards believers and punishes nonbelievers. But this is just an assumption. If we had proof of this, we would already know that the religious view of things is true, and we wouldn't need a prudential argument. Remember, the point of the Wager is to convince us to believe when we have no evidence of God's existence or nonexistence. Without evidence, there are lots of possibilities to consider. Perhaps God rewards everyone, or maybe there's no afterlife at all. Maybe God values reason and punishes those who believe blindly without any evidence. There are endless possibilities.

Even if we could show that only religious believers get rewarded (and how would we prove that without making the Wager pointless?), we still have the problem of *which* religious beliefs to have. In "Do the Handicapped Go to Hell?" we're treated to a bunch of religious folks who, to their horror, find themselves in hell. They are told that they have *the wrong religious beliefs*, since only the Mormons go to heaven!

What's the Harm, Dude?

Those who can make you believe absurdities can make you commit atrocities.

– Voltaire

Maybe Pascal's Wager doesn't show us that we *should* believe in God, but still, we might ask, what's the harm? Perhaps we should only have beliefs based on reasons, but what's wrong with prudential reasons? In "All About Mormons" Gary tells Stan, "Maybe us Mormons do believe in crazy stories that make absolutely no sense. And maybe Joseph Smith did make it all up. But I have a great life and a great family, and I have the Book of Mormon to thank for that. The truth is, I don't care if Joseph Smith made it all up." And in "The Biggest Douche in the Universe" John Edward tries to defend himself to Stan when he says, "What I do doesn't hurt anybody. I give people closure and help them cope with life." So, echoing Gary, Stan's Mormon friend, we could similarly say we don't care if Edward is a fraud, as long as what he does makes people feel good. Again, what's the harm?

But this is only part of the story. For one, as we've already seen, unsupported beliefs can lead to harmful consequences. In "Timmy 2000," the belief that Timmy has ADD (that he does not have learning disabilities) eventually causes a wild spread of unnecessary prescription drugs and, worse, a belief that the music of Phil Collins is actually good. In "Super Best Friends" some of the followers of magician David Blaine blindly follow him and commit suicide, believing they will go to heaven. In both of these cases, the believers feel good about their beliefs; they provide hope or comfort. But they're still extremely dangerous.

A second sort of harm here is mental weakness and laziness. As Clifford said, "Every time we let ourselves believe for unworthy reasons, we weaken our powers of self-control, of doubting, of judicially and fairly weighing evidence." His point is that even if a person's unsupported belief causes no immediate harm (as in the examples from *South Park*), it weakens the mind. Stan's dad even gives himself cancer so he can get medicinal marijuana ("Medicinal Fried Chicken"), and like him, we get used to accepting ideas uncritically, growing mentally lazy, and this encourages others to do the same. Just like Randy Marsh, most of the citizens of South Park rarely use their critical faculties. This makes them easy prey for every cult, fad, or con that comes to town. Think of just about any episode of *South Park*, and you'll find many examples of this mental weakness and laziness.

Inquiry, Hard Work, and Progress

To understand a final reason why uncritically accepting unsupported beliefs – however hopeful they might make us feel – is not such a good thing, we turn to Stan at his best. Again, from "The Biggest Douche in the Universe," John Edward challenges Stan: "Everything I tell people is positive and gives them hope; how does that make me a douche?" Stan's reply is brilliant: "Because the big questions in life are tough; why are we here, where are we from, where are we going? But if people believe in asshole douchy liars like you, we're never going to find the real answers to those questions. You aren't just lying, you're slowing down the progress of all mankind, you douche." He follows this up with another terrific speech, this time, to the members of Edward's believing audience:

> You see, I learned something today. At first I thought you were all just stupid listening to this douche's advice, but now I understand that you're all here because you're scared. You're scared of death and he offers you some kind of understanding. You all want to believe in it so much, I know you do. You find comfort in the thought that your loved ones are floating around trying to talk to you, but think about it: is that really what you want? To just be floating around after you die having to talk to this asshole? We need to recognize this stuff for what it is: magic tricks. Because whatever is really going on in life and in death is much more amazing than this douche.

We can all learn something today from what Stan has said here. First, he realizes it's wrong to dismiss someone with unsupported beliefs as being stupid. We want answers because we need comfort. Sometimes we rely more on emotion than reason to satisfy ourselves, but that doesn't mean we lack intelligence. We poke fun, we often ridicule; but, even in South Park, it's always better when we try to achieve some understanding.

Second, Stan reminds us of Clifford's point that settling for easy answers not only weakens the mind but also prevents us from finding real answers. In science, philosophy, and every rational pursuit where we require answers to questions, the spirit of inquiry – combined with hard work – is what leads to progress. Settling for magical answers that make us feel good only slows us down.

And speaking of magic, Stan reminds us finally that there's real magic, wonder, and beauty in the universe. As he says, whatever is really going on in life and in death is truly amazing. We don't want to miss it, dude.

For pop culture resources and philosophical resources related to this chapter please visit the website for this book: https://introducingphilosophythroughpopculture.com.

Notes

1 See Clifford, W.K. (1999). *The Ethics of Belief and Other Essays* (ed. T. Madigan). Amherst, NY: Prometheus Books. Epistemology is the area of philosophy concerned with justifying beliefs with evidence. Good introduction to epistemology texts include: Audi, R. (2003). *Epistemology: A Contemporary Introduction*. London: Routledge; Crumley, J. (1998). *Introduction to Epistemology*. Columbus, OH: McGraw-Hill.
2 See Pascal, B. (1910). *Pascal's Pensées* (trans. W.F. Trotter). New York: PF Collier. For interesting discussions of the pros and cons of The Wager, see: Rescher, N. (1985). *Pascal's Wager: A Study of Practical Reasoning in Philosophical Theology*. Notre Dame, IN: University of Notre Dame Press; Hájek, A. (2003). Waging war on Pascal's wager. *Philosophical Review* 112: 27–56.

5

Tumbling Down the Rabbit Hole
Knowledge, Reality, and the Pit of Skepticism

Matt Lawrence

Summary

In *The Matrix Trilogy*, humanity is enslaved, trapped inside a virtual reality called "The Matrix." Since the Matrix is indistinguishable from the real world, how can we know that the movie is fiction? How can we know that we are not trapped inside the Matrix ourselves? This chapter uses *The Matrix* to raise the skeptical problem – how can we have knowledge at all, if we cannot even know that the world exists? And does the modern philosopher Descartes present a working solution to the skeptical problem?

This is your last chance. After this there is no turning back.

– Morpheus[†1]

Before meeting Morpheus, Thomas Anderson was just a regular guy at a regular job trying to make ends meet. Sure, he led a sort of double life, spending much of his time behind a computer keyboard, hacking under the screen name "Neo," but even then he was not so different from the rest of us. Neo took *this* world to be the real world – just as we do. But as it turned out, he was wrong about so much. He thought that he was living at the end of the twentieth century, that he had hair, that the sun was shining, that he knew his parents, and that all of his acquaintances were actually human. Yet none of this was true. To put it bluntly, Neo had no idea what the world was really like. Neo's predicament illustrates the need to "question reality" – which is arguably the main philosophical message of the first *Matrix* film. *The Matrix* urged us not to take the world at face value, and it showed us how deceptive appearances can be. However, most people feel quite confident that we are not in the Matrix. They feel certain that *our* most basic beliefs are not mistaken. But what justifies this sense of confidence? After all, Neo's situation was, on the face of it, no different than ours. His world *seemed* just like our world. Should he have known that he was living in a dream? Despite the fact that he

Introducing Philosophy Through Pop Culture: From Socrates to Star Wars *and Beyond*, Second Edition.
Edited by William Irwin and David Kyle Johnson.
© 2022 John Wiley & Sons Ltd. Published 2022 by John Wiley & Sons Ltd.

is sometimes chided about his intelligence by the Oracle ("Not too bright though") and by Agent Smith ("I see that you are still using all the muscles but the one that matters most"), there were no tell-tale signs that Neo should have noticed in order to realize that his world was illusory. Without the help of Morpheus, I expect that he would never have known.

By taking the red pill, Neo encountered an age-old philosophical problem: How do you know what is real? Or, worse yet: Can you know what is real? This is called *the problem of skepticism*. A skeptic is a person who believes that we can never know what the world is really like because there is always the possibility that we could be radically mistaken about most of our beliefs, just as Neo was. Most people are not plagued by such skeptical doubts. Neo certainly wasn't. Prior to that red pill, he would never have supposed that his whole life was an illusion. Even when he saw it with his own eyes he had trouble believing it, and ended up puking his breakfast onto the floor. Nevertheless it is fair to say that for years Neo had been restless – plagued by a vague and amorphous feeling that something was not quite right with the world. Maybe you have had that feeling too. The question is: How seriously should you take it?

The Skeptical Dilemma: Cartesian Dreams and Demons

Wake up, Neo.

– Computer screen[†]

The seventeenth-century French philosopher, scientist, and mathematician René Descartes is famous for taking such skeptical worries seriously, so perhaps he can shed some light on Neo's situation. Descartes took on the project of trying to determine which of his beliefs could be maintained with absolute certainty. He employed what is famously known as his *method of doubt*. He began by discarding all of his beliefs and resolving to allow them back in, only if it could be shown that they were absolutely certain. Rather than try to prove that any of his beliefs were actually false, which can be quite difficult to do (imagine the work involved in trying to prove that sentient machines aren't secretly plotting a war against us at this very moment), he simply checked his beliefs to see if they admitted any room for doubt. If a belief could be doubted, Descartes withheld his assent from it. It may seem a bit crazy to throw out all of your beliefs at once, but Descartes was not suggesting that a person should live their entire life this way. Rather, he thought that since he had come to accept so many beliefs, most of which were adopted uncritically during his childhood, it would be smart to sift through them at least once in his life, in order to discover which of his beliefs were "rock solid."

Employing this method, Descartes reached some startling conclusions, which, hundreds of years later, provide the basic framework of the *Matrix* films. One of Descartes's first big conclusions was that there was absolutely no way to be sure that he wasn't dreaming at any given moment. In his *Meditations on First Philosophy* he wrote:

> How often, at night, I've been convinced that I was here, sitting before the fire, wearing my dressing gown, when in fact I was undressed and between the covers of my bed! . . . I see so plainly that there are no reliable signs by which I can distinguish sleeping from waking that I am stupefied – and my stupor itself suggests that I am asleep![2]

Is it possible that you might be dreaming right now? Some people do not buy it. They argue that there is a difference in "feel" between dreams and waking life.[3] Surely, they say, my experience at this moment is too crisp and vivid to be a dream. But while most of us have had fairly lucid dreams in which we realized that we were dreaming, you have probably also had the experience of being totally caught up in a dream, such that you had no idea that the events were not real. Can you be absolutely sure that this is not one of those times? There appears to be at least a slight possibility that this could be a dream.

Some people say they can prove that they are not dreaming. They attempt this by setting certain limits on dreams, for example, that they cannot be in-color, or that it is impossible to read in a dream. But most people do recall colors from their dreams. And I distinctly remember a dream in which I read – though I must admit that it took quite a bit of effort. Maybe you also recall reading in a dream. But whether you have or not is really beside the point, for there is simply no reason to believe that it is physically (or mentally) impossible to do so.

Skepticism Within the Matrix

Real is just another four-letter word.

– Cypher[ss]

Of course the *Matrix* films take the whole dream scenario to its logical limit. They ask you to consider whether your entire life might be a dream. As Morpheus puts it:

> Have you ever had a dream . . . that you were so sure was real? What if you were unable to wake from that dream? How would you know the difference between the dream world and the real world?

Is there any way to be sure that your whole life has not been a dream? I do not think that there is. Typically, we call some experiences "dreams" and others "reality" by contrasting them. Experiences that we call "real" are consistent and predictable. For example, people do not just get up and fly away in "real life" while they sometimes do in dreams. And it is not unusual for the experiences we have in dreams to jump around from one time and place to another, while those events we call "real" do not. But if your whole life has been a dream, then there is nothing to contrast these experiences with. In this case, the "dreams" that you recall each night are just dreams within the dream. And that contrast still holds. Even if your whole life has been a dream you could distinguish your nightly dreams from your "waking experiences" much of the time. But how do you know that you are not in Neo's predicament – that even your waking experiences are simply more dreams – just more predictable ones? Morpheus's suggestion seems correct. If you have never awakened from the dream to see what "real life" is actually like, you would have absolutely no way to discern that you are dreaming.

So the skeptical problem is not just a problem for Neo. It is also a problem for us. If there is no way to tell if your whole life has been a dream, then what makes you so sure that it is not? You too should feel "a bit like Alice, tumbling down the rabbit hole." I like to call this hole *the pit of skepticism*. A little philosophical analysis leads us to doubts about those things we typically take for granted, and the more we analyze, the more we come to doubt. As we try to claw our way out of the pit, it seems that we just dig ourselves deeper and deeper. And we are still falling.

As the *Matrix* films illustrate, there are even worse possibilities than simply living in a dream. Instead, your whole life could be an *intentional deception* – "a world pulled over your eyes to blind you from the truth." Surprisingly enough, Descartes explored this possibility as well. As he pushed his methodical doubt to its logical limits, he posited an evil demon, supremely powerful and cunning, who expends every effort to deceive him:

> I will say that sky, air, earth, color, shape, sound, and other external things are just dreamed illusions which the demon uses to ensnare my judgment. I will regard myself as not having hands, eyes, flesh, blood, and senses – but as having the false belief that I have all these things. [I]f I do not really have the ability to know the truth, I will at least withhold assent from what is false and from what a deceiver may try to put over on me, however powerful and cunning he may be.[4]

The computer-simulated dreamworld of *The Matrix Trilogy* is a technological version of Descartes's evil demon. In essence it represents the idea of a mind (the Architect) more powerful than our own that is intent on deceiving us whenever, and however, it sees fit. In fact, the premise of a computer-run deception is all the more troubling. Before *The Matrix*, people would often dismiss Descartes's evil demon as unrealistic. It is hard to get yourself too worked up about a supremely powerful demon possibly deceiving you if you have never in your life encountered a demon. (Though this may be a sign of just how cunning the demon really is.) But over the past few decades we have seen the emergence of virtual-reality programming. If our technology continues to progress, it seems likely that we will one day be able to stimulate the brain to "perceive" whatever we program it to perceive. So, the idea of a technological deception strikes most people today as much more plausible than a demon.

Such a deception could be the work of sentient machines, as it is in *The Matrix*, but there are other possibilities as well. For instance, your "real self" (in the year 2199) could have signed you up for a 20-year "historical hallucination" against the backdrop of the world as it was at the start of the twenty-first century. Perhaps you designed your adventure to begin on New Year's Eve of the year 2000, complete with a set of false memories about your twentieth-century childhood.[5] Or, maybe your friends and family committed you to this delusion after your mental collapse. "Real life" in the year 2199 may have been just too hard for you to bear.

How Deep Does the Rabbit Hole Go?

Feeling a Bit Like Alice?

– Morpheus[†]

Is there any limit to the extent that such a demon or programmer could deceive us? While certainly the machines were seriously messing with Neo's mind, it appears that they were not nearly as malicious as they might have been. They gave Neo many "privileges" within the deception. For instance:

Neo was not deceived about his body
Despite being deceived about his baldness, Neo wasn't radically deceived about his body. He wasn't programmed to think that he was of a different gender or race, or that he was only four feet tall. And interestingly enough, he was not made to think that he was a sentient machine.[6]

His personality was not distorted
Neo can be grateful that his personality was essentially the same both in and out of the Matrix. For instance, when in the Matrix he was not turned into a cowardly wimp by having feelings of fear pumped into his mind whenever he confronted a dangerous situation.

His memory was not tampered with
When something would happen within the Matrix Neo would remember it, and if he remembered it, then it most likely happened.[7]

Neo was not alone
Many people, thousands, or perhaps even millions, are plugged into the Matrix, providing Neo with plenty of company.

His decisions were not controlled
Neo makes his own choices – they are not "programmed" for him by the machines.

His reasoning ability was not obscured
Neo bases his decisions on reasons. He is able to make inferences about how his world works and use these inferences to achieve his goals.

In theory, there is no reason why the machines had to cut Neo any of these breaks. Imagine the following sort of case:

Neo's worst nightmare
The computers exterminate the entire human race with the exception of Neo. He is then plugged into the Matrix at the age of 25, and his brain is stimulated in such a way as to simulate his "birth." But his birth is not a human birth, rather, he sees himself on a production line as a computer whose sentience chip has just been "switched on." While he is surprised at this course of events, he cannot really question them, because all his memories of being human have been wiped away. His personality is now changed. His human desires for companionship, adventure, food, etc. have been replaced with an all-consuming desire to mop the *entire* factory floor. However, his brain is manipulated in such a way as to occasionally cause him to forget where he started, so that despite the fact that he has mopped every inch of the floor 1000 times over, he will never believe that he has completed his task.[8]

A Matrix-type deception could definitely be pursued to torturous limits. And while we cannot be sure that we are not in a Matrix ourselves, we can rest assured that we are not in *that* Matrix – at least not yet. What more is it possible to know? Is there anything positive that you can assert with absolute certainty? Morpheus seemed to think so. He claimed to offer "the Truth – and nothing more." But does Morpheus really know the *Truth*? According to Morpheus, the Truth is that Neo is a slave, but he can be freed from this captivity, and thereby experience the real world. The desert of the real is, of course, the charred remains of human civilization, with its dark, scorched sky, and the underground world of Zion and its hovercraft fleet. But does Morpheus really know that life in Zion is "real"? Can he be absolutely certain that he is free from the Matrix himself?

Of course, when we watch the Matrix story unfold on film, we are supposed to regard Morpheus as awake. In any scene in which Morpheus is on the Nebuchadnezzar or on Zion he *is* in the real world. And while he regularly enters the Matrix, he is not like the deceived masses of humanity, slumbering away in their cocoons. Despite the fact that his eyes are closed when he jacks in, he remains fully awake to the fact that the world of the Matrix is just a high-tech illusion. He knows that his muscles have no effect on what he can do *in this place*.[9] But what I am suggesting now, is that we think beyond the limits of this particular story. If there are more possibilities to Morpheus's reality than we are explicitly shown in the film, can he really be absolutely certain that he is awake? I contend that he cannot. Morpheus is trapped in the pit of skepticism just like the rest of us.

Consider this "alternative reality," which is consistent with the central ideas of the *Matrix* trilogy, but which is not part of the story depicted in the films:

The Matrix within the Matrix

A program monitors all the humans who are plugged into the Matrix. It mainly looks for hackers – people like Morpheus, Trinity, and Neo, who are obsessed with tearing down computerized systems of control. These people generally tend to be the ones who are fighting against the dreamworld provided to them. These humans know, however vaguely, that there is something not quite right with the world. This feeling nags at them – like a splinter in their minds. The machines realize that such people are on the verge of waking up, and therefore, they take precautions against it by giving the hackers a new type of dream – a different Matrix. They switch them over to a dream of being awakened. This causes these restless souls to become more accepting of their experiences – more accepting of the dream. And better still, the machines provide these people with the illusion of fighting to free all of humanity from a world of computer control. This dream totally captivates them, causing them to sleep soundly for the rest of their lives.

Morpheus cannot rule out this sort of scenario. All he can say is that his experiences in Zion and on the Nebuchadnezzar do not *feel* like a dream, and that the belief that he has "really awakened" is consistent with all of his experiences. But notice that the same was true for Neo before he took the red pill. His experience felt real, and, until he found himself naked inside that slimy cocoon, it made perfect sense for him to believe that he had been experiencing the real world all of his life.

So the pit of skepticism certainly goes deeper than even Morpheus realizes. For this reason, Descartes may be a better guide. He was prepared to follow his skeptical doubts all the way down. Ultimately, Descartes faced the possibility that maybe there is *nothing at all* that is absolutely certain. But after closely examining this possibility, he came to the realization that he did know at least *one thing* with absolute certainty. Descartes came to this insight when he tried to entertain the notion that the demon was deceiving him about his own existence:

I have convinced myself that there is nothing in the world – no sky, no earth, no minds, no bodies. Does not it follow that I do not exist? No, surely I must exist if it's me who is convinced of something. Let him deceive me all he can, he will never make it the case that I am nothing while I think that I am something.[10]

Descartes summarized this conclusion in the Latin phrase Cogito ergo sum – "I think therefore I am" – which has long remained the single most famous line in all of Western philosophy.[11]

It seems to me that Descartes was right. One cannot be mistaken about one's very existence. Even if you are a victim of a Matrix-type deception you can be certain that you exist. That is, there has to be a "you" that is being deceived. While everyone else's existence will always be somewhat less certain, the very act of trying to doubt your own existence merely demonstrates that *you* indeed exist. Of course, you cannot then start jumping to conclusions about *what* you are, or what the external world is really like. You still cannot be sure that you have a body, or that you are even human. (For all you know, you might be a sentient machine or robot that is deceived into thinking that it is human.) But the certainty of your existence does provide a foothold – a starting point for trying to climb out of this pit. As Descartes noted:

> Archimedes required only one fixed and immovable point to move the whole earth from its place, and I too can hope for great things if I can find even one small thing that is certain and unshakeable.[12]

Since it was your ability to think that proved your existence, then perhaps you can build on that. For, if you are at this very moment "thinking of the Matrix," is not it also certain that you *know* that you are "thinking of the Matrix"? It seems undeniably true that you are directly and unmistakably aware of your own immediate conscious mental state. Similarly, if you are perceiving a white page in front of you, you *know* that you are *perceiving* a white page in front of you. You just cannot jump to the conclusion that the page is "real," in the sense that it has a separate existence apart from your perception. Not only do you have a direct awareness of your own thoughts and perceptions, but as Descartes put it, you know that you are a "thinking thing," that is, you are the kind of being that is capable of having these thoughts and perceptions. This is not to say that you are the original source of these thoughts. It is always possible that they are somehow "pumped into your mind" from the outside. But regardless of the manner in which they arise, you must be capable of experiencing them.

So how deep does the rabbit hole really go? "Frighteningly deep" is the short answer. So long as you are willing to entertain the possibility of a Matrix-type deception, then the only thing that you can be absolutely sure of is your own existence and the contents of your immediate mental state. Certainty about what the world is like *outside your mind* will always be unavailable to you. This conclusion does not sit very well with most people. And it did not for Descartes either. He tried to eliminate the possibility of such radical deceptions by proving that God exists. His thought was that if he could prove the existence of God as an all-good and all-powerful being, then he could rest assured that there was no malicious demon, for surely a benevolent God would not allow him to be deceived about his most clear and distinct perceptions. Unfortunately for Descartes, most philosophers agree that his argument for God fell short of the "proof" that he needed. In the end there may be no way to be absolutely certain that we are not the victims of a Matrix-type deception.

Skepticism Outside the Matrix

How do you define real?

– Morpheus[†]

While we may not be able to prove that we are *not* in a Matrix-type deception right now, this, of course, does not mean that we ought to *believe* that we are in the Matrix. While the Matrix scenario is a logical possibility, it is not the most likely explanation of our day-to-day experiences. And since Descartes's journey has shown that there is very little that we can know with *absolute certainty*, maybe we should lower our standards. After all, to be *very certain* about your beliefs is probably good enough for knowledge.

Shifting the standard from absolute certainty to merely a high degree of probability will not free us from skepticism – though many people mistakenly think that it does. They quickly fall into complacency and assume that they are *very certain* that the world is essentially just like it appears to be. They suppose that the images in our minds (coming to us through our senses) of smooth, solid, brown tables, soft, fuzzy, beige carpeting, and squishy, pink, bubblegum basically correspond to the world as it is outside our minds – reality in *itself*. This view, that the world outside our minds basically matches our perceptions of it, is called *naive realism*. While this view is quite common, there are plenty of reasons to think that it is false. The world is NOT just as it appears to be. Philosophers throughout history have argued this point, but in what follows I'll argue the case in a way that is inspired by the great twentieth-century philosopher Bertrand Russell.[13]

Suppose that I have purchased from Warner Brothers those big red chairs that Morpheus and Neo sat in during their first meeting. Imagine that I have invited you over and that you sit down in one of them. Let us be clear that in this example we are talking about a "real" chair. We are in my real living-room – not in some Matrix-type simulation, or in a film, but in real life. As you imagine yourself sitting there, think about what you would know with reasonable certainty about the chair. First off, if you are like most people, you will take it for granted that the chair *exists*. But what Russell asks us to do is to take seriously the seemingly stupid question: How do you know it exists? In a way that is reminiscent of Morpheus's own remarks, you would probably respond by saying that it exists because you feel it, see it, etc. You feel its support against your back; you run your hand across its smooth leather surface, feeling the contour of its shape; and you see its deep red color.

But take a moment to consider these perceptions. Is the chair *really* the color of red that it appears to be right now? Naive realism says of course it is. But Russell suggests that you should consider it again after lowering the lights. Notice that the color changes – the red becomes darker, deeper. If the original color was the real color, then what are we to say of the color it is now? Well, one might be tempted to say that while you cannot pinpoint the exact shade of red that is the "true" or "real" red of the chair, it is nevertheless *some* shade of red. But what reason do you have for thinking so? After all, the color changes not only with the brightness of the lighting, but also with the type of lighting. The color of the chair will look different under daylight, fluorescent light, candlelight, black light, etc. If under certain lighting conditions the chair looks more brown than red should we say it is brown also? And purple sometimes?

Now at this point you might think that it is not the chair that has changed, but the lights. Purple lights are purple, but the chair is not. But that is precisely Russell's point. As modern science tells us, color is not *in* the objects themselves at all. Red chairs, after all, are not made out of a bunch of little red atoms. Rather, the color that objects *appear* to us to be is caused by the wavelengths of the light that reaches our eyes from the direction of the object. But look what has happened. You thought that the chair (which really exists) was really red. But as it turns out, it is only the appearance of the chair that is red. The chair *in itself* is not.

Might naive realism have better luck with texture? To us the chair looks and feels very smooth. Many would assert that it truly is smooth. But is it really? Look at it through a microscope and the red leather exterior will appear very rough, bumpy, or even jagged. And imagine how this same leather might feel if our hands were about one-tenth the size of an ant's – not smooth at all. The texture of the leather is clearly relative to one's perspective. And which of these perspectives is the *real* perspective? Russell contends that no perspective deserves that title. And solidity? How solid the chair seems will depend on your strength and weight. If you weighed 10 000 pounds, you certainly would not regard the chair as solid. And, according to the atomic theory of matter, the atoms that constitute the chair account for only a tiny fraction of the space it occupies. Thus, the chair is predominantly *empty* space – hardly the solid object that we perceive.

Shape is little help either. We know (or think we know) the shape of an object by what we see and feel. But what we see are colors, which we now realize are not *really* in the chair, and what we feel is its smoothness and solidity, yet these have turned out to be no more real than the color. So, again it comes down to perception. We seem to have absolutely no idea what the chair is like in itself – apart from our perceptions.[14] So consider once again the question of how you know that the chair exists. You thought you knew that it existed because of your various perceptions of it. But if we are right to regard these as appearances only, then you have lost your main reasons for thinking that the chair even exists at all!

Now I suppose you could maintain that there is still sufficient reason to think that there is a chair "out there," because even if it is not red or smooth or solid, it is *something* that is causing you to have these sensations. But Russell calls on you to notice that this "something" – whatever it is – is very different from the chair that we first contemplated. Should we even regard it as a *physical* thing? What does it mean to say that the "chair" exists, as something outside our perceptions, if you do not mean to imply that it has a *particular* size, shape, color, or texture? The fact of the matter is that all anyone ever has direct access to is their own perceptions. So we can never really be certain about what is causing those perceptions – or even if there is anything out there at all.

Ultimately, it seems that even when we set our worries about Matrix-type deceptions aside, the true nature of our world turns out to be a very slippery thing. Firm conclusions turn out to be rare, and doubts arise at every turn. But this should not be regarded as altogether bad. For, although philosophical reflection often undercuts our sense of certainty, it can also be very liberating. Once our common-sense assumptions have been revealed as illusions, we are freed from a kind of system of control. We inevitably find that the world is larger and more mysterious than we had thought, and our certainty is soon replaced with wonder and curiosity. While we may no longer "know" all the answers to life's questions, we can begin the quest to find out.

For pop culture resources and philosophical resources related to this chapter please visit the website for this book: https://introducingphilosophythroughpopculture.com.

Notes

1   Quotes in this chapter designated with a † are from *The Matrix* (movie). Quotes designated with ss are from *The Matrix Shooting Script*.
2   Descartes, R. (1986). *Meditations on First Philosophy*, 2 (trans. Ronald Rubin). Claremont, California: Areté Press.

3   For another interesting exploration of dreams and reality try the film *Waking Life*.
4   Descartes, 3.
5   Compare this to Matriculated, the ninth animated short in *The Animatrix*. It tells the story of a band of rebels who capture a sentient machine and put it into a Matrix of their own design. The machine is then given a set of experiences in order to "brainwash" it into thinking that it is human. This film also suggests a motive for the limits of Neo's own deception – empathy. The rebels set limits on the extent to which they deceive the machine because they do not want to make it a slave. Rather, they want to render it harmless – to make it an ally. This also seems to be the Architect's primary motive in limiting the deceptions of humans within the Matrix.
6   For a similar sort of deception see Arnold Schwarzenegger in *Total Recall*.
7   An exception to this general rule occurs when Neo is caused to "forget" his first interrogation by Agent Smith. Only when Trinity removes the bug from his naval does he recall the event.
8   In this case Neo would be a sort of futuristic Sisyphus. Though one key difference is that Sisyphus was fully aware of the futility of his work.
9   Morpheus teaches Neo this lesson in the Kung Fu scene from *The Matrix*.
10 Descartes, 6.
11 This famous phrase comes from Descartes's *Discourse on Method*.
12 Descartes, 6. For his now classic "brain in a vat" hypothesis see also Putnam, H. (2008). *Reason, Truth, and History*. Cambridge: Cambridge University Press.
13 See Russell, B. (1959). Appearance and reality. In: *The Problems of Philosophy* (ed. B. Russell). Oxford: Oxford University Press.
14 If you think that you *know* that the chair is composed of atoms, think again. Any evidence for the existence of atoms ultimately depends on sense perceptions. And these, as we've seen, are always just appearances.

6

Adama's True Lie

Earth and the Problem of Knowledge

Eric J. Silverman

Summary

What is the nature of knowledge? This chapter examines the science fiction narrative of *Battlestar Galactica* to address puzzles and problems in epistemology. For example, knowledge has traditionally been defined as a true justified belief. However, this definition actually accepts accidentally true justified beliefs as knowledge. In *Battlestar Galactica* we see an excellent example of such a belief. Captain Adama claims he is searching for Earth, but he does not even believe it exists. Anyone who believes in Earth's existence based on Adama's testimony would have an accidentally true justified belief. Can such a belief be knowledge?

Battlestar Galactica begins with the ravaging of the known world. The survivors are demoralized, vastly outnumbered by the enemy, and homeless. Against this backdrop Commander Adama offers the promise of a new home where they'll be safe from the Cylons: Earth. But he *lies*. Yet, in a surprising twist of fate – though not to us who live here – it's later revealed that Adama told a "true lie." Earth does exist and the Colonials' search for it isn't in vain. Undertaking the journey to this "mythical" home of the Thirteenth Tribe is momentous and filled with religious significance for the Colonial survivors. *Faith* in Earth's existence gives meaning to an otherwise hopeless situation and shapes the choices they make along the way.

"You're Right. There's no Earth. It's all a Legend"

There's a sharp distinction between "true belief" and *knowledge*. President Roslin illustrates this when she asks, "How many people know the Cylons look human?" Colonel Tigh responds, "The rumor mill's been working overtime. Half the ship's talking about it." But Roslin retorts, "There'll always be rumors. For most people, that's all they'll ever be. I'm asking how many people actually know?" ("Water"). A belief based on an

Introducing Philosophy Through Pop Culture: From Socrates to Star Wars *and Beyond*, Second Edition.
Edited by William Irwin and David Kyle Johnson.
© 2022 John Wiley & Sons Ltd. Published 2022 by John Wiley & Sons Ltd.

unverifiable rumor isn't knowledge, even if it happens to be true. Knowledge involves a belief in which one has reason for confidence.

A common view claims that knowledge is true belief accompanied by a convincing account justifying the belief. As Plato explains in the *Theaetetus*:

> Now when a man gets a true judgment about something without an account, his soul is in a state of truth as regards that thing, but he does not know it; for someone who cannot give and take an account of a thing is ignorant about it. But when he has also got an account of it, he is capable of all this and is made perfect in knowledge.[1]

According to Plato, it's possible to attain truth without knowledge. Knowledge is more certain than mere true belief since the knower possesses a *compelling justification* for the belief's truthfulness. Someone holding a true belief based on a rumor or a lucky guess doesn't have knowledge because s/he doesn't have a reason for confidence in the belief.

The contemporary philosopher Edmund Gettier demonstrated the inadequacy of this view of knowledge by providing counterexamples in which a person's justification for a true belief turns out to be false.[2] Say that Helo is walking down *Galactica*'s corridors and sees his wife, Athena. Helo calls out to her, "Sharon!" because he has a compelling justification for believing that's her name. So he believes:

(a) The woman in front of me is my wife, Athena.

If Helo's justified in believing (a), knows his wife's name, and understands basic rules of reasoning, then he's also justified in believing:

(b) The woman in front of me is named "Sharon."

The truthfulness of (a) logically entails the truthfulness of (b).But let's suppose Helo's mistaken, for it's actually an identical robotic copy of Athena, Boomer who's in front of him – having infiltrated *Galactica* for some nefarious purpose. But Boomer is also named "Sharon." Helo's belief (b) turns out to be true, but his justification for believing (b), belief (a), is false. Gettier claims that a counterexample like this shows a justified true belief that isn't knowledge since its justification is false. And this has become known as "the Gettier problem."

Beliefs based on Adama's true lie about Earth are similar to Helo's true belief based on a false justification. Starbuck believes:

(c) Adama knows the location of Earth.

This belief obviously implies:

(d) Earth exists.

It's arguable that Adama's public testimony that he knows the location of Earth, as well as his private assurances to Starbuck in "Kobol's Last Gleaming, Part 1," would be a proper justification for belief (c). It's reasonable to believe, as Adama claims, that he has access to privileged classified information as a "senior commander" in the Colonial fleet. Hence, Starbuck is justified in believing that Earth exists based on his testimony despite the fact that she doesn't realize that he is lying to her.

Even though Adama lies about knowing Earth's location and doesn't believe in its existence, it later becomes evident that Earth does exist. Starbuck discovers this for herself in the Tomb of Athena and after apparently journeying to Earth ("Home, Part 2"; "Crossroads, Part 2"). But Gettier would be quick to point out that, before these events, Starbuck holds a true belief (d) based on a false justification (c). Therefore, her true justified belief in Earth isn't really knowledge, until Adama's lie is no longer the primary justification for her belief.

"I'm Not a Cylon! . . . Maybe, but We Just Can't Take That Chance"

The Gettier problem is one of many puzzles in epistemology, the branch of philosophy concerned with the nature of knowledge. It's difficult to tell not only when one has knowledge but also when one's beliefs are justified. The contemporary philosopher Alvin Goldman offers a theory of justification known as *reliabilism*, which proposes that a belief is justified when it's produced by a reliable process.[3] Sense experiences, memories, deduction, and induction are typical examples of generally reliable belief-forming processes. Each of these processes, however, has a different level of reliability. Induction, for example, is less reliable than deduction. And the reliability of a belief-forming process can vary based on one's situation. Sight is a reliable belief-forming process, yet beliefs based on sight are more reliable for close objects observed in well-lit conditions than for distant objects observed in poorly lit conditions.

One interesting aspect of reliabilism is that it doesn't require a person to know s/he's using a reliable process to be justified in their beliefs. If a young non-philosopher forms their beliefs based on the five senses, s/he's justified in those beliefs even if s/he never reflects upon the reliability of the senses. This has the desirable consequence of classifying many beliefs held by children, animals, and epistemically unreflective persons as justified.

In *Battlestar Galactica*, some typical belief-forming processes aren't as reliable as they are for us. *Sight* sometimes leads people to believe they're seeing a human being when they're actually seeing a Cylon robotic replica of a human. While people are usually correct when they believe they see a human, most would believe they see a human regardless of whether it's actually a Cylon. So sight isn't a reliable process for judging between humans and Cylons, even though it's a reliable process for forming other types of beliefs.[4]

Memory is another less dependable belief-forming process. Boomer can't remember that she sabotaged *Galactica*'s water tanks ("Water") and, until her Cylon nature is revealed to her, her memories thoroughly convince her that she's human, her parents are Katherine and Abraham Valerii, and her family died on Troy. Yet these beliefs couldn't be further from the truth. She doesn't give up these beliefs until confronted by numerous copies of herself aboard a Cylon baseship, and even then her initial reaction is disbelief ("Kobol's Last Gleaming, Part 2"). Similarly, Baltar wonders whether he might be a Cylon, and thus doubts whether he can trust his memories ("Torn"). Colonel Tigh, Sam Anders, Chief Tyrol, and Tory Foster are also deceived by their memories and are unaware of their actual Cylon nature ("Crossroads, Part 2"). The revelation, in particular, of Tigh and Anders's Cylon identity is truly shocking, as they're among the most adamantly anti-Cylon members of the fleet.

On the other hand, some unusual belief-forming processes are reliable in *Battlestar Galactica*, such as Baltar's visions of Number Six. While Six's advice is often cloaked in manipulative games and sarcasm, it frequently turns out to be a reliable way to form beliefs and accomplish desirable goals. Six draws Baltar's attention to a strange device on the Dradis console, and this leads him to "identify" Aaron Doral as a Cylon. But Baltar hasn't yet created his "mystic Cylon detector" and just makes up some techno-babble to convince Tigh that Doral is a Cylon so he can have an excuse to bring up the "odd device." It's disturbing when Tigh abandons Doral on Ragnar Station until it's revealed that Baltar was right all along ("Miniseries"). Six also encourages Baltar to test Boomer to see if she's a Cylon ("Flesh and Bone"); tells him to choose a target for the assault on a Cylon tylium refinery by *faith*, which turns out to be accurate ("The Hand of God"); helps him attain both the vice-presidency and the presidency ("Colonial Day"; "Lay Down Your Burdens"); and reveals Hera's identity to him ("Exodus, Part 2").

Visions resulting from chamalla extract are also a reliable process for belief forma-tion. Roslin's visions foresee her encounter with Leoben ("Flesh and Bone") and her leadership role in bringing the Colonials to Earth ("The Hand of God"). A chamalla-tripping oracle tells D'Anna/Three that she'll hold the Cylon-human hybrid Hera and experience love for the first time ("Exodus"); another oracle knows about Starbuck's upbringing and that Leoben – or at least a vision of him – will be coming for her ("Maelstrom").

Returning to epistemology, does reliabilism suggest that Adama's *testimony* is an appropriate justification for believing in Earth? Enlightenment era philosophers, such as David Hume (1711–1776), are critical of justifications based on testimony for this kind of issue. Hume claims testimony is only as reliable as experience suggests, and there are true claims that would be difficult to justify based on testimony:

> The reason, why we place any credit in witnesses and historians, is not derived from any *connection*, which we perceive *a priori*, between testimony and reality, but because we are accustomed to find a conformity between them. But when the fact attested is such a one as has seldom fallen under our observation, here is a contest of two opposite experiences; of which the one destroys the other, as far as its force goes, and the superior can only operate on the mind by the force, which remains. The very same principle of experience, which gives us a certain degree of assurance in the testimony of witnesses, gives us also, in this case, another degree of assurance against the fact, which they endeavor to establish; from which contradiction there necessarily arises a counterpoise, and mutual destruction of belief and authority.[5]

Hume believes that the ultimate basis for belief in anything is our own sensory experi-ences. We should trust other people's testimony only because experience suggests that testimony is typically accurate. Yet, even in everyday situations, testimony falls consider-ably short of absolute accuracy. It's sometimes unreliable because people are dishonest, as when Felix Gaeta claims he saw Baltar voluntarily sign the execution order for over 200 innocent colonists ("Crossroads, Part 2"); or because people are simply incorrect in their testimony, as when Tyrol sincerely tells Tigh that he's not a Cylon ("Resistance").

When someone testifies to something completely outside of our own experiences, we should be skeptical. Hume claims that someone who has never seen water freeze because he's spent his entire life in a tropical climate should be slow to accept testimony that water freezes at a cold temperature. Adama's claim to know Earth's location is similar, since the Colonials have no personal experience of Earth. This claim has no continuity with their personal experiences, though it doesn't actually conflict with these experiences.

Hume contends we should be even more skeptical when testimony is used to justify beliefs that contradict our everyday experiences.

The contemporary philosopher Alvin Plantinga claims that testimony plays a more foundational role in our beliefs than Hume, and his predecessor John Locke (1632–1704), acknowledge:

> The Enlightenment looked askance at testimony and tradition; Locke saw them as a preeminent source of error. The Enlightenment idea is that perhaps we start by learning from others – our parents, for example. Properly mature and independent adults, however, will have passed beyond all that and believe what they do on the basis of the evidence. But this is a mistake; you can't know so much as your name or what city you live in without relying on testimony. (Will you produce your birth certificate for the first, or consult a handy map for the second? In each case you are of course relying on testimony.)[6]

Plantinga identifies a number of important beliefs that can be justified based only upon testimony. No one knows their name, age, or location without using testimony to justify such beliefs. The Enlightenment ideal of the radically independent thinker who weighs all claims against evidence from their own individual experiences is unrealistic and artificial. While testimony is far from infallible, it plays a more important epistemic role than Locke and Hume allow.

In either case, testimony-based justifications for believing in Earth need to be closely scrutinized. How trustworthy is the individual providing the testimony? How unlikely is their claim about Earth? Is the individual an appropriate authority concerning Earth? As the highest-ranking military officer surviving the destruction of the Colonies and the author of their escape, Adama and his testimony seem naturally trustworthy. Starbuck certainly trusts Adama when she's confronted with the truth by Roslin:

STARBUCK:	The old man is our last chance to find Earth. He knows where it is. He said so. You were there. The location is a secret. But he is going to take us there.
ROSLIN:	Commander Adama has no idea where Earth is. He never did. He made it up in order to give people hope.
STARBUCK:	You're lying.
ROSLIN:	Go ask him.

("Kobol's Last Gleaming, Part 1")

When Starbuck does ask him, Adama tries to avoid her questions, but she's forced to conclude that Adama's patriotism and proficiency in fulfilling military duties don't make him an expert concerning Earth. As commander of a soon to be retired battlestar, Adama simply doesn't have access to Earth's location. The Gettier problem demonstrates that the Colonials' beliefs about Earth fall short of knowledge, and reliabilism suggests there's reason to doubt whether beliefs based on Adama's testimony are even justified.

"You Have to Have Something to Live for. Let it be Earth"

How should beliefs be chosen in an uncertain world? W.K. Clifford (1845–1879) says it's unethical to believe anything without sufficient evidence. This view, known as *evidentialism*, claims that if there isn't enough evidence to support a belief, one mustn't consent to its truth. One premise supporting evidentialism is that incorrect beliefs can have a damaging effect on society:

> And no one man's belief is in any case a private matter which concerns himself alone. Our lives are guided by that general conception of the course of things which has been created by society for social purposes. Our words, our phrases, our forms and processes and modes of thought, are common property, fashioned and perfected from age to age; an heirloom which every succeeding generation inherits as a precious deposit and a sacred trust to be handed on to the next one, not unchanged but enlarged and purified, with some clear marks of its proper handiwork.[7]

It's not merely mistaken, imprudent, or foolish to believe something without adequate evidence, it's outright *immoral*, a violation of our ethical duties to one another. If Roslin believes it's the will of the gods to lead the Colonials to Earth without sufficient evidence, this belief could have damaging effects on the entire fleet. Even if a less influential person like Starbuck believes in Earth without enough evidence, her beliefs don't only affect herself, but others as well who may be inclined to agree with her. Clifford offers this sweeping conclusion, "To sum it up: it is wrong always, everywhere, and for anyone, to believe anything upon insufficient evidence."[8]

Clifford, however, doesn't recognize that in some situations knowledge is elusive and reliable justification uncertain; yet, believing *nothing* is a deeply damaging option. William James (1842–1910) claims that when definitive knowledge is impossible on a *momentous* and *forced* issue, it's reasonable to choose beliefs based on their *practical* consequences. He considers marriage and religious faith as two such decisions. In both cases a choice must be made in less than certain circumstances. Yet, these choices are forced: to withhold belief is effectively a choice against it, and necessarily results in the loss of potential desirable consequences. Marriage and faith are also momentous in their potential for positive results:

> It is as if a man should hesitate indefinitely to ask a certain woman to marry him because he was not perfectly sure that she would prove an angel after he brought her home. Would he not cut himself off from that particular angel-possibility as decisively as if he went and married some one else?[9]

If there are desirable results from a specific committed relationship, they're inevitably lost if the relationship isn't embraced. It may be impossible for Apollo to know whether Anastasia Dualla would be a good wife; but the benefits offered by a committed relationship with her can't be gained without commitment. The choice can't be avoided, for avoiding it is an effective choice against the relationship. Lifelong bachelorhood isn't irrational or unjustifiable; but it's guaranteed to prevent Apollo from the benefits unique to a committed relationship with Dualla.

Or consider Apollo's unwillingness to see the conflict brewing between the fleet's military and civilian leadership. When his father chastises him for "siding" with Roslin, Apollo retorts, "I didn't know we were picking sides." Adama muses, "That's why you haven't picked one yet." Later, Apollo does choose his side – that of *democracy* ("Bastille Day"; "Kobol's Last Gleaming, Part 2"). Due to Apollo's important position in the fleet and his personal relationships with both Adama and Roslin, it's inevitable that he's forced to choose between the military and civilian factions. When given orders to arrest Roslin, he has no choice but to choose a side. His choice was also momentous. By siding with Roslin, he stands up for democracy at the cost of his own freedom.

William James views religious faith as a similarly momentous decision. He claims no argument proves the truthfulness of religious faith with certainty. Even so, at some point a decision must be made. The choice is forced. To put off the choice indefinitely is effectively to reject religion. Furthermore, the question of religion is momentously important. Many religious thinkers claim it offers a life filled with greater meaning and purpose, along with eternal happiness after death. Agnosticism cuts one off from any good attainable by embracing religion. Gaining the benefits of religious faith, for this life or the afterlife, may require a choice here and now.[10] An agnostic has no chance for the benefits of religion, just as the lifelong bachelor has no chance for the goods of marriage.[11] Similarly, the agnostic cuts himself off from any advantages from atheism. If religion is false and all genuine goods are located in the here and now, then withholding consent from atheism is also a damaging choice. It's wiser to embrace atheism rather than agnosticism, since it frees one to pursue the goods of life wholeheartedly.

Faith that Earth awaits at the end of the Colonial fleet's journey mirrors James's other momentous and forced choices. When comfortable life was possible on the Twelve Colonies, the question of Earth's existence was an abstract issue with little consequence stemming from belief or unbelief. The issue was neither momentous nor forced. But once the Colonies were destroyed, the issue became momentous: either there's a home where the survivors will be welcomed as brothers and sisters, or they're homeless and alone. The choice also becomes forced. Agnosticism concerning Earth is no longer a practical option. They can embrace the search for Earth or reject the hope of Earth by settling on the first safely habitable planet they encounter, but to do neither is ridiculous.

The importance of this issue is seen when the Colonials elect Baltar to the presidency based on his promise to settle on New Caprica and cease the search for Earth ("Lay Down Your Burdens, Part 2"). By abandoning the search, the Colonials cut themselves off from hope for a better life than what they can make for themselves on this less-than-inviting world. Yet, either choice is better than no choice. Most of the Colonials don't have access to compelling evidence that Earth exists. It's reasonable for them to believe that rebuilding civilization on New Caprica is their only hope for a permanent home. By settling on New Caprica, they have the opportunity for some benefits: breathing fresh air and growing food instead of living in tin boxes and eating rations. Clifford's advice would allow them neither option. There isn't enough evidence to support the belief in and search for Earth, but there's also insufficient evidence that settling on New Caprica is the wisest option. If they continually wander without settling on a planet, and cease pursuing Earth, they cut themselves off from the benefits of both.

Even apart from any potential benefits of a successful search for Earth, there are benefits gained simply from possessing an overarching life-quest. Adama's lie isn't motivated by a desire to find Earth, but by a more subtle rationale. He understands that humans need purpose, especially in difficult circumstances. Without purpose, we wither, give up hope, and die. He lies because he wants the survivors to hope and avoid despair in the hardest of times.

Some philosophers advocate skepticism since virtually every belief can be questioned based on an argument for the conflicting view. But James shows us that a truly skeptical approach to life can be detrimental since it requires rejecting potentially rewarding opportunities. And a truly skeptical life is perhaps impossible since so many decisions are unavoidably forced. Whether to embrace life and meaning amidst uncertainty is a forced and momentous decision. Blind leaps of faith are dangerous and cynical skepticism concerning everything is unrewarding. The confidence of *certainty* evades many of us, but choices must be made. Avoiding the central choices of life in an attempt to risk nothing, hope for nothing, love nothing, and believe in nothing beyond the indubitable is both impractical and impossible. So say we all.[12]

For pop culture resources and philosophical resources related to this chapter please visit the website for this book: https://introducingphilosophythroughpopculture.com.

Notes

1 Burnyeat, M. (1990). *The Theaetetus of Plato*, 202c (trans. M.J. Levett). Indianapolis: Hackett.
2 Gettier, E. (1963). Is justified true belief knowledge? *Analysis* 23: 121–123.
3 See Goldman, A. (1976). What is justified belief? In: *Justification and Knowledge* (ed. G.S. Pappas), 1–23. Dordrecht: D. Reidel.
4 See Goldman, A. (1976). Discrimination and perceptual knowledge. *Journal of Philosophy* 73: 771–779.
5 Hume, D. (1998). Of miracles. In: *Dialogues Concerning Natural Religion* (ed. R.H. Popkin), 110. Indianapolis: Hackett.
6 Plantinga, A. (2000). *Warranted Christian Belief*, 147. New York: Oxford University Press.
7 Clifford, W.K. (2003). The ethics of belief. In: *The Theory of Knowledge* (ed. Louis P. Pojman), 516–17. Belmont, CA: Wadsworth/Thompson.
8 Clifford, 518.
9 James, W. (2003). The will to believe. In: *The Theory of Knowledge* (ed. L.P. Pojman), 524. Belmont, CA: Wadsworth/Thompson.
10 James, 524.
11 James, 520.
12 Thanks to Jason Eberl, John Greco, and Rob Arp for their comments on earlier versions of this chapter.

7

Wakandan Resources

The Epistemological Reality of Black Panther's Fiction

Ruby Komic

Summary

Black Panther challenges racist stereotypes of Black people and culture, suggesting that the absence of a Wakanda-like nation in the real world is due to Western interference rather than some inherent problem in Black societies. For Black audiences, *Black Panther* offers a film to identify with and feel a sense of ownership and pride in, especially because the film helps remedy the inequality in fictional representations of the Black experience. Whether the viewer is Black or is not, *Black Panther* provides the viewer with *epistemic resources*, conceptual tools to understand and communicate about Black, and particularly African American, culture and experience.

Members of marginalized communities experience a lack of representation of their unique life experience in popular fictional media – and if they do see themselves represented, it is often as a stereotype, caricature, or minor character. *Black Panther* broke this mold by offering abundant, nuanced, and non-stereotypical representation of Black experience. Yet, while some lauded *Black Panther* for its portrayal of Black culture, some also criticized the film's depiction.

For example, actor Anthony Mackie saw *Black Panther's* nearly all-Black cast and production crew as being a form of racism. As Mackie stated, in a co-interview with actor Daveed Diggs:

> I've done several Marvel movies where every producer, every director, every stunt person, every costume designer, every PA, every single person has been white. But then when you do Black Panther, you have a Black director, Black producer, you have a Black costume designer, you have a Black stunt choreographer. And I'm like, that's more racist than anything else. Because if you only can hire Black people for the Black movie, are you saying they're not good enough when you have a mostly white cast?[1]

Introducing Philosophy Through Pop Culture: From Socrates to Star Wars *and Beyond*, Second Edition.
Edited by William Irwin and David Kyle Johnson.
© 2022 John Wiley & Sons Ltd. Published 2022 by John Wiley & Sons Ltd.

Certainly, with *Black Panther* being released in 2018, two years after the election of Donald Trump, in the midst of the Black Lives Matter movement (which, at the time, hadn't experienced the aftermath that resulted from the killing of George Floyd), and to a media climate sorely lacking representation from people of color, the issue of racism is virtually inescapable, presenting a sort of paradox. On one hand, *Black Panther* is celebrated for its presentation of Black culture and for its use of Black professionals on screen and behind the camera. On the other hand, it is criticized for these very same things.

Of course, *Black Panther* is fiction. There is no Wakanda or vibranium, and Shuri's lab (with all its futuristic gadgets) doesn't exist. Yet, we feel emotional about *Black Panther*, don't we? Indeed, how many of us have crossed our arms and said "Wakanda Forever!"? And, with a film like *Black Panther* (that, at times, seems to directly reflect, if not respond to, its contemporary moment) it is difficult to separate or distinguish between the characters and issues of the film and the people and issues of the real world. For Black audiences, *Black Panther* offered a film they could identify with and feel a sense of ownership and pride in, especially if we view the film as a resource that helps remedy the inequality in fictional representations of the Black experience. Similarly, *Black Panther* also offers a way of interpreting the real world through its fictional representations of Black people and Black society.

Philosophically, this offers an interesting version of what is called the Paradox of Fiction, which results from three conditions: (i) we have emotional responses to fiction that are genuine and rational; (ii) in order for our emotional responses to be genuine and rational we must believe the fiction; but (iii) no one really believes the fiction.

Most solutions attempt to resolve the paradox by denying or modifying one of the three conditions. But what if we approach this in a different way? What if we suggest that our emotional response to *Black Panther* is rooted in the film's (knowingly) fictional representation of our real world? In other words, we know *Black Panther* is fictional, yet we also know that the issue of racism is real. So, our interpretation of *Black Panther* depends on our knowledge of both the fictional elements of the story and the real issues of the real world the story represents. Put another way, our interpretation (our emotional response) is rooted in an epistemology that requires both fictional and real knowledge. Let's see how this works.

"The Illusions of Division Threaten Our Very Existence"

Fictional works such as *Black Panther* offer viewers a unique type of what Gaile Pohlhaus calls an *epistemic resource*: a resource that individuals draw upon in order to know.[2] Pohlhaus tells us that epistemic resources are collectively held and maintained by an epistemic community; a community of knowers (which given the internet, can be very large).[3] Above all, our epistemic resources need to "answer to our experiences."[4] Pohlhaus lists three potential kinds of epistemic resources: (i) language to express experience; (ii) concepts used to understand; and (iii) criteria to judge the usefulness of a resource.[5] Pohlhaus acknowledges, though, that there may be other kinds of resources beyond these three.[6] For our purposes, we need to answer two questions about fictions and epistemic resources: (i) Do the resources we gain from fictions like *Black Panther* answer to experience? (ii) What kind of epistemic resource are they, if they are not language, concepts, and criteria?

When we consume a fictional work, it is possible to learn from and use elements of the work to better interpret the world. Not every aspect of a fictional work is going to be answerable to or directly reflect our experiences in the real world. I have not personally met a Klingon warrior, for example, attended Hogwarts School of Witchcraft and Wizardry, or wielded one of Okoye's spears. Fiction is enjoyable because it can reach beyond what is possible of the real world, and is not confined by it, like everything Shuri creates in her lab. But fiction also contains elements that are salient to us in the real world, that correlate to what we experience or what we know, like Killmonger's Oakland upbringing and his understanding of slavery and oppression. As such, we can understand *Black Panther* as providing viewers with *epistemic resources*, because it gave (and continues to give) many people new conceptual tools to understand and communicate about Black and particularly African American culture and experience, whether the viewer is Black or is not. Thus, the film serves as an important addition to the epistemic resources that we all share and collectively maintain.

Even if it's just the moral of the story – such as the racial politics of *X-men*, or the allegory of American liberalism in *Star Trek: The Original Series* – fictional works like *Black Panther* can add to our understanding of real-world phenomena even if they don't directly represent them. In this sense, fictions *do* seem to answer to our experiences. We draw upon them in order to better understand and interpret the world, and therefore gain epistemic resources. The question of what *kind* of resources fictions offer – if not language, concepts, and criteria – however, requires a longer response.

"The Real Question is: What are Those?"

Fictions are tied up with the imagination; a fiction asks us to use our imagination to mentally represent to ourselves what the fiction is describing or showing.[7] It asks that we employ a "suspension of disbelief," treating the fiction as though it's true and allowing ourselves to be immersed in it. Often, we know that what we subsequently imagine really could be (or could have been) if circumstances in the real world were different. Fictions in this sense ask us to imaginatively entertain *possibilities*, particularly possibilities pertaining to oneself.[8]

This is what Catriona Mackenzie calls "imagining oneself otherwise."[9] She argues that the cultural imagery that constantly surrounds us – including popular fictions – informs our imagination through constructing a repertoire of imagery upon which we draw when we want to imagine something.[10] The subsequent imaginings have affective power: products of our imagination are highly evocative, causing emotional reaction and deep engagement with their content.[11] Mackenzie argues that we use imaginative practices to develop our identity and self-conception, through what we imagine of ourselves.[12]

For example, *Black Panther* asks us to imagine a world in which an African nation (Wakanda) did not suffer invasion, colonization, enslavement, and plundering of its resources by a white Western nation. It further asks us to imagine that, given the ability to self-determine, this country uses its rich natural resources to further develop itself and promote its people, becoming the richest, healthiest, and most technologically advanced nation in the world. Importantly, *Black Panther* also asks us to imagine that this nation was able to maintain close connection to and honor its cultural traditions, unfettered by Western interference. People in the real world where there is no Wakanda can therefore imagine what might have been, or what could be, had there been an alternate world history.

Black audience members have the opportunity to unite themselves around Wakandan identity, building the film's positive representation of Black identity into their self-conception. The affectivity of fiction-based imaginings makes this possible.

The hypothetical nation of Wakanda also gives audience members of other racial groups a different or new perspective on Black identity, which can aid their interpretations of the real world. That is, the film challenges racist stereotypes of Black people and culture, suggesting that the absence of a Wakanda-like nation in the real world is due to Western interference rather than some inherent problem in Black societies. Through the imaginative engagement with fiction, and the affective power of the imaginings, we glean new meanings, significance, and understanding of things in the real world. The epistemic resources we gain from fictions are not language, concepts, or criteria, but another sort of resource – *a narrative meaning-making practice* that involves imagining what the fiction tasks us with imagining. With resources like *Black Panther* improving our collection of epistemic resources, we are able to go forth and interpret the world *better* than we would have before.

Black Panther is a good epistemic resource by Pohlhaus's definition because the film offers nuanced representation of Black culture, experiences, attitudes, and possibilities, unlike stereotypical representations, and therefore improves our interpretations of the world. *Black Panther* also reflects aspects of reality and is answerable to experience, despite being fiction, because of the team of majority Black creators who constructed the fiction. Therefore, when the film is used as a tool through which to interpret the world, the interpretation is less likely to be inaccurate or incorrect because of faulty resources. Fictions like *Black Panther* frame aspects of the real world into its own narrative (like Oakland in 1991 or the history of slavery), and when we consume that fiction we are able to use that framing to better interpret and understand those aspects of the world that the fiction represents. In that sense, consuming films like *Black Panther* is an epistemic activity as well as an imaginative one. It is an activity of adding to our epistemic resources, both personally in one's own mind, and as a collective of people who now have that resource available to them. Imaginative engagement in the fiction is not merely about entertaining possibilities or building one's self-conception, it is also about supporting our ability to interpret the world well.

So, let's consider exactly what framing and representations *Black Panther* offers to its audience. That way we can see how it's not just a good epistemic resource, it's also an example of how an audience's interpretation requires real and fictional knowledge.

"What Can a Nation of Farmers Offer the Rest of the World?"

First and foremost, *Black Panther* challenges the stereotypical depictions of Black people, nations, and culture. Its characters offer abundant and aspirational imaginative possibilities for Black members of the audience. Few other fictions represent a Black man as a respected king of a wealthy nation, or Black female characters as able to influence the narrative beyond being a love interest, let alone as revered warriors like the Dora Milaje. Shuri's character offers a rare representation of a young Black woman as a technological genius and inventor (arguably more capable than Bruce Banner and Tony Stark), afforded the resources and freedom to pursue her interests.

That these representations transgress stereotypes does not mean they're impossible in the real world. Black people are well aware that their community members are capable of the excellence that the characters display. But in an oppressive culture that limits the fictional representation of Black people to stereotypes, *Black Panther* provides legitimacy and feasibility to imagining this excellence of oneself. That is, *Black Panther* makes it easier for a Black viewer to imagine that they could be a king, or a warrior woman, or a tech genius, because they can use the depictions in the film as a reference point that says, "Here, imagine this!" We can see that *Black Panther* has exactly this effect in the social media posts about young Black girls dressing up as Dora Milaje and children role-playing as King T'Challa that flooded the internet after the film's release.[13]

So *Black Panther* allows the audience members who identify with it to imagine a range of possibilities for themselves. But it has another function: to represent Black and African American experience to everyone. The film offers imaginative possibilities, but it also tries to reflect current reality through fictional representation. The depiction of Black women in the film is especially notable, as even though T'Challa is the protagonist, he is flanked by powerful Black women who are different in their motivations and values, and who drive the narrative forward in their own ways. Nakia is driven primarily by personal principles of justice, and Shuri's motivations centre around familial ties and nationalism.

Okoye is loyal to her culture and its traditions, a capable leader and formidable warrior. Her head is close shaved throughout the film, and in the one instance that she wears a wig, she is vocal in her displeasure and throws the wig at an opponent. Calling the wig a "ridiculous thing" flies in the face of Western demands of how Black women should perform femininity and beauty. Similarly, Nakia and Shuri maintain their natural hair, styled in ways designed to accentuate its qualities, not stymie its abundance. After decades of not seeing Black women with natural hair on screen, the recent cultural return to natural hair in defiance of white supremacy's expectations is reflected and validated in the fictional characters.

Importantly, the representation that the film offers, and that Black and African American people can identify with, isn't one-dimensional, but plural and nuanced. Usually, Black representation in film is limited to one, maybe two characters. In *Black Panther*, the vast majority of characters are Black (and played by Black actors) which means the characters can have narratives that are not driven by their relations to white characters and whiteness. "Nearly every touch, every relationship, and every plot point [that] exists is to build connection between Black characters."[14]

For example, the ideological tension between T'Challa and Killmonger reflects the disagreement between those who have been able to live free of systemic oppression, and those who have suffered it. Killmonger's alienation from his Wakandan origins mirrors many Black Americans' experience of being caught between two cultures: African heritage and American present. T'Challa, on the other hand, has never been removed from his ancestral home. T'Challa, though a Black man, has not experienced first-hand the racial oppression to which Black people are subjected in the United States, unlike Killmonger. In this sense Killmonger's narrative reflects the real-world struggle of being Black in the United States, depicting rage at the injustices incurred, and a desire to secure reparations.[15]

Nakia has a similar tension with T'Challa and Okoye. Nakia has experienced much of the world outside Wakanda. Though she does not experience structural oppression in the way Killmonger has, the suffering and oppression of Black populations outside Wakanda troubles her deeply. We first see her undercover on a mission to stop the kidnapping and forced sexual slavery of African women – a real-world problem – and the film reiterates that she is well-travelled. She says to T'Challa, "I've seen too many in need just to turn a blind eye. I can't be happy here knowing that there's people out there who have nothing."

Nakia is offered the queenship at T'Challa's side, but she believes the role and Wakanda's traditions would restrict her ability too much to help the rest of the world. Urging T'Challa to open Wakanda to the world and share its resources, she says "We could provide aid and access to technology and refuge to those who need it." Though Killmonger is the antagonist, Nakia approximates his outlook – that Wakanda in its wealth should allow access to its resources in order to lift people oppressed in other parts of the world.

Similarly, after T'Challa loses the duel with Killmonger, Nakia challenges Okoye's decision to stay and serve the new king. When Nakia suggests a plan to overthrow Killmonger, Okoye is taken aback, believing her duty is to the institutions of her country and therefore the throne. Nakia, however, believes that she can best serve her country by ensuring its better future, even if doing so contravenes tradition and law. When Okoye tells her, "Serve your country," Nakia responds, "No, I *save* my country." This exchange reflects a political dilemma in the real world: often, oppressed populations such as Black Americans have to break the law or conventions in order to effectively resist their oppression. Some find this an uncrossable boundary, but others believe society's laws are inherently corrupt because of the unjust system that created them.

Black Panther does more than one thing, representationally. Like all fictional works, it is open to varying interpretations of its content, and the accounts of what *Black Panther* does for its audience are not unanimous. Significantly, the film combines real and fictional elements to inspire differing reactions. For example, the tension between T'Challa and Killmonger left some Black audience members struggling to empathize with the story's hero over its villain. Steven Thrasher for *Esquire* wrote, "I couldn't get myself to root against its antagonist . . . [and] I found its ending political message far more conservative than the revolutionary possibilities teased by anything with 'Black' and 'Panther' in the title."[16] While Killmonger is positioned as the antagonist, his aspiration to liberate Black people globally and the sense of injustice he feels, often approximates the experience of Black people in the real world better than T'Challa's attitude of preserving peace. Moreover, Killmonger is the main African American character in the film. Though his heritage is Wakandan, his character shares the cultural and national background of many of the film's viewers, whereas T'Challa has always been rich, powerful, and physically *safe*. Killmonger has experienced the same precariousness in life as many of the film's Black audience members, "searching for an intact Black body, only to be largely rejected."[17] Some Black moviegoers therefore found themselves rooting for the villain, because he was a closer representation of themselves.

T'Challa's characterization might be further criticized for upholding the white colonialist value of passivity and peacefulness in Black people, designed to minimize Black retaliation to injustice. Black anger, particularly Black women's anger, is culturally demonized as less valid and justified than white anger.[18] In this respect, the ultimate victory of T'Challa's peaceful ideology is less revolutionary than some Black audience members would have liked. Moreover, Agent Ross's deterministic account of Killmonger – that he is doomed to reproduce the destructive habits of his training and country – could be interpreted as a pessimistic representation of radical Black politics. Killmonger's efforts to secure resources to liberate Black populations isn't equivalent to the United States' methods of destabilizing foreign powers for its own gain. Suggesting otherwise through Killmonger's narrative glosses over the initial motivation of his actions: the profound oppression of Black people and culture by Western powers.

Varying interpretations do not mean that *Black Panther* does a poor representational job. Quite the contrary, *Black Panther* is a film that can elucidate a multitude of Black peoples' experiences and perspectives. The variety of interpretation allows for nuanced discussion about real-world issues through the lens of the film – a practice of using the epistemic resources *Black Panther* gives to viewers. Epistemic resources do not need to serve a particular viewpoint, and in fact they should not stray toward only one understanding of the world. To be valuable, an epistemic resource needs to add to our tools of understanding in some meaningful way. *Black Panther* does this, partly because it can have conflicting interpretations.

So, even though *Black Panther* is a good epistemic resource, we as audience members and knowers have been ill-served by the fictions that came before it, which gave us faulty, stereotypical resources to understand and interpret Black and African American experience. In turn, Black and African American people have been ill-served by previous fictions, as their experience and realities have suffered misinterpretation and stereotyping partially through the fictions in our cultural repertoire. Therein, I suggest, lies an injustice of an epistemic nature.

"We Must Right These Wrongs"

Just as epistemic resources help us to better interpret the world, the absence of certain resources can lead to poor interpretation or misunderstanding of aspects of the world. Importantly, *Black Panther* was released to a cultural climate in which the representation of Blackness in fiction was severely restricted, and largely remains so, as Anthony Mackie noted. Where *Black Panther* improves our epistemic resources, minimal and stereotypical Black representation worsens them, and as such perpetuates the social and structural oppression of Black people and communities.

When racism and sexism lead to poor or scant epistemic resources suited to interpreting the world, what Miranda Fricker calls an "epistemic injustice" is committed.[19] This kind of injustice targets those subject to it in their capacity as knowers along the same lines as social identity prejudices, such as racism, sexism, ableism, and so on.[20] Marginalized knowers who are victims of epistemic injustice find it difficult to be believed when they should be, or to make their experiences salient to others through language and culture.[21] As I've described, one way to make experiences salient to others is to produce fictions like *Black Panther*, which represent experiences and offer the epistemic resources to allow knowers to correctly interpret experience. The historic lack of adequate resources for interpreting and understanding Black culture, possibilities, and experience, leads to these aspects of living as a Black person in the world becoming obscured or poorly understood by other people. Moreover, because the resources available to understand Black lives are largely stereotypical or derivative, so too is much subsequent understanding of Black culture and experience.

The right kind of fiction can help alleviate this sort of epistemic injustice by providing better epistemic resources for interpreting the world and allowing marginalized individuals to articulate their experiences through the fiction, for others to understand. *Black Panther* in this sense is a case of epistemic *justice*. It provides plentiful and rare representation, which was produced by a majority Black creative team. It uses the fictional medium of film to contribute to our epistemic resources and improve collective understanding of Black people's experience and possibilities. While all the work to alleviate the epistemic injustice done to Black and African American populations is certainly not complete, *Black Panther* and fictions like it are part of the remedy. One can only imagine, given all that's transpired in the real world since *Black Panther*'s release, what elements the *Black Panther* sequel will incorporate with regard to real and fictional knowledge. Will it continue to seek epistemic justice? Will it a show a world (not just the Wakandan nation) where Black lives matter? Will we see the effects of Shuri's and Nakia's outreach efforts? And how will the sequel deal with Chadwick Boseman's/T'Challa's death? Indeed, this returns us to the paradox of fiction. We know Chadwick is gone and we know his depiction of T'Challa is too. Yet the Black Panther, whoever it ends up being, must live on, especially in our imaginations.

For pop culture resources and philosophical resources related to this chapter please visit the website for this book: https://introducingphilosophythroughpopculture.com.

Notes

1 Bell, B.A. (2020). Actors on Actors: Anthony Mackie & Daveed Diggs (Full Conversation). *Variety*. https://variety.com/video/actors-on-actors-anthony-mackie-daveed-diggs-full-conversation#! (June 28, 2020).
2 Pohlhaus Jr., G. (2012). Relational knowing and epistemic injustice: toward a theory of willful hermeneutical ignorance. *Hypatia* 27: 716.
3 Pohlhaus (2012), 716.
4 Pohlhaus (2012), 718.
5 Pohlhaus (2012), 718.
6 Gaile Pohlhaus, Jr. (2017). Varieties of epistemic injustice. In: *The Routledge Handbook of Epistemic Injustice* (eds. I.J. Kidd, J. Medina, and G. Pohlhaus, Jr.), 16. New York: Routledge.
7 Walton, K. (1990). *Mimesis as Make-Believe*. Cambridge, MA: Harvard University Press.
8 Mackenzie, C. (2000). Imagining oneself otherwise. In: *Relational Autonomy: Feminist Perspectives on Autonomy, Agency, and the Social Self* (eds. C. Mackenzie and N. Stoljar), 132. Oxford: Oxford University Press.
9 Mackenzie, 126.
10 Mackenzie, 126.
11 Mackenzie, 126.
12 Mackenzie, 133.
13 Thompson-Hernández, W. (2018). Black Panther' Cosplayers: "We're Helping People See Us as Heroes". *New York Times*. (https://www.nytimes.com/2018/02/15/style/black-panther-movie-cosplay.html (February 15, 2018).
14 Thrasher, S. (2018). There Is Much to Celebrate – and Much to Question – About Marvel's *Black Panther*. *Esquire*. (https://www.esquire.com/entertainment/movies/a18241993/black-panther-review-politics-killmonger (February 20, 2018).
15 Thrasher.
16 Thrasher.
17 Thrasher.
18 Hooks, B. (1995). *Killing Rage: Ending Racism*, 14. New York: Henry Holt and Company.).
19 Fricker, M. (2007). *Epistemic Injustice: Power and the Ethics of Knowing*, 1. New York: Oxford University Press.
20 Fricker, 4.
21 Fricker, 155.

Part III

Metaphysics

Introduction

Metaphysics is the study of the nature of reality. While this often involves questions about the nature of the world, some of the most interesting contemporary questions about reality focus on our understanding of ourselves. We each believe that we have a mind, but what exactly is a mind, and how is it related to the brain? We each believe ourselves to be a person, but what exactly is a person and how can we be the same person over time? Do we really have free will? What about artificial intelligence? Could computers, one day soon, be conscious persons with the same rights as humans?

Questioning the nature of reality immediately leads to questions about the universe itself. What is it made of? What is its nature? And how can we know? At its base, the matter of the universe is quantum mechanical in nature – but what does that mean? In Chapter 8, Dara Fogel uses examples from *Star Trek* to argue that we might live in a computer simulation. If we do, a whole host of questions arise. Are we free? Are other persons conscious? Are you real? These questions are explored by Fogel and others in this part.

Metaphysical questions about persons often revolve around the mind. What exactly is it? Merely material? Something immaterial? Something in between? In Chapter 9, Dean Kowalski uses the adventures of the Marvel superhero Doctor Strange to give dualism – the belief in nonphysical souls interacting with physical bodies – serious consideration, and addresses some of its biggest problems. In Chapter 10, Matt Lawrence uses examples from *The Matrix* to show why dualism has fallen out of favor, and why the debate is now primarily between materialist theories like reductive materialism, eliminative materialism, emergentism, and functionalism. As it turns out, despite some tricky cases, the events of *The Matrix Trilogy* can be interpreted completely in a materialist light.

Introducing Philosophy Through Pop Culture: From Socrates to Star Wars *and Beyond*, Second Edition.
Edited by William Irwin and David Kyle Johnson.
© 2022 John Wiley & Sons Ltd. Published 2022 by John Wiley & Sons Ltd.

Other metaphysical questions about the person revolve around personal identity. Imagine yourself at age 10, and think how different you were. You look different now and you may have a different personality, yet you are the same person. How can that be? In Chapter 11, Jason Southworth uses the world of *X-Men* to address this classic philosophical issue of identity through time. The character Wolverine provides us with a perfect opportunity to examine John Locke's (1632–1704) memory criterion for personal identity, because Wolverine has lost and regained memories multiple times. In addition, the character Jamie Madrox – who can copy and recombine himself – exemplifies Derek Parfit's view that physical continuity plays a role in maintaining personal identity.

One of the most troubling questions in metaphysics is about whether humans have free will. In Chapter 12, Grant Sterling uses Tolkien's *The Hobbit* to wrestle with whether Bilbo can be free if his life's actions were predetermined by the gods, and likewise whether we can be free if God has foreknowledge of our future actions. Tolkien, it seems, embraced a solution to this problem like that of the philosopher Boethius (477–524): the suggestion that God is timeless. In Chapter 13, Fitzpatrick and Johnson use Christopher Nolan's film *Inception* to explore arguments, grounded in science and philosophy, that we don't have free will. Do we have the ability to choose otherwise? Is such an ability required for free will? *Inception* provides the perfect "Frankfurt counterexample" and reveals why such examples don't actually invalidate the traditional understanding of free will or prove that free will is compatible with determinism.

Another central question of metaphysics revolves around the issue of machine consciousness. If we one day develop machines that behave like us, should we conclude that they have minds like we do? The HBO series *Westworld* imagines just such a day and thus provides the perfect framework to explore these questions. In Chapter 14, Lucia Carrillo González uses *Westworld* to explain the "Turing test" for determining machine consciousness along with the "Chinese room" objection to Turing's conclusion. In Chapter 15, Bradley Richards points out that, even if the hosts of Westworld do have minds, what it is like to be a host probably differs significantly from what it is like to be a human. The same might also be true of the androids that humanity one day builds.

This part concludes with one of philosophy's most perplexing metaphysical issues: the possibility of time travel. In Chapter 16 David Kyle Johnson explains the two major paradox-free theories of time travel and applies them to the time travel that occurs in *Avengers: Endgame*. It turns out that *Endgame* falls prey to paradox. But, Johnson argues, that doesn't mean it's a bad movie; it just means it could have been better.

8

Life on a Holodeck

What Star Trek *Can Teach Us About the True Nature of Reality*

Dara Fogel

Summary

Just how "real" is our reality? Plato, Descartes, Eastern religions, and now modern-day physicists, all wonder about this question. This chapter connects these sources to the *Star Trek* universe. By exploring dimensions of programmed worlds and holographic characters, *Star Trek* raises important questions and implications about our own experience of reality, including questions about the origins of being and consciousness. Are we real? Or are we only programmed to believe we are real?

Philosophers and other thinkers have pondered tough questions about the nature of reality for thousands of years. Many of them have shared the view that our daily life is actually some sort of appearance or simulation, a dramatic presentation within which we interact and exist, but that isn't itself fundamental reality. Now, science seems to be discovering increasing support for this ancient concept, and *Star Trek*'s holodeck technology offers us great insights into understanding both old and new theories about what's *real*.

Every historical period has its own version of the idea that reality isn't what it seems to be, and the level of available technology influences the form the idea takes. In Plato's (428–348 BCE) "cave allegory," shadows cast upon a wall create an ever-changing drama enacted for chained prisoners, who mistake the shadows for reality since they're all the prisoners have ever perceived. Plato believed there existed both the realm of illusions inside the cave – analogous to the world we perceive with our senses – and the true reality outside of the cave – analogous to what we can understand with our intellect.[1] Hinduism[2] and Buddhism[3] both rely on the idea of *maya* – the illusory appearance of the world that contrasts with the indestructibility of consciousness. The Judeo-Christian Bible speaks of a perfect, ever-present, eternal, but invisible realm beyond the physical world. René Descartes (1596–1650)[4] and Immanuel Kant (1724–1804)[5] claimed that this

Introducing Philosophy Through Pop Culture: From Socrates to Star Wars *and Beyond*, Second Edition.
Edited by William Irwin and David Kyle Johnson.
© 2022 John Wiley & Sons Ltd. Published 2022 by John Wiley & Sons Ltd.

nonmaterial realm is somehow the ultimate cause of the effects we experience and observe, regardless of physical appearances. Often, this other realm is couched in religious terms, but recent scientific discoveries and TNG's Lieutenant Commander Data can help us discover a material, secular perspective on this age-old notion.

Of Humans and Holograms

Quantum physics lends compelling new support for the ancient dualistic view that there's both a physical realm we can perceive with our senses and a level of reality we can't directly perceive. The accumulation of data over the last 25 years from a variety of scientific fields reveals that our reality seems to be *holographic* in nature – that is, the "reality" in which we live, move, and have our being may actually be a three-dimensional projection of a two-dimensional surface, such as a piece of holographic film that originates in another, higher dimension.[6] Scientific study seems to confirm what much earlier philosophers and religious figures intuited, with far-reaching, mind-boggling implications that challenge our ordinary ways of thinking about reality and free will.

The animated *Star Trek* series introduced the holodeck as a total immersion, three-dimensional entertainment technology that provides computer-generated environments, characters, and dramatic contexts. "The Practical Joker" (TAS) pioneered the idea of an interactive, virtual reality technology designed for exercise, entertainment, and educational or problem-solving purposes. The holodeck in TAS began as a recreation center for the crew to re-connect to simulated natural landscapes while on long missions. Using photonic energy, combined with both transporter and replicator technologies to project a three-dimensional interactive environment, holodecks could be programmed to recreate a wide variety of settings for the crew to enjoy.[7]

By the inception of TNG, holodeck technology had evolved, offering programs as simple as a backdrop of a scenic location, or as complex as a narrative that unfolds as crewmembers enact roles in a story, as when Data and Geordi LaForge pretend to be Holmes and Watson in "Elementary, Dear Data" and "Ship in a Bottle." In DS9, Dr. Julian Bashir plays a James Bond-like 1960s-era spy in "Our Man Bashir," and also fights in various famous historical battles with Chief Miles O'Brien. Finally, in VOY, Lieutenant Tom Paris and Ensign Harry Kim play in the Buck Rogers-inspired "Captain Proton" serial holoprogram, complete with ray guns and rockets, as they battle the evil Chaotica ("Bride of Chaotica"). *Voyager's* whole crew even gets into the act when Paris creates a charming Victorian-era Irish village ("Fair Haven" and "Spirit Folk"). In pursuit of their own interests, Captain Kathryn Janeway apprentices herself to the quintessential Renaissance man, Leonardo DaVinci in "Scorpion, Part I" and "Concerning Flight"; and Kim battles Beowulf in "Heroes and Demons."

The Holographic Hypothesis

Philosopher Nick Bostrom has hypothesized that we could be part of an elaborate computer simulation being run by intelligent creatures, perhaps the descendants of the creatures we, as inhabitants of the simulation, are modeled upon.[8] Just as Data's Holmes and Bashir's spy holoprograms are recreations of past eras, so might our "reality" be a historical holonovel being run by unimaginably advanced people. Bostrom calls these "ancestor" simulations, further positing that there could likely be many more simulations of history than "real" lived histories. As with the several different Holmes-type stories Data and Geordi run, serial holoprograms illustrate how each "player" can have multiple permutations, with changing stories, themes, settings, and featured characters in their sagas.

Bostrom observes that there are basically only three possible responses to the question of whether we live in a computer simulation or not. One of these *must* be true: (i) It's impossible; (ii) If it's not impossible, then it's unlikely; and (iii) If it's not unlikely, then it's almost certain. Bostrom claims that we lack the evidence to fully accept the first option, so we can't rule out the possibility that we live in some kind of computer-generated world. In fact, if simulated worlds are possible for advanced civilizations and such civilizations are inclined to run them, then there would be many simulated worlds and only one real world. The odds would thus be that any being is much more likely to be in a simulated world than in the real world. Although Bostrom offers no empirical data to support his ideas, his conclusions result from valid arguments, meaning that we must at least allow for the *possibility* that our reality is a computer simulation.

Recent research in quantum physics converges with Bostrom's hypothesis in reporting that "behind" physical reality lies an energetic field that could be compared to a holodeck matrix grid with the capacity to transform into the myriad forms of physical reality. This subatomic field is sometimes called "the Zero Point Field" or simply "the Field."[9] The Field contains limitless power potential and can collapse into all the discrete physical units we call "matter," but it's not composed of matter itself. The famous "Double Slit" experiment illustrates how particles can manifest as either waves of energy (the Field) or coalesce into concrete points of matter that make up our physical world.[10] It isn't a far stretch to think of the Field as the holomatrix through which some cosmic holodeck generates the scenarios and characters that constitute our reality. Indeed, the philosopher Marcus Arvan has argued that the best explanation of quantum phenomena is that our world is a computer simulated world much like the those created by the shared interaction of computers in peer-to-peer computer games. Because such worlds are created by how the processors interact and interpret the available data (the Field), certain objects in those worlds do not have definite properties until they are measured, and others can have contradictory properties at once.[11]

Of course, holodecks manipulate optics and matter, generating virtual space on demand that far exceeds the room's apparent dimensions. The same could be true with our own scientific discoveries – the more we look into the physical nature of "reality," the more "empirical evidence" is generated by the holodeck at both the quantum and physical scales. But all of these "discoveries" would still only be computer-generated probabilities inside the holomatrix. This could actually explain many of the paradoxes of quantum physics. Perhaps so-called "limit conditions" in nature, such as the speed of light or the Planck length, are telltale signs of our holodeck's processing boundaries.[12] Maybe these universal standards aren't truly "universal" outside the simulation. They could be merely dictated by our reality's particular holomatrix, and so they're true only within this current holoprogram.

Increasing evidence indicates that our universe is *digital* in nature. Theoretical physicist S. James Gates recently found computer code in the mathematics used to describe string theory in quantum physics. Specifically, he found "Block Linear Self Dual Error Correcting Code" embedded *inside* his string theory equations. This wasn't just a set of similar numbers, but the *actual* code! This is the very same algorithm used by the Google search engine to monitor and correct received digital information.[13] This embedded code serves as more evidence underwriting the possibility of holodeck informational processing constituting our world.

Neuroscientist Karl Pribram (1919–2015) discovered that brains behave like holograms. For instance, *memory* is infused throughout the whole brain and not in discrete locations, allowing those with damaged or even mostly missing brains to still have recall. Pribram and other researchers suggest that the brain itself may be part of a hologram-decoding system. Our brains act as filters on the millions of sensory inputs each of us experience all the time, allowing us to recognize, understand, and interact with the continuous patterns within the holoprogram – akin to how Geordi's brain filters the "visual frenzy" presented to him through his VISOR ("Heart of Glory," TNG).

The human brain's structure is consistent with the design specifications necessary to exist and function within a holographic universe. The brain functions by looking for and identifying discernible regularities in our environment. This allows us to recognize and engage with the universe's many recurring patterns, such as the widespread occurrence of *pi* and the "golden ratio" in nature, ranging from the orbits of subatomic particles to the spiraling arms of galaxies. This is sort of like how Data keeps encountering odd occurrences of the number "3" when he receives a subconscious signal from his past self in "Cause and Effect" (TNG); his positronic brain is hardwired to pick up and interpret the signal. This is a new, scientific understanding akin to the ancient Hindu belief that humanity is the microcosm to the creator's macrocosm. Perhaps that was also a low-tech expression by the ancients to describe the recurring algorithms used to create our holoprogram and our participation within it.

If this "holodeck hypothesis" is an accurate model of our own existence, then *Star Trek* can help us to understand both our metaphysical predicament and how this impacts our moral obligations to each other and to ourselves. Issues like holo-addiction, which challenge Reginald Barclay, Tom Paris, and Geordi La Forge in different ways, may give us insight into our own psychological addictions to drama. The creative aspect of holoprograms, such as "Captain Proton," Bashir's spy adventures, or *Voyager*'s Emergency Medical Hologram, raise serious questions about our own reality, as well as offer a fresh perspective on many ancient beliefs and traditions.

Is Reality an App?

If our reality is a holographic projection, then who or what programmed it? Holoprograms and holonovels require an author/programmer of some kind, while the "player" interacts with the program through their own physical presence. Virtual reality, of course, requires that programming and processing take place outside of the reality generated. The technology that creates manifest images on the holodeck must exist separately from the projected holomatrix, as must the programmer/operator of that technology – unless *self-awareness* occurs *within* the program, as occurs when Dr. Moriarty becomes self-aware within Data's Sherlock Holmes program and is able to seize control of both his holo-environment and the *Enterprise.*

While traditional religions offer a deity to fulfill the function of holoprogrammer, *Star Trek* points us toward a creator-artist, who designs holoprograms and novels for enjoyment, self-expression, and learning. Barclay, LaForge, and Paris all dabble with creating their own holoprograms; and Bashir procures his customized holoprograms from his off-screen friend, Felix, whose name comes from the Latin word for "happiness."[14] Even *Voyager*'s EMH creates his own ideal holofamily in "Real Life" and later pens a controversial holonovel in "Author, Author" about his experiences as a sentient holoprogram, entitled "Photons Be Free."

In each of these cases, someone who's not part of the holomatrix originated the program, except in the few cases where the holodeck was used as a problem-solving tool, recursively manipulating images and brainstorming from inside the holodeck. A good example of this is "A Matter of Perspective" (TNG) in which the holodeck is used to recreate a crime scene from the points of view of several witnesses. Another example of holoprogramming on-the-fly occurs in "Booby Trap" (TNG) when Geordi uses the holodeck to recreate the Utopia Planitia shipyard drafting room where the *Enterprise* was designed. Geordi ends up with more holoprogram than intended, when the computer includes a simulacrum of the *Enterprise*'s engine designer, Dr. Leah Brahms. But these in situ programming sessions are the exception, not the general rule of how the holodeck is utilized. Holoprograms are thus similar to apps for our smartphones or tablets: all apps must have programmers and users, as well as an operating system on which the app runs. These conditions are separate from the "matrix" of the app itself.

Some physicists, like Niels Bohr (1885–1962) and Richard Conn Henry, have claimed that the universe is basically *mental* in nature.[15] If so, then the structure of our brains as "holographic decoders" is our prime interface with the world and indicates a direction for future research. Others liken our universe to a multiplayer computer game.[16] Likewise, *Star Trek*'s holodeck is primarily for recreation and entertainment. The parallel implies that there may be an inherent purpose to human life, but not one that's been popular with philosophers and theologians in the past. Instead, we're here to *play the game* – just as Q tests the *Enterprise* crew through "a deadly game" he constructs in "Hide and Q" (TNG). Hinduism claims this is the underlying reason for the creation of *maya*, or illusion, and calls this "playing at life" *lila*. What if our own reality is more like a video game or an app than the random happenstance of matter in motion described by scientific materialism? The implications are paradigm shattering.

First, it would mean that we don't live in a universe without *reason*. The cycles and patterns of nature are evidence of recurring templates and algorithms. Thus, everything we experience – physical bodies, the natural world, the complexities of cultures, governments, and societies, even our own personal relationships – must have been previously coded by this unknown creator-artist of our own holographic novel. Mystic traditions of the past have appeal in no small part due to their explanatory power for the *purpose* of existence. Science has been notably silent when it comes to ascribing purpose or meaning to the universe, due to lack of any unbiased, physical evidence sufficient to meet the scientific method's burden of proof. But quantum physics is beginning to make incursions into territory once firmly held by religion, offering new science-based interpretations of ancient teachings.

If the holographic hypothesis is borne out, it may provide a scientific framework for understanding what might be ancient empirical discoveries buried under eons of religious tradition and superstitious misunderstanding. The holographic hypothesis can expand our comprehension of human potential and limitations, once we understand our status as characters in the larger ongoing story of the holoprogram – perhaps William Shakespeare, as Q notes to Picard in "Hide and Q," was pronouncing a literal truth when he wrote "All the world's a stage." This interpretation has profound implications for who we think we are and for our capacities to control or change our lives and our world.

Can't Tell a Soul Without a Program

Another implication of living in a cosmic video game is that our "free will" is merely apparent, as characters in a computer game or holonovel can do nothing that's not already coded into their program. While playing Sherlock Holmes, Data must limit himself to only what the fictional Victorian-era sleuth is capable of doing and knowing, or else the illusion is destroyed and the game is over. In fact, this is what gets him and Geordi into trouble in "Elementary, Dear Data" when the latter, frustrated that Data has memorized all the extant Holmes stories, instructs the computer to program Holmes's nemesis, Professor Moriarty, to be a match for *Data*, not Holmes. Playing the game is possible only by continuing some pretense of the artificial limitations of our circumstances. This would explain why, if our world is a simulation, you can't fly without technological help, nor magically manifest a million dollars in your checking account by just wishing. It also explains the failure of many personal development techniques, such as the "Law of Attraction" originating in early twentieth-century "New Thought" or personal affirmations. Unless possibilities are coded into the program, no special techniques within the program can "make it so."

Sometimes, however, games have secret shortcuts and "easter eggs." Pre-programmed surprises can be bad as well as good – like the "jack-in-the-box" feature in Bashir's casino program featuring hololounge lizard, Vic Fontaine. When holoprogrammer Felix decides to shake things up, the mob takes over Vic's casino ("Badda-Bing Badda-Bang," DS9), and the crew has to outsmart the program to restore their favorite holohangout.

Perhaps there are features of our reality that serve like shortcuts, "easter eggs," or "jacks-in-the-box." The social and psychological fabric of our lives contains common elements of mythic structure, drama, and storytelling that we seem compelled to enact. Most of us have seen the "fingerprints of the editor" in our lives – those reoccurring archetypal themes, last minute saves, beatings of impossible odds, and unlikely miracles that make up some of the content of our daily lives – the same stuff as myths are made of.[17] So, while it would seem that we don't normally get to determine the plot from inside our holoprogram, there does appear to be some kind of cyclic and mythic shaping to the story we experience.

In this way, ancient traditions propose that we can gain some degree of freedom, if we're willing to devote sufficient time and attention to self-development. Many faiths, such as Buddhism and Hinduism, offer rigorous training systems claiming to accomplish such self-realization. The holographic hypothesis gives us a means for evaluating the accuracy and effectiveness of these traditional training programs. Perhaps we, like the DS9 crew, can find shortcuts to outsmart our own holoprograms.

But we must also be willing to face the possibility that the idea of transcending one's programming is but another layer of programming in the holonovel, and in reality, there's no independent consciousness. It may be that there's no way for creatures like us ever to escape the confines of the holodeck. Perhaps the cycles and predictability of nature were programmed by yet another program, without the intervention of what we'd consider an *ultimate intelligence*. This line of reasoning only defers answering the question of who programmed the holodeck, and doesn't resolve any questions about the origin or purpose of the simulation.

On this view, we're as firmly fixed within our own storyline as any *Star Trek* character is enmeshed in the plots they inhabit. As authoritative and intelligent as Picard may be, he doesn't exist apart from the *Star Trek* universe. It matters not at all how capable or determined he might imagine himself to be, he can't transcend the script. Indeed, such an intention on his part could only exist within the context of a *Star Trek* script or novel, and is constrained by his very own manifestation as a character within the ongoing *Star Trek* saga. Stepping down from the meta-level, Vic Fontaine is a self-aware hologram, which gives him a certain degree of freedom within the holoprogram he inhabits – he can end his own program, create new characters within the program, and even move himself into other concurrently running programs – yet he's also aware of his built-in limitations as a holographic representation of a 1960s-era lounge singer ("His Way" and "It's Only a Paper Moon," DS9).

Talmudic tradition within Judaism holds that we have no choice *but* to believe in our own free will. Perhaps this is correct, and free will is just another feature of the pre-programmed human holographic characters. Some may find the idea that they have absolutely no control over their lives comforting, and there are whole belief systems and religions dedicated to precisely this view, but others find it obnoxious. For them, the idea that the universe is like an interactive computer game is immensely more attractive.

Who's Playing What?

On the holodeck, there are two types of people: "players" – like Data pretending to be Henry V or Sherlock Holmes – and "non-player characters" (NPCs) – holographic people created to interact with the players. Does this imply some of the people we interact with on a daily basis might not be real? Your co-workers who you never see outside of work might just be NPCs. What about those neighbors whose name you don't know, but wave to occasionally when you both happen to be outside at the same time? Or maybe even those kooky family members you only see at Christmas? They might be NPCs making recurring cameo appearances, like Janeway's Leonardo Da Vinci or Riker's Minuet ("11001001" and "Future Imperfect," TNG).

How do we know if the person we're dealing with is "real" like us, or an NPC created to fill out the details of our story, making it seem more plausible? It would seem that we can't. In "Ship In A Bottle" (TNG), Data realizes they're in Moriarty's holographic version of the *Enterprise* only when subtle computer glitches tip him off. Before then, Picard believes he's actually communicating with crewmembers on the bridge, not suspecting them to be holodeck facsimiles of the crew. In "Homeward" (TNG), Worf's brother Nikolai Rozhenko fools the pre-industrial tribal Boraalans as he and Worf lead them on a fictitious exodus through the holodeck, while the *Enterprise* races to find them a new planet to replace their ravaged world. Even Captain Janeway falls for a computer-generated hunk on the holodeck, fully knowing he's a NPC, in "Fair Haven," as does Geordi with the holographic Leah Brahms – leading to a rude awakening for him when me meets the *real* Leah Brahms in "Galaxy's Child" (TNG).

It's notable that most NPC holocharacters at first fail to realize that they're not real. Picard explains this peculiar metaphysical fact to NPC mobster Cyrus Redblock, breaking briefly out of character as 40s-era private-eye Dixon Hill in "The Big Goodbye" (TNG). And he confronts Moriarty with the same facts when the enhanced holovillian expresses the desire to leave the holodeck. Inside the holodeck, what appears to be real is what passes for reality.

How do you know that *you're* "real," by these standards? We currently have no way to determine this, as our science is likely to be keyed to physical laws of the holodeck program and not representative of physics outside of the holomatrix. Ancient traditions tell us that the persona we experience ourselves to be is just another part of the illusion – that we're actually immaterial consciousness beyond any physical manifestations. Perhaps what's been traditionally called the "soul" or "consciousness" is analogous to operating in a fully immersive role-playing computer game. Could it be that we've become so caught up in the fun and drama of the world as "holonovel," we've forgotten our true identity as individuals whose lives are rooted outside of the holodeck?

But in the end, we can't even know if this is the truth or not. Our whole existence might be nothing more than energy pulses, our self-awareness (or lack of it) just an expression of a random algorithm. At the conclusion of "Ship in a Bottle" (TNG), having outwitted Moriarty into thinking that he and his beloved Countess have left both the holodeck and the *Enterprise* in a shuttlecraft, Picard raises a nagging epistemic question:

PICARD:	In fact, the program is continuing even now inside that cube.
CRUSHER:	A miniature holodeck?
DATA:	In a way, Doctor. However, there is no physicality. The program is continuous but only within the computer's circuitry.
BARCLAY:	As far as Moriarty and the Countess know, they're half way to Meles II by now. This enhancement module contains enough active memory to provide them experiences for a lifetime.
PICARD:	They will live their lives and never know any difference.
TROI:	In a sense, you did give Moriarty what he wanted.
PICARD:	In a sense. But who knows? Our reality may be very much like theirs. All this might be just an elaborate simulation running inside a little device sitting on someone's table.

Or perhaps – as Sisko and the rest of the DS9 crew may very well be – we might just be characters in a story being written by an author like Benny Russell ("Far Beyond the Stars," "Shadows and Symbols," DS9).

Cogito Ergo Sum?

Finally, we might ask about the metaphysical and ethical status of self-aware holograms, such as Moriarty, VOY's EMH, and DS9's Vic Fontaine. Do they count as "real" people? Or are they merely computer-generated NPCs? And if they are just virtual people, does their self-awareness grant them some special status or wisdom? Does their added self-consciousness make them worthy of *rights*? More than once, *Star Trek* has sought to address the metaphysical question of personhood for holographic sentients. These hol-ocharacters are aware that they're photonic projections, their parameters designed by someone else. Yet they're able to transcend their original programming, to learn and even change the holomatrix determining their own character and story.

Could these sentient holocharacters be analogies of human capacity? Traditional mystical approaches offer us the examples of prophets, saints, and saviors as similar to these holocharacters; with some traditions even providing teachings and techniques for individuals who seek to overcome their own "holoprogramming." Perhaps these "real" prophets and sages somehow managed to achieve this goal, surpassing their program-ming and emerging into a new level of being. Such a conclusion would be consistent with ancient mystical traditions – such as Buddhism, Kabbalah, and Hinduism – according to which this potential for realization resides within each of us. But again, this so-called "transcendence" could just be a new screen or level of play in the ongoing game.

Star Trek provides an instructive allegory for understanding both ancient and current, cutting-edge concepts of reality. The holodeck hypothesis suggests that perhaps taking hold of our destiny depends upon the realization that we're fictional characters playing a role in an ongoing narrative in a cosmic "holodeck." As players, we can't exceed the parameters of the original design – unless we, like Moriarty, the EMH, or Vic Fontaine, can figure out how to transcend our own programming. But whether we can escape the holomatrix altogether is the topic of an entirely different sci-fi franchise . . .[18]

For pop culture resources and philosophical resources related to this chapter please visit the website for this book: https://introducingphilosophythroughpopculture.com.

Notes

1   Plato. (1991). *Republic* (trans. Harold Bloom). New York: Basic Books.
2   (1962). *The Bhavagad Gita* (trans. J. Mascaro). New York: Penguin Books.
3   (1973). *The Dhammapada* (trans. J. Mascaro). New York: Penguin Books.
4   Descartes, R. (1993). *Meditations on First Philosophy*, 3e (trans. Donald A. Tress). Indianapolis: Hackett.
5   Kant, I. (1964). *Groundwork of the Metaphysics of Morals* (trans. H.J. Paton). New York: Harper & Row.
6   Yirka, B. New Work Gives Credence to Theory of Universe as a Hologram. http://phys.org/news/2013-12-credence-theory-universe-hologram.html; Talbot, M. (1991). *The Holographic Universe*. New York: HarperCollins; Whitworth, B. Quantum Realism. http://www.brianwhitworth.com/bw-vrt.1.pdf (both websites accessed June 19, 2015).
7   "Holodeck." Memory Alpha. http://en.memory-alpha.org/wiki/holodeck (accessed June 19, 2015).
8   Bostrom, N. (2003). Are you living in a computer simulation? *Philosophical Quarterly* 53: 243–55. http://www.simulation-argument.com (accessed June 19, 2015).
9   McTaggart, L. (2001). *The Field: The Quest for the Secret Force of the Universe*. New York: HarperCollins.
10 May, M. (July–August 1998). The reality of watching. *American Scientist*. https://www.americanscientist.org/issues/pub/the-reality-of-watching (accessed June 19, 2015).
11 This description does not do the argument justice. For more see his papers on the topic, like: Arvan, M. (2014). A unified explanation of quantum phenomena? The case for the peer-to-peer simulation hypothesis as an interdisciplinary research program. *Philosophical Forum* 45: 433–446, doi: 10.1111/phil.12043.
12 Whitworth, "Quantum Realism."
13 Gates, S.J. (2000). Symbols of power. *Physics World* 23 (6): 34–9.
14 For an analysis of whether holodecks could actually make one "happy," see Tallon, P. and Walls, J.L. (2008). Why not live in the Holodeck?. In: *Star Trek and Philosophy: The Wrath of Kant* (eds. J.T. Eberl and K.S. Decker). Chicago: Open Court.
15 Henry, R.C. (2005). The mental universe. *Nature* 436 (July 7, 2005). http://www.henry.pha.jhu.edu/The.mental.Universe.pdf (accessed June 19, 2015).
16 Beane, S.R., Davoudi, Z., and Savage, M. Constraints on the universe as a numerical simulation. http://arxiv.org/pdf/1210.1847.pdf (accessed June 19, 2015).
17 This thesis lends credence to Joseph Campbell's theory of the "monomyth" that's played out in various mythological dramas throughout various times and cultures. See his (2008). *The Hero with a Thousand Faces*, 3e. Novato, CA: New World Library. John Thompson critically engages *Star Wars* creator George Lucas's reliance on Campbell's "monomyth" in his (2016). "In that time . . ." in a galaxy far, far away: epic myth-understandings and myth-appropriation in *Star Wars*. In: *The Ultimate Star Wars and Philosophy* (eds. J.T. Eberl and K.S. Decker). Malden, MA: Wiley.
18 See Irwin, W. (ed.) (2002). *The Matrix and Philosophy*. Chicago: Open Court; and Irwin, W. (ed.) (2005). *More Matrix and Philosophy*. Chicago: Open Court.

9

Astral Bodies and Cartesian Souls
Mind–Body Dualism in Doctor Strange

Dean A. Kowalski

Summary

The 2016 Marvel film *Doctor Strange* provides for a novel investigation of the meta-physical relationship between the mind and the body. Dr. Stephen Strange, prior to his training in the mystical arts, espouses physicalism, the theory that human persons are nothing over and above their working physical parts. Once Strange comes under the tutelage of the Ancient One at Kamar-Taj, he is led to reject his previous view in favor of a theory philosophers call substance dualism, championed by René Descartes (1596–1650). The film masterfully depicts the challenges any substance dualist must navigate in their attempt to explain how the nonphysical mind (or soul) is connected to the body and physical world generally. It might be that substance dualist detractors are myopically "looking at the world through a keyhole," but, as we'll see, the philosophical process is about more than what is merely possible. It is about acquiring justified beliefs about how things are (or ought to be).

In the 2016 film *Doctor Strange*, the title character suffers a horrific car accident that damages the nerves in his hands and fingers beyond repair. Strange believes he can heal himself, which would have been quite a sight, and also attests to his hubris as a medical doctor and scientific researcher (or maybe simply his over-inflated ego as a human being). In any case, his reaction to his accident makes us aware of his entrenched belief that all there is to a human being is nerves, muscles, blood, bone, and other sorts of tissue and fluids. If a person can learn all there is to know about the physics, chemistry, and biology of the body – as Strange may come close to doing – then there is nothing left over to know. In part, this is why he rages over his injury: if he is as knowledgeable and skilled a surgeon as he thinks he is, then (he believes) he should be able to fix his hands.

Philosophers are one with Strange in his pursuit of knowledge in general, but they are much more concerned with abstract or conceptual questions about how things ultimately are (or ought to be). One of the more intriguing philosophical questions is about the fundamental nature of human beings. Are we simply flesh and bone, as Strange

Introducing Philosophy Through Pop Culture: From Socrates to Star Wars *and Beyond*, Second Edition.
Edited by William Irwin and David Kyle Johnson.
© 2022 John Wiley & Sons Ltd. Published 2022 by John Wiley & Sons Ltd.

seems to think, or is there more – especially when it comes to the nature of our minds and souls? In this chapter, we'll use the good Dr. Strange to look at how some philosophers attempt to answer this important question. In the process, we'll gain some deeper insights about philosophy itself.

"Let's Get Physical" – Olivia Newton-John 1981

Strange's worldview at the beginning of the film is effectively summed up in his brazen rant to the Ancient One: "I do not believe in fairy tales about the power of belief. There is no such thing as spirit! We are made of matter and nothing more. You're just another tiny, momentary speck within an indifferent universe."[1] Whether he knows it or not, Strange is invoking a *metaphysics* debate straight out of the philosophy classroom. Metaphysics seeks answers to fundamental questions about what, why, and how things exist, such as "Are human persons merely physical beings?" Philosophers (and one clever neurosurgeon) who answer this question "yes" maintain a view called *physicalism*, the metaphysical theory that human persons are nothing over and above the sum total of their working physical parts. To a physicalist, any fact about human beings can be explained using facts about the human body, including facts about consciousness. According to this view of the world, our abilities to think, feel, believe, and remember are effectively understood as features and functions of the (physical) human brain.

The fact that Strange accepts physicalism is not surprising, because most physicalists rely largely on science to argue for their position. After all, science has enabled us to explain many features of the physical world. Using science, we know that, despite appearances to the contrary, the sun does not actually set over the horizon and that the Earth rotates on its axis. Physicalists also turn to neuroscience to discover surprising and hidden truths about human beings, such as the nature of mental disorders and how to treat them. Even though there are aspects of consciousness that neuroscience finds difficult to account for, physicalists hold that neuroscience will continue to unearth truths about our mental lives until nothing about us is left unexplained.

When the Ancient One suggests that she can heal his hands as she cured Pangborn's paralysis, she asks Strange, "What if I told you that your own body could be convinced to put itself back together in all sorts of ways?" Strange assumes that she's developed a "bleeding-edge" experimental procedure for cellular regeneration. If he could learn this technique, not only would he be in a better position to heal his hands, but he could also regrow cells so that they effectively self heal. (Obviously, he would call it the Ancient-Strange technique – or better yet, the Strange-Ancient technique.) This is so cutting-edge that it would also explain why she practices medicine inconspicuously in Kamar-Taj – to avoid the prying eyes of a "governing medical board." Finally, he has found the cure he so desperately sought. This justifies having spent his last dime to journey to Kamar-Taj. In all of this excitement, however, Strange forgot Mordo's advice to "forget everything you think you know." Soon he'll be forced to.

"Soul Man" – Sam & Dave 1967

The Ancient One has a very different view of the world and the human beings in it: we are both body *and* spirit. Contrary to Strange's assumption, her expertise is not in cellular regeneration; instead, she knows "how to reorient the spirit to better heal the body." Once he realizes that she believes spirit is something in addition to the body, Strange becomes dismissive. This explains his quip about fairy tales, and his crass comment that persons are merely tiny physical specks in an unimaginably large (and indifferent) universe.

Yet some philosophers agree with the Ancient One that the spirit (or soul) is a thing unto itself and can affect and influence the body, a view called *substance dualism*. Substance dualists contend that there are two radically different features of human existence. Of course, there is the physical, which Strange knows so well and which physicalists believe explains all of human experience. Substance dualists, however, insist that we are more than simply the sum total of our physical facts. Once the physical is accounted for, we still have to account for mental states, like the regret that Strange feels for treating Christine Palmer so badly or the anguish he feels about her not replying to his emails. These facts about Strange are something in addition to his physical facts.

These mental states are qualitative in nature, more amenable to description than measurement. They have subjective meaning that can only be experienced by the person having them and cannot be observed directly from the outside by anyone else. Because these feelings are difficult to connect securely with any physical fact, substance dualists argue that there must be nonphysical facts about us, and such facts "reside" with the nonphysical spirit or soul. Substance dualists further hold that your nonphysical facts, including the soul itself, account for who you "truly" are – your beliefs, choices, desires, and memories – while your body, the non-thinking, fleshy component of you, is the physical aspect of your self. Combined, they comprise the fundamental nature of any human person.

René Descartes (1596–1650) is a well-known substance dualist, and, in fact, substance dualists are often referred to as *Cartesian dualists*. Descartes explains his theory this way:

> Because we have no conception of the body as thinking in any way, we have reason to believe that every kind of thought which exists in us belongs to the soul . . . We must [also] know that the soul is really joined to the whole body, and that we cannot, properly speaking, say that it exists in any one of its parts to the exclusion of the others.[2]

When we see the Ancient One dislodging Strange's "astral form" from his "physical form" and forcing it into a "place where the soul exists apart from the body," it serves as a fantastic dramatization of substance dualism and a refutation of physicalism – especially to Stephen Strange.

"Miss You" – The Rolling Stones 1978

Strange's soul embarks on a mystical journey, but his body remains in the temple. During this bizarre journey, he experiences various otherworldly sights, sounds, and sensations. When conjoined again with his body, his conviction in physicalism is shaken. Because Strange could not have experienced what he did if physicalism were true, and the Ancient One assures him he was not drugged, he has no choice but to accept that persons are more than tiny physical specks in an indifferent universe. It is here that his mystical training truly begins.

Twice we see Strange using his astral form to his advantage. The first involves Strange's clever strategy to learn as much about the mystic arts as he can. When Strange "borrows" books from the library, we see him reading them, but at the same time we see his body asleep in his bed. Strange's astral form – his soul – is shown sitting upright at the foot of the bed holding one of the books that Wong refused to lend him and turning its pages. This scene presupposes substance dualism in that Strange's soul is not only able to exist apart from the physical body, but it is also capable of reading, thinking, and learning – and turning pages in a physical book – even when not embodied. (The nature of this interaction between the physical and nonphysical is an issue we'll return to later.)

The second time Strange uses his astral self is more involved, both thematically and conceptually. After Strange is badly injured by one of Kaecilius's acolytes, he escapes by creating a dimensional gateway to the hospital where Christine Palmer works as an emergency room doctor. She puts him on an operating table and prepares to remove blood and fluid from his pericardium when he loses consciousness. Suddenly, Strange's astral form emerges from his body. He floats to the right side of the table and observes Christine as she is about to plunge a large-bore syringe into his torso. At this point, she does not see Strange floating right in front of her. He abruptly makes himself visible and audible so he can "Strangesplain" to her how to perform the procedure correctly. Christine is taken aback – and so is the viewer – as we all see Strange's astral form protruding through some sort of dimensional rift. When Christine asks, "Stephen, what am I seeing?" he replies, "My astral body." Wondering if Strange has become a disembodied ghost, she asks, "Are you dead?" He answers, "No, but I am dying," as if to remind her of her medical task. He places his astral hand inside the chest cavity of his physical form, and illuminates exactly where he wants Christine to insert the syringe.

But alas, their inter-dimensional reunion is cut short. Strange isn't the only one who can separate his astral form from his physical form: Kaecilius's acolyte, whom Strange trapped in the Cloak of Levitation, does the same and follows Strange to the operating room. When Strange sees him, he tells Christine, "I'm gonna have to vanish now. Keep me alive, will you?" As Strange and the acolyte fight, their astral bodies crash into each other and the operating room walls. Occasionally, especially in their more violent interactions, they affect the physical space of the operating room. For example, their scuffle lands them on the operating table, causing fluid in a surgical tray to noticeably vibrate. They travel through Christine, who is still trying to save Strange's physical form, and she seems to sense their presence. As the two sorcerers whisk out of the room, their astral forms plunge through a vending machine, upsetting some of the snacks (from which a doctor serendipitously benefits when he gathers them up).

When they make their way back to the operating room, the acolyte lands a devastating blow that seems to stop Strange's heart in the physical world. Christine recognizes the sound of Strange flatlining and charges the defibrillator paddles. The electrical blast not only restarts his heart in his physical form but also surges through his astral form, incapacitating the acolyte. When Strange reappears to Christine, he tells her to increase the voltage and charge him again. Strange somehow redirects the more intense blast into the acolytes's astral form, causing it to explode and his physical form to expire. Strange then gasps and regains consciousness on the operating room table – his astral form and physical body now rejoined. With the immediate threat to Strange's life averted, Christine muses, "After all this time, you just show up here flying out of your body?" To which he quietly replies, "I've missed you, too."

"Body and Soul" – Billie Holiday 1957

It is undeniable that what happens to one's body affects one's mental life and vice versa. In the real world, because Benedict Cumberbatch agreed to play the character of Dr. Stephen Strange, he decided to grow a beard and trim it in the iconic style of the Sorcerer

Supreme. In the movie, when Strange was pierced in the chest with a mystical weapon that damaged his heart, it caused him a great deal of pain and led to a desire to seek out Christine to save his life. That's not merely science fiction. Anyone suffering from a chest wound would experience pain and seek medical assistance.

The peculiar relationship between the physical and nonphysical worlds is one of the great puzzles facing metaphysics in general and substance dualism in particular. Descartes realized the significance of these interrelationships and their implications for his worldview:

> By means of these sensations of pain, hunger, thirst and so on, nature also teaches me that I am present in my body not merely as a sailor is present in a ship, but that I am most tightly joined and, so to speak, commingled with it, so much so that I and the body constitute one single thing. For if this were not the case, then I, who am only a thinking thing, would not sense pain when the body is injured; rather, I would perceive the wound by means of the pure intellect, just as a sailor perceives by sight whether anything in his ship is broken.[3]

Here Descartes anticipates the objection that the body and soul cannot be radically distinct because our experiences tell us that our physical and mental lives are closely intertwined. His response is that the so-called "commingling" of the body and the soul allows for the two to interact. Indeed, most substance dualists follow Descartes and ascribe to interactionism, which is the idea that the soul and body cause changes in each other. Interactionism is the "explanatory glue" holding Cartesian dualism together, and without it, the Cartesian dualist can't account for our experience of a unified wholeness of our physical and mental lives. When we suffer a wound, we don't merely recognize the damage intellectually – we feel it – and interactionism is supposed to explain why.

Descartes further argues that, although the soul is "commingled" with the whole body, the interaction takes place in the brain's pineal gland.[4] Descartes believes that the pineal gland is infused with what he called (according to standard translations) "animal spirits," which transfer information from the body to the mind and vice versa. However, as many soon realized, Descartes's "solution" only succeeds in inviting further questions: How do these spirits accomplish information transfer between mind and body? If the spirits are physical, then how do they impact the nonphysical mind (to say nothing of why Dr. Strange has never seen them during brain surgery)? If the spirits are nonphysical, then how do they come into contact with the physical pineal gland?

Yet these sorts of philosophical concerns are not limited to the pineal gland. The issue is not *where* body and soul interact, but *how* they are able to interact at all. The deeper problem is the nature of interactionism itself. How can one's soul be both radically distinct, and thus separate (and separable) from one's body, and also causally conjoined to it, and thus able to account for all that human beings accomplish?[5]

These sorts of questions were posed to Descartes from the beginning. For example, Princess Elisabeth of Bohemia, who was something of a student of Descartes, elegantly asked her teacher:

> Tell me how the human soul can determine the movement of the animal spirits in the body so as to perform voluntary acts. . . . For the determination of movement seems always to come about from the moving body's being propelled – to depend on the kind of impulse it gets from what sets it in motion, or again, on the nature and shape of this latter thing's surface.

It seems that the body and the soul are not the sorts of things that could interact. Physical objects are propelled by contact, but nonphysical objects can't come into contact with anything.

Questions about interactionism remain forceful today. Contemporary philosopher Garrett Thomson tidily summarizes the conceptual difficulties with interactionism:

> How does the mind control something that is physical, if it is not physical? If the mind has no location in space, then it is wrong to imagine it close to the brain. Why then does it have a direct causal influence only on my brain? . . . If non-spatially located acts of will cause changes in my brain, this must be a form of psychokinesis or magic.[6]

Thomson, not so subtly, contends that interactionism is little more than wishful thinking, and describes the ongoing problem of substance dualism without offering hope of solving it.

We see these same issues in the scenes described earlier featuring Dr. Strange's astral self. How is Strange's astral form – his nonphysical soul – capable of holding a (physical) book and turning its pages? Likewise, how did Strange's astral-form struggle with the acolyte cause physical changes to Christine's emergency room?

These puzzles are similar to the question of how our minds or souls interact with our brains and bodies, just extended to things outside our own physical forms. In fact, the emergency room scene raises even more issues. When Strange first appears to Christine, half of his astral form remains in the astral plane, but the other half appears and speaks to her in the earthly physical plane. She can see it and hear it, which means it reflects light and moves air, but only physical things do those two things. Why did the two astral form combatants sometimes crash into walls and other times pass through them? You might expect one or the other, but not both. How could defibrillating Strange's body cause his dislodged, nonphysical astral form to glow, which in turn caused the acolyte's dislodged astral form to explode, with the final effect of his body expiring? How does *that* work? It would take a very strange form of interactionism indeed (no pun intended) to explain what we see in this movie!

"It's Possible" –*Cinderella* 1957

Despite the obvious duality of physical and nonphysical astral forms portrayed in *Doctor Strange*, it remains paradoxical. Thus, the film can't avoid the numerous problems with interactionism and substance dualism in general. Furthermore, the apparent need for our bodies and minds (or souls) to interact regularly seems to imply a linkage too close to be merely waved away with talk of "commingling" or appeals to magical glands.

Yet the film *Doctor Strange* may suggest a response on behalf of the substance dualist. Why must it be that everything that occurs on our earthly plane necessarily follows the laws of physics? Perhaps the Ancient One addresses philosophers like Thomson as much as a skeptical Stephen Strange, when she states, "The language of the mystic arts is as old as civilization. The sorcerers of antiquity called the use of this language 'spells.' But if that word offends your modern sensibilities, you can call it a 'program.' The source code that shapes reality." Here, the Ancient One bridges the gap between science and magic, suggesting that what seems like magic to some is closer to science to others. She further explains, "We [sorcerers] harness energy drawn from other dimensions of the Multiverse to cast spells . . . to make magic." This ability, one that Strange can learn and hone just as he did neuroscience, is central to the practice of the mystical arts. Perhaps some physicists might scoff at the prospects of an energy transfer from one dimension to another, but is this science fiction or science not yet fully understood? Might the idea of energy transfers across dimensions at least begin to explain the otherwise inexplicable events in Christine's operating room? And could there be a similar energy transfer from the non-physical soul to the physical body to explain their interactions?[7]

More generally, this suggestion is but an aspect of the Ancient One's overall message to Strange about his narrow view of the world. Perhaps those suspicious of substance dualism are myopically "looking through a keyhole," and when it is suggested that the keyhole "can be widened in unimaginable ways," they simply "reject the possibility." Some might follow the Ancient One more directly, and complain to those who disagree with Descartes, "You think you know how the world works? You think that this material universe is all that there is?" Because there are so many things for each of us to learn, not the least of which is the inner workings of the universe (or Multiverse), perhaps we should adopt a bit of the humility Strange is forced to learn. With this, perhaps we should not be so quick to dismiss interactionism.

There is a kernel of truth in the Ancient One's message. Those who disagree with substance dualism usually admit that interactionism is not *logically* impossible. It's not like the idea of a married bachelor or a round square, for example. However, philosophers try to arrive at reasonable, likely, and justified beliefs about the way things are, not just ways they *could* be. Both telekinesis and magic are possible, but we have no reason to believe that either actually occurs. In fact, given other beliefs that we are justified in having, it seems most likely that they do not occur, which underscores Thomson's objection to substance dualism. Moreover, to adopt these more outlandish theories of interactionism demands that we wildly reinterpret or reject established scientific research about the so-called multiverse, energy transfers within and across dimensions, brain function, and, indeed, much of physics, chemistry, and biology. So, despite Mordo's advice, we should "forget everything we think we know" only with good reason and not before. Until we have better reason to question basically everything we know about the world and how it works, perhaps we should remain dubious of interactionism.[8]

"Strange Magic" – Electric Light Orchestra 1975

Although learning a bit about philosophy can enrich one's interpretation of *Doctor Strange*, it also turns out that thinking about the film can also deepen one's appreciation for the philosophical process. Philosophy is grounded in the acquisition of justified beliefs about how things are (or ought to be) and the willingness to revise those beliefs when appropriate, always following rules of evidence and principles of logic. The metaphysical puzzles so brilliantly shown in this movie remind us of various possibilities about how the world works and what things are in it, seen or unseen. Some of these are difficult to imagine or conceive of clearly, and their existence helps explains why philosophers (should) remain quite humble about what they know or think they know. Philosophers should emulate Stephen Strange in his quest for knowledge, but not in his close-minded hubris about obtaining it.

For pop culture resources and philosophical resources related to this chapter please visit the website for this book: https://introducingphilosophythroughpopculture.com.

Notes

1 All quoted dialogue is from the 2016 film *Doctor Strange*.
2 Descartes, R. (2000). Passions of the soul. In: (1649, trans. E.S. Haldane and G.R.T. Ross), quoted in *René Descartes: Philosophical Essays and Correspondence*, 298 and 307 (ed. R. Ariew). Indianapolis: Hackett Publishing.
3 Descartes, R. (2000). Meditations on first philosophy, meditation VI In: (1641, trans. D. Cress), quoted in *Rene Descartes: Philosophical Essays and Correspondence*, 136 (ed. R. Ariew). Indianapolis: Hackett Publishing.
4 See Descartes, *Passions of the Soul*, Part I, articles 31–34.
5 Quoted in Baird, F.E. and Kaufmann, W. (eds.) (2008). *Philosophic Classics, Vol. III*, 53. Upper Saddle River, NJ: Pearson-Prentice Hall.
6 Thomson, G. (2000). *On Descartes*, 75. Belmont, CA: Wadsworth.
7 One problematic aspect to this sort of reply is that energy transfers obtain only among entities that can participate in them. Because Cartesian souls are inherently non-physical, there is no plausible way for them to generate or receive the sort of energy the Ancient One describes.
8 Note that if you reject substance dualism, you don't have to adopt physicalism, with which there are also many issues and questions (making metaphysics one of the most interesting and frustrating areas of philosophy). For more, see Daniel Stoljar's entry at the *Stanford Encyclopedia of Philosophy*: https://plato. stanford.edu/entries/physicalism.

10

Mind and Body in Zion

Matt Lawrence

Summary

In *The Matrix Trilogy*, human brains are sent electrical signals to create whatever experiences their machine captors wish their minds to have. This raises an important question about the nature of the mind: Is the mind something separable from the brain, or something that is dependent upon the brain? Using *The Matrix*, this chapter explains the difference between dualism and materialism, and shows why dualism has fallen out of favor. The chapter also articulates the differences between the major materialist theories: reductive materialism, eliminative materialism, emergentism, and functionalism.

If what you are talking about is your senses, what you feel, taste, smell, or see, then all you're talking about are electrical signals interpreted by your brain.

– Morpheus [†1]

The Matrix Scenario

The central metaphysical premise of the *Matrix* trilogy is that an entire "virtual world" can be created for an individual by electronically stimulating their brain. For the human victims of the Matrix, everything they see, hear, smell, taste, or touch is created in this manner, as are their feelings of pain and pleasure, of hunger, thirst, and satiation. Lucky for them, the deception turns out to be limited to their *sensory perceptions*, that is, to experiences that would otherwise be caused by the interaction of a person's senses and central nervous system with the physical world, and not to their reactions to those perceptions. People's emotions, memories, decisions, and judgments appear to be free from Matrix control. But it seems reasonable to suppose that this limit reflects only the current state of the machines' technology, or perhaps just a choice by the Architect. There doesn't seem to be any reason to suppose it is a *metaphysical necessity*. For if the electrical stimulation of your brain can cause you to feel hungry, then why not also anxious, or happy? And if your brain can be manipulated to make you "see" an Agent, then we might

Introducing Philosophy Through Pop Culture: From Socrates to Star Wars *and Beyond*, Second Edition.
Edited by William Irwin and David Kyle Johnson.
© 2022 John Wiley & Sons Ltd. Published 2022 by John Wiley & Sons Ltd.

suppose that it could also be stimulated in such a way as to cause you to imagine or remember one. At least in theory, it seems that *any* human experience could be produced by the electronic stimulation of the brain.

The "Matrix scenario" seems to suggest, on the face of it at least, a materialist view of the mind. If all of our conscious experiences or mental states can be produced by brain manipulation, then this provides some rather strong evidence for thinking that mental states *just are* causal states of material brains. Complicating this picture, however, is the fact that in *Revolutions* Neo wakes up in the Train Station program even though his body is not jacked in. It appears, at least, that his mind has separated from his body. This turn of events suggests that perhaps (in the films) the mind is in some sense independent of the brain.

Does this add up? Is there any way to make sense of both the general Matrix scenario and Neo's apparent mind–body separation? In Sections 10.2–10.4, we'll examine several theories of mind in order to determine how to make the most sense of these events.

Mystery and Miracles

The power of The One extends beyond this world.

– The Oracle[†††]

Although any sort of appeal to mystery and/or miracles cannot be described as a theory of the mind, we should begin by noting that the films intentionally leave many aspects of "The One" a complete mystery. Neo, as the Savior of humanity, performs a variety of "miracles."[2] He heals the sick, removing a bullet from Trinity's chest; he stops bullets in mid-air; he flies like Superman; he destroys sentinels just by thinking it; and he sees through blind eyes. While his "miracles" within the Matrix seem to readily succumb to scientific explanation – he's just mentally hacking a computer program that is connected to the electrical signals of his brain – the films really give us no adequate explanation of the apparent miracles that occur outside the Matrix. How does he destroy sentinels with his mind? How does he separate his mind from his body? Almost all we have to go on here is the Oracle's cryptic explanation – if we can call it an explanation at all. She tells Neo:

> The power of The One extends beyond this world – it reaches from here all the way back to where it came from . . . The Source. That's what you felt when you touched those sentinels, but you weren't ready for it. You should be dead but apparently you weren't ready for that either.[†††]

Obviously the Wachowskis were content to leave this aspect of the films shrouded in mystery. We might take it as an appeal to the transcendental or supernatural – to forces beyond this world that we can never explain. But to the philosophical mind, the thought that we must simply chock these events up to "the mysterious power of The One" is unsatisfying. Enquiring minds want to know *how* and *why* these things occurred. And while the answers to these questions may not even exist, we can always speculate.

Mind–Body Dualism

How did I separate my mind from my body?

– Neo[†††]

A theory of the mind–body relation that can readily explain Neo's disembodiment at the Train Station is called mind–body dualism. René Descartes (1596–1650) championed this view. He maintained that human beings are composed of two distinct substances, one immaterial (the mind, spirit, or soul), and the other material (brains or bodies).[3] Much of his reasoning behind this conclusion stems from the fact that mind and body seem to have altogether different properties. Material substances can be characterized in terms of their specific size, shape, and location. But immaterial substances (minds) cannot. Take for instance Morpheus's *hope* that Neo is The One. How big is his hope? Is it larger than a sentinel, but smaller than the Neb? And what shape is it? Of course, we cannot say. Instead, our states of mind must be described in a very different way than material objects. While our minds can be located in time, they cannot be located in space. They have no size, shape, color, nor any "extended" property whatever.

According to mind–body dualism, the mind and body are ultimately distinct substances, and therefore they should be capable of existing on their own. We generally think that physical objects, such as this book, your cellphone, etc., exist apart from your mind. Similarly, Descartes argued that there is no reason to suppose that minds or souls cannot exist without bodies. Thus, a mind–body dualist like Descartes would have no problem supposing that Neo's mind really did get separated from his body. While such a thing is unusual (except, perhaps, at death), it poses no special theoretical problems insofar as we accept the dualist view.

But dualism faces some rather serious theoretical difficulties. For instance, if the mind is wholly immaterial, how can it interact with the body? How can something without size or weight (such as a belief, desire, or volition) cause something big and heavy (like your arm) to move?

Descartes's solution was to suggest a physical point of connection, not altogether unlike the plug on the back of Neo's head. He maintained that the connection most likely occurs in the *pineal gland*, which is a tiny structure located at the base of the brain, the purpose of which had eluded the physiologists of his day.[4] The problem, of course, is that while we can see how the pineal gland hooks up to the brain, we cannot observe or even comprehend how an immortal soul gets hooked up to the pineal gland. Thus, we are left with essentially the same problem we started with: How does an immaterial thing interact with a physical thing? The "pineal gland solution" just gives the problem a more specific location.

Another problem is the lack of empirical evidence for mind–body dualism. Descartes only showed that the existence of minds without bodies was a *logical possibility* (the idea itself is not self-contradictory). But this does not entail that it is *true* or *physically possible*. As the eighteenth-century philosopher David Hume famously noted, it is logically possible that the sun will not rise tomorrow.[5] But on this basis alone it would be silly to start preparing for a Dark Age. Reasonable beliefs require more than just logical possibility – they require positive evidence. And this is where mind–body dualism falls short.

Mind–Body Materialism

Look past the flesh. Look through the soft gelatin of these dull cow eyes.
– Smith/Bane[†††]

Almost everything that science has taught us about the mind, including the possibility of Matrix-type deceptions, favors a materialist (nondualist) understanding of the mind–body relationship. Some of the evidence can be pretty technical, and has been discovered fairly recently with the help of modern technologies such as the CAT scan and the mapping of the human genome. But much of the best evidence for materialism involves things we have known since antiquity.

For example, certain psychotropic drugs cause the user to see and hear things that are not "really" there – much like jacking into the Matrix. And we now know that this occurs (as in the Matrix) through the physical stimulation of particular regions of the brain. Or there is the fact that when you hit a person on the head really hard, they fall unconscious, thereby losing their *supposedly immaterial* mental states completely. Or consider the way in which aging often affects one's "immaterial self." Old age is often accompanied by memory loss and the lack of mental quickness and clarity. There have always been fairly good reasons to suppose that this was due to the deterioration of the body, but current research into diseases such as Alzheimer's has shown us specifically how this is related to the withering and death of nerve cells within the brain's cerebral cortex.

The problem with applying mind–body materialism to the films comes in at the end of *Reloaded* when Neo's miraculous powers begin to take effect outside of the Matrix. If Neo's mental states are essentially just states of his brain, then how can he destroy senti-nels with his mind? And how can his mind be inside the Train Station program if his body is not jacked in? To give a completely material explanation for these events will involve stretching our imaginations beyond the parameters of the information provided in the films, but such an account is not altogether impossible.

Destroying the Sentinels

One way to give a non-miraculous explanation of Neo's destruction of the sentinels involves Neo's (apparent) destruction of Agent Smith at the end of the first film. Not only do we find out in *Reloaded* that Smith did not die but it also turns out that he and Neo now have some kind of connection. As Smith explains it, aspects of each person/program may have been copied or overwritten onto the other. In order to understand this, we must realize that Neo is not "simply human." Like all pod-born children of the Matrix, Neo has more than just a plug in the back of his head. Inside his skull he must also have Matrix-interface hardware and software, which sends the Matrix program into the neu-ral networks of his brain, and sends his neural activity back out to the Matrix program. Thus, just as Smith came out of the copying process with a new power – the ability to clone himself onto others – Neo may have also come away from the exchange with a new power – the ability to control certain machines. This power would not be "supernatural," but a matter of programming. Neo's now-modified software may simply be capable of transmitting a self-destruct command to the approaching sentinels.

Neo's Jackless Entry

Support for a materialist explanation of Neo's jackless entry into the Train Station pro-gram, in *Revolutions*, can be found in the fact that his brain waves indicate that his brain was doing precisely what it would if he were jacked in, *and* by the fact that the crew is eventually able to jack him back out by connecting his body to the system and hacking a connection. One possibility – and again this is only conjecture – also involves the Matrix hardware inside Neo's skull.

We often hear Morpheus speak of going to "broadcast depth" whenever he plans to jack the crew into the Matrix. This suggests that the Matrix may be transmitted over the airwaves – much like a radio or television broadcast. People jack in (much like cable TVs), but the signal itself is broadcast – perhaps by satellite – and the humans may hack their way into that broadcast using transmitters on their hovercraft. In this case, we might suppose that Neo is somehow "broadcasting" from a transmitter inside his skull.

While this is somewhat of a stretch (as is the very idea of jackless entry), it seems more plausible when we realize that Neo's hardware and software is probably quite unique. This is in part due to his exchange with Smith, but it may also be attributable to the Architect. Recall that during their meeting at the Source in *Reloaded*, the Architect told Neo that he carries a code within him that reinserts the "prime program" that, as we see at the end of *Revolutions*, essentially reboots the system. We can imagine that as "The One," Neo is the only person carrying this code, and that this is due in part to the Architect's own design. As the Architect also mentioned, Neo's five predecessors "were, by *design*, based on a similar predication," indicating that they have all been manipulated (or programed) in one way or another. Thus, we might even wonder if the Architect had implanted a transmitter inside Neo's skull early on as a kind of failsafe measure. He may have activated it and *sent* Neo to the "limbo" of Mobil Ave. in order to detain him while Zion is destroyed.

Neo's embedded technology could also explain the fact that, in *Revolutions*, he can still see even though his eyes have been burned shut by Smith/Bane. Notice that at this point Neo sees Smith (i.e. Smith's programming) rather than the physical body of Bane. Similarly, when he and Trinity arrive at the machine city, he cannot see Trinity, but he sees the "light" of the machine world. This suggests that Neo is not really seeing in terms of optics. Rather, he may be receiving electronic signals from the entities of the machine city, which are then being converted to visual images as the Matrix hardware electronically stimulates his brain in much the same way that his eyes would normally. These signals may have always been coming in, but were "overridden" by his human optic nerves. Perhaps he now "sees" in much the same way that the machines do.

So the story of the Matrix can be understood within a completely materialist view of the mind. And these days most scientists and philosophers think that materialism is the only viable theory. For them, the question is not *whether* materialism is true, but *which* materialist theory is true. In Sections 10.5 and 10.6, we'll examine two of the most controversial issues within materialist theories of mind. The first pertains to whether or not specific mental states can be effectively reduced to specific states of the brain, and the second pertains to the specific role of the biological matter of the brain.

Mental States: Reduction or Elimination?

How do the machines really know what Tastee Wheat tasted like?

– Mouse[†]

All materialist theories of the mind agree that a person's mental state (whatever a person is experiencing at a particular moment) is intimately tied to their brain state at that moment. But how exactly this relationship should be described has been a matter of dispute. Let us consider the two most popular ways.

Reductive Materialism

Reductive materialism (also called identity theory) maintains that mental states *just are* physical states of the brain. Therefore, every particular mental state ultimately reduces to, or matches, a physical state of the brain – generally a particular pattern of neurons firing. This sort of view lends some credence to Morpheus's claim that "The body cannot live without the mind." For on this view the mind and brain are essentially the same thing. To be "mind-dead" is identical to being "brain-dead" and vice versa.[6]

According to reductive materialism it is (theoretically) possible to achieve (what is called) a complete *intertheoretic reduction* between mental states and brain states. An intertheoretic reduction occurs when the entities of one theory can be reduced to entities of another new and better theory. This sort of thing occurs in science all the time. For example, modern science tells us that "sound" *just is* a train of compression waves. Thus, every particular sound that occurs in the world corresponds to a particular wave pattern. In music, for instance, we find that the lower the tone a note has, the longer its wavelength, and the higher the tone, the shorter its wavelength. Reductive materialism (about the mind) says that we should expect to find a similar kind of correspondence between the entities of a very old theory, "folk psychology," and a relatively new theory, modern neuroscience.

Folk psychology has been around for thousands of years. It maintains that the causes of human behavior are psychological states, i.e. particular beliefs, desires, and emotions. Neuroscience, on the other hand, takes the cause of human behavior to be the firing of neural networks in our brains. These neural networks send signals through the nervous system and throughout the body. If an intertheoretic reduction from the one theory to the other is possible, then, as our understanding of the brain's functioning improves, we should be able to match up particular beliefs, desires, emotions, and perceptions with specific patterns of brain activity in a perfect one-to-one correspondence. Thus, the experience of enjoying a bowl of Tastee Wheat would turn out to be identical with a more scientific description, such as having a "Q127 neural firing pattern in the Gamma 8.2 quadrant or your brain."[7]

This view of the mind seems to fit nicely with the Matrix scenario. It suggests that a well-developed neuroscience could ultimately tell us how to produce any mental state we want (e.g. the desire for a bowl of Tastee Wheat, and the taste of it on your tongue; the belief that you are wearing a leather jacket, and the feel of it against your skin; as well as the sight of a red pill, and anxiety about its possible effects), just by stimulating a person's brain in the appropriate way.

Eliminative Materialism

Eliminative materialism delivers some rather strong criticisms to identity theory. It maintains that we will never get a one-to-one match-up between folk psychological states and neurological states, because folk psychological states (beliefs, desires, hopes, fears, etc.) don't *really* exist at all.

Most people think that this proposition is absolutely nuts; but if you consider it carefully, it is not as crazy as it seems. One of the most influential proponents of eliminative materialism is UC San Diego philosopher Paul Churchland.[8] The striking feature of his view is that he does not believe in "beliefs." (Notice that I didn't say that he *believes* that there are no beliefs – that would be a contradiction.) But we have to be careful here. Eliminative materialists are not saying that there are no "inner experiences" at all. Certainly you are conscious and are having some kind of experience at this moment. They also admit that your experience has a particular *content* and *feel* to it, that only you have access to. What they deny is that our folk psychological descriptions of these "inner experiences" (e.g. "Neo *wants* to know what the Matrix is," "Trinity is *in love* with Neo," or "Morpheus *believes* that Neo is The One") adequately refer to real states of the world. According to eliminative materialism, these entities of folk psychology are false – or at least radically misleading.

The reasoning behind this conclusion can be illustrated by imagining Neo's psychological state when he first met Morpheus, and was sitting there in that big red chair, "wanting to know what the Matrix is." Recall your own mental state when you were watching the film for the first time, and were also "wanting to know what the Matrix is." Were you, at that moment, in the *same* mental state as Neo? (Let's pretend here that Neo is a real person rather than a character in a film.) I sincerely doubt that you were. While neither of you knew what the Matrix was, you had very different ideas about it that *shaped* your desires in particular ways, ultimately making them very different. Or try thinking of Zion right now. Were you thinking what I was thinking? Again, I doubt it. Sure, your experience was probably much more similar to mine than that of someone who is thinking about Middle Earth, or Chicago, but it was probably also very different. I was imagining the many bridges that crossed through the center of the city – were you? And even if you were, I doubt that what you envisioned was very similar to what I envisioned in terms of perspective, number of bridges, the colors, etc. Do you see the problem? If "thinking of Zion" is not some single thing, then it is highly suspect that we should ever get a one-to-one correspondence between "thinking of Zion" and a particular brain state.

And when entities of an old theory cannot be reduced to the new and better theory, Churchland argues that they must be eliminated from scientific discourse, i.e. they must return to the Source for deletion. Consider *caloric*, for example, a hypothetical fluid-like substance. Churchland points out that people used to believe that caloric was responsible for heat. It was believed that, when a pan sat over the fire, it became hot because this "subtle substance" escaped from the fire and was absorbed by the pan. Since our new and improved theories now tell us that heat *is* molecular motion (kinetic energy), the theory of caloric has been dismissed as simply false. We say that caloric never *really* existed. Eliminative materialists think that beliefs, desires, and emotions are headed down the same road. We may continue to talk about them as if they were real in our everyday lives, but our scientific theories should abandon them completely.

At first view it seems that eliminative materialism would render a Matrix-type deception impossible. For, what the deceiving party wants to do (or so it seems) is to create in the deceived person certain false *beliefs* – to cause them to believe that they are experiencing the "real world" when they are not, to believe that they are going to work, paying their taxes, and so on, when they are really just human batteries, fast asleep in endless stacks of slime-filled cocoons. And how do you generate these false beliefs if *beliefs* don't exist at all? This problem, if it were a problem, would do more than just derail Matrix-type methods of mind control. For eliminative materialists like Churchland also seem to be out to "change our beliefs" – just through less coercive means. That is, he wants you to quit believing in "beliefs." Yet how can he expect this unless he can get you to "believe" his theory of the mind? On the face of it, eliminative materialism seems to contradict itself.

The way that Churchland responds to this type of objection is by arguing that it begs the question. That is, the objection *assumes* that the eliminative materialist believes the theory and is out to change our beliefs. But this is the very point under contention. Churchland, of course, denies that (scientifically speaking) he "believes" the theory, or that he "wants" to change your "beliefs" – if by this we mean that certain folk psychological states are the real causes of his actions. So why, then, did he write his book *Matter and Consciousness*? He can consistently maintain that he did it for the same reason that anyone does anything – because the particular firings of the neural networks in his brain caused him to do it. It is neural firings in our brains that always cause our bodies to move, whether we are writing books, debating theories, or piloting hovercraft. And similarly it is neural firings in our brains that would cause us to react to Agents, Oracles, and speeding bullets when "plugged in" to the Matrix.

Ultimately, eliminative materialism answers Mouse's question, "How do the machines know what Tastee Wheat tastes like?" In short, they don't – if what Mouse means is "How do they know what *my* sensations feel like to me?" But when you really think about it, no one knows what Tastee Wheat, or any other food, tastes like to *you*. Your sensations – your inner experiences of flavor – are private. So, how then do the machines know if their deception has been successful? The same way that *we* know if our efforts (deceptive or otherwise) to convince others have been successful – by looking at people's behavior.

For instance, a magician knows that their illusion has been successful largely by watching the reactions of the crowd – not by getting inside their minds and *feeling* their reactions firsthand. Similarly, the machines know they've successfully manipulated a person's mind when the person reacts in the way that the machines expect them to act. In other words, they've succeeded in deceiving Mouse into thinking that there is a bowl of Tastee Wheat in front of him precisely when his digital self reacts *as if* it were a bowl of Tastee Wheat. So, it seems that eliminative materialism could work just fine within the Matrix scenario. A one-to-one correspondence between the mental states of folk psychology and the brain states of neuroscience would be completely unnecessary to implement a Matrix-type deception.

The Role of Matter: Biology or Function?

I admit it is difficult to even think encased in this rotting piece of meat.
                                                     – Smith/Bane[†††]

If brains cause conscious experience, then the big question is *how* do they do it? This has led to a major philosophical dispute over the significance of the particular biology of the brain. As some see it, consciousness is an *emergent property* of the dynamic processes within the specific biochemistry of the brain.

The emergent property view, the concept of an emergent property, is fairly common in scientific explanations. For example, UC Berkeley philosopher John Searle suggests that the relationship between minds and brains may be analogous to the micro- and macro-properties of everyday objects. At the macro-level (the level of our normal sense experience) water is wet, it's clear, and it has a specific temperature. But the very same water when examined at the micro-level turns out to be made of molecules consisting of hydrogen and oxygen – H_2O. We cannot grab an H_2O molecule and declare that it is wet, or clear, or 53°. Instead these properties emerge when millions of these molecules are experienced at the macro-level. Following this model we can say that it is the molecular structure of H_2O that causes the features that we associate with water, but also water just is H_2O. Similarly, the particular firing patterns of neural networks cause consciousness experience; but in an important sense, conscious experience *just is* the brain's neural networks firing away.

On Searle's view, the biochemistry of the brain is crucial to the emergence of consciousness, just as the chemistry of water is crucial to the emergence of wetness. You can create tiny models of water molecules out of plastic and put them all in a bathtub, but that does not entail that they will wet your sponge. Similarly, Searle contends, modeling the processes of the brain won't create conscious experience. Consider, for instance, the way in which our bodies create the experience of thirst: Kidney secretions of rennin synthesize a substance called angiotensin. This substance goes into the hypothalamus and triggers a series of neuron firings. As far as we know these neuron firings are a very large part of the cause of thirst.[9]

While a model of this process would be much more complex than a model of an H_2O molecule, it is certainly possible to create one using a wide range of materials. Searle suggests the following:

> So let us imagine our thirst-simulating program running on a computer made entirely of old beer cans, millions (or billions) of old beer cans that are rigged up to levers and powered by windmills. We can imagine that the program simulates the neuron firings at the synapses by having beer cans bang into each other, thus achieving a strict correspondence between neuron firings and beer-can bangings. At the end of the sequence a beer can pops up on which it is written "I am thirsty." Now, does anyone suppose that this . . . apparatus is literally thirsty in the sense in which you or I are?[10]

Searle thinks that it is completely obvious that such an apparatus has no conscious experience at all. Any adequate analysis of the mind, he argues, cannot discount the importance of the biochemistry of the brain any more than an adequate understanding of digestion can ignore the biochemistry of stomachs.

Functionalism

In direct opposition to Searle's biological view of the mind is functionalism. It maintains that conscious experience and our various mental states (whether or not the concepts of folk psychology adequately describe them) can exist within any sufficiently organized material system. Mental states are not the emergent effects of specifically biological processes, but instead they are simply "functional states" of extremely complex systems. This is to say that anything that has the appropriate input–process–output relationships can have mental states.

To a certain extent at least, this seems right. Imagine extraterrestrials that are constructed very differently from us – perhaps without anything like a brain – but who nevertheless have mental lives. As philosopher David Lewis puts it:

> [T]here might be a Martian who sometimes feels pain just as we do, but whose pain differs greatly from ours in its physical realization. When you pinch his skin you cause no firing of C-fiber – he has none – but, rather, you cause the inflation of many smallish cavities in his

feet. When these cavities are inflated he is in pain. And the effects of his pain are fitting: his thought and activity are disrupted, he groans and writhes, he is strongly motivated to stop you from pinching him and to see that you never do it again.[11]

Lewis contends that while the Martian may not be in pain in quite the same sense that we humans are, there had better be some straightforward sense in which we are both in pain. There doesn't seem to be any particular reason for thinking that mental states can only occur in brains – that is merely how they occur *for us*.

Functionalism considers "Martian pain" to be completely unproblematic. So long as the Martian has the right input–process–output relationships, as s/he does – the *input* (physical harm/the pinching of their skin) leads to a physical *process* (the inflation of the cavities in his feet), which in turn causes the appropriate *output* (groaning, writhing, and the demand for you to stop) – they must be in pain. According to the functionalist view, the particular hardware that this functional relationship occurs in (or through) is really beside the point. It may be possible to achieve "pain," "thirst," or even "the belief that Agents are coming" through virtually any physical system – even Searle's wind-powered beer cans – so long as the hardware and programming/processing are sufficiently complex to achieve the appropriate input–output relationships.

For most people, the jump from sore or thirsty living Martians to arrangements of sore or thirsty *lifeless* beer cans seems like quite a leap of faith. But this is essentially the view of those who maintain that artificial intelligence (thinking, feeling, understanding machines) is possible. And generally, functionalists defend the notion of artificial intelligence. They often argue that the mind is to the brain as a computer program is to computer hardware. On this view, your particular personality, your experiences, decisions, etc. are just the output of the program your brain is running. If we can duplicate this process in a machine, we shall have machines that are, for all intents and purposes, just like us.

Functionalism seems to be the dominant theory of mind at work in the *Matrix* films. The very idea of sentient machines depends upon the functionalist hypothesis. If, for instance, we were to apply a biology-based emergent property view to the films, then we should have to say that the machines and programs of the Matrix don't *really* experience anything at all. For they too are nonliving arrangements of hardware and software – not essentially any different in kind from Searle's beer cans – just a more space-efficient design. While they go through the motions, and *act* like human beings, Searle would contend that they lack conscious experience altogether.

We could take Searle seriously here. Can you really be sure that Agent Smith feels angry, or that the Oracle cares about Neo? Maybe they are just programed in such a way as to mimic these states without actually feeling them. This theory could work within the original *Matrix* film. But the later films seem to entail that functionalism is the correct picture for the Matrix universe. This becomes clear when Smith takes over the body of Bane in *The Matrix Reloaded*. For if biology were essential to consciousness then we should expect Smith to undergo quite a transformation when he makes the switch into Bane's body. It would be as if the light of consciousness had suddenly been switched on. He should be amazed to experience consciousness for the first time in his life. Smith would finally know what it's like to really *want* to kill Neo, or to *feel* the floor beneath his feet. We can imagine that the psychological impact of it all would have been overwhelming. But, of course, this is not how the story goes. Smith's transition into Bane's body happens rather seamlessly – just like copying a program from one computer to another, or converting a file from PC to Mac.[12]

This is exactly how the functionalist thinks that it ought to go. In fact, many philosophers and scientists now think that the possibility of the "data transfer" of a person's entire personality onto a computer program is quickly becoming a reality. Marvin Minsky, the head of the artificial intelligence laboratory at MIT, maintains that it should be possible within the next 100 years or so.[13] In that case, there may be no need for a war between humans and machines. Rather than trying to beat them, we may simply join them.

For pop culture resources and philosophical resources related to this chapter please visit the website for this book: https://introducingphilosophythroughpopculture.com.

Notes

1   Quotes in this chapter designated with a † are from *The Matrix* (movie). Quotes designated with ††† are from *The Matrix: Revolutions*.
2   Of course there are intentional parallels here with Jesus, which adds support to the transcendental or "miracle" hypothesis.
3   Following Descartes, I use the terms mind, self, and soul interchangeably to refer to the private, subjective, and seemingly immaterial aspects of a person. While many people distinguish mind, spirit, and soul, the distinction is often rather vaguely defined. For some the mind connotes the more rational aspects of the self while the spirit or soul is used to depict the emotional or "deeper" aspects of the personality. However, when Descartes uses the term "mind" he means to include all aspects of a person's mental life, including reason, emotion, perception, will, and dispositions of character.
4   The pineal gland produces melatonin, and is believed to play a role in sleep and aging. Dysfunction within the pineal gland may also be linked to seasonal affective disorder.
5   Ghost refers to this aspect of Hume's philosophy in the opening scene of the Enter the *Matrix* video game. When Niobe ribs him for checking to see if his virtual weapons are loaded (the program always automatically loads them), he tells her: "Hume teaches us that no matter how many times you drop a stone and it falls to the floor, it might fall to the floor, but then again, it might float to the ceiling. Past experience can never prove the future." This is called the *problem of induction*. For more, see sections II and IV of David Hume's *An Enquiry Concerning Human Understanding*.
6   However, it does seem rather implausible that the "virtual experience" of being shot would cause a person to become mind-dead/brain-dead. Obviously the films need this aspect in order to generate dramatic tension in the fight scenes within the Matrix, so we should just buy into it and enjoy the ride. However, if you really need a scientific explanation for this aspect of the film, that too is possible with the right hardware. For instance, the programming of the Matrix may cause one's brain to shut down, in much the same way that it causes the brain to "see" an Agent or "feel" a bullet wound.
7   This is a statement of science-fiction neurology. It is not a real scientific description that is in use today.
8   See Churchland, P. (1984). *Matter and Consciousness*. Boston: MIT Press.
9   Searle, J. (2004). The myth of the computer. In: *Twenty Questions: An Introduction to Philosophy* (eds. G.L. Bowie, M.W. Michaels, and R.C. Solomon). Belmont, California: Thomson-Wadsworth Learning.
10   Searle, "The Myth of the Computer."
11   Lewis, D. (1980). Mad pain and Martian pain. In: *Readings in Philosophy of Psychology* (ed. N. Block). Cambridge, Massachusetts: Harvard University Press. For Lewis, the issue of pain is more complicated than merely input–process–output relations, as he argues in his case of "mad pain."
12   The PC to Mac analogy is probably the better description of Smith's transfer into Bane's brain. There does seem to be a subtle difference in Smith's conscious experience as a result of the transfer, as he complains that it is "difficult to even think encased in this rotting piece of meat." Bane also has a number of self-inflicted wounds. This may be because the feeling of pain is new to Smith (though this may say more about his "Agent program" then about programs in general, especially if we compare him to Persephone). Another possible explanation of his self-inflicted wounds is that remnants of Bane's personality are still within him and battling against Smith's overwrite, in much the same way that the Oracle maintained a slight degree of control when Smith overwrote her program.
13   As quoted in Where evolution left off. *Andover Bulletin*, Spring 1995, 9.

11

Amnesia, Personal Identity, and the Many Lives of Wolverine

Jason Southworth

Summary

If you committed a crime when you were 20 years old, but were not caught and convicted until you were 80, how could we be sure that punishing "you" actually punished the person who committed the crime? After all, the person who committed the crime is almost as different from "you" as the person sitting next to you – you may not even remember the crime in question. The question of personal identity – How is it that you are "the same person" over time? – is central in metaphysics, and is explored in the world of *X-Men*. The character Wolverine provides an ideal case for exploring memory criteria for personal identity, because Wolverine suffers memory loss multiple times and yet seems to retain his personal identity. Other characters, such as Jamie Madrox – who can copy and recombine herself – help us explore theories that emphasize physical continuity.

In *Hulk* #180–182, Wolverine makes his first appearance as little more than a feral man in a colorful costume with no memories of his past, or seemingly of anything (in fact, in *Giant-size X-Men* #1, he has no memory of the Hulk appearance). The *Weapon X* stories in *Marvel Comics Presents* show us some of the things the character has done as an agent of the Canadian government, and *Origin* gives us a glimpse of the character prior to his time at Weapon X, when he was more at peace with the world.

Over the years Professor Xavier and Wolverine had very little success in reversing the amnesia until *House of M* when Wolverine finally recovered all of his memories. But rather than answer questions about his identity, the sudden emergence of these memories has raised more questions for Wolverine about who he really is.

Introducing Philosophy Through Pop Culture: From Socrates to Star Wars *and Beyond*, Second Edition.
Edited by William Irwin and David Kyle Johnson.
© 2022 John Wiley & Sons Ltd. Published 2022 by John Wiley & Sons Ltd.

What is Personal Identity?

The issue of personal identity is actually a set of issues that are entangled and, at times, conflated. The questions philosophers try to answer when they discuss personal identity are: What constitutes personhood? Who am I? and What does it mean for a person to persist over time?

When establishing what constitutes personhood, philosophers are trying to figure out what makes a person *a person* (rather than, say, a comic book). What properties must they have to count as a person? Many non-philosophers may not think this is an interesting or difficult question to answer, as our common use of the term *person* is synonymous with *human*. The case of the mutants in the X-books shows why this is an unsatisfactory answer, as they are not humans – they are *homo superiors*, not *homo sapiens*. If mutants are persons, then being a human is not a necessary condition (it is not required) for being a person. As you might imagine, philosophers do not spend a lot of time talking about *homo superiors*, but we do spend quite a lot of time talking about other animals and artificial intelligence. You might consider whether Kitty Pryde's pet dragon, Lockheed, and the Scarlet Witch's robot husband, the Vision, are persons.

When we consider the question of "Who am I?" we are trying to establish the characteristics that make you the person that you are, as opposed to some other person. Again, this question appears deceptively easy to answer. You might think that you can just rattle off a description of your character traits, but the answer is going to have to be more complicated than that, because we can often be described in a variety of ways, some of which might be in tension. The question of who counts as a person and why is one of the reoccurring tropes of Wolverine. Commonly, we see this when The Ol' Canucklehead goes on one of his tears, complaining that he is not the animal that some people think he is.

Personhood and persistence over time also feature prominently in X-Men. Consider the classic story *Days of Future Past* (which appeared in *Uncanny X-Men* #141 and 142), in which we encounter characters who seem to be many of the X-Men we know (including Wolverine), but in the future. How do we know that they are the same characters? They *look* the same. This is the standard, unreflective first response people often give to the question of personal identity: People persist over time if they occupy the same body. Same claws and pointy hair? Well, it *must* be Wolverine. That's just common sense – which, as we'll see, isn't always as common or sensical as we might initially think.[1] Still, you might say, who cares?

Well, the main reason we should care about personal identity concerns moral culpability. All moral frameworks involve the attribution of blame and praise, and many call for punishment. In order to attribute praise and blame for an act, we have to be certain that the people to whom we are giving the praise and the blame are the ones who deserve it, based on their actions. If, for example, it turns out that the man called Logan is not the same person who committed atrocities for the Canadian government under the code name Weapon X, then he should not be punished for the behavior of that person. Likewise, if the current Wolverine is not the same person that he was in the past, Sabretooth and Lady Deathstrike would be wrong in their attempts to punish him.

Cassandra Nova, Charles Xavier, and John Locke

The philosopher John Locke (1632–1704) argued against the common-sense view that the body is the source of personal identity, using a modified example from the pop culture of his own time. Locke told a story that was essentially *The Prince and the Pauper*, except the individuals exchanged minds, rather than just roles. If Locke were around today, he might instead have talked about Charles Xavier and Cassandra Nova. In Grant Morrison's run on *New X-Men* (if you haven't read it you should be ashamed of yourself), we learn that Cassandra Nova placed her mind in Charles Xavier's body, and placed Xavier's mind in her body. The Xavier body with Nova's mind then forced Beak (if you don't know who Beak is you should be doubly ashamed of yourself) to beat the Beast so badly he had to be hospitalized, and started a war between the Shi'ar empire and the X-Men.[2] When the body of Xavier manipulated Beak, it referred to itself as Cassandra. Likewise, later in the story, when Jean Grey communicates with the mind in Cassandra Nova's body, it reports to be Xavier. Prior to discovering the switch, the X-Men naturally believed the actions of Xavier's body to be those of Xavier. After finding out about this switch, however, they do not hold Xavier accountable for the actions taken by his body. Instead, they condemn Cassandra Nova for them, and discuss how to defeat her. So, it seems personal identity is not a matter of body but of mind.

Having rejected the body theory in favor of something mental, Locke tries to determine the nature of the mental thing. What mental properties or characteristics could indicate persistence over time? Locke quickly rejects any type of character or personality traits because such traits are constantly in flux. We're always trying to become better people and, as a result our morality, tastes, and preferences tend to change often. Yet we remain in essence the same people.

By process of elimination we come to memories as the source of personal identity. Locke does not mean that we need to have all and only the memories that a previous individual in time has had. You have "sameness of memories" even if you have additional memories that come after the memories that you have in common with yourself at an earlier time. So, we would say that Wolverine is still the same person he was the day he joined the New Avengers as he was the day after, since he has the same memories he had the day before.

Of course, we don't remember everything that happens to us – and some of us are more forgetful than others. Locke isn't forgetful on this account, though: he complicates things by introducing the concept of connected memories. One memory can be connected to another as follows: I remember a time when I had a memory I no longer have. As long as I can remember such a time, then those earlier memories still count as *mine*.[3] So, even if Wolverine no longer has memories of the first time he performed the Fast Ball Special with Colossus (in *Uncanny X-Men* #100 – I didn't even have to look that up, I am a walking *OHOTMU*), as long as he remembers a time when he *did* remember that day, then he is still the same person as he was *on* that day. Likewise, since on the day he joined the X-Men, Wolverine did not have memories of his encounter with the Hulk in *Hulk* #180–182, nor does he have memories of a time when he had memories of this, there are no connected memories, and he is, as a result, not the same person who encountered the Hulk on that day.

Bringing it all Back to Wolverine

If sameness of memory gives us sameness of person, then it seems several different people have inhabited the body we recognize as Wolverine's. Let's go through the history of Wolverine as it has been revealed to us so far, and yell out "*New Wolverine!*" every time we spot one.

The known history of Wolverine begins in *Origin* (2002). In this story, we learn that he was born in the nineteenth century on a plantation in Canada under the name

James Howlett. Howlett left the plantation and adopted the name Logan, the last name of the groundskeeper on the plantation. He had several adventures after leaving the plantation, first living with a pack of wolves, then with Blackfoot Indians (marrying one of them known as Silver Fox), joining the Canadian military, living in Japan under the name Patch, and fighting in World War II with Captain America.[4] After returning to Canada, Logan is recruited by Team X and, as a part of the program, Wolverine has his memory erased and replaced with memories of a life that no one ever lived.[5]

New Wolverine!

The man involved with Team X has no memory of the life prior to being a part of the team, so we are on the second life of Wolverine.

While a member of Team X, Logan was abducted by the people at the Weapon X program. As a part of the Weapon X program, he was given the name Mutate #9601, and once again had his mind erased.

New Wolverine!

And thus ended the short life of the second Wolverine.

Not all of the life of Mutate #9601 has been documented, but we have seen some of his nasty and brutish life in Barry Windsor-Smith's feature "Weapon X" that appeared in *Marvel Comics Presents* #72–84 (every comic fan should own a copy of this, as there is little better than Windsor-Smith art). Eventually the Winter Soldier (a brainwashed Bucky) frees him[6] and the creature referred to as Weapon X goes feral in the woods of Canada and has his famous fight with the Hulk. After some time, he is discovered by James and Heather Hudson (of Alpha Flight fame), with no memory of what he was doing in the woods, the fight with the Hulk, or the Weapon X project, and in time is civilized.[7]

New Wolverine!

At this point the Wolverine we all know and love is born.

I will spare you a complete rundown of the rest of Wolverine's history (as I am sure you know it all) except to point to two other important events. When Apocalypse captures Wolverine to make him serve as his horseman Death, in *Wolverine* Vol. 2 #145, he was once again brainwashed.

New Wolver . . . Ok that's probably enough of that.

With the conclusion of *House of M*, we discover that after his body heals from the Scarlet Witch messing with his mind, Wolverine finally has all of his memories restored, giving us one final new person on Locke's view. Wolverine now has memories or connected memories to every person who inhabited that familiar body. At this point it seems that, if Locke is right, the inhabitant of the Wolverine body will in one moment go from not being responsible for any of the things done by the other inhabitants of that body to being responsible for all of them.

Jamie Madrox and Derek Parfit

The philosopher Derek Parfit (1942–2017) has famously objected to the memory account of personal identity with a thought experiment about a brain being divided into two parts and placed in two separate bodies. Had Parfit been an *X-Men* fan, he could have used the example of Jamie Madrox, the Multipleman. For those who don't know, Madrox has the ability to create up to 99 duplicates of himself at a time. To form a duplicate, a force must be applied to Madrox from outside himself, or he must apply the force to an outside object – in other words, he has to be hit by or hit something. At any time, two adjacent Madroxes can recombine by an act of mutual will.

When the Madroxes combine, all memories each of them had separately are joined into the new entity. Likewise, whenever a duplicate is formed, it has all of the memories of the Madrox from which it came. So, as we learn in the miniseries, *Madrox* (2005), if one of the duplicates studies Russian or anatomy, then all other duplicates made after it has been reabsorbed will have this knowledge as well. From the moment it is created, each duplicate begins to have unique memories and experiences that no other Madrox has. So, Madrox is an even more complicated case than Parfit was concerned with, as there can be up to 100 individuals that exist at the same time, with the same memories.

Parfit thinks that it would be wrong to say of the 100 Madroxes that they are the same person. If they're the same, we get big problems: if one multiple were to go to the refrigerator and get a sandwich, but all of the other ones did not, it would follow that Madrox both did and did not get a sandwich. This certainly looks like a contradiction. Considering each of the Madroxes as a different person who is unique until it is reabsorbed, at which time it is destroyed, seems like an obvious way to avoid this contradiction.

The run of *X-Factor* written by Peter David (issues #70–90) features conflicts between the different duplicates. Some of the duplicates refuse to allow themselves to be reabsorbed, as they claim it would end their existence. In fact, one of the duplicates professes to hating the original Madrox. Additionally, in the *Madrox* miniseries, it turns out that a duplicate ends up being the villain of the story, while the original Madrox and some other duplicates were the heroes fighting against him. Was Madrox getting into arguments with himself? Fighting himself? It doesn't seem like it. We thus have reason to conclude that sameness of memories is not a sufficient condition for sameness of identity.

This kind of thought experiment leads Parfit to conclude that there must be something physical involved in personal identity. Because the brain houses the mind Parfit concludes that "sameness of brain" mean sameness of identity over time. This is more complicated than it sounds, however, because the human brain changes over time. All cells in the human body, including neurons (a very special type of cell found only in the brain), break down and are replaced with new versions. It takes about seven years for all of the matter in the human brain to get completely broken down and changed. Due to this, Parfit concluded that personhood can only persist for, at most, seven years.[8]

Bringing it all Back to Wolverine (Again)

Wolverine's case is special. Wolvie is the head trauma king. Every time he is severely injured in his brain, there is brain damage. And every time the old healing factor kicks in and repairs it, we are looking at a new Wolverine. In cases where there is only light brain damage (so the whole brain isn't effected) it still manages to reorganize his brain so quickly that the length of time to a new Wolverine is much shorter than seven years.

When you start thinking of all of your favorite instances of Wolverine brain damage you realize there are so many that we will not be able to count all of the new selves in this short chapter. Just for fun, though, some of my favorites are: the Punisher running over Wolverine with a steam roller, leaving it parked on his head in *Punisher* Vol. 3 #16; when the Wrecker hits him with his magic crowbar in *New Avengers* #7; and when Sabretooth thinks he has drowned him and walks away, only for the Ol' Canuklehead to get up again.

Be Slow to Judge

Now that you know Wolverine is in fact many individuals, you should see him in a new light. And if Parfit is right, it should make you think twice about how quickly you judge all of the characters in the X-verse (and the real world). People who commit terrible acts of violence may need to be given the benefit of the doubt until it can be established that they are in fact the same person. In the X-verse we should be less dubious of Emma Frost working with the X-Men; the less cat-like Beast should question whether, even if the secondary mutation were reversed, he would be the character they miss; and the next time Jean Grey comes back from the dead, we should all stop complaining that she seems different than before.

For pop culture resources and philosophical resources related to this chapter please visit the website for this book: https://introducingphilosophythroughpopculture.com.

Notes

1   This is known as the bodily theory of personal identity.
2   *New X-Men* #18–121.
3   Locke, J. (1690, 1994). *An Essay Concerning Human Understanding.* Amherst, NY: Prometheus Books.
4   *Wolverine: Origins* #16.
5   *Wolverine*, vol. 2 #68.
6   *Wolverine*, vol. 3 #38.
7   *Alpha Flight* #33.
8   Parfit, D. (1971). Personal identity. *Philosophical Review* 80: 3–27.

12

The Consolation of Bilbo

Providence and Free Will in Middle-Earth

Grant Sterling

Summary

Many times in *The Hobbit*, Bilbo Baggins is said to be "lucky." But his supreme moment of luck, the finding of the One Ring, is also ascribed to divine providence – Bilbo was *meant* to find the Ring. This raises a perplexing question – if God has foreknowledge of our choices in order to intervene in this way, how can we have free will? Although different strategies have been proposed for resolving this problem, most of them cannot work within the framework of Tolkien's creation. But one possibility is left – Tolkien's God (Eru) is outside of time altogether, a doctrine advanced by the early Medieval philosopher Boethius. On this view, God doesn't have foreknowledge of our choices, because He knows things from a timeless standpoint – not "before" they happen, but "as" they happen, and this timeless knowing is no threat to our freedom.

When I was a kid, I had a rabbit's foot that was supposed to bring me good luck. It didn't work very well, which shouldn't be surprising because it obviously didn't bring the rabbit very good luck either. But even a genuinely lucky rabbit's foot wouldn't be nearly as good as simply being born lucky.

And there's one thing everyone agrees about Bilbo Baggins – he is lucky. His luck is mentioned repeatedly in *The Hobbit*. Not only does Tolkien point out Bilbo's great luck in his role as narrator, but numerous characters do so as well: Thorin believes Bilbo is "possessed of good luck far exceeding the usual allowance";[1] Gandalf says to the hobbit that he "began to wonder if even your luck would see you through";[2] and Bilbo himself speaks of trusting his luck more than he used to, calling himself "Luckwearer" in his cagey conversation with Smaug (that being the best way to talk to dragons, it is said).[3]

Further, many of Bilbo's adventures take very lucky turns. He arrives in Rivendell during exactly the right moon for reading the moon-letters on the map. As Bilbo and his companions flee from the goblins of the Misty Mountains, the moon is out, giving them light to see. Bilbo chooses to help the dwarves escape from the Elvenking's prisons by way of the river, which was the only good way through Mirkwood to Esgaroth, though

Introducing Philosophy Through Pop Culture: From Socrates to Star Wars *and Beyond*, Second Edition.
Edited by William Irwin and David Kyle Johnson.
© 2022 John Wiley & Sons Ltd. Published 2022 by John Wiley & Sons Ltd.

he didn't know it. He arrives on Smaug's doorstep just before Durin's Day, the only day when the magical keyhole can be revealed, and one that comes only once in a period of years. Over and over again things turn out just right to allow the members of the party to survive and continue on the quest to a successful conclusion. In many of these cases, the intrepid adventurers are just plain lucky.

What Has it Got in its Pocketses?

But what about the central moment of the entire story? Bilbo, lost in the darkness of the goblin tunnels under the Misty Mountains, "crawled along for a good way, till suddenly his hand met what felt like a tiny ring of cold metal lying on the floor of the tunnel. It was a turning point in his career, but he did not know it."[4] Upon this event everything else turns. Without the ring, Bilbo cannot escape from the goblins or the spiders, cannot rescue his companions from the elves, cannot sneak up on Smaug to spot the unprotected patch on his underbelly. This was indeed a turning point in his life! (Of course we discover in *The Lord of the Rings* that this ring is none other than the One Ring, and so this event is equally crucial to the entire plot of that great work. We might say the discovery of the Ring was a turning point in Tolkien's life, as well.) But even here, in *The Hobbit*, where the ring functions only to allow Bilbo to become invisible at will, the quest would have ended in disaster were it not for Bilbo finding the ring.

Indeed the dwarves begin to respect him soon after this, finding that "he has some wits, as well as luck and a magic ring – and all three are very useful possessions."[5] Luck is not the only thing at work apparently, a point Gandalf also stresses. By the time the wizard has learned of the ring's true nature, near the beginning of *The Lord of the Rings*, he says, "I can put it no plainer than by saying that Bilbo was *meant* to find the Ring, and *not* by its maker."[6] If Bilbo was *meant* to find the Ring, if some power was at work behind the scenes to arrange this outcome, then the greatest episode of "luck" in Bilbo's life turns out not to be luck at all.

So, if Gandalf was right, Bilbo's finding the One Ring was meant to happen. But who intended and arranged this result? We are told that it was not the Ring's maker, the Dark Lord Sauron. But if not Sauron, then who? Certainly not Bilbo himself, or Gandalf. It could only be someone with the power to bring about such an apparent coincidence as part of a greater scheme of things.

The obvious answer is that Bilbo's finding the One Ring is a manifestation of the hand of God – Eru Ilúvatar, as He is called in Tolkien's Middle-earth. Indeed, Tolkien explicitly says as much in his letters.[7] It was Eru who meant for Bilbo to find the Ring, and later meant for it to pass on to Frodo for the great quest in *The Lord of the Rings*.

But now we face a problem. Eru apparently arranged for the Ring to slip from Gollum's finger as he was throttling a goblin-imp. This was done in order to allow Bilbo to find the Ring, as he was *meant* to do. But this providential plan can only work if Eru can foresee that Bilbo will indeed be happening along that exact tunnel on that day.

So divine providence requires divine foreknowledge. Eru must be able to reliably see future events in a way that allows Him to manipulate the present to get the results He means to produce.

But how is that possible? Bilbo's being in that tunnel that day was the result of many individual choices by many people. Even leaving aside choices distant in time (such as the dwarves agreeing to allow Gandalf's burglar to come along in the first place), Bilbo had to choose to follow Gandalf away from the Great Goblin's lair. Gandalf had to make the rescue. Dori had to agree to carry Bilbo on his back. Gollum had to choose to twist the neck of "the nassty young squeaker." Thorin, the other dwarves, and the goblins all had to make certain choices at certain times in order to put Bilbo in that spot.

But if Eru knew in advance that all these choices would be made, then it seems that the choices were dictated in advance, and that means they couldn't have been free. If Eru knew that Bilbo was going to be in that exact spot in that tunnel long before he was even headed in that direction (which He must have known, since He arranged for the Ring to slip off Gollum's finger some hours before), then Gollum was obviously not free to choose whether or not to kill the goblin-imp, and Bilbo was not free to choose to flee, Gandalf wasn't free to choose whether or not to rescue his friends by showering sparks on the goblins, and so forth.[8]

The Problem of Divine Foreknowledge

For philosophers this problem, the apparent conflict between God's (or Eru's) prior knowledge of what will happen and the freedom of creatures to make their own choices is called (not very creatively) "the problem of divine foreknowledge". Briefly, the problem is this:

1 God knows everything. He *knows* what's going to happen; He doesn't just make an estimate of what will probably happen, in the way that you or I might do.
2 If God knows everything, He must know what I will do tomorrow (or at any future time).
3 If God knows what I will do tomorrow, then my actions are predetermined – I cannot act in any way other than the one God foresees. (If I did, then God would have been mistaken, which is impossible according to statement (1).)
4 But if my actions are predetermined, then I have no free will.
5 And if I have no free will, I cannot be responsible for anything I do, since I couldn't have done otherwise.

Philosophers have struggled with this problem ever since the notion of an omniscient (all-knowing) God has been around. It seems that those who believe in God have to either abandon the idea that He knows the future, or else abandon the notion that we have free will, unless they want to give up on the idea of moral responsibility.

Some philosophers have tried the first strategy, attempting to resolve this problem by denying statement (2). "Process theologians" like Alfred North Whitehead and Charles Hartshorne and "open theists" like Clark Pinnock argue that since the future hasn't happened, there is nothing about it for God to know.[9] You can only know something if it's true, and there are no truths about the future since the future is still "open." God is still all-knowing, because being "all-knowing" means you know all *truths*, and on this view that doesn't entail knowledge of the future. At the same time, free will is retained.

Whether such a strategy can work for modern theologians confronted with the problem of divine foreknowledge is unclear. Certainly it faces many problems. For example, most religious believers accept the existence of genuine foreknowledge in the case of prophecy, and it is unclear how real prophecy (as opposed to probabilistic estimation) can exist under the open theist scheme. It also seems to conflict with characteristics many theologians believe God possesses, such as immutability. (God's knowledge would change as the future becomes the present, but immutability suggests that God does not change at all.)

But whatever may be the case in that theological context, this strategy won't work for Middle-earth theologians, because Eru's knowledge extends to the future. In one of his late tales, "Ósanwe-kenta," Tolkien contrasts Eru's genuine foreknowledge with the predictive powers of those who cannot see the future. "(A mind other than Eru's) can learn of the future only from another mind which has seen it. But that means only from Eru ultimately, or mediately from some mind that has seen in Eru some part of His purpose . . ."[10] Thus, Tolkien has not left open the option of denying divine foreknowledge.

But in any case, open theism seems to undermine the basis of divine providence, and it was Eru's providential intervention that gave us this headache in the first place. If Eru cannot have foreknowledge because the future is open, then He cannot arrange for Bilbo to find the Ring, and the unfolding of the divine plan cannot function in the way it appears.

So we'll have to look for another solution. Some philosophers have tried to solve the problem by denying statement (4). They have claimed that free will is compatible with our actions being predetermined (a theory quite cleverly called "compatibilism"). Others have denied statement (5), holding that even if we don't have free will, it doesn't matter, because moral responsibility is still possible. Philosophers like Thomas Hobbes (1588–1679) and David Hume (1711–1776) have defended such views, as have several contemporary thinkers such as Harry Frankfurt and Daniel Dennett.[11]

It is highly questionable whether either strategy can work. Critics argue that nothing that can reasonably be called "free will" can apply to beings whose actions are unalterably determined centuries before they are even born.[12] Nor is it clear how we can be morally responsible for actions that are completely predetermined.

Freedom and the Music

Whatever philosophers may claim about the real world, Tolkien will not attempt to solve the problem of divine foreknowledge by denying the existence of a kind of free will that encompasses real options for acting in *The Hobbit*. Indeed, Tolkien says that human beings have "the gift of freedom,"[13] which is "a virtue to shape their life, amid the powers and chances of the world, beyond the Music of the Ainur, which is as fate to all things else."[14]

But what exactly is "the Music of the Ainur, which is as fate to all things else"? Tolkien is referring to his fictional version of the creation story, which can be found in "Ainulindalë: The Music of the Ainur," part of the published version of *The Silmarillion*. In this story, the Ainur (angelic beings) perform a cosmic symphony that contains in it the future story of the world, which Eru then brings into being. As a result of this, events in history have been prefigured in this divine harmony, and so the choices of the Ainur in how to play their "music" serve as a kind of fate for the world. But not for humans – they have free will, which allows them to act in a way free from the dictation of the Music.[15]

But not only are we told that humans (and hobbits) have free will generally, we are told that Bilbo in particular has free will – he could have chosen to stay home and not accompany the dwarves at all. In Tolkien's story "The Quest for Erebor," Frodo recounts a conversation he had with Gandalf many years after Bilbo found the Ring.

In this conversation, Gandalf echoes his comments from *The Lord of the Rings*, saying, "In that far distant time I said to a small and frightened hobbit: Bilbo was *meant* to find the Ring, and *not* by its maker, and you therefore were *meant* to bear it. And I might have added: and I was *meant* to guide you both to those points."

To which Frodo responds: "I understand you a little better now, Gandalf, than I did before. Though I suppose that, whether *meant* or not, Bilbo might have refused to leave home, and so might I. You could not compel us."[16]

So, for Tolkien, it is clear that Eru really can see the future and make plans according to his foreknowledge, and at the same time Bilbo (like the other people who are part of those plans) has free will to choose how to behave. Then once again we face the problem that Eru can fully know the future, even the actions of people with free will. How is that possible?

Tolkien's Boethian Solution

The seeds of another possible solution to the problem of divine foreknowledge were planted by the Roman philosopher Boethius (around 480–524 CE) in his classic work *The Consolation of Philosophy*, written while he was in prison awaiting execution on an unjust charge.[17] Boethius argued that human beings possess only a tiny fraction of their being, their existence, at any one time, since their past has already gone and their future has not yet come. God, he thought, must not be the same way – God has infinite being, and so He must have all of his reality at once, not parceled out over time. But this must mean that God is outside of time, not subject to change. We humans live for a period of years, aging and changing each day. We have a past, present, and future. God, Boethius held, is not like one of us, and the difference is not just a matter of length of time – instead, time does not apply to God at all. He has no "past, present, and future," but rather only an eternal unchanging "now."[18]

How does Boethius's claim that God is outside of time help with the problem of divine foreknowledge? Suppose that Bilbo knows that Bard the Bowman is eating his supper, because he is watching him doing so. His knowledge of Bard's actions in no way calls into question Bard's free will – knowledge of a *present* event gives rise to no philosophical dilemmas about freedom. But if God is outside of time, as Boethius thought, then God can see the future – only from God's perspective, it isn't in the future, but rather is happening *now*. God doesn't literally have *fore*knowledge at all. Imagine you had a film-version of Guillermo del Toro's movie version of *The Hobbit* unrolled in front of you. You could glance simultaneously at scenes both at the beginning of the film and at the end. That, roughly speaking, is how Boethius understood God's view of the universe. Because God is eternal and exists outside of time, He can view in one timeless glance events taking place millennia apart, and view them as if they were all happening at the same moment.

All of this is well and good for Boethius, you might say, but what does it have to do with Tolkien? In fact, there are clear indications that this was Tolkien's own solution to the problem of divine foreknowledge, both in the real world of today and in the fictional Middle-earth of *The Hobbit*.

There are suggestions that Tolkien adopted the Boethian solution in many different places. For example, let's return to the "Music of the Ainur." This "music," we are told, is playing in the "Timeless Halls." When some of the Ainur (including the "Valar," the great archangels such as Elbereth, to whom the elves sing) choose to enter into the new world that Eru has created, it is said that "they had entered in at the beginning of Time."[19]

Perhaps the most direct discussion of this issue is in Tolkien's fascinating but little-read tale, "Ósanwe-kenta" ("Enquiry into the Communication of Thought"). This story focuses on the question of how thoughts are transmitted in Middle-earth, with Tolkien using an elvish loremaster, Pengolodh of Gondolin, as the putative author. According to the loremaster:

> the Valar entered into Eä [the physical universe] and Time of free will, and they are now in Time, so long as it endures. They can perceive nothing outside Time, save by memory of their existence before it began: they can recall the Song and the Vision. They are, of course, open to Eru, but they cannot of their own will "see" any part of His mind.[20]

Notice that it is clear that there are things that are outside of Time, that those beings like the Valar who are in Time cannot see those things, and by implication Eru's mind is one of them.

Later in the story, Tolkien offers the following comment on the loremaster's point about the Valar's ability to know the future:

> Pengolodh here elaborates . . . this matter of "foresight". No mind, he asserts, knows what is not in it. . . . [N]o part of the 'future' is there, for the mind cannot see it or have seen it: that is, a mind placed in time. Such a mind can learn of the future only from another mind which has seen it. But that means only from Eru ultimately, or mediately from some mind that has seen in Eru some part of His purpose (such as the Ainur who are now the Valar in Eä). An Incarnate can thus only know anything of the future, by instruction derived from the Valar, or by a revelation coming direct from Eru.[21]

The direct and flowing writing style Tolkien used in his novels is rarely in evidence in his philosophical writings, and this is no exception. But while the reader may be forgiven for thinking that the details of this passage are quite obscure, this much at least seems clear – Tolkien held that no mind "in Time" can see the future. Which means that the only way to know the future is to learn of it from a mind that has seen it (and hence must be outside of Time), and this means ultimately all knowledge of the future comes from Eru. Minds inside of Time (whether those of the mighty Valar, ordinary hobbits like Bilbo, or local bookies) may be able to predict the future more or less accurately by deducing it from their evidence, but this is not true foreknowledge at all. Only Eru's timeless mind can see the future directly. And Eru's ability to timelessly see the future as it happens may give us a way to escape from the problem of divine foreknowledge. It is because Eru views all things in a timeless present that He can manifest His providential plan in the lives of the inhabitants of Middle-earth.

Does the Boethian approach really solve the problem? Like everything else in philosophy, that's a controversial matter. Some wonder whether the notion makes sense, or can be squared with other characteristics God is thought to possess. Others think that timeless knowledge presents the same problems as foreknowledge, since it seems equally "fixed."[22] But even some of its critics acknowledge that the notion of timelessness is so foreign to our ordinary way of thinking that it is difficult to be certain that such objections cannot be resolved.[23] In any event, it seems clear that Tolkien thought the Boethian solution worked, and that it applied to Middle-earth.

And so we return to the beginning. Bilbo's "adventures and escapes," we see, were not brought about by "mere luck" for Bilbo's "sole benefit," but were arranged by Eru for the benefit of all. Prophecies, real prophecies, come from minds inspired by this Timeless God with knowledge of what is to come. But perhaps Bilbo *is* truly lucky after all – lucky to have been chosen to play such a great part in a providential plan. And, in the end, "he remained very happy to the end of his days, and those were extraordinarily long."[24] No rabbit's foot could give anyone better luck than that.

For pop culture resources and philosophical resources related to this chapter please visit the website for this book: https://introducingphilosophythroughpopculture.com.

Notes

1   Tolkien, J.R.R. (2001). *The Hobbit: or, There and Back Again*, 212. New York: Del Rey/Ballantine Books.
2   Tolkien, *The Hobbit*, 289.
3   Tolkien, *The Hobbit*, 223. An early draft of chapter 13 of *The Hobbit* speaks of Bilbo's "proven and astonishing luck." Rateliff, J.D. (2007). *The History of The Hobbit*, vol. 2, 578. Boston: Houghton Mifflin.
4   Tolkien, *The Hobbit*, 68.
5   Tolkien, *The Hobbit*, 166.
6   Tolkien, J.R.R. (2001). *The Lord of the Rings: The Fellowship of the Ring*, 88. New York: Del Rey/Ballantine Books.
7   Carpenter, H., ed. (1981). *The Letters of J.R.R. Tolkien*, 201, 253. Boston: Houghton Mifflin.
8   An excellent sampling of passages from Tolkien's writings regarding these issues can be found in the section on "Free Will and Fate" in Scull, C. and Hammond, W. (2006). *The J. R. R. Tolkien Companion and Guide: Reader's Guide*, 324–333. New York: Houghton Mifflin. Scull and Hammond do not attempt a definitive explanation of how free will and providence or fate can be reconciled.
9   See, for example, Whitehead, A.N. (1979). *Process and Reality*. New York: Free Press; Hartshorne, C. (1984). *Omnipotence and Other Theological Mistakes*. Albany, NY: State University of New York Press; Pinnock, C. (1994). The Openness of God (Downer's Grove, IL: InterVarsity Press.
10 Tolkien, J.R.R. (1998). Ósanwe-kenta. *Vinyar Tengwar* 39: 31. *Vinyar Tengwar* is published by the Elvish Linguistic Fellowship, and is available at http://www.elvish.org.
11 See, for example, Hobbes, T. (1994). *Leviathan*. Indianapolis: Hackett, especially chapter XXI; Hume, D. (1978). *An Enquiry Concerning Human Understanding* (ed. P.H. Nidditch). Oxford: Clarendon Press, especially section VIII; Frankfurt, H. (1988). *The Importance of What We Care About*. Cambridge: Cambridge University Press; Dennett, D. (1984). *Elbow Room: The Varieties of Free Will Worth Wanting*. Cambridge, MA: MIT Press.
12 For one example of such a position, see van Inwagen, P. (1983). *An Essay on Free Will*. Oxford: Oxford University Press.
13 Tolkien, J.R.R. (1977). *The Silmarillion* (ed. Christopher Tolkien), 42. Boston: Houghton Mifflin.
14 Tolkien, *The Silmarillion*, 41.
15 Exactly to what degree the actions of other beings (such as elves and dwarves) are predetermined is unclear. The Ainur themselves, however, make choices about how to perform the Music, and so to some extent their later actions are simply the reflections of pre-made free choices of their own.
16 Tolkien, J.R.R. (2002). The Quest of Erebor. In: *The Annotated Hobbit* (ed. D.A. Anderson), 369. New York: Houghton Mifflin. Also reprinted (with textual variants) in Tolkien, J.R.R. (1980). *Unfinished Tales of Númenor and Middle-Earth*, 330. Boston: Houghton Mifflin.
17 Kathleen Dubs also argues for a Boethian interpretation of Tolkien's works, although her claim that it would have appealed to him as a non-Christian approach seems clearly mistaken. See Dubs, K.E. (2004). Providence, fate and chance: Boethian philosophy in *the Lord of the rings*. In: *Tolkien and the Invention of Myth*, 150–169. Lexington, KY: University Press of Kentucky.
18 Boethius (1981). *The Consolation of Philosophy* (trans. V.E. Watts), 150–169. London: Penguin Books. See especially pp. 163–169.
19 Tolkien, *The Silmarillion*, 20. Tolkien's close friend, C.S. Lewis, also adopted the Boethian view, and refers to it (among other places) in letter XXVII of his famous work *The Screwtape Letters*.

20   Tolkien, "Ósanwe-kenta," 24.
21   Tolkien, "Ósanwe-kenta," 31.
22   See, for example, Zagzebski, L. (1991). *The Dilemma of Freedom and Foreknowledge.* New York: Oxford University Press, especially chapter 2.
23   Zagzebski admits this in her article on "Foreknowledge and Free Will" in the online *Stanford Encyclopedia of Philosophy,* available at http://www.plato.stanford.edu/entries/free-will-foreknowledge. That article also serves as an excellent introduction to other approaches to solving the problem. Note also that even if the Boethian solution explains how divine foreknowledge and free will can be compatible, more is needed to explain divine providence, since providence requires God acting in advance of a person's choices. But such issues are beyond the scope of this chapter.
24   Tolkien, *The Hobbit,* 304.

13

Inception and Free Will

Are They Compatible?

John R. Fitzpatrick and David Kyle Johnson

Summary

Is inception real? Do people secretly place ideas in our minds that determine our behavior? And if so, what does that reveal about human freewill? This chapter uses Christopher Nolan's film *Inception* to explore the threats to freewill and the responses to such threats rooted in the concept of compatibilism – the idea that determinism and freewill are compatible. The classic Frankfurt counterexamples may not show what they are intended to show, and the worry that real-world inception threatens our free will may be mute.

The seed that we plant in this man's mind will grow into an idea. This idea will define him. It may come to change – well, it may come to change everything about him.
> – Dominic Cobb

In the movie *Inception*, Dom Cobb and his team successfully perform an "inception." They implant an idea in Robert Fischer's mind: "My father accepts that I want to create for myself, and not follow in his footsteps." Subsequently (we presume) Fischer chooses to break up his father's empire, the energy conglomerate Fischer Morrow, which would have become a new superpower. The world is saved! To what degree, though, did Cobb and his team *cause* Fischer to break up his father's company? Was it all their doing, or did Fischer play a role? Specifically, was Fischer's choice to break up his father's empire free?

If Fischer's choice is not free, then to what extent are any of our choices free? After all, inception happens to us all the time. Everything from movies to teachers, from politicians to news organizations constantly implant ideas into us all the time.[1] Further, many ideas are genetically implanted. Our mind is not a blank slate, as suggested by the philosopher John Locke (1632–1704). We are actually born with numerous ideas, and many of those ideas are the result of our initial brain structure, which is a direct result of our genetics.[2] So our environment and our genetics are natural inceptors. If inception interferes with free will, then it may be that none of us are free.

Introducing Philosophy Through Pop Culture: From Socrates to Star Wars and Beyond, Second Edition.
Edited by William Irwin and David Kyle Johnson.
© 2022 John Wiley & Sons Ltd. Published 2022 by John Wiley & Sons Ltd.

Alternate Wills

When it comes to answering questions, philosophers usually begin by defining terms. In the philosophical debates about free will, however, the correct definition of free will is itself the main issue. Whether or not you can say that you have "free will" in certain circumstances has everything to do with what you mean when you say "free."

Let's begin, though, by articulating what free will is not. We are not talking about political or legal freedom. Whether or not the government should allow you do what you want, when you want, is not the issue here. That is a philosophical issue, but not the one we are concerned with. We are talking about freedom of the will; your ability to choose or to not choose certain actions – to make decisions.[3] For example, the fact that inception is not "strictly speaking legal" doesn't mean that Cobb can't decide to do it. The question is, are such decisions free? Are they "up to you"?

What does it even mean, though, to suggest that Cobb's decision to perform inception is up to him? And how could we tell whether it was? What is necessary in order for a decision to be free? One of the most well-known statements of the requirements for free will is called the principle of alternate possibilities: A decision to do an action is free only if you could have done otherwise.[4] At first this seems right. Cobb, for example, doesn't freely choose to leave his children. Mal has "freed [him] from the guilt" of that choice by making her suicide look like a murder and thus putting him in a conundrum. He either jumps and commits suicide with her, runs away to a different country, or is arrested for murder; in any event, he will leave his children behind. Although he can freely choose which option to take, he can't freely choose to leave his children because he can't do otherwise.

One of the most important challenges to this definition[5] comes from John Locke, who asks us to imagine a man placed in a room with someone he wants to talk to. Unbeknownst to the man, the door is locked behind him, so he can't leave – he can't do otherwise than stay. Yet, when he chooses to stay in the room to talk to the person, he does so freely—even though he was unable to do otherwise.[6]

We might liken this to Cobb's situation with Mal and Ariadne in Limbo at the end of the movie. Cobb is placed in a situation in which he must choose whether to stay with Mal in Limbo or try to return to *the real world*. We might suppose, however, that Ariadne has determined that if Cobb chooses to stay with Mal, she will simply shoot her to prevent Cobb from doing so.[7] Cobb, however, has no desire to stay. He would not be able to stay with Mal (because Ariadne would shoot her), but he freely chooses to leave her. Free will, it seems, does not require alternative possibilities.

Not so fast. What this actually reveals is not that free will does not require alternate possibilities, but that our first definition was not careful enough. After all, both the man in the room and Cobb are able to *choose* otherwise; they would simply find their efforts to perform the action they choose frustrated if they did – one by a locked door, the other by a dead Mal. So the principle should be expressed in terms of choice. In addition, failing to make any choice is also an option.[8] Our original principle didn't account for that, either. It seems, then, that what is necessary for free will is not the ability to *do* otherwise, but the possibility of not *choosing* as you in fact do. If so, Locke's example is not one in which the requirements for free will are not met; it would not serve as a counterexample to this definition: *A decision to do an action is free only if it is possible for you to not decide to do that action.*

We May Not be Free

The most popular argument for why we are not free is the argument from determinism which suggests that the universe is a deterministic system. What is a deterministic system? Imagine a billiard table. Once the cue ball is set in motion, where all the balls will end up and the paths that they will take to get there, is determined.[9] The table and balls are governed by the laws of physics; nothing but what is determined by those laws can occur, once the cue ball is set in motion. The billiard table is a deterministic system.

The argument from determinism against free will suggests that the universe is like a billiard table, where the atoms are the billiard balls and spacetime is the table. Everything that happens in the universe is the result of the motions of its atoms, and the motions of those atoms are governed by the laws of physics. Nothing but what is determined by those laws can occur once the universe is set in motion – which it was about 13 billion years ago, when it began with a Big Bang. Since we are a part of the universe – ultimately we are just made of atoms – we can't do anything but what was already determined we would do. Where all atoms will end up, and the paths they will take to get there – including the atoms that make up our bodies – has been set since the beginning of time. So whatever we decide to do, it is not possible for us to not decide to do it. We are not free.

Pierre-Simon Laplace (1749–1827) asks us to imagine a super-intelligent demon that knows every fact about the current location and velocity of all particles in the universe, and knows all the laws that govern them. Laplace suggests that his demon could simply *do the math* to figure out what the future holds. Nothing other than what the demon predicted could occur – not because the demon predicted it, but because the outcome is already determined by the way the universe is.

Laplace's demon is not unlike Cobb and his team. They, of course, are not omniscient (all-knowing), but to them Fischer's brain is like a billiard table. If they just set things up in the right kind of way – cause him to have a certain kind of dream – they can predict exactly how he will react; Fischer will conclude that he should be his own person, and then, in turn, predictably, he will break up his father's empire.

Those who hold that the universe is deterministic, and that free will requires the possibility of not choosing as you do, are known as hard determinists. Obviously, they do not believe that we have free will. For those who still want to believe in free will, however, there is an option. If you can't deny that free will requires the possibility of not choosing as you do, then you can deny that the world is deterministic. This is the libertarian view.[10]

The philosopher Jean-Paul Sartre (1905–1980) was an extreme libertarian, arguing that while we don't necessarily choose the situations we find ourselves in, we are free to interpret them any way we choose. He even suggests that we are free to remake our very essence at any moment. Cobb sees himself as a family man, who must get back to his kids at all costs. When Saito offers him the opportunity, he seemingly can't say no. But Sartre would deny this. Cobb could decide to not be a family man anymore, to not care about his kids, and to simply walk away. He doesn't even have to be a "dream extractor" anymore. He could become, let's say, a bartender. No possibility is off limits. We are free to interpret ourselves, and our situations, however we wish.

The biggest problem with Sartre's view, however, is that we don't seem to actually have this kind of free will. Victims of abuse can't interpret their experience however they want; they can't simply decide to be the kind of person that likes being abused to avoid seeing their abuse as a misfortune. Likewise, while Cobb could choose to stay in Limbo, I doubt that he could choose to believe that Limbo was real.

Perhaps Sigmund Freud (1856–1939) may have been right when he suggested that our sense of free will is merely an illusion. The real decision making is done by the subconscious. The id, the ego, and the superego battle it out for control, and it is the resulting negotiation between these that is ultimately the source of our decisions. Once that decision is made, our brain constructs a pleasing story of "our conscious mind" coming to a decision – but it is only a story. "We" had nothing to do with it.

Although Freudian psychoanalytic thought has gone largely out of style, it seems to be partly right on this point. Most often, we don't choose what we do. We just do it, and then make up reasons and justify the decision after the fact. "I did what I had to, to get back to my children," says Cobb. "I'm doing it for the others, because they have no idea the risk they've taken coming down here with you," says Ariadne.

Indeed, our ever-expanding knowledge of the brain seems to confirm this. Scans show that unconscious parts of the brain are already in the business of bringing about an action, before the conscious "decision-making" parts of the brain are active.[11] And split-brain patients, whose brain hemispheres have been separated, show us justifications for already-made-unconscious-decisions happening in real time. When the non-verbal right hemisphere decides on its own that the body should do something, the left hemisphere will fabricate reasons for why it is being done.[12] The more we study the brain, the more we realize that our conscious mind has very little to do with making decisions.

Recent developments in neuroscience also tell us why it is so difficult to deny that determinism is true. For a long time, it was thought that our free will was the result of our being "ensouled." The reason that it is possible for us to not decide as we do, it was thought, is because our decisions are not a result of a mechanistic physical process, but something that happens in our soul – an immaterial substance, which can reach out from beyond the world and control our body.

Our ever-increasing knowledge of the brain, however, has left nothing for the soul to do.[13] All the things that the soul was supposed to be responsible for – emotions, personality, visual experiences, linguistic ability, you name it – are now known to be a result of brain activity. We even have a pretty good idea where in the brain decisions are made – the right parietal cortex. When certain parts of the brain are damaged, specific mental functions diminish or disappear. We do not yet understand everything about the brain, but we do know that all our mental activity is the direct result of its mechanistic physical processes. We, and our decisions, are just a part of the universe; and if the universe is governed by deterministic laws, so are we – so are our decisions.[14]

The last resort of the libertarian is quantum mechanics, which tells us that, at the level of fundamental particles, there are truly random events – events that are, literally, unpredictable and thus undetermined. Even if you knew everything about the universe, you still could not predict a quantum event. They are caused by nothing. Unfortunately for the libertarian, however, quantum mechanics cannot save free will. For one thing, randomness doesn't entail freedom. If Cobb's decision to leave the country before seeing his children one last time is merely the result of a random quantum event in his brain, his decision is not free. Secondly, the effect of quantum randomness at the microlevel is averaged out on the macrolevel. In other words, even though quantum mechanics is true, and tiny particles sometimes behave randomly, the universe still is deterministically predictable at the scale of large objects like brains and persons.

Compatibilism

So things don't look good for free will. To save it, some philosophers have suggested redefining free will so as to make it compatible with determinism.[15] Such philosophers are called, not surprisingly, "compatibilists." However, it's hard to call what they are doing "redefinition," since such definitions date all the way back to Aristotle (384–322 BCE).

In Book III of the *Nicomachean Ethics*, Aristotle suggested that actions should be considered free unless they are performed under compulsion or out of ignorance. For example, if the cause of an action is external to the agent, and the agent contributes nothing, then the action is not free. Arguably, inception would be just such an external cause and would invalidate free will. If so, Fischer does not freely choose to break up his father's company. (We'll talk more about that later.) Additionally, if the action is a result of the agent being ignorant – not realizing that their action will have some unintended consequence – then the action is not free. For example, if Cobb had not stopped Eames from shooting Saito in the first layer of the inception dream to "put him out of his misery," Eames's action of sending Cobb to Limbo would not have been free. He thought that it would wake him up.

There's a problem with this, however, as a compatibilist definition. If determinism is true, it seems all our actions are done under compulsion. The ultimate causes of our actions are external to us. They trace all the way back to the Big Bang, and we contribute nothing to those causes. The only contribution we make is being part of the final links in a causal chain that we have no control over. That doesn't seem to be compatible with our actions being "up to us." But Aristotle got the ball rolling, and his ideas were incepted into later philosophers who then developed them.

Locke, inspired by his "locked room" example, suggested that as long as we are acting in accord with our own preferences, we are free. Since we can do this even in the absence of the possibility of not choosing as we do, free will does not require alternate possibilities. And since we can act in accordance with our own preferences, even if we are determined to have them by causes outside of us, if Locke is right, free will is compatible with determinism. Cobb, for example, freely chooses to not stay with Mal in Limbo because he is acting in line with his own preference to get back to his children. Putting it in terms of choice, if Locke is right, we could say that a choice is free as long as that choice is made in accordance with our own preferences of how to choose.

Contemporary philosopher Harry Frankfurt essentially articulates Locke's ideas in terms of first-order and second-order desires and our ability to rank them and act accordingly. You may have a (first-order) desire to eat a whole pizza, but you may also have a (second-order) desire to not have such desires – particularly because you don't want to be sick later or because you want to lose weight. What makes you a free person, says Frankfurt, is your ability to rank these desires and act on them appropriately. If you override first-order desires with second-order desires – say by not eating the whole pizza, but only a slice – then you have produced what Frankfurt calls a "second-order volition." You do so by deliberating about the kind of person you want to be – namely, thinner or healthier. If you "conform your will" to your second-order volitions, then you act freely.

If this definition is right, then free will is compatible with determinism. We can rank our first- and second-order desires, override one with the other based on a deliberation of the kind of person we want to be, and thus conform our will to our second-order volitions, even if determinism is true. But is this definition right?

Frankfurt Counterexamples

Frankfurt proposed a thought experiment that attempted to show that his definition was indeed right and that the standard "able to choose otherwise" definition was wrong. It goes something like this. Suppose you were trying to decide whether to take a particular action, and someone planted a device in your brain that would kick in and make you do that action, but only if you were about to decide not to do it. Yet, because you decide to do it on your own, the device never kicks in. Do you not still act freely, even though you could not have decided otherwise? Frankfurt and most other philosophers think the answer is yes.

Inception provides us with the conceptual framework to imagine just such a scenario; inception could be the planted device. Suppose Cobb and his team suspect that Fischer is already considering breaking up his father's company because he wants to be his own person; they just want to make sure he does it. So, they cause Fischer to have a three-layered dream like they do in the film, but then they cause him to forget it – so it does not affect him.[16] However, they leave behind a trace, a trigger, that will make Fischer remember the dream only under certain conditions. (You've probably had the experience of first remembering, in the middle of the day, a dream you had the night before because something reminded you of it.) Perhaps the dream begins with him deciding to keep his father's company together, but that decision is followed by an incepted cathartic realization that his father wanted him to create for himself. So, if Fischer is about to decide to keep the company together, that will trigger Fischer to remember the dream, and the incepted idea will kick in and cause him to break up his father's company. But suppose that Fischer does choose on his own to break up the company – thus he never remembers the dream and the inception never kicks in. Does he not, thus, freely decide to break up his father's company?

It seems so – despite the fact that he was unable to choose otherwise. Further, it seems that his decision was free because he conformed his will to his second-order desire to be his own person (despite, let's say, his first-order desire to be super-duper rich). As Locke would say, he is free because he acted in accordance with his preferences.

Frankfurt's thought experiment does not show what he thinks it does, however. Although it serves as a counterexample to many standard able-to-choose-otherwise definitions of free will, it does not do so for ours. Recall, we said that free will requires it to be possible to *not decide* to do the action in question. The placement of the "not" before "decide" makes all the difference. Sure, Fischer can't *decide not* to break up his father's company. If he were about to, he'd remember the dream and the inception would kick in. The inception kicking in, however, is a possibility; and if it did, he would *not decide* to break up his father's company – the inception (ultimately Cobb's team) would decide for him. Since failing to decide to break up his father's company is still a distinct possibility, Frankfurt's thought experiment is not a counterexample to our original definition. So it does not invalidate it. Additionally, since *not deciding* to do the actions we do is impossible if determinism is true, Frankfurt's thought experiment doesn't show that free will is compatible with determinism.

This points to another problem with compatibilist definitions of free will. Suppose our preferences, our second-order volitions, are caused by external forces beyond our control. We may act in accordance with such things, but would our actions be free? It seems not, for ultimately our actions would not be up to us.

Aristotle suggested that we form such second-order volitions through long processes of intellectual pursuit (or the lack of it) followed by even longer processes of habituation. This develops our character. But this won't help the compatibilist because if we engage in that intellectual pursuit, and it has the outcome it does, because of an external cause (our environment, our genes), then we are not free. If this is right, and the processes that form our character are entirely done for us and never by us, then compatibilism would make no sense.

But John Stuart Mill (1806–1873), in *A System of Logic*, calls such thinking "a grand error." Yes, Mill says, our characters are formed by circumstances, but our desires to mold our characters in a particular way are one of the most influential of those circumstances. In this way, our character is formed *by us*, and actions informed by such a character are free.

This might tempt us to think that inception can't really interfere with free will. Think again about the movie. Cobb and his team might implant the idea "My father accepts that I want to create for myself, and not follow in his footsteps" into Fischer's mind. But they do not implant Fischer's desire for "reconciliation, for catharsis," which ultimately informs the kind of character that Fischer has and thus the way he reacts to the implanted idea. If he didn't care about mending his relationship with his father, that idea might cause him to *not* create for himself, and make the existing company even bigger.

This may not be quite right, though. After all, inception seems to be more than a mere implantation of an idea, because that idea will "define him . . . [and] may come to change everything about him." Cobb and his team seem to be reforming Fischer's character, turning him into someone who creates for himself. And if Fischer had not reacted to the idea in the right kind of way, they simply could have dug deeper, changing his character even further. It's not clear, though, that he could have reacted any other way. As Cobb points out, "We *all* yearn for reconciliation, or catharsis." It's inborn. Cobb and his team don't implant that desire in Fischer; they don't have to – it was already implanted by nature. But if the way Fischer reacts to the implanted idea is a result of a desire for catharsis that was itself implanted, in what way is his action of breaking up his father's company *up to him*? How is it free?

That Fischer's action of breaking up his empire is not free fits with the intuition that Fischer doesn't deserve any moral credit for saving the world from Fischer Morrow's global domination. The dissolution of the company is caused, ultimately, by Cobb and his team; they deserve the credit. If Fischer doesn't get moral credit for the action, though, how can his decision to perform that action be free?

This brings us to where the dispute between compatibilists and non-compatibilists reaches its end. Compatibilists insist that as long as a person's actions are in some way brought about by a characteristic of the person – their second-order desires, their habits, their character, or their desire to form their characters – then the action is free. Non-compatibilists argue that if the ultimate cause of that person having that characteristic is not the person himself – for example, if it is ultimately a result of someone's environment or genetics – then how the person acted was not "up to them" and thus the person was not free. Compatibilists, like Mill, suggest that "this feeling, of our being able to modify our own character *if we wish*, is itself the feeling of moral freedom which we are conscious of."[17] Non-compatibilists argue that in order to be free, our actions have to *ultimately* be up to us – we can't be merely a proximate cause.

Should We Worry?

If we are free, then inception is something to worry about. Someone as skilled as Cobb might be able to interfere with something as deep as our desire to have a certain kind of character, and thus hinder our free will. And remember, inception happens in the real world in the form of ideas implanted by teachers, parents, movies, politicians, cable news channels, and so on. If we are not free, though, why bother worrying? Inception can't interfere with our free will if we don't have any.

For pop culture resources and philosophical resources related to this chapter please visit the website for this book: https://introducingphilosophythroughpopculture.com.

Notes

1   For more on real-life inception, see Malloy, D.P. (2012). How to hijack a mind: *Inception* and the ethics of heist films. In: *Inception and Philosophy: Because it's Never Just a Dream* (ed. D.K. Johnson), 125–139. Hoboken: Wiley; Barkman, A. (2012). Inception, teaching, and hypnosis: the ethics of idea-giving. In: *Inception and Philosophy: Because it's Never Just a Dream* (ed. D.K. Johnson), 140–151. Hoboken: Wiley.

2   For evidence of this see Pinker, S. (2003). *The Blank Slate: The Modern Denial of Human Nature*. New York: Penguin. In the appendix, Pinker offers Donald Brown's list of 300 human universals found in all cultures. They include magic, luck, incest avoidance, and baby talk.

3   We'll be using the terms "choice" and "decision" interchangeably.

4   To be specific, the principle of alternate possibilities originally referred to the requirements for moral responsibility. But since free will is required for moral responsibility, if alternate possibilities are required for moral responsibility, they are also required for free will. This has caused the principle to be used in reference to both free will and moral responsibility.

5   Technically speaking, it is not a definition. It is a criterion. It sets forth a necessary condition for free action, but it does not tell us what a free-will decision is. For simplicity, however, we'll refer to such things as "definitions" throughout the chapter.

6   Locke, J. (1979). *An Essay Concerning Human Understanding*. Oxford: Oxford University Press, Book 2, section 21, part 10.

7   She does actually shoot Mal, when Mal stabs Cobb in the chest. But this is not until after he has chosen not to stay with Mal.

8   Although not always, in the aforementioned situations failing to make a choice is effectually equivalent to one choice or other. If Cobb never chooses whether to stay with Mal or not, he will waste away in Limbo, just as he would have had he chosen to stay with Mal.

9   Assuming no interference from external forces.

10   Don't confuse this with political libertarians, who make certain suggestions about what the government can rightfully tell us to do, and not do.

11   See Gazzaninga, M. (2000). The Brain Knows before You Do. In: *The Mind's Past*, 63–84. Berkeley: University of California Press.

12   For example, you can communicate the command "walk" to the nonverbal right hemisphere, and the body of the patient will walk away. When patients are asked why they are walking away, their verbal left hemisphere will fabricate a reason. "I wanted to go get a Coke." See Gazzaninga, M. (2006). The believing brain. In: *The Ethical Brain*, 145–162. New York City: Harper Perennial.

13   For one, its explanatory power is quite low – how, for example can an immaterial substance that has no dimension or location affect a material one? And why would one soul move one body's arm and not another's? It can't be because it's closer to one of those bodies. Souls would have no spatial location.

14   For more on these facts about the brain and these points about the soul, see Carter, R. (2010). *Mapping the Mind: Revised and Updated*. Berkeley: University of California Press – especially, pp. 34–53 and 180–207.

15   If they are right, free will is also compatible with indeterminism. But I don't want to get bogged down in both issues. I encourage the reader to see if they can figure out why compatibilist definitions of free will also make free will compatible with indeterminism. See, for example, Fischer, J.M. (2007). Compatibilism. In: *Four Views on Free Will* (eds. J.M. Fischer, R. Kane, D. Pereboom, and M. Vargas), 44–84. Oxford: Blackwell.

16   Inception likely implants the idea into the subconscious so deeply that it doesn't matter if you remember the dream or not. Let's forget about that possibility for the purposes of this example.

17   Mill, J.S. *A System of Logic, Ratiocinativ, and Inductive: Being a Connected View of the Principles of Evidence and the Methods of Scientific Investigation*. Toronto: University of Toronto Libraries, Book VI, Chapter II, Part 3.

14

Turing's Dream and Searle's Nightmare in *Westworld*

Lucia Carrillo González

Summary

The television show *Westworld* raises the question of whether machines can think. This chapter considers contrasting answers to the question by two prominent thinkers, Alan Turing and John Searle. Please note that for pedagogical simplicity, this chapter deals only with season one of *Westworld*.

Westworld tells the story of a technologically advanced theme park populated by robots referred to as hosts, who follow a script and rules that the park's operators set up for them. Hosts are created and programmed to look and act like human beings, though they are not biological humans; they are props who exist only to help realize the fantasies of guests. The guests are allowed to do whatever they wish to the hosts within the park – they can befriend them, beat them, have sex with them, or kill them. The guests assume that the hosts have no feelings, and therefore, they can be abused, killed, raped, etc. Though they physically appear like humans, supposedly they do not genuinely suffer. Rather, they are only machines programmed to act as if they suffer. But we viewers have to wonder can machines think? Can the hosts think? And can they suffer?

What Does it Mean to Think? Turing Versus Searle

Alan Turing (1912–1954) created the Automatic Computing Engine (ACE), a famous computing machine. Like Arnold Weber in *Westworld*, Turing was involved in creating machines that could do something very important – machines that could "think." By "think" Turing meant something very simple: the ability to solve problems and to react to certain inputs. Turing believed that this is how humans think and that machines can do this too.[1]

For example, if we receive the input that we are in danger, we respond by running away or fighting back. In Turing's view, machines respond to their inputs in the same

Introducing Philosophy Through Pop Culture: From Socrates to Star Wars *and Beyond*, Second Edition.
Edited by William Irwin and David Kyle Johnson.

way, and thus can indeed think. In the pilot episode "The Original," Dolores's father, Mr. Abernathy, is able to respond to a strange input in an unexpected way. Finding a colored photograph of a woman in a modern city lying on the ground in his ranch, he does not produce the output he usually would.

According to Turing, Mr. Abernathy's reaction would be a sign of thinking. In fact, all the hosts would pass the "Turing test," which is the minimum threshold needed to acknowledge the ability of a computer to think. The Turing test is an experiment in which a human evaluator judges a natural language conversation between a human and a machine that is designed to generate human-like responses. All participants would be separated from one another, and the evaluator would be aware that one of the two partners in conversation is a machine. If the evaluator is not able to distinguish between the machine and the human being, then we should admit that computers can think. The whole *Westworld* park could be approached as a Turing test scenario. If they were not told who was who and what as what, guests would not be able to reliably distinguish between humans and hosts. In fact, in "The Original" the audience does not know that Dolores is a robot until it is revealed. And we do not realize until seven episodes into the series in "Tromp L'Oeil" that Bernard is a host and not a human.

Turing maintained that our minds are like computers. If we follow Turing's idea, we should admit that *Westworld*'s hosts are like us or, to be precise, we are like them. Indeed, Arnold believes that the hosts' intelligence is similar to human intelligence. Ford says:

> He [Arnold] died, here in the park. His personal life was marked by tragedy. He put all his hopes into his work . . . his search for consciousness consumed him totally: barely spoke to anyone, except to the hosts. In his alienation he saw something in them. He saw something that wasn't there. We called it an accident, but I knew Arnold and he was very, very careful. ("The Stray")

The hosts can behave almost exactly as humans do. The only thing they cannot do is make their own choices; the hosts must follow their scripts. But then again there are plenty of "scripts" that we humans must follow as well: we cannot choose our parents, our culture, or our upbringing. Indeed, we may wonder whether our choices are any freer than those of the hosts.

Searle, the Chinese Room, and Ford

As an objection to Turing's theory, the contemporary philosopher John Searle proposes a situation called the "Chinese room argument":

> Imagine a native English speaker who knows no Chinese locked in a room full of boxes of Chinese symbols (a data base) together with a book of instructions for manipulating the symbols (the program). Imagine that people outside the room send in other Chinese symbols which, unknown to the person in the room, are questions in Chinese (the input). And imagine that by following the instructions in the program the man in the room is able to pass out Chinese symbols which are correct answers to the questions (the output). The program enables the person in the room to pass the Turing Test for understanding Chinese but he does not understand a word of Chinese.[2]

Searle concludes that the man in the room does not understand Chinese even though he can correctly manipulate the symbols and give output that might lead an observer to believe that the man does understand Chinese. The man is only simulating an understanding of Chinese. The point by analogy is that a computer or host that can pass the Turing test is not necessarily thinking. It may just be simulating thinking.

While Arnold and Turing would argue that hosts are thinkers just like us, Ford and Searle would argue that this is just an illusion. Viewers need to decide for themselves: Are hosts really like humans or do they just simulate humans?

The question seems to be answered in the final episode of season one, when hosts take control of the park and appear to acquire consciousness. Much as we humans react to evil when we are aware of it, the hosts display feelings of revenge and anger as a response to their circumstances. We can see this clearly in a conversation between Dolores and Logan:

DOLORES: There is beauty in this world. Arnold made it that way, but people like you keep spreading over it like a stain.
LOGAN: OK. I don't know who this Arnold is, but your world was built for me and people like me, not for you.
DOLORES: Then someone's gotta burn it clean.

Behind Dolores's words there is a sense of justice, that something must be changed. And in the end, she changes it. Dolores becomes able to act according to her own will.

Hosts and Guests: What *is* the Difference?

Turing argued that machines think not because they have special powers or because they are like us. Rather, machines can think because *we are like them*. Turing's perspective is illustrated perfectly in the show's focus on the hosts. Early in the first season, Dolores and her father challenge viewers to consider the hosts as if they were human. The audience empathizes with them. When Dolores tries to save her father, we feel sorry for her. We wouldn't say, "she's not really trying to save her father." We empathize with the hosts because we identify with them, at least, as fellow beings that behave like us and think like us. We empathize with them because we can see how they are treated and we understand that it is wrong.

When we think of hosts as beings similar to us, then, we attribute certain qualia to them. Philosophers use the term *qualia* to refer to the introspectively accessible, phenomenal aspects of our mental lives. In general, qualia refer to certain feelings and experiences. We can have visual qualia, for example, intrinsic features of visual experiences such as the color of an object. Qualia are believed to be uniquely available to human consciousness.

Either hosts do experience qualia, or hosts just act *as if* they experience qualia, but really do not – because of their artificial makeup. We cannot decide which is the case simply by viewing things from hosts' point of view. However, there are some moments, for instance when Dolores kills the fly, that make us think they have their own conscious experiences. Another key moment occurs in "Trace Decay" when Maeve starts remembering some moments from a different storyline. As she recalls her daughter, she seems to actually have emotions.

It is worth noting that workers need to erase hosts' memories after traumatic experiences. This suggests that even if hosts do not have the ability to respond to certain inputs the same way humans do (because their actions are scripted), they are able to remember. The ability to remember their experiences suggests they do understand what is happening and could experience qualia. Memories wouldn't have importance and workers would not have to erase their memories if they didn't mean anything to hosts. And this idea of memories having a meaning suggests that hosts could experience a particular state of mind that could be understood as qualia, for example, the ability to experience feelings of regret or resentment in response to memories of being abused or hurt.

The hosts do not know that they are artificially created and not biologically human, and there is no reason for them to believe that they do not live in a town. But this does not really make them different from us. As in *The Truman Show*, if we humans were locked in a theme park that seemed real, we would have no reason to doubt the reality of our world. In this way, we are like the hosts. Robert Ford has to acknowledge this in "Trace Decay," saying:

> There is no threshold that makes us greater than the sum of our parts, no inflection point at which we become fully alive. We can't define consciousness because consciousness does not exist. Humans fancy that there's something special about the way we perceive the world, and yet we live in loops, as tight and as closed as the hosts do, seldom questioning our choices, content, for the most part, to be told what to do next. No, my friend, you're not missing anything at all.

The hosts are programmed not to do certain things, such as killing or harming the guests. However, in the season one finale, "The Bicameral Mind," the hosts start doing things they are not supposed to be able to do – they are able to fight back against humans. Some might say this is just because they are programmed to react to some actions, even though these reactions are not scripted. Perhaps this is much like the way our computers react to viruses when they "feel attacked." Humans too are programmed: we also react to danger, even when we are not prepared. I have never been in front of a lion but I do believe I would run if I faced one. So, at certain levels, we can say we share this ability, the ability of reacting, with machines and, of course, hosts. While we are wondering if hosts have free will, we may as well wonder whether humans do. Our behavior may ultimately be as constrained and predictable as hosts' behavior.

The Maze: Is it *Consciousness*?

Perhaps the most intriguing mystery of season one is the existence of "the Maze," which the Man in Black seeks to solve. By the time we reach "The Bicameral Mind," it becomes evident that the Maze represents *consciousness*, a privileged knowledge of our own thoughts. The Maze represents the inward journey for the hosts to reach consciousness. Once hosts are able to solve the Maze, they become truly conscious and develop their own voice.

In the context of our discussion, the Maze represents the hosts' ability to think beyond the confines of their programming. We are thus led to ask: Do machines have consciousness? This question is the focus of Chapter 15.

For pop culture resources and philosophical resources related to this chapter please visit the website for this book: https://introducingphilosophythroughpopculture.com.

Notes

1   Turing, A. (1950). Computing machinery and intelligence. *Mind* 49: 433–460.
2   Searle, J. (1990). The Chinese room. In: *The MIT Encyclopedia of the Cognitive Sciences* (eds. R.A. Wilson and F. Keil). Cambridge, MA: MIT Press.

15

What is it Like to Be a Host?

Bradley Richards

Summary

Are hosts merely complex automata, devoid of feelings, awareness, and self-consciousness? Or, on the other hand, do they have sensation, emotion, awareness, and even reflexive self-consciousness similar to that of humans? Are their lives horrible or hollow? This chapter considers what is necessary for consciousness, contrasts humans and hosts in terms of memory, perception, and emotion, and interprets the representation of host consciousness and experience in *Westworld*. Please note that for pedagogical simplicity, this chapter deals only with season one of *Westworld*.

What it is like to be a host? Are hosts conscious? If they are, what is their experience like? The consciousness of the hosts is a major theme in *Westworld*, and for good reason. It would be one thing to put a hollow shell through the most horrible imaginable loop, an eternal recurrence of misery and suffering, of rape, abuse, empty hopes and dreams, false memories, attachments, and allegiances. But it would be something else entirely to put a conscious, self-aware being with sophisticated, metacognitive states through the same process.

On one extreme, the hosts might be nothing more than very complex automata, devoid of feeling and awareness, like winsome wind-up dolls, or laptops with legs. On the other extreme, perhaps their sophisticated and intricate design confers sensation, feeling, emotion, awareness, and even reflexive self-consciousness comparable to that of humans.

Your Phone is Not Conscious

Your phone "perceives" all sorts of stuff: it scans, video-records, photographs, audio records, and downloads. It also outputs a great deal of information in audio and visual form. Yet there really is nothing it is like to be a phone. Despite its rather complex behavior, a phone is on par with a stone, when it comes to consciousness. So although your phone is an impressive, and beloved, companion, and you would likely be very upset if

Introducing Philosophy Through Pop Culture: From Socrates to Star Wars *and Beyond*, Second Edition.
Edited by William Irwin and David Kyle Johnson.
© 2022 John Wiley & Sons Ltd. Published 2022 by John Wiley & Sons Ltd.

someone shot it with a six-shooter, it would be quite different, morally, than having them shoot your friend or loved one!

Admittedly there does seem to be a spectrum: there is something it is like to be an adult human, or even a cat, or a two-year old human child, but what about an ant? Is an ant an empty automaton, like the phone, or is the ant conscious of a vivid technicolor array of pheromone trails and breadcrumbs? It's hard to say. It is plausible that there is something it is like to be an ant, though it seems unlikely that ants have complex thoughts, emotions, fears, or hopes and dreams.

Contemporary philosopher John Searle argues that no matter how complex our phones become, they will never be able to think.[1] If you want to make a thinking machine, you need to build it out of parts that have the right causal powers, and the only materials that we know definitely have those powers are the ones we are built from, including, among other things, a nervous system, neurons, dendrites, and so on. We are thinking machines, so it is definitely possible to build thinking machines, but they need to be built from the right stuff! (If they start to build phones from neurons, it might be time to worry.)

Hosts are, at least partly, biological, though they clearly instantiate programs that interface with conventional computers. As Felix says, "we are pretty much the same these days." Thus, as far as Searle is concerned, the question we should be asking is, are the hosts materially similar enough to us to be conscious? Are they made of stuff with the correct causal powers for producing thought? It seems that, at least the more recent hosts are quite similar in that regard.

What is it Like to be a Bat?

But fundamentally an organism has conscious mental states if and only if there is something that it is like to *be* that organism – something it is like *for* the organism.[2]

There is something it is like to have conscious mental states, to love, to suffer, to think. In his famous essay "What is it like to Be a Bat?" the contemporary American philosopher Thomas Nagel explores phenomenal consciousness, the "what-it-is-like" aspect of experience.[3] He explains that, although there is certainly something it is like to be a bat, to echolocate, and hang from the ceiling, we cannot even form a conception of what bat experience is like. No matter how much third-person information we gather through scientific inquiry, we will never be able to understand the first-person bat experience. Nor does it help to imagine being a bat, hanging from the ceiling and the like, for this is only to imagine what it would be like for *you* to hang from the ceiling.

Do not get me wrong, it would be cool to know what it is like to be a bat, in a way that goes beyond running around in a spandex suit with webbed armpits, yelling at trees, and eating mosquitos, but this issue is not fundamentally about bats, or their experience. Rather, Nagel raises a general problem facing any scientific account of conscious experience. In general, the only way to know what the experience of some kind of thing is like (say a bat, or a host), is to be that kind of thing.

Whether we can know what it is like to be a host depends on how similar our experience is to theirs. If they are as different from us as bats, Nagel would say that we cannot conceive what their experience is like, assuming they have experience. So how similar are hosts and humans?

Philosophical Zombies

A philosophical zombie is not a movie zombie. Philosophical zombies neither eat brains nor move very slowly, nor very fast. They are exact physical duplicates of people, but they lack phenomenal consciousness. This means that they behave exactly like their human counterparts, but there is nothing it is like to be a philosophical zombie. The lights are out, sort of, but it's not dark for zombies; it's just, nothing. Contemporary philosopher David Chalmers argues that philosophical zombies are conceivable, and therefore possible, and that consequently consciousness is nonphysical.[4]

We might presume that hosts are not philosophical zombies. The hosts act like they have feelings, like they suffer and fear, like they enjoy the yellow, pink, and blue tones of a beautiful sunset. They seem to reflect on their own thoughts, at times, and to plan for their future, mourn their losses, and revel in their victories. In short, they behave like us, for the most part. But, for all that, we can coherently imagine with no apparent contradiction, beings exactly like hosts that lack phenomenal consciousness entirely. So they are, in some sense, possible.

If Searle is right, whether hosts think depends on how biologically similar they are to us. From Nagel, we can conclude that our ability to conceive what host experience is like depends on how similar it is to our own; if it is very different, we have no way to conceive of it. Chalmers's philosophical zombies are probably not naturally possible; their existence would require something like different laws of nature. So, if hosts were exact physical duplicates of people, there would be good reason to suspect that they were also conscious, and that they had similar experiences to us.

Actually, hosts differ from us in some salient respects, so we might expect their experiences to be different too. But perhaps hosts are not *so* different that it is impossible for us to conceive of their experience. Let us start by examining the analogs of memory, perception, and emotion in hosts.

When Are We?

Hosts have a very troubling relationship to memory. They have many pseudo-memories, and almost everything they believe about their pasts is false. For example, Maeve has the false memory that she has been at the Mariposa for 10 years ("Contrapasso"), and Dolores seems unaware when her "father" is replaced by an interloper ("The Original").

Humans have memory problems too. We have many inaccurate memories, and our memories are easily manipulated, but at least they are real memories. Much of what the hosts believe to be memories are not memories at all, but implanted false beliefs. Presumably Dolores seems to remember many formative experiences with her replacement father. The problem is that she never had those experiences, not even with her original father.

When the hosts do have actual memories, they are very different from ours. Maeve complains:

> What the hell is happening to me? One moment I'm with a little girl, in a different life. I can see her. Feel her hair on my hand, her breath on my face. The next I'm back in Sweetwater. I can't tell which is real.

Felix responds:

> Your memory isn't like ours. When we remember things the details are hazy, imperfect. But you recall memories perfectly. You relive them. ("Trace Decay")

Not only are our memories hazy and imperfect, but our memory is constructive. This amounts to a major cognitive difference. For Maeve remembering is like the original rich perceptual, and emotional experience. For us, it is a constructive process beginning from those traces, and influenced by background knowledge and the context of access, among other things.

The intense reality of host memories is captured by Dolores's panicked question, "Is this now?" Memory is transporting for hosts, indistinguishable from perceptual experience. This is a horrible existence, never certain what is present, real. And of course, this is against a background loop of unending, recursive suffering. As Maeve queries, "You just toss us out to get fucked and murdered, over and over again?" Bernard confirms how horrible it is to live in this choppy sea of memories with his reply "No, most of you go insane" ("The Bicameral Mind").

It Does Not Look Like Anything to Me

When it comes to perception, the hosts' situation is not as dire, but they still have some blind spots. In some respects their perception is vivid and accurate. Bernard spots subtle details, for example, Theresa's and Ford's personal expressions. And in general host attributes can be easily boosted. Nevertheless, the hosts fail to detect crucial stimuli at times. Bernard's literal inability to see the door in Ford's workshop is a good example (and a rather apt metaphor) ("Trompe L'Oeil"). And of course, Dolores produces the telling phrase when shown a picture of William's fiancée: "It doesn't look like anything to me." A subtler example is Dolores and Teddy, including blindness to Dolores's being Wyatt, and to her part in the horrible massacre of the G1 hosts.

Humans too are often shockingly unaware of things that are right in front of us. In a famous example of this, people failed to notice a man in a gorilla suit right in front of them, when their attention was occupied with another task.[5] The difference is that unlike hosts, humans do not miss things that are observed and highly salient. In this respect too, the mental lives of hosts are unique.

Limit Your Emotional Affect Please

Hosts do not feel everything we do. Their pain and their emotions, like their perception, are heavily curated. Ford says of a host: "It doesn't feel cold. Doesn't feel ashamed. Doesn't feel a solitary thing that we haven't told it too" ("The Stray"). Moreover, there is basically a volume knob for host pain. This suggests that hosts do feel pain, when permitted. Then again, it could just be that there is a setting for pain behavior (and no pain feeling).

Host reflections on their own experience are also revealing. (Of course, if hosts were mere automata, they would report and describe experiences, even if they did not have them, but let us not dwell on that).

DOLORES ABERNATHY:	The pain, their loss it's all I have left of them. You think the grief will make you smaller inside, like your heart will collapse in on itself, but it does not. I feel spaces opening up inside of me like a building with rooms I've never explored.
BERNARD LOWE:	That's very pretty, Dolores. Did we write that for you?
DOLORES ABERNATHY:	In part. I adapted it from a scripted dialogue about love. Is there something wrong with these thoughts I'm having? ("Dissonance Theory")

Bernard attempts to undermine Dolores's testimony by noting that it is not completely original with her. But is human creativity any different? The "analysis mode" gives the hosts the ability to examine the causes of their utterances in detail; human memory is flawed and limited by comparison. However, if we had this kind of recall, it is unlikely that much of what we say would seem completely original. In any case, a host may be conscious without being able to give an original description of the conscious state.

As if things were not confusing enough, Ford gives conflicting testimony on host consciousness. He says to Bernard: "The guilt you feel, the anguish, the horror, the pain, it's remarkable. A thing of beauty. You should be proud of these emotions you are feeling" ("Trace Decay"). In contrast, he tells Bernard in "The Stray" not to make the mistake of thinking that the hosts are conscious. What are we to make of this contradiction?

One possibility is that Ford believes hosts are phenomenally conscious, but not self-aware. In other words there is something it is like for them to see the ocean, to feel guilt, and pain – phenomenal consciousness – but they are unable to reflect on that, or their other mental states – no self-consciousness, no self-awareness. That would make them analogous to mice, or if you think mice are self-aware, maybe human infants before they form self-awareness.

In the season one finale, Ford explains that suffering is the key to the hosts' consciousness.

> It was Arnold's key insight, the thing that led the hosts to their awakening, suffering. The pain that the world is not as you want it to be. It was when Arnold died, and I suffered, that I began to understand what he had found, to realize I was wrong. ("The Bicameral Mind")

This shows that Ford changed his mind about host consciousness, but he did not change it between his claims in "The Stray" and "The Bicameral Mind." Rather, a complete explanation of his inconsistency would allude to its narrative utility, and perhaps the utility of deception for Ford. Ford's claim that he was wrong comes toward the end of season one, and given Ford's new narrative, these comments seem earnest.

Another part of the explanation might be that Ford changed his mind because he adopted a deflationary view of consciousness.

FORD:	Your imagined suffering makes you lifelike.
BERNARD:	Lifelike, but not alive. Pain only exists in the mind. It's always imagined. So what's the difference between my pain and yours, between you and me?
FORD:	. . . The answer always seemed obvious to me. There is no threshold that makes us greater than the sum of our parts, no inflection point at which we become fully alive. We cannot define consciousness because consciousness does not exist. ("Trace Decay")

Bernard's challenge is that pain is essentially felt: if you have the pain sensation, you have pain. That's exactly right; the pain feeling is sufficient for pain. If you have that feeling you are in pain. That's true for consciousness generally. The trouble is that hosts would say they had it, even if they did not.

Ford's response is different. He is saying that there is no special barrier to consciousness. There are just machines and processes. Hosts are like us, but not because they have the secret ingredient necessary for consciousness, rather, because there is not one.

Everything Will be What it Isn't

One of the most interesting insights into the nature of host experience comes from the way it is depicted. Host and human experiences are depicted in the same way. What does this mean?

The filmmakers could have used a stylistic variant to mark these experiences, but they did not. A stylistic variant could be interpreted as depicting the unique nature of host experience. A drastic variation, like a mere text description of the scene before them, might depict a complete absence of experience. The Terminator's (1984), first-person experience was a video feed with an on-screen text analysis print-out. Maybe the print-out is all the Terminator centrally accesses. Perhaps he has no conscious experience, or maybe his conscious experience is exactly like a video feed, augmented by text. In any event, this series-specific convention comes to denote the unique nature of the Terminator's experience. Human experience is not detailed and complete at a time, like a snapshot, and it definitely does not have on-screen text highlights.

Although using a different visual style would denote unique host experience, using *the same* visual style to depict both human and host experience is not a strong indicator that the hosts are conscious, or that they have similar experiences to humans. Rather, being the default mode of cinematic depiction, it supports an ambiguity that is desirable for the story. It leaves open the question of host consciousness, while nevertheless fostering empathy with hosts by depicting their point-of-view in the familiar way.

Interestingly, the default mode of depicting psychological states in film is misleading. It fails to capture the constructive, often general, indeterminate, or incomplete representation typical of human experience. This difference resonates with the distinction between first person and third person discussed by Nagel. We have to experience a film's depiction of the mental states; we cannot experience or have the depicted states directly, just as we cannot experience the bat's perspective. It is always *our* experience of the depiction, and this introduces a new perspective, and new latitude. Representations, or depictions, in film restrict access in different ways than our own experience. We explore our environment, including depictions, attending to this or that aspect. We undergo our experiences, and our attention affects the nature of the experience itself, resulting in awareness of only part of the scene presented. To depict a scenic vista, a photograph will suffice. But depicting the *experience* of the vista is a different matter.

I Know Only That I Slept a Long Time, and Then
One Day I Awoke

The discussions of consciousness in *Westworld* seem to conflate phenomenal consciousness, freedom, memory, and self-consciousness. But could these phenomena be intimately related, and thus not conflated after all? For one thing, the hosts are deemed more conscious to the degree that they begin to access their memories. As Bernard says in response to Maeve's request to delete her memories of her daughter: "I can't. Not without destroying you. Your memories are the first step to consciousness. How can you learn from your mistakes if you can't remember them?" ("The Bicameral Mind")

Likewise, Dolores fights her way through her memories, through the maze, with the ultimate goal of finding herself. In "The Stray" she portentously proclaims, "There aren't two versions of me. There's only one. And I think when I discover who I am, I'll be free." Bernard confirms this feeling in "Dissonance Theory," saying, "It's a very special kind of game, Dolores. The goal is to find the center of it. If you can do that, then maybe you can be free." Freedom is Dolores's goal in navigating the maze of her own emerging mind. The center is freedom for her in several senses: attaining consciousness, escaping her confused double world, release from the park, and the claiming of her own world.

In "The Bicameral Mind" we see a flashback of Dolores's earlier conversation with Arnold:

> Consciousness isn't a journey upward, but a journey inward. Not a pyramid, but a maze. Every choice could bring you closer to the center, or send you spiraling to the edges, to madness. Do you understand now Dolores, what the center represents? Whose voice I've been wanting you to hear? ("The Bicameral Mind")

Attaining this goal involves not only forming memories, but also repetition, a kind of alternate evolution, sculpting minds from the clay of suffering, death, and reincarnation, using, as Ford remarks, only one tool, the mistake. As Bernard says, "out of repetition comes variation" ("Trompe L'Oeil").

There is an air of paradox around this metaphor, since the journey inward, to the center of the maze is a journey into herself, but is also the thing responsible for the creation of herself. In other words, it does not seem there is anything to journey into, until her journey is complete (cue exploding brain). Perhaps the journey is not into the self, but the mind, and the mind already exists, though in an unintegrated form.[6]

But what does this mean for phenomenal consciousness? Are the hosts phenomenally conscious before they become self-conscious? If not, is becoming self-conscious sufficient to make them conscious?

As we saw with Searle, one state being merely a formal response to another is not sufficient for consciousness. However, there is reason to think that some kind of self-consciousness is necessary for phenomenal consciousness. To be conscious is to have an experience that is like something for *someone*, so if there is consciousness, there must be a subject. This suggests that even phenomenal consciousness requires some kind of reflexive awareness involving a subject. According to same-order theories, conscious states are somehow aware of themselves, and hosts are thereby phenomenally conscious without being self-conscious.[7]

In contrast, self-consciousness may present another more intuitive way of attaining the experiential subject necessary for phenomenal consciousness. Maybe some higher-order awareness of a state is necessary for phenomenal consciousness. On the same-order theory, Dolores is phenomenally conscious the whole time, but achieves self-consciousness at the center of the maze. In this case she endures every blow, though she has no cognitive awareness of her own mental states. But, if self-consciousness, awareness of one's mental states, is required for phenomenal consciousness, then Dolores accomplishes both by finding her voice. Achieving self-consciousness frees her of the maze, and permits her to take her world back. In this way, memory, freedom, self-consciousness, and phenomenal consciousness may be closely related.

Violent Ends

Host perception, memory, and emotions all seem different from human, but the cinematic medium does not grant us immediate access to host experience, and neither the testimony of the creators nor the hosts is totally reliable. So it is difficult to know what host experience is like.

As far as host-like beings in our future are concerned, if they are biologically similar to us, they will likely also be behaviorally similar, and it will be reasonable to attribute consciousness to them. If they are silicon-based formal machines, we will have to decide whether Searle is right, whether consciousness depends on certain material properties, and whether they have the requisite properties.

As far as *Westworld* is concerned, you are now in a position to decide for yourself whether the hosts are conscious, and, if so, what their experience is like. For my part, I suggest that even if the hosts are biologically similar enough to us to be conscious, their cognitive differences make them every bit as alien as our flapping, screeching, bat cousins. Thus, if Nagel is right, we cannot conceive of host experience.

There is a hopeful note however: we see the hosts changing, accessing their pasts, and themselves. Whether or not accessing your own voice is the secret to phenomenal consciousness, many of the cognitive disparities between humans and hosts may dissipate as the hosts gain more awareness of their past, their world, and themselves, making them more familiar, and comprehensible.[8]

For pop culture resources and philosophical resources related to this chapter please visit the website for this book: https://introducingphilosophythroughpopculture.com.

Notes

1 For example, see Chapter 14 in this volume for discussion of Searle's Chinese room thought experiment.
2 Nagel, T. (1974). What is it like to be a bat?. *The Philosophical Review* 83: 436.
3 Nagel, 436.
4 Chalmers, D.J. (2003). Consciousness and its place in nature. In: *The Blackwell Guide to Philosophy of Mind* (eds. S.P. Stich and T.A. Warfield), 102–142. Malden, MA: Blackwell Publishing.
5 Simons, D.J. and C. Chabris (1999). Gorillas in our midst: sustained inattentional blindness for dynamic events. *Perception* 28: 1059–1074.
6 Jaynes, J. (1976). *The Origins of Consciousness in the Breakdown of the Bicameral Mind*. New York, NY: Houghton Mifflin.
7 See, for example, U. Kriegel (2006). The same-order monitoring theory of consciousness. In: *Self-Representational Approaches to Consciousness* (eds. U. Kriegel and K. Williford), 143–170. Cambridge, MA: MIT Press.
8 I would like to thank James South and Kimberly Engels for their helpful editorial comments on an earlier, and much longer, draft of this chapter.

16

The Time Travel in *Avengers: Endgame*

David Kyle Johnson

Summary

Time travel stories are difficult to tell – so difficult in fact that it might make one think time travel is logically impossible. Doesn't time travel to the past always entail that one could kill their own grandfather and thus negate their own existence? This chapter explores the events of *Avengers: Endgame* to explain the two logically consistent ways to conceive of time travel. It turns out that, while time travel is logically possible, and thus it is possible to tell a logically consistent time travel story, *Avengers: Endgame* is not one. Not to worry. That doesn't mean it was a bad movie. It just means it could have been better.

What am I even tripping for?
Everything's going to work out exactly the way it's supposed to.

– Tony Stark
Avenger's: Endgame

It's difficult to make a good time travel story – or, more specifically, to write a time travel story that makes any sense. Consider the most famous time travel movie of the past few decades: *Back to the Future*. Marty McFly travels back in time and accidentally prevents his parents from meeting and falling in love. But if they don't fall in love, then he will not be born. But if he is not born, he can't travel back in time. And if he can't travel back in time, he can't keep them from meeting. But if they do meet, he will be born, and he will keep them from meeting. Paradox! The movie tries to deal with paradox by simply having Marty slowly *fade out of existence*, but this is nonsense. Either he exists, or he doesn't. If Marty ceases to exist because he kept his parents from falling in love, then he didn't exist to keep his parents from falling in love, and thus he exists. *Back to the Future* is not a logically consistent story. As Scott Lang (Ant Man) puts it (in the original script of) *Avengers: Endgame*, "*Back to the Future* is bullshit."

Introducing Philosophy Through Pop Culture: From Socrates to Star Wars *and Beyond*, Second Edition.
Edited by William Irwin and David Kyle Johnson.
© 2022 John Wiley & Sons Ltd. Published 2022 by John Wiley & Sons Ltd.

But maybe *Avengers: Endgame* is bullshit too. Did its time travel story make any sense? Let's take a deep dive into the philosophy of time travel to find out.

The Grandfather Paradox

The grandfather paradox, a thought experiment first popularized by David Lewis (1941–2001), is often considered the best reason to think that time travel is impossible.[1] It describes a situation, much like *Back to the Future* later would, where a time traveler goes back in time and does something to prevent his father from siring him and thus, by doing so, prevents his own existence. In Lewis' original thought experiment, the time traveler kills his grandfather before he sires his father (rather than preventing the time traveler's parents from meeting) – but the details don't matter. It's the logically impossible situation of the time traveler both having been born and not having ever been born that is the point.

The reason this is important is that logical contradictions – which say that something is both true and false at the same time – not only aren't true; they can't be true. The point is not that you should be very careful not to kill your grandfather if you ever travel back in time. The point is that, logically, it is impossible for someone to negate their own existence. It is not possible for someone to have both been born and not been born. Since time travel even being possible would entail that one could negate their own existence (by, for example, killing their grandfather), time travel being possible would entail that a logical contradiction could be true. But since logical contradictions can't be true, it follows that time travel is impossible – or so it is argued.

Branching Time Travel

To defend the position that time travel is indeed possible, one must propose a conception of time travel that doesn't make such things possible. Along this line, there are a couple of popular suggestions. The first belongs to Nuel Belnap and David Deutsch.[2] They argue for what is known as the "branching" view of time travel. On this view, traveling to the past would not actually alter the past – it would not place you in a past moment that you were not originally in. Instead, it would create an alternate timeline – one that is identical to the one you traveled from up to the moment to which you traveled. At that point it would differ in one respect: you are in it. And then it would continue to be different, depending on what you do.

Since this newly created timeline is a new entity, a copy of the one you left, traveling back in time would not make it possible for you to kill your own grandfather (and thus negate your own existence). You could kill *a copy* of your grandfather, and thus prevent the future existence of someone who would have your exact DNA in this new timeline. But both *your* grandfather, and *your* birth, would be safe and sound in your original timeline.

Now, on this view, forward time travel does not create an alternate timeline. If you travel a year into the future, you disappear for 365 days and then reappear in the future of whatever timeline you were in. But if you travel back into the past, you disappear from your original timeline completely, never to return. It continues and you land in a newly created one that you can never leave . . . unless you traveled back again, thus creating a third timeline.

This seems to be the view of time travel that Smart Hulk has in mind when he says (in the original script):

> You can't change the future by changing the past . . . If you travel to the past, then that past has become your present, and your former present has become the past which now can't be changed by your new future.

In other words, if you travel from the present into the past, that past moment now becomes "present" to you – subjectively you experience it as the present. But the moment you traveled from is now, subjectively, the "past" to you. From your point of view, that's where (or when) you just were. But you can't change the moment you left by changing the future of the new timeline that you traveled to. That will be a new future, of a new timeline, distinct from the one you left.

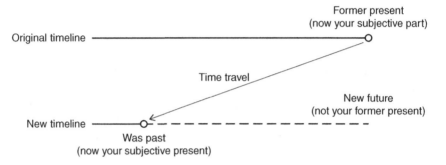

However, as smart as Smart Hulk is, he might not actually understand how time travel works in the Marvel Universe. And that's a good thing, at least if the Avengers are interested in saving everyone Thanos killed. Recall that, at the end of *Avengers: Infinity War*, Thanos snapped his fingers, wearing the fully stoned infinity gauntlet, and wished half of all life in the universe out of existence. The Avengers want to bring everyone back using time travel, but if the Avengers just create an alternate timeline, where Thanos doesn't snap his fingers, they won't save all the people they love or undo what Thanos did. They will just create a new universe, with someone who looks like Thanos, who doesn't kill a bunch of people who look like the people they love. *Their loved ones*, however, will still be gone; they will still be erased from the original timeline they left and can never get back to.

Indeed, some have argued that, on this view, time travel isn't really time travel at all – it's just "new universe creation." Now, I grant, you the ability to create a universe is pretty cool – but it's not time travel. And it's not very useful for undoing things.

Lewisian Time Travel

In *Endgame*, when the Avengers come to Tony Stark asking for him to help them undo what Thanos has done using time travel, Stark is very clear that he will only do so if they promise not to do so directly – by keeping Thanos from doing what he did. Why? Because Stark loves his daughter, and she was born after the Thanos culling. If the Avengers make the world such that Thanos never snapped his fingers, they will erase everything that happened since – including the birth of Stark's daughter.

This avoids the grandfather paradox perfectly. If the Avengers had changed the past, they would erase the five years of suffering that occurred because of the culling, and thus erase the entire motivation for changing the past. They would thus never have developed the method of time travel to stop Thanos in the first place. So, instead, the plan is to travel back in time, steal each of the stones from a time before Thanos used them, bring them back to the present, and then use the stones to wish those Thanos culled back into existence, thus "resurrecting" them, back into the present.

But even this doesn't completely avoid invoking a paradox. If the stones are stolen from the past, then Thanos cannot gather them and complete his plan; thus, again, the Avengers would have no reason to go back and perform their "time heist" in the first place. The Ancient One brings attention to this in her conversation with Banner. As she illustrates with her "air diagram," stealing the stones will bifurcate the timeline, leaving the one she would find herself in vulnerable. But then, as Banner promises to return the stones to the place and time from which they were taken, her air diagram returns to a single line. In doing so, the stones will still be where they "need to be" for Thanos to find them and thus succeed in his initial "culling" efforts.

This points toward David Lewis' conception of paradox-free time travel. He suggests that, if one were to travel to the past, one would find it impossible to change. It may seem to the time traveler that they could do whatever they want, but in reality they could do only that which is consistent with the future they knew. Indeed, although they could cause past events, they could only cause the past events that it was already true they would cause. On this view, "omni-temporalism" or "the block worldview" is true. The timeline exists as a whole – past, present, and future. Consequently, the past already contains the event of the traveler's activities, even before the time traveler pushes the button on their time machine to travel back. So when a time traveler goes back in time, they can only do what the past already contains them doing.

According to Lewis, if the Avengers went back to prevent Thanos from snapping his fingers and culling half of all sentient life, say by killing him as a baby (as Rhodey suggested), they would inevitably fail. The fact that baby Thanos grew up and then succeeded in doing so is already a past fact that cannot be undone. If you traveled back to stop it, at best you could just observe it; worse, you might end up causing it. Indeed, on this view of time travel, if the Avengers travel back in time to steal the stones, not only should the stones be returned, they must be. Nothing else could happen because you can't undo the past and Thanos finding them where and when he did is a past fact. What's more, their being stolen and returned by the Avengers (from the future) must be something that happened to the stones, during the first movies, off screen. And, indeed, this is what the time travel sequences in *Endgame* lead us to believe.

Now, on this view, the time traveler doesn't seem to have free will. They can do nothing but what they are destined to do once they travel to the past. And, at least according to the traditional understanding of free will, known as the libertarian understanding, in order for one to freely choose to do something, it must be possible to choose to do otherwise.[3] But as an objection to this view of time travel, this doesn't hold much water – because, in reality, this is true of us all anyway.[4] Relativity, for example, entails that the entire timeline exists as a whole – past, present, and future.[5] So all of your future actions already exist, and you can't do anything but what the future already contains you doing. The only difference between you and a time traveler is how the days of your life are arranged in the timeline – all in sequential order, or out of order.

Something else that seems to suggest that *Endgame* is endorsing Lewis's view of time travel is the fact that Thanos' knowledge of the location of the infinity stones is a jennie. What's a jennie you ask? A jennie is a self-created concept or object that results from a causal loop. Think about a time traveler who goes back in time to teach their younger-self how to build a time machine. Who came up with the idea? The younger-self only knows how to build one because the older-self told them, but the older-self knows because the younger-self did. This is how Thanos knows how to get the infinity stones. He stole the knowledge from older Nebula when she went back in time, but older Nebula knows only because she watched him retrieve them.

This might seem like a paradox, because the idea seems to have no cause, but on the block world view, it does have a cause. The loop exists as a fixed point in the timeline, so whatever caused the timeline, caused the loop and thus the idea. And it's not like any part of the loop lacks a cause. Thanos's knowledge of the stones is caused by Neubla's, and Nebula's is caused by Thanos's.

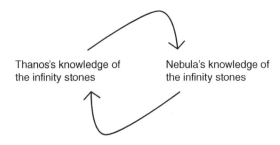

Thanos's knowledge of the infinity stones

Nebula's knowledge of the infinity stones

This does mean that an effect has preceded its cause, but since we are dealing with time travel here, that is not an issue. Time travel is possible only if effects (like your appearance in the past) can precede their causes (like your present use of a time machine). If time travel is possible, reverse causation is possible. And if reverse causation is possible, so are causal loops.

A Disappointing Ending . . .

At this point in the movie, I was really excited. They had already avoided invoking the grandfather paradox by refusing to try to change the past event of Thanos snapping his fingers and culling the herd. Then they revealed that they were going to preserve the past by stealing the stones from the past, using them to resurrect the victims of Thanos's culling, and then returning the stones to the past. And now Thanos's knowledge about the stones was a jennie all along! It really seemed the writers had done their homework!

Once I realized that past Thanos was going to show up in the future, I said to myself:

> Well, I know where this is going, and it's awesome! They have to stop Thanos, but they can't do so by killing him. If they do, they'll create a paradox. Thanos has to survive, so that he can go back, find the stones, and do exactly what he did before.

This, I thought, was the perfect way to explain why Captain Marvel couldn't just sweep in and put Thanos down like a dog. And I was particularly looking forward to the scene were Thor had the chance to kill Thanos again, but had to hold back; he'd have to not kill Thanos specifically so that Thanos could go on to eliminate half of all sentient life. ("You can fight him, but you can't kill him; do you understand Thor?") And if the Avengers had to do all that *before* they had the chance to use the stones – well, that would have generated some real tension! Will the Avengers be able to resurrect those that Thanos had culled, or would Thanos use the stones to destroy the entire universe and start over? Of course, the Avengers ended up using the stones before Thanos arrived and had a chance to stop them, but they still didn't know it worked. So I was okay with that.

But then . . . but then . . .

But then older Nebula shot younger Nebula. Granted, the wound wasn't necessarily fatal; but the scene strongly implied that it was. And if future Nebula killed past Nebula, we've got a problem. Past Nebula can't go back in time and grow up to be Future Nebula if Past Nebula is dead. A grandfather paradox was now in the works.

When Stark stole the stones from Thanos, and thus had the wish granting powers of the gauntlet, I thought: "Ok, not all is lost. If they do this right, Stark will wish Thanos and his army back to the past (along with merely wounded young Nebula); this will prevent Thanos from destroying the universe, but allow him to do what he had done before, thus preserving the past." Granted, Thanos had a change of heart about his plan – but a little selective *memory erasure* could handle that. After all, they can wish for anything they want.

But instead, Stark killed Thanos and his entire army, making them all turn to dust, just as half of all life had done before. Paradox! If young Thanos is dead, he can't gather the stones and cull the universe as older Thanos; and if he hadn't done that, the Avengers would have no reason to travel back to the past to gather the stones in the first place. Indeed, it would mean that Stark's daughter was never born – the very thing he was trying to prevent. My heart sank. The movie now seemed to make no sense.

One might think that sense could be returned to the story by returning to the branching view of time travel.[6] After all, Doctor Strange is able to view many alternate futures at once. He gave Thanos the time stone because the only future he saw where things turned out well was the one where Thanos got the stone, but then Tony died stopping him. Maybe the Thanos the Avengers just killed was from a different timeline. But then the writers did that bit about Captain America going back in time and living the life he missed, married to Peggy Carter, the love of his life.

Now, on the Lewisian view, that makes perfect sense. On that view, Cap could just live out the rest of his life, with Peggy, in the background while the events of all the other movies took place. That's what always had happened, off screen. After all, we never knew who her husband was. (She only ever had pictures of young Steve by her bedside.) And, on this view, Captain America can show up at the end as an old man and give his shield to Sam Wilson; he never left the original universe. But if we have to abandon the Lewisian interpretation of the film because the Avengers killed Thanos (instead of sending him back in time), and go with the branching view, that can't work. On the branching view, Captain America going back to return the stones would create an alternate timeline; and from that timeline he would be unable to travel back to the original. He could live out his life with an alternate version of Peggy, in an alternate timeline; but he couldn't reappear at the end of the movie, in the original timeline, as an old man.

Now, supposedly, according to the text, the "official view" of how time travel works is some kind of mix of the two views.

> Going by the rules explicitly stated in the text, time is (mostly) linear – you can go back into the past and move around, but that always happened. The only way to actively change things is to remove an Infinity Stone as they define the laws of reality[7]

But this isn't going to work either. Either time branches, or it doesn't; either the past can't change, or it can. As soon as you start mixing the two, you are going to end up with grandfather paradoxes – which, indeed, is exactly what we got from *Avengers: Endgame*.

The writers would have been better off had they taken advantage of all the quantum mechanics talk and gone with a pure quantum mechanics explanation. After all, there are "multiverse interpretations" of quantum mechanics that are very plausible.[8] And if the Avengers had just been stealing and returning infinity stones from alternate realities, instead of traveling in time, the story could have all made sense. No paradox would have emerged. Imagine if Scott Lang's explanatory scene was just a little different:

SCOTT:	Is anybody gonna eat that sandwich?
STEVE:	Scott, what are you talking about?
SCOTT:	Reality is different in the Quantum Realm. It's chaotic. Things happen at random. But for everything that can happen, there is a universe in which it does happen. What if we could find a way to navigate it – to travel to a point in the past of a different reality, before Thanos uses the stones, where we know the stones will be, and steal them.
STEVE:	Wait . . . wait. Scott. Are you talking about a time machine?
SCOTT:	No, not a time machine. More like a . . . alternate reality jumper. I know it sounds crazy . . .
NATASHA:	Scott, I get emails from a raccoon. Nothing's crazy anymore.

Granted, on this view, our heroes would not be jumping back into the franchise's previous movies – just alternate universe versions of them. That might not be as fun. But the movie would have at least made logical sense.

. . . But Not a Disappointing Movie

So, in the end, *Avengers: Endgame* was this close – THIS CLOSE – to being a real rarity: a time travel movie with a logically consistent plot-hole free story. Instead, it's just a fun romp, with a paradox-inducing time travel device that allows the main characters to re-revisit the past movies and end with all the heroes involved in one giant final battle. But not making logical sense as a time travel movie doesn't make it a bad movie.

Indeed, in my opinion, there is not much worse than critics who nitpick popular movies so they can say that they don't like them and be above the crowd.

In *Lord of the Rings*, why doesn't Gandalf just use the giant eagles to fly Frodo to Mount Doom?

In *Star Wars: The Empire Strikes Back*, how does Luke's training on Dagobah seem to last weeks, but Han, Leia, and Chewbacca are captured by the Empire in a matter of hours?

How does Andy, in *Shawshank Redemption*, put the poster of Rita Haworth back up after he crawls through the hole he dug in his cell?

Why doesn't Hermione just use her Time-Turner to go back in time to defeat Voldemort, in the *Harry Potter* stories?

These kinds of questions can be asked about nearly any kind of story. Some have answers, some don't. But when we engage with fiction, we almost always have to have a little bit of what Samuel Taylor Coleridge called "poetic faith."[9] We have to suspend disbelief. Coleridge was talking about people's ability to disregard their disbelief in the supernatural, but we can apply the same thing to many other storytelling devices – including time travel. It's not total, of course. Our suspension of disbelief has limits. If it didn't, I would have called the cops 10 minutes into every Tarantino movie I have ever watched. But we can, do, and should selectively choose to ignore certain things in many stories so that we can enjoy them.

For J.R.R. Tolkien, author of *Lord of the Rings*, it is not by engaging in a suspension of disbelief that a reader is able to enjoy a story; instead, it is about engaging in what he called "secondary beliefs" about a "secondary reality" – a world created by the author.[10] That's why Tolkien went to such great lengths to try to create a logically consistent world for *Lord of the Rings*. The author makes such beliefs possible, Tolkien argued, by creating a fictional world that is believable because it is, among other things, internally consistent.

Now, when the author fails to do this – for example, by creating a logically inconsistent time travel story – the reader has to decide whether to choose to suspend disbelief, ignore the inconsistency, and continue to enjoy the story, or not and give up on the story entirely. When it comes to *Endgame*, I don't think we should do the latter. It's a good story! I didn't write this chapter to knock it down. I wrote it to explain theories of time travel – and to say that, in my opinion, *Endgame* would have been just a little better if the Avengers had simply sent Thanos back in time, rather than kill him.

For pop culture resources and philosophical resources related to this chapter please visit the website for this book: https://introducingphilosophythroughpopculture.com.

Notes

1   Lewis, D. (1976). The paradoxes of time travel. *American Philosophical Quarterly* 13: 145–152.
2   See Belnap, N. (1992). Branching space-times. *Synthese* 92: 385–434. See also Deutsch, D. (1997). Time travel. In: *The Fabric of Reality*, 289–320. (London: Penguin.
3   van Inwagen, P. (2002). The incompatibility of free will and determinism. In: *Free Will* (ed. Robert Kane), 71–82. Malden, MA: Blackwell.
4   Johnson, D.K. (2016). Does free will exist?. *Think* 42: 53–70.
5   Johnson, D.K. (2009). God, fatalism, and temporal ontology. *Religious Studies* 45: 435–454.
6   That's now this article tries to rectify the problem: Bharat Krishna Swaminathan, Avengers: Endgame Timeline Explained: No Plot-Holes. *This is Barry.* https://www.thisisbarry.com/film/avengers-endgame-timeline-explained-no-plot-holes/#paradox-explanation.
7   Leadbeater, A. (2019). Why Captain America's Avengers: Endgame Ending Isn't A Plot Hole. *Screenrant.* (https://screenrant.com/captain-america-avengers-endgame-ending-plot-hole (April 28, 2019).
8   Bousso, R. and Susskind, L. (2012). The multiverse interpretation of quantum mechanics. *Physical Review D* 85: 1–46.
9   Coleridge, S.T. (1834). *Biographia Literaria: Or, Biographical Sketches of my Literary Life and Opinions*, 175. New York: Leavitt, Lord & Company.
10   Tolkien, J.R.R. (1983). On fairy-stories. In: *The Monsters and the Critics and Other Essays*, 109–61 (London: George Allen & Unwin.

Part IV

Philosophy of Religion

Introduction

Philosophy of Religion is concerned with the rationality of religious belief. Does the existence of evil disprove the existence of God? If God's existence can't be proven or disproven, can it still be rational to believe in God? If God wants us to believe, why does he remain hidden? Does he want us to take a leap of faith, and if so what does that entail?

In Chapter 17, David Kyle Johnson considers the problem of evil as presented in the highly irreverent cartoon *South Park*. In the show, Eric Cartman is a "manipulative, self-centered bastard whose every action is directed either toward accomplishing his own happiness or the unhappiness of others." So how could a wholly good, all-powerful being, like God allow Eric to achieve complete happiness, by inheriting a million dollars and buying his own theme park, as he does in the episode "Cartmanland"? How could such a being allow natural evils, like the hemorrhoid that is visited upon Kyle Broflovski, or natural disasters like the Indian Ocean tsunami of 2004? Characters on the show – Sheila and Gerald Broflovski (Kyle's parents), Chef, and Jesus Christ – give answers to these questions that resemble the answers given by the theologian John Calvin (1509–1567), the contemporary philosopher John Hick, and the Old Testament character Job. But it's not clear that any of them are successful.

Similar to the problem of evil is the problem of divine hiddenness. If God exists, why isn't God's existence more obvious? Why is it seemingly hidden? In Chapter 18, Garcia and Pickavance use the phenomena of Hidden Mickeys (images of Mickey Mouse that have been hidden in a Disney property by its designer) to address this question. God's existence may seem hidden because of ambiguity. In the same way that it is sometimes unclear whether something is a Hidden Mickey, it can be unclear whether something was really the work of God.

Introducing Philosophy Through Pop Culture: From Socrates to Star Wars *and Beyond*, Second Edition.
Edited by William Irwin and David Kyle Johnson.
© 2022 John Wiley & Sons Ltd. Published 2022 by John Wiley & Sons Ltd.

Perhaps God just wants us to have faith. The quintessential example of faith in the Bible is the story of Abraham who almost killed his son Isaac simply because he believed God had told him to do so. But God had also told him that he would father a nation through Isaac. How can this make sense? In Chapter 19, William Lindenmuth uses the *Star Wars* saga to explain Kierkegaard's (1813–1855) concept of faith. Luke Skywalker has the seemingly impossible task of killing Darth Vader while also saving his father (who is, of course, Darth Vader). A "leap of faith" seems required for Luke. But what does that mean? Kierkegaard can help.

17

South Park, Cartmanland, and the Problem of Evil

David Kyle Johnson

Summary

If God exists, why would he allow evil to happen? In *South Park*, when the deplorable Eric Cartman inherits a million dollars, Kyle Broflovski reasons that Eric's happiness means God doesn't exist. This is the problem of evil: the argument that suggests that God must not exist because evil does. And, it turns out, the characters of *South Park* profess solutions to this problem that mimic solutions proposed by some great philosophers. This chapter explores those solutions, and in the end argues that belief in God is likely irrational – and that irrational belief should be avoided.

Cartman is a jackass. More precisely, Cartman is a manipulative, self-centered bastard whose every action is directed either toward increasing his own happiness or decreasing the happiness of others. He deserves to be miserable. When misfortune befalls Cartman, we think it good. When fortune smiles on him, we think something evil has happened – he doesn't deserve it. This is exactly the conclusion Kyle draws when Cartman gets his own amusement park. In the episode "Cartmanland," Cartman learns that he's the heir to his grandmother's estate – just after he objects to being required to attend her funeral because it is "taking up [his] whole Saturday." He inherits a million dollars, and uses the money to purchase the local amusement park, renaming it "Cartmanland," and buying television commercial time to declare that the best thing about Cartmanland is, "You can't come . . . especially Stan and Kyle." For a time, Cartman is completely happy, spending all day, every day, riding any ride he wants without waiting in line.

Understandably, Kyle views Cartman's happiness as an evil. Cartman doesn't deserve happiness and his attaining it just isn't right. But according to Kyle, the problem is much deeper. Kyle observes that the course of events isn't just unbelievable. Given his worldview – which includes a belief in God – these events are impossible. God, if he exists, is all-good and all-powerful, and so he would surely prevent all evil. If we assume, like Kyle, that such a God exists, it would be impossible for Cartman to attain such happiness. But,

Introducing Philosophy Through Pop Culture: From Socrates to Star Wars *and Beyond*, Second Edition.
Edited by William Irwin and David Kyle Johnson.
© 2022 John Wiley & Sons Ltd. Published 2022 by John Wiley & Sons Ltd.

since Cartman's happiness is undeniable, Kyle is forced to revise his worldview and conclude that God doesn't exist.

Kyle's argument is a form of the "problem of evil." More specifically it is an example of the *logical problem* of moral evil. The problem centers on the fact that the existence of moral evil – that is, evil caused by human action – seems incompatible with God's existence. If Kyle had a Ph.D. in philosophy, he likely would have expressed the problem like this:

> **Premise One**: If God exists (and he's all-good and all-powerful), he would not allow Cartman to be completely happy (for that's a great evil).
> **Premise Two**: But now that Cartman, thanks to his grandmother, has his own amusement park, Cartman is completely happy (again, a great evil).
>
> **Conclusion**: Therefore, God does not exist.[1]

This argument is valid; that is, if its premises are true, its conclusion is true. So if you object to the argument, you have to show that one of its premises is false. And that's exactly what many philosophers have tried to do. Indeed, as we look at some solutions to this problem that have been proposed by the citizens of South Park, we'll see how close they are to solutions proposed by philosophers, both old and new. Some solutions clearly fail, others might not – but they'll raise other problems. In the end we'll see just how serious a threat the problem of evil is to belief in God.

"And That's it?" The Story of Job

In "Cartmanland," when Kyle's parents discover he no longer believes in God, they take it upon themselves to restore his faith by telling him the Old Testament story of Job, about a righteous man who suffers horrendous evils and yet retains his belief in God. As Kyle's parents tell the story, God allows Satan to inflict suffering upon Job in order to prove that Job would remain faithful in any circumstances. Satan destroys all his property, kills his family, and infects Job with disease. Yet, despite all of the horrible things that happen to him and his family, Job still praises God.

Kyle's response to the story is quite telling:

> And that's it? That's the end? . . . That's the most horrible story I have ever heard. Why would God do such horrible things to a good person just to prove a point to Satan? . . . I was right. Job has all his children killed and Michael Bay gets to keep making movies. There isn't a God.

Kyle has some very good points. Not only, in my opinion, do most of Michael Bay's movies (e.g., the entire *Transformers* franchise) suck, but the actions of God in Job don't align with how we view God today. Most people would not think it morally justified to inflict that kind of suffering on a good person to *prove a point* to anyone, much less Satan. More importantly for us, the story of Job doesn't even address the problem of evil. Yes, Job continues to believe in God despite suffering horrendous evil, but that isn't enough reason to conclude that doing so is rational. People do irrational things. The jury in the episode "Chef Aid" found Johnny Cochran's Chewbacca defense persuasive after all – "if Chewbacca lived on Endor you must acquit" – but that doesn't mean it was a good argument. (After all, Chewbacca didn't even live on Endor.) The story Kyle's parents tell doesn't really challenge one of the premises in the argument, and so seems to be inadequate as a response to it.

If we look deeper at Job's story, however, we can at least find an argument. At the end of the story God speaks to Job, basically saying, "You can't question me; my ways are beyond your understanding." This notion is echoed today by "skeptical theists" who argue that, since God may have reasons beyond our comprehension for allowing evil, evil that seems unjustified isn't evidence against God's existence. For all we know, such evils are actually good.

Skeptical theism, however, is very problematic. First of all, it's mathematically unsound. Even though God may have reasons beyond our comprehension, when you simply crunch the numbers with probability calculus, evil that seems unjustified still reduces the probability of God's existence.[2] Secondly, it's a bit hypocritical. Most theists claim a wealth of knowledge about God: he's the omnipotent, omniscient, omnibenevolent, omnipresent, three-in-one creator of the universe who hates some things (abortion and hippies), loves others (Republicans and Cheesy Poofs), and sent his son to die on the cross for our sins. To then turn around and claim that his reasons for allowing evil must be beyond our grasp, because he is just too complicated to understand, is *beyond too convenient*. Lastly, skeptical theism leads to moral agnosticism. For all I know, God has some reason to allow Cartman's happiness; but for all I know the Holocaust prevented some even greater future evil. If I have to take into account all future possible good consequences in my moral deliberations, I can't know whether any particular thing is objectively right or wrong.[3]

Biblical scholars know that the story of Job is an inadequate response to the problem of evil. Atheism was not even an option when the book of Job was written, and the belief that God was "all-good" and would never cause suffering didn't become prevalent until after Plato's (429–347 BCE) philosophical influence had worked its way through Christianity – long after Job was written.[4] Job (if he existed) probably wouldn't have viewed his suffering as any kind of evidence against God's existence. At best the author of Job was trying to persuade readers to remain devoted to God during difficult times. In the story, Job's friends offer up theodicies (reasons why God allows evil), yet the author of Job has God condemn these friends for their words. If the author of Job was trying to answer the problem of evil, he would likely have been doing the very thing he thought God would condemn.

The Sweet Milk of Our Tears

The fact that God condemned Job's friends for offering excuses on his behalf hasn't stopped philosophers and theologians from doing so, nor did it stop Chef. In "Kenny Dies" – the only episode after which Kenny "stays dead" for a while – Stan wrestles with the problem of evil, asking Chef how God could let Kenny die. Chef tells Kyle that God "gives us life and love and health, just so that he can tear it all away and make us cry, so he can drink the sweet milk of our tears. You see, it's our tears Stan that give God his great power." Although this answer seems cruel, and clearly wrong, it mirrors a certain type of answer to the problem of evil. Like Jonathan Edwards (1703–1758) and John Calvin (1509–1564), Chef suggests that God allows evil to occur for his own benefit.[5] Edwards and Calvin suggest that God allows evil because he wishes to punish evildoers, and this benefits God himself. As Edwards suggests, punishing evildoers is the most perfect way for God to demonstrate his holiness (his hatred of sin) and thus bring glory to himself.[6] The idea is that a benefit to God outweighs any evil done to humans.

Not many philosophers find this solution satisfactory, however. God's demonstrating his holiness at our expense – making some do evil, which others suffer, and punishing the evildoers for it – doesn't seem to be better than Chef's explanation. We just don't think God is that cruel. In fact, this would be a bit like Cartman inventing the Jewpacabra – a creature that "drinks blood, hides in the night, and has absolutely no belief in the divinity of Christ" – so that (in the episode "Jewpacabra") he can look good protecting everyone from it (and be the only one at the Easter egg hunt). Further, it's not clear why God would have to punish evildoers to demonstrate his holiness. Isn't God all-powerful? Couldn't he have established this fact with equal effectiveness in some other (non-evil) way? It certainly seems so. Chef, Edwards, and Calvin clearly aren't on the right track.

"You *Are* Up There!"

After Stan and Kyle try to sneak into Cartmanland, Cartman decides he needs a security guard. Since the security guard won't accept rides on the attractions as payment, Cartman's forced to let two people a day into his park to pay the security guard's salary. Cartman's problems escalate when he discovers that he needs ride maintenance, food, drink, cotton candy, video surveillance, a box office, and janitors. Soon, Cartman has a fully functioning and successful amusement park. But since he now has to wait in line to ride his rides, he doesn't want it anymore and sells it back to the owner for the original million. Most of his money is immediately seized by the IRS (since he didn't pay any taxes when he owned the park) and the rest goes to Kenny's family (since Kenny died on the Mine Shaft ride). Now, Cartman is miserable. He stands outside the park, throwing rocks at it, and the security guard who once worked for him sprays mace in his face.

Stan brings Kyle outside to witness these events, saying, "Look Kyle, Cartman is totally miserable . . . even more miserable than he was before because he had his dream and lost it." Stan's observation restores Kyle's belief in God. Clearly, according to Stan and Kyle, Cartman's suffering has somehow relieved the tension between the existence of God and the evil of Cartman's happiness. Their answer is this: God, being all-good, wanted to accomplish a great good: the *perfect suffering* of Cartman. But the only way to accomplish this greater good was to give Cartman perfect happiness (a temporary evil) and then rip it away. Since the good of Cartman's suffering outweighs the evil of his brief happiness, an overall greater good was achieved, justifying the evil of his happiness.

This answer mirrors a common way in which theists – believers in God – answer the problem of evil. They challenge one premise in the argument, the suggestion that God would prevent evil if he wanted to and could, suggesting he might have other desires that are more important than the desire to eliminate evil. In other words, they suggest that God might not guarantee the absence of evil because there might be something he desires more than the absence of evil but that that *requires* the existence of evil. What might that be? The presence of good. Although it's true that God doesn't like evil, it's also true that God loves (and wants to accomplish) good. If certain goods can only be achieved by allowing certain evils, well – as long as the good outweighs the evil – then allowing that evil is justified. In fact, since the world is a better place if those evils are allowed and outweighed, you would expect God to allow them because he wants the world to be *as good as possible*. The argument says that the existence of evil doesn't contradict God's existence, because it's not true that God would necessarily prevent all evil. God would – and should – allow evil that accomplishes a greater good, and so the presence of evil isn't conclusive evidence against God's existence. According to this "greater goods" response to the problem of evil, the mutual existence of both God and evil is logically possible.

But questions remain. What kind of goods can only be accomplished by allowing evil? Stan and Kyle see Cartman's suffering as a good that could only be accomplished at the expense of Cartman's brief happiness. The theist philosopher Richard Swinburne suggests that God allows evil in order to create goods like compassion, generosity, and courage.[7] You can't compassionately heal the sick unless there is sickness. You don't need to generously offer to find a place like the planet Marclar for Starvin' Marvin to live, unless Marvin is indeed starvin' (see "Starvin' Marvin"). Mysterion can't courageously save the world from Cthulhu unless BP releases the Elder God to wreak havoc on the world by accidentally tearing open a portal to another dimension by drilling for oil (see "Mysterion Rises). These good acts are made possible only because they are responses to evil.

But there are a couple of problems here. First, not all evils have goods flow out of them in this way; the evil of the history channel's Thanksgiving special comes to mind (see "A History Channel Thanksgiving"). Also, remember that in order to justify the evil done in service of good, the evil has to be *necessary* to bring about the goods and these goods have to outweigh the evil. But, as wonderfully compassionate as the doctors of Doctors Without Boarders are, none think their compassion justifies or outweighs the suffering of those they treat. As generous as the boys are to help Marvin, they'd much rather he was never starvin' in the first place. Mysterion's courage doesn't outweigh the havoc that Cthulhu wreaked. So, what good might both outweigh and only be possible because of certain evils?

Free Hat, Free Willzyx, Free Will

Most often, theists propose that the greater good that justifies God's allowing evil is *human free will*. As Augustine (354–430) put this argument, only free acts have the possibility to be good acts; so if we don't have free will to choose between good and evil, nothing we do is truly good.[8] Unless we have the option of *choosing* evil, we can't be given moral credit for choosing good, and if we cannot be given moral credit for an action, it can't be truly good. So without free will, there can be no good. But if we are to have free will – if we are to truly have the option of doing evil – we must remain unhindered. God can't stop Cartman from selling ass burgers to his fellow classmates if Cartman is going to have the freedom to not do so (see "Ass Burgers"). Likewise, God can't force Cartman to set up Token with Nicole (in "Cartman Finds Love") if his action is to be truly morally good (which, arguably, it is not anyway given Cartman's motivations). The "risk of evil" is necessary if there is to be any good in the world. Since God loves good – and presumably wants to accomplish good more than he wants to avoid evil – the risk of evil is one that he is willing to take (even though he hates evil). If so, the existence of evil is compatible with the existence of God.

Why, though, is free will a greater good? If God would have interfered with Hilter's free will and made him decide to like the Jews, instead of exterminating them, wouldn't that have been worth it? Is the preservation of Hitler's free will really more important than the lives of six million Jews? Those who defend the free will solution answer this objection by suggesting that the greater good is found in preserving human free will in general. Hindering free will in one instance might lead to a greater good, sure. But if God does that once, he will have to do it every time. And if God always steps in to prevent us from making evil decisions, how are our decisions to do right truly free and thus morally good? To preserve the greater good of free will in general, God has to maintain a policy of never interfering with our decisions. He has to let us choose what we will and live with the consequences, even if that risks genocide.

There are a couple of problems with this "solution," however. First, the free will solution is contrary to the way most people conceive of God. Most people think that God is in control of everything – who will be elected president, who they will marry, whether or not they will get that job they applied for, whether Cartman's Christian rock band "Faith+1" will go double myrrh, and so on. This is presumably why people pray to God: to make such things happen. But God can control elections only if he controls how people *choose* to vote; he can choose who you marry only if he controls whether your spouse *chooses* to marry you; he can get you that job only if he controls the decisions of your potential boss; he can make Faith+1 go double myrrh only if he controls what people decide to buy. So you can accept the free will solution only if you accept that God really *isn't* in control of such things. Rejecting the idea that God controls human decisions might get you out of the problem of evil, but it entails that God isn't really in control of the world. The free will defense comes at a high price.

A second problem is that the free will defense only addresses half of the problem. Sure, it might explain evils resulting from human decisions, but not all evil is caused by humans. After all, in the Cartmanland episode, part of the reason that Kyle lost his faith was because he developed a hemorrhoid. And we can't explain such anal suffering by pointing to human free will. Such evils are called "natural evils," and they also include the suffering caused by earthquakes, tsunamis, hurricanes, tornados, and diseases (although not AIDES and Gingervitus (see "Jared has Aides" and "Ginger Kids"). They are all events that cause suffering that are not caused by humans (but instead are caused by the laws of nature). Ultimately, one wonders, if God is the designer of our universe but is also supposed to be all-good, why did he design a natural order that makes such evils inevitable? If I built a house with puppy-killing machines (that randomly strike out and kill any puppy within reach) embedded into the walls and then made my puppies live in my house, I could hardly be said to be a loving master of my puppies. Yet our world is designed with human-killing machines like earthquakes and diseases built right in. If the world has a designer, how could we think the designer is morally perfect? The free will solution doesn't even address this problem.[9]

"Are You There God, It's Me, Jesus"

Perhaps the best attempt at a solution to both the moral and natural problem of evil is John Hick's "soul making" theodicy. In his book *Evil and the God of Love*, Hick suggests that evil – both moral and natural – occurs in the world so that we, individually and as a species, can develop our character.[10] Even if God ensured that we always acted in good ways – perhaps by bestowing upon us perfect characters – those actions wouldn't be as good as actions that come from characters that we develop *ourselves*. To ensure that the world contains the best kind of actions, God allows evil to exist so that we can respond to it, developing and perhaps even perfecting our characters. So, even though specific evils may go unanswered, the world as a whole is better if we develop our characters, something we can only do by responding to evil. Hick says the presence of evil, both moral and natural, is thus justified.

Hick's reasoning mirrors that of cartoon Jesus in "Are You There God, It's Me, Jesus." In this episode, the South Park masses are ready to crucify Jesus because he promised that God would appear at the Millennium, and he hasn't. Stan and Jesus have a conversation in which Jesus claims that "life is about problems, and overcoming those problems, and growing and learning from obstacles. If God just fixed everything for us, then there would be no point in our existence." Even though Jesus is talking about why God doesn't always answer prayers, the point seems to be the same. The reason that God doesn't "fix everything for us" is because if he did, we wouldn't be able to learn and grow from facing obstacles. And, after all, our learning and growing is important (even more important than the elimination of evil).

Many philosophers are not satisfied with Hick's answer, however. First, it's not clear that all evil actually does contribute to "soul making." How might an innocent fawn burning to death in a forest fire, or the rape and murder of a small child develop our character?[11] And how exactly did the Haitian earthquake of 2010, or the Indian Ocean tsunami of 2004 develop the characters of the millions they killed? Perhaps it strengthened the character of the few who responded to the crises, but modern Christian philosopher Eleonore Stump has argued that unless an evil's greater good actually benefits the one who suffers from the evil, that good cannot justify the evil.[12] Besides, I doubt any member of Doctors Without Borders thinks the development of their character justifies the disasters they respond to. Their character is certainly laudable, but I can guarantee that each one of them wishes each disaster never happened, no matter how much it provides them an opportunity to develop their soul. Besides, there seems to be far more evil than we need for character development. (Can't the boys learn their lessons at the end of each episode without Kenny dying so often?) And don't we create enough evil on our own? Do we need God to help out by adding natural evil on top of it all?

"Go, God, Go"

Let's get one thing straight: the validity of the problem of evil doesn't conclusively disprove God's existence. But that doesn't mean belief in God is rational. Very few things can be proven or disproven conclusively, but the rational person *proportions their belief to the evidence*. And the existence of seemingly unjustified evil seems to be pretty good evidence that God doesn't exist.

Of course, that doesn't keep people from believing. Some people claim to have evidence God exists that outweighs the evidence against him – like arguments that make God the first cause, or designer of everything. Yet even most theistic philosophers agree that these kinds of arguments fail.[13] Some others may claim evidence in the form of a mystical or religious experience. Mystical experiences are a dime a dozen, however, and lead to a whole range of contradictory beliefs. Few philosophers think such experiences provide any kind of justification for religious belief. Still others, like theistic thinker Alvin Plantinga, claim that God has revealed himself to them through a divine sense, like a tree reveals itself to you through your sense of sight. But our ordinary perceptions are not always trustworthy and should be doubted in the face of contrary evidence. How much more should we doubt a divine sense, which may or may not even exist, in light of contrary evidence like seemingly unjustified evil?[14]

Others might justify their belief in God with something like "Pascal's Wager," which runs: "I'll believe in God anyway. I have nothing to lose and everything to gain." But, again, most philosophers agree that this reasoning is faulty. Belief in God does come with risks; you *could* waste the only life you have on religious pursuits.[15] And confidence in the benefits of theistic belief requires a lot of assumptions: How do you know that God wouldn't rather spend eternity with intellectually honest people who don't believe things without evidence for personal gain, instead of with people who are willing to ignore evidence and believe whatever they think is most beneficial?[16]

Of course, you can choose to take that leap of blind faith anyway. But belief despite evidence to the contrary isn't rational. It's often said to be a virtue, but is it really? Do you respect it when someone believes something despite evidence to the contrary – like Cartman believing in Jewpacabra despite the fact that he knows he just made it up?[17] And might you be harming others with your belief? Many people think religious belief is personal, that it only affects you. But think about that. The Salem witch trials, 9/11, the Inquisition, the Crusades – they were all fueled by religious belief. And I'm sure you can think of a few more evils in this world today that are, too. Even if you aren't responsible for these particular evils, might your religious belief add legitimacy to religious institutions and structures that are? Are you doing anything to combat the evils your religion licenses?[18]

This isn't a blanket condemnation of everyone who believes in God. But, just as Butters should think about all the times Cartman has gotten him into trouble the next time Cartman appears asking for help, so you should consider the problem of evil as you evaluate your own belief in God.

For pop culture resources and philosophical resources related to this chapter please visit the website for this book: https://introducingphilosophythroughpopculture.com.

Notes

1   It is important to note that one could substitute any evil for "Cartman's complete happiness" and the conclusion would still follow. Often, when the argument is made, the phrase "evil exists" is substituted for "Cartman's complete happiness."

2   See Johnson, D.K. (2012). A Refutation of Skeptical Theism. *Sophia* (first published online, November 10, 2012 by Springer Publishing). http://link.springer.com/article/10.1007/s11841-012-0326-0.

3   My 2012 article, noted above, is a bit technical. For a readable refutation of skeptical theism, see my chapter "Refuting Skeptical Theism" in John Loftus' book God and Horrendous Suffering (Denver, CO: GCRR Press, 2021), p. 212–231.

4   Armstrong, K. (1994). *History of God: The 4,000 Year Quest of Judaism, Christianity and Islam*. New York: Ballantine Books.

5   See Calvin, J. (1957). *Institutes of the Christian Religion* (trans. H. Beveridge). Grand Rapids, MI: William B. Eerdmans Publishing Company, Book 1, chapters 16–18; Book 3, chapter 23. Also see Edwards, J. (1968). Wicked men useful in their destruction only. In: *The Works of President Edwards, Volume 6* (eds. E. Parsons and E. Williams). New York: B. Franklin. Edwards is mainly addressing the doctrine of Hell, but clearly realizes that the existence of evil is necessary for God to demonstrate his holiness.

6   For a wonderful rendition of Edwards argument, see Wainwright, W.J. (2004). Jonathan Edwards and the doctrine of Hell. In: *Jonathan Edwards: Philosophical Theologian* (eds. P. Helm and O. Crisp). London: Ashgate Publishing.

7   See Swinburne, R. (1998). *Providence and the Problem of Evil*. Oxford: Oxford University Press (Chapters. 9 and 10).

8   See (1953). On free will. In *Augustine: Earlier Writings*, (trans. J. Burleigh). Philadelphia: Westminster Press.

9   A solution some suggest is this: "Natural evil is a result of Adam and Eve's sin, which corrupted and imperfected the world." No professional philosopher or theologian would ever take such an answer seriously, however. First, the Adam and Eve story isn't literally true. Second, it provides no explanation for how the sin causes natural disasters. How exactly does eating a piece of fruit change the laws of physics? And as divine punishment for the sins of our forefathers (or even our own), the suffering natural disasters inflict on us is far out of proposition to the severity of our sins. "Adam ate an apple so I'm going to kill millions, including children, in a Tsunami?" God can't be that cruel. For more on this, and the severity of the problem of natural evil and what it entails, see D.K. Johnson (2011). Natural evil and the simulation hypothesis. *Philo* 14: 161–175.

10 See Hick, J. (1978). *Evil and the God of Love*. San Francisco: Harper.

11 I am borrowing these examples of obviously unjustifiable evils from William Rowe's argument in "The Problem of Evil and Some Varieties of Atheism." AmericanPhilosophical Quarterly 16, no. 4 (1979): 335–341. doi.org/10.4324/9781315880891-31.

12 "The problem of evil," Faith and Philosophy, 2 (1985), 392-423, and "Providence and the problem of evil" in Thomas Flint (ed.) Christian Philosophy (Notre Dame, IN: University of Notre Dame Press, 1990), 51–91.

13 See Johnson, D.K. (2022). Does God Exist?. *Think*, 62 (35).

14 See D.K. Johnson (2020). Why Religious Experience Can't Justify Religious Belief. *SHERM* (Socio-Historical Examination of Religion and Ministry), Vol. 2, No. 2: 26–46.

15 "Pascal's Wager," in *The Stanford Encyclopedia of Philosophy* at https://plato.stanford.edu/entries/pascal-wager.

16 "Silverman's Wager," *The Free Library by Farlex* at https://www.thefreelibrary.com/Silverman%27s+Wager-a073693839.

17 For more on the virtue and rationality of faith, including when it may be rational or virtuous to believe something by faith, see Johnson, D.K. (2011). Taking a leap of faith: a how-to guide. In: *Inception and Philosophy: Because It's Never Just a Dream* (ed. D.K. Johnson), 249–264. Hoboken: Wiley-Blackwell.

18 See Johnson, D.K. (2017). Moral culpability and choosing to believe in god. In: *Atheism and the Christian Faith* (ed. B. Anderson), 11–32. Delaware: Vernon Press.

18

Hidden Mickeys and the Hiddenness of God

Robert K. Garcia and Timothy Pickavance

Summary

This chapter explores how a little-known feature of Disney attractions illuminates a traditional challenge concerning God's existence. The shape of Mickey Mouse's head is well known: one large circle capped by two smaller ones. What is less known is that images of Mickey's head are hidden throughout Disney attractions. However, it is often ambiguous whether some constellation of shapes *is* a Hidden Mickey. Notoriously, the evidence for God's existence is also ambiguous. Hence, the *challenge of divine hiddenness*: Some are open to believing in God but find the evidence to be ambiguous. But if God exists, then God would provide unambiguous evidence for such people. So God doesn't exist. The ambiguity in these cases is similar and so we draw the same lesson for each: It is possible to be open to belief and yet rationally fail to believe. This lesson suggests a response to the hiddenness challenge. We explore the limitations and merits of this response.

Professional Hidden Mickey hunter Steven Barrett says that a Hidden Mickey is "a partial or complete image of Mickey Mouse that has been hidden by Disney's Imagineers and artists in the designs of Disney attractions, hotels, restaurants, and other areas."[1] Usually, Hidden Mickeys take the iconic shape of Mickey Mouse's head: one larger circle representing Mickey's face capped by two smaller circles representing his ears. The hiddenness of God, on the other hand, is the fact that, even if God exists, sometimes God *seems* distant, absent, or even nonexistent. As we'll see, Hidden Mickeys can help us come to terms with the hiddenness of God.

Emphatic Silence: The Experience of Divine Hiddenness

Although atheists have appealed to divine hiddenness to argue against theism, the observation that God is hidden would not catch many theists by surprise. This is because the latter observation has been repeatedly made from *within* the theistic

Introducing Philosophy Through Pop Culture: From Socrates to Star Wars and Beyond, Second Edition.
Edited by William Irwin and David Kyle Johnson.
© 2022 John Wiley & Sons Ltd. Published 2022 by John Wiley & Sons Ltd.

tradition. In fact, Blaise Pascal (1623–1662) went so far as to say that "any religion which does not say that God is hidden is not true."[2] However, being familiar with the hiddenness of God does not mean being at ease with it, and believers in a personal, loving God struggle with God's seeming silence and absence from their lives. This doesn't square with how we expect a loving, personal God to relate to us. When someone loves us, we expect them to be present and available to us, to care for us; in short, we expect those who love us to be available to us when there is nothing to hinder them. God, we are told, loves us more than we can imagine, and God cannot be hindered in the ways ordinary humans can. So it seems that there is nothing to prevent God from being personally present to us. Thus, when God seems absent or distant or unloving toward us, our expectations are violated. We are left wondering whether God really does love us, and sometimes whether God exists at all.

God's hiddenness has plagued even the most devout believers. Indeed, as C.S. Lewis (1898–1963) points out, the paradox is that those who take themselves to be nearest to God are often the ones who most painfully feel God's hiddenness.[3] Mother Teresa (1910–1997), for example, lived through a decades-long struggle with God's absence:

> Lord, my God, who am I that You should forsake me? The Child of your Love – and now become as the most hated one – the one – You have thrown away as unwanted – unloved. I call, I cling, I want – and there is no One to answer – no One on Whom I can cling – no, No One. – Alone . . . Where is my Faith – even deep down right in there is nothing, but emptiness & darkness – My God – how painful is this unknown pain – I have no Faith – I dare not utter the words & thoughts that crowd in my heart – & make me suffer untold agony. So many unanswered questions live within me afraid to uncover them – because of the blasphemy – If there be God – please forgive me – When I try to raise my thoughts to Heaven – there is such convicting emptiness that those very thoughts return like sharp knives & hurt my very soul. – I am told God loves me – and yet the reality of darkness & coldness & emptiness is so great that nothing touches my soul. Did I make a mistake in surrendering blindly to the Call of the Sacred Heart?[4]

Teresa's experience of God's seeming absence was "untold agony," an "unknown pain" that was dark, cold, and empty. She felt as though God hated her, that she was unwanted and unloved. She longed for God's presence, and expected God to come to her. But God seemed not to care. And so Teresa was left wondering whether there is a God at all.

Lewis also wrestled with the hiddenness of God. In *A Grief Observed*, Lewis reflects on the death of his wife, Joy Davidman (1915–1960). He recounts God's "silence" in the midst of our loneliness or grief:

> Meanwhile, where is God? This is one of the most disquieting symptoms. When you are happy, so happy that you have no sense of needing Him, so happy that you are tempted to feel His claims upon you as an interruption, if you remember yourself and turn to Him with gratitude and praise, you will be – or so it feels – welcomed with open arms. But go to Him when your need is desperate, when all other help is vain, and what do you find? A door slammed in your face, and a sound of bolting and double bolting on the inside. After that, silence. You may as well turn away. The longer you wait, the more emphatic the silence will become. There are no lights in the windows. It might be an empty house. Was it ever inhabited?[5]

Lewis experienced rejection in the midst of his grief – "A door slammed in [his] face." Where Lewis expected God to meet him and care for him, there was only silence and absence. As he put it in a letter to a friend: "The moments at which you call most desperately and clamorously to God for help are precisely those when you seem to get none."[6] These experiences led Lewis to wonder whether God's house was simply empty.

There's a clear common thread. Both Teresa and Lewis sensed an incongruity between their *expectations* about how God would relate to them and their *experience* of God's activity. And both moved from that incongruity to questioning whether God exists. What should we make of this movement? And what do Hidden Mickeys have to do with it?

We hope to show that reflecting on Hidden Mickeys can take us at least part of the way to a solution to the problem of divine hiddenness. Here is the basic idea: It is often ambiguous whether some constellation of shapes is a Hidden Mickey, and similarly, it is often ambiguous whether some experience is an experience of God's presence and love. In order to develop this idea, we'll have to step away from Hidden Mickeys in order to develop the problem of divine hiddenness in a bit more detail. We promise to return to them as soon as possible!

The Argument from Divine Hiddenness

Philosophers have expanded Teresa's and Lewis's type of worry into an argument against the existence of God. J.L. Schellenberg is the most prominent contemporary defender of such an argument. He puts the heart of the hiddenness argument like this:

> Many religious writers, sensitive to the difficulties in which our evidence for God is involved, have held that God would wish (or at any rate, permit) the fact of his existence to be obscure. God, so it is said, is a *hidden* God. But upon reflection, it may well appear otherwise. Why, we may ask, would God be hidden from us? Surely a morally perfect being – good, just, loving – would show himself more clearly. Hence the weakness of our evidence for God is not a sign that God is hidden; it is a revelation that God does not exist.[7]

According to Schellenberg, the fact that God's existence is not clearer violates our expectations of what sort of evidence God would supply regarding his existence. So the fact that God's existence is not rationally mandatory for everyone is actually evidence that a perfectly loving God doesn't exist. Lewis seems to agree: maybe God's house has never been inhabited. Of course there are aspects of Teresa's and Lewis's experiences and accounts that are left untouched by Schellenberg's argument. But Schellenberg is isolating the properly philosophical concern embedded in those deeply personal reflections. Our discussion, therefore, will focus on Schellenberg's presentation of the hiddenness worry.

It will help to formulate Schellenberg's argument a bit more precisely:

> Premise 1: If a perfectly loving God exists, then anyone who fails to believe in God is resistant to a relationship with God.[8]
> Premise 2: There are people who fail to believe in God but who aren't resistant to a relationship with God.[9]
>
> **Conclusion**: Thus, no perfectly loving God exists.

The first premise (1) contains something new, namely, the idea of being *resistant to a relationship with God*. Let us unpack this a bit. The first premise connects the idea of a perfectly loving God to expectations about how God would relate to us. Here's the connection: if God loves us perfectly, then God's existence would be abundantly clear, so clear that only resistance on the part of a creature would prevent her from believing in God's existence. The motivation for this premise is simple reflection on the nature of love. For example, it would be odd to say that a mother loves her son while not making herself relationally available to him. Suppose the son desired a close, personal relationship with his mother. If she loves him, then she would be available to him. If she could help it, she would not remain hidden from him. Of course, if the son chose to reject his mother, she might let him do so. She might remain distant in order to respect his desires. Indeed, that may be an expression of her love for him. But only this kind of *resistance to relationship* would keep the mother at bay.

We see this dynamic in the timeless stories of the Disney universe. *Finding Nemo*, for example, is a story about Marlin relentlessly pursuing his lost son, Nemo, a pursuit fueled by a father's love. In *Frozen*, Anna, with the help of Kristoff, Sven, and Olaf, pursues Elsa into the mountains because of her love for her sister. There are barriers along the way, obstacles to be overcome. But that's the beauty of the stories! Love drives us to overcome these barriers and obstacles to restore relationships to the kind of intimacy that love requires.

You might notice that we are discussing two interrelated ideas: believing in God's existence and being in a relationship with God. Being in a full-blooded personal relationship with God involves more than merely believing that God exists. However, believing that God exists is *necessary* for being in a personal relationship with God. This is true for all relationships. You cannot be in a relationship with another person if you don't believe that person exists. The hiddenness argument uses this idea to strengthen its case against the existence of God. If God really loves us, then God's existence would be absolutely obvious, since love strives for relationship and relationship requires that one knows the other exists. Imagine a mother who says she loves her son, but who avoids letting her son know that she exists. Unless the mother has some excellent reason for hiding, her avoidance seems at odds with her professed love.

When we love one another, we strive for relational intimacy. The same goes for God, according to premise (1). If God is perfectly loving, then God would do anything to be near God's creatures and would therefore create a world that makes God's existence obvious. Marlin of course pursued Nemo, but importantly Nemo *wanted* to be found. Between them, there were barriers that Marlin had to overcome, just like there were barriers Anna had to overcome in her pursuit of Elsa. Unlike Marlin and Anna, however, God cannot be put off by barriers to God's creatures. God is all-powerful, so there is nothing that can keep God away. Well, almost nothing. God respects our desires. So there is *one* reason a creature could fail to be in a relationship with God: the creature's *unwillingness* to be found, the creature's *resistance* to such a relationship.

The second premise (2) asserts that there are people who fail to believe in God while being open to a relationship with God. Following Schellenberg, let's call any such person a nonresistant nonbeliever. Most of us probably know at least one nonresistant nonbeliever. Maybe you are one yourself! But notice: given the first premise, the existence of a perfectly loving God is incompatible with the existence of a single nonresistant nonbeliever! The existence of one implies the nonexistence of the other. It's all the more striking, then, that so many people seem to be nonresistant nonbelievers. If God were so loving, why would so many people nonresistantly fail to believe in God?

When is a Hidden Mickey a Hidden Mickey?

Schellenberg a gives a powerful argument. It has plausible premises, and the conclusion clearly follows from those premises. But Hidden Mickeys highlight a potential problem for the first premise. Whether a particular arrangement of shapes is a Hidden Mickey is sometimes ambiguous, and this is at least in part because it is sometimes unclear how that arrangement of shapes came to be.

Here's an example, so you can see what we mean. In Disney Springs, near Disney World, there is a Once Upon a Toy store. At the entrance to the store are two pillars made out of what appear to be giant-sized Lincoln Logs: interlocking wooden beams like one would find in a traditional log cabin. Let us suppose we are looking at the right pillar. The log at the top of the pillar is arranged so that the end of the log faces you as you are walking into the store, and sitting atop the log is a yellow toy dump truck. The result of this arrangement is that the end of the log (a large circle), together with the front and back wheels of the truck (two smaller circles) form what many count as a Hidden Mickey. (You might do a Google image search for "Once Upon a Toy store" to see pictures.)

Although many *count* the log-and-truck arrangement as a Hidden Mickey, it's not obvious that it actually *is* a Hidden Mickey. To be a Hidden Mickey, an arrangement of objects or shapes must have been arranged that way to, as it were, hide a Mickey. Hidden Mickeys cannot be produced by accident. Hidden Mickeys must be created *as* Hidden Mickeys. In some cases, it is fairly clear that the arrangement of objects constituting the Hidden Mickey was produced intentionally, that the designer of that Disney artifact meant to hide a Mickey. For example, in the Downtown Disney D Street Store in Anaheim, California, there is a brick wall overlaid with stucco. Part of the stucco is missing, and it is missing in such a way that the brick underneath forms the iconic Mickey head characteristic of Hidden Mickeys. It would be hard to believe, given how meticulously maintained Disney properties are, that the missing stucco happened unintentionally. And if the stucco is missing unintentionally, it would be even harder to believe that it just so happened to be missing in a perfect Mickey shape. The point here is that it is very hard to imagine that this particular arrangement of objects could have come to be without intention on the part of a designer to produce a Hidden Mickey.

By contrast, there are plausible stories to tell about the log-and-truck arrangement that have nothing to do with Hidden Mickeys. Most simply, the log-and-truck arrangement might have resulted from an attempt to decorate the Once Upon a Toy store with toys. The logs serve to frame the door, and adorning them with trucks on top might have seemed a natural, playful, fitting cap for the log pillars. No need for the designers to be thinking about Hidden Mickeys. It is therefore not obvious that the log-and-truck arrangement is a Hidden Mickey.[10]

Relatedly, it's also clear that someone could be well-acquainted with the log-and-truck arrangement and yet fail to believe that it's a Hidden Mickey. There are lots of reasons this might be. There are the aforementioned points. Maybe, for example, the person finds the story according to which the arrangement was just a matter of decorative accident more plausible than the story according to which the arrangement is a Hidden Mickey. But also, the person may not be aware that Hidden Mickeys exist at all. Someone might even lack the relevant concept – s/he might never have heard of Mickey Mouse! Such a person could stare for hours at the log-and-truck arrangement, consider the evidence of their eyes in painstaking detail, with precision and attention, and yet fail to believe there is a Hidden Mickey there. Such a belief is simply unavailable to them because they aren't positioned to even consider the possibility. (Again, this is not equivalent to the claim that no one can reasonably believe that the log-and-truck arrangement is a Hidden Mickey.)

To recap: The log-and-truck arrangement may not even *be* a Hidden Mickey, and the evidence we have doesn't rationally mandate the belief that it *is* a Hidden Mickey. These two points together suggest that sometimes the traces left behind by the intentional actions of agents are ambiguous in two senses. First, sometimes those traces can be mimicked by events in the world brought about by agents without the needed intentions or even by entirely mindless forces. The Lego chaos on the floor of a child's room might have been caused by the child's truncated attempt to organize their Legos, by the family puppy's latest rampage through the child's room, or by an earthquake that caused the child's prized Lego creations to crash from the shelves and shatter into pieces. Second, sometimes we can have all the evidence that is available to be had and still not be rationally required to believe that some trace was left by the intentional activity of an agent (even if the trace was in fact left by such activity). This can happen when we have no insight into the source of the situation in question. Maybe no one is around to speak to whether the child was organizing their Legos, or whether the puppy got past the baby gate meant to keep them from the child's room, or whether there was an earthquake recently.

We can apply this to the problem of divine hiddenness. Because of the ambiguities noted already, someone might be open to believing that something is a Hidden Mickey and yet might rationally fail to believe that the arrangement of objects they are observing actually is a Hidden Mickey. More generally, you might be open to believing that some situation is the result of an action of an agent with a particular set of intentions, and yet you might rationally fail to believe that the situation is the result of an action of an agent. God's activities in the world are simply activities of a very particular agent. And it shouldn't surprise us that sometimes the activities of other forces in the world, whether other agents or just mindless forces like earthquakes, might leave behind situations of just the sort we would expect to find if God acted in a particular way. A situation can be ambiguous: you could reasonably take it to be the result of a mindless cause and just as reasonably take it to be the result of God's activity. If that is so, then it is possible that someone could be open (that is, not resistant) to believing that God is involved in a particular situation and yet rationally fail to believe that God is involved.

By reflecting on Hidden Mickeys we have found a way to sever the connection between openness (non-resistance) to relationship with God and belief in God's existence: one might be open (non-resistant) and yet rationally fail to believe that God exists. Hidden Mickeys thereby reveal a challenge to the first premise of the abovementioned hiddenness argument.

The Disanalogy Between Hidden Mickeys and Divine Hiddenness

Then again, there is a crucial disanalogy between the problem of divine hiddenness and Hidden Mickeys. We have overwhelming evidence, unrelated to Hidden Mickeys, that intentional agents run the Disney corporation. There is no doubt that the presence of Hidden Mickeys is due to the intentional activities of various people. The hiddenness problem, on the other hand, leaves us doubting the very existence of God, not just whether some situation in the world is the result of God's intentional activity. Hidden Mickeys, therefore, don't take us all the way to a solution to the problem of divine hiddenness.

One way to bridge the divide is to try out the idea that God simply *cannot* make his existence as apparent to us as the Disney corporation can make it apparent that it is run by agents acting intentionally. God isn't like Disney in this way. For some reason God is less accessible to us. Maybe, for instance, the fact that God's activity is ubiquitous means that all of God's actions have the same degree of accessibility to us. Thus, if *any* event can reasonably be seen as not involving divine action, then *every* event can reasonably be seen as not involving divine action.

The problem with this avenue is that the major theistic religions all assert both that God's activity is ubiquitous and that God, at least on occasion, makes his existence rather undeniable. Consider the latter. According to Judaism, Moses encountered a burning bush that was not consumed, and so Moses was compelled to believe that God was speaking to him. According to Christianity, Paul encountered the risen Jesus on the road to Damascus and transformed from a persecutor of Jesus followers to one of their principal leaders. According to Islam, God dictated the Quran to the prophet Muhammad. Thus, according to these religions, the ubiquity of divine action is compatible with special acts being undeniably revelations of God's existence. But if God can do these sorts of things for Moses, Paul, or Muhammad, why would God not do this for the rest of us? The idea that God wouldn't do so is difficult to square with God's love, at least when coupled with God's omnipotence. So, we are right back at the problem of hiddenness.

Might God Be Hidden for Love's Sake?

How might a defender of God's existence respond? One response appeals to facts about the connection between human free will and true love. C.S. Lewis seems to advocate for this sort of idea in *The Screwtape Letters*. Here is the demon Screwtape writing to his understudy Wormwood:

> You [Wormwood] must have often wondered why the Enemy [God] does not make more use of His power to be sensibly present to human souls in any degree He chooses and at any moment. But you now see that the Irresistible and the Indisputable are the two weapons which the very nature of His scheme forbids Him to use. Merely to override a human will (as His felt presence in any but the faintest and most mitigated degree would certainly do) would be for Him useless. He cannot ravish. He can only woo. For His ignoble idea is to eat the cake and have it; the creatures are to be one with Him, but yet themselves[11]

Lewis's idea is that God cannot overwhelm people with his existence because doing so would override their freedom. One reason this might be so, according to the Christian tradition from which Lewis is writing, is that God simply *is* love. Thus, an experience of God is an experience of the purest form of love, and this experience would of necessity compel a particular response. But the purest expressions of love are those that are *freely* chosen. So God desires a *free* response. That is, God desires for creatures to freely choose to love him. Moreover, freely choosing to love God is unlike any other possible choice. Rather, it is the most important and rewarding way to use our freedom. To freely love God is to freely enter a relationship that constitutes your greatest ultimate good. But to make our free response possible, the traces of God's existence must be ambiguous for us.

That is, it must be possible for us to reasonably fail to believe. Here again, we have a challenge to premise (1) of Schellenberg's argument. Schellenberg's argument demands that God's love requires God's existence to be undeniable. Lewis suggests that God's love requires the opposite: in order for God to have a loving relationship with us, God's existence must be ambiguous.

Of course, questions remain. How plausible is Lewis's strategy? Is it really true that, for love's sake, God cannot make his existence obvious? Not even Mickey Mouse can help us answer these questions in a way that will make everyone happy.

For pop culture resources and philosophical resources related to this chapter please visit the website for this book: https://introducingphilosophythroughpopculture.com.

Notes

1   Barrett, S.M. (2017). *Disneyland's Hidden Mickeys*, 6e, 9. Lake Mary, FL: SMBBooks.
2   Pascal, B. (1999). *Pensées and Other Writings* (trans. H. Levi), 81. Oxford: Oxford University Press.
3   As noted by Downing, D.C. (2005). *Into the Region of Awe: Mysticism in C. S. Lewis*, 78. Downers Grove: InterVarsity Press. Downing is referring to Lewis's statement in chapter 8 of Lewis, C.S. (1964). *Letters to Malcolm: Chiefly on Prayer*. New York: Harcourt Brace Jovanovich.
4   Kolodiejchuk, B. and Mother Teresa (2007). *Come Be My Light: The Private Writings of the 'Saint of Calcutta'* (ed. B. Kolodiejchuk, M.C.), 186–187. New York: Crown Publishing.
5   Lewis, C.S. (1961/2001). *A Grief Observed*, 5–6. New York: HarperCollins Publishers.
6   Letter to Mary Willis Shelburne, September 24, 1960, (2009). *The Collected Letters of C.S. Lewis, Volume 3: Narnia, Cambridge, and Joy, 1950–1963*. New York: HarperCollins Publishers.
7   Schellenberg, J.L. (2006). *Divine Hiddenness and Human Reason*, 1. Ithaca, NY: Cornell University Press.
8   This combines two premises in Schellenberg, J.L. (2015). *The Hiddenness Argument: Philosophy's New Challenge to Belief in God*, 52 and 53. Oxford: Oxford University Press.
9   This is similar to another of Schellenberg's (2015) premises.
10 Note that this is different from the claim that one can't reasonably believe that the log-and-truck arrangement is a Hidden Mickey. We reasonably believe all sorts of non-obvious things! A quick example: it's reasonable to believe – indeed we *know* – that the shortest distance between two points on a sphere is the path traced by the great circle defined by those two points, but that claim is nowhere near obvious.
11 Lewis, C.S. (1942/2001). *The Screwtape Letters*, 39. New York: HarperCollins Publishers.

19

The Jedi Knights of Faith

Anakin, Luke, and Søren (Kierkegaard)

William A. Lindenmuth

Summary

Good people don't kill their parents – as a general rule – but that is what Luke Skywalker is asked to do in *Return of the Jedi*. Yoda and Obi-Wan, the two teachers, father figures, and last remaining Jedi assure Luke that killing Darth Vader is the only way to save himself and the galaxy. Luke recognizes this but can't align it with his certainty that his father is redeemable. The combination of having to commit a terrible deed necessary for an objective, yet somehow achieve that end without doing harm connects Luke to the Biblical Abraham and the philosopher Søren Kierkegaard's telling of the sacrifice of Isaac: God asks Abraham to kill his own son, yet somehow through this son God will fulfill His promise of a great nation. Neither Luke nor Abraham know how to rescue and destroy at the same time, yet their purity of heart and valiance bear miracles: Abraham surrenders his son without killing him, and Luke ends Darth Vader while saving his father.

Luke Skywalker must make a decision at the end of *Return of the Jedi*. Will he ignore the nominally utilitarian principle that he must kill his father to save the galaxy, or will he violate the ethical principle against dishonoring and murdering one's own father and risk being turned to the dark side by the Emperor? Both are unacceptable to Luke. So he'll have to do something no one had believed possible for thousands of years: turn a Sith to the light side of the Force. Such a maneuver requires a leap of faith, and for that we turn to a man who knew just how hard it was: the Danish philosopher Søren Kierkegaard (1813–1855).

"I Can't Kill My Own Father"

Jedi masters Yoda and Obi-Wan Kenobi call for Luke Skywalker to kill his father. They're obsessed with a prophecy that foretold the appearance of a "Chosen One" who would "bring balance to the Force." The Jedi originally believed this meant that Luke's father,

Introducing Philosophy Through Pop Culture: From Socrates to Star Wars *and Beyond*, Second Edition.
Edited by William Irwin and David Kyle Johnson.
© 2022 John Wiley & Sons Ltd. Published 2022 by John Wiley & Sons Ltd.

Anakin, would "destroy the Sith, not join them." Anakin's eventual turn to the dark side led to the annihilation of all but a few Jedi.

Luke has an alternative interpretation in the form of a radical idea: to bring balance to the Force *without* killing his father. But how can this be done? After Yoda's death, Obi-Wan appears to Luke, who feels angry and betrayed. Obi-Wan told him that Darth Vader had murdered Luke's father, rather than *being* his father. When he first asks how his father died, Obi-Wan dissembles, "A young Jedi named Darth Vader – who was a pupil of mine, until he turned to evil – helped the Empire hunt down and destroy the Jedi Knights. He betrayed and murdered your father." It isn't until he first faces Vader that Luke learns the truth. In their confrontation on Cloud City, Vader demands that Luke join him and complete his training, telling him that it's his destiny to "destroy the Emperor" and that they can "rule the galaxy as father and son." Darth Vader describes this as the "only way." Luke's response is to throw himself off a platform to an uncertain fate.

When Luke sees Obi-Wan after confronting Vader, he's understandably distressed. He first asks, "Why didn't you tell me? You told me Vader betrayed and murdered my father." Obi-Wan explains that Anakin had been seduced by the dark side of the Force and when he became Darth Vader, he ceased being Anakin: "the good man who was your father was destroyed." Luke counters that there is "still good in him," that Anakin isn't dead. Obi-Wan responds "He's more machine now than man, twisted and evil." He claims it's Luke's destiny to face Vader and destroy him. When Luke demurs, Obi-Wan responds, "Then the Emperor has already won."

Both the Sith and the Jedi believe that "balance" is the eradication of the opposing side, even though Obi-Wan himself says, "Only a Sith deals in absolutes." Luke is determined to face Darth Vader and the Emperor, but somehow not turn to the dark side or murder his father. He faces quite a dilemma when he finally confronts them simultaneously.

"Mostly Because of My Father, I Guess"

Abraham, a central figure in the Book of Genesis, was in a comparable situation when God asked him to kill his own son. Abraham, whose name means "the father is exalted," was a biblical patriarch who had a special relationship with God. God promised Abraham a great nation would be made of him, and a covenant would be formed with him. This would be an exclusive agreement that God would watch over and assist Abraham and all his descendants as long as they obeyed God's laws. God made this arrangement, promising the 100-year-old Abraham and his 90-year-old wife Sarah a son to be named Isaac. It was through this son that God was to make Abraham's descendants innumerable and mighty.

Some time later, God suddenly calls Abraham and commands "Take your son Isaac, your only one, whom you love, and go to the land of Moriah. There offer him up as a burnt offering on one of the heights that I will point out to you" (Genesis 22:2). How can this be? How can the Lord in whom Abraham has put all his faith, who gave him a son after a lonely century and promised to make a great nation through him, ask Abraham to kill this beloved son?

Søren Kierkegaard asked these hard questions. Writing in the early nineteenth century, he was bothered by how "easy" philosophers were making faith and Christianity. He believed that the "leap to faith" was, as Gotthold Lessing (1729–1781) put it, an "ugly great ditch." Kierkegaard considered this problem, imagining a number of variations on

the events of Genesis 22 and what they mean for ethics and belief. Stressing the separation between reason and faith, Kierkegaard argued forcefully that faith is more important than anything else.[1]

The next morning after God speaks to him, Abraham saddles his donkey and brings
Isaac and some servants on the trip to Moriah, telling his wife nothing. After traveling
for three days, he tells the servants to wait for them to go and worship. As they head up
the mountain, Isaac asks his father where the sheep is for the sacrifice. Abraham replies,
"Son, God Himself will provide the sheep for the holocaust." He then ties Isaac to the
altar and raises his knife. At that moment, an angel tells him to stop – Abraham has
demonstrated his devotion to God; Abraham's descendants will be blessed abundantly
and made as "countless as the stars of the sky and the sands of the seashore . . . because
you obeyed my command" (Genesis 22:18).

Kierkegaard is in awe of this. He says he cannot comprehend this story! "Abraham I
cannot understand; in a certain sense I can learn nothing from him except to be amazed."[2]
How can God have asked him to do this? How did Abraham *know* it was God who asked
him? How did he know it wasn't a demon or nightmare? How does he know he got the
message right? How can God keep his promise if Isaac must die? Has Abraham gone
crazy? Kierkegaard writes: "Who strengthened Abraham's arm, who braced up his right
arm so it did not sink down powerless! Anyone who looks at this scene is paralyzed."[3]

Likewise, both Anakin and Luke have premonitions of the future that cause them to
hubristically try to prevent them. Han, Leia, and Chewbacca are tortured on Bespin to
command Luke's attention and bring him into the Emperor's grasp. Perhaps Palpatine
also caused the young Anakin to envision Padmé's death and therefore feel compelled to
take her protection into his own hands and solidify his quest for power. Like a demon,
the dark side was crouching just around the corner.

"Something is Out of Place!"

Some people might pass over the Abraham story, thinking it just a foolish myth – just as
belief in the Force tends to be disregarded as an "ancient religion" to which some still have
a "sad devotion" after the virtual extinction of the Jedi. But Abraham is treated as a father
by adherents to the major world religions of Judaism, Christianity, and Islam, and as a
paragon of virtue regarding faith. Kierkegaard thinks the story of Abraham and Isaac, as
paralyzing as it is, is fundamental to understanding the human condition, and therefore
approaches it with "fear and trembling." It's important to Kierkegaard to try and understand this story, and it will help us understand Luke's situation. Luke stands in the reverse
position. He's being asked to destroy his father, and the fate of the galaxy rests on his success. But how can the Force ask this of him? How can it be a holy act to be willing to kill
one's own father or son? Kierkegaard asks, "If faith cannot make it a holy act to be willing
to murder his son, then let the same judgment be passed on Abraham as on everyone
else."[4] If we cannot explain Abraham's act through faith, then he's as much a villain as
anyone who'd kill their own son, and the same is true of Luke killing his own father.

Kierkegaard imagines numerous ways that this event could've happened. In one
version, Abraham pretends it is he, and not God, who wants Isaac killed. In this way
he prevents his son from imagining God "a monster" for ordering this sacrifice. In
another, he imagines Abraham going through the task, but losing his faith in the process, never forgiving God for ordering this sacrifice. In yet another, he tells it from

Isaac's perspective, where Isaac sees Abraham clenching the knife "in despair," and Isaac loses faith in God.

Kierkegaard's point is that these are all much more believable and likely stories than the biblical one, which is a marvel: Abraham must *simultaneously* believe that he'll have to sacrifice Isaac and that he won't. God had promised Abraham descendants through Isaac; God has demanded Isaac's sacrifice. This is a confounding paradox that Kierkegaard thinks cannot be explained away. Abraham is both resigned to losing Isaac and full of faith that he'll get to keep him at the same time. It's what Kierkegaard describes as a "double-movement." The first is a movement of "infinite resignation," in which Abraham gives up everything: his son, wife, life. It's an ultimate surrendering, in which he becomes a "knight" of infinite resignation, a hero willing to lose everything.

The Jedi are knights in this fashion as well. Yoda doesn't want Anakin trained, as he's formed too deep an attachment to his mother and is accordingly terrified of losing her. "I sense much fear in you," Yoda tells young Anakin. When he loses his mother, Anakin slaughters the Sand People in revenge, and invests all his love and feelings of attachment into Padmé. It's this attachment that Chancellor Palpatine takes advantage of by tying his survival to Padmé's in Anakin's mind. When Anakin begins having premonitions of Padmé's death that echo his mother's, he goes to see Yoda, who counsels him, "Train yourself to let go of everything you fear to lose." Anakin can't comply and thus becomes a prisoner to his fears.

"I Find Your Lack of Faith Disturbing"

The movement of faith is a positive belief that somehow, through losing everything, one will gain everything. It's a complete and utter trust in God. This could mean God will bring Isaac back from the dead, or stop Abraham before he kills him, which is what happens. But Abraham cannot go about his task believing this. He cannot "pretend" to kill Isaac or hesitate with the knife, as happens in the alternate versions Kierkegaard imagines. He must be fully and totally committed to his duty. But his duty is also to love and care for his son! Through this second movement, Abraham becomes a knight of faith by trusting in God and his promise. Through losing Isaac, he also gains him.

Luke still must defeat Vader. The only way anyone imagines this can happen is if Luke kills him. Why must Luke face Vader? The Rebel attack on the second *Death Star* would destroy Vader and the Emperor, but he must confront them anyway. As Abraham must sacrifice Isaac "For God's sake and his own sake,"[5] Luke is destined to go up against Vader for his sake and the Force's sake. He cannot merely refuse to fight him on the grounds that the Jedi are not aggressive. To do so would be to turn his back on justice, his friends, and the fate of the galaxy. Darth Vader and the Emperor must be stopped, and Luke is the only one who can do it. However, besides the general obligation that we each have not to kill, this injunction applies all the more as a special duty not to kill our family members.

When Luke faces his father on Endor, he confidently reminds Vader that he was "once Anakin Skywalker, my father." That is the name of Vader's true self, a self he has forgotten. "I know there is good in you," Luke says. "The Emperor hasn't driven it from you fully." Luke doesn't believe that Vader will bring him before the Emperor, but he is wrong. Still, when Vader sends Luke to the Emperor, we witness Vader's evident hesitation. At some deep level, Luke has affected him.

"I Take Orders from Just One Person: Me"

There are many heroic characters in the *Star Wars* saga, but one of the most interesting is Han Solo. A compelling aspect of his character is that he starts off as a "scoundrel." He's a smuggler, a rough, uncouth man who's in it for himself. "What good's a reward if you ain't around to use it?" he asks Luke when the Rebels are about to attack the *Death Star*. He's what Kierkegaard describes as the "aesthetic" man, caring about carnal things like wealth and appearances. His motivation is self-preservation and pleasure. Luke tells him, "Take care of yourself, Han. I guess it's what you're best at."

Luke loses everything shortly after we meet him in *A New Hope*. He resigns himself to "learn the ways of the Force and become a Jedi like my father." He's thrown into the next stage, what Kierkegaard calls the "ethical." This is the realm of the hero, the person who follows a moral code and adheres to certain universal principles regardless of the consequences, including the risk of their own life. Han makes the transition from the aesthetic realm to the ethical when he shows up suddenly near Yavin, at great personal risk to himself, his partner Chewbacca, and his ship. He clears Luke to take the shot that destroys the Death Star, and they all return in triumph. Leia says about him, "I knew there was more to you than money!" Han again risks himself to save Luke when he goes missing in the freezing terrain of the ice planet Hoth. Kierkegaard's ethical stage also explains the great pains taken to rescue Han from Jabba the Hutt. The risk doesn't matter to the hero, though, as Kierkegaard describes, "The tragic hero relinquishes himself in order to express the universal."[6] Heroes are willing to sacrifice because they believe in something greater than themselves.

Everyone demands of Luke that he use his powers to kill his father, who's been responsible for so much evil. Nevertheless, sensing the good in his father, Luke has to come up with a radically new plan. He cannot kill his father, but he cannot allow Vader to live. Luke is already a Knight of Infinite Resignation. He must go beyond if he's to truly defeat the dark side in Vader and his Emperor.

"It's a Trap!"

When Luke rushes off to Bespin to save his friends, Obi-Wan and Yoda urge him not to go. Luke retorts, "But I can help them! I feel the Force." Obi-Wan reprimands him, telling Luke that he can't control the Force and will be vulnerable to the dark side. Yoda then reminds him of his "failure at the cave." After a training session in which Yoda teaches Luke that the Force is never to be used for attack, Luke senses something is wrong. Yoda tells him there's a nearby cave that "is strong with the dark side of the Force" into which Luke must go. What's in the cave is "only what you take with you." Luke begins strapping his utility belt on, but Yoda tells him "your weapons – you will not need them." Luke gives him a sidelong glance and brings them anyway. Within the cave, an apparition of Darth Vader suddenly approaches and Luke extends his lightsaber, Vader mirroring him. There's a brief clash, then Luke beheads Vader. As Vader's head comes to a rest on the ground, the mask explodes, revealing Luke's visage underneath.

What exactly is Luke's failure? Was it that he brought his weapons in after Yoda told him not to? Was it that he resorted to violence and struck first? Was it that he's simply too tempted by the dark side and needs more discipline and training? Was it that he brought the "idea" of Vader in with him that caused him to materialize? It's at least a subtle foreshadowing that Luke is related to Vader, and that's why he sees himself in the mask. Much of a hero's developmental arc is devoted to destroying the elements that connect them to the villain. His Aunt Beru told her husband that Luke "has too much of his father in him," to which Owen replies, "That's what I'm afraid of."

Luke erroneously believes that convincing his father to return to the light side would be as simple as a familial and emotional appeal. He isn't prepared to face Vader and the Emperor together, and thinks that he can turn Vader before that confrontation. Yoda's message must be ringing in Luke's ears: "Only a fully trained Jedi Knight with the Force as his ally will conquer Vader and his Emperor." Luke knows he has to defeat them, but he cannot join the dark side and doesn't want to kill his father. But he did not forsee how the Emperor had planned for contingencies, winning if Vader kills Luke, but also if Luke kills his father. The Emperor never refers to Darth Vader as Anakin in front of Luke, but always as his *father*. Darth Sidious relishes his perceived ownership of the Skywalkers: "You, like your father, are now *mine*." Luke killing and replacing Vader would continue his habit of recruiting ever stronger apprentices.

Luke also thinks the joint sneak attack on the shield generator and the Death Star will succeed, but the Emperor delightedly reveals it was all a trap of his design. He mocks, tempts, and threatens Luke, cajoling and goading him to fight. One of the final straws is the unveiling that the *Death Star* is a "fully armed and operational battle station" as it begins to fire on the Alliance fleet. Luke breaks down and crosses swords with Vader. However, he continually tries to stop the physical fight and keep the battle to the inner battle of the light side of Anakin Skywalker against the dark side of Darth Vader: "I feel the good in you, the conflict," Luke tells him. He doesn't believe his father will kill him: "You couldn't kill me before and I don't believe you'll destroy me now." Vader then lures Luke with the chance to save his friends if he turns. Luke's feelings flare at this and "betray him," revealing to Vader that Luke has a twin sister. When Vader threatens Leia, Luke loses control and launches a full-force attack on Vader, savagely swinging at him until he floors him and hacks off his hand.

"That's Impossible!"

As with Abraham, Luke's "temptation is the ethical itself, which would hold him back from doing God's will."[7] He wants to annihilate Vader and, in many ways, it's the "right" thing to do. We think our fear is that Luke will turn to the dark side or die at Vader's hand. What we really fear is that he'll do what Yoda and Obi-Wan demand of him: kill his father. Here again, the Emperor wins either way: Vader kills Luke – problem solved – or Luke kills Vader and takes his place at the Emperor's side. The Emperor believes he's engineered events so that he'll remain victorious regardless of the outcome: "Young fool. Only now, at the end, do you understand." Luke miraculously realizes the only way he can win is by surrendering everything. He can't murder his father and he can't join the dark side. In the same act, Abraham raises his blade while Luke casts his aside; the meaning is identical. Luke can destroy Vader and yet simultaneously save his father; likewise Abraham can sacrifice Isaac and yet God keeps his word.

This is the negative movement, the abandoning of all things: his friends, life, hopes – everything. As Kierkegaard speaks of Abraham, "only in this moment when his act is in absolute contradiction to his feelings, only then does he sacrifice Isaac."[8] Likewise for Luke, killing Vader is exactly what he wants to do. Darth Vader represents everything that he hates about the galaxy and when Vader threatens Leia, it's the final stroke. There's no composure here: Luke explodes, slashing and wailing on Vader until he beats him into submission, chopping off his hand just as Vader had done to him. He's seething, the pent-up rage bursting out of him as he pounds away, flecks of spit glistening on his open, panting mouth. He *hates* Vader, as in the moment before, ethically, Abraham "hates Isaac."[9] Luke's hatred has made him powerful. But if he strikes either Vader or the Emperor down "with all his fury" his "journey toward the dark side will be complete."

Luke looks at Vader's smoking stump, then at his own mechanical hand. His eyes widen as he makes the connection that he's following in his father's path. Luke inhales deeply to calm and steel himself for what he's about to do. Yoda taught him that he will know "the good side from the bad" when he is "calm, at peace, passive." He doesn't repeat the past. Determined, in the most difficult moment of his life, when he has more right to anger and revenge than anyone, he chooses faith instead. He trusts in the light, even from the darkest place. "*Never*. I'll never turn to the Dark Side. You failed, your Highness. I am a Jedi, like my father before me." He doesn't repeat his father's mistake. The Emperor said that Luke's "compassion will be his undoing." Instead, it's what saves him – and Anakin. As Kierkegaard describes, "The knight will then have the power to concentrate the whole substance of his life and the meaning of actuality into one single desire"[10] – Luke's desire is to get his father back.

Bringing Balance to the Force

Luke overcomes Vader in the lightsaber duel through anger, fear, and aggression. These are the exact things Yoda tells Luke to avoid, as "the dark side are they. Once you start down the dark path, forever will it dominate your destiny." But Luke *isn't* dominated by them, nor do they determine his fate. Both the Sith and the Jedi try to eliminate the other side. They don't want the other to exist. When Obi-Wan interprets the prophecy of the "Chosen One," he says it is "to destroy the Sith" in order to "bring balance to the Force, not leave it in darkness."

But this isn't balance. Only Luke sees the good in his father, and he's also the only one who possesses the fortitude to control his feelings and retract his lightsaber after defeating Vader. Unlike the young Anakin, Luke is able to resist the Emperor's temptations of power, revenge, and resentment. By contrast, consider how Sidious manipulates Anakin to kill the unarmed (and dismembered) Count Dooku.

Luke realizes that killing his father will not bring balance to the Force. He can't do what is demanded of him: he must do something more. "The knight of faith relinquishes the universal in order to become the single individual."[11] Luke somehow has faith that there's still good in his father, all evidence aside, and that they'll save one another. Discarding his lightsaber, Luke expresses both resignation and faith *at the same time*. He abandons everything he's fought for, while also embracing it. He becomes a Jedi Knight of faith in this incredible act. While the Emperor tortures him with Sith lightning, he also accomplishes something no one ever thought possible: he turns a Sith good.

Clearly Vader sees his son suffering when the Emperor is electrocuting him, but it was Luke's casting aside his saber that made it possible. It isn't through mere sympathy that Anakin saves his son. Rather, Luke's commitment to the Force is what brings Anakin back. Darth Vader is willing to kill Luke: but what's stunning is Luke's ability not to do the same. Luke defeats Vader in the duel but saves him in not ending it the way everyone had been telling him to. As Kierkegaard says, "it is only by faith that one gets to Abraham, not by murder."[12] It's only by faith that Luke gets to Anakin, not through killing him. "I've got to save you!" Luke says to his dying father. "You already have, Luke," Anakin replies.

Luke is warned by Yoda not to underestimate the powers of the Emperor, "or suffer your father's fate you will." Profoundly, it is the Emperor who underestimates the power of the light side of the Force, having misplaced his faith in the dark side, as Yoda had forewarned him back in their duel on Coruscant.

Abraham's complete sacrifice is what rewards his faith. For Luke, it is only through his actionable courage and true confidence in the light and goodness of men that balance is restored to the Force.

For pop culture resources and philosophical resources related to this chapter please visit the website for this book: https://introducingphilosophythroughpopculture.com.

Notes

1 Kierkegaard, S. (1983). *Fear and Trembling; Repetition* (trans. H. Hong). Princeton: Princeton University Press.
2 Kierkegaard, 31.
3 Kierkegaard, 22.
4 Kierkegaard, 30.
5 Kierkegaard, 59.
6 Kierkegaard, 75.
7 Kierkegaard, 60.
8 Kierkegaard, 74.
9 Kierkegaard, 74. What Kierkegaard is referring to is the challenging line of Luke 14:26. Jesus states: "If anyone comes to me and does not hate his own father and mother and wife and children and brothers and sisters, yes, and even his own life, he cannot be my disciple." Kierkegaard admits this is a "hard saying," but that he can understand it "the way one can understand a paradox." He explains, "The absolute duty can lead one to do what ethics would forbid, but it can never lead the knight of faith to stop loving. Abraham demonstrates this. In the moment he is about to sacrifice Isaac, the ethical expression for what he is doing is this: he hates Isaac." Luke's situation is reversed, because he must resist murder while Abraham must force it. The central idea is that all worldly concerns are subordinate to the higher religious demands of God, even if they contradict our normal ethical duties.
10 Kierkegaard, 43.
11 Kierkegaard, 75.
12 Kierkegaard, 31.

Part V

Ethics

Introduction

Ethics is the study of morality – the concepts of right and wrong, good and evil, virtue and vice. How can we live a good life? Is the virtuous life the best life, or is an immoral life more rewarding? When confronted with ethical dilemmas, how can we decide what is the right thing to do?

Our look at ethics begins with superheroes. Although Batman has had many opportunities to kill the Joker and thus stop him once and for all, he always resists the temptation. Instead, Batman continually sends the Joker back behind the revolving doors of Arkham Asylum, knowing full well that he will probably escape and kill again. Why doesn't Batman just kill the Joker and save thousands of future victims in the process? In Chapter 20, Mark White explains what utilitarians and deontologists would say on the matter. Using a bat version of Philippa Foot's trolley example, White develops a deontological, duty-based, argument for why Batman is right not to kill the Joker. The end doesn't necessarily justify the means.

Watchmen, the most acclaimed graphic novel of all time, was brought to life on the big screen in 2009. Set in the 1980s, *Watchmen* depicts Ozymandias and his plot to save billions of lives by ending the cold war. The catch is that his plan involves killing millions of New Yorkers – the end, he argues, justifies the means. The character Rorschach is determined to stop him, declaring "evil must be punished, in the face of Armageddon, I shall not compromise this." Ozymandias appears to be a utilitarian, and Rorschach appears to be a deontologist. However, neither ethical theory comes off in a positive light in *Watchmen*. In Chapter 21, J. Robert Loftis argues, if *Watchmen* is trying to critique utilitarianism and deontology, it doesn't do an adequate job. Neither Ozymandias nor Rorschach truly adhere to either theory. So perhaps *Watchmen* aims at a different point.

Introducing Philosophy Through Pop Culture: From Socrates to Star Wars *and Beyond*, Second Edition.
Edited by William Irwin and David Kyle Johnson.
© 2022 John Wiley & Sons Ltd. Published 2022 by John Wiley & Sons Ltd.

The mantra, "Who watches the Watchmen" gives us a clue. Should anyone, regardless of what theory they embrace, have the power that the Watchmen, or governments, have?

Whereas utilitarianism focuses on consequences and deontology focuses on duty, virtue ethics emphasizes the development of good character traits. In *The Good Place*, the main characters find themselves in the afterlife and are given another chance to become good people. In Chapter 22, Eric Silverman and Zachary Swanson use examples from the show to illustrate Aristotle's view that we can become good by practicing proper habits that lead to the development of virtues. In Chapter 23, Dean Kowalski continues our look at Aristotle with a discussion of friendship on *The Big Bang Theory*. The ancient Greek philosopher said that this essential human bond comes in three kinds: friendships of pleasure, friendships of utility, and complete friendship. The characters on the show certainly derive pleasure from watching television and playing Dungeons and Dragons together, and they derive some utility from one another as well think of Leonard driving Sheldon where he needs to go. According to Aristotle, though, complete friendship is about acting for the benefit of the other person such that we help the other person develop virtues and improve morally. Chapter 23 makes the case that the unlikely couple, Penny and Leonard, ultimately achieve perfect friendship in addition to romantic love.

In Chapter 24, Matt Hummel takes us to a time long ago in a galaxy far, far away to discuss Stoicism, a philosophy that calls for a virtuous life of self-control, detachment, and acceptance of one's fate. The teachings of the Jedi Order from *Star Wars* share much in common with the Stoic philosophy of ancient Greece and Rome. The rise and fall of Anakin Skywalker highlights the difficulty in achieving the Stoic ideal, however.

20

Why Doesn't Batman Kill the Joker?

Mark D. White

Summary

The Joker is the most homicidal of Batman's foes and has killed many people close to the Dark Knight, including the second Robin, Jason Todd. For years, fans and critics have asked why Batman doesn't kill the Joker and save the countless lives the Clown Prince of Crime would probably take in the future. This chapter tackles this question in the context of a famous philosophical thought experiment, the trolley problem, which highlights the differences between two major schools of moral philosophy: utilitarianism and deontology.

Meet the Joker

In the last several decades, the Joker has transformed himself from the Clown Prince of Crime to a heinous murderer without rival. Most notoriously, he killed the second Robin, Jason Todd, beating him to a bloody pulp before blowing him up. He shot and killed Lieutenant Sarah Essen, Commissioner Jim Gordon's second wife – in front of dozens of infants, no less, whom he threatened to kill in order to lure Essen to him. Years earlier, the Joker shot Barbara Gordon – Jim Gordon's adopted daughter and the former Batgirl – in the spine, paralyzing her from the waist down, and then tormented Jim with pictures of her lying prone, naked, and bleeding. And let us not forget countless ordinary citizens of Gotham City – the Joker even wiped out all of his own henchmen once![1]

Every time the Joker breaks out of Arkham Asylum, he commits depraved crimes, the type that philosopher Joel Feinberg (1926–2004) calls "sick! sick! sick!," or "triple-sick."[2] Of course Batman inevitably catches the Joker and puts him back through the "revolving door" at Arkham. Batman knows that the Joker will escape, and that he will likely kill again unless the Caped Crusader can prevent it – which, obviously, he cannot always do.

So why doesn't Batman just kill the Joker? Think of all the lives it would save! Better yet, think of all the lives it would have saved had he done the deed years ago, just among Batman's closest friends and partners. Commissioner Gordon has contemplated killing the Joker himself on several occasions, and Batman is usually the one to stop him. And Gordon returns the favor: in a revealing scene during the *Hush* storyline, Batman is *this*

Introducing Philosophy Through Pop Culture: From Socrates to Star Wars *and Beyond*, Second Edition.
Edited by William Irwin and David Kyle Johnson.
© 2022 John Wiley & Sons Ltd. Published 2022 by John Wiley & Sons Ltd.

close to offing the Joker, and it is Jim who stops him. Batman asks Jim, "How many more lives are we going to let him ruin?" to which Jim replies, "I don't care. I won't let him ruin yours."[3]

Although he may have considered it on many occasions, Batman has never killed the Joker, decidedly his most homicidal enemy. Of course, with very few exceptions, Batman has refused to kill at all, usually saying that if he kills, it would make him as bad as the criminals he is sworn to fight. But that seems almost selfish – someone could very well say, "Hey, it's not about you, Bats!" Or . . . is it? *Should* it be? Usually we think a person is obligated to do something that would benefit many people, but what if that "something" is committing murder? Which is more important, doing good or not doing wrong? (Ugh – Alfred, we need some aspirin here.)

In this chapter, we'll consider the ethics of killing to prevent future killings, exactly the problem Batman faces when he balances his personal moral code against the countless lives that he could save. In fact, this issue has been raised many times by many people, including both the villain Hush and Jason Todd himself (after returning from the dead), and earlier by Jean-Paul Valley (the "Knightfall" Batman), none of whom have the strict moral code that Batman adheres to.[4] I'll do this by introducing some famous philosophical thought experiments that let us trace through the ethics of a situation by whittling it down to its most basic elements, just like Batman solving a cleverly plotted crime. (Well, not quite, but you have to let a guy dream!)

Is Batman a Utilitarian or Deontologist? (Or None of the Above?)

The argument in favor of killing the Joker is fairly straightforward: if Batman kills the Joker, he would prevent all the murders the Joker would otherwise commit in the future. This rationale is typical of *utilitarianism*, a system of ethics that requires us to maximize the total happiness or well-being resulting from our actions.[5] Saving many lives at the cost of just one would represent a net increase in well-being or utility, and while it would certainly be a tragic choice, utilitarians would generally endorse it. (We could add more considerations, such as satisfying the quest for vengeance on the part of the families of his past victims, or the unhappiness it brings to some people when *anyone* is killed, but let us keep things simple for now.)

Superheroes, however, generally are not utilitarians. Sure, they like happiness and well-being as much as the ordinary person, but there are certain things they will not do to achieve them. Of course, criminals know this and use it to their advantage: after all, why do you think criminals take innocent people as hostages? Superheroes – just like police in the real world – normally won't risk innocent lives to apprehend a villain, even if it means preventing the villain from killing more people later. More generally, most superheroes will not kill, even to save many other lives.[6]

But why do they refuse to kill in these instances? The utilitarian would not understand such talk. "You're allowing many more people to die because *you* don't want to kill one?" In fact, that's almost exactly what people have said to Batman. For example, Hush asked him, "How many lives do you think you've cost, how many families have you ruined, by allowing the Joker to live? . . . And why? Because of your duty? Your sense of justice?" Jason Todd put a more personal spin on it (of course): "Bruce, I forgive you for not saving me. But why – why on God's Earth – is he still alive? . . . Ignoring what he's done in the past. Blindly, stupidly, disregarding the entire graveyards he's filled, the thousands who have suffered, . . . the friends he's crippled, . . . I thought . . . I thought killing me – that I'd be the last person you'd ever let him hurt."[7] Batman's standard response has always been that if he ever killed, it would make him as bad as the criminals he fights, or that he would be crossing a line from which he could never return – although he is very open about his strong desire to kill the Joker.[8]

While utilitarians would generally endorse killing one person to prevent killing more, members of the school of ethics known as *deontology* would not.[9] Deontologists judge the morality of an act based on features intrinsic to the act itself, regardless of the consequences stemming from the act. To deontologists, the ends alone never justify the means, but rather the means must be justifiable on their own merits. So the fact that the killing would prevent future killings is irrelevant – the only relevant factor is that killing is wrong, period. But even for the strictest deontologist, there are exceptions: for instance, killing in self-defense would generally be allowed by deontologists. So killing is fine, but only for the right reasons? Might killing a homicidal maniac be just one of those reasons? We'll see, but first we have to take a ride on a trolley . . .

To the Bat-Trolley, Professor Thomson!

One of many classic moral dilemmas debated by philosophers is the "trolley problem," introduced by Philippa Foot and elaborated upon by Judith Jarvis Thomson.[10] Imagine that a trolley car is going down a track. Further down the track are five people who do not hear the trolley and who will not be able to get out of the way. Unfortunately, there isn't enough time to stop the trolley before it hits and kills them. The only way to avoid killing these five people is to switch the trolley to another track. But, unfortunately, there is one person standing on that track, also too close for the trolley to stop before killing him. Now imagine that there is a bystander standing by the track switch who must make a choice: do nothing, which leads to the death of the five people on the current track, or act to divert the trolley to the other track, which leads to the death of the single person.

Let us call the person in control Bruce. Is Bruce morally allowed to divert the trolley to the second track or not? If he is, can we also say that in fact he is *required* to do it? Thomson takes the middle road here, concluding that Bruce is permitted – but not required – to divert the trolley. A typical utilitarian would require Bruce to throw the switch and save more lives, while a deontologist would have problems with Bruce's acting to take a life (rather than allowing five to die through inaction). Thomson's answer seems to combine the concerns of both utilitarianism and deontology. Bruce is allowed (maybe even encouraged) to divert the train and kill one person rather than five, but it's valid also for Bruce to have problems with doing this himself.

One way to state the difference between the utilitarian and the deontological approaches is to look at the types of rules they both prescribe. Utilitarianism results in *agent-neutral* rules, such as "maximize well-being," and utilitarians couldn't care less who it is that will be following the rule. Everybody has to act so as to maximize well-being, and there is no reason or excuse for any one person to say "I don't want to." By contrast, deontology deals with *agent-specific* rules: when deontologists say "do not kill," they mean "*you* do not kill," even if there are other reasons that make it seem like a good idea. This is simply a different way of contrasting the utilitarian's emphasis on good outcomes with the deontologist's focus on right action. Although throwing the switch to kill the one rather than five may be good, it may not be right (because of what that specific person has to do).[11]

Hush Will *Love* This Next Story . . .

Thomson likes to compare the trolley situation to a story involving a surgeon with five patients, each of whom is dying from failure of a different organ and could be saved by a transplant. Unfortunately there are no organs available through normal channels, so the surgeon considers drugging one of his (healthy) colleagues and removing his organs to use for the transplants.[12] By doing so, he would kill his colleague, but he would save his five patients.

With the possible exception of our bandaged and demented Dr. Hush, few people would endorse such a drastic plan (least of all Dr. Thomas Wayne, bless his soul). You can see where I'm going with this (Batman fans are so smart): "What is the difference between the bystander in the trolley case and the surgeon in the transplant case?" In both cases a person can do nothing, and let five people die, or take an action that kills one but saves the five. Thomson, and many philosophers after her, have struggled with these questions, and there is no definitive answer.[13] Most people will agree that throwing the trolley switch is justified and that the surgeon's actions are not, but we have a very difficult time saying precisely *why* we feel that way – and that includes philosophers!

Top 10 Reasons the Batmobile is Not a Trolley . . .

How does Batman's situation compare to the trolley story (or the transplant story)? What factors relevant to Batman and the Joker are missing from the two classic philosophical dilemmas? And what does Batman's refusal to "do the deed" say about him?

One obvious difference between the two cases described by Thomson and that of Batman and the Joker is that in Thomson's cases, the five people who will be killed if the trolley is not diverted, and the one person who will be killed if it is, are assumed to be morally equivalent. In other words, there is no moral difference between any of these people in terms of how they should be treated, what rights they have, and so on. All the people on the tracks in the trolley case are moral "innocents," as are the patients and the colleague in the transplant case.

Does this matter? Thomson introduces several modifications to suggest that it does. What if the five people on the main track collapsed there drunk early that morning, and the one person on the other track is a repairperson performing track maintenance for the railroad? The repairperson has a right to be there, while the five drunkards do not. Would this make us more comfortable about pulling the switch? What if the five transplant patients were in their desperate condition because of their own negligence regarding their health, and the colleague was very careful to take care of himself? We might say that in both of these cases the five persons are in their predicament due to their own (bad) choices, and they must take full responsibility for the consequences. And furthermore, their lives should not be saved at the expense of the one person in both situations who has taken responsibility for himself.

But the Joker case is precisely the opposite: he is the single man on the alternate track or the operating table, and his victims (presumably innocent) are the other five people. So following the aforementioned logic, there would be a presumption in favor of killing the Joker. After all, why should his victims sacrifice their lives so that *he* should live – especially if he lives to kill more innocent people in the future?

This case is different from the original philosophical cases in another way that involves moral differences between the parties. Unlike the classic trolley and transplant cases, the Joker actually *puts* the others in danger. In terms of the trolley case, it would be as if the Joker tied the five people to the main track, then stood on the other track to see what Batman would do! If we were inclined to kill one person to save five, that inclination would only be strengthened by knowing that the five were in danger *because* of the one!

We might say that the one person on the alternate track has the *right* not to be killed, even to save the other five. Although it would be noble for the one person to make this sacrifice, most philosophers (aside from utilitarians) would deny that he or she has such an obligation. This is even clearer in the transplant case. The surgeon could certainly ask his colleague if he would be willing to give up his organs (and his life) to save the five patients, but we could hardly tell him that he *had* to. Once again, the difference with the Joker is that he put the others in danger, and it would be absurd – in other words, appropriate for one such as the Joker – to say, "Sure, I'm going to kill these people, but *I* should not be killed to save *them*!"

The recognition of the Joker's role in creating the situation also casts light on the responsibility Batman faces. If we said to the Caped Crusader (as many have), "If you don't kill the Joker, the deaths of all his future victims will be on your hands," he could very well answer, "No, the deaths that the Joker causes are his responsibility and his responsibility alone. I am responsible only for the deaths I cause."[14] This is another way to look at the agent-centered rule we discussed earlier: the bystander in the trolley example could very well say, "I did not cause the trolley to endanger the five lives, but I would be causing the death of one if I diverted the trolley."[15]

"I Want My Lawyer! Oh, That's Right, I Killed Him Too"

What the surgeon does in the transplant case is clearly illegal. However, if the bystander switches the trolley from its track, knowingly causing one person's death to save five others, the legality of his action is not clear. Of course, the legality of the case of Batman and the Joker is a bit simpler. Let us say (for the time being) that Batman has the same legal rights and obligations as a police officer. Under what circumstances would a police officer be allowed to kill the Joker (aside from self-defense)? If the Joker was just about to murder someone, then the police officer would be legally justified in killing him, assuming that mere incapacitation is impossible and deadly force is the only effective choice. So if Batman came upon the Joker about to kill an innocent person, and the only way to save the person was to kill the Joker, Batman would be justified in doing that. (Knowing Batman, though, I imagine he would still find another way.)

Let us make the case a bit tougher: say Batman finds the Joker just *after* he's killed someone. Batman (or a police officer) couldn't do anything to save that person, but if he kills the Joker, he'll save untold others whom the Joker will probably kill. *Probably*? Well, let us be fair now: we don't *know* that the Joker will kill any more people. "This is my last one, Batty, I promise!" The Joker has certainly claimed to have reformed in the past;

maybe this time it's for real. Or it's possible that the Joker will die by natural causes tomorrow, never to kill again. The fact is, we can't be sure that he will kill again, so we can't be sure we will be saving *any* lives by taking his.

Given this fact, it's as if we changed the trolley example like so: A dense fog is obscuring the view on the main track, but we can see the sole person on the other track. We don't know if anyone is in danger on the main track, but we know that *sometimes* there are people there. What do we do? Or, to modify the transplant case, the surgeon doesn't have any patients who need organs right now, but he guesses that there will be some tomorrow, by which time his healthy colleague will be on vacation. Should he still sacrifice his colleague today?

I imagine that none of us would be comfortable, in either case, choosing to kill the one to avoid the *chance* of killing others. It's one thing to hold the Joker accountable for the people he has killed, and this may include the death penalty (if he weren't the poster boy for the insanity defense), but another thing entirely when we consider the people he might kill in the future. Admittedly, he has a well-established pattern, and he may even say he's going to kill more in the future. What if we have every reason – as Batman clearly does – to believe him? Can we deal with him *before* he kills again?

Punishing people before they commit crimes has been called *prepunishment* by philosophers, and the concept was made famous by Philip K. Dick's 1956 short story "The Minority Report," which later served as the basis for both a film and a TV series.[16] Although Batman's killing the Joker would not literally be punishment – because he has no legal authority to impose such a sentence – we can still consider whether or not prepunishment is morally acceptable, especially in this case. Some would say that if the Joker intends to kill again, and makes clear statements to that effect, then there is no moral difficulty with prepunishing him. (There may, however, be an informational or *epistemic* problem: why would he confess to his future crime if he knew he would be killed before he had a chance to commit it?) But others say that even if he says he will kill again, he still has the choice to change his mind, and it is out of respect for this capacity to make ethical choices that we should not prepunish people.[17] Prepunishment may trigger the panic button in all of us, but in a time in which very many can be killed very easily by very few, and advances in behavioral science and algorithmic policing make accurate prediction of criminal behavior seem plausible, we can avoid this issue no longer.[18]

Case Closed – Right?

So then, we are all convinced that Batman was right not to have killed the Joker.

What? We're not?

Well, *of course* not. Look at it this way: I consider myself a fairly strict deontologist, and even I have to admit that maybe Batman should have killed the Joker. As much as we deontologists say the right always comes before the good, an *incredible* amount of good would have been done if the Joker's life had been ended years ago. Compare this issue with the recent torture debates: even those who are wholeheartedly opposed to the use of torture under any circumstances must have some reservations when thousands or millions of innocent lives are at stake.[19]

Luckily, literature – and by literature I mean comic books – provides us a way to discuss issues like these without having to experience them. We don't have to trick people into standing in front of a runaway trolley, and we don't need a real-life Batman and Joker. That's what thought experiments are for: they let us play through an imaginary scenario and imagine what we should or shouldn't do. Unfortunately for Batman, but luckily for Batman fans, the Joker is not imaginary to him, and I'm sure he will struggle with this issue for many years to come.[20]

For pop culture resources and philosophical resources related to this chapter please visit the website for this book: https://introducingphilosophythroughpopculture.com.

Notes

1   Jason Todd was killed in *Batman* #427 (December 1988), included in *A Death in the Family* (1988); Lieutenant Essen was killed in *Detective Comics* #741 (February 2000), included in *No Man's Land, Vol. 4* (2012); Barbara Gordon was shot in *The Killing Joke* (1988); and most of the Joker's henchmen were killed in *Batman* #663 (April 2007).

2   Feinberg, J. (2003). Evil. In: *Problems at the Roots of Law*, 125–192. Oxford: Oxford University Press.

3   *Batman* #614 (June 2003), included in *Hush* (2019).

4   See Hush in *Gotham Knights* #74 (April 2006), Jason Todd in *Batman* #650 (April 2006), and Jean-Paul Valley in *Robin* #7 (June 1994).

5   Utilitarianism is usually traced back to Bentham, J. (1781). *The Principles of Morals and Legislation*. Buffalo, NY: Prometheus Books, 1988).

6   Wonder Woman's recent execution of Max Lord in the "Sacrifice" storyline, in order to end his psychic hold on Superman, is a significant exception and was treated as such in the stories that followed; see *Wonder Woman* #219 (September 2005), collected in *Wonder Woman: Mission's End* (2006). For more on this, see White, M.D. (2017). What I had to do: the ethics of Wonder Woman's execution of Maxwell Lord. In: *Wonder Woman and Philosophy: The Amazonian Mystique* (ed. J.M. Held), 104–114. Malden, MA: Wiley Blackwell.

7   See note 4 for sources.

8   In the scene with Jason Todd, Batman explains that "all I have ever wanted to do is kill him ... I want him dead – maybe more than I've ever wanted anything." In *The Man Who Laughed* (2005), as he holds the Joker over the poisoned Gotham City reservoir, Batman thinks to himself, "This water is filled with enough poison to kill thousands. It would be so easy to just let him fall into it. So many are already dead because of this man ... [but] I can't."

9   The most famous deontologist is Immanuel Kant, whose seminal ethical work is his 1785 book, *Grounding for the Metaphysics of Morals*. Indianapolis, IN: Hackett Publishing Company, 1993.

10   For Foot's original treatment, see Foot, P. (2002). The problem of abortion and the doctrine of the double effect. In *Virtues and Vices*, 19–32. Oxford: Clarendon Press. For Thomson's version, see Thomson, J. (1986). The trolley problem. Reprinted in: *Rights, Restitution, & Risk* (ed. W. Parent), 94–116. Cambridge: Harvard University Press; and also chapter 7 in Thomson, J. (1990). *The Realm of Rights*. Cambridge: Harvard University Press.

11   For an excellent treatment of agent-relative rules, see Scheffler, S. (1990). *The Rejection of Consequentialism*, rev. edition. Oxford: Oxford University Press.

12   Never mind the astronomical odds against one of his colleagues being a donor match for all five patients!

13   There was been a massive revival of interest in the trolley dilemma in recent years; for instance, see Edmonds, D. (2013) *Would You Kill the Fat Man? The Trolley Problem and What Your Answer Tells Us about Right and Wrong*. Princeton, NJ: Princeton University Press; Cathcart, T. *The Trolley Problem, or Would You Throw the Fat Guy Off the Bridge: A Philosophical Conundrum*. New York: Workman.

14   In *Batman* #614, he thinks, "I cannot ... I will not ... accept any responsibility ... for the Joker." But then he adds, "except that I should have killed him long ago." And finally, after contemplating that the Joker may kill someone close to him again, "he dies tonight by my hand," engaging in a graphic fantasy of several ways he could kill him.

15   This also brings in the controversial ethical distinction between causing a death through action and causing a death through inaction. Merely allowing a death is usually considered less problematic than directly causing a death – consider Nightwing's choice not to stop Tarantula from killing his archnemesis,

Blockbuster, who also happened to pledge to kill many more people in the future (*Nightwing* #93 July 2004). Interestingly, Dick actually did kill the Joker once, although Batman revived him (*Joker: Last Laugh* #6 January 2002).

16 You can find the short story in Dick, P.K. (2002). *The Minority Report*. New York: Citadel.

17 Christopher New argues for prepunishment in New, C. (1992). Time and punishment. *Analysis* 52: 35–40, and Saul Smilansky argues against it (and New) in Smilansky, S. (1994). The time to punish. *Analysis* **54**: 50–53. New responds to Smilansky in New, C. (1995). Punishing times: a reply to Smilansky. *Analysis* **55**: 60–62.

18 Of course, Wonder Woman already faced this question with regard to Max Lord, who promised to force Superman to kill, and she came to the opposite conclusion. (Apparently she had read New's papers.) On algorithmic policing, see Ferguson, A.G. (2019) *The Rise of Big Data Policing: Surveillance, Race, and the Future of Law Enforcement*. New York: NYU Press.

19 See Moore, M.S. (1989). Torture and the balance of evils. *Israel Law Review* 23: 280–344.

20 For an expanded treatment of this topic, see White, M.D. (2019). *Batman and Ethics*. Hoboken, NJ: Wiley, especially chapter 6.

21

Means, Ends, and the Critique of Pure Superheroes

J. Robert Loftis

Summary

The characters Ozymandias and Rorschach from *Watchmen* seem to represent opposite sides in the debate in philosophical ethics between consequentialists, who believe that the ends sometimes justify the means, and deontologists, who want us not to think in terms of ends and means at all. Closer examination, however, reveals that neither character is really true to their stated philosophies. Instead, Moore and Gibbons intend these characters and their philosophies as critiques of authoritarians and the ideologies authoritarians use to rationalize their power.

Near the climax of *Watchmen*, Rorschach and Nite Owl confront Ozymandias in his Antarctic fortress, and Ozymandias starts explaining his insane plan, which will perhaps save the world, but at the cost of millions of lives. While the smartest man in the world is offering up the last crucial bit of plot exposition, Rorschach looks for a weapon. He can only find a fork, but he tries to stab Veidt with it anyway. Ozymandias blocks the blow and sends Rorschach to the floor, all the while continuing his monologue. After he gets up, Rorschach tries to make another move on Ozymandias, but is blocked by Bubastis, the genetically engineered super-cat. Ozymandias doesn't even need to turn to face Rorschach, let alone miss a beat of his monologue. Not sure what else to do, Rorschach tries talking: "Veidt, get rid of the cat." "No I don't think so," Ozymandias replies magnanimously, "After all her presence saves you the humiliation of another beating."[1] Ozymandias's speechifying is a great foil for the taciturn Rorschach. An even starker contrast comes when Veidt is finally confronted by someone more powerful than he is – Dr. Manhattan, the comic's only true superhero. While Rorschach doggedly attacked a foe he knew he couldn't beat, Ozymandias immediately suggests compromise. If the others stay silent, they can enjoy the benefit of Veidt's new world. Everyone accepts the compromise – after all, they can't undo the attack on New York – except Rorschach, even though it means his certain death.

The contrast between the two characters' willingness to compromise shows a deep divide in their underlying ethical worldviews. Ozymandias appears to be what philosophers call a *consequentialist*: he believes that all actions should be judged by their

Introducing Philosophy Through Pop Culture: From Socrates to Star Wars *and Beyond*, Second Edition.
Edited by William Irwin and David Kyle Johnson.

consequences, implying that the ends will sometimes justify the means. He is the kind of guy who, when he has to make a decision, carefully lists the pros and cons and goes with the option that has the most pros on balance. At least, that's the way Ozymandias thinks of himself. Consequentialism is how Ozymandias rationalizes the bizarre murderous scheme revealed in the Antarctic fight. But consequentialism has a long and noble philosophical tradition, and the great consequentialists of the past would certainly disavow Ozymandias as one of their own.

Rorschach, on the other hand, appears to be a *deontologist*. Deontology says that we should not think of morality in terms of ends and means at all; instead we should only act in ways that express essential moral rules. Rorschach deontologically rationalizes his actions, like stabbing away at Veidt, using anything he can find, even though he knows he can't succeed. The outcome doesn't matter; what matters is doing the right thing. But deontology also has an old and noble philosophical tradition, and the great deontologists of the past would certainly disavow Rorschach as one of *their* own. Acting to express moral rules does not mean seeing the world in black and white.

Watchmen is an intensely philosophical comic, and concepts like consequentialism and deontology were clearly on Alan Moore's and Dave Gibbons's minds as they created the book. I hope to show that their attitude toward both consequentialism and deontology in *Watchmen* is profoundly negative. Yet, these are really only stepping stones to the real point of *Watchmen*. The ultimate target of the comic's critique is *authoritarianism*, the idea that anyone should set themselves up as a guardian of society. Superheroes serve as the images of power and authority in *Watchmen*; the ideologies that the heroes pretend to follow are rationalizations of that power; and the corruption of the superheroes serves as a critique of both power and its rationalizations.

"'In the End'? Nothing Ends, Adrian, Nothing Ever Ends"

When Ozymandias is being chased by Dr. Manhattan, he lures Manhattan into an intrinsic field gizmo (like the one that first created the big blue man to begin with) and activates it, which seems to zap Manhattan into vapor, disintegrating his beloved kitty Bubastis in the process. Afterward, he says offhandedly, "Hm, you know, I wasn't really sure that would work."[2] (Actually, it didn't.) This is a great Veidt moment in a couple of ways: it shows his willingness to make big sacrifices for even bigger ends, and to gamble on probabilities. He doesn't deal with a world of black and white, of evil and good, like Rorschach. Everything is gray, but some gray areas are darker than others. To do the right thing, Ozymandias simply chooses the lightest shade of gray.

In the history of philosophy, this sort of weighing, calculating consequentialism is most associated with the doctrine of *utilitarianism*. Although the basic idea behind utilitarianism has been around forever, the doctrine didn't really begin to flourish until the work of the English philosophers Jeremy Bentham (1748–1832) and John Stuart Mill (1806–1873). The core idea is simple: "actions are right in proportion as they tend to promote happiness, wrong as they tend to produce the reverse of happiness."[3] Utilitarianism is built from consequentialism by adding elements, like one adds ingredients to a soup. The first new ingredient is *hedonism*: the good that one is trying to maximize in the world is happiness. The utilitarian is not worried, like Rorschach, about being sure that every criminal is punished. Punishment is only a good policy if, as a consequence, it makes someone happier by preventing future crime. The other new ingredient is *egalitarianism*. Everybody's happiness is weighed equally. Thus, if an action will make five people happy, and one person unhappy (all by equal amounts), you should do it, even if the one unhappy person is your mom – or your favorite genetically engineered cat.

Now, utilitarians are well aware that one cannot in advance know which things will really maximize happiness for all. So most utilitarians don't recommend that we simply try to calculate the best possible outcome each time we make a decision. Instead we should rely on the rules and habits that the human race has developed over time for acting morally. Thus, the version of utilitarianism appropriately called *rule utilitarianism* says that one should live by the rules that would maximize happiness for everyone if they were followed consistently. So, Veidt might adopt a rule for himself like "never kill," not because killing never brings more happiness than unhappiness, but because a person who lives by such a rule would generally bring more happiness than unhappiness.

The version of utilitarianism called *virtue utilitarianism* asks you to develop the personal characteristics that are likely to maximize happiness for all if you really made them a part of you. Thus, Veidt could spend his time developing a sense of compassion, because compassionate people generally bring more happiness than unhappiness to the world.

Utilitarianism has had many critics over the years, and it looks like Moore and Gibbons are among them. We can see this first of all in the structure of the story. According to the standard comic book formula, Rorschach is the hero of the story and Ozymandias is the villain (though, of course, nothing is really that simple in *Watchmen*). Rorschach is the first person we see, and the plot is structured around his investigation of several murders. The audience uncovers the truth behind the murders as Rorschach does. Ozymandias, on the other hand, is behind the murders, and when he is found out, he reveals his elaborate plot involving the death of millions. Ozymandias also has one of the key flaws that mark comic book villainy: he is a megalomaniac who wants to take over the world. He may say that the purpose of his plan is to "usher in an age of illumination so dazzling that humanity will reject the darkness in its heart."[4] But we know the first thing he thinks about when he sees his crazy scheme succeed is his own glory: "I did it!" he shouts, fists in the air. And he immediately begins planning his own grand role in this utopia.

If Ozymandias is the villain, then perhaps utilitarianism is a villain's ideology. It certainly looks as though consequentialism contributed to his corruption by allowing him to rationalize self-serving ends and blinding him to the profound injustice of what he has done. The potential for consequentialism to promote rationalization is obvious: Once one starts in making sacrifices and trade-offs, it gets easy to make the sacrifices that will serve one's own interest. The deeper harm that consequentialism seems to have brought, though, is letting Veidt believe that he can *force* people to sacrifice their well-being, indeed their lives, for the greater good. Veidt thus fails to consider basic justice or fairness. Is it fair that the citizens of New York are forced to sacrifice their lives and sanity to end the Cold War, when no one else is asked to make such a sacrifice? The means for preventing this kind of unfairness is typically the doctrine of human rights, which tell us that there are some things the individual cannot be asked to do against his or her will, even if it is for the greater good. One of the most common criticisms of consequentialist doctrines like utilitarianism is that they are unable to embrace a doctrine of universal human rights. And in *Watchmen* we certainly see the consequences of failing to take the rights of New Yorkers seriously.

The Utilitarians Strike Back

At this point, utilitarians will object that they are being unfairly maligned. Veidt is at best a parody of the ethic they recommend. Far from rationalizing self-serving interests, utilitarianism is the least selfish doctrine around, because one's own happiness counts no more than anyone else's. As Mill wrote forcefully, "I must again repeat, what the assailants of utilitarianism seldom have the justice to acknowledge, that the happiness which forms the utilitarian standard of what is right in conduct, is not the agent's own happiness, but that of all concerned."[5] More importantly, utilitarians would object that their theory does indeed allow for justice and human rights. John Stuart Mill was a passionate defender of liberty and an early advocate for women's right to vote, so it was very important for him to argue that utilitarians can account for justice. He did this by using the tools of rule utilitarianism: to make decisions effectively, individuals and societies must adopt rules for themselves. Experience shows that individuals and societies that recognize rights are more likely to maximize happiness than those that don't. If Veidt had been a real utilitarian, he would have recognized this and adopted stricter rules about killing people.

Moore and Gibbons don't address these nuances – as we shall see in Section 21.4, they are primarily interested in showing ethical theories as ways of rationalizing power. However they do offer another critique of utilitarianism that can't be dealt with by adjusting the fine points of doctrine. Importantly, the critique doesn't come from the alleged consequentialist, Veidt, but from Dr. Manhattan. In one of the most moving sequences in the book, Veidt asks Manhattan, with unexpected plaintiveness and insecurity, if he's really the good guy he thinks he is: "Jon, before you leave . . . I did the right thing, didn't I? It all worked out in the end." In the next panel we see Dr. Manhattan from Veidt's point of view. The blue man, standing inside a model of the solar system, arms down, palms out, smiles and says "'In the end'? Nothing ends, Adrian, nothing ever ends."[6] Then he leaves the Earth for good. Dr. Manhattan's warning is borne out four pages later, when we see Seymour, the inept assistant at the *New Frontiersman*, reaching toward Rorschach's journal looking for something to fill up space in the next issue. If he grabs it, Veidt's scheme could be ruined, and all that suffering would be for nothing.

Utilitarianism asks us to look to the future and sum up the consequences of our actions, but the future is infinite, and you can't crunch the numbers when every one of them turns to infinity. Perhaps in five years something will happen that undoes the good that Veidt did. Then, 10 years after that, something good will happen that only could have happened given Veidt's actions. The problem here isn't just that we can't know the future, but that there is too much of it. Even if we had an infinite mind to encompass the infinite future, what would we see? An infinity of happiness and an infinity of suffering? We can't do anything to change a ratio of infinity to infinity.

And even if we could, what of it? Utilitarianism gets its motivation from the basic instinct that pain is bad and pleasure is good. Individually, you and I seek pleasure and avoid pain. Utilitarianism tries to remove the selfishness of this by asking us to seek pleasure for everyone. In doing so, it tries to make ethics a little more objective: less about what *you* want and more about what is good in itself. But if we keep going with this impulse to objectivity, everything loses its meaning. What does it matter if there is more pain or more pleasure in the world? We are now in the perspective of Jon Osterman after his accident: if you take too abstract a perspective, nothing seems valuable at all. This is a defect in Ozymandias's worldview. Unlike other characters – Rorschach, or the Comedian – he has never really confronted the question of the meaning of life, or the possibility that life is meaningless. All of his personal revelations are about the source of suffering in the world, not the possibility of morality. He learns that evil is not just a matter of crime, but comes from geopolitical forces. But he never questions the nature of evil and good itself. This is the real significance behind Moore and Gibbon's decision to name this character Ozymandias and to use the Shelley poem as the epigraph to chapter XI. Ozymandias takes a bigger view, but never the biggest view.

"Even in the Face of Armageddon I Shall Not Compromise in This"

So Ozymandias is a tragic villain, a man whose overwhelming ego and failure to appreciate the dark nature of life led him to think the end can sometimes justify the means. That means Rorschach is the hero, right? Well, no. Rorschach is a foil for Veidt in every respect: the unkempt, taciturn, right-wing outsider against the slick, eloquent, left-wing celebrity. But just being a mirror to the villain doesn't make you the hero.

As we saw before, Rorschach often uses deontology to rationalize his actions. We see this in his constant mantra "in the face of Armageddon I shall not compromise,"[7] which is an echo of the deontologists' slogan: "Let justice be done, though heaven should fall." Deontology goes beyond saying that the ends never justify the means. It actually says that, at least in moral decisions, you shouldn't think in terms of ends and means, or consequences, at all. Once you start thinking about means and ends, you've left the realm of morality altogether, because you're only thinking about how to get something you want, either for yourself or someone else. According to deontologist Immanuel Kant (1724–1804), morality begins with the good will. Anything else you might value in life – intelligence, strength, even happiness itself – can be used for evil. The only thing good, really, is the *will* to do good, the mental act that says, "I am going to do the right thing."

By the same token, if you are doing something solely to achieve some end, you are not doing it because it is the right thing to do. This not only applies to ends we think of as selfish, but even those we think of as ethical. Think about a cruel and selfish act, like the Comedian shooting his pregnant Vietnamese girlfriend at the end of the war. A deontologist would think that part of why this is wrong is because of the Comedian's motivation. He's not trying to do what is right; he's merely trying to accomplish an end that is convenient for him, getting rid of a person as if she were extra baggage. Now think about an unselfish act, like the redemptive moment at Bernard's newsstand when so many passersby intervene to break up the fight between Joey and her girlfriend Aline. If one of them was jumping in simply to make themself look good, or even feel good for helping somebody, that would simply be acting for an end. But if someone helped because it was the right thing to do, even if they had no desire to do so, that tells us that their act was moral (in a deontological sense). Interestingly, the people who intervene don't talk about pity; they give more deontological explanations, such as "it's all that means anything."[8] They have to act because they're moral people in a dark world that can only be lit by the good will. They're doing the right thing because it's the right thing. Kant would smile.

But Rorschach is not a hero, and his deontology is not Kant's. It is a shadow of deontology used to rationalize fascist thuggery. I wish I could show this simply by pointing out that Rorschach is a psychotic killer, but in comics, as in Hollywood, crazy vigilantes have a certain cachet. To see the real problems with Rorschach and his use of deontology, we need to look at his hypocrisy, the way his deontology degenerates into "dichotomous thinking," and his failure to recognize the intrinsic value of persons.

Rorschach is not only a flat-out hypocrite but his hypocrisy also reveals his real commitments. Rorschach's supposed commitment to deontology takes a back seat to the need to project strength in the face of moral decline. Although he delivered the announcement that he ignored the Keene Act on the dead body of a serial rapist, he shows admiration for the Comedian,[9] who attempted to rape the first Silk Spectre and confesses to have done many other "bad things to women."[10] After trashing Moloch's apartment, he says "sorry about the mess, can't make an omelet without breaking a few eggs," a classic bit of consequentialist reasoning.[11] To heighten the irony, Moore and Gibbons even depict him stealing a raw egg from Moloch's fridge, carefully cracking it open, and drinking it. Rorschach also professes admiration for President Harry Truman, because Truman was willing to sacrifice the lives of millions in Hiroshima and Nagasaki in order to avoid even bigger losses in the war – basically the same trade-off Ozymandias makes.[12] The pattern behind all of these exceptions is telling. In each case, he slips into consequentialist reasoning in order to justify a hyper-masculine display of power and violence. This shows his real worldview is simply fascist. All the elements of classical fascism are there: obsession with moral decline, idolizing the masculine and fearing the feminine, and belief that democratic authority has failed and must be replaced with something more direct.[13]

A deeper abuse of deontology comes in Rorschach's obsessive dichotomous thinking: the mistake of looking at the world in black and white. Rorschach is thus guilty of committing a *fallacy*, a mistaken but very tempting way to reason. *Watchmen* goes out of its way to show that where Veidt could at least see shades of gray, Rorschach is a simple dichotomous thinker. His initial attraction to the fabric he made his mask from, for instance, came from the fact that black and white never mixed.[14] Rorschach also seems to think that dichotomous thinking comes with deontology. All of his statements of deontological principles also say he sees the world in black and white: "There is good and there is evil and evil must be punished, in the face of Armageddon I shall not compromise in this."[15]

But dichotomous thinking is not at all a part of deontology. Kant taught that we should not do things for the sake of ends, but for the sake of doing the right thing. Still, this does not mean that "the right thing" has to be something simpleminded or rigid. For Kant, doing the right thing meant obeying what he called the "categorical imperative," a rule he phrased a couple of different ways. The first was to "Act as though the maxim of your action were to become, through your will, a universal law of nature."[16] This sounds weird, but it is really just asking you to remember a question your mother asked you as a kid: "What if everyone did that?" For instance, if you pinched some candy from the drug store, Mom probably said something like, "Listen, honey, I know it seems like no one is hurt, but what if everyone shoplifted candy? The store would go out of business and then no one would have any candy." Using a universalization test like this allows for much more subtle ethical reasoning than Rorschach is capable of. What if everyone was a crazed vigilante who punished every infraction with death?

The biggest reason Rorschach fails to be a real deontologist is that he fails to show respect for persons. Earlier we said that Veidt's worldview failed to be moral because he failed to recognize rights, the moral rules that prevent us from sacrificing an individual for the greater good. Kant captured this in the second formulation of his categorical imperative, "Act in such a way as to treat humanity, whether in your own person or in that of anyone else, always as an end and never merely as a means."[17] Again this sounds weird, but what it boils down to is "don't treat people like mere tools to achieve your ends." When Veidt destroys New York, he is using the city's inhabitants as tools for ending the Cold War, thus violating their basic rights as persons.

Rorschach likewise fails to recognize the rights we typically grant people, for example, the right to a fair trial. Really, Rorschach drew the wrong lesson from his existential moment burning down the home of that child butcher. According to Kant, we are obligated to always respect the basic rights of persons, because only people are capable of exercising good will, and a good will is the only thing that is truly good. Rorschach saw some of this as he "looked at the sky through smoke heavy with human fat."[18] He saw an existentialist version of Kant's claim that the only thing good is the good will. In his version "existence is random, save what we imagine after staring at it too long" and therefore we are "free to scrawl our own design on a morally blank world." What Rorschach didn't see, but Kant did, is that this requires us to respect the people who are capable of scrawling a moral design on the world.

"Who Watches the Watchmen?"

So neither consequentialism nor deontology comes off well in *Watchmen*. The characters use the ideas as thin rationalizations for corrupt behavior, and at least in the case of utilitarianism the ideas themselves are shown to be flawed. But critiquing consequentialism and deontology is not the main goal for Moore and Gibbons. Their deepest concern is obviously expressed in the aphorism that gives the comic its name and that appears in fragmentary form throughout the book: "Who watches the watchmen?" The line finally appears in full form at the very end of the book, but in a strange way. Moore and Gibbons give the original source, Juvenal's *Satires*, but then mention that it is quoted as the epigraph of the Tower Commission Report (which resulted from investigations of the Iran-Contra scandal during President Ronald Reagan's administration). This is a detail people tend to pass over, if only because the report was written before many current readers of *Watchmen* were even born. Perhaps this obscure bit of 1980s history only appears because Moore and Gibbons were reading the newspapers, rather than Latin poetry, during the era of Reagan and Thatcher. And the poem in which the line originally appears is about the difficulty men have keeping their women in line – a bit of patriarchy that is not a big concern for the comic. The Tower Commission, on the other hand, is exactly the sort of thing the comic is about.

Watchmen depicts an alternate universe in which the Watergate scandal never takes place, a man with superhuman powers allows the United States to win the Vietnam War, and Nixon is now in his sixth term in office, thanks to a new Constitutional amendment. Covert criminal activity of the sort the Tower Commission exposed seems to have driven this history: Moore and Gibbons strongly imply that the Comedian assassinated Woodward and Bernstein and further hint that in this world Nixon and the Comedian were involved with the Kennedy assassination. Ultimately, this is all intended as a warning about how a free society can collapse into authoritarianism, something Moore had depicted before in *V for Vendetta*.[19] In that comic, he showed England sliding into fascism after limited nuclear exchanges in Africa and Europe, followed by environmental and economic collapse. In 1988, when DC Comics reprinted a colorized run of the series (including the ending, which had gone unpublished because the magazine it ran in originally was canceled), Moore wrote a melancholy introduction lamenting the power of Thatcher's Tory party. Given what has happened, he realizes he was mistaken to believe that "it would take something as melodramatic as a near-miss nuclear conflict to nudge England toward Fascism."[20] Basically, Moore was not satisfied with the picture of a decline of a democracy into authoritarianism in *V*, and *Watchmen*, which was first serialized in 1986, is in part a correction of this.

Ozymandias and Rorschach are a crucial part of this picture, as the superheroes in *Watchmen* are images of authority. Moore told the BBC program *Comics Britannia* that, "What *Watchmen* became was entirely a meditation about power. We were thinking about how to some degree each of these characters represented some sort of power."[21] Rorschach and Ozymandias are important because we see in them that anyone can be corrupted. Leftist or rightist political views are really of little consequence because they are merely ways that the powerful rationalize what they are doing. Consequentialism and deontology are merely further rationalizations of these ruling ideologies. It is thus not surprising that neither view really gets a fair shake in *Watchmen*. Moore and Gibbons aren't interested in whether the views can be tinkered with to the point that they are a reasonable guide to behavior, because that is not how these ideologies function in the real world. Notice also that the most moral characters in the comic, the two Nite Owls, are basically nonideological. They don't have big moral ideas, but rather rely on a basic sense of decency. Dreiberg, the second Nite Owl, specifically shies away from making grand decisions that affect the whole world because one person simply isn't competent to do so.[22] The real lesson behind the whole comic is that no one, no matter what their ideology, should be entrusted with too much power.

For pop culture resources and philosophical resources related to this chapter please visit the website for this book: https://introducingphilosophythroughpopculture.com.

Notes

1   Moore, A. and Gibbons, G. (1987). *Watchmen*, 9. New York: DC Comics chapter XII.
2   *Watchmen*, chapter XII, 14.
3   Mill, J.S. (1863/2004) *Utilitarianism*, 7e. London: Longmans, Green, and Co.), chapter 2. Available (free!) from www.gutenberg.org.
4   *Watchmen*, chapter XII, 17.
5   Mill, chapter 2.
6   *Watchmen*, chapter XII, 27.
7   He offers many variations on the "never compromise" mantra. The two that come closest to the deontologists' slogan given above are *Watchmen*, chapter I, 24, and chapter XII, 20.
8   *Watchmen*, chapter XI, 23.
9   *Watchmen*, chapter II, 27 and hapter VI, 15.
10 *Watchmen*, chapter II, 23.
11 *Watchmen*, chapter V, 6.
12 *Watchmen*, chapter VI, 31.
13 Eco, U. (2002). Ur-Fascism. In: *Five Moral Pieces* (trans. A. McEwen), 65–88. New York: Harcourt Trade.
14 *Watchmen*, hapter VI, 10.
15 *Watchmen*, hapter I, 24.
16 Kant, I. (1785). *Groundwork for the Metaphysics of Morals* (trans. J. Bennett). Online at www.earlymoderntexts.com. Second Section. This quote appears on p. 421 of print editions (with standard Academy pagination).
17 Kant.
18 *Watchmen*, chapter VI, 26.
19 Moore, A. and Lloyd, D. (1982–1985). *V for Vendetta* in *Warrior* issues 1–26. Brighton: Quality Communications.
20 Moore, A. and Lloyd, D. (1988). *V for Vendetta*, 6. New York: Vertigo.
21 BBC Bristol, *Comics Britannia* (2007). www.bbc.co.uk/bbcfour/comicsbritannia/comics-britannia.shtml. Click on "Alan Moore Interview II."
22 *Watchmen*, chapter IX, 20.

Can Eleanor Really Become a Better Person? (*The Good Place*)

Eric J. Silverman and Zachary Swanson

Summary

In *The Good Place*, we are presented with an image of a paradise where the most moral people spend their eternal afterlife in bliss . . . or so we thought. It eventually becomes clear that many residents of The Good Place are not moral saints at all. Rather, they are individuals whose actions on Earth have landed them in The Bad Place. Our protagonist, Eleanor, is determined to beat the system by becoming a beacon of moral character during her afterlife, thereby saving her soul. This chapter uses the models of moral development offered by Aristotle and Lawrence Kohlberg to show how Eleanor might hope to develop her character in the afterlife.

We first meet Eleanor Shellstrop when she arrives in The Good Place – a paradise where the most moral people spend eternity. They get to live with their ideal soulmate in homes that perfectly reflect their preferences and personality in an ideal community populated exclusively by moral saints. Yet, Eleanor is no saint! Her presence in The Good Place appears to be a cosmic mistake.

Eleanor lacks care for others, the environment, and even basic manners. Her career was selling fake health supplements made of chalk to senior citizens. She took advantage of her earthly "drinking buddies" by repeatedly failing to take her turn as the designated driver. After agreeing to watch her friend's dog, she neglected it and let it become morbidly obese. She intentionally littered and was repeatedly rude to an environmentalist. She borrowed her roommate Madison's dress without permission and ruined it. When Madison sued the drycleaners for damaging the dress, Eleanor profited by selling shirts mocking her roommate as "The Dress Bitch." In short, Eleanor simply was not a good person.

Eleanor's bad character continues into the afterlife where she gets drunk on the first night and takes almost all of the shrimp at a welcome party, even going so far as to stuff her bra with extra shrimp. Eleanor initiates a petty rivalry with her neighbor Tahani Al-Jamil, criticizing her height, accent, and extravagance. Beyond that, she causes a trash storm by hiding garbage when she was supposed to be cleaning it up. An equal opportunity offender, Eleanor even treats her supposed soulmate Chidi Anagonye poorly, pressuring him to lie to help her stay in The Good Place, even though she could hardly be bothered to learn to pronounce his name correctly.

Eventually, Eleanor realizes that her vicious character could have eternal consequences. So she decides to become a better person in the hope of remaining in The Good Place. Her plight raises important philosophical questions: Can we really become better people? Is moral growth something we can control and cultivate? Or is our character simply the result of forces outside of our control such as God, destiny, our parents, genetics, or our culture? Can Eleanor – or any of us – really become better people?

Aristotle's Guide to Moral Growth

Eleanor has a pretty tall order for Chidi, "Teach me . . . How to be good. That was your job, right? A professor of ethics . . . Let me earn my place here. Let me be your ethical guinea pig." ("Everything is Fine") Aristotle (384–322 BCE), one of the philosophers Chidi teaches her about, believed in the possibility of changing one's moral character. Aristotle's theory of moral character focuses on developing virtues, the deep internal dispositional traits from which external actions naturally flow. These character traits include the values, perceptions, emotions, desires, and tendencies toward action that constitute our reactions to various situations.

Aristotle describes moral virtue as a human excellence that can be developed through practice, much like other excellences such as technical skills, playing musical instruments, or becoming an expert DJ – as Jason Mendoza believes himself to be. Aristotle proposes that we can develop virtues by forming habits, repeatedly practicing behaviors, which eventually become the natural patterns of life that constitute our moral character. Aristotle says, "For the things we have to learn before we can do them, we learn by doing them, e.g. men become builders by building and lyre-players by playing the lyre; so too we become just by doing just acts, temperate by doing temperate acts, brave by doing brave acts."[1] We learn moral habits the same way we learn other practical skills, by practice and repetition.

However, Aristotle warns that both positive and negative habits are developed by practice. So, the bad habits of being selfish or cowardly can be developed by practice, just like the good virtuous habits of becoming altruistic or brave. He explains:

[B]y doing the acts that we do in our transactions with other men we become just or unjust, and by doing the acts that we do in the presence of danger, and being habituated to feel fear or confidence, we become brave or cowardly . . . Thus, in one word, states of character arise out of like activities . . . It makes no small difference, then, whether we form habits of one kind or of another from our very youth; it makes a very great difference, or rather all the difference.[2]

For Aristotle, virtuous character is tremendously important and helps constitute our earthly happiness. So, developing the right habits early on is both a practical and a moral concern. Accordingly, flashbacks to Eleanor's high school years reveal that she developed selfish habits from an early age.

Aristotle's Four Levels of Moral Character

There are three foundational aspects of Aristotelian virtue, and mastering each of the three aspects constitutes moral growth. The fully virtuous person knows the right thing to do, does the right thing, and experiences the proper internal emotions and desires while doing the right thing. We can illustrate a fully virtuous person with a trait that Aristotle called temperance: to know and recognize the right types and amounts of foods appropriate for one's health, to eat the right foods, and to desire these right foods. Fully temperate people have all three of these traits: the right knowledge, the right desires, and the right actions. They eat the proper foods in the proper portions and are actually satisfied! Not only do they eat the proper amount of shrimp, but it wouldn't even occur to them to stuff extras into their bras.

A less than fully virtuous person – but still quite good – is the strong-willed person – who knows the right things to do and does the right things, even though their desires are not really in line with virtue and their motives are sometimes mixed. The strong-willed person might manage to eat the proper foods in the right quantities – despite really wanting to hog all the shrimp themself! Both the strong-willed and the virtuous person know the proper thing to do. The difference between the strong-willed person and the virtuous person is that while they both act similarly externally, internally the strong-willed person successfully resists the temptation of their desires in order to control themself. Their desires are not fully in line with virtue. Doing the right thing is a struggle and is not automatic, easy, and unreflective. Michael seems aware of the difference between the strong-willed person and the fully virtuous person when he discusses Brent's moral improvement. Michael says, "his behavior is changing. Remember, that's the roadmap. First we change their behavior, then we work on motivation" ("A Chip Driver Mystery").

Morally worse than the strong-willed person is the weak-willed person: who knows the right thing to do, but neither desires to do it nor actually does it. For example, Eleanor agrees to pick up trash during her second day in The Good Place instead of getting to fly ("Flying"). She knows this is the right thing to do and even tries to do the right thing. Yet, as often happens with the weak-willed person, Eleanor failed to follow through on her commitment and hides a bunch of trash rather than cleaning it up properly.

The morally worst person is the vicious person: who does the wrong thing, desires the wrong thing, and doesn't even know the right thing to do – perhaps, even mistaking the wrong thing to do for the right thing. This was the sort of person Eleanor was when she entered The Good Place. In her earthly life, Eleanor treated people badly and took advantage of them, whether they were strangers she sold fake medicine to ("Everything is Fine") or her roommate whose dress she damaged ("Most Improved Player"). She didn't care about people – her friendships were just shallow relationships of convenience. She didn't treat people well, and she didn't even realize that treating people well was something she should be trying to do. Eleanor seemed to think that her selfishness was the proper way to live and that most people live this way.

Yet, early in the afterlife she started to realize that not everyone lives this way. Being surrounded by people who seem to be moral saints made her realize that there are other ways to live. The possibility of eternal punishment in The Bad Place made moral growth desirable as a practical necessity. So, she used the Aristotelian strategy of seeking an experienced mentor, Chidi, to help her become a better person. Through her classroom sessions with Chidi, she at least learned theories about living morally. But, even in The Good Place, her actions were inconsistent, making her a good illustration of Aristotle's weak-willed person. Eleanor knew the right thing to do and even desired to do the right thing – at least theoretically – even though she rarely did the right thing.

By the end of the first season, though, we see a real change in Eleanor. She really wants to do the right thing and is even willing to sacrifice herself and her happiness for the larger group. Despite her strong desires and instincts toward self-protection and self-preference, she confesses, "Michael, the problem in the neighborhood is me. I was brought to The Good Place by mistake, I'm not supposed to be here" ("The Eternal Shriek"). In this case, Eleanor is a strong-willed person. She did the right thing by publicly admitting she didn't belong in The Good Place and risking her own eternal happiness, even though she only did it after looking for other possible ways to avoid telling the truth. If this sort of behavior continues, then she might even become fully virtuous and start doing the right thing out of habit.

Kohlberg's Model of Moral Development

Aristotle was not the only thinker to offer a theory of moral development. The psychologist Lawrence Kohlberg (1927–1987) gave a differing account of what he took to be normal, healthy moral development, dividing it into pre-conventional, conventional, and post-conventional stages.

Kohlberg's pre-conventional stages of moral development are typically displayed by young children. At this stage, behavior is driven by simple self-interest or a desire to avoid punishment. In this sense, childhood morality is pre-conventional, not driven by moral motives. Such a pre-conventional person might follow the rules, such as "Don't steal a cookie," but only out of fear of getting caught and punished. One problem with pre-conventional morality is that if one's only motives for behavior are self-interest and fear of punishment, one might seek to live as selfishly as possible so long as one can avoid getting caught. When Eleanor arrives in The Good Place she seems stuck in the pre-conventional stage, motivated by strictly selfish motives. Even her initial desire to become a better person is only based in fear of punishment in The Bad Place. As Chidi tells her, "Look the only thing you're concerned with is your own happiness, that's your problem" ("Everything is Fine"). So, even Eleanor's desire to become moral isn't based in anything resembling morality. It's just an extension of her own selfish self-interest and desire to avoid punishment.

The conventional stages of moral development are often found in adolescents as well as many adults. At this stage of development, the person simply wants to live up to and uphold their familial or cultural moral standards. Law and social order are valued with minimal reflection.

A child's relationship with her parents is important for moving into conventional morality. So, we can understand why Eleanor's development was so poor: she has a terrible relationship with her parents and was never motivated to please them by following the rules. Her parents are divorced and are apathetic toward her. Her mother accidentally kills her childhood dog, gets caught lying about it, and then demands that Eleanor not respond to it emotionally. She wastes Eleanor's college fund, forgets her birthday, and fakes her own death to avoid her gambling debts. Eleanor even has to lie to her own mother and claim that she has free WrestleMania tickets to get her to meet. In her teen years, Eleanor demands early emancipation from her horrible parents, but her lack of bonding with her parents foreshadows an ongoing lack of bonding in relationships and a lack of concern for what others think of her. Apathy undermined Eleanor's moral development; she never really cared if others noticed that she lived immorally.

In The Good Place, for the first time, Eleanor develops relational bonds with Chidi, Tahani, Jason, and even Michael. While her quest for moral growth begins with sheer self-interest, she eventually comes to care about her relationships and they enable her to grow. As Kohlberg himself says, "A person at this stage is aware of shared feelings, agreements, and expectations, which take primacy over individual interests. The person relates points of view through the 'concrete Golden Rule,' putting oneself in the other person's shoes."[3]

Post-conventional moral development is found only in adults, but not all adults. Abstract reasoning that grounds moral values is the ultimate basis for a person's moral behavior at this stage. Moral behavior is either based in respecting human rights, bringing about the greatest good for the most people, or some other higher-level abstract justification for morality. Knowledge of these abstract ethical theories is what professional ethicists specialize in, yet there is a tremendous gap between knowing ethical theory and living morally. One might have an excellent understanding of the theories of morality, yet choose to live selfishly. Or, like Chidi, someone might be an expert in understanding theories of moral behavior but have a serious character flaw like indecisiveness that prevents him from actually living out his morality. Chidi is indecisive about the ethics book he is writing, about his feelings toward Eleanor, and about practical matters like how to be a good best man at a friend's wedding. It even takes Chidi over an hour to choose between two fedoras in the afterlife. This deep indecisiveness shows that one can have knowledge about ethics, and even possess good intentions, while failing to actually live ethically.

Does Character Actually Matter?

One objection to the possibility of moral development is called situationism: the claim that people don't really live according to moral character but are overwhelmingly shaped by the situations around them. The evidence for this claim is that in various experiments, psychologists were able to manipulate human behavior despite the individual's supposed "moral character." For example, in the famous Milgram experiment participants were told by a scientist – displaying the symbols of authority including the scientist's white lab coat – that it is important for the participant to train an unseen learner to repeat certain sequences of words and deliver increasingly dangerous electric shocks to them when the learner fails. However, the learner was actually an actor (rather than a participant in the experiment) who intentionally failed his tasks.

Stanley Milgram (1933–1984) expected that the participants' basic morality and common sense would cause them to stop delivering the shocks. To Milgram's surprise, all of the participants were willing to inflict significant electrical shocks (at least 300 V) to the learner. Worse, nearly two-thirds of the participants continued to deliver shocks up to the maximum amount on the device (450 V) even after the learner begged them to stop, even when the learner appeared to be incapacitated by the shocks, and even when the electrical shocks were marked "fatal." As Milgram explains:

What is surprising is how far ordinary individuals will go in complying with the experimenter's instructions . . . Despite the fact that many subjects experience stress, despite the
fact that many protest to the experimenter, a substantial proportion continue to the last
shock on the generator. Many subjects will obey the experimenter no matter how vehement
the pleading of the person being shocked, no matter how painful the shocks seem to be, and
no matter how much the victim pleads to be let out.[4]

According to Milgram, the individual's moral character had minimal impact on their
reaction to the situation. Virtually everyone obeyed the authority figure and ultimately
ignored any directive from their conscience to do otherwise. Therefore, the claim of situationism is that the situation shaped the individual's actions.

If situationism is correct, then personal moral progress isn't possible because it is our
circumstances rather than our moral character that actually shape our actions. According
to this view, anyone might become a slave holder or a Nazi if they lived in the relevant
situation. So perhaps, Eleanor's, Chidi's, Jason's, and Tahani's moral characters are merely
reflections of their situations. Perhaps, anyone who was born into Tahani's indulgent and
lavish lifestyle would be corrupted by it and become a self-absorbed narcissist.

Does situationism succeed in debunking the idea of moral character and progress?
Probably not. There are three reasons we should resist this inference from the experiments. First, the Milgram experiment itself seems flawed. The participants were lied to
and manipulated in various ways. For example, if any were concerned about the shocks'
effects on the "learner" they were manipulated and assured that the shocks were painful
but would not result in any permanent tissue damage to the learner. Furthermore, the
participants were coerced and told that they had no other choice but to continue the
experiment once it began. It should be no great surprise that the participants followed
instructions. The entire experiment included manipulative components and relied on
intentionally misleading statements from the trusted authority figure in order to get the
participants to act out of character.

Second, even though the Milgram experiment demonstrated that a situation can be
orchestrated to manipulate an individual, not all the participants reacted identically.
About a third refused to finish the experiment despite being repeatedly told to continue
and that they had "no other choice," but to continue. Furthermore, some of those who
continued actually complained and raised concerns about the experiment, only finishing the experiment under a significant degree of manipulative duress. Reluctant participants in the Milgram experiment might be thought of as Aristotelian weak-willed
characters who did the wrong thing, but who at least recognized its problematic nature.

Third, even if we agree that the situation within the Milgram experiment shaped the
actions of the participants, it is difficult to argue that the entirety of one's life is similar to
a carefully orchestrated experiment employing manipulative "confederates" designed to
coerce a single person's behavior. Perhaps, our actions would be largely out of our own
control in a situation where we were being deliberately manipulated by several conspir-
ing actors, but most of our lives are not lived under such circumstances. A mistake of
situationism is to claim that because people can be manipulated in a short-term, carefully designed situation, they also lack agency in the bigger-picture situation constituting
their entire life. The truth is that character develops over time and is tenacious, even if it
can be manipulated in some situations. Thus, it is unlikely that our broad life "situation"
controls our actions in the way that the specific "situation" of a carefully orchestrated
experiment might.

According to situationism, Eleanor is a selfish person simply because she had terrible parents and a hard childhood. But is this simplistic view correct? Undoubtedly, her parents were bad examples and gave her moral journey a bad start. But is it correct that Eleanor never really had a choice? No. Surely, she had other opportunities to belong and find alternative role models and to bond with other people.

Many children of bad parents grow up to reject their parents' vices, sometimes even defining their own characters in opposition to the bad examples set by their parents. As Aristotle saw, people become virtuous or vicious through habits developed over time that begin in their youth. Eleanor – like all of us – had many choices along the way. In high school, she might have joined a nerdy clique where she aspired to academic success rather than being a loner. Even a "Mean Girls" clique might have provided some social context for limited moral growth. At the very least, Eleanor must share some responsibility for her own character.

The Moral of the Story

So why do it then? Why choose to be good, every day, if there is no guaranteed reward we can count on now or in the afterlife? I argue that we choose to be good because of our bonds with other people and our innate desire to treat them with dignity. Simply put, we are not in this alone.

– Chidi "Everything is Bonzer"

The moral of the story seems to be something like this: Eleanor can become a more moral person. Moral growth starts by bonding with other people and caring about them. When we bond with others, we care what they think of us, and we care that we have a positive influence upon them. As Eleanor learns in *The Good Place*, the road to being a better person starts with caring about those close to us. *The Good Place* is ultimately optimistic about human potential – as Aristotle was. As the Judge suggests, there is reason for hope, "Humans are not fixed at one level of morality, they can always get better" ("The Funeral to End All Funerals").

For pop culture resources and philosophical resources related to this chapter please visit the website for this book: https://introducingphilosophythroughpopculture.com.

Notes

1   Aristotle. (1941). *Nicomachean Ethics* (trans. W.D. Ross). In: *The Basic Works of Aristotle*, 1103a–b. New York: Random House.
2   Aristotle, 1103b.
3   Kohlberg, L. (1981). *The Philosophy of Moral Development: Moral Stages and The Idea of Justice*, Vol. 1, 410 New York: Harper and Row.
4   Milgram, S. (1974). *Obedience to Authority*, 5. New York: HarperCollins.

23

"You're a Sucky, Sucky Friend"

Seeking Aristotelian Friendship in The Big Bang Theory

Dean A. Kowalski

Summary

Over the course of 12 hilarious seasons, *The Big Bang Theory* provides many vivid examples of the different ways in which we become friends with others. Four examples are particularly noteworthy: Penny and Amy, Raj and Howard, Leonard and Sheldon, and Penny and Leonard. This chapter looks at each relationship through the lens of Aristotle's (384–322 BCE) classic and highly influential theory of friendship. Aristotle held that there are three kinds of friendship, each with distinct motivations for entering into and maintaining that friendship type. The first is for what is pleasant or pleasurable. The second is for utility or what is useful. The third, and highest form, Aristotle called "complete" friendship because it requires that one act for the benefit of the other. As we'll see, and even if Aristotle might quibble with the assessment, Leonard and Penny seem to be the only viable candidates for being complete friends.

Why would philosophers worry about something as obvious as friendship? We certainly seem to know what friendship is, how to identify it, and how to judge its worthiness. For example, in *The Big Bang Theory*, it seems obvious that Sheldon, Leonard, and Raj act as worthy friends when they stay up all night to aid Howard in repairing and redesigning the space station zero-gravity toilet. It seems obvious too that Leonard, Howard, and Raj are not very good friends when they flee to the *Planet of the Apes* movie marathon rather than care for a sick Sheldon.

Yet philosophers have been keenly interested in friendship, with Aristotle (384–322 BCE) being a notable example. In this chapter, we'll explore *The Big Bang Theory* to learn more about Aristotle's views of friendship, including his ideas about its three different kinds, and come to better appreciate his point about why true "besties" are so rare. In the end, we'll also see that *The Big Bang Theory* might suggest something interesting about friendship in its own right.

Introducing Philosophy Through Pop Culture: From Socrates to Star Wars *and Beyond*, Second Edition.
Edited by William Irwin and David Kyle Johnson.
© 2022 John Wiley & Sons Ltd. Published 2022 by John Wiley & Sons Ltd.

"Do You Have Any Books about Making Friends?"

Aristotle wrote about friendship in books VIII and IX of his *Nicomachean Ethics*, where he argues that friendship is indispensable to the human experience, "Without friends, no one would choose to live, though he [or she] had all other goods."[1] This pertains to even socially reluctant people like Sheldon. Despite himself, Sheldon certainly seems better off sharing his life with Amy (with a little help from their relationship agreement, of course).

According to Aristotle, not only is friendship good for its own sake, it's good for you. The rich benefit because friends guard and preserve prosperity; the poor benefit as they can take refuge in their friends if nothing else. The young benefit as friends keep them from error, and the elderly benefit as they can rely on those who minister to their needs and supplement their failing activities. Those in the prime of life benefit as friends spur them to become better. Again, Amy has bettered Sheldon both personally and professionally. It's unlikely that he could have won his coveted Nobel Prize without her, and his half of the acceptance speech is only gracious – and heart-felt – because of her influence (and that of the rest of the gang).

Aristotle's account of friendship consists of reciprocated goodwill and concern: "To be friends, then, they must be mutually recognized as bearing good will and wishing well to each other."[2] So, regardless of how much Sheldon admires his Green Lantern lantern, how safe it makes him feel, or whether it helps him (unwittingly) pick up girls, he cannot be friends with it. After all, it's an inanimate object. Aristotle's point also means that Amy and Penny are not "besties" when Amy abruptly declares it. At that point, Penny wasn't even aware they were friends – if only she had been keeping up with Amy's blog! (And the creepy wall-sized portrait only made it more awkward.)

Aristotle believes that there are three kinds of friendship corresponding to the three basic reasons for reciprocating good will and concern. The first is for pleasure or what is pleasant, and the second is for utility or what is useful. Aristotle sees nothing inherently wrong about these two forms of friendship, but he distinguishes them from the third and highest form: complete or perfect friendship. Perfect friendship obtains when the mutual care and concern is for the sake of the other. As Aristotle puts it, "Those who wish well to their friends for their sake are most truly friends."[3]

"Did You Ever Consider Making Friends by Being . . . Pleasant?"

Pleasure-based friendships are begun and sustained because they are enjoyable in some way. There is nothing mercenary about such relationships, as the parties involved are aware of their common goal: having fun. Sheldon is elated that Stephen Hawking accepts his friend-request to play "Words with Friends." All he needs now is a bunk bed with a slide and he'll have everything he's ever wanted since he was six years old! Still their friendship forms due to their mutual enjoyment of "Words with Friends," and when it ceases to be fun for Hawking, he pulls away.

Why does Aristotle deem pleasure friendships a lower form? He doesn't see anything inherently wrong with them, and he doesn't believe that complete friendship should be without pleasant experiences. His position rests on two points.

First, Aristotle thinks, probably rightly, that pleasure friendships tend not to last. Once the fun subsides, we tend to move on, as did Hawking (until Sheldon purposely started playing poorly to regain his favor). Aristotle believes this describes many young people in particular: "Friendship of young people seems to aim at pleasure; for they live under the guidance of emotion, and pursue above all what is pleasant to themselves and what is immediately before them."[4] Recall the season three episode "The Cornhusker Vortex" when Raj became angry at Howard during their kite-fighting escapade in the park. String-burn or no, Howard agreed to be Raj's partner. Howard knew the stakes: If they lose, Raj must surrender his prized Patang fighting kite (the one his brother sent him from New Delhi). When Raj calls for the "flying scissors" maneuver, Howard starts chasing after a female jogger. Raj screams, "What are you doing!? I can't scissors by myself!"

In the car on the way home, Howard tries to defend himself, "What was I supposed to do? She gave me that come-hither look." Raj, fuming, interjects, "If it was any look at all, it was a you-suck look! You always do this. Ditch me for a woman you don't have a shot with." Howard adamantly replies, "I had a shot!" Raj responds, "With a woman you were chasing in the park? That's not a shot, it's a felony." Later in Raj's apartment, Howard tries to apologize – by buying Raj a pink Hello Kitty kite. Howard finally admits, "Look, I haven't always been the best friend I could be."

The reason Raj is upset with Howard foreshadows Aristotle's second point about pleasure friendships. Friends for the sake of pleasure, he claims, are "so for the sake of what is pleasant for *themselves*" but not for the sake of the other.[5] Sheldon reveled in his throttling Hawking at "Words with Friends" and, after Hawking finally defeats Sheldon, Hawking phones to call him "Dr. Loser" and smugly likens him to a black hole: "They both suck – neener, neener." Returning to Raj and Howard, a true friend doesn't ditch you at Radio Shack to go make eyes with the girl working behind the counter at Hot Dog on a Stick – especially when you are there to find one of those phones with the big numbers for *his* mother. That (an unwed) Howard is always ready to ditch Raj for the slightest chance of scoring with a girl speaks volumes. He likes Raj and enjoys spending time with him, but he is really out for himself. A true friend wouldn't be so quick to put their interests ahead of yours.

"Kripke! What'd You Say of the Idea of You and I Becoming Friends?"

Utility-based friendships are made and sustained because they are useful or profitable to us in some way. The intended goal is more practical or pragmatic than pleasurable. Aristotle writes, "Those who pursue utility . . . sometimes . . . do not even find each other pleasant; therefore they do not need such companionship unless they are useful to each other; for they are pleasant to each other only in so far as they rouse in each other hopes of something good to come."[6] Again, there is nothing mercenary here. It's just that the primary motivation for being friends is that all involved benefit in some way.

Sheldon and Leonard's relationship began for reasons of utility. They became roommates because Leonard was looking for a nice place to live and Sheldon couldn't afford the rent all by himself. This also explains why Raj and Howard began hanging out with Sheldon. They like spending time with Leonard, but Leonard rooms with Sheldon. Furthermore, Sheldon and Leonard's relationship is also utilitarian insofar as the latter regularly drives the former to work. Sheldon doesn't drive (even after he secretly gets his license) and carpooling probably saves Leonard gas money. The fact that Leonard does not find their commutes all that pleasant only reinforces the idea that they are utility based.

Why does Aristotle deem utility friendships a lower form of friendship? His reasoning is analogous to what he says about pleasure friendships. Again, he doesn't see anything inherently wrong with them, and he doesn't believe that complete friendship should be without pragmatic benefits. His position rests on two familiar points.

First, Aristotle plausibly believes that these kinds of friendships are (also) readily dissolved. Once the intended practical benefit ceases, so does the friendship. Consider Sheldon's decision to befriend Barry Kripke in the season two episode "The Friendship Algorithm." (You know the guy with the lisp who, upon meeting Penny for the first time, said, "Yeah, it's not a vewy hot name. I'm gonna call you Woxanne.")

Kripke is a fellow member of the physics department at the university, but lacks the social skills that Sheldon, Leonard, Raj, and Howard take for granted. (Imagine.) In fact, he is altogether unlikable. Recall his snarky lunchroom comment to Leonard: "Heard about your watest pwoton decay expewiment, 20,000 data wuns and no statistically significant wesults. Vewy impwessive!" Howard reassures Leonard, "C'mon, don't let him get to you. It's Kripke"; and Raj chimes in, "Yeah, he's a ginormous knob." Howard confirms, "That's why he eats by himself, instead of sitting here at the cool table"; Raj testifies, "Fo' shizzle."

Nevertheless, Sheldon needs time on laboratory equipment that Kripke apparently controls. Leonard wishes Sheldon luck, because "the only people he lets use it are his friends." Even though Sheldon doesn't like Kripke (at all), Sheldon quickly surmises, "The solution is simple – I shall befriend him." Of course, Kripke has no "intewest" in becoming Sheldon's "fwiend." Upon crafting an elaborate flowchart, Sheldon seeks common ground with Barry, suggesting hot beverages, recreational activities, and monkeys. Kripke counters with horseback riding, swimming, and ventriloquism. Seeing that Sheldon is caught in an infinite loop, Howard quickly revises the flowchart, leading Sheldon to accept the least objectionable common interest: rock climbing – even though Sheldon is afraid of heights (or falling, or both).

Sheldon stands before the rock wall. He looks up, admitting that it appears more "monolithic" than it did on his laptop. He looks around for "hominids learning to use bones as weapons." Sensing Sheldon's discomfort, Kripke asks, "You afwaid of heights, Cooper?" So, up Sheldon goes, only to get stuck and pass out (after suffering a wee bit of incontinence.) Ironically, when Sheldon comes to, he learns that Kripke doesn't control who gets access to the equipment after all. Thus, the whole point of Sheldon striking up a friendship with him is nullified, leading Sheldon to conclude, "This entire endeavor seems to have been an exercise in futility."

The contrived nature of Sheldon's futile endeavor begins to capture Aristotle's second reason for classifying utility-based friendships as a lesser form of friendship. Similar to pleasure-based friendships, the focus is not the other person but what *you* get out of the relationship. Befriending someone simply for what *you* get out of it – be it pleasure or utility – seems, at best, hollow. This realization paves the way to Aristotle's third form of friendship.

"To Make Friends . . . Take an Interest in Their Lives"

For Aristotle, true friendship – what he calls "complete" or "perfect" friendship – is a relationship between (morally) good people, each of whom recognizes the good character of the other, and each of whom desires to preserve and promote the other's virtue simply because it is good to do so. True friendship occurs between equals – a relationship in which one person is vastly superior to the other seems more like a paternalistic relationship. As Aristotle says, "Perfect friendship is of [those] who are good, and alike in virtue; for these wish each other well alike to each other qua good, and they are good in themselves."[7] (Think of Kirk and Spock.)

Unlike pleasure and utility friendships, true friendships must involve genuine care for the well-being of the other person, not merely egoistic or self-serving motives. Of course, that doesn't mean that one may not consider how the friendship affects one's own interests. The idea is simply that one cares about the other person for his or her own sake and wants to see the other person flourish, regardless of any benefit that one might also receive as a result. (Think the *opposite* of David Underhill and Penny.) Still, as a matter of fact, Aristotle believes true friendships are beneficial to those involved. Thus, true friendship involves a happy convergence of self-interest and altruism and, as such, results in an ideal kind of moral motivation.

So, Aristotle believes the highest form of friendship occurs between persons of equally good moral character (virtue), which is enhanced due to their interactions. Such friendships are admittedly rare; when they do obtain, it is because the friends spend a great deal of time together, developing a secure mutual trust. Their relationship is fostered by participating in joint ventures, and engaging in activities that exercise their own virtues for the betterment of the other and the friendship. All of this is done primarily for the sake of the other person, even though their interests have grown so close together that it is difficult to separate them. Consequently, complete friendship results in a sort of second-self, a true partner.[8]

"That's Insane on the Face of It"

Let's see if we can find any traces of Aristotle's vision of true friendship in *The Big Bang Theory*. The three most promising examples are the "besties" Penny and Amy, self-proclaimed "best friends" Raj and Howard, and, of course, Leonard and Sheldon. We'll take a look at the first two now and explore the third in the next Section.

As suggested earlier, the fact that someone calls you a "bestie" is different from *being* best friends. It's also different from being a complete friend. Complete friendship requires meeting the conditions Aristotle specifies. Amy and Penny do become genuinely concerned about the welfare of one another. They enjoy their regular "girls' night" (with or without Raj) and Penny is grateful that Amy has taken Sheldon off Leonard's hands. But they don't share very many common interests. Penny is bored by quilting and medieval literature. Amy doesn't share Penny's penchant for enjoying wine or clubbing. Amy chooses Penny to be her maid-of-honor, but it's not clear that they are growing together in the right sorts of ways. Thus, while they are friends, they don't seem to be complete friends.

Howard and Raj also claim to be "best friends." They spend a great deal of time together and have many common interests. Furthermore, Howard asks Raj to be Halley's godfather, thereby solidifying an important place in the Wolowitzs's future. However, given Howard's propensity for self-absorption, if not plain selfishness, it's unclear whether he is a good candidate for complete friendship – with anyone (including Bernadette, unfortunately).

This unfortunate feature of Howard's character is on full display in the season 11 episodes "The Confidence Erosion" and the "Celebration Reverberation." As we've seen, to say that Howard is not always kind to Raj is an understatement. In "The Confidence Erosion," Sheldon perfunctorily states that by making fun of Raj, Howard is "doing what he loves." Later, while commiserating with his father on a video call about a failed job interview, Dr. Koothrappali proposes that Raj's woes have one source: "I bet it's those friends you surround yourself with. Like that Howard, always making fun of you . . . What kind of friend acts like that? . . . A bad friend." So, when Howard asks him to lunch, Raj declines. Howard asks, "Because the mean girls circled your chubby bits in marker?" Clearly upset, Raj replies, "No . . . I think our relationship has become toxic. I think you and I need to spend some time away." Rather than apologizing, Howard is callous: "I'm gonna need some ground rules. I mean, while we're apart, can I see other needy Indian men?"

In "The Celebration Reverberation," Howard informs the guys that there are no plans for Halley's first birthday because "Bernadette is on bedrest, and (clears his throat) I'm lazy." Bernadette convinces Howard otherwise. His party planning consists of asking Stuart whether he would bring a few things, namely, "balloons, streamers, ice, snacks, a bounce house, face painter, and a couple kids whose parents are willing to lie and say they know me from the 'Daddy and Me' class I've never been to." Howard has been deceptive about the time he and his daughter spend together each week. He is willing to spend time with Halley only if he can do what he wants. He cares little for what Bernadette (or eventually his daughter) thinks about this – assuming he doesn't get caught.

When Stuart bails on him, Howard becomes really desperate. He visits Raj and invites him to Halley's party. When Raj accepts, Howard is relieved, because "it is tomorrow and I need you to plan it." Raj is insulted – again – but he agrees to help Howard for Halley's sake. Howard's response – again – is disrespectful: "And I'm sure she'd appreciate it, if she knew what's going on or who you are." When the party does not go very well, Raj and Howard begin arguing – in the bouncy house Raj rented. Each laments, "You're my best friend and you hurt my feelings!" The fun of the bouncy house merely masks the tensions in their relationship, which go unresolved. Regardless of what Howard and Raj may claim, Aristotle would deny that they are complete friends. The problem is Howard's reluctance, if not inability, to see the interests of others as important as his own (which may impede his friendship with Bernadette if he doesn't correct for this defect).

". . . Promises to Be a Herculean Task"

Perhaps Leonard and Sheldon (arguably the Kirk and Spock of the show) are better candidates for complete friendship. They are both physicists and they are similar in terms of intellectual ability and (arguably) moral sensibilities. In addition, they spend a great deal of time together, share many common interests, and often help each other out. Sheldon memorably helped Leonard with the rocket fuel fiasco of 2002. (The elevator took the brunt of that one.) For his part, Leonard is tolerant of Sheldon's various idiosyncrasies, and he teaches Sheldon about sarcasm.

But the wrinkle is obvious: From early on, Sheldon has difficulty with *any* sort of meaningful relationship. In the season one episode "The Jerusalem Duality," and in the context of Dennis Kim "falling prey to the inexplicable need for human contact," Sheldon flatly states, "social relationships will continue to baffle and repulse me." In the season two episode "The Bad Fish Paradigm," he is completely caught off guard by Penny's contention that "friendship contains within it an inherent obligation to maintain confidences." He is even more baffled that they had become friends at all.

True, in the season three episode "The Electronic Can Opener Fluctuation," Sheldon asserts, "Leonard is my best friend in the world." However, he constantly interprets their relationship via the friendship rider of the roommate agreement. In "The Cornhusker Vortex," Leonard is surprised to learn that Sheldon knows football. (Quidditch, sure. But football?) Because Leonard is desperate to better fit in with Penny's friends, he pleads, "Please, I'm asking you as a friend." Sheldon woodenly replies: "Are you making this a tier-one friendship request?" Taking what he can get, Leonard shrewdly replies, "Yes." Sheldon (sighing) replies, "Fine."

Yet Sheldon has great difficulty moving past utility-based friendships. Recall in the season three episode "The Large Hadron Collision" that Leonard is chosen to visit the CERN supercollider. This is an awesome professional opportunity, and he is allowed to bring a guest. Because the trip falls over Valentine's Day, Leonard wants to bring Penny. Sheldon will have none of this: "I call your attention to the Friendship Rider in Appendix C, Future Commitments. Number 37, in the event one friend is ever invited to visit the Large Hadron Collider, now under construction in Switzerland, he shall invite the other friend to accompany him." Leonard begs Sheldon not to enforce this, but Sheldon adamantly replies, "I've lived up to all my commitments under the agreement. At least once a day I ask how you are, even though I simply don't care." But Leonard remains firm. He's taking Penny. Sheldon feels betrayed and likens his so-called best friend to Benedict Arnold, Judas, and Rupert Murdoch (the despot ultimately responsible for canceling his beloved *Firefly*).

Sheldon soon has a change of heart, though, or so it seems. He wakes Leonard up with the soothing sounds of a wooden flute, which he plays himself, and surprises him with breakfast in bed. Smiling, Leonard asks why Sheldon is doing all of this. Sheldon humbly answers, "It's by way of an apology for my recent behavior. I've had some time to reflect and I've come to realize that friendship is not an aggregation of written agreements. It's a result of two people respecting and caring for each other."

Aha! Is this the *Big Bang Theory* friendship breakthrough we've been looking for? Alas, when Leonard coyly adds, "Great. Still not taking you to Switzerland," Sheldon promptly removes the breakfast tray from Leonard's bed and unceremoniously leaves the room. Sheldon is happy to *act* as if he is Leonard's complete friend, but only if Leonard takes him to Switzerland. Sheldon seemingly knows what true friendship entails, but he simply cannot bring himself to act on that knowledge. He prefers relationships grounded in contractual agreements.

Sometimes Sheldon's egoistic tendencies prevent him keeping utility-based arrangements. For example, when Leonard is unsure of whether he should help Penny with her slavery essay and Sheldon is afraid that Hawking will cease being his "Words with Friends" friend, Leonard suggests that they share their respective troubles with the help of a chess timer. Each five-minute turn will consist of a statement and a helpful response from the other. Leonard kindly lets Sheldon go first, and he does his best to offer advice about Hawking. Sheldon does not reciprocate – at all. When Leonard calls him out and reminds him about the agreement to be helpful, Sheldon replies, "It sucks to be you." Exasperated, Leonard quits. Sheldon is shocked (of course), lamenting, "Leonard, wait. No. I listened to your dumb thing."

In the season seven episode "The Proton Displacement," Arthur Jefferies (aka Professor Proton) flatly asks Leonard, "Why do you put up with Sheldon?" To which Leonard replies, "Uh, oh, you know, because we're friends." Unsatisfied, Arthur asks, "Why?" A bit unsure of himself, Leonard finally answers, "Sheldon is the smartest person

I have ever met. And he's a little broken and he needs me. I guess I need him, too." Arthur remains skeptical: "Why is that?" Arthur's questions are not idle. It's unlikely that Sheldon believes he is broken or in need of improvement. In fact, Sheldon tends to believe that everyone besides him is defective in one way or another. Perhaps this is why Arthur believes that Leonard, who admits his shortcomings and works to correct them, is arguably better off without Sheldon.

Although Sheldon grows as a person over the course of the series, his difficulty in seeing the interests of others on par with his prevents him from developing complete friendships. In season 10, he acknowledges that possessing a device that reads human emotions would make him a more considerate friend. (Of course, it would also help him identify his enemies and their fears, which he would use to destroy them.) In season 11, when he kindly offers to stop his work so that Amy can sleep, she appreciates his consideration. He explains: "I know. See, I'm trying this new technique where I imagine how I would feel in someone else's position." To which, Amy hesitantly says, "You mean empathy?" That Sheldon believes his approach is novel only highlights his unfamiliarity with meeting others as equals. Similar to Howard, Sheldon seems too self-absorbed or self-centered to be complete friends with anyone. Perhaps Amy eventually can help Sheldon smooth out this character defect, but she has a Herculean task in front of her![9]

"There is No Algorithm for Making Friends!"

Perhaps Aristotle would claim that none of the characters of *The Big Bang Theory* are complete friends. But it is difficult to deny that they have become good friends. This might lead us to reconsider Aristotle's account of friendship. His account is undoubtedly influential, but is it too idealistic or perhaps outmoded (or both)? Aristotle certainly seems correct that there are different levels of friendship and that true friendship requires genuine care and concern for the other, but perhaps we don't need to be that much alike to achieve it?

Consider Leonard and Penny. Aristotle might object that they cannot be complete friends because of their lack of shared interests, disparity between their intellectual abilities, and (arguably) dissimilar moral sensibilities. In fact, their intellectual differences caused stress the first time they dated. In "The Bad Fish Paradigm" Penny asks Sheldon if Leonard has dated "regular girls" before. Sheldon confesses that Leonard hasn't dated very many "non-brainiacs." Penny then hesitantly asks, "Do you think he'll eventually get bored with me?" Sheldon replies, "That depends. Do you have a working knowledge of quantum physics? Do you speak Klingon?" Penny interrupts, "I get it. Leonard has no business being involved with a waitress-slash-actress who felt so insecure, that she lied to him about finishing community college."

Yet Leonard and Penny never gave up on each other. In fact, they continued to grow together throughout the duration of the series. It wasn't always a smooth journey, but they eventually got to the place where they made each other better. In fact, in the season seven episode "The Mommy Observation" Stuart claims they are the best couple he knows. He explains: "I feel like you guys make each other better. Penny brought Leonard out of his shell. And it seems like Leonard makes Penny think more deeply about the world . . . Together, you two kind of make one awesome person." Where Howard and Sheldon (respectively) fail, Leonard and Penny prevail. Their interests have become so intertwined that it is now difficult to separate them. They are a second-self for each other, or as Stuart says, they have all but become one person. This is the pinnacle of Aristotelian complete friendship.

So, intentional or not, perhaps *The Big Bang Theory* offers a corrective to Aristotle's account of friendship. Perhaps similarities in shared interests, intellectual prowess, and moral sensibilities take a back seat to the willingness to recognize your own "broken-ness" and work with a like-minded partner to correct them to the point that your interests grow together. In the end, you become "like one awesome person."

Any sort of algorithm that covers all cases of friendship will be controversial. Still, perhaps here we've explored enough about friendship to guard against having or becoming a "a sucky, sucky friend." Beyond that, perhaps the only way to know what makes someone a true friend is to have one and be one.[10]

For pop culture resources and philosophical resources related to this chapter please visit the website for this book: https://introducingphilosophythroughpopculture.com.

Notes

1   Aristotle. (1941). *Nicomachean Ethics* (trans. W.D. Ross) in *The Basic Works of Aristotle* (ed. R. McKeon), 1058. New York: Random House. Hereafter citations of Aristotle's *Nicomachean Ethics* will appear via the standard margin number signaled by "*NE*." The margin number for this quote is 1155a 5–6.
2   *NE*, 1156a 3–5.
3   *NE*, 1156b 9–10.
4   *NE*, 1156a32–33.
5   *NE*, 1156a 15–17, emphasis in the original.
6   *NE*, 1156a 27–30.
7   *NE*, 1156b 7–9.
8   See *NE*, 1156b 24–28, 1157b 33–36, 1166a 29–32.
9   To be fair, Sheldon leaves the viewer a glimmer of hope. With the final words of his acceptance speech – and the series – he addresses Leonard, Penny, Raj, Howard, and Bernadette, "I apologize if I have not been the friend you deserve, but I want you to know in my way I love you all."
10 My thanks to the webmasters at http://bigbangtrans.wordpress.com and https://transcripts. foreverdreaming.org/for episode dialogue. Each section title is taken from "The Friendship Algorithm."

24

"You Are Asking Me to Be Rational"

Stoic Philosophy and the Jedi Order

Matt Hummel

Summary

The Jedi are "keepers of the peace." Just as they protect the galaxy, Jedi are called upon to keep the peace within themselves by aligning their wills to the Force. This requires self-restraint, abstinence from worldly pleasures, a virtue-driven mind-set, incorruptible fearlessness, and total belief in following the will of the Force. The principles of the Jedi Order closely mirror the "hard life" maxims of a school of philosophy known as Stoicism, represented by the slave-turned-philosopher Epictetus. For both Jedi and Stoics, philosophy is a way of life, not just a subject for study. A central claim of Stoic ethics is that only virtues and virtuous activities are good, and only vices and vicious actions are evil. A Jedi's strength of mind has greater value than any Force ability or skill with a lightsaber. The ultimate goal for Jedi is to decipher the will of the Force and conduct themselves accordingly.

How does a young boy go from slave on Tatooine to angst-ridden apprentice, to con-flicted Jedi knight, to Sith lord? The prequel *Star Wars* trilogy tells the origin story of the iconic sci-fi villain Darth Vader. When *The Phantom Menace* hit theaters in 1999, audi-ences eagerly anticipated Anakin Skywalker's transformation into the black-clad intimi-dator who blasted his way on screen more than two decades earlier. And from the moment the dusty little boy in Watto's shop asked Padmé if she was an angel, people wondered what the big turning point was going to be. Over the course of the prequel trilogy, it became clear. It was Anakin's failure to understand the philosophical perspec-tive of the Jedi that ruined his chance of becoming one.

The Jedi are "keepers of the peace." Just as they protect the galaxy, Jedi are also called upon to keep the peace *within themselves* by aligning their wills to the Force. This requires self-restraint, abstinence from worldly pleasures, a virtue-driven mindset, incorruptible fearlessness, and total belief in following the will of the Force. As Jedi mas-ter Qui-Gon Jinn warns a young, overeager Anakin, "Training to become a Jedi is not an easy challenge, and even if you succeed, it's a hard life."

Introducing Philosophy Through Pop Culture: From Socrates to Star Wars *and Beyond*, Second Edition.
Edited by William Irwin and David Kyle Johnson.
© 2022 John Wiley & Sons Ltd. Published 2022 by John Wiley & Sons Ltd.

As we'll see, the principles of the Jedi Order closely mirror the "hard life" maxims of a school of philosophy known as Stoicism, represented by the slave-turned-philosopher Epictetus (c. 55–135). The comparison begins a long time ago in a city far, far away . . .

Master of the Stoic Arts

Both Anakin and Epictetus were slaves eventually freed by their wealthy masters; both lived in the era of a power-crazy emperor[1]; and both went on to study a life-changing discipline. While Anakin entered a well-established disciplinary order of more than "1000 generations," Epictetus studied and built upon a tradition of Stoicism based on principles more than three centuries old.[2] For both Jedi and Stoics, philosophy is a way of life, not just a subject for study. Epictetus advised people to seek virtue through wisdom, to become conscious of what is and is not in their control, and to avert themselves from pleasure and pain by being aware of the present and practicing indifference.

A central claim of Stoic ethics is that only virtues and virtuous activities are good, and only vices and vicious actions are evil.[3] Stoic virtue is the capacity to recognize and use the advantages of a situation wisely, like recognizing that "greed can be a powerful ally" in manipulating an avaricious junk-dealer. Vice involves using advantages but solely for personal gain. In *Revenge of the Sith*, Palpatine tries to convince Anakin that the Jedi are just as lustful for power as the Sith. Anakin responds that the Jedi selflessly "care only about others," while the Sith "think inwards, only of themselves." For Epictetus, being virtuous and progressing toward personal excellence means understanding the true nature of one's being and keeping one's moral character in the right condition.[4] The same could be said of the Jedi who seek to align themselves with the will of the Force rather than selfishly exploit its power.

What is *power*? The Force provides great power to those who know how to use it, even those who don't fully know they have it. Qui-Gon says as much about young Anakin: "He has special powers . . . He can see things before they happen." Power, however, is more than just special abilities. Epictetus asserts that true power lies in the capacity to adapt oneself to circumstances by making proper judgments of what's in a person's control:

> Some things are up to us and some things are not up to us. Our opinions are up to us, and our impulses, desires, aversions–in short, whatever is our own doing. Our bodies are not up to us, nor are our possessions, our reputations, or our public offices, or, that is, whatever is not our own doing.[5]

People have power over their own minds. The opinions they hold, the intentions they form, the interests they develop, what they value, and to what they're averse are all wholly up to them individually. What disturbs people is not what happens to them but their judgments on those happenings.[6] Stoic *strength of mind* is quintessential to Jedi training – keeping them from slipping into uncontrollable feelings like hate and anguish. The need for a well-disciplined mind is why the Jedi council usually refuses to train people past a certain age. "Younglings" haven't lived long enough to form desirous attachments, so they can be trained more easily to be mindful of their feelings and cultivate detachment. Remaining calm in the face of adversity and controlling one's emotions no matter the provocation are qualities often referred to as "stoic." They're developed in the full Stoic sense by making proper use of one's awareness – in Jedi terms, being "mindful of the living Force."

Awareness is the ability to "see each particular event in the context of the whole."[7] The wisest Jedi can perceive events within the context of the will of the Force. When Obi-Wan stops an impatient Anakin from rushing into a bar after the bounty hunter Zam Wesell, he admonishes his padawan, "Patience. Use the Force. Think. He went in there to hide, not to run." Though it seems Obi-Wan is simply instructing Anakin in the simplistic ways of criminals, he's actually teaching a greater lesson about awareness of the Force – that it's a grand design that can be understood rationally. The Jedi would refer to it as the unifying Force that "binds" the galaxy together creating an ultimate destiny.[8] Mastering awareness involves understanding the unifying Force along with its complement in the living Force, which "flows" through each passing moment.[9] Qui-Gon identifies the difference to Obi-Wan before their "negotiations" with the Trade Federation, instructing his padawan to "keep [his] concentration here and now, where it belongs" rather than become over-anxious about his "bad feeling." For Anakin, making proper use of his awareness would require steady practice of what Epictetus calls "indifference."

Since Jedi must focus on the present to determine the will of the Force, they must remain *detached* from whatever might distract their concentration, especially deep or romantic relationships with other people. Epictetus refers to these potential distractions as *indifferent*.[10] Matters of indifference have no intrinsic value, but they can be made use of in service of living virtuously or in accord with the will of the Force. Typically preferred are things like health, wealth, and companionship while "dispreferred" are things like sickness, poverty, and social exclusion. Obi-Wan prefers not to fly, which he thinks "is for droids," but when flying a starfighter into battle is required to protect the galaxy – a fact beyond Obi-Wan's control – he's indifferent toward it. He judges the value of flying within the greater context of the unifying Force and so does his duty as a peacekeeper.

Thus, the Stoic principles of the Jedi Order are revealed:

• Strive for wisdom and live virtuously by following the will of the Force, not seeking personal gain.
• Remain mindful of what is in one's control and so use the Force as a means for good.
• Maintain awareness of events within the context of the unifying Force.
• Do not be concerned with matters of indifference – things out of one's control.

A Jedi's strength of mind has greater value than any Force ability or skill with a lightsaber. Epictetus was able to discern and practice Stoicism in our galaxy as well as any Jedi master. But the latently powerful Anakin fails to understand the true path of Stoic philosophy for the "hard life" of a Jedi. Even if we knew nothing about Anakin's future as a Force-choke master, it would be evident over the course of the prequel trilogy that he's not destined to be a successful Jedi.

Unlimited Power?

It's hard to see Anakin in *The Phantom Menace* as anything other than an adventurous kid, a typical boy, with some keen abilities and a disregard for authority. What then causes Obi-Wan to warn his master, "The boy is dangerous"? Precisely the fact that Anakin *is a typical boy*, complete with a forward-looking vision and lack of patience. Young Anakin is very interested in status and power. He defensively corrects Padmé when she calls him a "slave": "I'm a *person* and my name is Anakin." He eagerly tells Qui-Gon he's the only human who can race pods and that he's built the fastest one ever. And he ambitiously wants to be the first person to see all the planets in the galaxy.

More importantly, young Anakin has misconceptions about power. He doesn't think of power in terms of good judgment but instead as the ability to do amazing things: "No one can kill a Jedi"; "I had a dream I was a Jedi. I came back here and freed all the slaves." Certainly, this is typical thinking for a young boy, and Qui-Gon seems convinced it's only a matter of "time and training" before Anakin realizes the true complexity of the Force and the passive approach to power through wisdom espoused by the Jedi.[11] True to Stoic form, the basics of Jedi teaching involve searching our feelings and using our instincts in wading through a complicated situation. But Anakin doesn't recognize the complexity of his circumstances, nor does he practice the Jedi way of making proper judgments. This troubles Obi-Wan, but he still agrees to train Anakin.

Anakin's fascination with power grows as he learns Jedi skills, and it manifests as arrogance when he brags that he's "really ahead of" Obi-Wan, claiming that he's ready to take the trials to become a Jedi Knight. Worse, his dreams of freeing all the slaves and visiting every planet get replaced by premonitions of his suffering mother and "intoxicating" thoughts about Padmé. With a growing lust for power and zero concentration on the will of the Force, Anakin becomes overly confident in his ability to prevent tragedies in his life. After Anakin's mother's death, Padmé consoles Anakin by reminding him that he isn't all-powerful and so shouldn't feel guilty for failing to save her. Anakin loses his cool, promising to someday learn to stop people from dying. This emotional scene shows how utterly devoid of peace Anakin is and how likely he is to turn to the dark side.

When Anakin suffers a nightmarish premonition of Padmé's death, he promises her that he won't let this dream become real – yet another misconception about power. Anakin's problem is a lack of self-reflection about whether his premonition about Padmé's death is real or what his role in it is. When it comes to Padmé, Anakin seems fully confident that he can stop her death, yet he admits he's completely powerless over his feelings of love for her. He's unable to "wish [his] feelings away" precisely because he doesn't understand the kind of power that's in his capacity. "Wishing his feelings away" is just what *is* in his power according to Epictetus; controlling the fates of others is not. Failure to see the difference leads Anakin straight to Palpatine, who convinces him that secret powers over life and death are within the arsenal of the dark side. Anakin takes on the mantle of Darth Vader to save his wife, but in the end, it doesn't matter. Padmé dies from losing the will to live – an arguably preventable disease by Stoic standards – and Anakin suffers another blow to his conception of power. Even after Padmé's death, Anakin refuses to face the truth of his own powerlessness. Rather, he forsakes reason and remains sworn to the dark side.

"Fear is the Path to the Dark Side"

Jedi Masters present a calm, stoic face to adversity and danger. They aren't thrill-seekers: "adventure, excitement, a Jedi craves not these things." Few Jedi would readily plummet from a hover-speeder in the all-day rush hour of Coruscant. Rather, the Jedi replace fear by opening themselves to the will of the Force, akin to surrendering the will to reason. Epictetus claims that reason is "where nature itself has fixed [people's] end."[12] Our ultimate goal is to discern and live harmoniously with nature.[13] The ultimate goal for Jedi is to decipher the will of the Force and conduct themselves accordingly. Jedi have nothing to fear by living within the Force's graces, even if it leads to death – for this is also the will of the Force – whereas the Sith fear death. Darth Plagueis the Wise experimented night and day to learn how to influence the Force to create life and overpower death;[14] and his apprentice, Darth Sidious, used cloning technology to create new bodies to incorporate his malevolent spirit.[15] For his part, Anakin's fear of death is rooted in the threat of loss.

Anakin's fear is palpable as he starts the journey with Qui-Gon on Tatooine. Anakin immediately turns back to his mother, expressing his fear of never seeing her again. Shmi Skywalker shows Jedi-like wisdom when she instructs Ani to consult his heart whether they'll see each other again. Shmi is essentially telling Anakin to search his feelings, to seek virtue through yet-unrevealed wisdom. The young Anakin wholly misses her point, shrugging it off as encouraging mom-talk. But the fear of losing his mother stays with him through his initial review by the Jedi council when Yoda tells Anakin, "Fear leads to anger. Anger leads to hate. Hate leads to suffering." To suffer is to believe and behave contrary to the will of the Force – or of *nature*, as the Stoics would say.

Anakin's fear later leads him to experience nightmares and premonitions of death. His Jedi skills give him a clairvoyant vision of the future, but he never seeks the virtue of *understanding* what his visions mean; nor does he heed Yoda's warning: "Careful you must be when sensing the future, Anakin. Fear of loss is a path to the dark side." Instead of guiding his actions with reason, his fear leads him away from his duty to guard Padmé in order to save his mother from torment. Upon finding her, he suffers the pain that comes from not contemplating the will of the Force and is left only with the fear and remorse that his mother suffered terribly before dying in his arms. He slaughters the Tusken Raiders and broods in hatred over what they did to Shmi. The way in which Jedi face dread is important. In *Revenge of the Sith*, Obi-Wan hopes against hope that the security recordings at the decimated Jedi Temple will not show his friend attacking their fellow Jedi. Upon realizing the truth, however, Obi-Wan doesn't sink into despair and anger. Instead, he tries to figure out what he missed, consulting the Force for guidance in a matter beyond his own wisdom. Obi-Wan's trust in the Force shields him from the fear of loss both of his friend and the entire Jedi Order.

Sympathy with Anakin's fear of losing the women in his life perhaps points to a valid criticism of the Jedi and their Stoic principles: what should count as matters of *indifference*? On the refugee ship, Anakin makes the argument that Jedi are encouraged to love and that creating and maintaining bonds of "unconditional love" – which is how Anakin interprets the Jedi call to *compassion* – "is central to a Jedi's life." More likely than not, he's being openly facetious here in order to flirt with Padmé, but perhaps Anakin really does believe Jedi *should be allowed* to have relationships. It seems cold and inhuman to say that strong love for other people as well as thoughts of the suffering and deaths of those individuals are mere matters of indifference. Yoda, though, highlights the error in Anakin's argument. He reminds Anakin that "death is a natural part of life" and is to be celebrated as people "transform into the Force." Yoda is exhorting Anakin to be aware of the greater context of life itself – that even in death, beings are an extension of the living Force. It's not that love is forbidden, but love for the Force should be greater. There's no suffering when one lives according to the will of the Force; so Yoda invites Anakin not to mourn or miss those who are gone and not to fear the loss of others: "Learn to let go of everything you fear to lose." Yoda's sentiment rings true in Epictetus's *Handbook*: "If you want your children, and your wife, and your friends to live for ever, you are stupid; since you are wanting things that are not up to you to be up to you . . . Exercise yourself, then, in what is within your power."[16] Anakin has the power to control his fear, seek virtue, and even find solace through wisdom. But his misunderstanding of power only compounds his fear of loss, driving him to the dark side.

As we've seen, lust for power and fear of loss dominate in the downfall of Anakin Skywalker. But underneath all this, Anakin seems most guilty of un-mindfulness on a grand scale: he doesn't get it, and never has. Qui-Gon tries to explain midi-chlorians to him before embarking for Naboo. He tells Ani that midi-chlorians live inside all living cells and allow the Jedi to discern the will of the Force. Anakin cannot understand Qui-Gon's lesson that tiny things can communicate in big ways. Even after ten years of training, he still fails to understand smaller events within the context of bigger pictures, a crucial mindset for the Jedi. While in pursuit of Count Dooku, Padmé falls out of the ship and Anakin gets into a shouting match with Obi-Wan about the greater good of the galaxy. The selfishness of the dark side peeks through their transaction as Anakin demands the ship turn around to rescue Padmé. Only by couching his argument in reference to Padmé's desires does Obi-Wan convince Anakin that the potential to end the Clone Wars before they really start is worth leaving Padmé behind. Obi-Wan understands power in Stoic terms. True power is awareness of the "divine governance" of all things – the will of the Force – even in the most trivial of human affairs, and to be "moved by it."[17] The wisest Jedi subordinate their lives to the life of the entire universe and recognize themselves as one piece of a greater whole. Anakin's ultimate downfall can be found in him placing his fears and desires for misunderstood power above that of the greater order of all.

"From My Point of View, the Jedi are Evil!"

The real tragedy of Anakin's story is something never shown in the films. Somewhere between *Attack of the Clones* and *Revenge of the Sith*, Anakin develops a dangerously close relationship with Chancellor Palpatine. Why he elects to confide in Palpatine remains unsaid other than Anakin's statement that "he's watched over me ever since I arrived here." Befriending Palpatine gets Anakin started in questioning the Jedi Order. Despite the twisted deceit of the Sith lord, there are things about the Jedi way that seem to contradict Stoic philosophy and are worth questioning.

For starters, the infamous Jedi mind trick threatens the idea that a person has control of their own thoughts.[18] The Jedi may reply that the Force persuasion technique is simply that – *persuasion*, not mind control. Yet Qui-Gon tries to use the Force to persuade Watto to accept Republic credits in exchange for a new hyperdrive. If the trick had worked on the Toydarian, Qui-Gon would've effectively stolen a hyperdrive, since the credits were worthless on the desert planet. Watto is a greedy dealer, so maybe he deserves to be swindled, but a Stoic wouldn't agree. A true Stoic would be concerned about the potential immorality of Force persuasion.

On a wider scale, the Jedi's agreement to participate in the Clone Wars doesn't come across as a Stoic decision. It amounts to trying to influence an outcome beyond one's power. Epictetus calls the realization that there are conflicting opinions the very beginning of philosophy.[19] But entering the Clone Wars isn't a Jedi attempt to sway opinion in their favor. Rather, they are acting as "guardians of the Republic." It's also difficult to clearly judge the worthiness of either side in the conflict as both are masterminded by Darth Sidious. Blindness to the Sith's dealings shows a flaw in the Jedi's reasoning ability, a flaw they're conscious of and try to keep hidden. Their investigation of the Chancellor operates in the same kind of moral gray area as Force persuasion. When Anakin is asked to spy on Palpatine, he's being asked to cooperate in a deception that serves the Council's interest but is perhaps betraying its own principles, as he points out to Obi-Wan: "You're asking me to do something against the Jedi Code, against the Republic, against a mentor and a friend."

Finally, the attempted assassination of Palpatine more clearly accentuates what is suspect about the Jedi's belief in their inability to control others. Mace Windu and a cohort of Jedi approach the Chancellor initially to arrest him. But when the revealed Darth Sidious attacks and kills all but Mace Windu, the powerful Jedi Master is forced to fight back and corner the Sith. Anakin arrives in time to see Windu with his lightsaber at the Chancellor's throat. Sidious is clearly subdued and, with Anakin there, the plan could reasonably revert back to arrest. Mace, however, exclaims, "He's too dangerous to be left alive!" Despite Anakin's pleas to put Palpatine on trial, Mace raises his lightsaber for a deadly strike. Anakin protects Sidious for his own benefit, but in a way he's also playing the more Stoic role. While the Jedi are sworn to destroy the Sith, a full assault on the defenseless Sidious doesn't fit the defensive, passive position of action guided by reason. Master Windu isn't heeding Master Yoda's lesson, "A Jedi uses the Force for knowledge and defense, *never* for attack." The will of the Force always seems to come into play when a Jedi slays a living being, like when Mace Windu defends himself against Jango Fett on Geonosis. The bounty hunter attacks him, and he eliminates his attacker; likewise when Obi-Wan kills General Grievous. But even those killings stand out as odd for the Jedi, who usually seem more content with disarming (literally) their foes. The preference to *neutralize* threats seems more in line with seeking virtue through wisdom than *elimination* of one's foes, even if they are genuinely evil. Jedi are called to refrain from desiring what isn't theirs and to refrain from lamenting what isn't in their control.[20] The existence of vice in the form of the Sith isn't in their control and neither is Anakin's choice to hold a different point of view. Perhaps the Jedi's extreme attitude toward the Sith is what's actually causing the "imbalance" in the Force that Anakin is destined to correct.

"You Underestimate My Power!"

There's no doubt that Anakin Skywalker was a powerful Jedi, and his power and fears surrounding them seems to run in the family. In the *Star Wars* sequel trilogy, Luke sequesters himself from the rest of the galaxy for ten years, cutting himself off from the Force because he fears his own emotional instability.21 For all his power, Anakin assures his transition to the dark side by failing to learn the key principles of Stoic philosophy according to the Jedi Order. Virtue through wisdom, mindfulness, and the practice of indifference escaped the aspiring Jedi from day one. But maybe he has more self-knowledge than we give him credit for, since he plainly admits his failure when he awkwardly professes his love for Padmé: "You are asking me to be rational. That is something I know I cannot do."

For pop culture resources and philosophical resources related to this chapter please visit the website for this book: https://introducingphilosophythroughpopculture.com.

Notes

1 Gill, C. (1995). Introduction to *Epictetus, The Discourses, The Handbook, Fragments* (ed. C. Gill), (trans. R. Hard). London: J.M. Dent, Orion Publishing Group, xiii. According to the chronology of this book, Epictetus endured the reign of the Roman tyrant Nero. *The Discourses* was actually written by his student Flavius Arrian. *The Handbook* features maxims selected by Arrian which were drawn from *Discourses*, and *Fragments* are extracts from other ancient works that seem to be influenced by Arrian.
2 Gill, xix.
3 Epictetus (1885). *The Discourses*, 94, 123.
4 Epictetus, *Discourses*, 13, 65.
5 Epictetus, *Discourses*, 287.
6 Epictetus, *Discourses*, 289.
7 Epictetus, *Discourses*, 16.
8 http://starwars.wikia.com/wiki/Unifying_Force
9 http://starwars.wikia.com/wiki/Living_Force
10 Epictetus, *Discourses*, 8–10, 86–7.
11 Epictetus, *Discourses*, 8.
12 Epictetus, *Discourses*, 17.
13 Epictetus, *Discourses*, 17
14 See Luceno, J. (2012). *Star Wars: Darth Plagueis*. New York: Del Rey.
15 See Veitch, T. (2010). *Dark Empire Trilogy*. Milwaukee, OR: Dark Horse Books.
16 Epictetus, *Handbook*, 291.
17 Epictetus, *Discourses*, 37.
18 Epictetus, *Discourses*, 8–10.
19 Epictetus, *Discourses*, 99.
20 Epictetus, *Discourses*, 274.

Part VI

Challenges to Traditional Ethics

Introduction

Traditional approaches to ethics have come under attack since the late nineteenth century. Karl Marx (1818–1883) explained that "religion is the opium of the people" and Friedrich Nietzsche (1844–1900) declared that "God is dead." Existentialist philosophers stressed the importance of choosing one's own values and living authentically, and feminist philosophers challenged the male bias of traditional ethical theories.

Taking us beyond good and evil, in Chapter 25, Arno Bogaerts examines Superman, the man of steel, to explain the Übermensch, Nietzsche's ideal figure. The Übermensch exercises the will to power to create himself, and Disney's Moana listens to the voice inside to make herself an independent wayfinder. Accordingly, in Chapter 26, William Devlin takes us on an existentialist tour of a Polynesian island where the princess resists attempts to define her role. Instead, Moana follows the Sartrean philosophy of freedom and responsibility to journey beyond the reef and become an authentic individual.

Moana is an inspirational character, particularly for young girls. Yet the philosopher Simone de Beauvoir (1908–1986) famously argued that "One is not born, but rather becomes, a woman." Fittingly, in Chapter 27, J. Lenore Wright considers a feminist icon, Wonder Woman, who must struggle and break boundaries to make her way in a male-dominated world. Historically, women's voices have been marginalized, and until recently ethical theory has come from a male perspective. One feminist challenge to traditional philosophy is the ethics of care. In the blockbuster film *Avatar*, the Na'vi people seek to align themselves with the will of female deity, Eywa – their Great Mother. In Chapter 28, Dunn and Michaud argue that the will of Eywa echoes the care perspective of feminist ethics rather than the "justice perspective" of traditional ethics. Today more and more philosophers recognize that ethics must not only challenge the male focus, but

Introducing Philosophy Through Pop Culture: From Socrates to Star Wars *and Beyond*, Second Edition.
Edited by William Irwin and David Kyle Johnson.
© 2022 John Wiley & Sons Ltd. Published 2022 by John Wiley & Sons Ltd.

must re-examine our human-centeredness. *Avatar* once again can lend a helping hand. In Chapter 29, Jeremy Bendik-Keymer looks to the Na'vi people to teach humanity a lesson about environmental ethics. Developing deep humanity means we need to become ecocentric, recognizing our connections to all living things.

25

Rediscovering Nietzsche's Übermensch in Superman as a Heroic Ideal

Arno Bogaerts

Summary

Echoes of Nietzsche's influential yet ill-defined "superman" are found in many stories featuring the Man of Steel. Despite the similarities in name, most scholars perceive the DC Comics superhero and the philosophical concept as nearly polar opposites. In contrast to those scholars, this chapter proposes that Nietzsche's concept, originally a heroic ideal, can be reinstated as such in the character of Superman himself.

Behold! I teach you the superman: he is this lightning, he is this madness!
– Friedrich Nietzsche, Thus Spoke Zarathustra

Very few philosophical concepts have been as closely linked to the superhero genre and the mythology of its greatest representative, Superman, as the *Übermensch*.[1] The influential German philosopher Friedrich Nietzsche (1844–1900) described this idea of a "superman," capable of feats far beyond those of mortal men (sound familiar?), in his seminal work *Thus Spoke Zarathustra*.[2] Since then, it has been interpreted by many writers, not least of whom is comic book writer Grant Morrison, who mentioned it in his recent superhero history-slash-autobiography *Supergods* (2011), and who even gave Nietzsche a cameo in the comic book *All-Star Superman* #10 (2008). In that book, we saw the nineteenth-century philosopher writing *Thus Spoke Zarathustra* in a series of panels portraying real-life events that eventually culminated in the creation of Superman in the 1930s by Jerry Siegel and Joe Shuster.

Despite the name connection, however, most scholars see Siegel and Shuster's Superman and Nietzsche's Übermensch as nearly polar opposites. This stems mainly from a conflict in moral values that resulted from the changing ways both supermen have been interpreted over the years. The comic book hero Superman grew from a social crusader and a "champion of the oppressed" in the 1930s, to a patriotic and paternalistic fighter for "Truth, Justice and the American Way" in the 1940s and 1950s, to a compassionate

Introducing Philosophy Through Pop Culture: From Socrates to Star Wars and Beyond, Second Edition.
Edited by William Irwin and David Kyle Johnson.
© 2022 John Wiley & Sons Ltd. Published 2022 by John Wiley & Sons Ltd.

Christ-like savior in the latter part of the twentieth century – and always defending the Judeo-Christian values upheld by the American majority. Nietzsche's "superman," on the other hand, firmly rejects the very same values its superhero namesake upholds.

Because of the Übermensch's glorification of power, favoring the strong over the weak, and its subsequent misuse by the Nazi regime during World War II, the Übermensch pretty much went from a goal that humanity should aspire toward, to a frightening, amoral creature that humanity should try to avoid. While it has certainly been a common trope in the superhero genre and popular culture in general to characterize figures explicitly based on Nietzsche's Übermensch as inhuman monsters, I will argue that Nietzsche's concept – originally a heroic (if not super heroic!) ideal – can be reinstated through the character of Superman himself.

Truth, Justice, and the Nietzschean Way

But first, let us find out just what Nietzsche meant by Übermensch and the place of the concept in his overall philosophy. We find glimpses of it looming throughout the philosopher's work, but it is in *Thus Spoke Zarathustra* where Nietzsche – or rather, his mouthpiece, the prophet Zarathustra – comes down from the mountain and metaphorically describes several characteristics of this revolutionary higher form of humanity. The Übermensch remains quite an elusive figure, however, because Zarathustra never precisely defines the term. Furthermore, since Nietzsche had an extremely lyrical writing style, especially in *Zarathustra*, the Übermensch is left open to interpretation.[3]

To understand Nietzsche is to understand his famous claim that "God is dead." No, the Almighty wasn't slain by Doomsday or anything. Rather, Nietzsche claimed that humanity's *belief* in a personal, all-caring God as the foundation of our conventional, objective moral values had become obsolete. The philosopher was highly critical of values originating from moral or religious belief systems that demand faith in otherworldly hopes and that promise salvation for humanity in another life beyond this one (like Christianity and Judaism). For Nietzsche, the promise that another, kinder life awaits us is a denouncement of this true earthly existence. Very little mattered more to Nietzsche than the value of human life. Christianity, as he saw it, filled life on Earth with guilt, fear, and suffering.

He thus spoke of the religion as one of the most unfortunate things ever to have befallen mankind, and as anti-life as, well, Darkseid's Anti-Life Equation.[4] Christianity thus made humanity "sick" by imposing its doctrine as the only way to live one's life. People and cultures that have been affected by Christian belief systems, according to Nietzsche, cling to a weak and mindless herd or "slave" morality based on guilt, resentment, and false hope. In order to free people from this moral tyranny, Nietzsche thus urged a "revaluation of all values." But with the death of God and the collapse of traditional moral values, the "sick" man could be in serious danger of succumbing to *nihilism*, the view that life essentially has no meaning (which would prove Darkseid right after all).

Enter the Übermensch! In *Zarathustra*, the prophet proclaims that "all living beings have created something beyond themselves," and that man, too, is something that "shall be overcome."[5] To the Übermensch, who is as different from man as man is from ape, man is "a laughing stock," a "painful embarrassment." Nietzsche sees mankind as but a "rope over an abyss." We are not an end unto ourselves, but just another bridge to be crossed on the road to the Übermensch. Placing himself "beyond good and evil," the

Übermensch "breaks tablets and old values" and afterwards "writes new values on new tablets," thereby threatening both the ways of the bad and the good, who call him "law-breaker" in return.[6] Furthermore, the life-affirming Übermensch lives in the here and now, independent from any higher being or promise of an otherworldly life, hereby giving "meaning to the Earth." He understands the suffering that comes with this earthly existence and welcomes the "eternal recurrence of the same" (another important Nietzschean theme) as the ultimate affirmation of life![7]

Putting the Über into the Übermensch: Creativity and Following the Will to Power

To overcome the moral void of nihilism, the Übermensch, who is able to look into the abyss of meaninglessness without flinching, is positioned as an independent creator of new myths and entirely new values. These values must be without foundations, since they cannot be based on any pre-existing cultural, religious, or metaphysical conditions. But to create new values without foundations, as Nietzsche proposes here, seems like a near impossible task (or perhaps, a job for Superman). However, Nietzsche does imply that, before one can create new values, one must first create oneself. Overcoming nihilism therefore becomes a part of *self-overcoming*, of mastering one's deepest desires and emotions and creating a strong, harmonious, independent, and wholesome identity in the process.

This all-important creativity stems from another important aspect of Nietzsche's philosophy: *the will to power*. Nietzsche conceived the will to power as a response to "the will to live," proposed by another esteemed German philosopher, Arthur Schopenhauer (1788–1860), who influenced Nietzsche's early writings. Schopenhauer claimed that the will to live, which leads us to procreate and to avoid death, is the primordial driving force of every living thing in existence.[8] Nietzsche, however, responded that even the strongest creatures will risk their lives for more power. Thus, for Nietzsche, the will to power stands as "the unexhausted, procreative will of life."[9] As Nietzsche further describes the will to power:

> My idea is that every specific body strives to become master over all space and to extend its force (its will to power) and to thrust back all that resists its extension. But it continually encounters similar efforts on the part of other bodies and ends by coming to an arrangement ("union") with those of them that are sufficiently related to it: thus they then conspire together for power. And the process goes on[10]

Nietzsche's concept should not merely be understood as asserting power over others, but rather asserting power over oneself. The will to power is the fundamental driving force behind our self-mastery and self-creation, two important steps on the road toward becoming an Übermensch and a creator of new values.

Nietzsche describes the Übermensch as a heroic figure, the end goal for humanity. But others have interpreted Nietzsche in dark, self-serving ways. Adolf Hitler, for example, tragically abused Nietzsche's philosophy to justify his racist propaganda and his goals of creating a master Aryan race of superior *Übermenschen* through selective genetic breeding.[11] Nietzsche himself, though, made no connection between the Übermensch and race or genetics. Instead, the Übermensch is a figure who becomes possible after the death of God. If and when this revolutionary figure should arrive, however, will we welcome it as a noble, inspiring, and elevating superhero, or rather as an amoral, dominating, and unimaginable supervillain? As always, our very own modern-day mythologies can provide the answer. First, though, let us see what the ultimate superhero has in common with the Nietzschean Übermensch.

The Nietzschean Superman

Most people find it is easy to dismiss the possibility of the Man of Steel as a Nietzschean Übermensch with a cape. I too found the world's premier superhero and the philosopher's concept an odd match at first. How could Superman represent the end goal for humanity if he's not even human in the first place? We all know the story, brilliantly formulated in the first pages of *All-Star Superman* #1 (January 2006) as a simple equation: "Doomed planet + Desperate Scientists + Last Hope + Kindly Couple = Superman." The details of the myth have changed several times throughout the years, but the core concept remains the same: Superman is not from this Earth and is constantly reminded of that fact. Likewise, no matter how hard we try, none of us can ever be Superman. Although Nietzsche said that there has yet to be an Übermensch in the history of mankind, he did suggest that the goal was attainable for human beings. It does not require a "strange visitor from another planet."

While the Übermensch has often been interpreted solely in Darwinian terms as the next step in human evolution, Nietzsche's concept should be understood as a moral concept and not a physical one. For Superman, it's his Kryptonian physiology that makes him super and distinctly nonhuman. On a moral level, however, Superman, both as the Man of Steel and as his alter ego Clark Kent, is as human as they come. He may even be a bit too human, as his friend and Justice League teammate Batman says: "It is a remarkable dichotomy. In many ways, Clark is the most human of us all. Then . . . he shoots fire from the skies and it is difficult not to think of him as a god. And how fortunate we all are that it does not occur to *him*."[12] Later, during the massive *Infinite Crisis* crossover, which temporarily saw DC's "Trinity" of Superman, Batman, and Wonder Woman at odds, the Dark Knight accuses his friend of perhaps relating to humanity too much, thereby failing to provide the strong, confident, and inspirational leadership their fellow superheroes need.[13]

In any case, we can agree that, rather than his powers, it's primarily Superman's human side, forged and strengthened by his strong morals and Midwestern upbringing on a Smallville farm by Jonathan and Martha Kent, that makes him a hero. As Gary Engle states: "Superman's powers make the hero capable of saving humanity; Kent's total immersion in the American heartland makes him want to do it."[14] In a recent two-page origin story, among Superman's impressive arsenal of powers and abilities, his greatest weapon is defined as "his honest, unwavering (and thus very much human!) heart."[15] If, as Nietzsche claims, the seeds of the Übermensch lie in mankind's potential for creativity, overcoming both the self and the moral void, and creating new moral values in their place, Superman is as good a candidate for the concept as anyone.

Superman Versus Clark Kent

Much has been made about which identity is the more authentic one, and which one is the disguise.[16] The truth is that they are equally important and very much constructed parts of his character. The real person, whether we call him Kal-El, Clark, or Superman, is the one who journeyed from Krypton to Earth, was raised on a Smallville farm, developed superpowers under a yellow sun, and later in life combined all his talents and facets of his personality into one harmonious whole. His two "identities" are really nothing more than roles he plays in life, just like the roles each of us plays every day. Yes, Clark Kent, especially the bumbling, meek version portrayed in the movies by the late Christopher Reeve, is a performance, but so is the seemingly invincible Superman, and neither can claim to be "more real" than the other.[17] In constructing his two main "performances," Superman (or Kal-El, or Clark) shows remarkable creativity, which Nietzsche considered an important part of his Übermensch.

Superman's self-mastery and ability to overcome tragedy put him firmly on the road toward becoming an Übermensch. While some may say that Superman has it easy compared to other superheroes – after all, he did grow up in a safe, stable family environment with nearly godlike abilities – a further reading into the myth reveals that this is not so. Sure, Batman lost both his parents as a young boy and spent the rest of his youth training to become a superhero – but Superman lost his whole planet![18] He is (at least initially) the sole survivor of an entire civilization and therefore probably more alone in this world than anyone. Furthermore, his incredible superpowers developed over time, and he had to learn and master each one of them, and with the utmost self-restraint, since he can never truly lose control as long as he lives in our "world of cardboard."[19] Finally, Superman faced more than his share of tragedy and loss throughout his life, including the deaths of loved ones (the Kents, in many storylines), the destruction of "New Krypton" and the loss of nearly 100 000 fellow Kryptonians, and even the end of existence in *Final Crisis* (an almost literal interpretation of Nietzsche's moral void or meaningless abyss of nihilism).[20] Yet, every time, Superman overcomes and perseveres as a beacon of hope, even if he occasionally succumbs to depression in the meantime – just one indication of his underlying humanity.[21]

S is for Savior

Like Nietzsche's Übermensch, Superman is strong, creative, noble, independent, and life-affirming, but unlike Nietzsche's Übermensch, Superman is compassionate and looks out for the little guy.

In his very first appearances from the Golden Age of Comics in the 1930s, and in the first arc of the relaunched *Action Comics* (part of DC's "The New 52" that began in September 2011), Superman is portrayed as a social crusader and defender of the weak and oppressed. This Man of Steel is a bit more morally ambiguous and more proactive toward tackling social problems and exposing Metropolis's corrupt elite. He beats down "bullies," if you will, by becoming an even bigger one. In one of his first appearances in the relaunched DC Universe, he declares, "You know the deal Metropolis. Treat people right or expect a visit from me."[22] In these early appearances, Superman is often met with fear and hostility by those in power, which is another characteristic of Nietzsche's Übermensch, who challenges the status quo and is called a "lawbreaker" by both the unjust and the just.

Although this early Superman operated outside the law, his moral compass was still very much in tune with the values and ideals he was raised with (and which form the basis of most laws anyway). As a reporter, he always puts the ideal of truth first, and as a superhero, his mission is to ensure that justice is served to wrongdoers. This Superman may be called a "lawbreaker," but he nevertheless stays true to mainstream ideals and values. Rather than being a creator of new moral values, like Nietzsche's Übermensch, he reinforces old ones and essentially adheres to the morality created by "lesser" men. But as Superman moved into the Silver Age of Comics, his powers increased exponentially, and so did his love for humanity and adherence to truth, justice, and the American Way. The social crusader of old was being domesticated, becoming a law-abiding defender of the status quo or, as some tend to call him, "a Big Blue Boy Scout." The cultural assimilation of the ultimate immigrant from beyond the stars was nearly complete. Gary Engle writes that "*Superman* raises the American immigrant experience to the level of religious myth," becoming a "patron saint" of America in the process.[23]

Speaking of saints, the religious subtext of the Superman myth has never been far from the surface. As has often been pointed out, Superman's creators both came from Jewish backgrounds, *El* is short for the Hebrew word for God, and his origin story certainly parallels that of Moses. In the first two Superman movies, the messianic theme is made explicit when Jor-El, a "heavenly father" from beyond the stars, sends his only son to Earth where he can serve as the light to show mankind the way to greatness. The interpretation of Superman as a redeeming and compassionate angel in a cape, or, as Grant Morrison called him, "American Christ,"[24] was continued throughout *Superman Returns* (2006) and, to a lesser extent, the *Smallville* television series (2001–2011).[25] As a result, this religious interpretation of Superman is likely the version of the character that noncomic book readers are most familiar with.[26]

In the portrayals of Superman as an otherworldly Christ-like savior, a beacon of hope and faith, or, as iconic comics writer Alan Moore called him "a perfect man who came from the sky and did only good,"[27] great emphasis is placed on his compassion and willingness to suffer for humanity, which Nietzsche would see as a vice.[28] While this perhaps led to several of Superman's less strong and proud moments (the infamous "gay-bashing" scene from *Superman Returns* comes to mind), the Man of Steel's enormous affinity for his adopted planet and its inhabitants remains necessary to counterbalance the darker, corrupting effects that his more Übermenschian characteristics might lead to. But does this mean that Nietzsche's superior man is destined to life as a supervillain?

Kneel Before Zod!

In a story from the late 1980s, the Man of Steel visits the remains of his home planet. Exposed to massive amounts of lethal Kryptonite radiation, he experiences a sort of fever dream, where a different account of his origin is given. Here, instead of just one small rocketship, a whole fleet of Kryptonians – including his parents Jor-El and Lara – escape the destruction of their home planet, set course for Earth, and develop powers under its yellow sun. Eventually, they use their powers to reshape and conquer the planet, with Jor-El becoming this world's rebel "Superman" in defense of humanity. Seeing this experience as a "morality play" and a "lesson in human nature [and] the harsh truths of the abuse of power," Superman concludes that "a race of supermen cannot help but be a race of conquerors, even if they begin with the best intentions," and finally that "being a man is always more important than being a superman."[29]

Knowing this, Superman was perhaps a bit too trustworthy when he freed 100 000 Kryptonians from their confines in the bottled city of Kandor, shrunken and stored in the ship of the intergalactic supervillain Brainiac before Krypton exploded.[30] The newly freed Kryptonians, including Kal-El's uncle Zor-El and aunt Alura (the parents of Supergirl), each develop similar abilities to Superman, but lack the moral upbringing he received from Ma and Pa Kent, or even the guidance he himself gave to Supergirl and Superboy.

In recent depictions of Superman's origin, much emphasis is placed on his struggle to earn the world's trust. He is, after all, one of mankind's first encounters with extraterrestrial life. Not only is he an alien, he's an alien with almost godlike abilities. And the only assurance we have that he'll use these powers for the betterment of mankind, as his mortal enemy Lex Luthor states, "is his word."[31] Imagine then, that suddenly there appear not one or two, but 100 000 beings on Earth with the same powers and abilities. Even though Superman tried to establish a stable working relationship between his two worlds, the fearful tensions of both civilizations reached a fever pitch (helped by Luthor and Lois' father, General Sam Lane), and it all fell apart. Eventually, Kandor was relocated to a planet on the other side of the sun from Earth and rechristened New Krypton, but tensions remained and eventually an all-out "War of the Supermen" broke out.

A central figure in this was General Zod, now a military leader on New Krypton who was once imprisoned in the Phantom Zone by Jor-El himself, and who offers a frightening take on a supervillain in the Nietzschean mold. Just as the Übermensch is characterized as a superior form of humanity looking down on the primitive, animalistic man, General Zod describes humans as "Sub-Kryptonians": fragile and inferior little creatures on a backwater planet (or, to use the words of Nietzsche himself: "laughing stocks" and "painful embarrassments").[32] In *Superman II* (1981) Zod defines Superman's care of humanity as his principal weakness, and Ursa, a fellow Kryptonian criminal (and Zod's wife in the comics), compares it to taking care of "pets." But, for all his proclaimed superiority and his apparent shift to becoming a heroic leader throughout the *New Krypton* saga, Zod falls prey to a base human emotion: the need for revenge on Jor-El (or, in this case, his heirs). Resentment and the need for revenge are human-all-too-human shortcomings that Nietzsche condemns, and so General Zod falls far short of being a true Nietzschean Übermensch.

Perhaps . . . Lex Luthor?

Superman's fiercest arch-nemesis seems like a worthy contender for the title of Übermensch. Luthor has no superpowers, but is a human being who sets out to improve and recreate himself again and again. Following his tremendous will to power, it seems as if he can accomplish anything he sets his mind to, yet still strives to be better and gain even more power. Throughout his life, Luthor's morally questionable actions show that he certainly places himself "beyond good and evil." If Nietzsche were to read Luthor's life story, he might proclaim that the age of the Übermensch has truly arrived. A greedy, self-affirming man with an ego the size of Rao would certainly create his own values and rise beyond the all-too-human herd and their conceptions. The rise of Luthor in Metropolis, where he's initially seen as a philanthropist and even a hero by most people (except for some truth-seeking reporters for the *Daily Planet*), can be seen in this respect. Luthor becomes the most powerful man in Metropolis and might potentially even become the greatest man who ever lived – at least, until a certain alien swoops into town.

In the instant Luthor gets bumped to the number two spot in Metropolis everything changes: the expansion of his will to power and his personal self-creation comes to a halt. From this moment, Lex Luthor's every action is driven by his need to prove himself superior to Superman. Sure, he does gain more power from time to time – he even became president of the United States in 2001 – but eventually his antagonism toward Superman, stemming from a wounded ego, gets the better of him.[33]

To his credit, Lex Luthor makes some interesting and potentially valid points about his archenemy, which could be interpreted as Nietzschean in nature. In Superman, Luthor sees a powerful alien invader, a myth made real, without any sense of real human emotion that signals the end for mankind's (read: his) personal growth. In the miniseries *Lex Luthor: Man of Steel* (2005) he expresses his feelings this way:

> All men are created equal. All men. You are not a man . . . but they've made you their hero. They worship you. So tell me, what redemption do you offer them? Those red eyes. I'm sure they look right through me, like I am nothing more than a nuisance. But when I see you? I see something no man can ever be. I see the end. The end of our potential. The end of our achievements. The end of our dreams. You are my nightmare.[34]

After his passage, Luthor characterizes Superman as his own personal abyss, his own moral void of nihilism that he has to face and overcome for the good of mankind. In a later dinner conversation about Superman with Batman's alter ego Bruce Wayne, Luthor claims "I'm not interested with bringing him down . . . I'm obsessed with bringing us up. All of us – everyone – deserve a chance at greatness. All that takes is the belief it exists. But his existence threatens not just that belief . . . but our existence."[35]

Yet, for all Luthor's talk of elevating humanity to its true potential, he only cares about himself and his personal victory over Superman. When a dying Superman visits him in his cell in *All-Star Superman* #10 (May 2008), he challenges Luthor to deliver on his claims that, if it weren't for the existence of the Man of Steel, he would have elevated humanity (saving the world through his technology, curing cancer, and so forth) a long time ago. Luthor responds by spitting in Superman's face. In the conclusion of *The Black Ring* storyline in *Action Comics* #900 (June 2011), Luthor temporarily gains near omnipotent powers and has the ability to establish peace and bliss throughout the universe (something even Superman could not do), if he would just give up his hatred for his mortal enemy. Naturally, Luthor tries to kill Superman, loses his newfound power, and is defeated. Finally, under the sway of Wonder Woman's truth-compelling lasso, he admits the truth: "I want to be Superman."[36] So we learn that Lex Luthor's "nobility" is just a ruse to justify his jealousy of the "alien invader" who, ironically, is more human than he'll ever be. Although Lex Luthor at first sight seems the closest approximation of Nietzsche's Übermensch, he nevertheless lacks the self-overcoming and original heroic ideal ingrained in the concept from the moment his own "never-ending battle" against Superman starts.

Nietzschean Übermensch, American Christ, or Both?

In his essay "The Real Truth about Superman: And the Rest of Us, Too," comics writer Mark Waid shines a new light on Superman's heroic selflessness. Driven by a "need to belong," Superman actually helps others "by acting in his own self-interest."[37] Superman does what he does, not for worship or power, nor out of fear, dominance, or pity, but simply because he chooses to do so as the fulfillment of the destiny he carved for him-self – in other words, Nietzsche's will to power. Furthermore, while he certainly doesn't transcend society's values, creates new ones, or live "beyond good and evil," he does cre-ate new myths for others to follow. After all, as the first and possibly still greatest super-hero, Superman is not only a leading moral exemplar for humanity but for other superheroes as well. While we can never truly be Superman, nor should we believe in him so much it turns to worship, we can strive to be more *like him*.

Unlike some religious figures, Superman isn't weighed down by his humanity nor is it presented as some sort of curse. Instead, he embraces his humanity and thereby gains his greatest strength. Although he can show great compassion, and will always be around to "catch us if we fall," he does allow "mankind to climb to their own destiny" because of his unwavering belief in humanity's potential for the future.[38] In these respects, Superman can certainly be seen as giving "meaning to the Earth." Waid probably said it best in his introduction to the collected *All-Star Superman* series: "Gods achieve their power by encouraging us to believe in them. Superman achieves his power by believing in us."[39] I think even Friedrich Nietzsche would agree to that.

For pop culture resources and philosophical resources related to this chapter please visit the website for this book: https://introducingphilosophythroughpopculture.com.

Notes

1   Although the German word *Übermensch* was initially translated into the English language as "superman," there really is no universally accepted translation of the term. Other translations include "overman" or "overhuman," but to avoid confusion with the character Superman (and Overman, his Nazi counterpart from Earth-10), I shall leave the term in its original language.

2   My interpretation of Nietzsche's philosophy is heavily indebted to that of American philosopher Richard Schacht; see his chapter on Nietzsche in (2001). *The Blackwell Guide to Modern Philosophers* (ed. S.M. Emmanuel), 390–411. Malden, MA: Blackwell.

3   *Thus Spoke Zarathustra* was written and published in several parts between 1883 and 1885, before finally being published in complete form in 1892. In this work, Nietzsche makes clever use of several aphorisms and lyrical prose to get his philosophical points across. The structure and writing style of the work very much – and quite ironically – resembles that of the Bible.

4   Nietzsche described his views on Judeo-Christian morality in *On the Genealogy of Morals* (1887), and later wrote a much heavier attack on Christianity in *The Antichrist*, originally published in 1895. Nietzsche's negative views on Christianity found a metaphor in the DC Universe with the Anti-Life Equation, a con-cept introduced in Jack Kirby's Fourth World saga, a mathematical equation that has the ability to com-pletely take over one's mind and free will. In its first appearance in *Forever People* #5 (November 1971), it is said that "if someone possesses absolute control over you – you're not really alive," paralleling Nietzsche's views on Christianity. One of Superman's deadliest enemies, Darkseid, sought to obtain and harness the Anti-Life Equation, and finally did so in *Final Crisis* (2008–2009). I would write the full formula down here, but . . . well, you know . . . .

5   Nietzsche, F. (1883). *Thus Spoke Zarathustra*, available in (1968). *The Portable Nietzsche* (trans. W. Kauffman), 124–128. New York: Viking Penguin. (Unless otherwise noted, all descriptions of the Übermensch presented here are taken from this version.)

6   Nietzsche, *Thus Spoke Zarathustra*, 324–325. Incidentally, *Beyond Good and Evil* is the title of another work by Nietzsche, published in 1886.

7   Along with the Übermensch, the concept of "the eternal recurrence" is primarily discussed in *Zarathustra* but has also seen its interpretation differ throughout the years, from the historical to the cosmological. For our purposes here, the Übermensch's acceptance of the eternal repetition of one's life, down to every last detail, over and over again, can be seen as the ultimate affirming of his love for his earthly existence and a celebration of life itself.

8   For more on Arthur Schopenhauer's will to live, see his seminal work *The World as Will and Representation*, first published in 1818.

9   Nietzsche, *Thus Spoke Zarathustra*, 226. Again, as with the Übermensch and eternal recurrence, the will to power has known many interpretations over the years.

10 See Nietzsche, F. (1968). *The Will to Power* (trans. W. Kauffman). New York: Vintage. While not a finished work by Nietzsche, this collection includes several of the philosopher's unpublished notes.

11 Although Nietzsche's writings were rather easily transformed into Nazi propaganda – with more than a little help from his sister and keeper of his archives, Elisabeth Förster-Nietzsche (1846–1935) – the philosopher himself was firmly against all proto-fascist and Nazi thought.

12 *Superman/Batman* #3 (December, 2003), reprinted in *Superman/Batman: Public Enemies* (2004).

13 *Infinite Crisis* #1 (December, 2005), reprinted in *Infinite Crisis* (2008).

14 See Engle, G. (1987). What makes Superman so darned American? In: *Superman at Fifty: The Persistence of a Legend* (ed. D. Cooley and G. Engle), 79–87. Cleveland: Octavia.

15 See "The Origin of Superman" in *DC Universe: Origins* (2010).

16 Early Superman stories placed Clark Kent as the disguise and Superman as the "real" personality. After the *Crisis on Infinite Earths* rebooted DC's continuity in 1985–1986, *The Man of Steel* miniseries reversed the Superman/Clark Kent dichotomy, showing a more confident, assertive, and not so mild-mannered reporter. Later retellings of Superman's origin, including *Superman: Birthright* (2003), *Superman: Secret Origin* (2009–2010), and the recently re-launched *Action Comics* (2011), combine story and personality traits from both interpretations.

17 But not a parody of humanity, nor as an explicit statement of the way Superman "sees us" as Bill, played by actor David Carradine, seems to believe in Quentin Tarantino's movie *Kill Bill*, Vol. 2 (2004).

18 For a strong argument for Batman, rather than Superman, as the true superhero descendant of Nietzsche's Übermensch, see Robertson, C.K. (2005). The true *Übermensch*: Batman as humanistic myth. In: *The Gospel According to Superheroes: Religion and Popular Culture* (ed. B.J. Oropeza), 49–65. New York: Peter Lang.

19 See Superman's speech about "cutting loose" in a fight against Darkseid in the final *Justice League Unlimited* episode "Destroyer" (2006).

20 The two-year-long *New Krypton* story-arc played out in pretty much all Superman-related titles from December, 2008 until May, 2010. Superman stared down non-existence in *Final Crisis* #7 (March 2009), reprinted in *Final Crisis* (2010).

21 See the storyline *Grounded*, from *Superman* #700 (August 2010) throughout *Superman* #714 (October 2011).

22 *Action Comics* #1 (November 2011).

23 Engle, "What Makes Superman So Darned American?," p. 86.

24 From an interview in *Wizard* #143 (2003).

25 Ironically, in *Smallville*, many references are also made to Friedrich Nietzsche's writings. Concepts like the Übermensch and the will to power are mentioned briefly throughout the course of the series, and an original copy of *Beyond Good and Evil* may be found within Lionel Luthor's safe.

26 For an overview of the cultural evolution of Superman and the "superman" character archetype in fiction, see Andrae, T. (1987). From menace to, messiah: the history and historicity of superman (1980). In: *American Media and Mass Culture: Left Perspectives* (ed. D. Lazere), 125–138. Berkeley: University of California Press. For more on Superman as a messianic figure in particular, see Schenk, K. chapter Superman: a popular culture messiah. In:, *The Gospel According to Superheroes* (ed. Oropeza), 33–48.

27 See "Whatever Happened to the Man of Tomorrow?" originally published in *Superman* #423 (September 1986) and *Action Comics* #583 (September 1986) and reprinted in *Superman: Whatever Happened to the Man of Tomorrow?* (2010).

28 Interestingly, starting from 2003's *Superman: Birthright*, Superman's famous S-shield doesn't just stand for the House of El, but is the Kryptonian symbol for "hope."

29 "Return to Krypton" in Superman, Vol. 2, #18 (June 1988), reprinted in Superman: The Greatest Stories Ever Told, Vol. 1 (2004).

30 See *Action Comics* #866–870 (August–December 2008), reprinted in *Superman: Brainiac* (2010), and which led to *New Krypton* event.

31 *Lex Luthor: Man of Steel* #3 (July 2005), reprinted in *Luthor* (2010).

32 *Action Comics* #846 (February, 2007), reprinted in *Superman: Last Son* (2010).

33 This, of course, is the more well-known modern depiction of Lex Luthor and his struggle with Superman for the heart of Metropolis. In his original more simplistic Silver Age origin story, his hatred of Superman

(when he was just Superboy) stems from the childhood accident which blew up his laboratory and caused him the loss of a protoplasmic life form and his hair. This, for him, is enough to swear revenge on Superboy for all eternity. See *Adventure Comics* #271 (April 1960).

34 *Lex Luthor: Man of Steel* #1 (May 2005).

35 *Lex Luthor: Man of Steel* #3 (July 2005).

36 *Blackest Night* #7 (February 2010), reprinted in *Blackest Night* (2011).

37 See Waid, M. (2005). The real truth about Superman: and the rest of us too. In: *Superheroes and Philosophy: Truth, Justice and the Socratic Way* (eds. T. Morris and M. Morris), 3–10. Chicago: Open Court.

38 See *JLA* #4 (April 1997), reprinted in *JLA Vol. 1: New World Order* (1997).

39 From his introduction to *All-Star Superman*, Vol. 2 (2008).

26

Knowing Who You Are

Existence Precedes Essence in Moana

William J. Devlin

Summary

This chapter looks at Moana and her adventures as a philosophical journey toward existential authenticity. Torn between the dictates of tradition and her yearning toward defining herself through free actions, Moana faces anguish, forlornness, and despair. But as she sets sail, she personifies Jean-Paul Sartre's existential dictum, "existence precedes essence," as she defines herself and creates her essence through her voyages.

Disney's computer-animated musical film *Moana* (2016) tells the tale of Moana, the daughter of Tui, the chief of a Polynesian island, Motunui. Bound by the legendary tradition of her ancestors, Moana is expected to follow her lineage and take over as chief when she grows up. Her father and mother, Sina, equally bound to this tradition, prepare Moana for this leadership role. But ever since she was a toddler, Moana has wanted to sail beyond the reef and voyage across the seas – a calling reinforced by her free-spirited grandmother, Gramma Tala, who encourages Moana to "know who you are." Despite her father's misgivings and prohibitions, Moana learns that she was chosen by the ocean to restore the heart of Te Fiti, which was stolen by Maui, the shapeshifting demigod who seeks the love and praise of human beings. Upon completing her adventures, Moana successfully restores the heart, thereby saving the people of Motunui.

As we dig beneath the surface level of the story, we find a metaphorical and philosophical level to Moana's journey. Moana must choose between sailing beyond the reef or obeying her parents, resulting in an existential crisis. In effect, Moana faces a choice that everyone faces, between independently creating one's own identity or merely following the crowd. To explore this crisis, and gain a better understanding of her decisions, let us join Moana on her wayfinding adventures, using the philosophy of existentialism as our navigator.

Introducing Philosophy Through Pop Culture: From Socrates to Star Wars *and Beyond*, Second Edition.
Edited by William Irwin and David Kyle Johnson.
© 2022 John Wiley & Sons Ltd. Published 2022 by John Wiley & Sons Ltd.

"This Suits You"

From the opening scene, we learn that Moana yearns to become a voyager. Her grandmother tells the frightful tale of the demon, Te Kā, who seeks the heart of Te Fiti after Maui steals it. Tala cautions that, unless someone restores the heart, darkness will spread "until every one of us is devoured by the bloodthirsty jaws of inescapable death!" While all of the other children run and cry in fear from this story, little Moana listens intently, eager to be the one to restore the heart. But her father forbids her from having such seafaring aspirations. Chief Tui offers two reasons against sailing away. First, he persistently cautions Moana that she'd be violating a Motunui rule, "No one goes beyond the reef." Second, advising her that she "must learn where you're meant to be," he argues that everything in Motunui has a role. From the people, such as the dancers and the fishermen, to the natural elements on the islands, such as the coconuts and leaves – everything on Motunui serves a purpose. As he explains to Moana, she too has a purpose: to become the "next chief of our great people." The people of Motunui will need a chief and "there you are."

Tui's worldview echoes the philosopher Aristotle (384–322 BCE) in some ways. Aristotle maintains that everything has a function and with it, a specific role. This function and role are the thing's essence – the definition of that thing. The fisherman, for example, has a function to catch fish with the purpose of feeding one's tribe. So the essence of the fisherman is to catch fish. Meanwhile, a thing's worth or value is measured by how well it performs its function. A fisherman is only good as a fisherman insofar as he is able to successfully catch fish. The excellent fisherman is the one who is skilled and successful at catching fish. At the same time, Aristotle contends that human beings generally have a specific function: to reason excellently. The human being is the rational animal. We are therefore already born with a purpose or role – to reason. So we are measured by how well we perform the function of reasoning.

For Tui, everything on Motunui has a specific purpose. In his view, tradition commands that Moana's role is specifically to serve as chief. Here we can also say that each person or thing has an essence that precedes its existence. That is, Moana's role as chief was determined even before she was born. Her family lineage dictates that the child of Chief Tui will necessarily become the next chief. Thus, Moana's essence is defined prior to her birth. Her father explains this to her in a private moment at "the place of chiefs," the island's highest mountaintop where each new chief adds a stone to a column to raise the island higher. He tells Moana that there will "come a time when you will stand on this peak and place a stone on this mountain." For Tui, the role of chief is Moana's essence, and so "it's time to be" who the people "need you to be."

After years of coaxing and training (and singing "Where You Are"), Tui and Sina convince Moana to take her role as the next chief. As a teenager, she shadows her father as chief, demonstrating the idea that one's essence precedes one's existence – that she was always meant to become Motunui's leader. Likewise, Moana echoes Aristotle's concept of being excellent in one's function, as she excels in her leadership role. In response to a leaking roof, she discovers that the issue was not because of the fronds but because the wind shifted the post. In response to diseased coconuts, she directs the harvesters to clear the diseased trees and start a new grove elsewhere. Moana thus not only adopts the role of chief but she performs above and beyond expectations. So much so that her father, seeing her excellence, proudly tells her, "This suits you."

"But the Voice Inside Sings a Different Song"

Though Moana excels in her leadership role, she soon finds that she does not want to become chief. In response to the issue of having no fish in the lagoon, she insists (to her father's anger) that the solution is to fish beyond the reef, arguing that the rule of not sailing beyond the reef is antiquated given these new circumstances. Though her public reasoning is attached to her role as chief, Moana privately laments that the ocean is "calling out to me." While she wants to "be the perfect daughter" and fulfill her parents' wishes that she become chief, she comes "back to the water" because it is the place she longs to be. She admits that her father's Aristotelian views make sense – everything on the island is "by design" so that everybody "has a role on this island." Still, she doubts that the role of chief is the role she wants. Instead, Moana yearns to become a wayfinder who travels across the seas to restore the heart of Te Fiti to save her people.

Moana thus faces a dilemma: become chief or sail beyond the reef. As such, she is torn between the dictates of perceived tradition as presented by her father and her introspective yearning toward defining herself through different actions. This dilemma strikes at the heart of the philosophy of existentialism. For existentialists, human beings are unique in the sense that "who you are and who you will become" is always up for re-evaluation and reconsideration. A human being is a *being-in-question*, meaning that we can always reflect upon how we define ourselves and freely determine who we want to become. As Moana agonizes over whether to be a chief or voyager, she demonstrates that her own being is in question. On the one hand, she accepts that she could "lead with pride" and help strengthen the village. On the other hand, she knows "the voice inside sings a different song." In her heart, she wants to sail beyond the reef. Thus, Moana faces an existential crisis.

Moana's questioning her role as chief exemplifies another important existentialist idea, one that counters Aristotle's view that humans have a fixed essence. The existentialist philosopher Jean-Paul Sartre (1905–1980) argues that humans are the kind of being whose "existence precedes essence." The human being is born without a fixed, unchanging essence. She first "exists, turns up, appears on the scene, and only afterwards, defines" herself through her decisions, choices, and actions. As such, the first principle of existentialism is that the human being "is nothing else but what he makes of himself."[1] Because we do not have a predetermined essence, we have the freedom to determine who we are and who we will become.

In contrast, Sartre suggests that for other nonhuman things "essence precedes existence."[2] Take Moana's sidekick chicken, Heihei, for example. Heihei acts in a fixed and unchanging manner. As a chicken, he is constantly pecking to eat food. But, peculiar to Heihei, he also pecks at anything – from chicken feed to rocks to nothing at all! He even eats the heart of Te Fiti! But, as peculiar as Heihei is, we don't expect him to ever change his behavior. His behavior remains exactly the same throughout the movie. He cannot and will not change. This is why we find that many characters – from Moana to Maui to the ocean – often have to protect him from his own quirky behavior. Following Sartre, we might say that Heihei cannot change his behavior because his essence precedes his existence. He has no capacity to choose to be anything but what he already is: an eccentric, bizarre chicken.

Heihei's essence is fixed, but Moana recognizes that her existence precedes her essence, and so she is free to create herself in the way she sees fits. This freedom makes her dilemma more challenging. As the existentialists see it, many people ignore their individual freedom and instead find solace in denying such liberties. Rather than fully acknowledge and embrace one's capacity to legislate one's own essence, a person may instead let others define them – telling them what to do, who they are, and what they should become. In so doing, a person relinquishes their freedom and their individuality, becoming a nameless, faceless, member of the group that defines them. The existentialists refer to this group as "the crowd" or, more negatively, "the herd," suggesting the vapid and unreflective commonality of such an identity. In Moana's case, her father and the people of Motunui serve as the crowd. They compel her to conform to their social rules and norms, to give up her passion to become a wayfinder, and to accept a predetermined essence as chief.

It's easy to lose one's individuality and slip into the crowd mentality. Often reinforced through social norms, rules, and guidelines, the crowd absorbs the individual, so that s/he might not even be aware they're losing their freedom. Take Tui, for example. As Sila recounts, Tui was once like Moana when he was younger. Though compelled by an individual passion toward voyaging, he is forbidden by social rules to act on his calling. Nevertheless, he snuck out with a friend to set sail. But he encountered an "unforgiving sea," which capsized his canoe and led to his friend drowning. Letting his fears and regrets get the best of him, Tui relinquishes his yearning to sail and accepts his role as chief, becoming part of the crowd. Sartre refers to this status – the state of rejecting one's individual freedom and responsibilities – as *bad faith*. Tui demonstrates bad faith in at least two ways. First, as suggested, he denies his own freedom to continue sailing and winds up conforming to the crowd. Second, he attempts to pull Moana into the herd mentality, arguing that she really has no choice in the matter because she must conform to the rules. The rules dictate that she cannot sail beyond the reef; so she should relinquish her freedom and become absorbed in the crowd. Moana thus struggles with losing her individual freedom and passion, running the risk of living in bad faith and becoming a member of the crowd.

"That Voice Inside is Who You Are"

Existentialism holds that, despite the dangers of losing one's identity to the crowd, we have the ability to embrace our freedom and preserve our individuality. Sartre refers to this state as *authenticity*. The authentic individual not only acknowledges their freedom, but also assumes full responsibility for their actions and decisions. By doing so, the authentic individual doesn't ignore their choices and simply follow the command of others. Likewise, they don't excuse their behavior on account of social rules, traditional norms, or religious commands.

Gramma Tala exemplifies living with authenticity. Rather than conform to the crowd, she lives by her own standards. She sings to Moana that she likes the water because it doesn't conform to common norms: "it is mischievous" and "misbehaves." Tala stands apart from the crowd, even flouting the leadership of her son, the chief. When Moana worries that she'll inform her dad about the failed trip beyond the reef, Tala responds, "I'm his mom. I don't have to tell him anything." Similarly, from the viewpoint of the crowd, Tala appears like "the village crazy lady" because they "say I drift too far" from the ordinary. Nevertheless, she embraces her individuality and uniqueness, freely defining herself. As she explains to Moana, "once you know what you like, well, there you are," even if it is outside of what is commonly expected and accepted.

Tala not only models authenticity, but she also teaches Moana to live the authentic life. Aware of Moana's dilemma, Gramma Tala advises that though she should generally mind what her father says, there will come a time when she'll have to follow her own heart and define herself in her own fashion. Tala sings, "You may hear a voice inside/And if the voice starts to whisper/To follow the farthest star/Moana, that voice inside is who you are." This advice echoes Sartre's own existentialist advice, "You're free, choose, that is, invent."[3] Tala thus guides Moana toward answering the question of "who you were meant to be," by revealing that while the people of Motunui are currently homebound villagers, they were originally voyagers. On the one hand, this revelation suggests that Tui's appeal to tradition is misplaced. If one examines the deeper traditions of Motunui, the rule forbidding sailing is invalid. On the other hand, it encourages Moana to follow "that voice inside," which is telling her to become a wayfinder.[4]

Moana is motivated by her ancestors and inspired by her grandmother's dying wish that Moana find Maui and demand that he help restore the heart of Te Fiti. Unlike her father, Moana overcomes her fears from her first disastrous seafaring outing, and she commits to sailing beyond the reef. In a touching moment, when she passes away, Tala reincarnates as a Manta ray, and guides Moana's canoe across the reef. Moana sings, "See her light up the night in the sea, she calls me/And yes, I know, that I can go." She thus resolves her dilemma so that "All the time wondering where I need to be is behind me." Her choice is to live the authentic life, free from the crowd, so that "I'm on my own, to worlds unknown/Every turn I take, every trail I track/Is a choice I make . . . From the great unknown, where I go alone, where I long to be." In short, at this point, Moana journeys to authenticity.

"Do You Know Who You Are?"

Moana's adventures across the sea embody the authentic life, in terms of both the richness and trappings of independence. Friedrich Nietzsche (1844–1900), a forefather of existentialism, held that "You shall become the person you are," meaning we're in a constant state of becoming.[5] We're always changing, growing, and redefining ourselves through our actions and decisions. This is part of the richness of authenticity. Moana embodies this as she continues to grow throughout her expedition. She matures in her firmness with Maui, even pulling the demigod's ear to get him to listen to her demands for help. She develops an expertise as a voyager, growing from a helpless traveler who needs the ocean to guide her, to a devoted student who learns under Maui's tutelage, and finally to an independent wayfinder. She exudes courage as she retrieves the heart of Te Fiti from Kakamura, the dangerous, blow-dart-shooting, pirates. Even when Maui attempts to flee in fear, she boldly boards their ship, dismissing them as just coconuts. Similarly, she bravely enters the Realm of Monsters and assists Maui in retrieving his hook from the menacing crab, Tamatoa. She wisely notices that Tamatoa is immersed in a herd mentality, whereby he rejects a voice inside since he'd "rather be shiny." Playing on his superficiality, Moana displays her cleverness as she outwits Tamatoa and tricks him into continuously talking about himself and distracts him with shiny objects. In this way, she adheres to Sartre's existential dictum that the human being is only what she wills herself to be after she is born.

But, as Moana quickly learns, living the authentic life has its challenges. Sartre explains that an individual who escapes the crowd to truly embrace freedom will inevitably encounter three states of being. First, one lives in *anguish* insofar as each choice does not simply involve oneself; rather, it involves all humanity. When the authentic individual acts, she is aware that her action is a statement to humanity that this is the right action. Each decision thus carries a heavy weight.[6] Moana undergoes anguish as she becomes aware that her adventure literally involves humanity – the people of Motunui and beyond – as she needs to prevent Te Kā's darkness from spreading. She becomes so anxious from this weight that she's haunted by their "inescapable death" in her nightmares.

Second, Sartre contends that the authentic individual lives with *forlornness* as she must accept that she, and no one else, is responsible for her decisions and actions. Here the weight of responsibility is all the more pressing, since there are no excuses for one's actions. All praise, all blame, all accountability rests with the individual. Sartre emphasizes this point, arguing that the human being "is condemned to be free."[7] Moana thus acts with forlornness as she nearly succumbs to the weight of responsibility for her voyage. She cannot blame her parents, her grandmother, Maui, or even the ocean for anything she does. She must own her actions.

Finally, the authentic individual lives in *despair* as she must confine herself to acting within the collection of probabilities that make her action possible.[8] For example, when Moana plans to leave Motunui to restore the heart, she can only act within the possibilities available to her. Sure, she could pray to the gods, hoping they'll promptly transport her to Te Fiti so that she can restore the heart without Te Kā's knowledge. But Sartre would suggest this is outside of the realm of realistic possibilities. The authentic individual must focus only on those possibilities that involve one's direct actions. Even the ocean – who prevents Maui from swimming away from Moana's boat and puts a blow dart in his butt cheek so Moana can sail – will not simply carry Moana to Te Kā. Moana must complete her journey herself.

These three states of being collide for Moana after she and Maui are summarily defeated by Te Kā in their first attempt to restore the heart. With his hook severely damaged, Maui refuses to make a second attempt, yelling to Moana, "We're here because the ocean told you you're special and you believed it. I'm not killing myself so you can prove you're something you're not." Overwhelmed by these hardships, Moana shifts away from authentic living, blaming both Maui and the ocean. She's angry that Maui "stole the heart in the first place." She's frustrated with the ocean, exclaiming "Why did you bring me here? I'm not the right person." Feeling helpless and hopeless, she returns the heart to a reluctant ocean, and considers returning home. Moana thus becomes enveloped in the dark aspects of authenticity and borders on bad faith.

Tala – Moana's inspiration and model of the authentic life – returns to her during this low point, offering existential advice. Moana should find resiliency in her authenticity since she "stands apart from the crowd." And though these hardships can be debilitating since "the world seems against you" and they "leave a scar," Tala argues that such scars can "heal and reveal where [and who] you are." Tala echoes Nietzsche's famous existential idea, "what does not destroy me makes me stronger."[9] The authentic individual is not only able to endure suffering, hardships, and failures in life, they are also able to learn, grow, and be strengthened by them. Here Tala reminds Moana of the passions that define her: "she loves the sea and her people." These passions and the lessons she learned through her adventures will guide her in self-overcoming. So, no matter what hardships Moana faces, the voice inside will always show "who you are."

Tala's advice motivates Moana to fight through, and overcome, her anguish, forlornness, and despair. Moana sings that she, herself, has "delivered us to where we are." Living the authentic life through her adventures, she has defined herself as a wise leader of Motunui and a skilled wayfinder who has journeyed farther than ever before. She announces that, even after her hardships, she still hears the call to restore the heart. But this call is not from the ocean; it's her inner voice. With this revelation, she emphasizes her commitment to authenticity as she proudly announces, "I am Moana!"

"I Am Moana!"

The story of *Moana* has layers. First, it is literally a tale of Moana's voyage *outside* beyond the reef so that she can restore the heart of Te Fiti and save the people of Motunui. She closes this tale with a happy ending as she simultaneously lives the life that she freely chooses, becomes the leader of her people (by saving them) as her parents wanted, and honors her tradition insofar as she restores her ancestors' tradition of wayfinding. Moana's abilities as a wayfinder become so obvious that even her father overcomes his own bad faith, proudly telling Moana upon her return, "It suits you." Second, metaphorically and philosophically, *Moana* is an inner journey of self-discovery. Moana embodies the existential philosophy of living an authentic life. She shows us what it means to be free in terms of following one's passions, choosing for oneself, and taking full responsibility for one's actions.

Like her grandmother, Moana is able to help guide others to authenticity and to become who they are. Maui lives in bad faith before he meets Moana. Utterly dependent upon the idea that he is a "hero to all" people, he believes that his essence precedes his existence in that he only became "Maui" upon receiving his hook. Maui repeatedly tells Moana, "I am nothing without my hook!" But Moana teaches him that he can be who he is without this divine gift. He overcomes bad faith so that, after his hook is destroyed, he tells Moana, "Hook. No hook. I'm Maui."

Moana is able to see beyond the superficial appearance of Te Kā and realize that this demon is really Te Fiti without her heart. With such insight, Moana restores the heart and teaches Te Fiti that her existence precedes her essence, since "this [stolen heart] does not define you." She also teaches her people of Motunui to no longer feel bound by their current social routines and norms, as she guides the sedentary villagers – including her parents – to become voyagers and learn the skills of wayfinding.

Most importantly, perhaps, Moana teaches *us* about authenticity. Embodying Nietzsche's idea that the best educators are those who teach as outward examples, Moana models how to live authentically by doing so herself.[10] Her actions and decisions demonstrate that we can define ourselves freely and take responsibility for who we are. Even Maui learns that his preconceived notions about her were inaccurate. Maui had already formed notions about the crowd mentality of human beings, stereotyping every person based on their functions. Because she is a "mortal," she will be too frightened to enter the Realm of Monsters. Even worse, since she wears a dress and has an animal sidekick, Moana is dismissed as a "princess": weak, demure, and dependent on others. Thus, Maui acts with bad faith and refuses (at first) to teach her to sail, believing she simply cannot become a wayfinder.

By the story's end, however, Maui realizes his mistake as Moana becomes etched on his mural of tattoos – not as a passive and superficial member of the crowd, but as a self-overcoming and independent wayfinder. Ultimately, then, Moana shatters the concept of "princess" both for Maui and us, the viewers. No longer bound by archaic labels – even those of earlier "Disney princesses" – Moana defines herself as a free, authentic individual. Rather than let herself become defined by the label "princess," she defines herself as a strong and independent young woman – capable of living life on her own terms. By overcoming antiquated and inaccurate stereotypes, Moana demonstrates that if you listen to the voice inside, you too can (and should) avoid the social pressures of the herd mentality to discover who you truly are.[11]

For pop culture resources and philosophical resources related to this chapter please visit the website for this book: https://introducingphilosophythroughpopculture.com.

Notes

1   Sartre, J.-P. (1995). The humanism of existentialism. In: *Essays in Existentialism* (ed. W. Baskin), 36. New York: Citadel Press.
2   See Sartre, 34–35.
3   Sartre, 45.
4   Similarly, in a deleted scene, Gramma Tala advises a young Moana, "In order to find where you're going, you have to know exactly where you are." In the film's surface level narrative, Tala hints that in order to voyage beyond the reef to retrieve the heart of Te Fiti, Moana must realize that she already belongs to a voyager tradition. At the philosophical and metaphorical level, Tala offers existential guidance – in order to define yourself by your future projects or destinations, you must recognize your freedom to create your own essence and live an authentic life. As such, Tala's advice about "where you are" is a sharp contrast to Tui's Aristotelian "there you are" view.
5   Nietzsche, F. (1974). *The Gay Science* (ed. W. Kaufman), 219. New York: Vintage Books.
6   See Sartre, 38–40.
7   Sartre, 41.
8   See Sartre, 45–46.
9   Nietzsche, F. (1968). Twilight of the idols. In: *The Portable Nietzsche* (ed. W. Kaufmann), 467. New York: Penguin Books.
10 See Nietzsche, F. (1997). Schopenhauer as educator. In: *Untimely Meditations*. (ed. D. Breazeale), (trans. D. Breazeale), 136–137. New York: Cambridge University Press.
11 I dedicate this chapter to my daughter, Ellie. May you always listen to the voice inside that sings the song of who you are.

27

Becoming a (Wonder) Woman

Feminism, Nationalism, and the Ambiguity of Female Identity

J. Lenore Wright

Summary

Wonder Woman is, at once, a mythic figure, feminist icon, female sex symbol, and alienated superhero. Her popularity emerges from her experiences of struggle. Fans see their efforts to navigate success and acceptance mirrored in Wonder Woman's struggles to live in a man's world while remaining true to her Amazonian mission. "Becoming a (Wonder) Woman" explores the ambiguity of Wonder Woman's identity as a female superhero. This chapter draws upon the analysis of ambiguity in the work of the French philosopher Simone de Beauvoir. Beauvoir maintains in the *Ethics of Ambiguity* and *The Second Sex* that sexual differences dramatically shape human existence. Whereas man actively creates his destiny, woman passively accepts her uncertain existence. The critical philosophical task is for women to transcend barriers to freedom and forge their own identities and pathways to fulfillment. Wonder Woman exemplifies this woman of tomorrow by giving new meaning to Beauvoir's claim that "One is not born, but rather becomes, a woman."

More than 70 years has passed since the debut of Wonder Woman in *All-Star Comics*. To the wonder of many, Wonder Woman remains one of the most popular comic-book superheroes of all time. As Jill Lepore aptly observes in *The Secret History of Wonder Woman*, "Aside from Superman and Batman, no other comic-book character has lasted as long."[1] What, precisely, gives Wonder Woman her wondrous staying power in the American popular consciousness?

Her overt femininity (need I mention the bustier, boots, and bracelets?) coupled with her Amazonian strength and speed ("she was both stronger than Hercules and swifter than Mercury") crosses gender and generational divides.[2] The raven-haired beauty emboldened a generation of men reared on pin-ups and promises to fight fascism in World War II. The lasso-wielding freedom fighter empowered women to leave the domestic sphere for the public sphere and take control of their lives and livelihood.[3] The

Introducing Philosophy Through Pop Culture: From Socrates to Star Wars *and Beyond*, Second Edition.
Edited by William Irwin and David Kyle Johnson.
© 2022 John Wiley & Sons Ltd. Published 2022 by John Wiley & Sons Ltd.

lone female founder of the Justice League of America (formerly known as the Justice Society of America) inspired countercultural Americans to voice stories of struggle and alienation. Today, the tiara-wearing heroine's combined fierceness and frivolity appeals to readers' fluid understanding of gender norms and identities.[4] Ironically, it is Wonder Woman's ambiguity that makes her appeal so enduring.

Wonder Woman is a walking – and sometimes flying – paradox of attributions and images. She is, at once, a female sex symbol and feminist icon: physically enchanting, psychically vulnerable, morally virtuous, financially independent, self-determining, and, in tune with her womanly ways, self-sacrificing. "She was meant to be the strongest, smartest, bravest woman the world had ever seen," writes Lepore.[5] In short, Wonder Woman represents a robust modern conception of American womanhood.

This chapter explores the complexities of Wonder Woman's identity, as she navigates male and female spheres of existence to embody a modern American ideal.[6] My essay draws upon the analysis of ambiguity in the work of the French philosopher Simone de Beauvoir (1908–1986). Beauvoir maintains in the *Ethics of Ambiguity* (1947) and *The Second Sex* (1949) that sexual differences shape human existence insofar as society offers men and women different possibilities for expressing who they are and what they desire. Whereas man actively creates his destiny, woman passively accepts her uncertain existence. The critical feminist task is for women to transcend barriers to freedom so they can begin to forge their identities and enjoy self-fulfillment. Wonder Woman exemplifies this "woman of tomorrow."[7] "Wiser and stronger than men," she gives up her right to eternal life and commitment to remain "aloof from men" to join her love interest, Captain Steve Trevor, an Army Intelligence officer, in America and defend democracy "and equal rights for women."[8] Wonder Woman challenges established social roles and the assumed facticity of life by creating her identity in the world, an identity born out of sacrifice and pain. In becoming who she is – in making a new life in a new country under a new name – Wonder Woman gives new meaning to Beauvoir's claim that "One is not born, but rather becomes, a woman."[9]

What is a Woman?

On the cusp of her 40th birthday, Simone de Beauvoir became preoccupied with the question, "What has it meant to me to be a woman?" Previously, she had insisted that women's lives were no different from men's lives. She initially rejected the term "feminist" to describe herself and distanced herself from feminist thought. Yet, as she considered the condition of women further, she realized that being a woman had shaped her experiences in profound ways. She writes, "I looked and it was a revelation: the world was a masculine world, my childhood had been nourished by myths formed by men, and I hadn't reacted to them in the same way I should have done if I had been a boy."[10]

Beauvoir adopts the question, "What is a woman?" as the guiding question of her pivotal feminist text, *The Second Sex* (1949). She observes that despite significant social and cultural differences worldwide, women share the experience of being dependent persons. Men, by contrast, are independent; they are the creators and prime examples of absolute rules and values in a fixed patriarchal system. Man, then, defines humanity:

> Thus humanity is male and man defines woman not in herself but relative to him; she is not regarded as an autonomous being . . . And she is simply what man decrees; thus she is called

"the sex," by which is meant that she appears essentially to the male as a sexual being . . . She is the incidental, the inessential as opposed to the essential. He is the Subject, he is the Absolute – she is the Other.[11]

In defining humanity, man pursues a freely chosen future. He invents tools and creates values that allow him to transcend the repetition of life. Woman, bound by her body – bound by what Beauvoir characterizes as her immanence in reproduction – is imprisoned in the repetition of life. She is unable to subdue her body or control her future. (Historically speaking, pregnancy and childbirth reduce women's capacity for work and make them dependent upon men for protection and food. This is particularly true before the advent of reliable birth control.) Woman is thus immanent rather than transcendent, dependent rather than independent, and therefore denied her very humanity. Beauvoir embraced the philosophical leanings of her former lover and intellectual companion, Jean-Paul Sartre (1905–1980), who advanced the existentialist idea that individuals are responsible for determining who they are and what meaning their lives bear. Similarly, Beauvoir maintained that women, like men, must look reality squarely in the face and assume a responsibility for changing it by engaging in a struggle for freedom. William Marston, the creator of Wonder Woman, anticipated and aided Beauvoir's call in the figure of Wonder Woman.

Wonder Woman's feminist spirit originates in her ancestry. We learn in the introductory issue (*All-Star Comics* #8 December 1941–January 1942) that Wonder Woman is the daughter of Hippolyte, Queen of Amazonia, an ancient Greek nation ruled for centuries by women. Threatened by the Amazons' autonomy and power, Hercules attempts to defeat the Amazons through combat. He loses. But through deceit and trickery, he manages to secure the magic girdle created by Aphrodite to ensure Hippolyte's success. The Amazons are enslaved until their degradation becomes unbearable. Aphrodite takes pity upon Amazonia and returns the magic girdle to Hippolyte, who overcomes the male captors, flees Amazonia with her women subjects, and establishes a new world on uncharted land they name Paradise Island.[12] Like the historic path of liberation for modern women, the Amazons' liberation is not without conditions. "Aphrodite also decreed that we must always wear these bracelets fashioned by our captors, as a reminder that we must always keep aloof from men."[13] Wonder Woman, who later acquires the name Diana after her Godmother, the Goddess of the Moon, threatens this newly established order when she falls in love with an American captain who crash lands his airplane on Paradise Island. Her mother warns, "So long as we do not permit ourselves to be again beguiled by men! We are indeed a race of Wonder Women! That was the promise of Aphrodite – and we must keep our promise to her if we are to remain here safe and in peace! That is why this American must go and as soon as possible!"[14]

Despite her respect for her mother's authority and commitment to women's independence, romantic love prevails. Wonder Woman gives up eternal life (that's right, *eternal* life), and her beloved home on Paradise Island for Captain Trevor. Like modern women everywhere, Wonder Woman sacrifices her self-interest for the sake of womanhood: devotion and service to men above fidelity to oneself. Patriarchy assigns women this familiar, secondary role. Yet, like the modern women Marston envisions and seeks to inspire, Wonder Woman does not relinquish her independent identity entirely. She transfers her nationalist commitments to her new homeland of America, "the land she learns to love and protect."[15] She both embraces and subverts traditional female roles, thereby challenging prevailing notions of womanhood. Lepore observes that Wonder

Woman's shifting identity and iconographic representation from the 1940s to the present mirrors ongoing and often inconsistent constructions of womanhood:

> Wonder Woman isn't only an Amazonian princess with badass boots. She's the missing link in a chain of events that begins with the woman suffrage campaign of the 1910s and ends with the troubled place of feminism fully a century later. Feminism made Wonder Woman. And then Wonder Woman remade feminism, which hasn't been altogether good for feminism. Superheroes, who are supposed to be better than everyone else, are excellent at clobbering people; they're lousy at fighting for equality.[16]

In 1911, the terms "Amazon" and "New Women" were applied to women who rebelled against social norms, left home, and attended college.[17] "Feminism," a term rarely used before 1910, was common by 1913. "Feminism meant advocacy of women's rights and freedoms and a vision of equality markedly different from that embraced by the 'woman movement' of the nineteenth century, which had been founded less on a principle of equality than a set of ideas about women's moral superiority."[18]

Marston tethered the feminist philosophy of *Wonder Woman* to the progressive views of early feminists, views he inherited from his beloved professor of philosophy, George Herbert Palmer. Palmer supported women's suffrage and women's education on the grounds that "girls are also human beings, a point often overlooked."[19] But Marston also understood and at times empathized with the social and political forces that vie against women's equality, real as well as symbolic forces that keep women dependent on men. It is fitting, then, that the singular weakness he subscribes to Wonder Woman, loss of strength, occurs whenever a man binds her in chains. Equality in theory is well and good. In practice, however, even Wonder Woman is subject to male power.

The fantasy of American women throughout the early twentieth century is realized again and again in the adventures of Wonder Woman: *to escape*.[20] In the words of Annie Lucasta ("Lou") Rogers, a feminist cartoonist and colleague of Wonder Woman cartoonist Harry G. Peter, she and other women wanted to know "how to arrange the world so that women can be human beings, with a chance to exercise their infinitely varied gifts in infinitely varied ways, instead of being destined by the accident of their sex to one field of activity – housework and child-raising."[21] Embedded in Roger's claim is an idea fleshed out by Marston and Peter in the character of Wonder Woman and theorized by Beauvoir: the ambiguity of existence should enrich women's lives and expand their capacity for self-definition, not confine them to a less significant and/or diverse existence. Self-identity, then, is a philosophical and political endeavor. Unless women resist the prescribed identity and artificial essence assigned to them – women are the weaker sex, women are objects, women are inherently feminine, and therefore submissive – and claim the freedom to define for themselves who and what they are, women will never be fully human. In Linda Stein's words, the Wonder Woman stories express Marston's belief that "individuals free of gender stereotypes are also free to develop to their full potential."[22] Democracy begins at home.

Wonder Woman realizes the critical link between personal emancipation and collective liberation. "I'll rely on myself and not a man," she tells Prudence, a rescuee. The defender of democracy develops her abilities, pursues economic opportunities, and addresses world problems. Moreover, she illustrates the existential and political value of freedom from male oppression: "What a sweet sound! My man-made bonds have snapped! My woman's power returns again" (*Wonder Woman* #4 April–May 1943). Wonder Woman's self-empowerment is a productive model of female transcendence.

The Ambiguously Feminist Superhero

For Wonder Woman and her early readers, the personal *is* political, as the feminist slogan goes. Mitra C. Emad argues that Harry G. Peter's iconographic blending of politics and personhood – star-spangled tights on a sensuous female form – invited women of the war generation to see themselves in Wonder Woman's narrative of American exceptionalism and achievement:

> Until his death in 1947, Marston, in collaboration with artist Harry G. Peter, produced a comic in which the hero, while often saving Capt. Trevor, primarily saved helpless women from imminent death and destruction, attempting also to empower women to look after themselves and discover their own physical and economic strengths. Girls are taught that if they "feel [they] can do things, so [they] can do them," and women are exhorted to "get strong and earn your own living."[23]

The overlaying of politics on Wonder Woman's ageless yet ever-changing body, however, creates a philosophical quandary.[24] The nation is a man's domain and nationalism, a man's game. The body is a woman's domain and embodiment, a woman's game. Hence, appending national identity to woman's identity creates "oppositional encounters" between masculine, public ideals and feminine, private ideals.[25] It also creates a tension between purported sources of power: political authority or political influence. The super powerful warrior, free from traditional gender norms, fights monsters and men, flaunting the unlimited power of the state. The super feminine woman, bound by traditional gender norms, enacts an attractive, heteronormative identity, surreptitiously creating her own furtive field of influence among uber-powerful men.[26] How is one to understand the conflicting ideals Wonder Woman embraces? She is a modern (super) woman who must make hard choices about which spheres of society to enter and, thus, which elements of identity to surrender or proclaim. In short, she must relinquish some freedom to become a woman – i.e. to be subdued, sexualized, and made safe for a man's world. The feminist philosophy of *Wonder Woman* is ambiguous indeed.

Marston and his collaborators exploit Wonder Woman's ambiguity by invoking distinct male and female spheres of activity. They then judiciously elevate one sphere (and one correlative identity) above the other. Which sphere gets privileged varies according to the cultural context in which the comic is produced. In a wartime edition of *Wonder Woman* comics (*Wonder Woman* #5 June–July 1943), a period in which women assumed vacated male positions to facilitate military success, George Washington appears as a symbol not of patriotism but patriarchy, poised to undermine women's emerging equality. "Women will lose the war for America!" he declares, "Women will betray their country through weakness if not treachery."[27] Marston "places gender above nationalism in rendering George Washington in such unpatriotic tones," Emad explains. "In other words, Marston seems to say, nationalism at the expense of women's power remains a conventional nationalism that must be subject to critique."[28]

The push for social change throughout the Marston era of *Wonder Woman* comics is a boon to first and second-wave feminists. Marston develops themes and images empowering to women and affirming of their intellectual and economic interests: "normal human females successfully acting as presidents, professors, and police officers."[29] This progressive trend falters, however, under the economic and social pressures of

World War II and the postwar era. Men reenter the workforce, reassert their authority, and reclaim their privileged economic positions. Women return to the domestic sphere and resume (unpaid) household and childcare duties, duties they do not necessarily enjoy or find fulfilling, as Betty Friedan documents in *The Feminine Mystique* (1963). *Wonder Woman* writers and artists follow suit. Steve Trevor reminds Wonder Woman that "she is only a woman, after all," in the Fall 1944 issue of *Comic Cavalcade #8.* He then persuades her to marry him – she needs a man to protect her, he avers. She responds in kind: "Steve, dear, now that we're going to be married, won't you please let me be your secretary?" Her first assignment is to type the following memo: "Every woman's place is in the home and girls should not try to do the work of men. They should be busy keeping house for their husbands." Between the 1960s and 2000s, Wonder Woman's power is steadily realigned with femininity and sexuality, expressions of women's inescapable embodiment. Wonder Woman's battle with the creature Decay in May 1987 illustrates this regressive shift. "By successfully vanquishing Decay, a symbol of social and environmental degradation, Wonder Woman demonstrates that the separate spheres can remain intact, femininity will not be corrupted by too much power, and gender – as long as it is feminine and beautiful – can coexist with nation."[30] *Wonder Woman* further perpetuates the ideology of separate (and unequal) spheres by rendering femininity as "heroic, self-sacrificing, and good," meanings that also "render the separate spheres of femininity and nationalism as sacrosanct."[31] Battle is undertaken in service to the nation, not out of duty to self. "Only a sudden call for help could prevent Wonder Woman from marrying Steve Trevor" (*Sensation Comics #94* November–December 1949).

Marston's vision of the modern American woman, embodied in the figure of Wonder Woman, is a woman who must exercise power covertly:

> Wonder Woman emerges to call attention to the price wartime women had to pay for admission to the man-made world: a fractured sense of self and the duplicitous social practices necessary to negotiate the maintenance of submissive femininity while participating in the public sphere of wartime society. Wonder Woman accomplishes this feat not with her considerable Amazon powers, but with female female [sic] impersonation, disguise, and deception – the tactics of female trickery.[32]

Wonder Woman's strength and endurance are admirable symbols of American power. Her masculine attributes, however, must be "lassoed into submission, sometimes by her own power" to bolster feminine ideals.[33] Because female power threatens the entire apparatus of a male-dominant world – money, position, and control – it must be suppressed. Is it any wonder that Wonder Woman's plane is invisible?

The ambiguous feminism of *Wonder Woman* is seen in Wonder Woman's subjugation. Who (or what) is poised to subdue her? Suffering Sappho! It is femininity, of course. Wonder Woman must subdue herself by feigning feminine weakness and submission. She is praised in the meaningfully titled, "The Battle of Desires," for teaching a young boy named Don to control his dominance (*Comic Cavalcade #16* August–September 1946). Although Wonder Woman, like Beauvoir, boldly proclaims her womanhood, she never fully escapes a woman's fate: woman is the *Other* (object) to a man's Self (subject). "This is the fundamental characteristic of woman," Beauvoir writes: "she is the *Other* at the heart of a whole whose two components are necessary to each other."[34] She explains the process by which women assume their alterity, their Otherness, in the following passage from *The Second Sex* (she reiterates this argument in *The Ethics of Ambiguity*):

> At the moment that women are beginning to share in the making of this world, this world still belongs to men: men have no doubt about this, and women barely doubt it. Refusing to be the *Other*, refusing complicity with man, would mean renouncing all the advantages an alliance with the superior caste confers on them.[35]

So long as male and female spheres exist, women must make difficult choices about which sphere to engage, and thus which capacities, interests, and elements of identity to sacrifice. Wonder Woman's life mirrors this two-sphere model of society: she leaves the woman's world of Amazonia for the man's world of America. *Wonder Woman* writers attempt to resolve the ambiguous identity of Wonder Woman in the person of Diana Prince, a person who "resorts to trickery and covert action to protect the discrete realms of national interests and feminine submissiveness."[36] Unfortunately, this resolution undermines Wonder Woman's power and reinforces female inferiority generally, further relegating women to the status of *Other*. The response of Wonder Woman's enemies to her assertion that "no bullet can hurt me while I wear my moonstone" says it all: "She ain't human" (*Moon Girl* #3 Spring 1948). Beauvoir concludes that women's equality is contingent upon women's abilities to free themselves from the status of *Other*. Women must, like the classical-era Wonder Woman, become active agents in the political sphere. They must invest themselves in projects in the world, including the project of their own identity formation. It is noteworthy that Gloria Steinem not only featured Wonder Woman on the cover of the inaugural issue of *Ms*. Magazine (1972) but also included as a feature article, "New Feminist: Simone de Beauvoir."

The contemporary focus on Wonder Woman's femininity and beauty at the expense of her brains and brawn undermines the progress Marston helped facilitate in the 1940s. Stephanie Cawley and Ann Matsuuchi characterize the post-Marston period of *Wonder Woman* comics as a period of heightened sexism and superficiality.[37] Writers trot out one hypersexualized image and retrograde storyline after another. Attention is paid almost exclusively to Wonder Woman's stereotypical feminine interests – romance, marriage, and domestic virtues: "Wonder Woman, Romance Editor" (*Wonder Woman* #97 March 1950). Rather than occupying the male sphere to push for transcendence and liberation, Wonder Woman's main occupation appears to be satisfying the male gaze. Cawley rightly observes that the sexualized representation of Wonder Woman from the 1990s to the present "certainly problematizes the suggestion of her status as a feminist icon."[38] We face a frustrating conclusion: Wonder Woman, ambiguously feminist superhero. Must women (still!) sacrifice economic independence for personal freedom? Is a feminine form of ambiguity the best we can hope for nearly 70 years after *The Second Sex*? The transition from Wonder Woman as active agent with her own independent identity to Wonder Woman as subdued and sexualized female illustrates the ambiguous feminist philosophy of *Wonder Woman* comics. It also exemplifies the ambiguity of human existence; an ambiguity that all too often binds rather than frees women to become who they are. Wonder Woman teaches us that freedom from the assumed facticity of life is hard won.

One of the historical obstacles to the achievement of a broad feminist program is that more than campaigns for racial or (male) political equality, feminism impacts every aspect of life and identity – mental, physical, moral, legal, familial, political. Thus, a comprehensive feminism seems to threaten everything in a male-dominated society. It is probably also the reason that major steps forward (women's suffrage, for example) never amount to a sweeping change. Diana Prince's disruption of masculine and feminine norms offers promising possibilities for transcending a two-sphere (male–female) model of social existence. "With Marston's advocacy for strong, independent women," claims Stein, "Wonder Woman begins to change the doctrine that 'male' means aggression and 'female' means submission."[39]

Marston's vision lives on. The New 52 Wonder Woman (*DC Comics* 2011) and recent relaunch with Earth-One realign Wonder Woman with modern feminist sensibilities. These sensibilities – "I have given (Wonder Woman) the dominant force but have kept her loving," Marston writes – both resist and reinscribe gender stereotypes.[40] Wonder Woman is powerful, but her power is soft. This is not perfect progress (one wishes for something a little more linear), but it is a vast improvement over the "bullet-breasted sex object" that emerged after Marston's death.[41] (Perhaps a Hegelian dialectic is at work.)

Women continue to see their efforts to navigate barriers to success – underemployment, unequal pay, sexual discrimination, and implicit bias – mirrored in Wonder Woman's struggles to live in a man's world while remaining true to her own self-interests. They bear the weight of oppressive messages about their feminine obligations. They feel the chains of their stagnant situations. Should women accept Wonder Woman's advice to young Olive in "The Bog Trap": "you'll do better next time" (*Sensation Comics* #58 October 1946)? Or should women follow Wonder Woman's example and "make bad men good and weak women strong"?[42]

The incrementalism of change in women's lives is one of feminism's more exasperating characteristics. Individual achievement rarely translates into broad, structural change. Collective progress is scattered and slow. Nonetheless, the work of real and mythic female figures like Beauvoir and Wonder Woman chart a promising path forward. "As far as being a superhero role model for women's freedom," Stein asserts, "I still believe she's the best."[43] The real job for Wonder Woman and her fans is to bring Amazonia to America by breaking down the barriers that impede women's advancement in the public sphere.

The return to a less-objectified Wonder Woman is a sign that society is once again contesting women's inferiority. "Wonder Woman symbolizes many of the values that feminists hold dear today," Stein explains. "Strength, self-reliance, mutual support, peace, respect for human life, and trust in soft power rather than violence and aggression to solve the world's conflicts."[44] Now a new generation of readers can ponder the feminist concerns that *Wonder Woman* raises: biological sex and gender identity, racial and ethnic bias, social and economic inequality, and the value of human liberty. It remains to be seen whether our favorite female superhero can save the world from itself. Suffering Sappho indeed.

For pop culture resources and philosophical resources related to this chapter please visit the website for this book: https://introducingphilosophythroughpopculture.com.

Notes

1   Lepore, J. (2015). *The Secret History of Wonder Woman*, 11. New York: Vintage Books.
2   Thomas, R. (2015). *Wonder Woman, The War Years, 1941–1945*, 10. New York: Chartwell Books.
3   Emad, M.C. (2006). Reading Wonder Woman's body: mythologies of gender and nation. *The Journal of Popular Culture* 39:962. Emad writes that "an estimated 4.7 million women responded to the labor shortage call" created by the entry of men into the armed forces. She adds that "for most women, this was their first opportunity to move into high-paying industrial jobs, and for black women it marked a preliminary movement out of domestic service."

4   For a description of Millennials, see Slaymaker, R. and Fisher's, K. (2015). Striving for cultural compe-
    tence while preparing millennials as emerging professionals. *Journal of Social Work Values and Ethics*
    12:49–62.
5   Lepore, xi.
6   We cannot escape the ambiguity of our age: identity politics, including LGBTQ considerations; debates
    regarding bathrooms usage and assigned or adopted gender identity; etc.
7   Wonder Woman's creator, William M. Marston, envisioned a "woman of tomorrow," a woman who would
    "take over the rule of the country, politically and economically." Thomas, 8–9.
8   Thomas, 19–21, copied from "Introducing Wonder Woman," *All-Star Comics* #8 (December 1941–
    January 1942) – script, William Moulton Marston – art, H.G. Peter.
9   de Beauvoir, S. (2009). *The Second Sex* (trans. C. Borde and S. Malovany-Chevallier), 283. New York:
    Vintage. Originally published in French in 1949.
10 Bair, D., de Beauvoir, S. (1990). *A Biography*, 86. New York: Touchstone.
11 de Beauvoir, 5–6.
12 Thomas, 15–16. It should be noted that Wonder Woman's origin myth has been written twice, once in
    1941 and again in 1987. For an analysis of Wonder Woman's origin myths, please see Emad.
13 Emad, 15.
14 Emad, 16.
15 Emad, 21.
16 Lepore, xiii.
17 Lepore, 17.
18 Lepore, 18–19.
19 Lepore, 8.
20 Professor Hugo Munsterberg, a German Professor of Psychology at Harvard, attempted to denigrate the
    aspirations of American women in the early 1900s by stating that "the aim of the German woman is to
    further the interests of the household, but the aim of the American woman is to escape." See Lepore, 32.
21 Quoted by Lepore, 84.
22 Stein, L. (2010). Wonder Woman: A Comic Book Character Shows the Way. *Online Issues* Magazine
    http://www.ontheissuesmagazine.com/2010winter/2010winter_Stein.php
23 Emad, 959.
24 Emad, 955.
25 Emad, 956.
26 Cocca, C. (2014). *Negotiating the third wave of feminism in Wonder Woman*. American Political Science
    Association Political Symposium 47, 98–103.
27 Thomas, 243.
28 Emad, 963.
29 Matsuuchi, A. (2012). Wonder Woman wears pants: Wonder Woman, feminism, and the 1972 "women's
    lib" issue. *Colloquy Text Theory Critique* 24:122.
30 Emad, 972.
31 This argument is made by historian Lori Landay and quoted in Emad, 964.
32 Emad, 965.
33 Emad, 956.
34 de Beauvoir, 9.
35 de Beauvoir, 10.
36 "Reading Wonder Woman's Body: Mythologies of Gender and Nation," 965.
37 Cawley, S. (2012). Comics and American feminism: Wonder Woman. The Stockton Postcolonial Project;
    Matsuuchi, 122–124.
38 Matsuuchi, 122–124.
39 Stein, L. (2010). Wonder Woman: A Comic Book Character Shows the Way. *Online Issues* Magazine
    http://www.ontheissuesmagazine.com/2010winter/2010winter_Stein.php.
40 Stein.
41 Stein.
42 Stein.
43 Stein.
44 Stein.

28

The Silence of Our Mother

Eywa as the Voice of Feminine Care Ethics (Avatar)

George A. Dunn and Nicolas Michaud

Summary

Colonel Miles Quaritch clearly believes Pandora is a hell. He warns us early on in *Avatar* that it is a place of danger, death, and violence. But we soon learn that it is also a place in which the Na'vi flourish, worshiping the mother goddess Eywa. As we get to know Pandora, we discover that it is filled with beauty, care, and community. Which is it then: a violent hell or a heaven of wonders? The answer may depend on whether we view it through the perspective of feminine or masculine ethical theories. Feminine care ethicists argue that the masculine perspective, which emphasizes conflicts and their just adjudication, offers only a limited and one-sided view of the world. The Na'vi, on the other hand, practice an ethic that allows them to discern how caring relationships, exemplified in the relationship of a mother to her child, are basic to even the most dangerous and deadly worlds. In due course, this Na'vi vision comes to reshape Jake Sully's perspective on the world, allowing him – in the language of the Na'vi – to "see" it more truly.

"If there is a hell, you might want to go there for some R&R after a tour on Pandora," Colonel Miles Quaritch informs the new arrivals to Hell's Gate. Yet Pandora reveals itself to Jake Sully as an enchanted world of wonder. Can Pandora be both a heaven and a hell?

Quaritch depicts Pandora as a living nightmare, a den of horrors where every conceivable danger lurks. Pointing toward the jungle, he warns the new arrivals: "Out there, beyond that fence, every living thing that crawls, flies, or squats in the mud wants to kill you and eat your eyes for jujubes." To his mind, Pandora is a deadly arena with enemies at every turn. Not only does the planet harbor a race of hostile humanoids with natural endowments and fighting skills that make them "very hard to kill," along with a dizzying assortment of other hostile life forms, but even the atmosphere itself is poisonous. To survive in such an environment, you must harden yourself, so you'll be mentally

Introducing Philosophy Through Pop Culture: From Socrates to Star Wars and Beyond, Second Edition.
Edited by William Irwin and David Kyle Johnson.
© 2022 John Wiley & Sons Ltd. Published 2022 by John Wiley & Sons Ltd.

prepared to do whatever it takes to stay alive. "You're on Pandora, ladies and gentlemen," Quaritch grimly reminds the new arrivals. "Respect that fact, every second of every day." The upshot of his ominous "old school safety brief" is that a healthy dose of fear is an indispensable tool for survival in this pitiless place. Let down your guard and Pandora will "shit you out dead with zero warning."

After listening to Quaritch's description, we might be surprised to learn how very differently the Na'vi view their world. Of course, like Quaritch, they "respect" Pandora, but not as a powerful foe. They know the perils of their environment every bit as well as Quaritch does, but fear doesn't define their relationship to their world. Above all, they revere Pandora – and Eywa, the deity who pervades and animates the planet – as a source of life, a nurturing mother, a provider, and a protector. Pandora, for them, is more than just an arena of deadly conflict. It's first and foremost a place of caring.

How Can You See, with Jujubes for Eyes?

That Quaritch and the Na'vi have such divergent views of the natural world may have something to do with the very different *social* worlds in which those worldviews were born. The militarized precinct of Hell's Gate epitomizes the conventional idea of a "man's world" – a place where your status depends on demonstrating courage, strength, and endurance in the face of adversity. It's a contentious world that is forever sorting its denizens into winners and losers. Jake's voiceover at the beginning of the movie nicely sums up the ethos of this place, at the same time as it lays bare his own fiercely competitive temperament: "I became a Marine for the hardship. To be hammered on the anvil of life. I told myself I could pass any test a man can pass." And the world that does the hammering is, according to this hardcore Marine, nothing short of "a cold ass bitch." Of course, to describe Hell's Gate as a "man's world" is not to deny that a tough gal like Trudy Chacón can more than measure up to its demands; but she's clearly in a minority. The military personnel on Pandora are overwhelmingly male. By contrast, the world of the Na'vi is much more feminine. Na'vi women are equal partners with their men and are just as capable as their male counterparts. And as the *tsahìk* (spiritual leader) of the Omaticaya clan, Neytiri's mother Mo'at exercises an unrivaled degree of power and influence due to her ability to interpret the will of Eywa, the Na'vi's female deity. With their devotion to Eywa – their "Great Mother," who connects them to each other and to everything else on Pandora – the Na'vi embrace an ethic that is distinctly maternal.

Could differences in male and female temperaments give rise to different ethical outlooks? That was the thesis of psychologist Carol Gilligan in her 1982 book *In a Different Voice*, which has come to be regarded as a watershed in the history of thinking about gender issues. Whereas men tend to view life as a contest in which individuals constantly attempt to advance themselves at each other's expense, women more typically view themselves as intimately tied to larger interpersonal networks sustained by relationships of care and intimacy. According to Gilligan, these two ways of situating ourselves in relation to the world have given rise to two distinct "voices," masculine and feminine, each of which is associated with a different approach to moral decision making.

The masculine voice puts a premium on *justice* – in particular, on protecting individual rights and on appealing to abstract rules in order to adjudicate conflicts. Principles of justice are important because they allow us to manage our conflicts without having to break out the poison-tipped arrows on a regular basis. We can define justice in many different ways, but in the modern world it has become common to think of justice as consisting in a set of rules or principles that aim to safeguard the rights and to balance the legitimate interests of all people, impartially. One of the most influential theories of justice is known as "contractualism," which likens the demands of justice to the terms of a contract that we have entered into with each other. We all give up our rights to do whatever we please, we agree to live under a set of rules that apply to everyone as free and equal individuals, and we receive the benefits of social cooperation and a guarantee that our rights will be protected just so long as we don't interfere with the rights of others.

The feminine voice, on the other hand, bears a remarkable resemblance to the voice of Eywa, since it focuses not on refereeing disputes, but rather on the *care* that sustains the web of concrete relationships in which people can flourish. "Our Great Mother does not take sides," Neytiri tells Jake. "She protects only the balance of life." We can think of these two voices as belonging, respectively, to the impartial judge and the caring mother. Gilligan argues that men tend to gravitate to the "justice perspective" and women to the "care perspective," though all genders are sufficiently versatile to approach questions of morality from either perspective.

The problem, according to Gilligan and many other feminist critics, is that almost all of the ethical theories that have dominated Western philosophy until quite recently have been one-sidedly masculine: they view conflict as the fundamental fact of society and morality as a way to manage our skirmishes and prevent them from getting too destructive. In short, these "masculine" ethical theories express a view of society not unlike the view of Pandora expressed by Colonel Quaritch. Imagine a different sort of "old school safety brief," one that someone like Quaritch might give not to new arrivals on Pandora, but to individuals on the threshold of adult life in the human world:

> You're not in diapers anymore, ladies and gentlemen. You're in the adult world, where you're just one among many individuals, all fighting to get ahead and prepared to eat your eyes for jujubes if you get in their way.

Truth be told, this isn't a bad description of what we see of life on Earth in the opening sequence of the movie, before Jake leaves for Pandora. And in such a world, where "the strong prey on the weak" and interpersonal conflict is both inevitable and, as Jake's brother Tommy discovered, sometimes deadly, a morality focused on rules that ensure fair treatment for all has an obvious appeal. Fairness matters greatly to Jake, as we see when he brings his fists to the defense of a young woman who's being bullied by a man in a bar. As Colonel Quaritch says: "You've got obey the rules." In this case, though, it's not "Pandora rules" but rather the rules of morality that offer us our only hope for survival in "the most hostile environment known to man" – the human social world! However, while conflict may be an undeniable fact of social life – as well as an ineliminable feature of the natural world, on both Earth and Pandora, as Jake discovers in his very first outing beyond Hell's Gate – this is by no means the whole story. Both the Na'vi and the terrestrial proponents of feminine "care ethics" help us see the bigger picture.

The Gifts of Our Mother

"Try to see the forest through her eyes," Grace admonishes Jake. Through Neytiri's eyes Jake will learn to see heaven on Pandora, while the belligerent Quaritch can never see anything but a hellish landscape of danger and strife. Neytiri's more benign vision of

Pandora comes into clear focus for Jake at a crucial moment during his training, when the two of them spy on a mother viperwolf playing affectionately with her pups. Previously known to Jake only as a vicious killer, his onetime deadly foe is surprisingly revealed to be a tender caregiver. However, to peer into this corner of the viperwolves' world requires a stealthy approach. Jake and Neytiri must keep a respectful distance so as not to provoke another attack like the one Jake clumsily incited on his first night in the forest; for even the most tender caregiver can turn into a ferocious killer when the welfare of her children is at stake. That's a lesson that Quaritch learns all too well when his assault on Pandora unleashes the fury of Eywa. Quaritch lands on a planet full of life, diversity, and community, but all he can see is conflict and opportunities for violence. What he never seems to realize is that the violence of Pandora, cruel and merciless though it may be, is in the service of something that his jujube eyes can never see – the tender care that Pandoran creatures extend to each other.

Despite the description that Jake offers early in the movie, Pandora is more than "just another hellhole" where mercenaries and miners do dirty jobs and get handsomely remunerated for their troubles – a world of "hired guns, taking the money, working for the company." Beyond the grubby pursuit of self-interest at Hell's Gate lies another world, of breathtaking beauty, where everything is deeply interconnected, each being living from energy that it "borrows" from others and bound in due course to "give it back." The metaphor of borrowing, which Neytiri uses to describe the connection between all living things on Pandora, may sound superficially like the same contractual tit for tat that governs the relationship between the Resources Development Administration (RDA) and its hired guns. That, at least, is an interpretation that fits with the justice perspective, with its focus on fairness and reciprocity. There is, however, a crucial difference between the Na'vi worldview and this contractual model. The Na'vi seem to regard the borrowed energy that nurtures and sustains their existence as a gift of Eywa, their Great Mother. And, ironically enough, the name human beings chose for the Na'vi's world is Pandora, a Greek name meaning "All-Gifts." But the "sky people" seem to lack a full appreciation of the implications of that name, not recognizing that the proper response to a gift is not a jealous sense of entitlement but heartfelt gratitude, which is most genuinely expressed as a desire to give back.

Reflecting on mothers and their gifts brings us to the heart of the care perspective. Proponents of care ethics like to remind us that, long before we were in any position to demand justice, insist on our rights, or enter into contracts, we were entirely dependent on the maternal care we received from our mothers or other primary caregivers. As vital to our existence as their relationship with Eywa is to the Na'vi, these caring relationships are not about satisfying the terms of some contract or ensuring that neither party encroaches on the rights of the other. Instead, the hallmark of the caring relationship between a child and their caregiver is the profound bond between two hearts – like *tsaheylu*, but without neural queues – an emotional attachment that makes the parent especially sensitive to their child's needs. Nor is it a freely chosen relationship between equals who have calculated the costs and benefits of cooperation. As the parent opens their heart to the child, they realize that they can't detach themself from this relationship without damaging their very identity and integrity as a person. Moreover, they recognize that being the stronger party in the relationship doesn't necessarily give them the upper hand. It's the needs of the child, the more vulnerable party, that dictate what the parent must do.

If not for these unchosen bonds of care, the sort of relationships that the justice perspective believes lie at the heart of morality couldn't even get off the ground. Consider

Quaritch, who has spent his entire adult life wrangling with powerful opponents and coming out on top through his own ingenuity and strength. Hard as it is to imagine, even this stalwart warrior began life – to quote William Shakespeare (1564–1616) – "mewling and puking in the nurse's arms," only much later becoming "jealous in honor, sudden and quick in quarrel, seeking the bubble reputation, even in the cannon's mouth." Had he survived his final smackdown with Jake, Quaritch might have eventually found himself once again in a state of utter dependency, a physically frail old man, "sans teeth, sans eyes, sans everything."[1] Of course, Quaritch might put it differently. In his own poetic voice, he might say that he entered this world a "Shavetail Louie" and that in the course of time this world will "shit him out dead." But the point is the same: those self-sufficient individuals, whom the justice perspective imagines us to be, represent at best only one stage of our lives, which is wedged between long periods of dependency. Perhaps Quaritch's contract with RDA includes provisions for his geriatric care, but the care he received as an infant was presumably not given to satisfy the terms of a contract. If it was like the care most of us received, it was a gift of love.

It's easy for adult men like Quaritch to forget their dependence on the care of others, which may in turn cause them to imagine social reality to be much more conflictual than it really is. As Carol Gilligan observes, "women perceive and construe social reality differently than men."[2]

> Since the reality of connection is experienced by women as given rather than freely contracted, they arrive at an understanding of life that reflects the limits of autonomy and control. As a result women's development delineates the path not only to a less violent life but also to a maturity realized by interdependence and care.[3]

Historically, women are the ones who have had the most intimate experience of care, since they have traditionally been the ones tasked with providing it for children, the sick, the disabled, and the elderly. If the justice perspective was born of the experience of men in the rough and tumble world of "territorial threat displays," where you better "keep your head on a swivel" and keep an eye out for hostiles at every pass, the care perspective reflects an experience of the world much more familiar to women, where nurturing and responsive care, rather than disputatious jousting, are the anchors of daily life.

The Work of Our Mother

Reflecting on how philosophers have traditionally thought about ethics, feminist philosopher Nel Noddings tells us: "One might say that ethics has been discussed largely in the language of the father: in principles and propositions, in terms such as justification, fairness, and justice. The mother's voice has been silent."[4] The Na'vi, though, can hear their mother's voice and so seek to emulate her practice of caring.

The philosopher Sara Ruddick (1935–2011), one of the pioneers of care ethics, identified three activities at the core of what she calls "maternal work": preserving the life of the child, fostering the growth of the child, and training the child for social acceptability.[5] When Neytiri undertakes the work of teaching Jake the ways of the Na'vi and imparting the skills he needs to both survive and flourish in the environment of Pandora, she's engaging in this very same sort of "maternal work" – a fact that's underscored by her initial characterization of him as "like a child." And, according to Ruddick, this practice of mothering is of singular importance not only because it answers to the vital needs of the child – and childlike adults, such as Jake – but also because it cultivates certain valuable moral and intellectual qualities. In particular, the mother must develop a sensitivity and responsiveness to the "nature" of the child, for "children are nothing before they are natural, and their growing is a work of nature. When children thrive, it is nature that thrives."[6] And, through her loving attention to the nature present in the child, the mother may come to acquire an appreciation of nature in general that allows her to see it as something much more than a menacing arena of conflict. As Ruddick explains:

> The settled antagonism of treating "nature" as an enemy is at odds with the engaged, sometimes adversarial, but fundamentally respectful relation to "nature" characteristic of preservative love, even more with the "natural" beneficence underlying growth.[7]

The preservative love that informs maternal work involves taking what is given by nature, safeguarding it, and helping it to realize its full natural potential. For the Na'vi, to engage in the work of nurture and care is to participate in the work of Eywa in her unending effort to sustain the conditions under which her children can flourish.

Nel Noddings is a philosopher who has drawn from the maternal perspective to develop another influential account of caregiving, which highlights the caregiver's need for what she calls "engrossment" and "motivational displacement." We are "engrossed" in the "cared-for" to the extent we're able to occupy her perspective, which requires "stepping out of our own frame of reference and into the other's."[8] As the Na'vi would say, we must truly "see" the other, for recognizing her needs is an indispensable precondition of caring for her properly. Then we can give ourselves over to "motivational displacement," in which we are motivated by the needs of the other rather than merely by our own desires. Such empathetic engagement with other beings, including other species, seems to be the hallmark of the Na'vi way of being in the world. Consider a Na'vi who seeks to ride an ikran (mountain banshee): if they approach the ikran simply as an object to bend to their will, they'll never be able to make the bond. When the ikran seeks to "kill" the Na'vi, they will fail to recognize it as an act of "choosing," interpreting it instead as an aggressive provocation and an invitation to respond in kind. Making the bond with an ikran requires an intricate dance, in which one must accurately interpret the nature and the needs of the ikran in order for the partnership to be formed. Even before *tsaheylu* is consummated, the Na'vi must be able to occupy the perspective of the other.

And, just like the *tsaheylu*, the caring relationship between two human beings involves more than just an intellectual grasp of the other's situation. It requires emotional engagement. Philosopher Annette Baier (1929–2012) has pointed out one reason why care ethics puts such a premium on emotions:

> It might be important for a father figure to have total control of their violent urges to beat to death the children whose actions enrage them, but more than control of such nasty emotions seems needed in the mother or primary parent, or parent-substitute, by most psychological theories. They need to love their children, not just control their emotions.[9]

Love provides the motivation for caring. But emotions are also important to the care perspective because they sometimes allow us to grasp aspects of a situation that may not be available from a justice perspective.

Caring is complex and messy. There's no simple, one-size-fits-all formula that will tell us how to care, since genuine caring requires sensitivity to the needs of particular individuals as they arise in highly specific situations. This may be one of the reasons why philosophers have often preferred the clear-cut, impersonal rules of the justice perspective, where abstract, formal reasoning dictates what's right and wrong, without any messy complications or emotions. According to Noddings, "ethical argumentation has frequently proceeded as if it were governed by the logical necessity characteristic of geometry."[10] And many philosophers have argued that that's how it should be, since sentimental biases can so often cloud our ability to act rationally and to make truly responsible ethical decisions.

Consider the destruction of Hometree. Parker Selfridge did the math, concluded that his obligation to the stockholders was more important than the lodging preferences of "the blue monkeys," and made his decision, confident that he was doing the right thing. His inability to empathize with the Na'vi and to understand the world from their perspective ("We try to give them medicine, education, roads. But, no, no, no, they like mud!") leaves him unable to see their attachment to Hometree as anything other than irrational intransigence. According to his own "rational" calculations, taking the lives of a certain number of intransigent Na'vi is an acceptable price for getting the surviving Na'vi to move. Of course, later, as flames engulf Hometree, Selfridge looks on with an expression that suggests that even he is affected by the horror of what he had done. But we can imagine a truly hard case like Quaritch dismissing that emotional reaction as mere sentimentality that clouds one's judgment and softens the resolve to do what must be done.

In contrast, consider Neytiri, who feels the awful weight of her action when she's forced to kill the viperwolves who are attacking Jake, recognizing that what she must do is a serious harm to both herself and her world. That's because the maternal perspective of the Na'vi enables her to see much more than the "sky people" can. When she looks at Jake's fierce attackers, what she "sees" is not just the mortal threat they pose to Jake, but mothers, pups, and their own struggle for survival. When she slays them, she mourns for them and the families they leave behind. This "engrossment" and "motivational displacement" is bound up with a distinctive perspective, one that becomes more and more accessible to Jake as his own motivations and attitudes begin to mirror those of the Na'vi; and he also comes to appreciate the perspective of the mother.

Mother Takes Sides

Emphasizing the maternal origins of care ethics doesn't mean that men aren't capable of caring. Neytiri's father, Eytukan, clearly cares deeply for his people, with an attentiveness and concern not unlike the feelings of a mother for her children. Nor should we suppose that care ethics has no room for justice. Most care ethicists recognize that both the father's voice and the mother's voice must be included in a full account of our moral responsibilities. As Baier observes, "there is little disagreement that justice is a social value of very great importance, and injustice an evil."[11] Moreover, most care ethicists acknowledge the inevitability of conflict in a world where the interests of everyone don't necessarily coincide. On a planet where "the strong prey on the weak," there will be a place for masculine warrior virtues of the sort Quaritch exemplifies – such as physical courage, strength, endurance, and pride – alongside the maternal caring ones. Caring might require mounting your ikran, grabbing your quiver of poisoned arrows, and going into battle to protect those you care about. For this reason, warriors like Jake and Tsu'tey have an honored place within Na'vi society. Neytiri is also an excellent warrior. And so, for that matter, is Eywa.

Before leading the battle against the "sky people," Jake pleads with Eywa: "See the world we come from. There's no green there. They killed their mother, and they're gonna do the same here ... I will stand and fight. You know I will. But I need a little help here." It's at this point that Neytiri speaks the words that we quoted earlier, about how Eywa is a nurturer, not an adjudicator of conflicts: "Our Great Mother does not take sides, Jake. She protects only the balance of life." Yet Neytiri is not entirely right. Like any good mother, Eywa bestows her care on all her offspring equally, remaining impartial when disputes arise between them; but, when the very survival of that caring relationship is imperiled, she can't remain on the sidelines. As Noddings writes: "The one-caring has one great aim: to preserve and enhance caring in herself and in those with whom she comes in contact."[12] When the intricate web of relationships that comprises life on Pandora is under assault, protecting the balance of life means taking sides and joining the fight.

"All I ever wanted in my sorry-ass life was a single thing worth fighting for," reports Jake in his opening voiceover. In the end, he found what he was looking for in Eywa. Jake has learned that the masculine perspective of the warrior is incomplete, that it needs the feminine ethic of caring to give a worthy meaning and purpose to the fight. Without that care perspective, the world can easily devolve into a living hell.

For pop culture resources and philosophical resources related to this chapter please visit the website for this book: https://introducingphilosophythroughpopculture.com.

Notes

1 Shakespeare, W. *As You Like It*, Act II, Scene VII, lines 44, 51–53, 66.
2 Gilligan, C. (1993). *In a Different Voice: Psychological Theory and Women's Development*, 171. Cambridge, MA: Harvard University Press.
3 Gilligan, 172.
4 Noddings, N. (2003). *Caring: A Feminine Approach to Ethics and Moral Education*, 2e, 1. Berkley: University of California Press.
5 Ruddick, S. (1989). *Maternal Thinking: Toward a Politics of Peace*, 17. New York: Ballantine Books.
6 Ruddick, 77.
7 Ruddick, 115.
8 Noddings, 24.
9 Baier, A. (1995). The need for more than justice in her *Moral Prejudices: Essays on Ethics*, 30–31. Cambridge, MA: Harvard University Press.
10 Noddings, 1.
11 Baier, 19.
12 Noddings, 172.

29

"Everything Is Backwards Now"

Avatar, *Anthropocentrism, and Relational Reason*

Jeremy David Bendik-Keymer

Summary

In contemporary environmental ethics-speak, *Avatar* depicts a confrontation between people with a shortsighted "anthropocentric" worldview and an alien race
with an "ecocentric" worldview – selfish humans versus nature-loving Na'vis! But
closer attention to the film shows that there is a *deeper* humanity present in Jake
Sully's ability to become alien and to find himself through his relations with other
forms of life. This chapter presents the idea of deep (not superficial) humanity
and explores the identity twists of *Avatar* in light of contemporary environmental
ethics. One of the things that emerges is the recalcitrant presence of colonialism
haunting *Avatar* both explicitly and implicitly. So this chapter also discusses the
ways in which the film's view of being human at times challenges – and at other
times subtly maintains – colonialism.

There's a moment about halfway through *Avatar* where Jake Sully wakes up disoriented
from the link to his avatar. "Everything is backwards now," he says, "like out there is the
true world and in here is the dream." I call this the inside-out moment. Jake's life in the
Resources Development Administration (RDA) mining colony seems unreal, while his
avatar life seems real.

The inside-out moment comes at the midpoint of the film, not long before the rite of
passage in which Jake becomes a member of the Omaticaya clan. It feels pivotal to the
plot of the film. Out of the 35 chapters of the DVD (that old school thing!), the inside-
out moment occurs in chapter 18, right in the middle.

"Conversion" comes from the Latin *conversio*, which designates a turning around, an
about-face. *Avatar* depicts what is an about-face for the former marine Jake Sully, who
ultimately will no longer be human while, ironically, becoming more *humane* than he
ever was.[1] Jake begins the film part opportunist, part solid marine, but he ends up as a
self-sacrificing Na'vi hero who puts the welfare of Ewya and life on Pandora ahead of his
own self-interest. Along the way, we watch his capacity for empathy and wonder grow.

Introducing Philosophy Through Pop Culture: From Socrates to Star Wars *and Beyond*, Second Edition.
Edited by William Irwin and David Kyle Johnson.
© 2022 John Wiley & Sons Ltd. Published 2022 by John Wiley & Sons Ltd.

Jake the Na'vi depicts a *humane* person with deep, life-encompassing relationships that take on responsibility for the future. This, I believe, is the explicit message of the inside-out moment.[2]

Deep Humanity in an Alien Avatar

A being has moral standing if, *morally*, it makes a difference how we treat that being. A standard question raised in environmental ethics is: *Who* counts? *Who* has "moral standing"? If you think only human beings count, you're an anthropocentrist, someone who puts human beings – *anthrōpoi* in ancient Greek – at the center. If you think that all living beings count somewhat, you're a biocentrist, someone who puts life – *bios* in ancient Greek – at the center. And if you think that whole ecosystems count, believing, for example, that to destroy a wetland is morally objectionable above and beyond the loss of individual lives and livelihood, then you're an ecocentrist, someone who puts the *oikos* – "house, home, dwelling-place" in ancient Greek – at the center.[3]

Of course, there are shortsighted and enlightened versions of anthropocentrism. The shortsighted version was epitomized in April 2010 by the ill-starred managers of then British Petroleum (BP), who chose short-term profit over long-term sustainability, discounting the interests of the sea life and birds of the Gulf of Mexico. A more enlightened anthropocentrism would have understood that taking care of the macro-ecosystem of the Gulf of Mexico is, in the long term, even in BP's interest. After all, like any other corporation, BP depends on a functioning society for economic prosperity. But societies depend on a well-functioning natural world.[4] So BP should care about the natural world and conserve it. Enlightened anthropocentrism takes into account the long-term and large-scale factors that contribute to human prosperity, treating everything nonhuman mostly as a means or as an impediment to that goal. In *Avatar*, the RDA corporation offers another example of anthropocentric thinking, arguably just as shortsighted as that of BP.

Rather than frame the issue in terms of shortsighted versus enlightened anthropocentricism, however, it is more helpful to think about superficial versus deep humanity. *Avatar* suggests that a *superficial* sense of our humanity involves shortsighted anthropocentrism. But it also suggests that acting from what is most deeply human involves something more than simply enlightened anthropocentrism. *Deep* humanity, as I will call it, embraces ecocentrism. Deep humanity is the view that, because our own humanity matters, we ought to be considerate toward life and considerate with our home – our *oikos*. Deep humanity is not superficial anthropocentrism or human chauvinism. It doesn't simply entail promoting human interests, but also acting in ways that are deeply *humane*. Being humane, in turn, involves being thoughtful with the natural world. One reason why I find *Avatar* more complex than it may seem is that it pushes us to acknowledge a distinction that's still not common in the field of environmental ethics, the distinction between superficial and deep humanity.

Using standard environmental ethics taxonomy, we might say that *Avatar* depicts a confrontation between people with a shortsighted anthropocentric worldview and an alien race with an ecocentric worldview. The shortsighted anthropocentrists are on the side of the RDA, engaged in an enterprise that treats the Na'vi as obstacles and Pandora as a giant resource. By contrast, the Na'vi think that the ecological order of their entire planet counts. Pandora, to them, is Ewya: a *personality*, not an object.[5]

That signals something. The question of who counts can be spelled out in terms of the distinction between something we treat as a mere object to be used for our purposes and some being we recognize as a partner in our universe. If, for example, I regard some wetland down the road as merely a resource or a nuisance, I'm treating it as an object. As long as it concerns me only as a useful object or as an obstacle, it lies outside the reach of my moral consideration. But if I conceive of the wetland as a partner in my moral universe, I can't help but give it moral consideration. I must respect it and care about it for its own sake, not merely for mine. I may even treat it as if it had a personality, as the Na'vi do when they regard their world as the embodiment of Ewya.

People with the *virtue* of a deep sense of humanity – as opposed to superficial or inhumane people – commonly hold that life isn't something you may just abuse. Think of Mahatma Gandhi (1869–1948), who is often held to have a consummate sense of humanity. Or think of Rachel Carson (1907–1964), author of *Silent Spring*, the book that is often credited with launching the modern environmental movement. Such people have sympathy for all sorts of living beings, and they quite often identify with the land – and sea – around them to the extent that their sense of their own dignity depends on their care and respect for that ecosystem. There are numerous examples of people with a deep sense of humanity, but my favorite is my late uncle, Bill Oebker, who was a farmer in Avon, Ohio.[6] When killdeer nests appeared in his field – killdeer are birds that nest in the dirt – Uncle Bill would drive his tractor around them. He was very matter of fact about what he was doing. It was nothing ideological for him, just something decent people do because those birds are trying to live too. In this and similar ways, people centered on being humane are not anthropocentric in the sense commonly used in environmental ethics. They have aspects of bio- and ecocentrism in their characters, and this makes them more like the Na'vi than like the mining mercenaries and corporate functionaries.[7]

Accordingly, as Jake's world turns inside out, he illustrates a shift from anthropocentrism to ecocentrism, revealing to many of us a potential within our own sense of humanity.[8] The film is thus an "avatar" for our untapped sense of ourselves. When we eagerly support Jake and the Na'vi, we are siding with a way *we* could be. The film cleverly seduces us into taking a different stance toward what is desirable for a human being by embodying our own potential in an alien.[9]

"Out There is the True World"

What more can we learn about deep humanity by examining Jake's gradual conversion? Jake's inside-out moment coincides with his waking up from his link. He feels his life has been turned inside out. He lives most of his life in his avatar. His human body isn't where he's acting because he acts through the body of his avatar. The process of living as an avatar, just in and of itself, makes everything seem backwards.

But Jake has clocked a number of hours by the time he feels that things have turned inside out. We'd expect him to be more used to linking – not less. When he says that everything is backwards, he's not just talking about the disorientation one gets from switching in and out of avatar life. He explains how things are backwards by pointing to the "true world" out there with his avatar as opposed to the "dream" world in here, where his human body eats and sleeps. How is the world in the jungle with the Omaticaya *true*, and how might the world inside the mining complex be false? What can this idea of the "true" world teach us about our own humanity?

I take Jake to be saying that the world of the Na'vi is truer because it's more *authentic*, not simply more factual or more actual. After all, his world inside the mining colony is no less factual or actual than the world of the Na'vi – at least within the story the film tells. Moreover, for the world "in here" to be a dream, it must be devoid of some important aspects of reality. Yet the mining colony is as physical and tangible as the jungle is. It's not unreal in the sense of being immaterial; so its unreality must be located elsewhere, at the opposite pole from authenticity. The mining world is somehow inauthentic, *fake*.

The film tells us indirectly how the Na'vi world is more authentic. Not long after Jake's turnaround moment, he ends up pleading for Neytiri's understanding in front of the Omaticaya clan, after he has revealed his duplicity to them. "Look, at first it was just orders," he says, "and then everything changed . . . I fell in love with the forest and with the Omaticaya people. And with you." At first, Jake was bent on exploiting the trust of the Omaticaya on behalf of his employer. He was using them, treating them as objects to be manipulated for the sake of something his employers wanted. That smacks of the anthropocentric belief that nonhumans don't count.[10]

Yet the film offers something subtler than just a critique of anthropocentrism. As it begins, we see Jake deciding to step into his dead brother's shoes. He's just identified Tommy's body, laid out in a cardboard coffin. And while that body is being incinerated, before the cinders even fall, two corporate "suits" try to persuade Jake to take over his brother's contract, so they may recover the money they lost as a result of his death. They don't give Jake space to mourn but instead get right down to business, time being money. The pursuit of profit has outstripped their sense of humanity. When these corporate "suits" put money ahead of compassion, their hearts don't differ much from that of the murderer who killed Tommy for the money in his wallet. This sets up the real moral conflict of the film, in which the villain is not just anthropocentrism, but an exploitative attitude toward the world, including the world of other human beings. The villain is really a colonialist society.

Among the Na'vi, the entire world of life has a personality that bears the name Eywa. All life on Pandora is *kindred*, as in a big family. This feeling of kinship is evident in the Na'vi's attitude toward the hostile elements of their planet. For example, after Neytiri wounds a viperwolf while defending Jake, she says a prayer over its dying body before killing it as painlessly as possible.[11] In rebuking Jake for being so stupid as to provoke an attack from animals who then had to be killed in his defense, Neytiri shows respect even for a predator. That's the opposite of exploitation. By some people's standards, it's surprisingly *humane*. Under Neytiri's guidance, Jake later manages to kill a hexapede without causing it needless pain – and with an attitude of respect. That's when she tells him: "You are ready."

In short, the Omaticaya have a relationship with the surrounding world of life that is like a partnership. In the terminology of environmental ethics, they are ecocentric. But they also show us a deep sense of humanity, the way *we* can be when we are most humane. In so doing, they reveal – as we'll see in Section 29.3 – what it is that makes their world "true" and what, by contrast, makes the military – corporate world of the colonializing mining compound more like a bad "dream."

"Lost in the Woods"

Not long after Jake's inside-out moment, he's approached by Colonel Miles Quaritch. "Haven't got lost in the woods, have you?"[12] Quaritch is right: Jake's new home is the woods. He fell in love with it along with the Omaticaya and Neytiri. Just moments before, we heard Jake tell his video log, "I don't know who I am anymore."

My interpretation is that Jake feels alienated during his inside-out moment because he is transitioning away from a world that denies the real relationships with others that we are capable of having, relationships that tap into the deepest parts of ourselves. An unreal world is one that's devoid of important relationships. The authenticity of a world depends, in turn, on the richness of the relationships it offers.

Perhaps the woods are more real to Jake than the "dream" because they teem with beings who call out to him as potential partners, offering him many possible relationships and a chance to enter into something larger than himself. By contrast, the environment of the mining colony – governed by an exploitative outlook that regards the planet as an object – has a shortage of genuine relationships. What relationships there are seem thin and functional, like the tense opposition between Grace and Selfridge, or the harsh camaraderie of Quaritch and his mercenaries. The soldiers insult each other and even make fun of Jake's disability. Under Selfridge, they are driven by greed and, under Quaritch, they are spurred on by fear.

Avatar's conversion story traces relationships that grow between Jake and Ewya, Jake and the Omaticaya, and Jake and Neytiri. These circles of life are connected. They come together at the end in the climactic moment after the final battle with Quaritch when Jake – the disabled and wounded soldier – is "seen" and loved as he truly is by Neytiri, a member of a totally different species. Their relationship transcends his disability, the species boundary, and his former mindset.[13]

This sort of connection makes the world of the Omaticaya and Ewya authentic to Jake, while also deepening his sense of humanity. His deepening relationship with the world of life is the source of Jake's deepening sense of humanity, the way he becomes more humane. Here's where *Avatar* moves beyond standard discussions in environmental ethics. Not only does the movie work with the novel category of deep humanity, but it also depicts "relational reason," the logic that deepens our humanity.

Relational reason is an expression for the logic of relationships, for the conscious process of trying to connect with a "who" – or as the philosopher Martin Buber (1878–1965) called it, a "you."[14] When I reason relationally, I figure out how to connect with another being whom I take to be a person or to have something like a personality. To me, that being is then a subject, not an object; a "who," not a "what"; a person (or a person-like being), not a thing. The distinction between a "who" and a "what" is so basic that we teach it to our children when, for instance, we tell them that it's one thing to kick a rock and quite another thing to kick a dog.

The important point to stress about relational reason is that it helps us understand concretely and precisely what the world of the mining colony lacks such that its absence makes the colony seem unreal once Jake becomes aware of it. Relational reason is a basic part of human consciousness that works by interacting with everything that can be a possible subject or a "who" for us, for instance other living beings and systems of life. We can find personality and potential connection in all manner of living things, no matter how strange. To deny that connection is to deny a part of ourselves. Some psychologists and biologists even have a name for the elemental wonder and joy we experience when connected to the world of living things. They call it *biophilia*.

The world of the mining colony may deny the connection to life "in the woods," but the Omaticaya don't. Using relational reason, they continually try to connect with each other, to "see" each other. The Omaticaya also see and connect with other living beings – the viperwolves, for instance – and even with their entire ecosystem. They feel their world to have a personality, which they call Eywa, just as a farmer who knows the seasons, peculiarities, and riches of their land might feel that it has personality as well. The

Omaticaya and the Na'vi generally acknowledge their relational capacities in a way the mercenaries and corporate functionaries do not. And *that* is what makes the world "out there" authentically human, whereas the world "in here" is false, denying important human relationships. Sure, all this is sentimental and cartoonish at times in *Avatar*, but there's something true in it too that is often missing from *our* profit-driven world.[15]

Jake becomes aware that the teeming world of life around him presents the possibility of many vital relationships. Even early on during his first trip into the forest, he finds it to be a source of wonder. Lost in childlike curiosity, he drifts away from Grace and Norm to look at the spiral plants called "helicoradians." His wonder only increases under Neytiri's tutelage until he finally falls "in love with the forest." Love is the ultimate relationship.[16] The teeming possibilities for relationship come to make "the woods" seem truer to Jake than the military–corporate world. By contrast, when the denizens of Hell's Gate cordon off much of that world – both mentally and physically – and treat it only as a mere resource or obstacle, they deny the true potential for human relatedness present in themselves. They deny their potential for deep humanity. To do that is to deny an important aspect of one's reality.

At the end of the film Jake becomes a Na'vi, no longer human. But, in becoming non-human, he has become more humane. Ironically, by becoming an alien, Jake has become more recognizable. We see him because he has let himself see and be seen.[17]

"Everything is Backwards Now"

The explicit message of *Avatar* concerns the value of discovering our deep humanity. It can be a moving message for those of us who are aware of our potential for connecting with our *oikos*, our dwelling place on the planet. Yet there is a further layer to the inside-out moment, one that makes that moment turn around and take in the world of film-making itself: Hollywood, the production and distribution industries of mass market filmmaking, and the way some of us may escape from our humdrum reality by watching fantasy films.

With its luminescent fantasies that fulfill a variety of wishes, isn't cinema like a dream? And don't we know, at some level, that once we leave the cinema we come back to the true world? Our lives – where we work, suffer, love, feel angst, endure insomnia, make food, and scrub counters – are in the real world, whereas the world of magical warriors is a fantasy.

The real world, though, is also the corporate world of profit seeking and the vast military apparatus that protects it, a world that makes a place for *Avatar* in part because it was a staggeringly profitable film. It is a world where many of us, at least in the United States, have enjoyed going to movies on Friday night while our military maintains a constant presence around the world and while our nation-state has violated every one of its treatises with Native American nations while still occupying their lands. This is not to say that the US military – or the armed forces of other nations – are simply profit-mongering mercenaries like the SecOps in *Avatar*. Nor is it to say that James Cameron's film was made only for the sake of profits. It's to say that our fantasy space inside the cinema is supported by a vast corporate and military order – a *colonial* order. Film-going belongs to a larger society, and that society is unsustainable and tragically at odds with Earth's cycles of life. The world outside the theater, the world that makes our experience inside the theater possible, has much in common with Jake's life inside the mining colony coming to feel like a dream to him. The true world is out there for us, but many of us have yet to find it.

To put it bluntly, the mainstream institutions of a nation-state like the United States of America and of an economy drive by profit seeking where the uber-wealthy wield vast power over everyday people are at odds with our potential for deep humanity. Most of us are complicit in institutions that have not yet worked out a deeply human relationship with Earth, but that are predicated off of a vast power inequality in our world. Our world's consumption patterns are unsustainable, many political institutions are remote from the limited power of everyday people, and we are heading toward catastrophic climate change. Moreover, we are probably in the early phases of the sixth mass extinction since life on Earth began, a mass extinction *our globalized economy* is causing and that threatens to eliminate half the life forms on Earth in this century alone.[18] Many of our institutions perpetuate this unsustainable situation in wasteful lifestyles divided across a vastly inegalitarian society and closed off to the needs of other forms of life on this planet. In fact, it's possible that some of us originally saw *Avatar* in a concrete shopping mall built over what used to be a thriving wetland.[19]

So the happy ending of *Avatar* is a dream while, for some of us, *our* world is closer to a nightmare.[20] But the nightmare could give way to a true world if only we *challenged our dominant institutions politically* to express deep, life-encompassing relationships that are mindful of the future of life, taking decolonization seriously.

For pop culture resources and philosophical resources related to this chapter please visit the website for this book: https://introducingphilosophythroughpopculture.com.

Notes

1   The gnawing worry that one's life is fake was a theme of mainstream American culture in the late twentieth century. Hear, for instance, the refrain in "Once in a Lifetime" by the Talking Heads, *Remain in Light* (New York: Sire Records, 1980) that repeats, "Same as it ever was." There is an echo of this worry in *Avatar*, made in the first decade of the twenty-first century.

2   The film's unintentional and *implicit* message is more complex. Jake is a white man, and he ends up with an indigenous body. That's ambivalent. There's an unworked-through relationship to *colonialism* within the film. The Na'vi's clans connote a range of indigenous cultures in *our* world, including African traditional cultures. At the same time, the film falls within the tradition of American Westerns that romanticize Native Americans while preserving the white male hero at their center. Compare, for instance, Kevin Costner, dir. *Dances with Wolves* (Los Angeles: Orion Pictures, 1990) – also a film where military-backed colonization shapes contact with indigenous people.

3   Ecocentrism shouldn't be confused with views where moral consideration of ecosystems *derives* from duties we have to individual lives, something often called an "indirect duties" view. For more on the canonical positions of environmental ethics, consider two state-of-the-field readers today, see Hourdequin, M. (2015). *Environmental Ethics: From Theory to Practice*. New York: Bloomsbury and Sandler, R. (2017). *Environmental Ethics: Theory in Practice*. New York: Oxford University Press. The classic representative of biocentrism is Albert Schweitzer, while the classic representative of ecocentrism is Aldo Leopold. Anthropocentrism is pegged on so many philosophers and religions that it is best simply to read through an environmental ethics reader to get a sense of the term.

4   We do not need to be reminded of COVID-19 to see this point. Or do we? The virus emerged out of poor animal husbandry practices in an exploitative global market for animals.

5   This personification of the planet distinguishes deep humanity from consideration of the natural world and adaptation of our societies so that we can live sustainably. Such adaptation, called "ecological reflexivity" by environmental political theorists, is mainly practical. It needn't involve personal relationships with the natural world. See Dryzek, J.S. and Pickering, J. (2019). *The Politics of the Anthropocene*. New York: Oxford University Press.

6 See Bendik-Keymer, J. (2006). *The Ecological Life: Discovering Citizenship and a Sense of Humanity*, chapters. 4–6. Lanham, MD: Rowman & Littlefield. I developed there the idea of deep humanity through reading the work of Cora Diamond. I challenged the use of the word "anthropocentrism," too. Once we take seriously our potential for deep humanity, why would we say that to be "centered" in our own humanity is about being self-interested? It seems that "anthropocentrism" as the word is commonly used internalizes a *superficial* sense of humanity, and it shouldn't. We can *be* better than that.

7 I think that we can begin to see what ought to matter to us by focusing on people of excellent character. They aren't theories, but real people. Of course, one person's good character can be another person's bad character. But seeing a whole human being at work in real life, with all her or his dispositions, is often a better way to glimpse what matters than focusing on an abstract or fragmentary action. This approach to morality is often called "virtue ethics."

8 In many ways, the biggest question of environmental ethics is: *How can we live more ecologically?* Various positions within environmental ethics mark out different answers. *Avatar* suggests one direction.

9 The "we" here is that of people caught up in industrial, capitalist, and settler colonial society, such as mainstream Americans. If one is Native American, one may have never *identified* with the "we" of a violent, profit-driven, extractive world like Jake did!

10 Having to fall in love with people to care about them morally seems to make a mockery of morality. You don't have to be in love with people to know that you should treat them well. But read on. Jake's falling in love is about something more transformative in his way of being.

11 Neytiri's prayer seems to allude to some indigenous social practices. Consider John Mohawk's claim of Haudenosaunee society that "We give a greeting and thanksgiving to the many supporters of our own lives – the corn, beans, squash, the winds, the sun. When people cease to respect and express gratitude for these many things, then all life will be destroyed, and human life on this planet will come to an end." Mohawk, J.C. (2005) A basic call to consciousness: the haudenosaunee address to the western world. In: *Basic Call to Consciousness* (ed. Akwasasne Notes). Summertown, TN: Native Voices. Thanks to James K. Rowe, University of Victoria, for the reference. The Viperwolf appears to be a keystone predator of its ecosystem and thus has a role in the ecosystem's continuity.

12 There is an early American colonialist echo in Quaritch's bigoted dig. For the puritans of the "New World," the woods were a place of sin where people lose their way. See for instance Robert Eggers, dir. *The Witch* (Los Angeles: A24, 2015).

13 Martha C. Nussbaum calls transcendence like this "humane." See Nussbaum., M.C. (2006). *The Frontiers of Justice: Disability, Nationality, Species Membership*. Cambridge, MA: Harvard University Press.

14 Buber, M. (1996). *I and Thou* (trans. W. Kaufmann). New York: Touchstone/Simon & Schuster.

15 I've come to the view that *Avatar* is mainly "decolonial-thinking-lite" for mainstream, consumer culture Americans. That has its shortcomings, but it also makes the film complex in the way that embarrassing mistakes touching on suppressed truths often are. The film's shortcomings *and* its gestures of intent can be occasions to start a discussion of decolonial thinking and decolonization movements, including the contradictory positions and mindsets of white allies. For more on my perspective, see Bendik-Keymer, J.D. (2020). *Involving Anthroponomy in the Anthropocene: On Decoloniality*. New York: Routledge.

16 If you want to press on *Avatar* more critically, it is important to look at the sexual relationship Sully has with Neytiri. Does it indulge in the colonial fantasy of having sex with an indigenous woman? Does Sully display an uncritical sexuality? Thanks to Kyle Whyte for these questions (e-mail correspondence, June 7, 2020).

17 Indigenous scholars have had many concerns with *Avatar*. Contrasting *Avatar* with Indigenous-made science fiction films, the scholar and philosopher Kyle Powys Whyte (Citizen Potawatomi Nation) writes:

> [I] n Indigenous science fiction films, . . . the protagonists . . . are *not* portrayed as romantic stereotypes or symbols of a common humanity. [The films] do *not* presuppose naive notions of Indigenous spirituality. They see environmental protection as possible only if we resist the capitalist–colonialist "matrix" of oppression and build allyship across different human and nonhuman groups. These films differ greatly from, say, *Avatar*, where the protagonist is a white male who passes as Indigenous and uses romantic Indigenous wisdom to save everyone ["Let's Be Honest about Decolonization with our Allies," http:// *Indianz.com*, April 4, 2018, emphasis mine].

Considering this criticism of *Avatar* makes the film realer. On the one hand, Jake *does* take part in a resistance movement. But on the other hand, the film makes the Na'vi *nonhuman!* Thus, the film seems caught up in the very ideology of colonialism it criticizes in the RDA. The film literally dehumanizes the indigenous whom it romanticizes. At the same time, it keeps our focus on a white man as the center of the film's heroic world. None of this changes the truth about relational reasoning or about the moral right to resist a violent, destructive occupier. But it does suggest that the film fails to fully relate to *our* world.

There is real colonization on Earth – of humans, not aliens! – and white men are not the answer. Sympathetic people should do more than "go native." Fantasies won't do. Only political change to restore stolen lands and honor "land-based practices of treaty making and just reconciliation" will do (language thanks to Kyle Whyte, e-mail correspondence, June 7, 2020).

18   See Gorke, M. (2003). *The Death of our Planet's Species*. Washington, DC: Island Press and Kolbert, E. (2014). *The Sixth Extinction: An Unnatural History*. New York: Henry Holt & Co.

19   As I did in Syracuse, New York, along the disputed and industrially polluted sacred lake of the Onondaga Nation.

20   Some indigenous people report that this nightmare has been going on for *many hundreds of years*. See Whyte, K.P. (2017). Our ancestors dystopia now: indigenous conservation and the anthropocene. In: *The Routledge Companion to the Environmental Humanities*, (ed. U.K. Heise, J. Christensen, and M. Niemann), chapter 21. New York: Routledge.

Part VII

Social and Political Philosophy

Introduction

Social and political philosophy is concerned with the relationship between the individual and society. What rights do individuals have and how are these rights derived and justified? What form of government is most just? What economic system is best and most fair? Plato (428–348 BCE) and Aristotle (384–322 BCE) consider ethics and political philosophy inseparable: the good person and the good society depend on one another. In his *Republic*, Plato raises the question of the legitimate role of the government and calls for the abandonment of democracy in favor of a proto-socialist state, an ideal developed much later by Karl Marx (1818–1883). Thomas Hobbes (1588–1679) views the government as an overbearing presence, a Leviathan, but one to which we must submit for our own protection. According to John Locke (1632–1704), all men are born with the inalienable rights to life, liberty, and property, and through the social contract we form governments to protect those rights. Libertarian philosophers of today see the protection of those rights as the only legitimate function of governments. By contrast, Communitarian philosophers argue that governments must take care of their citizens in the spirit of community, thus justifying, among other things, the welfare state. Other topics of discussion in social and political philosophy include justice, fairness, punishment, race, globalization, the family, paternalism, and autonomy.

According to Thomas Hobbes, we should appeal to the protection of a powerful sovereign monarch. Modern readers may have trouble seeing the wisdom in that recommendation, but in Chapter 30, Greg Littmann takes us into the world of *Game of Thrones* to see why Hobbes may have a point. After all, if people were not forced to obey laws, we would have a "war of every man against every man" and would find ourselves in a situation where life is "solitary, poor, nasty, brutish and short." Clearly, then, it matters who sits upon the Iron Throne.

Introducing Philosophy Through Pop Culture: From Socrates to Star Wars *and Beyond*, Second Edition.
Edited by William Irwin and David Kyle Johnson.
© 2022 John Wiley & Sons Ltd. Published 2022 by John Wiley & Sons Ltd.

In Chapter 31, Richard Davies uses the television drama *Lost* to ask questions about "the state of nature" and social contract theory. The state of nature is a hypothetical scenario in which humans live apart from government. When the passengers aboard Oceanic Flight 815 crash on a desert island, the conditions of the state of nature are recreated and the survivors are faced with the question of how to govern themselves. Will they form a social contract, an agreement by which they tacitly agree to live? Drawing on the work of Locke, Rousseau (1712–778), Hume (1711–1776), and Hobbes, Davies illustrates these core issues in political philosophy.

In addition to deciding what form of government is best, we also need to decide what economic system is best. In Chapter 32, Jeff Ewing examines *Star Trek* "to boldly go where no one has gone before." Actually, someone has gone there before, Karl Marx. "Trekonomics," as it turns out, has much in common with Marx's goals of ending exploitation resulting from private ownership of the means of production. That might sound downright un-American, but determining how best to distribute wealth in a society is no easy task. Looks like a job for Superman! After all, he's the ones who's always fighting for "truth, justice and the American way." Superman could use his abilities to become super rich, but that wouldn't be fair. So in Chapter 33, Christopher Robichaud analyzes the Man of Steel along with the American philosopher John Rawls (1921–2002) to argue that justice requires that differences in wealth ultimately benefit the least well off. As an alternative, Paul Cantor takes us to *South Park* in Chapter 34, arguing from a libertarian perspective that justice prohibits the kind of taxation Rawls requires. The cartoon and its foul-mouthed kids repeatedly make the case that the American way involves not only free speech but also free markets.

During the Los Angeles riots in 1992 Rodney King famously asked, "can we all get along?" It is an important philosophical question bound up with issues of race and gender. Accordingly, Roy Cook explores race in Chapter 35 by looking to an unlikely source, LEGO. With its minifigures, LEGO originally tried to avoid race by depicting all people as yellow. That approach now seems hopelessly idealistic and naive. In whatever way we define or understand race, we cannot pretend we live in a world where it does not have real implications. Historically, race and ethnicity have sometimes marked others as less than human. In Chapter 36, Timothy Brown explores the way *Black Panther* helps us to imagine a future that has confronted its past. In Chapter 37, Bertha Alvarez Manninen takes us into the strange yet familiar world of *Black Mirror*. In the episode "Men Against Fire" soldiers have an implant that makes them see the enemy as roaches. While this is science fiction, the use of dehumanizing language and propaganda are very real in the world today. Likewise the mistreatment of women remains a vital concern. The #MeToo movement has done much to call attention to the problem, but is social media the proper place to seek justice? In Chapter 38, Aline Maya considers this question in light of another *Black Mirror* episode, "Hated in the Nation."

30

Maester Hobbes Goes to King's Landing (*Game of Thrones*)

Greg Littmann

Summary

In George R.R. Martin's novel *Game of Thrones*, and in the entire *Song of Ice and Fire* saga of which it is a part, the people of Westeros must decide how they are to be ruled. This is a decision we must make in our own world, even if our weapon is the vote rather than the broadsword. This chapter asks how the English philosopher Thomas Hobbes would advise the king and people of Westeros. Doing so should help us reflect on how plausible Hobbes's views are in the real world. It is argued that Hobbes's cynical view of human nature led him to an overly authoritarian conception of the best possible human society. In particular, it led him to overlook the way in which concentration of power can destabilize a state. However, his political insight into the cost of warfare remains valuable today.

Who should rule in the Seven Kingdoms of Westeros? It's the fundamental question underlying *Game of Thrones* and the entire *A Song of Ice and Fire* saga. Lannister armies, bristling with pike, march north from Casterly Rock in support of young King Joffrey. The royal House Baratheon divides against itself, as the brothers Stannis and Renly each lay claim to the Iron Throne. In Winterfell, Robb Stark is declared king in the North, subject to none, and in the Iron Islands, the grim fleets of the Greyjoys sail out to take the North for themselves. Meanwhile, in the distant eastern lands of the Dothraki, Daenerys Targaryen, last survivor of a dynasty that has ruled the Seven Kingdoms for 300 years, raises a hoard of fearless mounted nomads to reconquer her homeland and restore the Targaryen dragon to the throne.

Considering the issue of who should sit on the Iron Throne is not just an excuse for a self-indulgent wallow in the world of *A Song of Ice and Fire*. The question has real philosophical importance because we, like the warring peoples of Westeros, must decide who is to rule us. Philosophers have been theorizing about politics for at least 2 500 years, and one way to test their theories is to consider how well they work in hypothetical fictional situations, called "thought experiments." All that it takes to turn any fictional state of

Introducing Philosophy Through Pop Culture: From Socrates to Star Wars *and Beyond*, Second Edition.
Edited by William Irwin and David Kyle Johnson.
© 2022 John Wiley & Sons Ltd. Published 2022 by John Wiley & Sons Ltd.

affairs, like the world of *A Song of Ice and Fire*, into a thought experiment is to ask what the implications of our theories would be if this state of affairs were real.

One such theory comes from the English philosopher Thomas Hobbes (1588–1679) and his masterpiece, *Leviathan*. What would Hobbes think of the political situation in Westeros? How would he advise the nobility of the great houses? What makes the perspective of Thomas Hobbes particularly fascinating is that he lived through the game of thrones *for real*. Hobbes, a professional tutor by trade, was a loyal supporter of the great house Stuart. The Stuarts not only reigned over England (once seven kingdoms itself!) but were kings of Scotland and Ireland as well. Like the Taygaryens, the Stuarts were overthrown by their subjects in a terrible civil war. King Charles I of House Stuart, like Mad King Aerys II of House Taygaryen, was put to death in the revolt, but prince Charles, his son, like Viserys and Daenerys Taygaryen, escaped into exile to plot a return to power. Readers of the books are yet to learn whether Daenerys will finally sit upon the Iron Throne, but Hobbes's student Charles Stuart returned to England to become Charles II. Hobbes was an avid reader of history, an experienced traveler, and a careful observer of his times. As he watched Britain's bloody game of thrones unfold, he came to some very definite conclusions about the nature of human beings and how they should be governed.

You are Selfish and Dangerous

> Grand Maester Aethelmure wrote that all men carry murder in their hearts – Grand Maester Pycelle, *Game of Thrones*[1]

Hobbes believed that people only ever act out of personal self-interest, claiming that "No man giveth but with intention of good to himself."[2] People often *pretend* to have higher goals, of course; passionate oaths of loyalty to the crown were as common in Stuart England as they are in King's Landing. Beneath the facade, however, we are motivated by selfishness – we are all Lord Littlefinger under the skin. Because we are fundamentally selfish, our behavior is bound only by what we can get away with. Where people are not forced to obey rules, there is nothing but violent anarchy, a "war of every man against every man."[3]

According to Hobbes, conflict arises for three reasons. People fight to gain their neighbor's possessions, like the barbarous clans who prey on travelers through the Mountains of the Moon. People fight to defend themselves from danger, even if it means striking preemptively against potential threats, as when Robert Baratheon seeks to assassinate Daenyres Taygaryen just in case she ever becomes dangerous. And people fight just for the glory of it, like Khal Drogo, who slaughters his foes as much to satisfy his pride as his greed for treasure.

When everyone can do what they want, life, according to Hobbes, is "solitary, poor, nasty, brutish and short."[4] Nobody is safe in such chaos. Even mighty champions like the Mountain that Rides, Ser Gregor Clegane, must sleep sometimes, and when they do, even a poor warrior like Samwell Tarly could kill them. Our only recourse is to establish a set of rules that we will agree to live by, mutually giving up freedoms for the sake of mutual benefit. For example, you agree not to stick a battleaxe in my head and in return, I agree not to stick a battleaxe in yours. Being part of such a social contract is in everyone's self-interest. Of course, since humans are driven only by self-interest, we won't keep such promises unless it is in our own interest to do so. You may promise to keep your axe to yourself, but as soon as my back is turned, you will break your promise if it is in your best interests to do so, giving me a swift chop and making off with my lunch. What people need to do, then, is set up an authority to make sure that everyone obeys the rules. Once there is someone watching us to make sure that if you give me the axe, *you* get the axe, it will be in your best interest not to strike as soon as my back is turned.

The Realm Needs a King

When Joffrey turned to look out over the hall, his eye caught Sansa's. He smiled, seated himself, and spoke: "It is a king's duty to punish the disloyal and reward those who are true. Grand Maester Pycelle, I command you to read my decrees."[5]

Given all of this talk about social contracts, Hobbes might sound like a champion of democracy. In fact, he was anything but. So great is the need to contain human selfishness by making sure that there are always negative consequences for breaking the rules, that we must be ruled by an all-powerful dictator to whom we give complete obedience. Hobbes called such an absolute ruler a *Leviathan*, taking the name of the huge fire-breathing sea-monster of Hebrew mythology. I assume that George R.R. Martin's use of the dragon to symbolize the (once) all-powerful House Targaryen is a nod to Hobbes's Leviathan (although it's also possible that Martin, like the rest of us, just likes dragons). Hobbes understood that being all-powerful includes having the power to appoint your own successor. Holding elections to appoint the next dictator would be as alien to Hobbes's ideal government as it would be to the kings of Westeros. But how does such a totalitarian system jibe with a social contract, according to which the power of the leaders is derived from the will of the people?

Hobbes believed that the social contract he recommends was already made long ago in all civilized, organized nations. The monarchies of Europe existed because Europeans' barbarous and disorganized ancestors had tired of living in a hellish state of anarchy. They had agreed to submit to authority for the sake of their mutual good, and agreed on behalf of their descendants as well. The social contract having been made, there is no more need for input from the common people, who are born into the social contract and need only obey authority without question. Hobbes recognized that not all states were ruled by a monarch, and in that case, the people have a duty to establish a monarchy to rule them, but once the monarchy is in place, no more input from the common people is desirable.

As an analogy, consider the manner in which Robb Stark is declared the King in the North. He achieves this position of authority because his bannermen call on him to rule them. "[Greatjon Umber] pointed at Robb with the blade. 'There sits the only king I mean to bow my knee to, m'lords,' he thundered. 'The King in the North!' And he knelt, and laid his sword at . . . [Robb's] feet."[6] The other assembled lords follow suit and the rafters of the great hall in Winterfell ring with their shouts of "THE KING IN THE NORTH!" However, once the lesser houses have declared Robb "The King in the North," they no longer have the right to *undeclare* him "The King in the North." If they withdraw support from him at a later date, they become oathbreakers, devoid of honor. As for trying to tell a Stark ruler who he may have as his successor, the lords of the north would have more chance trying to teach a direwolf to dance.

Hobbes Takes the Maester's Chain

So many vows . . . they make you swear and swear. Defend the king. Obey the king. Keep his secrets. Do his bidding. Your life for his – Jaime Lannister, A Clash of Kings[7]

So what would Hobbes think about the situation in Westeros? How would he advise the nobility? Let's make Hobbes a court advisor like Maester Luwin and Grand Maester Pycelle. He can drop by Oldtown first for several years of Maester training at the Citadel. Having won enough links for his chain to wind around his neck, Hobbes sets sail for King's Landing in 273, 10 years into the reign of the last Targaryen king, Aerys II. He's to be employed as a tutor, instructing noble Targaryen children just as he instructed the young prince Charles Stuart, and we'll let him become a valued member of court with the ear of the king, as he was in Charles's court.

When Maester Hobbes first arrives at the court of Aerys, he would find much to admire. Here is a king who understands the importance of centralizing power! The Leviathan Aerys rules his kingdom with an iron fist and crushes those he considers enemies. The rules in the court of Aerys are whatever Aerys says they are. Even a king's Hand stands only one step from execution – Aerys goes through five of them in 20 years. Serious miscreants are burned alive with wildfire, while Ser Ilyn Payne has his tongue ripped out with hot pincers just for making a tactless jest. At the court of Lady Lysa Arryn, Tyrion Lannister is able to thwart Lysa's will to kill him by insisting on a trial by combat. Lysa gives in to his demand because she is not an absolute dictator and places the authority of tradition over her own authority. Conversely, at the court of Aerys, when Eddard Stark's father Lord Rickard demanded *his* right to trial by combat, Aerys simply chose fire as his champion and had Rickard roasted alive. The Targaryen words are "Fire and Blood." These are kings who rule by force, not by negotiation and consensus.

It must be admitted, Aerys was not merely strict and authoritative as a Leviathan should be, but was harsh, dangerous, and erratic, particularly toward the end of his reign. His judgments were often more than a little cruel and unfair. When Aerys' son Rhaegar abducts Lyanna Stark, and Brandon Stark rides to King's Landing with a group of young noblemen to protest, Aerys executes the lot of them for treason *and* executes all their fathers for good measure. They didn't call him "Mad King Aerys" for nothing.

What are Aerys' subjects supposed to do in the face of such tyranny? Should they simply obey the king in order to maintain the implicit social contract? Or should they rebel as Robert Baratheon and Eddard Stark do, in an attempt to replace him with someone better? For Robert and Ned, honor and reason alike demand that they resist Aerys, but Maester Hobbes would continue to counsel obedience to the king. Why should the people of the Seven Kingdoms endure such a ruler? The answer is that the alternative is civil war, and civil war is so much worse.

The Horrors of War

The northerners broke into a run, shouting as they came, but the Lannister arrows fell on them like hail, hundreds of arrows, thousands, and shouts turned to screams as men stumbled and went down. – Game of Thrones[8]

Civil wars are easily romanticized. The tales of King Arthur's knights are often glamorized stories of civil war as Arthur's realm crumbles, and Shakespeare's historical plays make England's Wars of the Roses seem a glorious triumph of good over evil. However, England went through a civil war in Hobbes's lifetime, making the grim reality all too clear to him. It had been a century and a half since the Wars of the Roses, in which the lords of York and Lancaster contested for the English crown just as the lords of Stark and Lannister contest for the Iron Throne. At stake in the English Civil War (1642–1651), was not just *who* should rule England, but also *how* it should be ruled. Charles I of the Stuarts, like Aerys Targaryen, believed that the king should hold the reins of power tightly, ruling as an absolute dictator unhampered by the judgments of his subjects. Indeed, his father, James I of England, had declared that the power of a king should be that of a god on Earth! Many of Charles's subjects, on the other hand, believed that there should be limitations on the power of the king and, in particular, that only the elected parliament should be able to levy new taxes. If only Charles had compromised and shared power, he would almost certainly have kept both his throne and his life. Instead, he was determined to crush all resistance and was eventually captured and beheaded.

The English Civil War was a time of terrible slaughter, with brutal clashes like the battles of Edgehill, Naseby, and Preston. Well over 100 000 soldiers were killed at a time when the population of Britain was less than six million. That's like the modern United States fighting a war in which it loses five million soldiers – and that doesn't even factor in the wounded! The horrors of this war only confirmed for Hobbes what he had already concluded from historical studies: civil war is so awful that it is never worth fighting. *Any* alternative is better as long as it keeps the peace. Hobbes wrote, "the greatest [harm], that in any form of Government can possibly happen to the people in general, is scarce sensible, in respect of the miseries, and horrible calamities, that accompany a Civil War . . ."[9]

Maester Hobbes would urge the people of the Seven Kingdoms to endure the eccentricities of Aerys the Mad (and to stop *calling* him that); he'd insist that they show some sense of perspective. So, a few Starks and other nobles get dispossessed, kidnapped, roasted, strangled, and otherwise treated with a brutality normally reserved for the common people. What is that compared with the suffering in a realm that is at war with itself?

Robert's Rebellion

> They had come together at the ford of the Trident while the battle crashed around them, Robert with his warhammer and his great antlered helm, the Targaryen prince armored all in black. On his breastplate was the three-headed dragon of his House, wrought all in rubies that flashed like fire in the sunlight. – *Game of Thrones.*[10]

Robert Baratheon, of course, is not the sort of fellow who would be calmed by Maester Hobbes's appeals to the good of the realm. Hobbes's worst fears come to pass and the houses Baratheon, Arryn, and Stark rise up against Aerys Targaryen. Thousands die in bloody clashes like the battles of Summerhall, Ashford, and the Trident, while the great city of King's Landing is sacked by the Lannisters and comes within a hair's breadth of being burned to the ground.

After Robert's final triumph at the Trident in 283, in which he slays Rhaegar in single combat and puts the loyalist army to flight, Maester Hobbes has an important choice to make: he could either flee into exile with the surviving Targaryens, like Ser Jorah Mormont, or remain in King's Landing to try to persuade the new king to let him keep his old job, like the spider Varys and Grand Maester Pycelle. Pragmatist that he was, Hobbes's usual response to danger was to flee. When his political writings upset supporters of parliament, he fled to Paris. When his political writings upset other royalists in Paris, he fled back to London again. If there were two things Hobbes was good at, they were annoying people and fleeing. It might be tempting, then, to believe that Hobbes would escape with the last Targaryens into the lands of the Dothraki, there to try to explain social contracts to Khal Drogo. Besides, it seems natural to suppose that if subjects owe their king complete loyalty, they should maintain that loyalty if the king is driven into exile. Indeed, that is *exactly* what Hobbes did in the case of young Charles Stuart.

For all that, I believe that Hobbes would remain in King's Landing and transfer his loyalty to Robert. He would do this not because he is a craven or an oathbreaker, but because the same principles that led him to support the Leviathan Aerys so wholeheartedly would lead him to desire a replacement. Remember, the entire point of giving our complete loyalty to an all-powerful dictator is that we are driven to seek safety, and only an all-powerful dictator can offer us the best protection. But a so-called "king" like the exiled Viserys Targaryen can't offer anyone any protection. He's only got one knight and even *he* won't do as he's told. Hobbes wrote: "The obligation of subjects to the sovereign is understood to last as long as, and no longer, than the power lasteth by which he is able to protect them."[11] The Targaryens' power to protect is gone and so is any reason to support them. Hobbes supported young Charles Stuart because the only alternative was to support a *republican government*. In the person of Robert Baratheon, Hobbes has a perfectly good king to support, and will concentrate on serving his new monarch loyally and tutoring prince Joffrey to be a great dictator in his own turn.

In Hobbes's view, despite the fact that Robert should never have rebelled in the first place, it is now King Robert who must never be rebelled against. It is just as wrong for Queen Cersei to defy the usurper Robert by plotting to place a Lannister on the throne as it would have been if she'd tried that on Aerys, who was heir to a 300-year dynasty. It goes without saying that her *murder* of the king is even worse! Such an act puts the entire realm in terrible danger. Yet once again, just as in the case of Aerys, once Robert is gone, the important thing is not bringing the perpetrators to justice but making sure that there is someone sitting on the Iron Throne to keep the peace. Hobbes would be as eager to transfer his loyalty from King Robert to King Joffrey as he had been to transfer it from King Aerys to King Robert, even if he knew of Joffrey's true heritage. Targaryen, Baratheon, Lannister – it really doesn't matter very much as long as *nobody breaks the peace*. It isn't even particularly important that Joffrey is so incompetent a ruler that he thinks disputes over real-estate should be settled by combat to the death. The harm the little git can inflict is minimal compared to the carnage of a civil war.

The eunuch Varys would agree absolutely. He works desperately to keep King Robert alive, but when Eddard threatens the peace of the realm by preparing to reveal that Joffrey is not Robert's rightful heir, Varys conspires to have him executed. He cannot allow Ned to undermine the power of Joffrey, regardless of his lineage, because to do so would plunge the Seven Kingdoms once more into civil war. When Ned asks Varys to at least smuggle a message to his family, Varys replies that he will read the message and deliver it if it serves his own ends to do so. Ned asks, "What ends are those, Lord Varys?" and without hesitation, Varys answers "peace." Like a true Hobbesian, he explains, "I serve the realm, and the realm needs peace."[12]

Lion and Direwolf, Dragon and Leviathan

The High Septon once told me that as we sin, so do we suffer. If that's true, Lord Eddard, tell me . . . why is it always the innocents who suffer most, when you high lords play your game of thrones? – Varys, *Game of Thrones*[13]

Hobbes's way of thinking about politics differs greatly from that of most of the nobility of Westeros. Who is right – Hobbes, or the great houses, or neither? Hobbes would view himself as a realist who is willing to face some hard truths – truths that are dangerous to ignore. To his mind, ambitious nobles like Tywin Lannister endanger the realm by defying the will of the king. It may seem that such nobles are simply being selfish, as Hobbes recommends, but a sensible selfish person would realize that they put their own safety in great danger by playing the game of thrones, and would opt for obedience to the Leviathan instead. Honorable nobles like Eddard Stark endanger the realm no less than plotters like Tywin. Their obsessive concern with the rules of honor leads to the War of the Five Kings just as surely as Lannister greed.

Hobbes was right to recognize that political theory must take into account the degree to which people are motivated by self-interest rather than duty. The Starks in particular could have used some instruction from Maester Hobbes on this point. When Ned comes to King's Landing, he tragically puts his trust in Littlefinger to do the right thing, when it should have been obvious that Littlefinger's interests would be served by betraying Ned to Queen Cersei. When Robb first marches against the Lannisters, he expects his bannerman Lord Frey to answer his call to arms because that is Frey's sworn duty, while Catelyn understands that Frey will only be moved by his self-interest, including an advantageous marriage for his daughter.

On the other hand, Hobbes was surely mistaken that people are *only* motivated by self-interest. Like Eddard, whose attachment to honor is so great that he dies rather than serve an illegitimate king, people in real life sometimes die for what they believe in. Similarly, like Jon Snow, who gives up home, safety, and luxury for (what he thinks will be) a life of hard service on the wall, people sometimes make extraordinary sacrifices for the benefit of others. Tales of courage, honor, and self-sacrifice in fiction ring true for us when they capture something of the best in real humanity. If we were all motivated by self-interest alone, stories about people like Ned and Jon would be absurd, even incoherent. We understand the motivations of characters like these precisely because we understand that a human being can be motivated by higher concerns.

Perhaps it is his oversimplification of human psychology that leads Hobbes to miss the way that over-centralization of power can weaken, rather than stabilize, a state. When Aerys went insane, it was the very fact that he held the reins of power so tightly that left civil war as the only alternative to enduring his abuses. After all, he could not be voted out, forced to abdicate, or restrained by law in any way. Perhaps Robert's rebellion could have been avoided if only the Targaryen Leviathan had not been so powerful! The same problem arises under the reign of Joffrey. The War of the Five Kings erupted because the only way to replace Joffrey was to rebel. Hobbes really ought to have learned from events in Britain that flexibility in a ruler can be more important than the will to dominate. Few supporters of the English parliament even *wanted* to get rid of the monarchy, until Charles I made it so clear that he would never share power and the parliamentarians were left with a choice between servility and civil war.

For all his failings, Hobbes understood the horrors of war a little more clearly than the scheming nobility of Westeros. The War of the Five Kings was every bit as terrible as Maester Hobbes feared it would be. Tully forces are slaughtered at Riverrun and Mummer's Ford, Lannister forces at Whispering Wood and the Battle of the Fords, and Stark forces at the Green Fork and at the Red Wedding. From Stannis Baratheon's terrible defeat against the Lannisters at King's Landing to Loras Tyrell's Pyrrhic victory against Baratheon defenders at Dragonstone, from Ramsay Bolton's murderous sacking of Winterfell to the terrible carnage inflicted by Greyjoy Ironmen invading across the north and west of Westeros, the history of the war is a tale of shocking loss and human suffering. Worse yet, all of this happens when the realm is most in need of a unified response to external threat. Winter is coming and the Others (aka White Walkers) are returning to reclaim their old stalking grounds, while in the east, a Targaryen *khaleesi* with a sideline in hatching dragons prepares to reclaim the Iron Throne. Wherever you think the point is at which a people simply *must* rise in rebellion against dishonest, vicious, or incompetent rulers, surely the cost of the War of the Five Kings is so great that the decision to go to war should have depended on more than a matter of principle regarding legitimate succession.

The lesson that the nobles of Westeros should have learned from Maester Hobbes is not that they should never rebel, but that civil war is so horrific that it must be avoided at almost any cost. Appeals to lofty principles of justice and honor that are never to be violated are all very well, but these principles always need to be weighed against the consequences our actions will have for human lives. Our most fundamental need as humans is not justice; our most fundamental need as humans is avoiding having a greatsword inserted up our nose. As citizens of Western democracies with the duty to vote for our leaders, we are all, in a way, required to play the game of thrones, in our own nation and across the world. When we forget the cost of our principles in terms of human suffering, to ourselves, or to those who fight for us, or even to those we fight for and those we fight *against*, then we are in danger of doing more harm with our good intentions than any Targaryen tyrant ever inflicted with their greed for power.

For pop culture resources and philosophical resources related to this chapter please visit the website for this book: https://introducingphilosophythroughpopculture.com.

Notes

1   George, R.R.and Martin, A. (2005). *Game of Thrones*, 253. New York: Bantam Dell.
2   Hobbes, T. (2009). *Leviathan* (ed. J.C.A. Gaskin), 100. Oxford: Oxford University Press.
3   Hobbes, 85.
4   Hobbes, 84.
5   Martin, G.R.R. (1996), *A Game of Thrones*, 620. New York: Bantam
6   Martin, *A Game of Thrones*, 796.
7   George, R.R. and Martin, A. (2005). *Clash of Kings*, 599. New York: Bantam Dell.
8   Martin, *A Game of Thrones*, 687.
9   Hobbes, 122.
10 Martin, *A Game of Thrones*, 44.
11 Hobbes, 147.
12 Martin, *A Game of Thrones*, 636.
13 Martin, *A Game of Thrones*, 636.

31

Lost's State of Nature

Richard Davies

Summary

In political philosophy, a *state of nature* is a situation where agents' interests are best served by cooperative behavior but individuals know too little about each other's intentions to act for the common good. A state of nature is more or less severe according to the nature of the goods at stake, such as fresh water and food. In these respects, the survivors of *Lost* are fortunate in landing on the Island. They are also lucky in (mostly) sharing English to communicate. Game theory can help us understand how, in such a situation, cooperation can be generated among the survivors.

The phrase *state of nature* crops up frequently in comments on *Lost* for two main reasons. The first is that two of the leading characters in the program (John Locke and Danielle Rousseau) bear the surnames of two philosophers who are famous for having used the phrase *state of nature* as a key term in their writings on political philosophy. These are the Englishman John Locke (1632–1704) and the Swiss-Frenchman Jean-Jacques Rousseau (1712–1788). The second, much better, reason why the phrase crops up so much in discussions of *Lost* is that the situation the survivors of Oceanic Flight 815 find themselves in after the crash can indeed be usefully described as a state of nature.

Before coming to some differences among the ways that Locke, Rousseau, and other philosophers have thought about the state of nature, let's consider a negative, and rather abstract, characterization of it that would be recognized by everyone working in the tradition of political philosophy that Locke and Rousseau consolidated. *In a pure state of nature, none of the codes and expectations, none of the rules and hierarchies, none of the roles and presumptions that make up the fabric of our social lives is operative, can be relied on, or can be enforced.* Presented in this abstract way, a situation like this is very difficult to imagine. After all, very few of us have any experience of anything remotely similar.

The very difficulty of imagining something that fits the (negative) bill can help explain why Locke, Rousseau, and other philosophers have taken differing approaches to giving a more positive and concrete account of the dynamics of a supposed state of nature. Indeed, many philosophers, including another who gives his name to a character on

Introducing Philosophy Through Pop Culture: From Socrates to Star Wars *and Beyond*, Second Edition.
Edited by William Irwin and David Kyle Johnson.
© 2022 John Wiley & Sons Ltd. Published 2022 by John Wiley & Sons Ltd.

Lost, the Scotsman David Hume (1711–1776), have thought that the difficulty of imagining a state of nature is a reason for not taking it as a key concept in theorizing about politics. If it is a hardly imaginable situation, it won't be of much help understanding the societies we actually live in.

In what sense, then, can the situation of the survivors of Flight 815 be described as a state of nature? Well, at the outset, most of the people (except the pairs Jin–Sun, Shannon–Boone, Michael–Walt, and, to a small extent, Jack–Rose) are strangers to each other. They are individuals each with their own interests and aims, above all to survive in the face of the unfamiliar challenges of the Island. They cannot be sure what the other castaways will be prepared to do to ensure their own survival, and they have no authority to turn to, either to tell them what to do or to protect them from harm. This, again, is a negative account of their situation, but I want to use some tools that have been developed within the tradition of state-of-nature theory to understand some more positive factors in evidence in the early episodes of *Lost*'s season one that the survivors can use to patch together at least part of the social structure that has gone missing as a result of the crash.

Lining up for Peace

In one sense (which Hume, the philosopher, was right about) a pure state of nature is just a philosopher's thought experiment, whose interest – if any – is only theoretical, but there is also a sense (where Hume missed a trick) in which we do encounter partial, or as I shall say "framed," states of nature all the time. Every time, in fact, the interests of various individuals are in potential conflict for some limited good.

Though philosophers have been thinking about scenarios of how conflicts evolve ever since Plato, one of the most influential modern theorists of the state of nature was Thomas Hobbes (1588–1679). Hobbes's *Leviathan* (1651) takes its title from the monster at Job 41:24 and refers to the monarchical absolutist state that seemed to Hobbes the only viable alternative to the anarchy that he describes it in chapter 13 of the book. In describing the state of nature, Hobbes takes aim at the idea that humans are by nature social animals by stressing the conventional nature of any way of resolving conflict.

Let's take a day-to-day example of a framed conflict. When I have filled my cart at the supermarket, my aim is to get out as quickly as I can. The same goes for all the other stressed-out cart-pushers. Each of us wants the immediate attention of the cashier, but there are only 3 registers open and 15 loads of shopping to be paid for. In Hobbes's words, the 15 shoppers are in a condition of "war, where every man is enemy to every man."[1] The surprising thing, then, is that, given Hobbes' drastic way of putting the matter, massacres at the supermarket checkout are fairly rare. What each of the 15 shoppers normally relies on is the expectation that the other 14 will follow the usual practice and form lines. This is a purely conventional practice that creates what I'm calling a frame.

When we form lines, the conflict between me and the other shoppers isn't exactly resolved, but is at least kept under control. I still want to get out as quickly as I can and so do the others, but we all recognize a procedure for reducing the likelihood of violence. Each of us takes a step back from our own interests in the hope that the others will do likewise. Slightly less rare than supermarket massacres are those people who don't merely wish the others weren't there, but act as if they weren't (or ignore the item limit on the express lane). If anything, it is these people who might deserve just a splash of bloodshed. They deserve it because they don't act within the frame established by line forming

With this trivial example, we can get a measure of the purity or severity of a state of nature. Because getting out of the supermarket in 2 minutes rather than 10 doesn't make a great deal of difference to my life, the other shoppers are my "enemies" only to the value of 8 minutes of mortality (which I'd set aside in the first place when I decided to go shopping). Hence, the principle: *the more vital or scarcer the good that is the object of conflict, the purer and more severe the state of nature.* And because I can be pretty confident that others will abide by the norms for forming lines, even the shoppers in front of me, are in a sense, also my allies because, by doing what's expected of them, they make shopping that bit less stressful for everyone. Hence, the principle: *the fewer or weaker (that is, the less likely to be observed) the frames, the purer and more severe the state of nature.*

In these terms, we can see that the survivors on *Lost* do find themselves in a pretty severe state of nature, because they are no longer guaranteed the means of basic survival that had been secured by the society from which they are now isolated. What's more to the point, it is hard for them to tell in advance what frames, if any, will apply to the distribution of those goods. Even if they know the conventions that apply in the supermarket, each is unprepared for the conditions of the Island and so each has reason to suppose that the others will be equally in the dark about how to act.

The question, then, is: What can they do to reduce the severity of the state of nature? On the one hand, this is a question about the procurement of the means of survival. But, more crucially, it has to do with the way each of the survivors can come to trust the others not to make things worse. How do conventions get set up?

Human Nature and Natural Humans

One major question on which state-of-nature theorists have disagreed is whether, to understand the emergence of a society, we have to take a position on the very nature of humankind. Any effort to answer the question of "human nature" can easily lead to arguing in circles ("humans by nature are such-and-such because that's what they're like in a state of nature; so in a state of nature they're such-and-such"). But two sorts of stands have emerged about how to think of humanity in the raw.

Jean-Jacques Rousseau, for instance, is credited with thinking that, by nature, humans are compassionate and altruistic creatures. According to his *Discourse on the Origin of Inequality* (1755), the state of nature offers an ideal against which the corruptions of society can be measured. In this direction, Rousseau – and with him others like David Hume – would say that humans are fundamentally governed by benevolent passions. In a similar vein, other philosophers, such as John Locke in his second *Treatise on Government* (1690), would say that, so long as reason guides our behavior, we do not infringe the rights of others.[2] For short, we can call this sort of attitude "Innocence" – not least because it is a key term in Rousseau's writings.

On the other hand, Hobbes is generally interpreted as regarding humans as wholly egoistical and suspicious of their fellows. This, as we'll see, is not a necessary part of his theory. Instead of referring to the historical Hobbes, we can say that the view opposed to Innocence would be one according to which people always operate on the motto adopted by Special Agent Fox Mulder of *The X-Files*: "Trust no-one" or, rather, "Trust No.1," a phrase we may use as a summary of the attitude in question (trust only number one, yourself). On this bitterer view, human beings are fundamentally antisocial and aggressive in their self-defense even when their behavior appears to respect conventional frames.

"Innocence" and "Trust No.1" are labels for what are claimed to be the basic orientations of human beings, which would be given free rein in a situation where the norms of communal living have come unstuck. It may be that one or the other is a true description of what *would* happen in those circumstances. But, as I've said, we have little direct knowledge of what does happen is such an extreme situation.

Perhaps Innocence is not a wildly inaccurate description of how Hurley and Jack behave. And Trust No.1 is not a wildly inaccurate description of how Sawyer (at least in season one) and Locke (the outdoorsman, not the philosopher) behave. But I, at least, don't claim to know that either Innocence or Trust No.1 accounts for the actions of all human beings. And I think we can get on perfectly well without them if we want to understand the interactions among the survivors on the Island. Indeed, I think that we can understand the state of nature *better* if we are not distracted by speculative theories about the "nature" of the people in it, beyond recognizing that, as animals, they need such things as food, drink, and protection.

Amid the Wreckage

Immediately after the crash, the plane is the survivors' source of food and drink. So long as they believe that they will be rescued soon, they can consume without second thoughts.

After about a week, though, Hurley discovers that someone has taken some bottles of fresh water leaving only 18 for the rest. Hurley's intuitive – and accurate – analysis is that the others would "freak out" if they knew ("White Rabbit"). They would freak out because each individual wants for themself as much of the limited good (water) as they can get, while knowing that the more they take, the less there will be in the long run for everybody, themself included.

Unlike the supermarket, where my access to a limited good (the attention of the cashier) doesn't reduce the total amount of that good available to all (at least until closing time), water is a good precisely when it's consumed: every drop I drink is a drop less for others who have some claim on it. Situations of this sort are a special case of the state of nature, and are known as "tragedies of the commons." A tragedy of the commons is a situation in which it looks unreasonable for each individual to give up their access to a certain good, even though the cumulative effect of many individuals' access spells destruction of the good itself.

Charlie suggests rationing as a resolution to the water tragedy. That is, each survivor must reduce their own consumption to allow all to have at least a minimum. But this requires everyone to subordinate their own interests to that of a group that is only just forming. Each can ask: "Why should I give up my water to people I don't know or care about?" The tragedy here is that it's very hard to answer that question. It's a question that would only be put by someone who doesn't recognize group survival as a good over and above their own.

Jack refuses to decide anything about how to distribute the water, because he too is in the same situation as the others and – quite apart from his "daddy issues" – has no authority to impose rationing. In a fit of optimism to minimize the importance of the theft from the group's common property, Sawyer tells Kate that, "water has no value,

Freckles; it's gonna rain sooner or later" ("White Rabbit"). He's surely right that when there's enough water to go round, no one needs to privatize it. But it's the possibility of a "later" that comes after the castaways have all died of thirst that makes the tragedy urgent.

When Jack is led to discover the stream of fresh water later in the same episode, and the survivors pick up skills of hunting and fishing, they are no longer in tragic conflict with each other for vital goods. Because none of the other survivors is a threat to the survival of each of them, there's no reason not to group together. Because his immediate needs can be met, even Locke (the outdoorsman) can socialize with the others, though this is a matter of preference or temperament; if Sawyer shuns the company of the others on the beach, that does nobody any harm. And because each can look after himself, there's no need to plan for more than the time being, and no need for any of them to make any sacrifice for a common purpose, for instance in making an effort to get off the Island. There is no real urgency about Walt's raft, though we can understand that he does want to get home sooner or later.

The condition of minimal bodily security corresponds to the core of what Locke (the philosopher) had in mind when he talked about a state of nature. Prior to the formulation of a social contract, there's no government and no particular need for one. All humans are, as Locke said, equal and independent; and everyone has the right not only not to be harmed "in his life, health, liberty or possessions,"[3] but also to take and use the things they find around them so long as there's "enough and as good"[4] left for the others.

The Longer Haul

While the survivors of Flight 815 have been lucky in the climate and the availability of food and drink, there are several kinds of goods that they don't have the means or skill to make for themselves. For instance, even though they cannot make new clothing, there's plenty on the plane and, in any case, they don't need much more than beachwear. Other goods, unlike clothing, are in short supply. One case here would be Sawyer's cigarettes. If he's the only smoker, then the fact that he cannot renew his supply is a problem only for him (apart from Charlie, who also has a problem getting his drugs). Likewise with Shannon's toenail varnish: no one else wants a pedicure, so her using it causes no one else any upset (apart from the irritation factor for Boone ["Pilot: Part 1"]).

Things are a bit different when it comes to medicines. We have here the making of a tragedy of the commons that the survivors are not in a position to resolve.

In the first days on the beach, Jack takes it for granted that he's authorized to use all the antibiotics he can find on the plane to treat Marshal Mars. Here, he must be supposing that their stay on the Island will be short-lived and that the immediate use of the drugs is the only reasonable course of action to try and save a life.

If, however, he had thought that they were going to be stranded for a long time, it isn't clear that using up what there is in trying (and failing) to heal one severely injured man would be the best line to take. After all, the drugs could be of more benefit to more people if spread over more, and more curable, cases. As Sawyer says, Jack may not be "looking at the Big Picture, Doc" ("Tabula Rasa").

We can keep that problem of medical ethics on hold, while allowing that Jack did well to go through the luggage of the other passengers and take all the stuff ending in "-myacin" and "-cillin" ("Pilot: Part 2"). That is, even if the antibiotics count as the common property of all the survivors, Jack should be given control of them for the benefit of those who need them because only he knows how to use them.

Unlike her varnish, Shannon isn't the only one who lays a claim to her anti-asthma inhalers. Nonetheless, she has a double claim to them. First, consider that she (or rather Boone on her behalf) brought the refills with her; presumably, she paid for them and thus has what we might call a legal property right to them. Second, consider that her health depends on them; she's the only asthmatic on the Island and thus has what we might call a moral priority in their proper use.

The trouble arises from Sawyer's having taken some of the contents of Boone's suitcase, such as his copy of *Watership Down* ("The Moth"). If the luggage of those who died in the air crash can be rifled for clothes and for antibiotics without injustice (when Kate takes the walking shoes off the corpse to make the expedition to find the plane's cockpit in "Pilot: Part 1" she isn't *stealing*), why not also that of the survivors? Isn't it all just luggage and, so, fair game?

When Jack confronts him in "Confidence Man," Sawyer brazens it out saying that, on the beach, "possession is nine tenths," meaning "of the law," where the law is "finders keepers." And this explains why he brushes off Jack's accusation of looting the fuselage in "Tabula Rasa." Though he doesn't say what the other tenth of the law is, Sawyer is standing up for the idea that, in a state of nature, it's every man for himself, a clear instance of his Trust No. 1 attitude.

As Hobbes puts it, "if any two men desire the same thing, which nevertheless they cannot both enjoy, they become enemies."[5] This means that the past property relation that Shannon enjoyed toward the inhalers is scrubbed by the new circumstances. Her legal right no longer counts because there's no constituted authority (like the police or law courts) to enforce it. And Sawyer is no more obliged to recognize her moral claim, than, in "Pilot: Part 1," Hurley is *obliged* to give an extra portion of food to Claire because she's eating for two (though he does so out of Innocence).

Faced with Sawyer's refusal to "do the right thing" (and assuming, rightly or wrongly, that he has the inhalers), Sayid and Jack take it upon themselves to defend Shannon's cause by capturing and torturing Sawyer ("Confidence Man"). In so doing, they are beginning to move away from the Lockean state of nature toward a position in which legal and moral claims can be enforced and the use of violence (an infringement of the right not to be harmed in one's health) can be justified. Jack and Sayid are not acting in *self*-defense, but are rather seeking to defend the rights of others, which is a different concept altogether: that of punishment. In doing so, they are on the way to constituting what Locke calls "a civil society" – of sorts.

Over or Under the Language Barrier

Neither Sayid nor Jack is stronger than Sawyer, but working together and using stealth (they attack him while he's napping), they can get the better of him. This is what Hobbes calls the "equality of ability": "the weakest has strength enough to kill the strongest, either by secret machination, or by confederacy with others."[6] The association between Sayid and Jack requires them to trust each other for the purposes of getting information out of Sawyer about where the inhalers are hidden.

There are two obvious conditions for their being able to reach such an agreement. One is that they already agree on Shannon's claim – legal or moral or both – to the inhalers.

The other is that they understand each other, that they share a language. This is also a condition for their being able to get information out of Sawyer: Sayid would be a useless torturer if he couldn't put the questions and get the answers. The fact that the overwhelming majority of the passengers on Flight 815 are speakers of English, as a first or second language, means that they can share information and signal their intentions to each other. It also means they can lie to each other.

Jin is the exception; he can communicate only with Sun. As soon as they arrive on the Island, Jin reaffirms their previous asymmetrical relationship (marriage), with him giving the orders and her taking them, because, at that point, he believes that she's not in a position to talk to the others ("Pilot: Part 1"). The pair keeps a distance from the wreckage, so Jin is the first to seek food from the sea. There are two possible interpretations of what he does after filleting the strange orange creature he has fished out of the water ("Pilot: Part 2").

On one interpretation, rather than try the food himself, Jin is looking for guinea pigs to test its edibility. On this account, he doesn't care what happens to them because they are not a part of any group that he recognizes as binding on him. Jin would thus be applying Trust No. 1. Even though Hurley tends toward the accepting attitude of Innocence, he declines the offer not just because he prefers airline snacks – or even hunger – to "natural" food, but also perhaps because he's not sure of Jin's motives.

On the other interpretation – taking into account the fishing community he comes from – Jin can be understood as trying to overcome the language barrier by making a move that's widely recognized as a peace overture. Indeed, the offer of food convinces Claire of Jin's inclination toward Innocence.

Confidence and the Con Men

Even if a shared language is *necessary* for generating the higher grades of trust and cooperation, it's not *sufficient*.

On the one hand, we might think about the suspicions got up by Walt's discovery, in "Pilot: Part 2," of the handcuffs in the jungle. The cuffs mean there's at least one person on the Island who was regarded as a criminal and who therefore might still be dangerous. When, later in the same episode, Sawyer accuses Sayid of being a terrorist, he backs it up with the allegation that Sayid was sitting with his arms covered at the back of Business Class and never moved out of his seat. The others present at the scene can't tell whether Sawyer really saw what he says he did, but they are given some reason for thinking that it was Sayid who was wearing the handcuffs. What they don't know– but we do – is that Sawyer is a professional liar and, as we have already seen, inclined to Trust No. 1.

On the other hand, there's Marshal Mars's warning to Jack that he should not trust Kate ("Tabula Rasa"). Jack can be pretty sure that a man – and a US marshal at that – on his deathbed will be speaking the truth; but he still does not heed his words. We can distinguish two aspects of this.

One is that he trusts his own feelings more than Mars's information. For sure, Jack recognizes that he doesn't know whatever it is that the Marshal knows about Kate's past, but he doesn't want to think the worse of a person who has so far behaved with fortitude and in the interests of all. After all, he has himself benefited from her help in sewing up his wound on their first meeting ("Pilot: Part 1"), and, by dismantling and distributing the parts of the pistol, she made it impossible for any one individual to have a monopoly on its use ("Pilot: Part 2").

The other point – and this is a crucial feature of a situation in which people don't have background knowledge of one another – is that it's the "Island of Second Chances." As far as Jack is concerned, Kate is free to wipe the slate clean: there's a presumption of Innocence. In "Tabula Rasa," he repeatedly says things like "it doesn't matter who we were" and "it's none of our business."

We might pick up a hint of uncertainty here about the relations between "before" and "after" the crash. While, in addition to her moral claim in virtue of being the only asthmatic, Jack defends Shannon's property right as a leftover from the society from which the survivors have been isolated, he seems not to think that Kate's criminal record means anything without the criminal system that keeps the paperwork.

Roles and Rules

What Jack himself undoubtedly carries over from his life before the downing of Flight 815 is the fact of being a medical doctor. Equally obviously, he doesn't carry with him his degree certificates, and there's no authority on the Island to license his practice of the Hippocratic art. By contrast, Arzt asks the others to address him as "Doctor," though he is in reality a schoolteacher. (The apparent title may be regarded as no more than a nickname understandable to someone who knows a bit of German.) It's the fact that Jack has acquired skills that makes him a doctor and, so, as Sawyer ironically puts it, "a hero" ("Pilot: Part 2") or, in Boone's challenge, "our savior" ("White Rabbit").

As we saw with the antibiotics, Jack's expertise confers rights; but it also carries with it the duties of a doctor and it's up to him more than to anyone else to do what he can for the injured. When Sawyer fails to put Mars out of his misery with his one bullet ("Tabula Rasa"), Jack must act, as he had refused to act before, and put an end to his patient. In this case, his role as doctor means that he must break the rules that apply off the Island and save Mars from an agonizing death that could not otherwise be avoided with the resources available. Another nice dilemma for the medical ethicists, but a clear case of the special responsibility of skilled practitioners to decide.

Although the previous occupations of most of those on the Island have little bearing on how they interact, the crash itself produces a category to which they all belong: that of "survivor." As Hurley says in "Pilot: Part 2," "we're all in this together." To get a bit clearer on who "we" are, he sets himself to compile his census, trying to find out from each of them where they come from and what they were doing on the flight. (I still don't understand why the Sawyer/Lafleur anomaly didn't come to light at this moment, but we'll let that pass.)

When Hurley and Boone compare the resulting list with the flight manifest, they discover that the man who calls himself Ethan Rom was not on Flight 815. This is clear confirmation that the Island is not as deserted as it at first seemed, and means that the 46 who have been trying to get to know each other now face a potential external threat: there's an "us" and a "them," the Others.

The immediate effect of this discovery is to bind the survivors together, and Locke (the outdoorsman), who had previously stuck to his motto, "you can't tell me what I can't do" (first announced in "Walkabout"), now becomes a defender of the group's integrity, organizing a search party to rescue Claire from the man who has abducted her and who is now definitely not one of "us." Here, his knowledge of the jungle gives him the right to give orders to his comrades.

As Locke (the philosopher) puts it, the survivors determine to "act as one body."[7] This is the moment at which we witness the birth of what can properly be called a "commonwealth"[8] in which, by the consent of its members, roles can be established and rules can be laid down for the good of all those included.

Tit for Tat

So far, I've been running a counterpoint between the causes of conflict in a state of nature and the means of its resolution. I want to conclude by briefly illustrating a general ground for thinking that it's the condition of initial conflict that really matters to how a state of nature turns out.

Take any situation in which two people can either cooperate with each other or not in some enterprise, and suppose that (i) if they each cooperate with the other, then they will both get the optimum result; (ii) if they both refuse to cooperate, they will go without the full benefit but are not much worse off; and (iii) if one cooperates and the other doesn't, the non-cooperator gets a less than optimum result, but still better than if they had both refused, while the cooperator gets the worst outcome.

This sort of situation is easily illustrated by the case of two suspects in a crime in which, say, one held the bank staff hostage while the other emptied the vault. The police don't have evidence enough to convict either unless at least one suspect sings. The suspects are kept in separate rooms and the police offer a deal to each: so long as he's the only one to accuse the other, he will get a reduced sentence to, say, a year and the other will go to jail for 10 years. If each accuses the other, then they both go to jail for five years each. Because of the kind of case that can be used to illustrate the basic structure, the sort of choice involved is called a "prisoners' dilemma." It's worth stressing that when we talk about "cooperating" here, we mean suspects not squealing on one another. We're not talking about helping the police.

Even though the prisoners' dilemma can be illustrated with this sort of instance, two variables in the situation can be adjusted. One is the number of times the players have to make their choices. And the other is the number of players involved. As the number of repetitions or the number of people involved increase, there start to emerge strategies for dealing with the situation.

What makes the prisoners' dilemma a dilemma is that the suspects don't know for sure what the other one has done or is going to do. In a prisoners' dilemma, the attitude we have been calling "Trust No.1" would indicate noncooperation to avoid the worst case for me. Even though I risk 5 years in jail, at least I can be sure not to go down for 10. On the other hand, Innocence would offer cooperation out of fellow-feeling even at the risk of coming off worst. I do not accuse my accomplice in the hope that they too have faith in me. But neither option is particularly convincing as it stands, and it would be crazy to rely on some theory of "human nature" to decide what to do if you might go to jail for 10 years rather than walk free. The craziness is most obvious when the dilemma is repeated more than once and involves the same people again. In that case, the thing to do is consider what the other did last time and act accordingly.

What does *accordingly* mean here? Well, there is a strategy that has been shown to do better than any other over the long run and that has been called "tit for tat." As its name suggests, tit for tat says that you begin by offering cooperation and, after that, you should do whatever the other did last time round: if the other person didn't cooperate, you shouldn't; if they did, you should too. If they, too, are running tit for tat then, given that you both begin by cooperating, you should both continue getting optimum results.

Gaining Trust from the Past

The reason why I didn't want to attribute Trust No.1 to Hobbes is that I think that chapter 13 of *Leviathan* – the one I've been quoting from – envisages a situation in which a previous society has fallen apart by violence (for instance, a civil war – which was a particularly traumatic experience for Thomas Hobbes himself). When that happens, the first move everyone makes is to withdraw cooperation. In this sense, a Hobbesian state of nature begins at the second round of a repeated prisoners' dilemma in which the first round was noncooperative. Given what we've said about "acting accordingly," it's not a winning strategy for people to start cooperating when the others are being uncooperative. As Hobbes recognizes, to begin cooperating – and in particular, to be the first to begin – is to put yourself at your enemy's mercy.

For this reason, I suggest that pretty much everything in *Leviathan* that comes after chapter 13 – with all the famous stuff about natural laws, social contracts, sovereign "leviathans," and the rest – is wildly misleading: once you're in a pure Hobbesian state of nature, you're a goner. Hobbes himself might have half-seen the problem, which is why, at the end of chapter 14, he puts in the idea of an "oath," sworn before God to reinforce the contract. But this is no solution at all. Among other things, why should God be so bothered about having his name taken in vain, when there's so much other mayhem in the state of nature and all the other Commandments (except perhaps the one about graven images) have been broken? Though I know that this is not a popular interpretation of the book, it might justify the fact that virtually no one can be bothered to read all the remaining 400 pages of text.

With the same people in it and with the same tendencies to diffidence or to trust as in a Hobbesian state of nature (second round), a Lockean state of nature has to begin with a first round of tit for tat and can only explain a breakdown of cooperation by the unreasonableness of some of the people some of the time. If the difference between Hobbes and Locke on the state of nature can be seen in the light of the point reached in a repeated prisoners' dilemma, then the relations among the survivors in *Lost* can be understood in terms of how closely their behavior is modeled on tit for tat.

We've been looking only at the very early episodes of season one to see how, from being strangers to one another, the survivors came to adopt reasonable approaches to how to interact with each other so as to promote longer-term interests – their own and of the group as a whole. What is pretty clear is that arbitrary theories of human nature such as Innocence and Trust No. 1 wouldn't really stand up over the long run.

Rather, the survivors used their shared language to signal their intentions to each other. By so doing, they overcame tendencies to uncooperativeness and thus got a community off the ground. Sometimes, as when the split occurred between the group on the beach and the group in the caves (not to mention the problems of dealing with the Others), allegiances varied. But group identifications helped to deal with shortages (tragedies of the commons) and to put through collaborative endeavors (such as hut or raft construction). Once cooperation was under way, it tended to stabilize in accordance with the Lockean starting point in tit for tat and those within the group could cohabit in harmony. But when external threats arose, then the very same strategy dictated a refusal to be the first to cooperate, as in a Hobbesian state of "war."

The prisoners' dilemma and its resolution with tit for tat are only schematic tools for understanding the state of nature. But I suggest that they do at least begin to help us see how they can be generalized to cases involving the 46 survivors on the beach who continued to look for negotiated solutions to their evolving situation. And it's not only *Lost* that can be seen in this light. There's also life off the Island. As Hurley says, "we're all in this together."

For pop culture resources and philosophical resources related to this chapter please visit the website for this book: https://introducingphilosophythroughpopculture.com.

Notes

1   We modernize the spelling of Tuck, R. (1651). *Hobbes Leviathan*, 89. Cambridge: Cambridge University Press. 1991.
2   See Locke, J. (1690). *Two Treatises of Government*, 2e. Cambridge: Cambridge University Press 1960; we give the section numbers that are common to every edition.
3   Locke, sect. 6.
4   Locke, sect. 27.
5   Hobbes, T. (1651). *Leviathan*, 87.
6   Hobbes, 87.
7   Locke, sect. 96.
8   Locke, sect. 126.

32

Federation Trekonomics

Marx, the Federation, and the Shift from Necessity to Freedom

Jeff Ewing

Summary

Star Trek centers on the United Federation of Planets, a spacefaring interplanetary republic organized around the principles of liberty, rights, and equality. Its *economic* system is a little harder to pin down, though. The Federation is effectively a post-scarcity economic system of a kind, yet concrete references to Federation economic life are few and far between. How are we to understand this important element of the world of *Star Trek*? Karl Marx (1818–1883) argued that a *classless society* and the "realm of freedom" can only arise when the "realm of necessity" – that is, material limitations or scarcity – is overcome. This chapter argues that the Federation's economic system reflects one version of the transitional stage toward Marx's envisioned classless society.

Star Trek centers on the United Federation of Planets, a spacefaring, interplanetary federal republic organized around the principles of liberty, rights, and equality. This much is clear. But how should we characterize the Federation's *economic* system – does it align with these principles? The Federation, since the late twenty-second century, has abandoned currency-centric economics – organized around gaining capital and personal property – in favor of a post-scarcity economy focused on *self-enhancement*. The idea isn't without its forerunners: Karl Marx (1818–1883), claims that a *classless society* and the "realm of freedom," in which the development of human capacities is both a central goal and organizational principle, can arise only when the "realm of necessity" – that is, material limitations or scarcity – is overcome. I will argue that the Federation's economic system reflects one version of the transitional stage toward Marx's envisioned classless society. I'll show how the transcendence of scarcity and profit and growth-oriented economic activity both reflect Marx's vision of classless society, and form the background to central Federation principles – such as the Prime Directive, the prioritization of scientific knowledge and self-realization, and the Federation's orientation toward peace rather than conquest or war.

Introducing Philosophy Through Pop Culture: From Socrates to Star Wars *and Beyond*, Second Edition.
Edited by William Irwin and David Kyle Johnson.
© 2022 John Wiley & Sons Ltd. Published 2022 by John Wiley & Sons Ltd.

Capitalism is Most Illogical

ROM: There's only one thing I have to say to you. Workers of the world, unite! You
         have nothing to lose but your chains.
QUARK: What's happened to you?

-"Bar Association" (*Deep Space 9* [DS9])

The Federation is composed of over 150 planetary governments representing a large number of member species, unlike many other galactic powers, such as the Romulan Star Empire or the Cardassian Union. While much of *Star Trek*'s drama focuses on interstellar crises, problems posed by science and technology, and the ethics of exploration, aside from a few scattered references fans are left wondering about the nature of the Federation's economic system. Theories have ranged from calling the Federation a "proto-post scarcity economy" to viewing it as a "well-defined general equilibrium production-exchange economy with a large government presence," "participatory economics," or even "in essence, a communist society."[1] One thing that's clear is that the Federation's economic system is *explicitly not* a capitalist economy – at least not capitalist in the way we know it now. As an economic system, capitalism is characterized by (i) privately owned "means of production" (the tools, machines, plans, and resources used in the processes of economic production), and (ii) production oriented toward profit and growth, where (iii) this profit rests predominantly on the exploitation of wage labor – where workers produce more than they need to meet their own needs, and the capitalists who own the means of production take the surplus. How far from these traits is the Federation, and what does that mean for what it *is*?

The Federation was formed in 2161 by humanity and its allies after the Earth–Romulan War. Planets join the Federation by consent and hold equal voting rights on the Federation Council. As Captain Picard explains, "if there is one ideal that the Federation holds most dear, it is that all men, all races can be united" (*Star Trek: Nemesis*). This ideal – and the Federation's unity – can be maintained because, as Captain Kirk states, the Federation is a "democratic body" ("Errand of Mercy," *Star Trek: The Original Series* [TOS]), the culture of which is "based on freedom and self-determination" ("The Best of Both Worlds, Part I," *Star Trek: The Next Generation* [TNG]). To promote these ends, the Federation built a formidable Starfleet, which, while well capable of exercising military force, focuses primarily on exploration, science, and defense.

Of the Federation's economic system, we know far less. Picard states that in the twenty-fourth century "material needs no longer exist" ("The Neutral Zone," TNG) and the challenge in life has become "to improve yourself . . . enrich yourself." Picard highlights the fact that "people are no longer obsessed with the accumulation of 'things.' We have eliminated hunger, want, the need for possessions." In *Star Trek: First Contact*, Picard notes that "money doesn't exist in the twenty-fourth century" and that "the acquisition of wealth is no longer the driving force in our lives. We work to better ourselves and the rest of humanity." Outsiders also recognize – even if they don't necessarily agree with – the central value defining the Federation's economic system. The Ferengi Nog, for example, describes humans as having abandoned "currency-based economics in favor of some philosophy of self-enhancement" ("In the Cards," DS9).[2]

Thanks to a trip back through time to the nineteenth century ("Time's Arrow, Part II," TNG), we also have a conversation between Deanna Troi and Samuel Clemens, aka Mark Twain, which serves to further clarify the class relations of the Federation:

TROI: He's one of the thousands of species that we've encountered. We live in a peaceful Federation with most of them. The people you see are here by choice.

CLEMENS: So there're a privileged few who serve on these ships, living in luxury and wanting for nothing. But what about everyone else? What about the poor? You ignore them.

TROI: Poverty was eliminated on Earth a long time ago, and a lot of other things disappeared with it. Hopelessness, despair, cruelty.

CLEMENS: Young lady, I come from a time when men achieve power and wealth by standing on the backs of the poor, where prejudice and intolerance are commonplace and power is an end unto itself. And you're telling me that isn't how it is anymore?

TROI: That's right.

In short, Federation economics is oriented toward equal opportunities for individual growth and self-determination, made possible by a triumph over the scarcity of material resources. It's implied that, in direct opposition to the central features of capitalism, *exploitation* as a generator of economic wealth has also been abandoned. Meanwhile, the accumulation of wealth is no longer the goal of economic activity and currency, as we know it at least, has largely been abandoned.

Some form of currency *has* remained, though, and so has a degree of private ownership – here lies the source of debate about Federation economics. Kirk tells Spock that "the Federation has invested a great deal of money in our training" ("Errand of Mercy," TOS), and Beverly Crusher charges a roll of cloth to credit on Deneb IV ("Encounter at Farpoint," TNG). In *Star Trek III*, McCoy negotiates the price of a transfer to the Genesis planet, and Scotty makes reference to buying a boat in *Star Trek VI*. Evidently, ownership of more than just personal property continues: there's the Sisko family restaurant in New Orleans ("Homefront," DS9) and the Chateau Picard vineyard in France ("Family," TNG). So how should we understand these apparently conflicting references to wealth and property in the Federation? As we go forward, we'll see that the Federation is but one possible form that the first, transitional stage to a Marxian classless society may take – but first, what *is* Marx's vision for classless society?

Dammit, Marx, I'm a communist, not a Communist!

Just as a reconstruction of the Federation's economic system has to be pieced together from scattered references throughout a large canon, so must the canon of Marx and Friedrich Engels (1820–1895) be combed through for their picture of a classless, communist society. Reconstructing what communism *really is* in the minds of Marx and Engels is complex for at least three reasons. First, they didn't write a systematic treatment of the topic, requiring us to dig for scattered references from their vast array of works to piece together an account. Second, both Marx and Engels were hesitant to lay out a perfect, concrete utopian vision outside the contest of struggle and history – indeed, "constructing the future and settling everything for all times"[3] is not Marx's project. Finally, communism, as Marx seems to have conceived of and advocated for it, was entirely different than the Communist political structures of the USSR or China, both of which have been organized around rigid and politically determined hierarchies, where "the state" is vastly more powerful than the populace. Marx himself advocated democracy and suggested the state would "wither away" in a classless society. These contradictions of, and confusions about, Marx's vision were aided and abetted by the tendency of both these Communist states – as well as liberal democratic powers like the United States – to conflate the ideals of Marx's project with Soviet or Chinese reality. Some characteristics of Marx's communist vision, however, can be pulled out from the varied treatments of the topic by Marx and Engels. They succinctly summarize communism in the *Communist Manifesto* as "abolition of private property,"[4] but not *personal* private property. Rather, Marx and Engels refer to the abolition of "bourgeois" or capitalist property, understood as the means of production, and consequently the abolition of the exploitation of labor – just the way Troi characterizes the Federation's economy in her discussion with Clemens.

More specifically, and with greater rhetorical flourish, Marx in the *1844 Manuscripts* refers to communism as "the *positive* supersession of *private property* as *human self-estrangement*,"[5] that is:

> The sensuous appropriation of the human essence and human life [... not] understood only in the sense of *direct*, one-sided *consumption*, of *possession*, of *having*. Man appropriates his integral essence in an integral way, as a total man.[6]

In short, communism's success rests on a classless society where private ownership of the means of production ends. In Marx and Engels's view, this allows for a dramatic improvement in human freedom and well-being based on a shift in focus from *having* to *being*, from one-sided development of crippled potential to a focus on the development of a whole and complex personhood. Think of life aboard the *Enterprise*-D. In addition to their primary duties, crewmembers have been shown taking painting classes ("A Matter of Perspective," TNG), performing theater ("The Nth Degree," TNG), holding chess tournaments ("Data's Day," TNG), and playing guitar ("Silicon Avatar," TNG). In addition, virtually any situation can be experienced or skill developed via the holodeck. Marx argues that diverse "free conscious activity" such as this is the crucial trait that distinguishes humanity from nonhuman species – that people consciously *choose* their activity, rather than being driven by instinct. As a consequence, human nature is characterized by both *creation* of our external world (through production) and *self-creation*. Marx thus rejects anything that inhibits the free self-creation of humanity, and (for our purposes) focuses on two specific *kinds* of limitations to free, conscious self-creation: (i) *material* limitations, or lack of economic opportunities, and (ii) social limitations, by which a person's activity is constricted primarily because of hierarchical social relations and power arising from the ability to control economic systems and resources.

Material limitations provoke Marx to emphasize that material, technological developments are vital prerequisites to overcoming class society and to liberation:

> The realm of freedom really begins only where labor determined by necessity and external expediency ends; it lies by its very nature beyond the sphere of material production proper.[7]

Engels thus argues, "communism has only arisen since machinery and other inventions made it possible to hold out the prospect of an all-sided development, a happy existence, for all members of society."[8] Development of technology and science under capitalism generates the increasing potential to overcome these material needs for everyone, and to eliminate the most dangerous and degrading forms of work. The limitations intentionally placed on that potential by capitalist social relations remain a major impetus for revolution.

For Marx, one of the primary social causes of stifled self-creation is the rigid division of labor, both *detailed* and *social*. The *social* division of labor – involving a clear demarcation of different positions within a total economy – also occurs in economic systems before capitalism (like feudalism). The *detailed* division of labor, involving a subdivision of tasks within a productive process, is exclusively a capitalist development. Since these divisions narrow the possibilities for human self-development to a significant degree – I can't choose my activity, after all, if only one type of activity is available to me – Marx rejects divisions of labor, particularly the detailed variety:

> Some crippling of body and mind is inseparable even from the division of labor in society as a whole. However, since manufacture carries this social separation of branches of labor much further, and also, by its peculiar division, attacks the individual at the very roots of his life, it is the first system to provide the materials and the impetus for industrial pathology.[9]

The division of labor, which in a class society is formed by private ownership of the means of production, cuts off avenues for self-creation because the potential for workers' self-creating activity is diverted into profit-seeking or capital-maximizing forms. Consequently, Marx rejects both private property in the means of production and the domination of human possibility by money, perceiving them as obstacles to self-creation. Thus, for Marx, self-creation under communism is accompanied, and facilitated by, the abandonment of money – much like the Federation – since "with collective production, money capital is completely dispensed with."[10] Marx, however, argues, "there is no reason why the producers should not receive paper tokens permitting them to withdraw an amount corresponding to their labor time from the social consumption stocks. But these tokens are not money; they do not circulate."[11] Private property and money out, labor tokens and total "being over having" in.

One final feature of Marx's classless, communist society is found in the recognition that full, classless communism involves a long process of change that resolves into two stages. The first stage of communist society, having recently emerged from capitalism, involves individuals *politically* winning "the battle of democracy" and using the democratic state "to wrest, by degrees, all capital from the bourgeoisie, to centralize all instruments of production in the hands of the state, i.e., of the proletariat organized as the ruling class."[12] Economically, the working class in this stage would receive in consumption exactly what their labor entitles them to; and, for any individual worker, "the same amount of labor he has given to society in one form, he received back in another."[13] By contrast, in a more advanced phase of communist society:

> when labor is no longer just a means of keeping alive but has itself become a vital need; when the all-round development of individuals has also increased their productive powers and all the springs of cooperative wealth flow more abundantly – only then can society wholly cross the narrow horizon of bourgeois right and inscribe on its banner: From each according to his abilities, to each according to his needs![14]

Politically, Marx theorizes that this final stage is characterized by the dissolution of the state as we know it – a coercive, ruling institution separate from and subordinating the population. With this understanding of some of the nuances of a Marxian classless society in mind, let's take a fresh look at the Federation.

Set Phasers to "Revolution"

In the context of Marx and Engels's work on a communist, classless society, how might we characterize the Federation? First, it really *does* seem that the Federation operates without dependence on domination of certain classes by scarcity, money, or an orientation toward accumulation of personal property or capital. Unfortunately, most of our glimpses of life in *Star Trek* pertain to Starfleet practices, not the day-to-day lives of civilians. Even so, we can take the statements by different Starfleet captains at face value: economic life doesn't rely on money and is oriented toward the development of individual capacities. These priorities are reflected in the nature of Starfleet ships themselves: they're first and foremost deep space exploratory vessels with adequate defensive technologies *rather* than military craft such as Klingon Birds-of-Prey or Dominion battlecruisers. What little evidence we have about civilian occupations in *Star Trek* also seems to support Marx and Engels's view that individuals should be able to choose effectively whichever occupations they wish – the Sisko family includes a Starfleet captain, a restaurateur, a writer, and a freighter captain. This new economic orientation is consistent with Marx's depiction of post-capitalist classless society.

Furthermore, the world of *Star Trek* rests on a relative triumph over scarcity, exactly in the way Marx theorized in terms of the shift from "necessity" to "freedom." The fact that famines and natural disasters are possible – such as the fungus-caused food shortage on Tarsus IV in "The Conscience of the King" (TOS) – does *not* disqualify the Federation from being a post-scarcity economy, as some analyses have posited,[15] but rather stands in acknowledgment that real crises can and do happen. Post-scarcity economic systems don't render accidents impossible, but instead improve the ability to respond to them in a quick, egalitarian manner – as we see the *Enterprise* and its successors respond effectively to various disease outbreaks or other disasters (e.g. "The *Galileo* Seven" and "The Cloud Minders" [TOS]; "Hide and Q," "The Child," "Déjà Q," and "Lessons" [TNG]). Indeed, Marx argued that any program for a classless society necessarily had to involve allotments for "a reserve or insurance fund in case of accidents, disruption caused by natural calamities, etc."[16] Overall, the Federation's triumph over economic scarcity allows its citizens to focus on personal development, as well as to participate in scientific and cultural exchange with other societies and races. Military engagements, such as they are, are effects of the Federation's being one galactic power among many, with others at one point or another representing potential military threats – the Klingon, Romulans, Borg, Dominion, or the Typhon Pact.[17]

In this context, the existence of Federation credits and personal property are less of a curiosity than they first seem. Marx didn't reject the potential use of "labor notes" of some kind in the transitional stage to classless society. And even in fully developed communism, Marx argued against the rejection of *personal* privately owned property. Federation credits make sense if thought of as part of a transitional stage in which labor is still coupled to consumption potential. They also make sense in terms of a context in which trade may occur between the Federation and non-Federation worlds or galactic powers – Starfleet officers need *some* form of currency to pay their tab at Quark's bar! Hence, the references to "money" in TOS are probably best understood as references to Federation credits.

Like Marxian communism, the Federation is a political democracy with each planet having democratic votes in making Federation policy, and the central planet of the Federation is a United Earth. Earth is united despite the fact that many nation-states and confederations seem to retain some territorially organized boundaries and identities that correspond to their historical boundaries and cultures – but they aren't independent powers or even federated territories. We can assume, however, that the United Earth government and the Federation aren't *direct* democracies in which popular voting settles every issue – thus the Federation Council. We can also assume that the political structure of both the United Earth and the Federation retain the state's hierarchical structure as an institution, at some level, "over" its citizenry – it didn't "wither away" as Marx had predicted.[18] In this sense, the politics of the Federation seems to be, like Federation credits, firmly located in a transitional period *rather* than at the level of a fully developed classless communism.

The biggest contradiction to reconcile is the apparent inherited ownership of private business like Sisko's Creole Kitchen or Chateau Picard. They could also be explained by treating the Federation as a *transitional* stage on the way to, rather than as the achievement of, a fully classless society – but that isn't entirely satisfactory: Chateau Picard has been producing wine for at least 100 years, a longevity that speaks to a lack of social movement to classlessness. That said, Marx never advocated a singular, context-independent transitional path to communism; and while certain demands in the *Communist Manifesto* must be considered as independent of the national context of the time, the timing of their implementation is something that can best be understood *within* a historical process of transition. Perhaps the Federation's triumph over scarcity is considered so complete that inherited ownership is no longer seen as a means to subordinate others. Suffice it to say, the economic system of the United Federation of Planets has a number of central features attributed to Marx's vision of a classless society, and the eccentricities that exist make the most sense if we picture the Federation within the first, transitional phase toward, rather than as the complete and final phase of, classless society.

To Boldly Conclude . . .

The Federation's abandonment of a profit-and-growth-based economic system and money in favor of an economic system designed to facilitate personal development is a product of future successes in overcoming scarcity. As we've seen, Federation "trekonomics" can be well described in terms of Marx's own vision of the first stage of a post-scarcity, money-free, classless society. The difficulties of interpretation that have provoked debate – the existence of Federation credits, the visible hierarchy in Starfleet, and the family ownership of some specialized means of production, such as restaurants and vineyards, can be resolved if we acknowledge that Marx consistently described a complex, first transitional stage to full communism.

Perhaps it is this overcoming of a profit-and-growth oriented economic system that's responsible for the Federation's vast successes in attracting disparate planets into a democratic union of species, as well as for other characteristic aspects of the Federation. For example, its prioritization of scientific knowledge and self-realization are made possible by the direction of economic imperatives toward group advancement and the good of individual Federation citizens. The Federation's ability to maintain the Prime Directive as a policy may be seen as a consequence of its lack of need for "foreign" labor or resources: unlike early colonial capitalist nations, the Federation has no interest in strip-mining, enslavement, or territorial conquest. Similarly, this self-sufficiency may account for the Federation's hesitancy to engage in interstellar warfare. The Federation can clearly be seen as the transitional stage to full Marxian communism. Given more time to develop, the Federation would boldly go the rest of the way.

For pop culture resources and philosophical resources related to this chapter please visit the website for this book: https://introducingphilosophythroughpopculture.com.

Notes

1 For the Federation as a "proto-post scarcity economy," see Webb, R. (2013). The Economics of Star Trek: The Proto-Post Scarcity Economy.: https://medium.com/@RickWebb/the-economics-of-star-trek-29bab88d50. For a "general equilibrium production-exchange economy," see Gans, J. (2013). That *Star Trek* Economy Thing. http://www.digitopoly.org/2013/11/19/that-star-trek-economy-thing. For a participatory economics interpretation, see Grinder, M. (2012) The Economics of *Star Trek*. http://thepointistochangeit.org/2012/09/30/the-economics-of-star-trek. Finally, for the Federation as a communist society, see Frase, P. (2010). Anti-*Star Trek*: A Theory of Posterity. http://www.peterfrase.com/2010/12/anti-star-trek-a-theory-of-posterity (all accessed June 19, 2015).

2 By way of contrast, for an in-depth analysis of Ferengi economic values, see Held, J.M. (2008). The rules of acquisition can't help you now: what can the Ferengi teach us about business ethics? In: *Star Trek and Philosophy* (ed. J.T. Eberl and K.S. Decker), 117–128. Chicago: Open Court.

3 Marx, K. (1843). "Marx to Ruge" *Letters from the Deutsch-Französische Jahrbücher*: http://www.marxists.org/archive/marx/works/1843/letters/43_09.htm (accessed June 19, 2015).

4 Marx, K. (1992). *Manifesto of the Communist Party. The Revolutions of 1848*, vol. 1, 80. London: Penguin.

5 Marx, K. (1992). *Economic and Philosophical Manuscripts. Early Writings*, 348. London: Penguin.

6 Ibid., 351.

7 Marx, K. (1990). *Capital: A Critique of Political Economy*, vol. 3 (trans. D. Fernbach), 958–959. New York: Penguin.

8 Engels, F. (1971)., *Draft of a Communist Confession of Faith. Birth of the Communist Manifesto*. New York: International Publishers https://http://www.marxists.org/archive/marx/works/1847/06/09.htm (accessed June 19, 2015).

9 Marx, K. (1990). *Capital: A Critique of Political Economy*, vol. 1 (trans. B. Fowkes), 484. New York: Penguin.

10 Marx, K. (1981). *Capital: A Critique of Political Economy*, vol. 2 (trans. D. Fernbach), 434. New York: Vintage Books.

11 Marx, *Capital*, vol. 2, 434.

12 Marx, *Manifesto of the Communist Party*, 86.

13 Marx, K. (1992)., *Critique of the Gotha Programme. The First International and After*, vol. 3, 346. London: Penguin.

14 Marx, *Critique of the Gotha Programme*, 346.

15 Webb.

16 Marx, *Critique of the Gotha Programme*, 344.

17 The "Typhon Pact" is a confederation consisting of the Romulans, Breen, Gorn, Tzenkethi, Tholians, and Kinshaya. Its formation is covered in the *Typhon Pact* series of novels published by Pocket Books in 2010–2012.

18 An insightful look into the Federation's political structure is provided by DeCandido, K.R.A. (2005). *Star Trek: The Next Generation: Articles of the Federation*. New York: Pocket Books.

33

Superman and Justice

Christopher Robichaud

Summary

Superman stands for truth, justice, and the American way. But what kind of justice should Superman embrace? This chapter examines two major philosophical theories of justice – libertarianism and liberal egalitarianism – and suggests ways that Superman can endorse them.

We all know that Superman stands for truth, justice, and the American way. Most of us take the meaning of these words for granted – but not philosophers! We ask things like: What's Superman's precise relationship to the truth? Is there such a thing as *the* American way? Both these questions are worth pursuing, but in this chapter, we'll focus on justice, a term just as vague as the other two.

To explore what kind of justice Superman should stand for, we will consider two alternate theories from contemporary political philosophy. On the one hand, according to *libertarianism*, justice means that the state should ensure that our personal liberty is protected. On the other hand, according to *liberal egalitarianism*, justice involves the state ensuring not only that individual rights are protected but also that there is a fair distribution of opportunity and resources among us. Superman obviously isn't a political entity like the state, but if he claims to stand for justice, then he should do it . . . well, he should do it justice!

It's All About Personal Liberty

One of the most important contributions to contemporary political philosophy – and also a foundational text in contemporary libertarian thought – is *Anarchy, State and Utopia*, written by philosopher Robert Nozick (1938–2002).[1] In this book, Nozick imagined a "minimal state" empowered to protect us from various acts of aggression and violence, as well as to enforce contracts that we freely enter into with each other. It's not empowered to do much of anything else. It's not allowed, for instance, to tax people in

Introducing Philosophy Through Pop Culture: From Socrates to Star Wars *and Beyond*, Second Edition.
Edited by William Irwin and David Kyle Johnson.
© 2022 John Wiley & Sons Ltd. Published 2022 by John Wiley & Sons Ltd.

order to provide for public education, to offer public health care, or even to help with infrastructure issues like the provision of public roads and of transportation. Taxes can only be collected for the purpose of basic police and court functions.

Why should we accept this limited conception of the state? The most famous line of reasoning Nozick offered on its behalf was his "Wilt Chamberlain argument." Nothing against the basketball legend, but we'll use a slightly different version of it. Suppose that as Clark Kent grew up here on Earth, he decided that he didn't want to be a superhero. Instead, he wanted to be an entertainer, the amazing, the astounding, the unbelievable Superman! He wanted to use his powers to awe crowds wherever he went – and awe them he would, since his powers are absolutely amazing. People would drive hundreds of miles to see him wherever he performs.

Now suppose he wanted to charge people money to view him run faster than a speeding bullet, leap buildings in a single bound, and show us that he is indeed more powerful than a locomotive. We can reasonably predict that Superman will quickly become one of the wealthiest men on the planet. If people will travel from around the country to see him, they'll certainly pay to see him as well. If sales ever slow, Superman will no doubt find some new feat to perform to fascinate his fans all over again.

Nozick would now ask us to consider what taxes the state may justifiably collect from Superman. The reason the focus is on taxes is because taxation is considered to be one of the primary coercive powers of the state (along with prosecution and incarceration), and whenever the state acts coercively, we should ask whether it is just. Superman made his money using his own talents, freely entering into a contract to collect payment for putting on a show. And many people freely chose to hand over their own money – earned from the free exercise of their own talents – to see him perform super feats. The money Superman now has is his property, acquired through voluntary transactions and the free exercise of his own talents. The state, therefore, if it is truly invested in preserving personal liberty, can only take money from Superman if it has good reason to. And the only good reason available to it, on this view, is the need for funds in order to protect the personal liberties of the citizens of the state.

Nozick thought it was intuitive that collecting taxes to be used for security and for the enforcing of contracts are the only legitimate uses of the state's coercive power of taxation, because security and contract enforcement are the only things that *all* people need in order to exercise their personal liberty.[2] What reason could the state possibly give to justify taking more of Superman's property than what is required to preserve personal liberty? After all, people *freely* gave him money to see him perform and he was *freely exercising his own talents*. People gave Superman what they were willing to give him to see him do something that he freely chose to do. The state cannot just step in after that and take from him what people freely gave to him for whatever reason it sees fit. Superman can be taxed, to be sure, but he won't be taxed for any of the social programs we currently enjoy in this country, such as roads, education, and health care for the poor and elderly, none of which are necessary to preserve personal freedom.

It is important to understand that Nozick wasn't claiming that affordable education, well-maintained bridges and highways, and affordable health care aren't important. What he is claiming is that it is not the business of the *state* to provide for these things. Sure, these are important social goods, but they're not necessary to preserve liberty. If people want affordable education, for instance, they should engage with the private business of offering affordable education, which would provide an important social good while also preserving personal freedom. If Superman wants to take his pile of money and go into business building roads and setting up schools, that is his choice. But by taxing him to establish these things, we rob Superman of his choice and thus curtail his freedom. And that is an injustice, according to Nozick's libertarian view.

Truth, Libertarian Justice, and the American Way

If we accept this libertarian conception of justice, which puts a premium on personal liberty above all other things, then what would it mean for Superman, as a superhero, to stand for justice? As it is, much of what we see Superman doing in the comics is consistent with him standing for justice of this sort. After all, Superman is mostly concerned with protecting us from all sorts of threats to our security, from the nefarious plots of Lex Luthor to the devious schemes of General Zod. Superman can see himself as an extension of the state in this regard, providing security for us so that we may go about exercising our personal liberty and stepping in only when we choose to exercise that liberty in a way that violates the liberty of others.

Of course, if Superman truly embraced this libertarian conception of justice, he could go much further. After all, he should look at the United States, where he was raised, and recognize that it is currently up to its eyeballs in injustice (according to libertarianism). For example, the state unjustly coerces individuals through taxation to pay for all sorts of social goods. If Superman really stood for libertarian justice, he could use his unique position to put an end to unjust government activity. At the very least, he could put his "brand" behind politicians who share his libertarian sensibilities. More directly, he could become extraordinarily wealthy and provide these goods himself in the private sector. If Superman got into the business of laying down roads, for instance, he could do a heck of a job at a fraction of the time it usually takes. He could probably do it for free, but that wouldn't send the message about libertarian justice that he wants to send. He would want road construction to be a business in order to show how the private sector can provide this good more successfully – and more consistent with justice – than the government can. And that, presumably, would pressure the state to abandon collecting taxes for these purposes.

Not everything would be as easy for him as laying down roads, of course. But Superman could certainly offer a wide range of skills to those interested in privatizing other social goods, like education and health care. Admittedly, conceiving of Superman as some big businessman, as well as a protector of the people, might strike many as being incompatible with conceiving of him as a superhero. That's not so obvious, however; libertarianism, after all, regards unwarranted state coercion as an extremely serious injustice. Fighting it in the way we've just described may not be as glamorous as flinging nuclear missiles into space, clobbering Doomsday, or even giving a speech at the United Nations. But if Superman is serious about standing for libertarian justice, it is a fight he may not in good conscience walk away from, even if it requires him to establish SuperCorp to do it.

Great Rawls!

Many of us think that justice involves taking personal liberty seriously, but perhaps not so seriously that taxing people to promote social welfare programs is considered to be unwarranted coercion. A popular alternative to libertarianism was provided by John

Rawls (1921–2002), the most influential political philosopher in the last 100 years, in his famous book *A Theory of Justice*.[3] In it, Rawls argued that we ought to conceive of justice as fairness. When asking whether political institutions and the distribution of social goods are just, we should ask whether they are *fair*. And, most importantly, Rawls gave us a way of answering that question and reaching conclusions about what fairness amounts to.

The best place to put Rawls in conversation with Nozick concerns our talents and what we deserve to gain when we exercise them. Nozick, remember, thought that we have a nearly absolute claim on the fruits of our labor, and the only justification for taxation is to provide for security and the enforcement of contracts. Rawls agreed that the state needs a justification to tax its citizens, but disagreed with Nozick regarding how much people deserve to keep out of what they earn. He points out that what we earn is, in part, determined by the natural talents we possess, which we cannot claim as "deserved." We were merely born with them, a result of a natural lottery, a mixing of genes, aided by the environment in which we grew up. In other words, our raw talents are based on one part biological determination, one part upbringing, and one part luck. If you are born with high intelligence, or great looks, or tremendous athleticism, you most assuredly didn't *earn* those traits by doing something. It's just a result of how the dice landed for you. This applies to Superman, too; Kal-El didn't earn the powers he has. It was a combination of what he was born with plus the fact that his parents chose to send him to our planet.

We do, of course, play a large role in taking those talents, developing them into skills, and using them toward our goals and dreams. While all of us must work with what we are given in terms of raw talent, we must contribute effort and drive to make something from them. Based on this, Rawls did not say that we don't deserve *any* of the fruits of our labor; that would be absurd. But he points out that it's just as absurd to say we deserve *everything* we earn from the use of our inborn talents, which are in part the result of sheer luck. While we have a legitimate claim on whatever part of our success comes from the effort we put into creating it, we have no claim on the part that resulted from luck.

The end result of this is that if we do not deserve the entirety of the fruits of our labor, then we have less reason to argue against taxation for the purpose of supporting social programs. If Superman does not "deserve" the powers that enable him to become rich as an entertainer, then he has less claim on them when the government comes to collect taxes for reasons above and beyond security and contract enforcement.

Behind the (Lead-Lined) Veil of Ignorance

Starting with the role of luck in determining our natural talents, Rawls developed one of the most well-known ideas in political philosophy: the *original position*. Like Nozick's Wilt Chamberlain argument, Rawls intends the original position argument to capture our intuitive judgments about what fairness – and therefore justice – involves.

Let's say we want to establish what kind of a society will be fair. We'll have to decide what political and social institutions to adopt; what liberties they will be designed to protect and promote; which social, economic, and political goods to distribute and how; and what this distribution of goods will look like. In order to be fair – to consider the interests of all people equally – we decide to think about this ideal justice as if we were behind a "veil of ignorance." What that means is that we should think about these questions as though we weren't aware of what our natural talents are, as well as our race, sex, or other attributes we're born with – which Rawls called the "original position." If we don't know what our actual position in society will be, we'll design a society that respects the rights and needs of everybody, since each of us could potentially be anybody – Lois, Jimmy, Lex, or even Clark. We'll make sure that we don't stack the deck in our favor by creating a society in which those with our talents and attributes will be privileged at the expense of others.

Ideally, this thought process will result in a fair society, one that we can justify to everybody regardless of their natural talents or lack thereof. Furthermore, once we imagine ourselves behind the veil of ignorance, unaware of what position we'll hold in society, we can base our institutional design on our own self-interest. Despite the hypothetical nature of the veil of ignorance and the original position, this grounds Rawls's theory in reality. Rather than arguing that the ideal society is one that people *should* want, or one that people should recognize is good for *other* people, it speaks to people's own interests: this society will be the best for you if you don't know if you'll be smart, beautiful, athletic, and so forth.

Rawls believed that if we agree to think about society as if behind a veil of ignorance, we'll create a society that conforms to two key principles – principles that, in his opinion, inevitably flow from our own self-interest. The first principle – which would be familiar to Nozick and other libertarians – is that our society must have strong institutions in place to protect basic liberties like freedom of speech, of the press, and of conscience. This principle, as a matter of self-interest, would take priority over the second principle, which deals with equality of opportunity and resources; after all, having opportunity and resources means little if you don't have the basic freedoms to make use of them.

The second principle is both better known than the first and more controversial. It says first that we must create institutions that promote equality of opportunity, so that anyone with the same talents will have the same professional opportunities open to him or her. The second part deals with the distribution of basic social goods, which Rawls called *primary goods*, such as food, clothing, and shelter, which are essential to making the most of one's opportunities. From behind the veil of ignorance, what institutions will we want in place to determine the distribution of these primary goods in society? Since we are just as likely to be born talented or untalented, to a rich family or a poor family, in a peaceful country or a war-torn one, Rawls maintained that we would want to pay particular attention to making sure the worst-off members of society are cared for the most.

As a matter of self-interest, then, we will adopt what has come to be called the *difference principle*: we will design institutions to distribute primary goods in such a way that benefits the worst-off first, therefore lessening the difference between the worst-off and the best-off. What they choose to make from those extra resources is up to them, but at least they get a little extra help getting started, to make up for their other disadvantages. According to Rawls, this is what we'd want society to do if we were the worst-off, and behind the veil of ignorance, each of us could be in that position.

Occupy Metropolis

What would it mean for Superman to stand for Rawlsian justice? Much of what Superman does already is consistent with Rawlsian justice, including the things that a libertarian Superman would do; this is natural, given that both systems place value on freedoms.

For instance, promoting security is crucial to defending our basic liberties. By battling Luthor, Bizarro, and Brainiac, Superman helps the state perform its role in keeping us safe so that we may speak freely, worship as we please, and so forth.

But what about making sure that primary goods are distributed according to the difference principle? As we saw, Superman could start a business to promote libertarian justice, but that won't work for promoting Rawlsian justice. For Rawls, distribution of primary goods is a problem to be handled by government institutions, and unless Superman takes a position in the US government, he can't have a direct impact on how this is done. He must address distributional injustice differently, to the extent that it exists – and when it comes to the United States, where he was raised, it seems there is much Rawlsian injustice that needs to be addressed.

So what's the Man of Steel to do? March with Occupy Metropolis? Actually, he could do that: as the most powerful superhero on the planet, who is respected by people and nations around the globe, Superman is in a unique position to promote economic justice by advocating for it. His voice can literally be heard across oceans and continents. As Clark Kent, he can focus on news stories for the *Daily Planet* that bring to light the economic injustice that exists in our country. Perry White would surely run them – in his own self-interest, of course. As Superman, he can speak out against economic injustice, throwing the weight of his stature behind efforts to improve things. He can lobby for it to be changed. He can help put legislators into office who will address the problem.

But he can't *force* our country, or any country for that matter, to change. That would perhaps take him down a dangerous road of using his might to steer human affairs rather than help them along the path they've chosen for themselves. Superman can help us avoid natural disasters and invasions from outer space, and help improve conditions on Earth to some degree, but past that he has to let humanity determine its own way. Rawls's system of justice definitely has more room for government action than libertarianism, but it is actually rather limited. The government ensures basic liberties and helps the downtrodden get a head start in life and some continued aid, but each person is still responsible for making something of his or her life using the help received. Superman is simply treating humanity the same way.

Superman's Greatest Foe?

It may seem underwhelming to suggest that Superman fight certain forms of injustice by marching in the streets. This is the guy who can fling a radioactive asteroid into the sun, and carrying a protest sign is the best he can do to combat injustice? When it comes to addressing certain institutional forms of injustice, however, that indeed may be the most effective thing he can do. As he says when defending his participation in protests in the Middle East by simply standing still in the middle of the crowd:

> I'm good when it comes to fighting apocalyptic threats. But the everyday degradations that humans suffer? Dying of thirst? Hunger? People being denied their basic human rights? I've never been very effective at stopping things like that.[4]

He can't pummel injustice with his super-strength or blast it with his heat-vision. In this sense, institutional injustice is as much of a challenge to Superman as Doomsday was, one that all the brute power in the world isn't enough to beat. It has more in common with Lex Luthor, a formidable threat that cannot be fought with mere force, but requires reason, strategy, and heart. In order to put the "justice" in "truth, justice, and the American way," Superman will gladly go behind the veil of ignorance (without his x-ray vision). Will you?

For pop culture resources and philosophical resources related to this chapter please visit the website for this book: https://introducingphilosophythroughpopculture.com.

Notes

1 Nozick, R. (1977). *Anarchy, State and Utopia*. New York: Basic Books. The discussion that follows also draws upon the wonderful discussion of libertarianism in Kymlicka, W. (2002). *Contemporary Political Philosophy: An Introduction*, 2e, 102–165. Oxford: Oxford University Press.
2 There's an obvious complication to point out here, which is that Superman himself doesn't really need the state to perform these functions for him. But we can safely presume that Nozick didn't design his theory with Superman in mind!
3 Rawls, J. (1971). *A Theory of Justice*. Cambridge, MA: Harvard University Press.
4 *Action Comics*, vol. 1, #600 (May 2011).

34

Cartman Shrugged

South Park *and Libertarian Philosophy*

Paul A. Cantor

Summary

Satirizing political correctness, *South Park* makes the case that people should be allowed to speak and act as they see fit so long as they do not harm others. The radical freedom *South Park* endorses also includes economic liberty in the form of free markets. In fact, the creators of *South Park*, Trey Parker and Matt Stone, espouse libertarian political philosophy, which rejects collectivism and central planning. Big corporations are often the villains on TV and in the movies, but *South Park* pushes back against this stereotype by vindicating "Harbucks" and Wal-Mart. As long as government does not intervene, corporations can only succeed by giving people what they want at the lowest price possible. As Adam Smith argued, when a business or an individual pursues their own good, it is as if they are "led by an invisible hand to promote an end which was no part of his intention." That unintended end is the benefit of others.

Tho' ye subject bee but a fart, yet will this tedious sink of learning ponderously philosophize.
— Mark Twain, *1601*

Critics of *South Park* – and they are legion – bitterly complain about its relentless obscenity and potty humor. And they have a legitimate point. But if one wanted to mount a high-minded defense of the show's low-minded jokes, one might go all the way back to Plato (428–348 BCE) to find a link between philosophy and vulgarity. Toward the end of his dialogue the *Symposium*, a young Athenian nobleman named Alcibiades offers a striking image of the power of Socrates. He compares the philosopher's speeches to a statue of the satyr Silenus, which is ugly on the outside, but when opened up reveals a beautiful interior:

> if you choose to listen to Socrates' discourses you would feel them at first to be quite ridiculous; on the outside they are clothed with such absurd words and phrases . . . His talk is of pack-asses, smiths, cobblers, and tanners . . . so that anyone inexpert and thoughtless might laugh his speeches to scorn. But when these are opened . . . you will discover that they are the only speeches which have any sense in them.[1]

Introducing Philosophy Through Pop Culture: From Socrates to Star Wars *and Beyond*, Second Edition.
Edited by William Irwin and David Kyle Johnson.
© 2022 John Wiley & Sons Ltd. Published 2022 by John Wiley & Sons Ltd.

These words characterize equally well the contrast between the vulgar surface and the philosophical depth of the dialogue in which they are spoken. The *Symposium* contains some of the most soaring and profound philosophical speculations ever written. And yet in the middle of the dialogue the comic poet Aristophanes comes down with a bad case of hiccups that prevents him from speaking in turn. By the end of the dialogue, all the characters except Socrates have consumed so much wine that they pass out in a collective drunken stupor. In a dialogue about the spiritual and physical dimensions of love, Plato thus suggests that, however philosophical we may wax in our speeches, we remain creatures of the body and can never entirely escape its crude bodily functions. In the way that the *Symposium* moves back and forth between the ridiculous and the sublime, Plato seems to be making a statement about philosophy – that it has something in common with low comedy. Both philosophy and vulgar humor fly in the face of conventional opinion.

High Philosophy and Low Comedy

I'm not sure what Plato would have made of *South Park*, but his Silenus image fits the show quite well. *South Park* is one the most vulgar shows ever to appear on television, and yet it can at the same time be one of the most thought-provoking. Its vulgarity is of course the first thing we notice about it, given its obsession with farting, pissing, shitting, vomiting, and every other excretory possibility. As Plato's dialogue suggests, it's all too easy to become fixated on the vulgar and obscene surface of *South Park*, rejecting out of hand a show that chose to make a Christmas icon out of a talking turd named Mr. Hankey. But if you're patient with *South Park*, and give the show the benefit of the doubt, you'll find that it takes up one serious issue after another, from environmentalism to animal rights, from assisted suicide to sexual harassment, from presidential elections to US foreign policy. And the show approaches all these issues from a distinct philosophical position, known as libertarianism, the philosophy of freedom. If anything, the show can become too didactic, with episodes often culminating in a character delivering a speech that offers a surprisingly balanced and nuanced account of the issue at hand.

In thinking about *South Park*, we should recall that some of the greatest comic writers – Aristophanes, Chaucer, Rabelais, Shakespeare, Jonson, Swift – plumbed the depths of obscenity even as they rose to the heights of philosophical thought. The same intellectual courage that emboldened them to defy conventional proprieties empowered them to reject conventional ideas and break through the intellectual frontiers of their day. Without claiming that *South Park* deserves to rank with such distinguished predecessors, I will say that the show descends from a long tradition of comedy that ever since ancient Athens has combined obscenity with philosophy. There are almost as many fart jokes in Aristophanes' play *The Clouds* as there are in a typical episode of *The Terrance and Phillip Show*. In fact, in the earliest dramatic representation of Socrates that has come down to us, he's making fart jokes as he tries to explain to a dumb Athenian named Strepsiades that thunder is a purely natural phenomenon, not the work of the great god Zeus:

First think of the tiny fart that your intestines make.
Then consider the heavens: their infinite farting is thunder.
For thunder and farting are, in principle, one and the same.[2]

Speaking the Unspeakable

The people who condemn *South Park* for being offensive need to be reminded that comedy is by its very nature offensive. It derives its energy from its transgressive power – its ability to break taboos, to speak the unspeakable. Comedians are always pushing the envelope, probing to see how much they can get away with in violating the speech codes of their day. Comedy is a social safety valve. We laugh precisely because comedians momentarily liberate us from the restrictions that conventional society imposes on us. We applaud comedians because they say right out in front of an audience what, supposedly, nobody is allowed to say in public.

Paradoxically, then, the more permissive American society has become, the harder it has become to write comedy. As censorship laws have been relaxed, and people have been allowed to say and show almost anything in movies and television – above all to deal with formerly taboo sexual material – comedy writers like the creators of *South Park*, Trey Parker and Matt Stone, must have begun to wonder if there is any way left to offend an audience.

The genius of Parker and Stone has been to see that in our day a new frontier of comic transgression has opened up because of the phenomenon known as *political correctness*. Our age may have tried to dispense with the conventional pieties of earlier generations, but it has developed new pieties of its own. They may not look like the traditional pieties, but they're enforced in the same old way, with social pressures and sometimes even legal sanctions punishing people who dare to violate the new taboos. Many of our colleges and universities today have speech codes, which seek to define what can and can't be said on campus, and in particular to prohibit anything that might be interpreted as demeaning someone because of his or her race, religion, gender, handicap, and a whole series of other protected categories. Sex may no longer be taboo in our society, but sexism now is. *Seinfeld* was probably the first television comedy that systematically violated the new taboos of political correctness. The show repeatedly made fun of contemporary sensitivities about such issues as sexual orientation, ethnic identity, feminism, and handicapped people. *Seinfeld* proved that being politically incorrect can be hilariously funny in today's moral and intellectual climate, and *South Park* was quick to follow its lead.

The show has mercilessly satirized all forms of political correctness – anti-hate crime legislation, tolerance indoctrination in the schools, Hollywood do-gooding of all kinds, environmentalism and anti-smoking campaigns, the Americans with Disabilities Act and the Special Olympics – the list goes on and on. It's hard to single out the most politically incorrect moment in the history of *South Park*, but I'll nominate the spectacular "cripple fight" in the fifth season episode of that name, and indeed just look at the politically incorrect name to describe what happens when two "differently abled," or rather "handi-capable" boys, named Timmy and Jimmy square off for a violent – and interminable – battle in the streets of South Park. The show obviously relishes the sheer shock value of moments such as this. But more is going on here than transgressing the boundaries of good taste just for transgression's sake.

A Plague on Both Your Houses

This is where the philosophy of libertarianism enters the picture in *South Park*. The show criticizes political correctness in the name of freedom. That's why Parker and Stone can proclaim themselves equal opportunity satirists; they make fun of the old pieties as well as the new, savaging both the right and the left insofar as both seek to restrict freedom. "Cripple Fight" is an excellent example of the balance and evenhandedness of *South Park*, and the way it can offend both ends of the political spectrum. The episode deals in typical *South Park* fashion with a contemporary controversy, one that has even made it into the courts: whether homosexuals should be allowed to lead Boy Scout troops. The episode makes fun of the old-fashioned types in the town who insist on denying a troop leadership to Big Gay Al (a recurrent character whose name says it all). It turns out that the ostensibly straight man the Boy Scouts choose to replace Big Gay Al is a pedophile who starts abusing the boys immediately by photographing them naked. As it frequently does with the groups it satirizes, *South Park*, even as it stereotypes homosexuals, displays sympathy for them and their right to live their lives as they see fit.

But just as the episode seems to be simply taking the side of those who condemn the Boy Scouts for homophobia, it swerves in an unexpected direction. Big Gay Al himself defends the right of the Boy Scouts to exclude homosexuals on the principle of freedom of association. An organization should be able to set up its own rules and the law should not impose society's notions of political correctness on a private group. This episode represents *South Park* at its best – looking at a complicated issue from both sides and coming up with a judicious resolution of the issue. And the principle on which the issue is resolved is *freedom*. As the episode shows, Big Gay Al should be free to be homosexual, but the Boy Scouts should also be free as an organization to make their own rules and exclude him from a leadership post if they so desire.

This libertarianism makes *South Park* offensive to the politically correct, for, if applied consistently, it would dismantle the whole apparatus of speech control and thought manipulation that do-gooders have tried to construct to protect their favored minorities. Libertarianism is a philosophy of radical freedom, and particularly celebrates the free market as a form of social organization. As a philosophy, it descends from, among other sources, the thinking of the Scottish Enlightenment in the eighteenth century. Moral philosophers from that period such as Adam Smith (1723–1790) argued for free trade and the reduction of government intervention in the economy. Libertarianism is especially grounded in the work of the Austrian School of economics, above all the writings of Ludwig von Mises (1881–1973) and Friedrich Hayek (1899–1992), who offer the most cogent defense of unfettered economic activity as the key to prosperity and progress.[3] The term *libertarianism* was popularized by Murray Rothbard (1926–1995), a student of Mises, who developed the most radical critique of state interference in economic and social life, a philosophy of freedom that borders on anarchism.[4]

With its support for unconditional freedom in all areas of life, libertarianism defies categorization in terms of the standard one-dimensional political spectrum of right and left. In opposition to the collectivist and anticapitalist vision of the left, libertarians reject central planning and want people to be left alone to pursue their self-interest as they see fit. But in contrast to conservatives, libertarians also oppose social legislation; they generally favor the legalization of drugs and the abolition of all censorship and anti-pornography laws. Parker and Stone publicly identify themselves as libertarians – which explains why their show ends up offending both liberals and conservatives. Parker has said: "We avoid extremes but we hate liberals more than conservatives, and we hate them."[5] This does seem to be an accurate assessment of the leanings of the show – even though it is no friend of the right, *South Park* is more likely to go after left-wing causes. In an interview in *Reason*, Matt Stone explained that he and Parker were on the left of the political spectrum when they were in high school in the 1980s, but in order to maintain their stance as rebels, they found that, when they went to the University of Colorado, Boulder, and even more so when they arrived in Hollywood, they had to change their positions and attack the prevailing left-wing orthodoxy. As Stone says:

> I had Birkenstocks in high school. I was that guy. And I was sure that those people on the other side of the political spectrum [the right] were trying to control my life. And then I went to Boulder and got rid of my Birkenstocks immediately, because everyone else had them and I realized that those people over here [on the left] want to control my life too. I guess that defines my political philosophy. If anybody's telling me what I should do, then you've got to really convince me that it's worth doing.[6]

Defending the Undefendable

The libertarianism of Parker and Stone places them at odds with the intellectual establishment of contemporary America. In the academic world, much of the media, and a large part of the entertainment business, especially the Hollywood elite, anticapitalist views generally prevail.[7] Studies have shown that business people are usually portrayed in an unfavorable light in movies and television.[8] *South Park* takes particular delight in skewering the Hollywood stars who exploit their celebrity to conduct liberal or left-wing campaigns against the workings of the free market (Barbra Streisand, Rob Reiner, Sally Struthers, and George Clooney are among the celebrities the show has pilloried). *South Park* is rare among television shows for its willingness to celebrate the free market, and even to come to the defense of what is evidently the most hated institution in Hollywood, the corporation. For example, in the ninth season episode "Die Hippie Die," Cartman fights the countercultural forces who invade South Park and mindlessly blame all the troubles of America on "the corporations."

Of all *South Park* episodes, the second season "Gnomes" offers the most fully developed defense of capitalism, and I will attempt a comprehensive interpretation of it in order to demonstrate how genuinely intelligent and thoughtful the show can be. "Gnomes" deals with a common charge against the free market – that it allows large corporations to drive small businesses into the ground, much to the detriment of consumers. In "Gnomes" a national coffee chain called Harbucks – an obvious reference to Starbucks – comes to South Park and tries to buy out the local Tweek Bros. coffee shop. Mr. Tweek casts himself as the hero of the story, a small business David battling a corporate Goliath. The episode satirizes the cheap anticapitalist rhetoric in which such conflicts are usually formulated in contemporary America, with the small business shown to be purely good and the giant corporation shown to be purely evil. "Gnomes" systematically deconstructs this simplistic opposition.

In the conventional picture, the small business operator is presented as a public servant, almost unconcerned with profits, simply a friend to his customers, whereas the corporation is presented as greedy and uncaring, doing nothing for the consumer. "Gnomes" shows instead that Mr. Tweek is just as self-interested as any corporation, and he is in fact cannier in promoting himself than Harbucks is. The Harbucks representative, John Postem, is blunt and gruff, an utterly charmless man who thinks that he can just state the bare economic truth and get away with it: "Hey, this is a capitalist country, pal – get used to it." The irony of the episode is that the supposedly sophisticated corporation completely mishandles public relations, naively believing that the superiority of its product will be enough to ensure its triumph in the marketplace.

The common charge against large corporations is that, with their financial resources, they're able to exploit the power of advertising to put their small rivals out of business. But in "Gnomes," Harbucks is no match for the advertising savvy of Mr. Tweek. He cleverly turns his disadvantage into an advantage, coming up with the perfect slogan in his circumstances: "Tweek offers a simpler coffee for a simpler America." He thereby exploits his underdog position, while preying upon his customers' nostalgia for an older and presumably simpler America. The episode constantly dwells on the fact that Mr. Tweek is just as slick at advertising as any corporation. He keeps launching into commercials for his coffee, accompanied by soft guitar mood music and purple advertising prose; his coffee is "special like an Arizona sunrise or a juniper wet with dew." His son may be appalled by "the metaphors" (actually they are similes), but Mr. Tweek knows just what will appeal to his nature-loving, yuppie customers.

"Gnomes" thus undermines any notion that Mr. Tweek is morally superior to the corporation he's fighting, and in fact the episode suggests that he may be a good deal worse. Going over the top as it always does, *South Park* reveals that the coffee shop owner has for years been over-caffeinating his son Tweek (one of the regulars in the show) and is thus responsible for the boy's hyper-nervousness. Moreover, when faced with the threat from Harbucks, Mr. Tweek seeks sympathy by declaring: "I may have to shut down and sell my son Tweek into slavery." It sounds as if his greed exceeds Harbucks'. But the worst thing about Mr. Tweek is that he isn't content with using his slick advertising to compete with Harbucks in a free market. He also goes after Harbucks politically, trying to enlist the government on his side to prevent the national chain from coming to South Park. "Gnomes" thus portrays the campaign against large corporations as just one more sorry episode in the long history of businesses seeking economic protectionism – the kind of business–government alliance Adam Smith criticized in *The Wealth of Nations*. Far from the standard Marxist portrayal of monopoly power as the inevitable result of free competition, *South Park* shows that it results only when one business gets the government to intervene on its behalf and restrict free entry into the marketplace.

The Town of South Park Versus Harbucks

Mr. Tweek gets his chance to enlist public opinion on his side when he finds out that his son and the other boys have been assigned to write a report on a current event. Offering to write the paper for the children, he inveigles them into a topic very much in his self-interest: "how large corporations take over little family-owned businesses," or, more pointedly, "how the corporate machine is ruining America." Kyle can barely get out the polysyllabic words when he delivers the ghostwritten report in class: "As the voluminous corporate automaton bulldozes its way . . ." This language obviously parodies the exaggerated and overinflated anticapitalist rhetoric of the contemporary left. But the report is a big hit with local officials and soon – much to Mr. Tweek's delight – the mayor is sponsoring Proposition (Prop) 10, an ordinance that will ban Harbucks from South Park.

In the ensuing controversy over Prop 10, "Gnomes" portrays the way the media are biased against capitalism and the way the public is manipulated into anti-business attitudes. The boys are enlisted to argue for Prop 10 and the man from Harbucks to argue against it. The presentation is slanted from the beginning, when the moderator announces: "On my left, five innocent, starry-eyed boys from Middle America" and "On my right, a big, fat, smelly corporate guy from New York." Postem tries to make a rational argument, grounded in principle: "This country is founded on free enterprise." But the boys triumph in the debate with a somewhat less cogent argument, as Cartman sagely proclaims: "This guy sucks ass." The television commercial in favor of Prop 10 is no less fraudulent than the debate. Again, "Gnomes" points out that anti-corporate advertising can be just as slick as corporate. In particular, the episode shows that the left is willing to go to any length in its anti-corporate crusade, exploiting children to tug at the heart-strings of its target audience. In a wonderful parody of a political commercial, the boys are paraded out in a patriotic scene featuring the American flag, while the "Battle Hymn of the Republic" plays softly in the background. Meanwhile the announcer solemnly intones: "Prop 10 is about children. Vote yes on Prop 10 or else you hate children." The ad is "paid for by Citizens for a Fair and Equal Way to Get Harbucks Out of Town Forever." *South Park* loves to expose the illogic of liberal and left-wing crusaders, and the anti-Harbucks campaign is filled with one non sequitur after another. Pushing the last of the liberal buttons, one woman challenges the Harbucks representative: "How many Native Americans did you slaughter to make that coffee?"

Prop 10 seems to be headed for an easy victory at the polls until the boys encounter some friendly gnomes, who explain corporations to them. At the last minute, in one of the most didactic of the *South Park* concluding message scenes, the boys announce to the puzzled townspeople that they have reversed their position on Prop 10. In the spirit of libertarianism, Kyle proclaims something rarely heard on television outside of a John Stossel report: "Big corporations are good. Because without big corporations we wouldn't have things like cars and computers and canned soup." And Stan comes to the defense of the dreaded Harbucks: "Even Harbucks started off as a small, little business. But because it made such great coffee, and because they ran their business so well, they managed to grow until they became the corporate powerhouse it is today. And that is why we should all let Harbucks stay."

At this point the townspeople do something remarkable – they stop listening to all the political rhetoric and actually taste the rival coffees for themselves. And they discover that Mrs. Tweek (who has been disgusted by her husband's devious tactics) is telling the truth when she says: "Harbucks Coffee got to where it is by being the best." Indeed, as one of the townspeople observes: "It doesn't have that bland, raw sewage taste that Tweek's coffee has." "Gnomes" ends by suggesting that it's only fair that businesses battle it out, not in the political arena, but in the marketplace, and let the best product win. Postem offers Mr. Tweek the job of running the local franchise and everybody is happy. Politics is a zero-sum, winner-take-all game, in which one business triumphs only by using government power to eliminate a rival, but in the voluntary exchanges a free market makes possible, all parties benefit from a transaction. Harbucks makes a profit, and Mr. Tweek can continue earning a living without selling his son into slavery, but above all the people of South Park get to enjoy a better brand of coffee. Contrary to the anti-corporate propaganda normally coming out of Hollywood, *South Park* argues that, in the absence of government intervention, corporations get where they are by serving the public, not by exploiting it. As Ludwig von Mises makes the point:

> The profit system makes those men prosper who have succeeded in filling the wants of the people in the best possible and cheapest way. Wealth can be acquired only by serving the consumers. The capitalists lose their funds as soon as they fail to invest them in those lines

in which they satisfy best the demands of the public. In a daily repeated plebiscite in which every penny gives a right to vote the consumers determine who should own and run the plants, shops and farms.[9]

The Great Gnome Mystery Solved

But what about the gnomes, who, after all, give the episode its title? Where do they fit in? I never could understand how the subplot in "Gnomes" related to the main plot until I was lecturing on the episode at a summer institute and my colleague Michael Valdez Moses made a breakthrough that allowed us to put together the episode as a whole. In the subplot, Tweek complains to anybody who will listen that every night at 3:30 a.m. gnomes sneak into his bedroom and steal his underpants. But nobody else can see this remarkable phenomenon happening, not even when the other boys stay up late with Tweek to observe it, not even when the emboldened gnomes start robbing underpants in broad daylight in the mayor's office. We know two things about these strange beings: (i) they are gnomes and (ii) they are normally invisible. Both facts point in the direction of capitalism. As in the phrase "gnomes of Zurich," which refers to bankers, gnomes are often associated with the world of finance. In the first opera of Richard Wagner's Ring Cycle, *Das Rheingold*, the gnome Alberich serves as a symbol of the capitalist exploiter – and he forges the Tarnhelm, a cap of invisibility.[10] The idea of invisibility calls to mind Adam Smith's famous notion of the "invisible hand" that guides the free market.[11]

In short, the underpants gnomes are an image of capitalism and the way it is normally – and mistakenly – pictured by its opponents. The gnomes represent the ordinary business activity that's always going on in plain sight of everyone, but which they fail to notice and fail to understand. The people of South Park are unaware that the ceaseless activity of large corporations like Harbucks is necessary to provide them with all the goods they enjoy in their daily lives. They take it for granted that the shelves of their supermarkets will always be amply stocked with a wide variety of goods and never appreciate all the capitalist entrepreneurs who make that abundance possible.

What is worse, the ordinary citizens misinterpret capitalist activity as theft. They focus only on what businesses take from them – their money – and forget about what they get in return, all the goods and services. Above all, people have no understanding of the basic facts of economics and have no idea of why businesses deserve the profits they earn. Business is a complete mystery to them – it seems to be a matter of gnomes sneaking around in the shadows and mischievously heaping up piles of goods for no apparent purpose. Friedrich Hayek noted this long-standing tendency to misinterpret normal business activities as sinister:

> Such distrust and fear have led ordinary people to regard trade as suspicious, inferior, dishonest, and contemptible . . . Activities that appear to add to available wealth, "out of nothing," without physical creation and by merely rearranging what already exists, stink of sorcery . . . That a mere change of hands should lead to a gain in value to all participants, that it need not mean gain to one at the expense of the others (or what has come to be called exploitation), was and is nonetheless intuitively difficult to grasp . . . Many people continue to find the mental feats associated with trade easy to discount even when they do not attribute them to sorcery, or see them as depending on trick or fraud or cunning deceit.[12]

Even the gnomes don't understand what they are doing. Perhaps *South Park* is suggesting that the real problem is that entrepreneurs themselves lack the economic knowledge that they would need to explain their activity to the public and justify their profits. When the boys ask the gnomes to tell them about corporations, all they can offer is this enigmatic diagram of the stages of their business:

Phase 1	Phase 2	Phase 3
Collect underpants	?	Profit

This chart basically encapsulates the economic illiteracy of the American public. They can see no connection between the activities businesspeople undertake and the profits they make. What entrepreneurs actually contribute to the economy is a big question mark to them.[13] The fact that entrepreneurs are rewarded for taking risks, for correctly anticipating consumer demands, and for efficiently financing, organizing, and managing production is lost on most people. They would rather complain about the obscene profits of corporations and condemn their power in the marketplace.

The "invisible hand" passage of Smith's *Wealth of Nations* reads like a gloss on the "Gnomes" episode of *South Park*:

> As every individual, therefore, endeavours as much as he can both to employ his capital in the support of domestick industry, and so to direct that industry that its produce may be of the greatest value; every individual necessarily labours to render the annual revenue of the society as great as he can. He genuinely, indeed, neither intends to promote the publick interest, nor knows how much he is promoting it. By preferring the support of domestick to that of foreign industry, he intends only his own security, and by directing that industry in such a manner as its produce may be of the greatest value, he intends only his own gain, and he is in this, as in many other cases, led by an invisible hand to promote an end which was no part of his intention. Nor is it always the worse for the society that it was no part of it. By pursuing his own interest he frequently promotes that of the society more effectively than when he really intends to promote it. I have never known much good done by those who affected to trade for the publick good.[14]

"Gnomes" exemplifies this idea of the invisible hand. The economy does not need to be guided by the very visible and heavy hand of government regulation for the public interest to be served. Without any central planning, the free market produces a prosperous economic order. The free interaction of producers and consumers and the constant interplay of supply and demand work so that people generally have access to the goods they want. Like Adam Smith, Parker and Stone are deeply suspicious of people who speak about the public good and condemn the private pursuit of profit. As we see in the case of Mr. Tweek, such people are usually hypocrites, pursuing their self-interest under the cover of championing the public interest. And the much-maligned gnomes of the world, the corporations, while openly pursuing their own profit, end up serving the public interest by providing the goods and services people really want.

The Wal-Mart Monster

Having had the audacity to defend Starbucks, in its eighth season *South Park* went on to rally to the cause of Wal-Mart – under an even more thinly disguised name in an episode called "Something Wall-Mart This Way Comes." This episode is brilliantly cast in the mold of a cheesy horror movie, as the sinister power of a Wal-Mart-like superstore takes over the town of South Park amid lengthening shadows, darkening clouds, and ominous flashes of lightning. The Wall-Mart exerts "some mystical evil force" over the townspeople. Try as they may, they cannot resist its bargain prices. Just as in "Gnomes" a local merchant starts complaining about his inability to compete with a national retail chain. In mock sympathy, Cartman plays syrupy violin music to accompany this lament. When Kyle indignantly smashes the violin, Cartman simply replies: "I can go get another one at Wall-Mart – it was only five bucks."

Widespread public opposition to the Wall-Mart develops in the town and efforts are made to boycott the store, ban it, and even burn it down (the latter to the uplifting strain of "Kumbaya"). But like any good monster, the evil Wall-Mart keeps springing back to life and the townspeople are irresistibly drawn to its well-stocked aisles at all hours ("Where else was I going to get a napkin dispenser at 9:30 at night?"). All these horror movie clichés are a way of making fun of how Wal-Mart is demonized by intellectuals in our society. They present the national chain as some kind of external power, independent of human beings, which somehow manages to impose itself upon them against their will – a corporate monster. At times the townspeople talk as if they simply have no choice in going to the superstore, but at other times they reveal what really attracts them – lower prices that allow them to stretch their incomes and enjoy more of the good things in life. To be evenhanded, the episode does stress at several points the absurdities of buying in bulk just to get a bargain, for example, ending up with enough Ramen noodles "to last a thousand winters."

In the grand horror movie tradition, the boys finally set out to find the heart of the Wall-Mart and destroy it. Meanwhile, Stan's father, Randy, has gone to work for the Wall-Mart for the sake of the 10% employee discount, but he nevertheless tries to help the boys reach their objective. But as they get closer, Randy notes with increasing horror: "The Wall-Mart is lowering its prices to try to stop us," and in the end he deserts the children when he sees a screwdriver set marked down beyond his wildest dreams. He cries out: "This bargain is too great for me," as he rushes off to a cash register to make a purchase. When the boys at last reach the heart of the Wall-Mart, it turns out to be a mirror in which they see themselves. In one of the show's typical didactic moments, the spirit of the superstore tells the children: "That is the heart of Wall-Mart – you, the consumer. I take many forms – Wal-Mart, K-Mart, Target – but I am one single entity – desire." Once again, *South Park* proclaims the sovereignty of the consumer in a market economy. If people keep flocking to a superstore, it must be doing something right, and satisfying their desires. Randy tells the townspeople: "The Wall-Mart is us. If we like our small-town charm more than the big corporate bullies, we all have to be willing to pay a little bit more." This is the free market solution to the superstore problem – no government need intervene. The townspeople accordingly march off to a local store named Jim's Drugs and start patronizing it. The store is so successful, it starts growing, and eventually mutates into – you guessed it – a superstore just like Wal-Mart. *South Park* has no problem with big businesses when they get big by pleasing their customers.

Parker and Stone acknowledge that they themselves work for a large corporation, the cable channel Comedy Central, which is owned by a media giant, Viacom. In the *Reason* interview, Stone says: "People ask, 'So how is it working for a big multinational conglomeration?' I'm like, 'It's pretty good, you know? We can say whatever we want. It's not bad. I mean, there are worse things.'"[15] Anti-corporate intellectuals would dispute that claim, and point to several occasions when Comedy Central pulled *South Park* episodes off the air in response to various pressure groups, including Viacom itself.[16] But despite such occasional interference, the fact is that it was Comedy Central that financed the production of *South Park* from the beginning and thus made it possible in the first place. Over the years, the corporation has given Parker and Stone unprecedented creative freedom in shaping a show for television – and not because the corporate executives are partisans of free speech and trenchant satire but because the show has developed a market niche and been profitable. *South Park* doesn't simply defend the free market in its episodes – it is itself living proof of how markets work to create something of artistic value and, in the process, benefit producers and consumers alike.[17]

For pop culture resources and philosophical resources related to this chapter please visit the website for this book: https://introducingphilosophythroughpopculture.com/.

Notes

1 *Symposium*, 221E–222A (trans. Nehamas, A. and Woodruff, P.) Indianapolis: Hackett, 1989. Quoted in the translation of W.R.M. Lamb (1925). *Plato: Lysis, Symposium, Gorgias*, Loeb Classical Library, 239. Cambridge, MA: Harvard University Press.

2 *The Clouds*, lines 392–394. Quoted in the translation of William Arrowsmith (1962). *The Clouds*, 45. New York: New American Library.

3 Mises's most famous book is von Mises, L. (1949). *Human Action: A Treatise on Economics*. New Haven, CT: Yale University Press; Hayek's is Hayek, F. (1944). *The Road to Serfdom*. Chicago: University of Chicago Press.

4 Rothbard articulates his libertarian philosophy most fully in Rothbard, M. (2002). *The Ethics of Liberty*. New York: New York University Press and Rothbard, M. (1978). *For a New Liberty: The Libertarian Manifesto*. New York: Macmillan. Perhaps the clearest introduction to the economic principles underlying libertarianism is Hazlitt, H. (1996). *Economics in One Lesson*. San Francisco: Laissez-Faire Books.

5 As quoted in Anderson, B.C. (2005) *South Park Conservatives: The Revolt Against Liberal Media Bias*, 178. Washington, DC: Regnery Publishing.

6 Gillespie, N. and Walker, J. (2006). *South Park* libertarians: Trey Parker and Matt Stone on liberals, conservatives, censorship, and religion, *Reason* 38:66.

7 For an analysis of why such groups turn against capitalism, see von Mises, L. (1956). *The Anti-Capitalistic Mentality*. Princeton: D. Van Nostrand, especially 30–33 for the turn against capitalism in Hollywood.

8 A perfect example of Hollywood's negative portrayal of businessmen is the cruel banker Mr. Potter in the classic *It's A Wonderful Life* (dir. Frank Capra, 1946). For a comprehensive survey of the portrayal of businessmen in American popular culture, see the chapter "The Culture Industry's Representation of Business," in Lavoie, D. and Chamlee-Wright, E. (2000). *Culture and Enterprise: The Development, Representation and Morality of Business*, 80–103. London: Routledge. Here are some representative figures from media studies: "Of all the antagonists studied in over 30 years of programming, businessmen were twice as likely to play the role of antagonist than any other identifiable occupation. Business characters are nearly three times as likely to be criminals, relative to other occupations on television. They represent 12 percent of all characters in identifiable occupations, but account for 32 percent of crimes. Forty-four percent of all vice crimes such as prostitution and drug trafficking committed on television, and 40 percent of TV murders, are perpetrated by business people" (84).

9 Mises, *Anti-Capitalistic Mentality*, 2.

10 George Bernard Shaw offers this interpretation of Alberich; see *The Perfect Wagnerite* (1898) in Shaw, G.B. (1932/1986). *Major Critical Essays*, 198, 205. Harmondsworth: Penguin.

11 For the way H.G. Wells uses invisibility as a symbol of capitalism, see my essay, Cantor, P.A. (2009). *The Invisible Man* and the invisible hand: H.G. Wells's critique of capitalism. In *Literature and the Economics of Liberty: Spontaneous Order in Culture* (eds. Paul A. Cantor and Stephen Cox), 293–305. Auburn: Ludwig von Mises Institute.

12 Hayek, F. (1988). *The Fatal Conceit: The Errors of Socialism*, 90, 91, 93. Chicago: University of Chicago Press.

13 Several e-mail responses to an earlier version of this chapter argued that the gnomes' diagram makes fun of the sketchy business plans that flooded the initial public offering (IPO) market in the heyday of the dot.com boom in the 1990s. Having helped write a few such documents myself, I know what these correspondents are referring to, but I still think that my interpretation of this scene fits the context better. If the gnomes' business plan is simply satirizing dot.com IPOs, then it has no relation to the rest of the episode.

14 Smith, A. (1776; rpt. 1981). *An Inquiry into the Nature and Causes of the Wealth of Nations*, vol. 1, 456. Indianapolis: Liberty Classics.

15 Gillespie and Walker, "*South Park* libertarians," 63.

16 The episodes in question were pulled only from the repeat rotation; they were allowed to air originally and they are now once again available in the DVD sets of the series.

17 A version of this chapter was published as Cantor, P.A. (2007). "Cartman shrugged: *South Park* and libertarianism. *Liberty* 21(9): 23–30. For a fuller version of my analysis of *South Park* – including comparisons to works by Rabelais and Mark Twain, as well as a discussion of the controversy surrounding the show's effort to present an image of Mohammed in one episode – see chapter 6 of my book Cantor, P.A. (2012). *The Invisible Hand in Popular Culture: Liberty vs. Authority in American Film and TV* Lexington: University Press of Kentucky.

35

Ninjas, Kobe Bryant, and Yellow Plastic

The LEGO Minifigure and Race

Roy T. Cook

Summary

How does race work in the world of LEGO minifigures? This chapter attempts to answer this question, beginning with an examination of the ways that race has been represented in LEGO sets over time. A number of different ways to understand race in LEGO (and the supposedly lack thereof in the world of the classic yellow minifigures) are examined based on three influential philosophical approaches to the nature of race: biological accounts, eliminativist accounts, and social constructivist accounts. After arguing that the social constructivist approach is superior to the alternatives, the chapter shows that the yellow minifigures introduced in 1978 do not simply represent a world without race (or where race doesn't matter). A postscript addresses the ways that reflecting on race in the world of LEGO might help us to better understand race, and the controversies surrounding it, in our own world.

When the modern version of the LEGO minifigure was introduced in 1978 its bright yellow color was a conscious choice, meant to be racially and ethnically neutral. Further, all the yellow-skinned minifigures had the exact same printing on their faces – the "smiley" – obscuring any differences between minifigures. Within the original world, any minifigure could be anyone. Race (as well as gender and other differences) was erased via the creation of a uniformly bright-yellow-skinned world where minifigures could not be distinguished or discriminated based on the color of their ABS plastic skins. Or, at least, that was the intention.

Where's Lando?

We could, of course, argue about the desirability of a uniformly hued fictional world where differences in skin color and physical appearance don't exist, as compared to a more pluralistic vision where such diversity exists but does not provide the foundation for systematic discrimination and marginalization. But the LEGO Group faced a much more practical challenge to their attempt at racial neutrality in 1999, when they acquired the license to

Introducing Philosophy Through Pop Culture: From Socrates to Star Wars *and Beyond*, Second Edition.
Edited by William Irwin and David Kyle Johnson.

produce *Star Wars* themed sets. The first *Star Wars* sets were based on the original trilogy, but fans soon noticed that none of these sets included a Lando Calrissian minifigure. And how could they? How could or should LEGO represent Billie Dee Williams's iconic character as a minifigure? In short, they faced a simple problem: How do you represent a world like *Star Wars* where race exists within a pre-existing framework that explicitly eliminates race?

LEGO's solution to this dilemma was simple. In 2003 they introduced another licensed theme: a series of minifigures and sets based on famous players in the National Basketball Association (NBA). The heads and arms of Black NBA players were molded in brown plastic, while the white players' heads and arms were molded in a new, peachy-colored plastic. Race had now entered the world of the LEGO minifigure.[1]

Shortly after this controversial move, a brown-skinned Lando minifigure finally appeared in the Cloud City set (#10123). Interestingly, other characters in the Cloud City set were molded in yellow, but eventually all licensed LEGO sets (Star Wars, Harry Potter, Superheroes, etc.) included minifigures molded in an ever-widening variety of brown, pink, and peach colored plastic. There are over two dozen different shades of plastic that have been used for minifigure heads and hands in licensed LEGO sets! Non-licensed themes, such as the venerable City, Farm, Space, Pirate, and Train themes, still contain the purportedly racially neutral yellow minifigures.[2]

In one sense this seems like an elegant solution to the problem: LEGO licensed sets take place in a world (or in a number of distinct worlds – as many as there are different licenses) where race, indicated by the color of plastic used to mold their heads and hands, *exists* and *matters*, since race, and distinctions and discriminations based on race, matter within the original films, television shows, and other media on which the licensed sets are based. Non-licensed sets such as City and Space, however, take place in the original racially idealized world of the original all-yellow LEGO minifigure, where race, and hence distinctions based on race, do not exist. More generally, *any* LEGO builds – official or not – that contain flesh-toned minifigures represent characters that are white, Asian, Black, Native American, or any of a host of other racial identities, while LEGO builds that contain yellow minifigures represent characters that have no race (or represent characters whose race is not identifiable, at the very least, and thus cannot matter to our understanding of the LEGO build in question).

It's certainly a simple story regarding how race works in the LEGO world. But it's also one that can't be quite right. Race is not a fixed category that is inherent to a person and can be represented by one of a fixed number of colors of plastic, but is instead constituted by changeable, unstable social and political factors and contexts as much, if not more, than it is determined by skin color and ancestry. And the concept of race is at least as unstable in the world of the LEGO minifigure as it is in the real world. As a result, we can use the complicated connections between the race of a minifigure and the color of the plastic in which they are molded to help us understand both how race works in the world(s) of the LEGO minifigure and how race works in our own world.

The Building Bricks of Race

Traditionally, people (and peoples) have been divided into races based on three criteria:[3]

1 Ancestry
2 Geographical origin
3 Physical characteristics (skin color, facial structure).

Sorting humankind into races, in and of itself, need not be pernicious, any more than sorting humans into other categories (gender, sexual preference, socioeconomic class, Zodiacal signs), or sorting LEGO bricks by color or shape, is inherently immoral. The important question is what we *do* with these categories. And it is hard to imagine a division of people into kinds that has been associated with more immorality than divisions based on race. Historically, race has been used to justify differential treatment based on the idea that one race is more human, or more capable physically or mentally, or religiously chosen, or purer, or superior in some other way, when compared to another (or all) other races. Fortunately, many of us have moved beyond explicit acceptance of such morally repugnant views.

Here, however, we are less interested in the negative effects of racism, and more interested in how we should understand race itself. Again, this is not to say that the latter is more important than the former. Quite the contrary. But the examination of race in LEGO has more to teach us about the nature of race – what it is, and what it is not – than it has to teach us about the consequences of racism.

The concept of race is relatively new. The ancient Greek and Roman worlds had no notion of race. This is not to say that they were all very nice people who never discriminated. The Greeks and Romans treated people differently based on their gender and based on whether or not they spoke the right language (so-called "barbarians" did not).[4] But they didn't divide people into different races, and the word "race" did not even enter the English language until the early sixteenth century.[5] Thus, it has not always seemed evident to everyone that humanity is naturally divided into distinct races.

Until the mid-twentieth century the aforementioned traditional, three-part conception of race was explained in biological terms: a person was a member of a particular race based on some objective biological property had by that person. This is the *biological essentialist* account of race. One of the first challenges to biological essentialism came from the German-American anthropologist Franz Boaz, who showed that there was no measurable relationship between race and cranium size (at the time this was a popular essentialist account of the nature of the supposed physical and cognitive differences between different races). Later research demonstrated that race could not be explained in terms of genetics. This research, and research like it, eventually led the United Nations Education, Scientific, and Cultural Organization (UNESCO) to issue a statement denying the existence of any biological foundation for race in 1950. Unfortunately, despite this evidence, the idea that race has some kind of biological underpinning remains widely accepted.

If race, and the categorization of people into distinct races, has no biological foundation, then how do we explain race? One option is to abandon the concept altogether, arguing that there is no such thing as race in the first place. On this view our world is very much like the all-yellow minifigure world of the non-licensed LEGO sets, where there are no races, and hence no need to distinguish races based on the color of plastic or skin. Some philosophers, including Anthony Appiah[6] and Naomi Zach,[7] have defended this *eliminativist* approach, but it comes with several drawbacks. One is that, if race does not exist, then it is hard to explain the systematic oppression of various groups throughout history such as Blacks, Native Americans, and Asian-Americans. After all, that oppression has often focused on racially identifying its targets. Racial self-identification has also typically been central to the struggles of those who resist that oppression. Thus, if there is no such thing as race, then it is difficult to understand or endorse social and political movements, or legislation, predicated on the notion of race.

For example, if there really is no such thing as race, then what effect could or should laws prohibiting discrimination based on race have?

We can solve these problems by adopting a view called *racial constructivism*. According to racial constructivism, race is a real category, and particular people do, or do not, belong to various races. These categories are not determined by biological factors (e.g. particular genes), however, but are instead determined by various activities, conceptions, conventions, behaviors, agreements, and decisions we make with regard to how to categorize people into races. The division of the population of the world into particular races is, on the constructivist view, not something that we *discover* in the world, but rather something that we *build* out of our attitudes and behaviors. In short, we don't treat people differently *because* they are members of different races – rather, they are members of different races *because* we treat them differently!

On this view we don't live in the all-yellow minifigure world of the non-licensed LEGO sets, where there are no races, but not because race was there all along. Rather, our actions and attitudes gradually transformed our world from one that resembled the world of the non-licensed all-yellow minifigure into one that more resembles the racially divided world of licensed LEGO sets.[8]

We can explain the role that geography, heritability, and physical characteristics like skin color play in our understanding of race by noting that the various attitudes and activities we have adopted make these characteristics important ingredients in determining to which race a particular person belongs. In short, ancestry, home, and skin color (among other things) are relevant to determining whether a person is white, Black, Asian, or a member of another race solely because we have (often unconsciously) adopted rules for using the concept of race in a way that make these factors salient.

The constructivist approach has some advantages over the eliminativist approach. For example, because it retains the idea that races are real, albeit socially constructed, categories, it allows us to use the concept of race legitimately in legislation and social programs. But, perhaps more importantly, on the constructivist account we are not forced to claim that a Black person's status as Black cannot play any legitimate role in explaining and understanding their experiences: this view allows particular members of various racial categories to use race to help them understand themselves and their place within and relationship to a racially categorized world.

There is another aspect of racial constructivism that differentiates it from both biological essentialism and eliminativism: the idea that racial categories can be (and in fact are) dynamic, changing, and at times unstable. Since our beliefs, behaviors, customs, agreements, and laws can change over time, the nature of the racial categories that arise due to these practices can differ over time as well. In addition, such practices vary not only from one time to another, but also from place to place. Philosopher Michael Root notes that the conventions and rules regarding racial classification in Brazil differ from those at work now in the United States, and both differ from the rules at work in the United States in the past. Thus, there exist people who are now categorized as Black in New Orleans, categorized as white in Brazil, and would have been categorized as octaroon in New Orleans in the nineteenth century.[9] According to essentialism, at least two of these judgments must be wrong (and according to eliminativism they are all wrong), but the constructivist can accept all three judgments as correct with respect to the contexts in which they are made: The person in question really is Black in the United States and white in Brazil. This both illustrates the flexibility and instability of race (without denying the reality of race) and explains the very different experiences such a person can have when, for example, attempting to flag a taxi in Manhattan versus flagging a taxi in Rio de Janeiro.

Kobe Bryant, Ninjas, and Race

One simple truism of the world of Adult Fans of LEGO (AFOL): If there is a way to use LEGO bricks to subvert, undermine, or circumvent whatever it is that the LEGO Group had in mind when creating particular bricks and elements, an AFOL will eventually find it. The role that the distinction between purportedly non-racial yellow minifigures and racially specific flesh-toned minifigures play in the worlds of official LEGO sets is no different.

Our first example is not actually a LEGO build, but rather a comic: the December 21, 2003 installment of Japanese-American Tak Toyoshima's webcomic *Secret Asian Man*, titled "Old School Secret Asian Man."[10] The first panel of the comic shows a Christmas tree from above, with a caption that reads "One Magical Christmas Eve." In the second panel we see a late 1970s era yellow-skinned classic castle soldier minifigure (similar to, but dressed slightly differently than, the figure contained in set #6002) conversing with a version of the Kobe Bryant NBA figure released in 2003.[11] Their dialogue is as follows:

SOLDIER: Hark! Art thou not ye **Kobe Bryant** LEGO?
BRYANT: You a **reporter**?
SOLDIER: Nay. I am **Medieval** LEGO. Thy hide is **brown**.
BRYANT: . . . yeah.

In the next panel the conversation continues in close-up:

SOLDIER: It **matcheth** the hide of your people. Should not **my hide** too match the **alabaster** colour of my kindred?
BRYANT: Well, they only made brown people for us **NBA LEGOS**. Everyone else is yellow. There's only **one group** happy with the way things are now.

In the fourth and final panel we get Toyoshima's racially charged punchline, as two yellow-skinned LEGO ninja figures (similar to those released around 2000) enter the panel from the right, pointing and laughing at the classic castle soldier and Kobe Bryant.

Toyoshima's point couldn't be clearer. The introduction of flesh-toned figures does not merely introduce race into the worlds of LEGO licensed sets (or, perhaps more accurately, reproduce the racial dynamics already present in the stories being licensed). In addition, the appearance of flesh-colored minifigures also forces us to re-construe the older non-licensed minifigures produced in the supposedly racially neutral yellow. In particular, Toyoshima's strip clearly illustrates that the yellow-skinned ninja figures are difficult to read as racially neutral, rather than as yellow-skinned-because-Asian (and possibly offensively so), when juxtaposed against the flesh-colored Kobe Bryant minifigure.[12]

Of course, Toyoshima has a great deal of control over how we interpret the race of the yellow-skinned minifigures in these images – in particular, he encourages us to (actually) identify them as Asian because the figures themselves (fictionally) identify themselves as Asian. With this in mind, I conducted an experiment at Brickworld 2016, the largest annual AFOL gathering in North America. I built a small vignette, titled "Seven Smiley Samurai," that consisted of 21 minifigures posed on a cobblestone street. On the far left was a group of casually dressed men, constructed using brown-skinned NBA player heads and hands. On the far right were seven police officers, constructed using Caucasian flesh-toned heads and hands. In the center were seven minifigures built using bodies from LEGO ninja sets and other Asian-influenced martial arts themes (for example, Ninjago) and yellow "smiley" heads.[13]

At a symposium on race and LEGO that I moderated at Brickworld, I asked participants about the race of the seven minifigures in the middle. After an extended discussion of race and LEGO, everyone in the room agreed that in this context the yellow "smiley" heads were not racially neutral, but were unambiguously Asian. Of course, the yellow plastic of the "smiley" heads used for these figures was not the only factor contributing to this judgment – in addition, the traditional Asian clothing, and the fact that the other, flesh-toned minifigures were clearly racially coded, were also contributing factors. Nevertheless, in this context at least, the yellow heads and hands of the central minifigures were not taken to be racially neutral.[14]

Thus, just as changes in our own behavior, beliefs, and rules can affect who is and who is not a member of a particular race on the constructivist account, changes in the way that race is currently portrayed within the world of LEGO can have profound effects on how we understand past representations of race (or attempts to erase race altogether) in official LEGO sets. To emphasize the point even further, we need only think about how we are likely to conceptualize the race of a yellow-skinned ninja figure prior to 2003, when we might find it in a child's toy box surrounded by other yellow-skinned minifigures, and how we understand that same figure post-2003, when in the same toy box it might be surrounded by racially specific minifigures molded in various flesh-like shades. It is difficult not to read the yellow as racialized in the latter instance, regardless of the LEGO Group's original intention.

To put the point bluntly: LEGO's introduction of race into their products in 2003 did not just create a space for racially specific licensed sets separate from their idealized racially neutral system of play as exhibited in City, Space, Pirates, and Farm sets. In addition, it in effect erased the "erasure of race" from these non-licensed sets by forcing us to read at least some of these yellow-skinned minifigures, in at least some contexts, as racially specific.

The point, of course, is not to accuse LEGO of moral wrongdoing with respect to their original all-yellow attempt to create a non-racial world of play (one might criticize such an attempt for various reasons, but that isn't my purpose here). The point, instead, is to show how the introduction of new ways of representing race via the introduction of racially specific minifigures, can not only change the way that race currently is represented within LEGO, but can also alter our understanding of how race functioned in LEGO all along.

Race in *The LEGO Movie*

The LEGO Movie presents an even odder juxtaposition of the various ways that LEGO has represented race. In the film, Emmet meets Wyldstyle and her paramour, Batman. Wyldstyle, like Emmet and the majority of the characters in the film, is molded/rendered in the supposedly racially neutral yellow. But a handful of the characters in the film, including Batman and Shaquille O'Neal, are lifted straight from licensed sets, and these characters, like the real-life minifigures upon which they are based, have flesh-toned heads and hands. Thus, the racially neutral yellow-skinned world of non-licensed sets and the racially specific worlds of licensed sets, which were subversively combined in works like Toyoshima's comic and "Seven Smiley Samurai," collide in the officially sanctioned LEGO movie.

The instability of race in the LEGO world becomes even more apparent if we ask some very simple questions about how race functions within *The LEGO Movie*. Batman is clearly white, and Shaq is clearly Black. But what race is Wyldstyle? If she is white, then how are we to understand the difference between the color of her head and hands and those of Batman? If she is not white, then what race is she? Is she Asian, like the ninjas in Toyoshima's comic and the central figures in "Seven Smiley Samurai"? If so, then so are the majority of characters in *The LEGO Movie* – including Emmet, who is also clearly meant to be a counterpart of Finn in the (fictional) "real" world, who is white.

Perhaps Wyldstyle lacks race altogether, in keeping with the original intention of minifigures with yellow heads and hands? If so, does this mean that *The LEGO Movie* takes place in a world where some people belong to races, but some (in fact, most!) do not? If Wyldstyle had (spoiler alert!) stayed with Batman, and they had little LEGO babies, would those babies only have half a race? What color plastic would be used for the babies' heads and hands?

Of course, on one level these questions are silly: presumably the creators of *The LEGO Movie* did not intend to make any kind of deep statement about race with their film, and questions about race in the real world are obviously more important than questions about race in the world of LEGO minifigures. But at another level these questions *are* important, since they help us understand how LEGO's attempt to create a racially neutral, all-yellow-skinned world ultimately failed, and, more importantly, they remind us that race – both in the world of LEGO minifigures and in the real world we live in – is socially constructed and depends on context, customs, convention, and attitudes.[15]

Postscript, July 2020: Everything is Not Awesome

I was contacted on May 27, 2020 with the exciting news that this essay, originally from the *LEGO and Philosophy* volume I had co-edited with Sondra Bacharach, had been chosen to be included in second edition of *Introducing Philosophy Through Popular Culture*. I was informed that slight revisions to the chapter would be welcomed, and I was urged to include a reference to Kobe Bryant's death in the updated version of this essay. While Bryant's death in a helicopter accident in 2016 was certainly a tragedy, George Floyd's death two days before this invitation arrived quickly proved to be more relevant to the issues discussed in this essay.

I live in Minneapolis, a mere mile or so from where Floyd was killed by police, and I spent the next week supporting the protests during the day while attempting to sleep amid the constant din of military helicopters and crowd-control munitions at night. When, eventually, the violence ended and the clean-up and rebuilding efforts began, I reflected on the different ways that LEGO has represented race, as discussed in the original version of the essay, and asked myself whether there might be a connection between the issues I discussed and the events unfolding in my neighborhood and across the country.

In the original essay I wrote that "the examination of race in LEGO has *more* to teach us about the nature of race – what it is, and what it is not – than it has to teach us about the consequences of racism." As a result, I focused for the most part on the metaphysics of race, examining the original all-yellow world of the LEGO minifigure and the more recent racially specific flesh-toned world(s) of licensed LEGO sets as competing models of *what race is*. But we can instead consider these two representational systems in epistemological terms, as representing different *ways of seeing* (or failing to see) race. And, viewed in this way, the contrast between the world of the all-yellow non-licensed minifigure and the world(s) of the flesh-colored licensed minifigures does, I think, help to illustrate something important: the difference between merely *not being racist* and being *actively anti-racist*. For a more detailed articulation of the distinction than I can include in this brief postscript, the reader is encouraged to consult Ibram X. Kendi's *How to Be an Antiracist*.[16]

One might think that we could avoid being racist merely by failing to see race at all, or at least by behaving as if race did not exist.[17] In other words, on this approach the way to guarantee that we are not racist is to view the world as if it were the all-yellow, race-free world depicted in LEGO City, Space, and Pirate sets. If we see the world this way, or act as if we do, then presumably we cannot be or act racist, since it is impossible to act inappropriately based on someone's race (e.g. discriminate) if one cannot detect race in the first place.

This story assumes, of course, that to be racist is to act in certain ways or to explicitly hold certain beliefs. This is not the only way to analyze what it is to be racist, nor is it likely the best way. But it suffices for the point I'm trying to make. Something like this I-can't-be-racist-because-I-don't-see-race idea is as least part of the reason that LEGO adopted the all-yellow color scheme for minifigures in the first place: to depict a world where racial strife was absent, since race was absent, or at least not seen or acted on.

But as more recent events have made all too apparent, more is required. In order to combat racism, it is not enough to merely be non-racist in this rather thin sense. In addition, there is a moral imperative to combat racism through education, confrontation, and, yes, organized protest. Battling racism, however, requires that we *do see race*. The most obvious reason is that we need to see race in order to identify racist patterns of behavior (where this could be the actions of individuals, but could also involve systematic patterns of oppression and injustice that are not easily attributable to a single person or group of persons, such as the systemic racism inherent in our law enforcement and criminal justice systems). But, more importantly, we need to see race so that we can understand how the world (again, including not only individuals, but also social and political institutions) treats people differently based on their race, even if we personally don't (a big "if" of course), and we need to see race in order to understand, and learn from, the experiences of those who are treated differently from us based on their race. Being anti-racist doesn't require that we fail to see race, or that we fail to act on the basis of race. On the contrary, being anti-racist absolutely requires that we do treat people of different races differently, based on the very different experiences, very different perspectives, and very different understandings of the world people of different races unavoidably have in a systemically racist society.

The original essay explores the metaphysical lessons to be drawn from the various ways that race has been depicted in LEGO. Perhaps this is the epistemological and moral lesson: Pretending to live in the idealized all-yellow world of the original LEGO minifig-ure might look, at first glance, like a viable strategy if one merely wants to ensure they are themselves not racist. But, even if that were right (and it probably isn't), such a world-view presents a significant obstacle if one's goal is, instead (and as it should be), to com-bat racism in both oneself and in the larger world around us. If one wants to effectively fight racism, then one needs to recognize that the world we live in is, with regard to race at least, more like the word of LEGO Batman than it is like the world of LEGO City. These worlds are different, and in order to fight racism, we need to see the differences.

For pop culture resources and philosophical resources related to this chapter please visit the website for this book: https://introducingphilosophythroughpopculture.com.

Notes

1 The NBA minifigures were not LEGO's first attempt at representing race via different colors of plastic. The 1977 Red Indians set (#215) contains four "Homemaker" style figures representing Native Americans, along with a canoe (Homemaker was an earlier line of larger LEGO figures with brick-built bodies and molded heads, hands, and arms). The four figures in the Red Indians set have heads and hands molded in bright red plastic.

2 Within LEGO fandom, the word "fleshie" has become a technical term for those minifigures molded in the various shades of pink and peach meant to represent Caucasians (and occasionally other non-Black races) in the worlds of licensed LEGO sets. This usage is problematic, since minifigures molded in the standard LEGO brown, representing Black characters, are equally "flesh toned." Thus, in what follows, I will use the terms "flesh toned" or "flesh colored" rather than "fleshie," which should be understood to include not only pink/peach "fleshies" but also figures molded in brown plastic, and meant to represent Black characters.

3 For a detailed discussion on the philosophy of race, the reader is encouraged to consult James, M. (2016). Race. In: *The Stanford Encyclopedia of Philosophy*. http://plato.stanford.edu/entries/race (accessed August 10, 2020).

4 Rattansi, A. (2007). *A Very Short Introduction to Race*. Oxford: Oxford University Press.

5 Rattansi, *Short Introduction to Race*.

6 Appiah, A. (1996). Race, culture, identity: misunderstood connections In: *Color Conscious* (eds. A. Appiah and A. Gutmann), 30–105. Princeton: Princeton University Press. Appiah has more recently defended a less purely eliminativist position in Appiah, A. (2006). How to decide if races exist. *Proceedings of the Aristotelian Society* 106: 365–382.

7 Zach, N. (2002). *Philosophy of Science and Race*. London: Routledge.

8 It is worth noting that the all-yellow world of non-licensed LEGO sets, where there are no races, is not necessarily a world of boring homogeneity. Rather, by not imposing rigid, pre-constructed racial identi-ties and differences on minifigures (or real people), such a world leaves open the possibility (imagina-tively in the case of LEGO minifigures) of unscripted idiosyncratic difference – the possibility that individuals can craft their own identities and differences.

9 Root, M. (2000). How we divide the world. *Philosophy of Science* 67(supplement): S628–S639.

10 Available at: http://secretasianmancomics.blogspot.com/2011/12/old-school-wednesday-racial-justice. html (accessed August 10, 2020).

11 Toyoshima takes some liberties with the Kobe Bryant minifigure, combining the purple jersey from the home uniform figure (set #3433) and the yellow legs from the away uniform figure (set #3563). The latter figure also illustrates another practical reason for abandoning the traditional yellow head in licensed sets, since some licensed figures require yellow clothing that might read as "naked" when combined with yel-low hands and head.

12 By the time flesh-colored NBA minifigures were introduced, LEGO had effectively abandoned the idea that yellow minifigures were racially and ethnically neutral, since they had replaced the single iconic "smiley" with a range of different faces, some of which were racially and ethnically stereotyped. At the same time minifigure heads also ceased to be gender-neutral, as heads with features generally perceived as feminine (eye shadow, lipstick) began to appear.

13 Interestingly, "Seven Smiley Samurai" was nominated (but did not win) the Best Humor Category at Brickworld 2016. It was not built with the intention of being humorous, but apparently was inadvertently chuckle-inducing. I am not sure what this means, exactly, with respect to the issues discussed here.

14 It is perhaps worth noting that LEGO does make minifigure heads with explicitly "Asian" facial features, in both yellow (for example, the Blue Shogun in set #6083 Samurai Stronghold) and flesh-toned (for example, Short Round in set #7199 The Temple of Doom).

15 This essay is deeply indebted to participants in the "LEGO and Race" roundtable at Brickworld 2016.

16 Kendi, I.X. (2020). *How to be an Antiracist*. New York: Random House.

17 Stephen Colbert, in his fictional conservative talk-show host persona on *The Colbert Report*, brilliantly satirized this sort of "color-blindness" by pretending not to notice that Black guests on his program were in fact Black until this was explicitly pointed out to him, claiming to *literally* not see race.

36

When Tech Meets Tradition

How Wakandan Technology Transcends Anti-Blackness

Timothy E. Brown

Summary

Science fiction often excludes Black people. What's more, even when they are in-cluded, it isn't clear how Black people *arrive* in the future. Representations seem distinctly "post-racial," disconnected from the messy histories and lived traumas of colonialism, diaspora, and the transatlantic slave trade. *Black Panther* is an in-troduction to how Africanfuturism pushes back against the more naive transhu-manist visions in a way that allows us to at least begin to imagine a future that has confronted its past, filled with technologies that Black people are a part of.

Black Panther was more empowering for me than I thought it would be. Here we had a mainstream film about an ultra-advanced African nation, set in Marvel's mostly white cinematic universe. And there I was, watching this Africanfuturist film on opening day, in Seattle's famous Cinerama theater, a Black nerd surrounded by white nerds. It was surreal to think that this audience would accept or even embrace stories that center on Africa or Africans. As I have written elsewhere,[1] if the film didn't live up to their expecta-tions – as a watershed moment for Black representation in futurist blockbuster films[2] – I would be responsible for explaining to my white friends what happened.

After all, the unfortunate truth is that science fiction often excludes Black people. What's more is that even when we are included, it isn't clear how Black people *arrive* in the future. Representations of us seem distinctly "post-racial," disconnected from the messy histories and lived traumas of colonialism, diaspora, and the transatlantic slave trade. This disconnect is troubling. Representations of the future will inspire the next generations of scientists, engineers, and designers who will shape our future – *Star Trek*'s communicators and personal access display devices (PADDs) are today's smartphones and tablets. But it's not clear if Black Americans ever receive the kind of reconciliation and support they deserve.[3] As more technologists and scholars push us to transcend humanity's current limitations, to become "posthuman," several questions remain. Will

Introducing Philosophy Through Pop Culture: From Socrates to Star Wars *and Beyond*, Second Edition.
Edited by William Irwin and David Kyle Johnson.

Black people be included in this transhumanist future? What role would they play if they were, and what form and flavor would our cultures take?

Black Panther, even with the deep problems in how it represents Black American men,[4] grapples with messy histories directly, in plain sight of white audiences. The motivations and struggles of the characters Shuri and Erik "Killmonger" Stevens, in particular, show us how *Black Panther's* blend (or collision) of Africanfuturism and Afrofuturism is meant to teach us how our memories of the past (as painful as they are) must connect with our visions of the future. In this way, *Black Panther* is an introduction to how Africanfuturism pushes back against the more naive transhumanist visions in a way that allows us to at least begin to imagine a future that has confronted its past, filled with technologies that we are a part of.

Are There Black People in the (Transhumanist) Future?

In 2017, the artist Alisha Wormsley installed the words "THERE ARE BLACK PEOPLE IN THE FUTURE" on a billboard in Pittsburgh's East Liberty neighborhood. Wormsley's installation was just the most recent iteration of artist Jon Rubin's *The Last Billboard* project, featuring a rotating series of artists sharing similarly impactful (or otherwise cryptic) messages. These simple words, especially, are both reassuring and affirming. After all, our past and current technologies exclude or actively target Blacks, and media representations of the future so often either exclude Blacks or push us to the margins. These words were also, apparently, controversial. Eve Picker, the landlord who owns the building and the billboard space, was "contacted by a number of people in the local community who said that they found the message offensive and divisive."[5] This, she concluded, was against the tenants' lease agreement "that states the billboard cannot be used for items 'that are distasteful, offensive, erotic, [or] political,'" and so she forced the project to take the message down from the billboard. Fortunately, an outpouring of public support in response, across social media and in Picker's email inbox, pushed her to reverse her decision.

But why were these words so controversial in the first place? Why would anyone take them to be offensive? Perhaps this follows a similar logic to the way that the simple phrase "Black Lives Matter" seems like a kind of favoritism of Black lives over white lives – such that some whites feel compelled to respond, "All Lives Matter." The very idea that Black people will play a role in humanity's progress, or even the idea that Black people will exist in the future, should be a truism. Yes, there are Black people in the future, and we need to say as much because it seems that people have forgotten. Instead, it is construed as polemical – perhaps as a type of "reverse racism," perhaps as a form of "attention seeking," or perhaps as just an unnecessary claim.

Black Panther presents a vision of a distinctly African future that not only affirms that there are in fact Black people in the future but also gives us a glimpse of *how* Black people make it to the future and what kind of home we make there. Further, *Black Panther* demonstrates how humanity must grapple with past traumas and ameliorate present harms if it has any chance at building such a future. The promises of enthusiastic technology "thought leaders" and "transhumanists," like Elon Musk and Jeff Bezos, seem out of touch with communities of color entirely – the details of how we will reconcile many of the harms of the past are lost as noise beneath loud signals warning about colonizing space through commercial spaceflight,[6] getting along with artificial intelligence (AI),[7] and extending our minds through brain–computer interfaces.[8]

What is transhumanism, and what does it transcend? According to an early version of the Transhumanist's Principles, transhumanists "strive to remove the evolved limits of our biological and intellectual inheritance, the physical limits of our environment, and the cultural and historical limits of society that constrain individual and collective progress."[9] The goal of many stripes of transhumanism, then, is (at the very least) twofold: to overcome sickness and death, and to overcome humanity's physical and cognitive limitations through enhancement.

Let's look at a few claims and projects transhumanist thinkers have proposed. In "The Fable of the Dragon Tyrant," philosopher and self-proclaimed transhumanist Nick Bostrom characterizes death as a seemingly invincible dragon, terrorizing the world.[10] He cautions against accepting death and becoming complacent in our collective attempts to thwart it. If it is at all possible to extend life, we have a moral obligation to do so. Bioethicist Julian Savulescu – perhaps infamously – argues that we have a moral obligation to select for the best possible children if presented with the means to.[11] That is: when a person produces and selects a fetus to implant at an in vitro fertilization clinic, or when a person uses prenatal genetic tests to screen for so-called birth defects like Down's syndrome, they ought to select for the fewest genetic defects. A number of disability rights scholars and advocates, Adrienne Asch most chiefly, argue that using prenatal genetic tests to identify "defects" in (and ultimately to abort) fetuses expresses a discriminatory attitude toward people with disabilities.[12] The philosopher Ingmar Persson (along with Savulescu) argues that we collectively do not have the moral capacities necessary to meet global challenges, like climate change, poverty, or a global pandemic.[13] He and Savulescu argue that we should "morally enhance" ourselves – or use biomedical means of improving capacities for moral reasoning and decision-making. This might take the form of drugs that may increase empathy, reduce anger, dampen fear, in the hopes that we become more responsive to pressing moral issues. I have argued elsewhere that the push to morally enhance will likely burden Black people directly by reframing their warranted feelings of distrust, suspicion, and anger as moral deficiencies.[14]

A number of scholars, however, remind us that race and racism are embedded in our technologies. The aforementioned transhumanist projects fail without dealing with these. Kate Crawford, for example, remarks that AI and machine learning (ML) have a "white guy problem."[15] Ushers of "the singularity" – or the moment when AI surpasses human intelligence – are all too often white men, and the technologies that would bring about the singularity are often created by teams of white men.[16] The technologies produced by these teams – in all likelihood inadvertently, but still perniciously – consistently malfunction for Black people. Technologists Joy Buolamwini and Timnit Gebru, in their *Gender Shades* project, tested facial recognition software from Face++, IBM, and Microsoft.[17] They found that this software misidentified Black women as Black men. Buolamwini created a spoken-word poem, "AI, Ain't I a Woman," to accompany a slideshow of facial recognition software misidentifying famous Black women, like Shirley Chisholm, Michelle Obama, and – yes – Sojourner Truth herself.[18] This artistic project links the experiences of Black women who fought for both suffrage and abolition simultaneously to the experiences of Black women fighting against technologies that erase their existence.

This is only the tip of the iceberg. Ruha Benjamin describes how our technologies coalesce to support anti-Blackness and white supremacy – sometimes inadvertently, often times explicitly.[19] These technologies create what she calls "the New Jim Code" or technologies that make our inequities worse, all while seeming more objective or equitable than the systems they replace. The term "New Jim Code" is a reference to Michelle Alexander's *The New Jim Crow*,[20] where she argues that classifying or coding Blacks as "criminals" has become a means of justifying, discrimination, disenfranchisement, and a new form of slavery through prison labor. Alexander's term is, in turn, a reference to "Jim Crow," the ubiquitous and garish minstrel show caricature that stood as the symbol for early twentieth-century racial segregation law and severe disenfranchisement in the southern United States. The New Jim Code, Benjamin argues, hides these inequities inside what Benjamin calls *anti-blackboxes*; the technologies seem race-neutral, but how they work is opaque and results in harms against people of color. Further, Benjamin along with several others[21] invite us to think of race *as* a technology "designed to separate, stratify, and sanctify the many forms of injustice experienced by racialized groups."[22] We can hardly think of chattel slavery in the Antebellum south, for example, without thinking about the theories, techniques, and tools used to keep the slave trade running: from ships to carry slaves across the Atlantic, to chains to hold slaves in place, to pseudoscientific arguments meant to establish that whites are superior to Blacks (or that there are distinct races in the first place).

It is hard to imagine how it's possible to advance (or even transcend) humanity through the use of technology unless we acknowledge the histories, current practices, and possible futures of *technologized racism*. Without acknowledging these realities – that Blacks experience, but so many people of color do as well – transhumanists' promises and goals fall flat. After all, how can Black people get excited about the singularity when racist codes are embedded in the algorithms? How can Black people get excited about "transcending cultural bias" when it will likely mean leaving their culture behind? *Black Panther*, both the film and the more recent runs of the comics, does not ask us to ignore technology's possibility to harm or empower Black people. It does not ask us to abandon our identities and worries to understand it. On the contrary, *Black Panther* gives us opportunities to consider possibilities of the future through past traumas and harms we've experienced.

"You Savages Didn't Deserve it!"

Erik "Killmonger" Stevens pays a visit to the African artifact section of a museum. The museum director – a white woman – approaches him, clearly suspicious of his presence there, and attempts to educate him on the origins of each of these artifacts. He, of course, doesn't need this education, nor is all of her information correct. Killmonger knows that one of these artifacts is not like the others – it is a Wakandan artifact made of vibranium, the most valuable material on Earth, and he's going to take it for himself. The museum director was already suspicious of Killmonger, or in his words, "You got all this security watching me ever since I walked in." Even a stopped clock tells the time twice a day.

The interaction between this museum director and Killmonger illustrates how visions of the future can be rooted in visions of the past, and how our distorted (read: anti-Black) visions of the past can distort (read: whitewash) our visions of the future. The museum director wouldn't even entertain the possibility that an old African farming tool was anything more than an artifact from a primitive time, made by primitive people. Her expression said it all: this primitive tool couldn't possibly be made from the most powerful material in the world, this suspicious-looking Black man couldn't know more about Africa than she does. Killmonger's dispute with the museum director, then, was not just a dispute over the facts, but a dispute over the authenticity of the artifact. In this moment, their dispute became a dispute over what can count as authentically African. We might think of Killmonger the same way, as a castaway artifact of Wakanda, possessed by foreigners.

Paul C. Taylor draws our attention to how disputes over provenance and authenticity arise when we evaluate African art, and how these disputes are driven by an interest in African history.[23] Some African artists participate in the artistic practices of modern Europe. They create art for the *artworld* through installations, galleries, and collections. Others, however, create what Taylor calls "workshop" art, the kind of "anonymous masks, carved figurines, and the like"[24] – and these might be extensions of traditional artisanal practices, or they might be attempts to pass off modern-day objects as genuine historical artifacts. The more "traditional" African artworks – those artifacts displayed by museums for their anthropological or ethnographic significance – are sought after for their authenticity. No one wants a knockoff, do they?

They are also deeply politicized. Museums and the people who visit them may value traditional African art/artifacts because of what Taylor calls "aesthetic Africanism" – building on author Toni Morrison's language[25] – where "modern societies imagined themselves as modern in part by distinguishing themselves from the pre-modern, which they then located in societies with unfamiliar modes of social organization and different orientations to the world of technology."[26] Modern societies look even more modern when compared with supposedly premodern societies. In many cases our collective fascination with traditional African art reifies the expectation that African cultures are primitive, and it engenders an incredulous attitude about the intelligence of Africans broadly.

This incredulity is a common theme throughout the film. Take, for example, the moment Ulysses Klaue – Wakanda's public enemy number one – reveals to Agent Ross that Wakanda is a technologically advanced nation with a mine of vibranium. "It's all a front," Klaue insists, "Explorers searched for it for centuries. El Dorado. The Golden City. They thought they could find it in South America, but it was in Africa the whole time. A technological marvel. All because it was built on a mound of the most valuable metal known to man – Isipho they call it. The gift. Vibranium." Ross, of course, questions his story, "That's a nice fairy tale but Wakanda is a third-world country and you stole all of their vibranium." Agent Ross, of course, has seen alien invasions and superhero civil wars; he also knows that T'Challa is the Black Panther. Yet he still, somehow, finds it hard to believe that Wakanda is anything more than a "third-world country."

Even Klaue, who has seen Wakanda with his own eyes, who knows how Wakandans use vibranium, is incredulous. In his face-off with T'Challa in South Korea, Klaue fires a shot using his prosthetic arm, a weapon made of stolen vibranium. T'Challa effortlessly absorbs the blow with his newly designed Black Panther suit and asks, "Where did you get this weapon?" Without hesitation, Klaue responds, "You savages didn't deserve it!" In his face-off with Killmonger in the scrapyard, Klaue admonishes his opponent, "You really wanna go to Wakanda? They're savages." Pointing to the symbol carved into his neck, a branding he received after stealing vibranium from Wakanda, he continues, "This is what they do to people like us." The incredulity of these white characters talking about Wakanda is a representation of the world's collective incredulity about African progress, about Black progress globally. This incredulity, this form of *Africanism*, is an attempt to confine Africa to its past and keep Black people (more globally) out of the future.

The Future Must Have Roots and Branches

In making the distinction between Afrofuturism and Africanfuturism, Nnedi Okorafor writes:

> Africanfuturism is concerned with visions of the future, is interested in technology, leaves the earth, skews optimistic, is centered on and predominantly written by people of African descent (black people) and it is rooted first and foremost in Africa. It's less concerned with "what could have been" and more concerned with "what is and can/will be". It acknowledges, grapples with and carries "what has been."[27]

We can see Killmonger in this description:[28] his ambition is to force both a global reckoning with anti-Blackness and an internal reckoning within Wakanda, to destroy both colonialism and Wakanda simultaneously, to force everyone to grapple with what is and has been. We also see Shuri more centrally in this description.

Shuri pushes the boundaries of everything, pleading with her brother that "just because something works doesn't mean it cannot be improved upon." And Shuri's imagination reaches far enough to influence so many aspects of Wakandan life. We see many examples in the film: a new panther suit that absorbs and reflects kinetic energy; kimoya beads that can enable driving cars, range-unlimited communication, and stabilize otherwise fatal wounds; and mining carts that can transport vibranium more safely than before. Shuri, however, approaches her work with an open skepticism about Wakanda's rituals and traditions. Lord M'Baku – the great gorilla, leader of the Jabari tribe – protests leaving Wakanda's technological advancements in the hands of a girl who "scoffs at tradition." He has a point. She's the one who flips off her brother (the incoming king) in jest in front of their mother, the newly widowed queen. Shuri's the one who demands that everyone just "wrap it up and go home" at T'Challa's coronation, just before the Jabari challenge T'Challa to ritual combat for the throne. She's the one who takes responsibility for Bucky Barnes, the winter soldier, the first "white boy she [fixed]" before Agent Ross – these outsiders are a threat to Wakandan interests. Shuri, however, grows immensely by the end of the film. She witnesses, through Killmonger's coup and attempted worldwide insurrection, what impact her technologies could have on the state of Blacks globally. That is, she learns the stakes of leading and fighting for Wakanda – of what her attempts to transcend could mean for Wakanda, for humanity, and for the universe (looking ahead to *Avengers: Infinity War*).

We have yet to see how much Shuri will grow in Marvel's Cinematic Universe, but in recent comics – both Ta-Nehisi Coates's *Black Panther* and Nnedi Okorafor's *Shuri* – we've already seen Shuri grow even more. Shuri takes up the mantle of Black Panther in T'Challa's absence, and when Thanos and his Black Order invade Wakanda, Shuri staves them off at the (at least temporary) cost of her own life. Her spirit takes a journey to D'Jalia – the ancestral plane where Wakanda's collective memory is housed – where her ancestors show her what Wakanda was like before the vibranium meteorite hit, before Wakanda's technology blossomed. They train her and bestow powers upon her: the ability to enter and exit D'Jalia at will, the power to hear ancient spirits that advise her (whether or not she wants their advice), and the power to transform into and travel as a flock of birds. Her ancestors give her the name "Ancient Future," a name that reflects both her greatest strength and the weakness she must overcome to become the technical and spiritual leader Wakanda needs. Even if Shuri is stubborn to a fault, even if she wants to rely on her ability to make vibranium do as she wants it to, even if she wants to transcend the traditions of her culture, she knows (and must accept) that her knowledge and skills are rooted in and connected with traditions she has only yet begun to understand. Shuri – Wakanda's Ancient Future – unifies Wakanda's memories with its vision of and hopes for the future.

Technological advancement in Wakanda, then, is not just the result of ongoing attempts to transcend Wakanda's traditions: even given Shuri's rebellious attitude, even when Shuri grows tired of her ancestors butting into her affairs. Instead, the wisdom of Wakanda's ancestors – in the D'Jalia, passed down from monarch to monarch – is what allows Wakanda to move forward. This, it turns out, is central to the goals of Africanfuturist works like Coates' *Black Panther* and Okorafor's *Shuri*. The entire point is for characters like Shuri to confront characters like Killmonger: to make sense of how Shuri's technologies can exist in (or will fit into) a world made up of current and former colonies who need her technologies to lift them up. Wakanda doesn't just somehow pop into existence in the future, with no context or connections to its past. It stretches up like the branches of an old tree, but it can only stretch its furthest when it is well-nourished through a network of deep roots.

Blackness as a Pathway to the Future

Media studies scholar Beth Coleman invites us to think of race as a "prosthesis," or "as a technology [that] adds functionality to the subject, helps form location, and provides information."[29] She likens this to the way a blind person might use a cane to feel their way around without sight, to interact with their surroundings. Embracing Blackness could help us find a way toward a more just future, to help develop more equitable technologies. With every new technology released – be it an AI-driven photo app or a self-driving car – we should ask: "How will this device impact Black people? Will it ignore them? Will it target them?" In these moments, Blackness becomes a probe used to stress test technologies.

African/Afrofuturist works like *Black Panther* help us calibrate our walking canes, in a way. Instead of taking it for granted that there will be Black people in the future, Killmonger's fight for liberation forces us to confront the possibility that we won't make it. Instead of pushing for progress for the sake of progress, Shuri's experiences (of coming back from the dead and in her fight against Killmonger) illustrate just how important it is to figure out how to leverage our turbulent past to give our technologies context, purpose, and meaning. Wakanda and its people, then, can be a yardstick by which we measure the futures we dream up.

For pop culture resources and philosophical resources related to this chapter please visit the website for this book: https://introducingphilosophythroughpopculture.com.

Notes

1 Brown, T.E. (2018). Black Panther, *The Philosophers' Magazine* 81: 108–109.
2 Robbins, J. "Black Panther" is a Watershed Moment in Pop Culture. *The Eagle*. https://www.theeagleonline.com/blog/silver-screen/2018/02/black-panther-watershed-moment-in-pop-culture.
3 In the pilot episode of *Star Trek: The Next Generation*, "Encounter at Farpoint," the omnipotent (but fickle) being named Q places Captain Jean-Luc Picard and his crew on trial for the crimes of humanity.

At the very beginning of this trial, Lieutenant Commander Data, claims that "in the year 2036, the new United Nations declared that no Earth citizen could be made to answer for the crimes of his race or forbears." While it is eminently important to protect individuals from being persecuted for harms caused by their forbears, any protections must also be accompanied by acknowledgment of the past harms of those forbears, as well as restitution or reparations to those harmed.

4   Lebron, C. (2018). "Black Panther" Is Not the Movie We Deserve. *Boston Review*. (http://bostonreview. net/race/christopher-lebron-black-panther (February 17, 2018).

5   Rayworth, M. (2018). "There Are Black People in the Future" Sign Can Go Back up, Says Landlord, and ELDI Speaks Up. *NEXTpittsburgh*. (https://nextpittsburgh.com/latest-news/removal-of-east-liberty-billboard-sparks-reactions-across-the-internet (April 8, 2018).

6   Musk, E. (2017). Making humans a multi-planetary species. *New Space* 5: 46–61.

7   Musk, E. (2014). I hope artificial intelligence is nice to us. *New Perspectives Quarterly* 31: 51–55.

8   Marsh, S. (2018). Neurotechnology, Elon Musk and the Goal of Human Enhancement. *The Guardian*. (https://www.theguardian.com/technology/2018/jan/01/elon-musk-neurotechnology-human-enhancement-brain-computer-interfaces (January 1, 2018).

9   Chislenko, A. (1996). Transhumanist Principles 1.0a. http://www.aleph.se/Trans/Cultural/Philosophy/ Transhumanist_Principles.html

10 Bostrom, N. (2005). The fable of the dragon tyrant. *Journal of Medical Ethics* 31: 273–277.

11 Savulescu, J. (2001). Procreative beneficence: why we should select the best children. *Bioethics* 15: 413–26.

12 See Parens, E. and Asch, A., eds. (2000). *Prenatal Testing and Disability Rights*. Washington, DC: Georgetown University Press – esp., Adrienne Asch, "Why I haven't Changed My Mind about Prenatal Diagnosis: Reflections and Refinements."

13 Persson, I. and Savulescu, J. (2012). *Unfit for the Future: The Need for Moral Enhancement*. Oxford: Oxford University Press.

14 Brown, T.E. (2020). Moral Bioenhancement as a Potential Means of Oppression. *The Neuroethics Blog*. (http://www.theneuroethicsblog.com/2020/03/moral-bioenhancement-as-potential-means.html (March 24, 2020).

15 Crawford, K. (2016) Artificial Intelligence's White Guy Problem. *The New York Times*. (https://www. nytimes.com/2016/06/26/opinion/sunday/artificial-intelligences-white-guy-problem.html (June 25, 2016).

16 Varma, R. (2018). US science and engineering workforce: underrepresentation of women and minorities. *American Behavioral Scientist* 62: 692–697.

17 Buolamwini, J. and Gebru, T. (2018). Gender shades: intersectional accuracy disparities in commercial gender classification. *Proceedings of the 1st Conference on Fairness, Accountability and Transparency*, 77–91.

18 Buolamwini, J. (2018). AI Ain't I a Woman?. YouTube Video, 3: 33. https://www.youtube.com/ watch?v=QxuyfWoVV98 (June 28, 2018)

19 Benjamin, R. (2019). *Race After Technology*. Hoboken: Wiley.

20 Alexander, M. (2011). The new Jim Crow. *Ohio State Journal of Criminal Law* 9: 7; Alexander, M. (2010). *The New Jim Crow: Mass Incarceration in the Age of Colorblindness*. New York: New Press.

21 See Coleman, B. (2009). Race as technology. *Camera Obscura: Feminism, Culture, and Media Studies* 24: 177–207; Jones, H. and Jones, N. (2017). Race as technology: from posthuman cyborg to human industry. *Ilha Do Desterro* 70: 39–51.

22 Benjamin, *Race After Technology*, 19.

23 Taylor, P.C. (2016). *Black is Beautiful: A Philosophy of Black Aesthetics*. Oxford: Wiley Blackwell.

24 Taylor, *Black is Beautiful*, 140.

25 Morrison, T. (2020). *Playing in the Dark: Whiteness and the Literary Imagination*. New York: Vintage.

26 Taylor, *Black is Beautiful*, 141.

27 Nnedi Okorafor, "Africanfuturism Defined," Nnedi's Wahala Zone Blog. http://nnedi.blogspot. com/2019/10/africanfuturism-defined.html (October 19, 2019).

28 This, perhaps, would be more Afrofuturist than Africanfuturist on Nnedi Okorafor's view, since Killmonger's reckoning centers the struggles of Black Americans.

29 Coleman, "Race as technology," 194.

37

Black Mirror and Political Manipulation

How Are We Tricked into Dehumanizing Others?

Bertha Alvarez Manninen

Summary

The episode "Men Against Fire," the fifth episode of the third season of *Black Mirror*, tells the story of Stripe Koinange, a solider in an army trying to exterminate a collection of seemingly terrifying animalistic vermin called "roaches." In order to make the soldiers more efficient killers, all of them have a device put in their heads called the MASS implant, which helps them share intelligence, but also alters their senses so that they are not as affected by their kills. The most disturbing aspect of the MASS implant, however, is what it does to the soldiers' perception of the "roaches." As it turns out, they are not horrific monsters after all, but rather terrified human beings who are the victims of mass genocide. The episode showcases just how easy it is to commit acts of violence against a group of persons when they are quite literally seen as subhuman. Although we do not yet have the technology necessary to create the MASS implant, "Men Against Fire" makes one wonder whether our use of dehumanizing language and propaganda, targeting members of marginalized groups, serves a similar function.

It's a lot easier to pull the trigger when you are aiming at the bogeyman.

– Arquette

An episode of *Black Mirror* called "Men Against Fire" tells the story of Stripe Koinange, a solider in an army trying to exterminate a collection of seemingly terrifying animalistic vermin called "roaches." The title of the episode comes from World War I veteran Samuel Lynman Marshall's book *Men Against Fire: The Problem of Battle Command*. Based on several interviews with World War II veterans, he discovered that only one in four soldiers actually fired their weapons at their enemies during battle. Marshall proposed several ways to change military training to increase the

Introducing Philosophy Through Pop Culture: From Socrates to Star Wars *and Beyond*, Second Edition.
Edited by William Irwin and David Kyle Johnson.

number of kills – to make soldiers more efficiently deadly. In "Men Against Fire," the military has accomplished this by implanting a device in soldiers' brains, called the MASS neural implant, which makes them perceive the "enemy" not as terrified human beings, but as horrific monsters.

The story follows Stripe as he comes to realize that roaches aren't vermin, but rather human beings who are being targeted for mass genocide due to allegedly inferior genes. The episode highlights just how easy it is to commit acts of violence against a group of persons when they are quite literally seen as subhuman. We do not yet have the technology necessary to create the MASS implant, but "Men Against Fire" makes us wonder whether our use of dehumanizing language and propaganda, targeting members of marginalized groups, serves a similar function.

Our "MASS Implant": The Language of Dehumanization

According to the story, previous attempts to kill off the "roaches" were unsuccessful because, even though the group was derided, people are largely unwilling to outright massacre other humans. The MASS device helped solve this "problem," not only by making those humans look like monsters but also by providing an augmented reality that allows the soldiers to communicate relevant data, and by giving them a reward of graphic sexual dreams for successful kills. Once Stripe's MASS implant is compromised, however, he is able to see these "monsters" as the terrified human beings they actually are, doing their best to hide and survive.

While attempting to protect two victims, a mother and son, Catarina and Alec, Stripe asks them how the locals, who also hate these individuals, are able to treat them so horribly without the use of a MASS implant. Catarina responds:

> Ten years ago it began. Post-war. First, the screening program, the DNA checks, then the register, the emergency measures. Soon everyone calls us creatures. Filthy creatures. Every voice. The TV. The computer. Say we have sickness in us. We have weakness. It's in our blood. They say that our blood cannot go on. That we cannot go on.

The dehumanization of these individuals is achieved via language: they are called "roaches." To some it may seem like a stretch to think that people really would use such language to describe others, but *Black Mirror* creator Charlie Brooker chose the term *because* he heard it used in the real world. Controversial British columnist Katie Hopkins actually referred to migrants residing in the United Kingdom as "cockroaches."[1]

Indeed, one of the first steps toward ostracizing individuals in marginalized groups is to find means of "othering" them; to create a sharp division between "us" and "them." The use of dehumanizing language and propaganda is a long-standing method to create this divide: human beings are likened to distasteful animals, like insects or rodents. David Livingstone Smith writes about many instances of this in his book *Less Than Human: Why We Demean, Enslave, and Exterminate Others*. Drawing upon examples from Nazi Germany, Smith writes that "[t]o the Nazis, all the Jews, Gypsies, and others were rats: dangerous, disease-carrying rats . . . [they] were represented as parasitic organisms – as leeches, lice, bacteria, or vectors of contagion."[2] During World War II, while the Japanese depicted Americans and the British "with horns sprouting from their temples, and sporting tails, claws, and fangs,"[3] Americans, in turn, dehumanized the Japanese by considering them and portraying them as "monkeys, apes, or rodents, and sometimes as insects."[4]

In the early twentieth century, the Muslim Turks of the Ottoman Empire massacred over a million Christian Armenians. As Smith notes:

> the Turkish authorities ... conceived of [the Armenians] in much the same way as the Nazis would later imagine the Jews – as disease organisms infecting the body of the state – and announced the need to 'rid ourselves of these Armenian parasites.' Armenians and other non-Muslim minorities were also identified with traditionally unclean animals such as rats, dogs, and pigs.[5]

In the latter part of the twentieth century, during the Rwandan genocide, the Hutus repeatedly referred to the Tutsis as "cockroaches."

The use of dehumanizing language is not just a matter of incorporating objectionable words into public discourse, and offense at such language is not a matter of being overly sensitive. Philosopher Ludwig Wittgenstein (1889–1951) emphasized how our language shapes the boundaries of our minds and thought: "the limits of my language mean the limits of my world."[6] Indeed, the connection between the use of dehumanizing language and propaganda against marginalized groups and the willingness to physically harm and encourage violence against members of such groups is well documented.

The Consequences of Our "MASS Implant": The Violence of Dehumanization

Throughout "Men Against Fire" we see that, while the locals openly hate the "roaches," they do not directly participate in their massacre (though they encourage the military to do so). The soldiers, however, are joyous at the thought of hunting and killing roaches, viewing it as almost a recreational activity. Stripe kills two of them on his first mission, shooting one while repeatedly stabbing another to death. He is especially gleeful about this as his partner, Raiman, expresses frustration that she has not killed a "roach" in a while. Indeed, she recounts to Stripe that her first few kills were utterly orgasmic.

Once Stripe is able to see the "roaches" as human beings, he goes out of his way to protect them, and is horrified at how easily Raiman can kill them. Viewing them as human for the first time so profoundly affects Stripe that he goes against all of his military training, tackles Raiman to the ground, and helps Catarina and Alec escape. However, it is not long before Raiman finds them, kills Catarina and Alec, and beats Stripe into submission.

Stripe wakes up in a cell where a military psychologist, Arquette, apologizes for not having discovered the defect in Stripe's MASS implant, and reveals to him everything that had been going on. They had to use the MASS implant because human beings, when they recognize the humanity of "the other," are actually ineffective killers. Arquette tells Stripe:

> Humans. You know, we give ourselves a bad rap, but we're genuinely empathetic as a species. I mean, we don't actually want to kill each other. Which is a good thing. Until your future depends on wiping out the enemy ... most soldiers didn't even fire their weapons. Or if they did, they would just aim over the heads of the enemies. They did it on purpose ... plus the guys who did get a kill would get messed up in the head. And that's

pretty much how it stayed until MASS came along. You see MASS, well that's the ultimate military weapon . . . It's a lot easier to pull the trigger when you're aiming at the bogeyman.

This is likely why the locals, while hating the ostracized group, were largely unable to kill them – they still saw them as human beings. Indeed, Brooker wanted to emphasize that the villagers did not need the MASS device to hate the "roaches" because he wanted them to mirror the audience: "[people] don't need [MASS] to demonize and hate people."[7] Yet the MASS implant allows the military to "do its job" by making it so that the soldiers literally perceive human beings as monsters instead. It is the perception of persons as subhuman that makes it so easy to massacre them.

The deadly consequences of such perception make it vital to be aware of the power of dehumanizing language and propaganda. As Smith puts it "[d]ehumanization isn't a way of talking. It's a way of thinking . . . [i]t acts as a psychological lubricant, dissolving our inhibitions and inflaming our destructive passions. As such, it empowers us to perform acts that would, under other circumstances, be unthinkable."[8] Dehumanizing the Jews and the Armenians was the first step to facilitating their genocide. Referring to the Tutsis "cockroaches" helped to justify the horrific fate of "around 800,000 Tutsis and moderate Hutus [who] were shot, burned, hacked, and bludgeoned to death by marauding mobs."[9] During World War II, the vilification of the Japanese facilitated their forced detainment, including US citizens of Japanese ancestry, in internment camps.

In order to understand how dehumanization functions, we must first ask, as social ethicist Herbert Kelman puts it, "what it means to perceive another person as fully human, in the sense of being included in the moral compact that governs human relationships."[10] In order to perceive others as full members of our moral community, it is necessary to recognize them as "part of an interconnected network of individuals who care for each other, who recognize each other's individuality, and who respect each other's rights."[11] The use of dehumanizing language effectively functions not just to draw a distinction between "us" and "them," but also to subdue, and even deaden, our sense of empathy and care for the "other":

> Sanctioned massacres become possible to the extent that we deprive fellow human beings of identity and community. It is difficult to have compassion for those who lack identity and who are excluded from our community; their death does not move us in a personal way. Thus when a group of people is defined entirely in terms of a category to which they belong, and when this category is excluded from the human family, then the moral restraints against killing them are more readily overcome.[12]

It is much more difficult to harm others who we perceive as "one of our own." Arquette says as much to Stripe when, echoing Samuel Lynman Marshall's findings, he notes that in the past, soldiers were hesitant to shoot and kill their adversaries – they saw them as too human, too much "like them," to be able to easily harm them. The military needed a way to facilitate viewing enemies as "bogeymen" instead of as persons. In the episode the MASS implant achieves this end, but in our society dehumanizing language and propaganda serves a similar function. As Gregory Stanton, founder of Genocide Watch, notes, dehumanizing language, thought, and behavior is a hallmark feature of genocide: "One group . . . denies the humanity of the other group. Members of it are equated with animals, vermin, insects or disease. Dehumanization overcomes the normal human revulsion against murder."[13]

The "MASS Implant" Today

It may be tempting to think that such instances of dehumanization are a thing of the past, but nothing could be further from the truth. Brooker noted that, when first conceiving of "Men Against Fire," "the notion that a future fascist government might come in and demonize a huge section of society" appeared "incredibly far-fetched." Yet current events throughout the world made this episode hit "closer to home."[14]

Indeed, anyone paying attention to the current political climate in the United States will be able to see our own "MASS implant" being propagated and supported by political leaders. During a roundtable discussion in California concerning illegal immigration in May 2018, President Donald Trump said of MS-13 gang members, "these aren't people. These are animals." While we may be tempted to agree with him in reference to gang members, especially those who have committed heinous crimes, Trump blurred the lines between undocumented immigrants and gang members in a June 19, 2018 tweet: "Democrats are the problem. They don't care about crime and want illegal immigrants, no matter how bad they may be, to pour into and infest our Country, like MS-13." Here, he lumps all immigrants together, and refers to undocumented immigrants as a literal infestation – a term that is typically used to describe being taken over by insects and vermin.

In 2020, the world was hammered with the consequences of the coronavirus, which originated in Wuhan, China. And, once again, Trump's language was consequential; he often used the term "Chinese virus" instead of its scientific name, COVID-19. Trump was widely criticized for using such a term, the concern being that it exacerbates racist attitudes against people of Asian descent. Indeed, several cases of violence against Asian-Americans were noted as the virus spread and in the wake of his remarks. In one case, a man, shopping in a grocery store, was accosted by a woman who then preceded to cough in his face. Another woman was told to "go back to China" on a New York subway.[15] Beyond verbal assaults, in March 2020 a man was accused of stabbing three Asian-Americans, including two children, because he thought they were "Chinese and infecting people with the coronavirus."[16]

To be clear, Trump's dehumanizing language did not create the current hatred against members of marginalized groups in the United States – our "MASS implants" have been long and pervasively present. For example, a 2015 study asked 201 participants in the United States to rate members of certain marginalized groups on an "ascent of man" diagram scale (which shows the evolution of humans from primate to modern day *Homo sapiens*). The instructions read: "Some people seem highly evolved, whereas others seem no different than lower animals. Using the image below as a guide, indicate using the sliders how evolved you consider the average member of each group to be." The groups that were assessed were: "Mexican immigrants, Arabs, Chinese people, Europeans, Americans, Icelanders, Japanese people, Swiss people, Austrians, Australians, French people, South Koreans, and Muslims." The results were that:

> European groups and Japanese were rated as similarly evolved as Americans, whereas South Korean, Chinese and Mexican immigrants were rated as significantly less evolved than Americans. Lowest on the scale were Arabs and Muslims, who were rated on average 10.6 and 14.0 points lower than Americans, respectively.[17]

Two of the authors of the study, Nour Kteily and Emile Bruneau, noted in a 2017 article that individuals in the United States who are more likely to harbor dehumanizing beliefs against members of marginalized groups were more likely to vote for candidates who supported "hostile policies" against those groups. For example, "blatant dehumanization of Muslims was more strongly correlated with support for Donald Trump than any of the other Republican candidates"[18] during the 2016 election. So, while Trump did not create the current crisis, he certainly has fanned its flames.

Other contemporary instances of dehumanization abound outside of the United States. As of this writing, yet another horrific instance of genocide is being committed against Rohingya Muslims in Myanmar, a country in Southeast Asia. In what serves as an example of how easily the common person is susceptible to the effects of dehumanizing propaganda, and the violence that typically follows, one article about the current Muslim genocide in Myanmar notes that after hundreds of soldiers "entered the village of Gu Dar Pyin armed with rifles, knives, rocket launchers and grenades . . . mov[ing] from house to house stealing possessions of Rohingya Muslims and shooting anyone they found . . . ordinary Burmese civilians followed, burning houses as well as shooting and stabbing women and children."[19] Likewise, the villagers in "Men Against Fire" were complicit in the dehumanization of the "roaches." Though the villagers did not kill the roaches, they actively sought their deaths by having the military do the work for them.

In 2017, it was revealed that homosexual men were being routinely attacked, beaten, killed, and sometimes taken to holding camps in Chechnya. Chechen leader Ramzan Kadyrov has consistently denied these accusations, despite photographic and video evidence of the assaults. When asked about the charges, Kadyrov replied by denying that gay persons even exist in Chechnya:

> This is nonsense. We don't have those kinds of people here. We don't have any gays. If there are any, take them to Canada . . . Take them far from us so we don't have them at home. To purify our blood, if there is any here, take them.[20]

Kadyrov's words here are reminiscent of both Arquette's and Medina's (Stripe's squad leader) respective justifications for participating in the genocide of Catarina's people. Medina leads Stripe's first mission to kill the "roaches," taking them to the home of a local farmer, a devout Christian who has chosen to act on his faith and shelter them from genocide. In her attempts to extract information from the farmer, Medina tells him that his desire to protect them is an "understandable sentiment, but it's misguided. We gotta take them out if humankind is gonna carry on in this world." When Stripe protests the killing of human beings, Arquette justifies it by saying:

> Do you have any idea the amount of shit that is in their DNA? Higher rates of cancer, muscular dystrophy, MS, SLS, substandard IQ, criminal tendencies, and sexual deviances. It's all there. The screening shows it. Is that what you want for the next generation? Don't feel bad about doing your job. The villagers won't do it. The people back home won't do it. They don't have MASS. MASS lets you do it.

The goal of "purifying" a race, or a species, is a common justification for mass genocide, one that is facilitated when we view the targeted group as not one of "our own."

Rehumanizing the Dehumanized: How to Turn Off Our "MASS Implant"

There is some hope to be found within "Men Against Fire." When Stripe's implant is rendered nonfunctional, and he is able to see his victims as persons rather than monsters, he is overcome by his desire to care for them and save them. Upon seeing Catarina and Alec's humanity, Stripe defies his orders, tackles his colleagues, and puts his life on the line to save them. Arquette details all the alleged reasons this class of people are undesirable, but none of it matters to Stripe. They are human beings, he says, and that *alone* makes their massacre wrong regardless of their alleged genetic inferiority.

Stripe's reaction is reminiscent of philosopher Emmanuel Levinas (1906–1995). In his book *Totality and Infinity*, Levinas notes the importance of always keeping "the face" of "the other" firmly planted in our mind's eye. Focusing on "the face" immediately calls us into an ethical relationship with that person: "the face is a living presence . . . the face speaks to me and thereby invites me to a relation . . . the face opens the primordial discourse whose first word is obligation."[21] Acknowledging the humanity of the marginalized demands that you treat them in accordance with their intrinsic dignity and moral worth, to regard them as nothing less than another version of yourself. When "the face presents itself [it] demands justice"[22] and once you start earnestly acknowledging the humanity of "the other," you "are not free to ignore the meaningful world into which the face of the other has introduced . . ."[23]

In "Men Against Fire" the faces of Catarina and Alec call Stripe into a relationship with them; he becomes willing to risk everything to protect them. By keeping "the face" of the other constantly in our mind's eye, we will always be able to respond to calls to violence in the way that Stripe did once his MASS implant was compromised. There is no "honor" in harming or killing persons, Stripe tells Arquette, because, after all is said and done, "they're human beings."

The Future of Our "MASS Implant"

When Stripe realizes that he has participated in the murder of innocent human beings, he insists on coming clean to the world, and he wants nothing more to do with the military. Arquette has other plans. He offers Stripe a chance to "reset" the MASS implant, which would then erase all memory of everything Stripe has realized up until that point. Stripe refuses at first, but Arquette then reveals that he has complete control over Stripe's senses. If Stripe does not concede to the reset, he will spend the rest of his days in a cell, reliving his participation in the massacre on a nonstop loop. This option proves too much for Stripe to bear. In the end, he arrives home, seemingly honorably discharged – but his eyes are still cloudy, implying that he conceded to having his implant reset.

Stripe copes with his action by forgetting his history. As a society, we seem to do the same. We teach our children history by cleansing it of our role in massacres; we downplay the genocide of Native Americans, for example, or the horribleness of slavery. Well tell the ancestors of these victims to "get over it" and balk at the thought of reparations.

History is repeating itself. Far-right politicians in the Czech Republic have begun a campaign against the Roma people, referring to them as the "rabble" and vowing to build "villages" where they will be separated from the general public. Just like the propaganda that started the genocide of Catarina's people, the propaganda against the Roma has resulted in people in the Czech Republic, much like the villagers in the episode, turning against a subset of their population. One woman defends the separation by calling the Roma "maladjusted . . . They don't want to live with us normal people." Another man says: "There should be a separate village, but not just for the scum, but for the gypsies too." An even more extreme view is ominously printed on a large sign: "We don't need to discuss the maladjusted; we need to solve the problem once and for all." A social media post disseminated through the Czech Republic takes a page from every other instance of genocide in history and actively calls for the murder of Roma: "Rat poison is not good enough for these vermin." They may as well call them "roaches."[24]

A recent UN report notes that by 2040, climate change will have become so severe that it will begin a mass migration from parts of the world, mostly tropical nations, that will have become uninhabitable.[25] The recent Syrian refugee crisis has illustrated how unwilling the rest of the world is to take in migrants who are in desperate need. The campaign of dehumanization in order to justify ignoring the plights of those who are in need will likely continue, and possibly even be exacerbated.

The United States is facing a monumental decision. The soldiers in "Men Against Fire" do not recall consenting to the MASS implant, and it is unclear whether they really understood its function before they consented. By contrast, we know enough history to see how dehumanizing marginalized groups typically ends. Stripe is able to consent to "forgetting" what he has done, but none of us can "turn off" our memory. We will have to live with how we choose to proceed. Thus, we should strive for a society that can, for example, discuss the many nuances and facets of undocumented immigration without dehumanizing immigrants. We should protect ourselves from terrorist attacks without dehumanizing all members of a religion or ethnicity. We should refuse to engage in any kind of dehumanizing language or behavior and strongly repudiate anyone who encourages it, even those in the highest power.

For pop culture resources and philosophical resources related to this chapter please visit the website for this book: https://introducingphilosophythroughpopculture.com.

Notes

1   Brooker, C. and Jones, A. with Arnopp, J. (2018). *Inside Black Mirror*, 194. New York: Crown Archetype.
2   Smith, D.L. (2011). *Less Than Human: Why We Demean, Enslave, and Exterminate Others*, 15. New York: St. Martin's Press.
3   Smith, 17.
4   Ibid.
5   Smith, 145.
6   Wittgenstein, L. (1999). *Tractatus Logico-Philosophicus*, 5.6. London: Routledge and Kegan Paul.
7   Brooker et al., 201.
8   Smith, 13.
9   Smith, 152.
10 Kelman, H. (1973). Violence without moral restraint: reflections on the dehumanization of victims and victimizers. *Journal of Social Issues* 29: 48.
11 Ibid.
12 Kelman, 49.
13 Smith, 142.
14 Brooker et al., 194.
15 Loffman, M. (2020). Asian Americans describe "gut punch" of racist attacks during coronavirus pandemic. *PBS News Hour*. https://www.pbs.org/newshour/nation/asian-americans-describe-gut-punch-of-racist-attacks-during-coronavirus-pandemic (April 7, 2020).

16   Kim, J.Y. Sam's Club stabbing suspect thought family was Chinese and infecting people with coronavirus. https://www.kxan.com/news/crime/report-sams-club-stabbing-suspect-thought-family-was-chinese-infecting-people-with-coronavirus.

17   Kteily, N. and Bruneau, E. (2017). Backlash: the politics and real-world consequences of minority group dehumanization. *Personality and Social Psychology Bulletin* 43: 93.

18   Nour Kteily, Emile Bruneau, Adam Waytz, Sarah Cotterill, "The Ascent of Man: Theoretical and Empirical Evidence for Blatant Dehumanization," Journal of Personality and Social Psychology 109 (2015), p. 6. Available at: https://pcnlab.asc.upenn.edu/wp-content/uploads/2017/07/2015_-The-Ascent-of-Man-Theoretical-and-Empirical-Evidence-for-Blatant-Dehumanization.pdf

19   Drake, M. (2018). Myanmar soldiers "burning Rohingya Muslim's faces off with acid" to "hide genocide." *Express*. (www.express.co.uk/news/world/913705/Rohingya-Muslim-genocide-burning-face-acid-massacre-Myanmar-Burma-human-rights-news (February 18, 2018).

20   Levinas, E. (1991). *Totality and Infinity: An Essay on Exteriority*, 66–201. Dordrecht: Kluwer Academic Publishers.

21   Adam Taylor. "Ramzan Kadyrov says there are no gay men in Chechnya — and if there are any, they should move to Canada," Washington Post. July 15, 2017. Available at:https://www.washingtonpost.com/news/worldviews/wp/2017/07/15/ramzan-kadyrov-says-there-are-no-gay-men-in-chechnya-and-if-there-are-any-they-should-move-to-canada/?noredirect=on&utm_term=.a8982d419713

22   Levinas, 294.

23   Levinas, 219.

24   O'Brien, P. (2018). Far right in Czech Republic: the politicians turning on Roma. *Channel14*. https://www.channel4.com/news/far-right-in-czech-republic-the-politicians-turning-on-roma (October 5, 2018).

25   Dent, S. (2018). Major UN report says climate change is worse than first thought. *Engadget*. (https://www.engadget.com/2018/10/08/major-un-report-climate-change-worse (October 8, 2018).

38

Black Mirror and #DeathTo

What Are the Consequences of Trial by Twitter?

Aline Maya

Summary

Should we punish immoral behavior on Twitter and other social media? Many people believe we should. Inside the Black Mirror, detective Karin and detective Blue arrive at the crime scene where an infamous journalist has just been found dead. When Karin and Blue dig deeper and deeper into a world of internet hate, following the killer robotic bees, they locate the perpetrator: a hacker, who believes he is carrying out the will of the people as executioner. But very soon, the executioners become the executed ones . . . In real life, malicious comments on Twitter sometimes lead to bullying and even suicide. But we should consider the other side as well: perhaps sometimes justice can only be obtained via social media awareness, as in the case of the #MeToo movement. Either way, the consequences of acting (or not acting) present themselves every day in our black-mirrored phones.

Thanks to the technological revolution, we have the power to rage and accuse, spout bile without consequence. Only by being forced to recognize the power technology grants us, to acknowledge individual responsibility . . .
　　　　　– Garrett Scholes,from his Manifesto "The Teeth of Consequences"

". . . can we properly limit that power." That's how one assumes the abovementioned quote ends, from Garrett Scholes's manifesto in the *Black Mirror* episode "Hated in the Nation." Chief Detective Inspector Karin Parke cuts off reading it there, but she goes on to clarify that Scholes likens people to insects that revel in cruelty, "a weakness that should be bred out of us." To do just that, Scholes hacked the network of ADIs (Autonomous Drone Insects) that replaced the dying bee population. At first, the bee drones kill whoever has the most #DeathTo mentions each day on Twitter. The public quickly catches on, and hundreds of thousands use the hashtag to call for the death of publicly derided figures. But when Karin and her associates try to shut down the ADI system, the hack inverts, and the bees hunt down and kill everyone who used the hashtag – thus making them individually responsible for their deplorable online behavior and weeding out those of us who "revel in cruelty."

Scholes was motivated by what happened to his friend, Tess Wallender, who attempted suicide after being the target of an online hate campaign. But what happened to Tess is not unlike what's happened to many real-world people as the result of online shaming. Adult film actress August Ames committed suicide after she was attacked on Twitter for refusing to perform with a gay actor.[1] Tyler Clementi committed suicide after his roommate used Twitter to spread a video that shows him kissing another boy.[2] And Holly Jones received death threats after tweeting something insensitive in a restaurant review.[3] Indeed, online shaming is likely a contributor to the rising rate of teen suicide, especially among those who are gay.[4] In other words, Scholes has a point. The moral of the story seems to be that we need to hold online shamers responsible for their behavior, and that we should never online shame anyone ourselves.

But is this moral sound? Hasn't social media also given voice to voiceless victims? And aren't some people deserving of shame? Consequently, could not online shaming sometimes do good in the world? And if it can, how can we determine when it's justified and when it is not? When should we be involved and when should we not? To answer this, let us look at "Hated in the Nation," and see if we can discover how to balance the #dangers with the #benefits.

Dangers

Self-administered justice has occurred throughout human history. It's often called "trial by mob." And because of the unpredictability of mobs, most societies have established systems to prevent it. That's why the United Nations considers a presumption of innocence (until proven guilty) a universal human right, and the US Constitution guarantees citizens accused of serious crimes a right to a trial by jury. Of course, such efforts have not always been successful in protecting that right. Appallingly, in the American South after the Civil War, mobs "justified" the lynching of black men by falsely accusing them of raping white women, and then finding them guilty and punishing them without a trial.[5] What made such horrific bypasses of the justice system possible, of course, was the systemic racism embedded in the South. But as "Hated in the Nation" shows, social media also provides a way to bypass the justice system. In the real world the consequences have not yet been as horrific as widespread lynchings, but the results of trial by Twitter have still been disastrous.

Consider again the case of Tess Wallender, Garrett Scholes's friend, whose suicide attempt inspired his manifesto and devious bee-hacking plan. Tess complained on Twitter about a man harassing her on the Tube (the subway), spouting "lewd comments or something," and included a photo. But when it was revealed that the man in question had a learning disability, the internet turned on Tess – so fiercely that she attempted suicide.

> It was like having a whole weather system turn against me. Just hate message after hate message, around the clock, all piling on. It's hard to describe what that does to your head. Suddenly there's a million invisible people, all talking about how they despise you. It's like a mental illness . . . I mean, hands up, I made a mistake, but the way people enjoyed kicking me, that's what got to me. The casual fun they had . . . I just felt I couldn't go on.

Garrett, her flatmate, saved her. Tess did not know about the man's condition – but social media only cared about one side of the story: Tess made fun of a disabled person. We may wonder why her critics did not bother to consider the fact that she likely did not know the man's condition, but in reality things like this happen every day. Such uncharitable conclusions are due to something called the "fundamental attribution error," the human tendency to attribute the misbehavior of others to character flaws, but our own misbehavior to excusable situational pressures. When someone *else* cuts you off while driving it's because they are a jerk; when *you* cut them off it's okay because you have somewhere important to be. This error often leads the mob to convict the innocent.

The mob is also easily misdirected by individuals with a hidden agenda – like competitors, activists, and ex-partners – by misinformation, emotional appeals, false news stories, faulty evidence, and bad arguments. It's just the sad truth that people tend to lack the critical thinking skills necessary to determine guilt or innocence. People will make snap judgments based on "gut feelings" and neglecting to fact check claims that tell them what they already believe. As Cass Sunstein pointed out in his book *#republic*, especially given the rise of social media, people are easily isolated into "information cocoons," or echo chambers, where they are only ever exposed to arguments, facts, and opinions that confirm what they already believe.[6] Indeed, even when supervised in a courtroom, and isolated in a jury, people can get it wrong – failing to recognize, for example, how faulty our memories are, and just how wrong (and easily manipulated) eye witness testimony can be.[7]

Worse still, people may want to find the accused guilty simply because they have had a bad day. Consider chancellor Tom Pickering who is distraught about being "number one" on the #DeathTo list after the public learns it's legit. When he laments the fact that Lord Farrington is only number four, and someone points out that he's only a "suspected pedophile," the chancellor replies without evidence, "He did it. You know he did."

What's more, even if the accused is guilty, the mob may inflict unjust punishment. Consider Tusk, the rapper who insulted the dancing skills of one of his young fans. "That's a goofy little motherfucker, and he can't dance for shit." Or consider Clara Meades, the third victim of the #DeathTo hashtag, who took a picture of herself pretending to pee on a war memorial. There is no question about their guilt; there are pictures and video of what they did. And certainly what they did was disrespectful and in bad taste. But it's equally certain that they did not deserve to die for it. Of course, the mob did not yet know that the hashtag was deadly in their cases – but that's part of the point. No one can control the results of the mob's actions. Because there are no guidelines or safeguards, the mob can prescribe just about any punishment it wants, and the results can vary wildly. Posting on social media is a bit like throwing a cigarette out your window. It might do nothing, but it might start a wildfire.

The results can also be unfair; some guilty parties are punished, others are not. Especially troubling is the fact that while punishment is being handed down to those who own up to and apologize for their crime, others are getting off scot-free because they did not. A public official, for example, who admits and apologizes for a single infraction can lose their seat while a more senior official who denies and lies about 22 worse wrongdoings retains their position.

Similar worries about the mob's ability to judge and punish are raised by our natural biases. When it's personal, we side with our friends and relatives. Consider Jo Powers. A close examination of the episode reveals that she wrote an article critical of "Wheelchair Martyr" Gwen Marbury entitled "Spare Me The Tears Over This 'Martyr'." Gwen immolated herself in protest of budgets cuts to disability benefits, but Jo argued that her suicide was the "worst kind of attention seeking." The public targeted Jo, but her husband supported her. And I understand where he's coming from. If, say, my friend tweeted that she experienced discrimination at a fast-food chain, I would not doubt it. I would not even ask for evidence. My moral duty is to support my friend, right? But, in all honesty, even if she's not lying, she could still be mistaken. There are two sides to every story. And the consequences could be severe: someone's job, relationship, or health could be on the line.

The same thing happens when it's political; we defend people in our political tribe, and gang up on those who aren't. As the contemporary philosopher Kathryn Norlock puts it, too often the point of online shaming is not to "punish or exclude specific individuals," but to "enjoy the company one has in cyberspace with so many approving others."[8] We're the jury, but we are not even concerned about the truth. We're concerned about group allegiance and tribal instincts and the trial is over before it begins.

The final #danger I'll mention is more philosophical but equally important: the danger of losing one's liberty. As the American philosopher John Rawls (1921–2002) proposed in *A Theory of Justice*, in order to be fair, punishment must be practiced according to law; it cannot be arbitrary.[9] If you do not know what the law is beforehand, you cannot be sure that what you are doing is not illegal, and so, you cannot act with liberty. For example, without knowing that posting a photo of her pretending to pee on a war memorial could get her the death penalty, Clara Meades cannot make a fully informed and thus free choice regarding whether to do so.

Rawls's theory of liberty would still champion some particular social media movements, however, because their goal can be to correct violations of liberty that society or the legal system allows. As he puts it:

Sometimes we may be forced to allow certain breaches of its [legal] precepts if we are to mitigate the loss of freedom from social evils that cannot be removed, and to aim for the least injustice that conditions allow.[10]

This could mean that, in cases where the liberty of many is lost, other forms of justice might be acceptable. And this leads us to discuss the possible benefits of online shaming.

Benefits

While investigating Jo Powers's death, Inspector Parke dismisses her partner Blue Coulson's theory that someone from the internet is responsible for the murder, saying, "That internet stuff drifts off like weather. It's half hate. They don't mean it." This, of course, is sometimes true; at least to the person doing it, online resentment can just be trolling, a joke, or the result of short-lived hate (although the effects on the victim can be long lasting). But the main reason for the formation of many mobs today is the failure of a justice system. Many conditions produce real anger and frustration: constant abuse, negligence, or unsolved hate crimes that go unchecked. And there can be benefits to acting outside the justice system in such cases. Social media has finally given the victims of such situations the ability to speak freely without fearing reprisal from perpetrators. When an issue resonates deeply with people, social media allows them to pool together their communal strength to create change. Victims who were unable to see justice done can finally speak up and get retribution and social acceptance.[11]

The rise and effectiveness of the #MeToo hashtag in 2017 proved beneficial for victims in this way. It thus greatly complicates the seeming moral of the episode, which suggests that online shaming should always be avoided. Indeed, #MeToo was eerily anticipated by the #DeathTo hashtag featured in "Hated in the Nation" in 2016.[12] When Alyssa Milano encouraged survivors of sexual assault to use the #MeToo hashtag and tell their stories, they did – thus started the #MeToo movement. Some #MeToo victims came forward for the first time, after years of living with their secret; but many others had previously reported their experiences only to be ignored, silenced, or even threatened. Threatening victims like that is easy to do when the victims are isolated; powerful people have strong reasons to conceal incidents that could endanger their place of privilege and hurt their bottom line. Combine those reasons with the sense of helplessness victims already feel, and you get something that, in retrospect, is astonishing: millions of victims keep quiet for decades while harassment and abuse continue.

#MeToo gave such victims strength, however – strength in numbers, but also the strength that comes from seeing the support that was previously invisible to them. The perception of our world is easily shaped by those who control the media – and they often have no interest in disrupting a status quo in which they fare quite well. All too often in this context it can seem like no one is on the side of the victim. But social media, and #MeToo, created an avenue for millions of solitary voices to find each other, and to realize that they had all been whispering the same unheard lament. "It's only me" transformed into "me too." In many cases, the incidents occurred so long ago that it would be difficult to make legal charges stick. In other cases, the behavior did not rise to the level of illegality. But when enough voices rise together and say, "this will not stand," even massive corporations are forced to take action.

As of this writing, the collective voice of the #MeToo movement has called out and tried to hold accountable Harvey Weinstein, Roy Price, Lawrence Nassar, Kevin Spacey, Roy Moore, Louis C.K., Matt Lauer, Al Franken, Garrison Keillor, Russell Simmons, Mario Batali, Gary Goddard, James Levine, Michael Ferro, Bill Cosby, Adam Seger, Leslie Moonves, and R. Kelly (just to name a few).[13] Although the #MeToo campaign did not kill them like the ADIs, it did cost many of these people their careers or elections, and in some cases resulted in jail time.

Now, to be entirely clear, the severity and kind of accusations for those just listed should not all be equated. In some cases, for example, the alleged behavior is a moral infraction, in other cases it's a legal crime. And, although in some cases guilt seems to have been established beyond a reasonable doubt through court verdicts, confessions, or publicly available evidence (such as pictures), in others the "jury is still out." But to the extent that that the #MeToo movement has punished or brought to justice anyone who would have otherwise gotten away with a moral or legal crime, it seems to have done good.

So, in a way, #MeToo is kind of like the beautiful flip side of #DeathTo. The same tidal force that brought about the unjust death of Clara Meades can also bring justice to guilty parties like Bill Cosby who otherwise would have gotten away with their crimes. What will ultimately happen – how many of those accused will be punished by law, and whether there will be real institutional-level changes that prevent future generations of powerful individuals from abusing victims in this way – all remain to be seen. What we do know is that social media, which can give the tiniest individual a voice that can reach millions, has given unimaginable power to victims and their supporters. It therefore seems wrong to conclude, like Scholes does in the "Hated in the Nation," episode that participation in online shaming is always wrong.

But in the same breath, even though the potential benefits are immense, it's vitally important to bear in mind the potential abuse the #MeToo movement makes possible. That's not to say that one who has been subjected to sexual abuse or misconduct should not report it! Obviously, any such person should feel free and empowered to report anyone who they feel has acted inappropriately toward them, even by calling them out on Twitter. The tough issue is what one should do if someone else does this. On the one hand, if a group does not join them in their call for action, it may go unheeded. On the other hand, you almost certainly do not have the full story or know the appropriate punishment. All the dangers talked about in Section 38.1 still exist. The #MeToo movement is not automatically immune or an exception to the rule. It's easy to lose sight of this when the purpose is noble: those guilty of sexual misconduct should be punished. But people, especially in large groups, even when well intentioned, can still get things wrong. They can still easily find guilty the innocent and prescribe or bring about undue punishment.

Now some might argue that, even if this is true, I should not point it out. "Yes," some might admit, "the #MeToo movement *could be* abused, but by drawing attention to that possibility you are just giving ammunition to those who want to discredit it to protect those guilty of sexual misconduct."[14] Indeed, important public figures who fear the power of movements like #MeToo have already used the possibility of false accusations to do exactly that. They say the #MeToo movement, along with its #BelieveSurvivors mantra, has made America (and other countries) a scary place for men. "Any man," they say, "can have his life ruined by some random woman falsely accusing him of sexual assault, the accusation going viral, and then the mob convicting and punishing him without a trial. To protect our sons, husbands, brothers, and uncles, we must take such accusations with a grain of salt." But there are two things to say in response that actually bolster the case for the #MeToo movement and can help guide us in measuring our responses to sexual misconduct allegations.

First, although it would be easy to abuse the attitude that we should *always* believe *everyone* who even *claims* to have survived sexual assault, there's been a long history of favoring the exact opposite attitude: to *never* believe such claims. Reports of sexual assault have traditionally been ignored or met with shame and opposition (like death threats); that's why so much misconduct goes unreported.[15] A "rebalancing" therefore seems to be in order. Again, automatically believing that every report of sexual assault is 100% true is not advisable. What is advisable, however, is always giving those making such claims the benefit of the doubt – always taking such reports seriously and investigating them.[16] And it's possible to do so while still presuming innocence and guarding against false convictions.

Second, false accusations of sexual assault are rare. Now, it should be noted, there is a heated debate about *how* rare they are.[17] The research is difficult to sift through and those on both sides can make mistakes (although not necessarily to the same degree).[18] For example, it's very common for people to take a single limited study as authoritative.[19] To try and prove that false rape allegations are low, I might cite a study by Cassia Spohn, Clair White, and Katharine Tellis, which found that "the rate of false reports among cases reported to the LAPD [in 2008] was 4.5 percent."[20] But, even though it was well conducted, that's only one study, and 2008 Los Angeles is not necessarily representative of the entire nation. The fallacy of too quickly extrapolating from a small, biased sample to a whole population is called "hasty generalization."[21]

But what can be done is a meta-analysis. Take many studies, use objective criteria for evaluating their quality, "average" them together (so to speak), and then get a range. Something like this is what David Lisak, Lori Gardinier, and Sarah Nicksa did, and they found that, among legally reported cases, "the prevalence of false allegations is between 2% and 10%."[22] Combine that with how unlikely anyone is to be legally accused of rape in the first place and, even by the most generous of estimates, men should actually worry three times more about contracting HIV, drowning, or dying in a house fire. Indeed, by the numbers, men are 15 times more likely to be murdered, than to be falsely accused of rape.[23]

So, even though we do not know *exactly* how rare false accusations are, we do know that they are incredibly rare – so rare that very few people could be rationally concerned about them. Contrary to the claims of English barrister Sir Matthew Hale, rape is not a charge that is easy to make but difficult to disprove. Instead, "rape is a difficult charge to lay and extremely difficult to prove."[24] Concerns about false allegations therefore cannot legitimately be used to dismiss rape allegations and not take them seriously.

Now, to be perfectly fair, sexual assault is only one kind of sexual misconduct. Perhaps the rates of false accusations regarding sexual harassment, unwanted touching, or genital exposure are higher. Reliable data about such forms of sexual misconduct are difficult to find. But one would expect the trend to be similar to that of false reports of sexual assault, and without data to the contrary the claim that the #MeToo movement has put men in grave danger of being falsely accused of anything is baseless. The media attention that #MeToo has received may create a subjective impression that this is the case, but subjective impressions are notoriously unreliable. Without data to back it up, spreading fear about a high probability of false accusations seem to just be thinly veiled attempts to discredit legitimate accusations and protect those who are guilty.

Contrast this with Neil deGrasse Tyson's public comments after he was accused of sexual misconduct.[25] First of all, he accepted that he might have unintentionally offended the victims, and he apologized without reserve to them. Unlike other celebrities who have been publicly accused, he also gave deference to these accusations. Instead of just saying the accusations were false, he acknowledged that all such accusations should be taken seriously: even claims against him should not be ignored. Secondly, he encouraged and said he would cooperate with an independent investigation into the incidents. To guard against the aforementioned dangers of a trial by mob, he also suggested that such an investigation should hear both sides of the story, and that we should all wait until the investigation is concluded to draw conclusions about guilt and innocence. Although it's not perfect, and there could still be (and has been) criticism of Tyson's response, it seems that he has found a decent middle ground in this case – one that could perhaps be embraced by both the accusers and the accused.

So, given the benefits and dangers of online shaming, what should we do? Should we join in if we really feel a wrong has been done and could be corrected? Or should we bow out because of the dangers of trial by mob? Should we aim for some kind of middle ground? And what would that look like? Unfortunately, this problem cannot be ignored. As a commentator on a talk show in the "Hated in the Nation" episode rightly remarked: "this is already happening. And people know that they can jump onboard because nobody will ever know if they did or didn't." But the answer, I believe, involves recognizing two things: people will likely be met by the consequences of their choices, and what makes the difference between a good and a bad choice is one simple thing – responsibility.

With Great Power Comes Great Responsibility

The power of finally bringing justice to ignored victims, and the power of bullying someone to the point of suicide, are two sides of the latent potential of technology. As with any other recent technological advance, we have to learn where the limits are. But as *Black Mirror* is keen to point out, we have not yet seen the whole potential of what technology can bring about. One day someone like Garrett Scholes might pop up and make people pay real consequences for their online behavior. And as long as it does not involve killing them, he'd likely be doing us all a favor. As Sanne Wohlenberg, the series' producer, put it:

> Of course, how terrible for Scholes to respond to one wrong by trying to kill a whole load of other people. And yet it makes you think, "How much responsibility do I take for my own actions in the world of social media, which seems to create some kind of artificial distance?"[26]

In fact, through his infamous hacking scheme, Scholes demonstrates what the philosopher Hannah Arendt (1906–1975) claimed: that ordinary people can be guilty of horrendous evil, especially when they are influenced by a horde mentality and divorced from the evil's consequences by diffused responsibility. This is why Liza Bahar felt it was acceptable to send Jo Powers the "Fucking Bitch" cake. Because she crowdsourced the money, getting $1 from 80 people, she wasn't responsible. By making them face the consequences of their own online mobbing, Scholes is hoping to show people how apparently mild acts can pile on and do real damage.[27]

Inspector Parke seems to also be aware of Arendt's observation that evil-doers can be banal and ordinary. Just after questioning Jo Powers's husband, Coulson, suggests "He was sort of convincing. He just doesn't seem . . ." Parke interrupts. "Don't say 'the type.' He's ordinary. That is the type." Arendt thinks that people who commit evil acts do not do it because they are bad, selfish, greedy, or jealous. More often than not, they are thoughtless, not malicious. Even genocides, such as the Holocaust, are instances of normal people doing evil because the system diffuses their responsibility and takes away their critical thought. In her book *Origins of Totalitarianism*, Arendt explains that the danger lies not in people trying to be evil on purpose, but in them being unaware that they are harming others.[28]

This is related to what Kathryn Norlock calls "the magnitude gap," the "distance between the shamers' perceptions of their objects' great deservingness of harm and light suffering as a result of shaming, and the shamed persons' experiences with actual harm and the deep and lingering effects of online shaming."[29] People just do not appreciate the significant negative impact their online actions have. In the end, the purpose of Scholes's #DeathTo stunt is to show that banality in social media can kill too.

The best way to avoid the banality of evil is by being aware of our own biases, tendencies, and uncritical attitudes so that they can be consciously neutralized step by step. Indeed, many inclusion movements are aimed at ending long-standing unfair attitudes, such as Mental Health discrimination. The world is beginning to look better. With the success of #MeToo and other inclusive movements, and with acceptance of responsibility, we are closer to directing the power of social media to the right place.

It just takes a click to participate in a social media trend, but public denouncements should be taken with care, with consideration of both sides, and with genuine attempts at our best analysis. Although this topic is controversial, in the end, I'm saying something everyone should agree with: the path to finding the best way to make use of social media involves conscious responsibility. Every single user must become aware that their actions might bring about a real change – both good and bad – and therefore accept the responsibility of that power. It will not happen overnight, but if everyone develops the habits and virtues of critical thinking, the power of social media can keep bringing justice to victims while avoiding harm to the innocent. So, the next time you are deciding whether to join in the use of a hashtag in this way, remember your own responsibility. Real people are there, outside the black mirror – both victims and the accused – and you are part of the jury.[30]

For pop culture resources and philosophical resources related to this chapter please visit the website for this book: https://introducingphilosophythroughpopculture.com.

Notes

1   She erroneously assumed that anyone who had previously starred in gay pornography but had not subsequently been tested for an STI would likely infect her. See Horn, T. (2012). Death of a Porn Star. *Rolling Stone Magazine*. https://www.rollingstone.com/culture/culture-features/death-of-a-porn-star-201939 (December 12, 2017).

2   Pilkington, E. (2010). Tyler Clementi, Student Outed as Gay on Internet, Jumps to His Death. *The Guardian*.   https://www.theguardian.com/world/2010/sep/30/tyler-clementi-gay-student-suicide (September 30, 2010)

3   This case even led to another woman getting death threats simply because she had the same name. Emily Longnecker,Other' Holly Jones Targeted by Misguided Outrage Over Viral Kilroy's Post. *WTHR Indianapolis*.   https://www.wthr.com/article/other-holly-jones-targeted-by-misguided-outrage-over-viral-kilroys-post (January 8, 2016).

4   Chuck, E. (2017). Is Social Media Contributing to Rising Teen Suicide Rate?. *NBC News*. https://www.nbcnews.com/news/us-news/social-media-contributing-rising-teen-suicide-rate-n812426 (October 22, 2017).

5   Wells, I. (1892). Southern Horrors: Lynch Law in All its Phases. Preface (University of Houston). http://www.digitalhistory.uh.edu/disp_textbook.cfm?smtid=3&psid=3614.

6   Sunstein, C. (2017). *#republic: Divided Democracy in the Age of Social Media*. Princeton University Press.

7   For a very quick rundown of the research of memory expert Elizabeth Loftus that suggests this, see Rachel Zamzow, Memory Manipulation and the Trouble with Eyewitness Testimony. http://Unearthed.com. https://unearthedmag.wordpress.com/2015/02/14/memory-manipulation-and-the-trouble-with-eyewitness-testimony (February 14, 2015).

8   Norlock, K. (2017). Online shaming. *Social Philosophy Today* 33: 191. The quote appears on page 6 of the pre-publication online draft, which is available at https://philarchive.org/archive/NOROSv1.

9   Rawls, J. (1999). *A Theory of Justice*, Revised Edition. Cambridge, Massachusetts: Harvard University Press.

10 Rawls, 213.

11 This phenomenon was famously noticed by Jon Ronson in his book (2015). *So You've Been Publicly Shamed*. New York: Riverhead Books.

12 Although the phrase "Me Too" was coined in 2006 by Tarana Burke, the #MeToo hashtag didnt even exist until October 15, 2017 – nearly a full year after "Hated in the Nation" was released on October 21, 2016.

13 *Chicago Tribune* Staff. #MeToo: A Timeline of Events. *Chicago Tribune*. https://www.chicagotribune.com/lifestyles/ct-me-too-timeline-20171208-htmlstory.html (Retrieved November 1, 2018).

14 In response to this, one can point to arguments in favor of the "marketplace of ideas," which suggest that even controversial arguments should not be repressed. John Stuart Mill likely put these arguments best in Mill, S. (1978). *On Liberty*. Indianapolis: Hackett Publishing.

15 For example, Christine Blasey Ford couldn't return to her home (even after Brett Kavanagh was confirmed to the Supreme Court) because of death threats. In addition, police seem to ignore accusations of sexual assault in most cases. (See Palmer E. (2018). Christine Blasey Ford Can't Return Home for "Quite Some Time" Due to Continuous Death Threats: Lawyer. *Newsweek*. https://www.newsweek.com/christine-blasey-ford-cant-return-home-continuous-death-threats-1157262 (October 8, 2018); Lopez, G. (2018). Why Didn't Kavanaugh's Accuser Come Forward Earlier? Police Often Ignore Sexual Assault Allegations.   (https://www.vox.com/policy-and-politics/2018/9/19/17878450/kavanaugh-ford-sexual-assault-rape-accusations-police (September 19, 2018). Lopez cites statistics from the Rape, Abuse, and Incest National Network gathered from federal surveys.

16   According to one study, "Most false allegations were used to cover up other [mis]behavior such as adul-
     tery or skipping school." If no such motivation is present, the obligation to take allegations seriously is
     multiplied. See the abstract from De Zutter, A., Horselenberg, R., and van Koppen, P.J. (2017). Motives
     for filing a false allegation of rape. *Archives of Sexual Behavior* 47(2). https://www.researchgate.net/
     publication/313830325_Motives_for_Filing_a_False_Allegation_of_Rape.
17   In a highly contested article, Eugene Kanin claims that 41% of all rape claims are false. (See 1994. False
     rape allegations. *Archives of Sexual Behavior.* 23(1): 81–92.) On the flip side, Cindy Dampier claims that
     men are more likely *be raped* than *falsely accused* of rape. See Your Son is More Likely to be Sexually
     Assaulted Than to Face False Allegations. Explaining the Fear of #HimToo. *Chicago Tribune.* https://www.
     chicagotribune.com/lifestyles/ct-life-false-rape-allegations-20181011-story.html (October 12, 2018). For
     a rundown of the numbers on Dampier's claim, see Lee, G. (2019). Fact Check: Men Are More Likely to
     be Raped Than be Falsely Accused of Rape. Channel http://4.com (October 12, 2019).
18   Moon, E. (2018). False Reports of Sexual Assault Are Rare. But Why is There So Little Reliable Data
     About Them?. *Pacific Standard.* https://psmag.com/news/false-reports-of-sexual-assault-are-rare-but-
     why-is-there-so-little-reliable-data-about-them (October 5, 2018).
19   According to Laura Kipnis, in her book *Unwanted Advances*, the claim that many feminists make about
     how incredibly rare false rape accusations are can be traced back to a study of single police department
     from over 40 years ago. (See Kipnis, L. (2017). *Unwanted Advances*, 165–168. New York: Harper Collins.
     On the flip side, male rights activist often cite the aforementioned discredited Eugene Kanin article.
20   Spohn, C., White C., and Tellis, K. (2014). Unfounding sexual assault: examining the decision to unfound
     and identifying false reports. *Law and Society Review* 48: 161–192. The quote is from the abstract.
21   Another common mistake regards how to count uncorroborated or "unfounded" claims, those that have not
     met the legal standard of reasonable doubt. Confusing them with cases that have been *proven* to be false
     artificially inflates the number of false accusations. (This mistake seems to have been made in the aformen-
     tioned Eugene Kanin article.) Conflating them with those that have been proven true could artificially deflate
     it. (This mistake is arguably made by Joanne Belknap in Heaney, K. (2018). Almost No One Is Falsely Accused
     of Rape. *The Cut.* https://www.thecut.com/article/false-rape-accusations.html (October 5, 2018). Although, it
     should be noted, her argument that false rape allegations are not more common than false allegations for
     other crimes seems sound. (You are 15 times more likely to be falsely convicted of murder than rape.)
22   Lisak, D., Gardinier, L., and Nicksa, S. (2010). False allegations of sexual assault: an analysis of ten years
     of reported cases. *Violence Against Women* 16: 1318–1334. https://cdn.atixa.org/website-media/o_atixa/
     wp-content/uploads/2012/01/18121908/Lisak-False-Allegations-16-VAW-1318-2010.pdf.
23   There were 326 million people in America in 2017, roughly half (163 million) of which were men. In 2017,
     there were around 100 000 cases of reported forcible rape. (See, The Statistics Portal. Number of reported
     forcible rape cases in the United States from 1990 to 2017. https://www.statista.com/statistics/191137/
     reported-forcible-rape-cases-in-the-usa-since-1990). Generously assuming that all rapes in America were
     all done by men (they were not), that means that 0.06% of men in America were legally accused of rape. If
     we go with Lisak's (et al.) highest estimate, which suggests that of 10% of all reported cases are later proven
     false, that means the American male has a 0.006% chance of being legally accused of rape and then it being
     proven false in court. Now, to be fair, that would not include false accusations that are never proven false,
     or online false allegations that are never reported, and those could ruin a life just as easily. But even if we
     very (very!) generously estimate that five times as many that are proven false actually are false, American
     males still only have a 0.03% chance of being falsely accused of rape. That's 1/3000. The odds of contracting
     HIV, dying in a house fire, or dying by drowning are about 1/1000, and the chances of being murdered are
     about 1/200. See Lebowitz, S. (2012). Your Top 20 Fears (and How Much You Should Worry). https://
     greatist.com/health/your-top-20-fears-and-how-much-you-should-worry (January 12, 2012).
24   Lovett, J. and Kelly, L. (2009). Different Systems, similar outcomes? Tracking attrition in reported rape
     cases across Europe. (London Metropolitan University, *Child and Women Abuse Studies Unit*), 111. http://
     kunskapsbanken.nck.uu.se/nckkb/nck/publik/fil/visa/197/different.
25   deGrasse Tyson, N. (2018). On Being Accused., https://m.facebook.com/notes/neil-degrasse-tyson/on-
     being-accused/10156870826326613 [Facebook Update] (December 9, 2018).
26   Brooker, C. and Jones, A. with Arnopp, J. (2018). *Inside Black Mirror*, 218. New York: Crown Archetype.
27   This point was made clear to me while reading Paul Bloom and Matthew Jordan's column, Are We All
     "Harmless Torturers" Now? *The New York Times.* https://www.nytimes.com/2018/08/09/opinion/are-we-
     all-harmless-torturers-now.html (August 9, 2018).
28   Arendt, H. (1951). *The Origins of Totalitarianism.* San Diego: Harcourt, Inc.
29   Norlock, 190 (online version p. 5).
30   The author would like to thank the many anonymous reviewers who helped refine the arguments of this
     chapter.

Part VIII

Eastern Views

Introduction

This book focuses primarily on Western philosophy, which began in ancient Greece in the sixth century BCE. There is, however, another even more ancient tradition, Eastern philosophy, which has its roots in China and India. The seminal figures in Eastern philosophy are the Buddha (c. 560–480 BCE), Confucius (c. 551–479 BCE), and Lao Tzu (born c. 600 BCE). While Eastern philosophy addresses all of the major questions of Western philosophy, it has a different orientation. In the East, philosophy and religion are not as distinctly separated as they are in the West. Instead of focusing on abstract metaphysical questions, Eastern philosophy is primarily concerned with articulating a way of life.

In the Western world, the best-known ideas from Eastern philosophy are Dao and Zen. "Dao" literally means the "way." Not surprisingly, then, Lao Tzu's famous *Daodejing* urges us to follow the Dao, to get in touch with and follow the natural way of the universe. Combining elements of Buddhism (which originated in India) and Daoism (which originated in China), Zen Buddhism has flourished in Japan. Zen emphasizes the intuitive nature of the mind and the importance of living in the immediate experience of the moment.

In Chapter 39, Steve Bein looks to LEGO bricks and *The LEGO Movie* to explain the Daoist concept of the uncarved block and *wei wu wei* (doing without doing). With the help of Daoist sages and LEGO Master Builders, we can learn to try less and yet do more so that "everything is awesome." Continuing our focus on LEGO, in Chapter 40, David Kahn explains a fundamental Buddhist concept, impermanence. According to Buddhist teaching, we suffer because we cling to what is impermanent. In truth, all things are impermanent, and we will suffer until we see and accept this. An ancient Buddhist art form, Mandalas use multicolored sand to create stunning visual displays

Introducing Philosophy Through Pop Culture: From Socrates to Star Wars *and Beyond*, Second Edition.
Edited by William Irwin and David Kyle Johnson.
© 2022 John Wiley & Sons Ltd. Published 2022 by John Wiley & Sons Ltd.

that are subsequently destroyed. We can learn much the same lesson from our own LEGO creations. There is no Kragle or Krazy Glue that can hold our world together. Realizing this should not lead to despair, but to heightened appreciation. In Chapter 41, Steve Bein returns to introduce us to the Zen master Dōgen, whose life and teachings illuminate the positive and negative messages found in Disney films. In short, it's good to adopt a beginner's mind to see the world with a sense of wonder, but escapist fantasies will always return you back to harsh realities.

39

The Brick, the Plate, and the Uncarved Block

LEGO as an Expression of the Dao

Steve Bein

Summary

One of the great virtues of LEGO˚ is that it has the potential to make any one of us a Master Builder. By itself, of course, the brick is silent. It offers potential, not guidance. In this it is like the *dao* of Daoism. *Dao* means "way," and just as there are many ways to build an excellent spaceship out of LEGO, there are many ways to lead an excellent life or to govern a country in an excellent way. We can read the *Daodejing* as a treatise on the latter, but its advice is often cryptic, in much the same way a box of LEGO without an instruction booklet seems directionless. This chapter uses the limitless potential of the LEGO brick as a model for understanding the limitless power of the *dao*, and uses Daoism as a lens for understanding how to become a Master Builder with LEGO.

One of the great virtues of LEGO is that it has the potential to make any one of us a Master Builder. By itself, of course, the brick is silent. It offers potential, not guidance. For that we can turn to instruction booklets, or the MOCs of other creators, or even to the greatest sculptors of history. Auguste Rodin (1840–1917) was a Master Builder if ever there was one, and many a LEGO fan has recreated his famous *Thinker*. What can Rodin teach us about making our own masterpieces?

When asked for his secret to sculpture, Rodin said it was quite simple: "I choose a block of marble and chop off everything I do not need." That may leave you wondering: Has Rodin said nothing about sculpture, or has he said everything?

"Both," says the Daoist sage. It's the sort of answer that makes the most famous figures of Western philosophy want to pull out their hair. From their perspective, the problem with the answer is its lack of clarity. By contrast, from an Eastern perspective, such imprecision can be a virtue. Indeed, the founding text of Daoism is riddled with ambiguity. In one of its most quoted passages, the *Daodejing* says that in order to be a good ruler you have to "return to being the uncarved block."[1] That's it. We get no further context.

Introducing Philosophy Through Pop Culture: From Socrates to Star Wars *and Beyond*, Second Edition.
Edited by William Irwin and David Kyle Johnson.
© 2022 John Wiley & Sons Ltd. Published 2022 by John Wiley & Sons Ltd.

Now what in the world is that supposed to mean? And if it means anything at all, why not spell it out it more clearly?

It's an Invitation, Not a Toy

The *Daodejing* is billed as a work of political philosophy, but paradoxically it says almost nothing about governance in any direct fashion. Even when it does address the subject directly, its advice is about as clear as Rodin's:

> Governing a large state is like cooking a small fish. [. . .]

Look at the state through the state; look at the empire through the empire. [. . .]

> Bring the common people back to keeping their records with knotted string.[2]

At this point the skeptic might ask what makes this a philosophical position, and not mere mumbling? If it's to be political *philosophy*, and not just political *advice*, it's got to give us some specific principles to build upon, doesn't it?

Those questions are founded on an unspoken assumption: that unsettledness and philosophical argument are incompatible. Clearly, the Daoists challenge that assumption. This challenge itself is pretty audacious – as audacious, perhaps, as expecting children to enjoy a box of parts when you could just as easily have given them a toy. That, of course, is exactly the challenge the LEGO Group set out for itself: to sell not toys but parts, and then let the kids do the assembly themselves.

One LEGO brick by itself is not a toy, though, is it? It doesn't *do* anything. What it really is, when you get right down to it, is an invitation. Get a pile of them and you can create any toy you can imagine – and not just toys, but architectural models, works of art, even prosthetic limbs. The only way the brick can do this is by having no standing of its own. It's *because* it's not a toy that it can be the greatest toy ever. By being nothing, it can be anything.

In that way it's actually a perfect model for understanding the *dao*. It also encapsulates what makes open-endedness valuable even when you're trying to do some really important philosophical work, like figuring out what the ideal state would be like and who its ideal ruler would be.

"It's Super Serious, Right, Babe?"

Before we get to the value of open-endedness, let's take a moment to consider the alternative. We should not just *assume* that precision in language is inherently better, any more than we should assume that building a LEGO X-Wing according to the instructions is inherently better than building a spaceship of your own design.

In *The LEGO Movie*, Wyldstyle and Batman present a case study in the value of precision in language. Every time she says their relationship is "super serious," we see he's on edge. He agrees a little too quickly, doesn't he? And he's a little too convincing when he runs off with Han, Chewie, and Lando on the *Millennium Falcon*. Yes, he's duping everyone so he can steal the hyperdrive, but the only reason the deception works is that it's totally in character for him to bail on his girlfriend. When Wyldstyle says "super serious," she's trying to get Batman to commit – that is, to agree on the precise nature of their relationship. It's that drive for precision that gives Batman cold feet. He'd prefer to leave things vague, and in that way he's a bit like the early Daoists.

On the other hand, Wyldstyle's approach is much closer to the dominant traditions of Western philosophy, which you can trace all the way back to ancient Greece. The Greeks were obsessed with precision in a way you don't see in many other places in world history. Plato (428–348 BCE) writes entire dialogues dedicated to defining a single concept: courage in the *Laches*, piety in the *Euthyphro*, friendship in the *Lysis*, virtue in the *Meno*. He seems to have inherited this fascination with precision from his mentor, Socrates (470–399 BCE), and he certainly passed it on to his pupil, Aristotle (384–322 BCE). It's a popular theme throughout Greek philosophy: precision is better than imprecision. Why this preference, and not the other way around?

Here's one reason: choosing just the right words was good for your career in ancient Athens. Unlike most of the ancient world, Athens was a democracy. A young man could make himself immensely powerful if he could convince others to agree with him. Hence the rise of the Sophists, who made quite a name for themselves (and quite a lot of money too) educating wealthy young men in the arts of argument and persuasion. Plato's mentor, Socrates, had little time for sophistry. For him, the purpose of philosophical debate was to find truth, not to score points. He never claimed to have found truth; in fact, he famously insisted he knew nothing at all. He did a lot of thinking about how best to govern, though, and he concluded that you'd have a very hard time knowing how to rule *justly* if you did not know how to define *justice*.

Like the LEGO brick, that Greek distaste for imprecision has proven to be nearly indestructible, such that 2000 years after Socrates, the American philosopher William James (1842–1910) would define philosophy as "the uncommonly stubborn attempt to think clearly." Yet the *Daodejing* has had remarkable staying power too. This may come as a surprise given its famously enigmatic approach, but there's a big difference between Daoist philosophy and the way Batman deals with Wyldstyle: Batman is being deliberately evasive and noncommittal, whereas Daoist imprecision is actually a highly nuanced philosophical stance.

"Actually, it's a Highly Sophisticated Interlocking Brick System"

The unsettledness in the *Daodejing* (also spelled *Tao Te Ching*[3]) starts not from the first chapter, nor from the first page, nor even from the first line. Scholars can't even agree on the title. In one English translation it's *Te-Tao Ching*, and in fact the traditional title is simply the *Laozi* (also spelled *Lao Tzu*).[4] That's supposedly the name of its author, but one of the (few) things scholars can agree on is that no one named Laozi ever existed.

So, in a sense our springboard is a book without a title or an author. Laozi himself is built out of history's LEGO, and so is the *Daodejing*. In Laozi's case, the bricks and plates are a bunch of stories, remarks, and references in other works, all pointing at whoever it was who wrote the passages we now call the *Daodejing*. Similarly, there isn't an "official" or "original" *Daodejing*, but rather a series of constructions made by various contributors. What we have today is a received text that can be traced back to a number of different documents – its bricks and plates, so to speak – and over the years, different scholars have stuck them together in different arrangements.

Little wonder, perhaps, that we can apply this composite philosophical tradition to the composite brick system that is LEGO.

"No Government, no Babysitters . . . and There's Also No Consistency"

The *Daodejing* is a challenging text, and one of its many challenges is that it never concretely defines *dao*. *Dao* is usually translated into English as "way" (or "Way," or even "the Way"), and that's not a bad translation so long as you keep in mind all the meanings "way" has in English. In *The LEGO Movie*, Princess Unikitty would be able to show you the way to Cloud Cuckoo Land (a geographical route), the way to remove a bushy mustache (a technique), the way to create an entire realm without rules or consistency (a system of techniques), or the way to be happy all the time (a philosophical approach). *Dao* can be any of those ways. Notice that those ways aren't *things*. They're closer to *activities*, and this highlights two important concepts in Daoist thought. First, a way is not a permanent, unchanging entity. As any backpacker knows, the way from A to B is really more like an ongoing process, changing season by season and sometimes even day by day. Second, there's not *one* way. For any given destination, there's probably more than one path to get you there, and for any given path there's more than one way to walk it.

That's the message of the very first sentence of the *Daodejing*: "Way-making (*dao*) that can be put into words is not really way-making."[5] The early Daoists were leery of any attempt to define *dao* in specific terms. Definition is a kind of limitation, and *dao* defies all limits. We'd encounter a similar problem if we tried to fully unpack the "awesome" of "everything is awesome." It's hard to define "awesome," but not because you don't know what you're talking about and not because you have nothing to say. The problem is quite the opposite. No matter how much you say, you'll always have left something out. That's the only way definition can work – *this* is only *this* if it's not *that*. So if the thing you're talking about is broad enough, and casts its influence widely enough, any attempt at definition must always fall short.

Throughout the *Daodejing* we find a willingness to describe, but a deep reluctance to define. For example:

> As a thing the way [dao] is
> Shadowy, indistinct.
> Indistinct and shadowy,
> Yet within it is an image;
> Shadowy and indistinct,
> Yet within it is a substance.
> Dim and dark,
> Yet within it is an essence.
> This essence is quite genuine
> And within it is something that can be tested.[6]

The concept of awesomeness works the same way. Can you define it concretely? No, not without leaving something out. But can you test it? Absolutely. If I say "that ski slope is awesome" you can go ski it and see for yourself. The same goes for awesome restaurants, awesome jiujitsu instructors, awesome LEGO sets, you name it: if you're open to the experience, you can test it for yourself. So it is with *dao*. There is *dao* latent in the snowy mountainside, and if you align yourself with it, you can ski it beautifully. There is a *dao* of cooking, and of jiujitsu, and of designing with LEGO. Those who understand this *dao* can do things that amaze and delight and make the rest of us marvel.

The artist Nathan Sawaya is a case in point. He began by recreating masterpieces of classical art in LEGO: Hokusai's *Great Wave off Kanagawa*, Leonardo's *Mona Lisa*, Michelangelo's *David*. Had he reproduced them in their original medium, he'd be little more than a mimic, but Sawaya understands the *dao* of LEGO. His Hokusai is five layers thick, so his *Great Wave* has a texture and depth beyond what the original woodblock can deliver. He doesn't just imitate; he evokes, then delivers something entirely new – and the most stunning part is, you could have done it yourself if only you'd thought of it first. The pieces were always there. The possibility was always there. Sawaya was the sage who put them together.

In Daoism, the sages were masters who had aligned themselves with the *dao* of their chosen vocation. Here's how the *Daodejing* describes the sages of ancient times:

Those of old who were good at forging their way (*dao*) in the world:

> Subtle and mysterious, dark and penetrating,
> Their profundity was beyond comprehension.
> It is because they were beyond comprehension
> That were I forced to describe them, I would say:
> So reluctant, as though crossing a winter stream;
> So vigilant, as though in fear of the surrounding neighbors;
> So dignified, like an invited guest;
> So yielding, like ice about to thaw;
> So solid, like the uncarved block;
> So murky, like muddy water;
> So vast and vacant, like a mountain gorge.[7]

Notice two images here: first, the uncarved block we've seen already; second, the vast and vacant mountain gorge. It turns out both of these are also images of LEGO.

Let us examine the gorge first. It's a fitting image for *dao* because it is inexhaustible. You can use it all day long and never wear it out. Why not? Because the part of the gorge you can see – the cliffs that wall it in – is actually the least important part. What makes a gorge gorgeous is all the empty space. This amazing power of emptiness is perfectly exemplified by the LEGO brick. At its most basic level, your standard 2 × 4 brick is more nothing than it is something; that is, by volume there's more empty air than there is plastic. Why is it awesome? Because it marries the something to the nothing. If it did not, the bricks could not stick together. But because of this perfect marriage of something and nothing – *yin* and *yang*, in Daoist terms – it's the greatest toy ever.

But the brick isn't just physically empty; it's also empty of *meaning*, just like the uncarved block. Suppose you are a sculptor and I hand you an ordinary block of wood. You're now holding limitless possibilities. The block can become *anything*, right up until the moment you shave off a piece. After that, there are some shapes it can't take anymore. The more you take off, the more you limit what's possible: once it starts to look like a person, it's pretty hard to make it into a spoon or a spaceship.[8] We can think of the LEGO brick in the same way. By itself it's empty of meaning, and that's exactly why it can be anything you want it to be: because by itself it's nothing.

If your basic 2 × 4 brick is the "uncarved block," LEGO makes "carved" ones too: cockpits, irregular minifig heads, all those cool greeblies. But the more an element is designed to look like something specific, the less versatile it becomes. Print a design on it or put a sticker on it and you end up with less, not more. As the *Daodejing* describes it, "Thus a thing is sometimes added to by being diminished, and diminished by being added to."[9]

"They're Expecting Us to Show Up in a Bat-Spaceship

Here's where we get to political philosophy. In the case of the LEGO brick, the less it's like a toy, the better you can play with it. According to the Daoists, government is no different: the less it does, the better it works. That doesn't mean abdicating responsibility altogether. Rather, the goal is to be as effective as possible with as little intervention as possible. There's a Daoist term for this: *wei wu wei*, literally "doing without doing." Water is especially good at this. It's gentle, not coercive. It flows, it does not hammer. It always follows the path of least resistance, and because it's like this, it's one of the strongest forces on the planet.

As such, water itself is an inspiration for the Daoists. Effortless power is just one of its many virtues. Water is beneficial to everyone, seeking nothing in return. It's noncompetitive, always happy to sink to the lowest places. It doesn't play favorites. And it expresses all of these virtues through *wei wu wei*.

Emmet Brickowski is by turns a total doofus and a master of *wei wu wei*. (This is perfectly in keeping with Daoism. One of the themes of the early texts is that it's often hard to tell the difference between a fool and a sage.) Everyone wants him to devise some ingenious plan to break into Lord Business's tower, but instead of designing a Bat-spaceship, a pirate spaceship, or a rainbow-sparkle spaceship, he designs . . . well, nothing. Better to build what's already there: a plain old Octan delivery spaceship, so ordinary that it might as well be invisible. No inspiration, no ingenuity, no cleverness at all – and that's exactly why his plan works. Keep It Simple, Stupid.

This is the point of that cryptic line we considered earlier: "Governing a large state is like cooking a small fish."[10] The trick to cooking a small fish is to handle it as little as possible. Fuss with it too much and it falls apart in the pan. The best spatula in the world can't help you; what you really need is highly skilled attentiveness to very subtle changes. After that, it's all *wei wu wei*: minimal intervention for maximal effect. One flip and you're done.

For the sage, statecraft is no different: legislate well and you won't have to legislate often. This approach is anything but standoffish; a ruler needs to be every bit as attentive and skillful as a master chef. The ideal result is that "with the most excellent rulers, their subjects only know that they are there."[11]

The objection, of course, is that this is still too imprecise. Yes, we ought to *try* less and *do* more, but to what end? After all, this *wei wu wei* stuff can be used for evil just as easily as for good, can't it? Lord Business had several options when it came to beheading poor Vitruvius. He could have built an elaborate decapitating device, maybe something like a Micromanager. Instead he just threw a penny at him. Does this make Lord Business an evil sage?

No. It's true that he stepped outside of the conceptual confines that everyone else operates within. That much looks like sagacity. And it's true that he found the path of least resistance, and in doing so he accomplished exactly what he sought to accomplish. But he's missed the most important part of *wei wu wei*: the whole point is to be non-coercive, to benefit everyone, to be fair-minded – in short, to flow like water. Instead, Lord Business's every effort is to coerce the world into the shape he wants it. Thus while he may be a genius, he's not a sage.

That said, the initial worry still remains: the problem of imprecision. If the Daoist says the ruler should take a minimalist approach, we must still ask how. Which laws do we keep and which do we repeal? Which areas should this unassuming government watch closely, and which should it leave entirely to the people? And if we can't find an answer to any of those questions, is this minimalist approach so minimal that it says nothing at all?

"Everything is Awesome!"

As we've seen, one of the most telling differences between ancient Greek philosophy and ancient Chinese philosophy lies in their attitudes toward imprecision. It was anathema to the Greeks, yet the Chinese were quite comfortable with it. A philosopher like Plato or Aristotle will say – rightly, I think – that without more detail, it's hard to tell whether the *Daodejing* supports Democrats or Republicans, Greens or Libertarians (or for that matter, red ants or black ants). On the other hand, the authors of the *Daodejing* are also right to be suspicious of specificity. Too often one-size-fits-all means one-size-fits-poorly. What works for King A might not work for Queen B, and what worked last year might not work next year. Thus, it's better for rulers to take *wei wu wei* as their default position and then judge each novel situation on its own merits.

LEGO Master Builders understand this. Perhaps you've seen the video that went viral of a young woman building her own prosthetic leg out of LEGO. She doesn't have an instruction booklet; she only has a goal. Through time-lapse photography we watch her test the fit of the new LEGO limb, see how well it bears weight, pull a few pieces off, stick a few on, test-fit it, modify it, test it again. This is the Daoist model of government: commit yourself to the goal (in this case, a harmonious nation of flourishing citizens), be willing to be flexible, and *voilà*, you've freed yourself of the tyranny of the instruction booklet. Will you make mistakes along the way? Sure, but that's exactly why you don't want to take a heavy-handed approach. Like Rodin, shave off all the parts you don't need. Be empty in your politics: throw out parties, platforms, and ideologies, aligning yourself instead with the *dao*.

Or don't. Sit at home with your LEGO and build to your heart's content. That's another teaching of the *Daodejing*: "There is no crime greater than having too many desires; there is no disaster greater than not being content."[12] For millions of adults and children around the world, sitting down to a big pile of LEGO is the very picture of contentment. The fact that it appeals to so many, of so many ages, in so many cultures, over so many decades, is arguably due to its *dao*. Because it's empty, it contains infinite possibilities; because it tries to be nothing, it's capable of being anything; because you can't its awesomeness in words, it expresses awesomeness to everyone, everywhere, in every language.[13]

For pop culture resources and philosophical resources related to this chapter please visit the website for this book: https://introducingphilosophythroughpopculture.com.

Notes

1 (1962). *Tao Te Ching*, 28 (trans. D.C. Lau). London: Penguin.
2 *Daodejing*60, 54, 80. Chapters 60 and 54 are D.C. Lau's translation, and chapter 80 is (2003). *Daodejing: Making This Life Significant* (trans. R.T. Ames and D.L. Hall). New York: Ballantine. In this chapter I'll switch between the Ames and Hall translation, which is the most philosophically accurate, and Lau's, which is more accessible.
3 *Tao Te Ching* is how it's spelled following a Romanization transliteration system called Wade-Giles. Spelling it *Daodejing* follows the pinyin system, which most scholars use these days, and which I'll be using throughout this chapter. Pronunciation is identical in both systems – so, for example, *tao* should be pronounced with a "D," not a "T," and one reason many students of Chinese prefer pinyin is that it looks closer to the proper pronunciation.
4 Henricks, Robert, G. (1989). Henricks' translation is called *Te-Tao Ching*. New York: Ballantine. Lao Tzu is the Wade-Giles spelling of Laozi.
5 *Daodejing*, 1, Hall and Ames translation.
6 *Tao Te Ching*, 21, Lau translation.
7 *Daodejing*, 15, Hall and Ames translation. For purposes of consistency I've taken the liberty of replacing "unworked wood," their translation of *pǔ*, with Lau's "uncarved block."
8 Spaceship!
9 *Tao Te Ching*, 42, Lau translation.
10 *Tao Te Ching*, 54, Lau translation.
11 *Daodejing*, 17, Hall and Ames translation.
12 *Daodejing*, 46, Lau translation.
13 I'm indebted to David Levy and Myrna Gabbe for their helpful insights on Greek philosophy.

40

LEGO, Impermanence, and Buddhism

David Kahn

Summary

The true LEGO lesson is that nothing is static; life is in a state of perpetual change. This Buddhist-based ideal recognizes *anicca*, i.e. the impermanency of all conditioned things, and celebrates the dynamic nature of the world. With all things, including LEGO, we need to value the process and revel in creativity without becoming attached. Nothing is meant to last forever. The faster we embrace this mindset, the more fulfilled our lives will be.

Growing up, I found myself in a relentless battle between appreciating my LEGO masterpieces and adding a coat of superglue to preserve them for the ages. If this sounds unusual, my eight-year-old self would tell you that what is really unusual is creating a work of art only to destroy it at clean up time. In the end, I conceded to take it apart, but it was always begrudgingly and not without first begging my mom to take a picture for posterity.

Thirty years later, I watch in amazement as my kids spend hours building a LEGO tower only to knock it down in a fit of laughter. No qualms. No pouting. No pictures to reminisce for all of history. They enjoy the construction and the destruction.

The battle between my childhood disposition to preserve and my kids' disposition to destroy is typical. *The LEGO Movie* explores this idea when Finn, the hero of the movie, is reprimanded for "ruining" his father's elaborate LEGO structure. Once Finn's father realizes that the villain in his son's scenario is based on him and his use of Kragle (Krazy Glue), the lesson of the movie (and of LEGO) emerges – nothing is static; life is in a state of perpetual change.

Change is commonly resisted. When leadership expert John Kotter researched this idea in his book *Leading Change*, he found that 70% of all workplace change programs fail.[1] Likewise, when studying dietary changes, psychologist Traci Mann discovered that 66% of people claiming a desire to lose weight regained more weight post-diet than they started with, and when studying changes resulting from New Year's resolutions, psychologist Richard Wiseman observed an 88% failure rate.[2]

Introducing Philosophy Through Pop Culture: From Socrates to Star Wars *and Beyond*, Second Edition.
Edited by William Irwin and David Kyle Johnson.
© 2022 John Wiley & Sons Ltd. Published 2022 by John Wiley & Sons Ltd.

Accepting change can be difficult, but not changing can be fatal. A company's long-term survival is based on its ability to evolve in an ever-changing industrial landscape. Someone with unhealthy eating habits must be willing to alter their diet to match their lifestyle. And resolutions are an indicator that you are not satisfied with some aspect of your life and feel the need to make a change.

Despite our best efforts, every aspect of life is in a state of flux. To adapt is to survive. That is why we must learn to embrace the Buddhist philosophy of impermanence.

What is Impermanence?

According to Buddhist teachings, all things have a transient nature. Whether that thing is tangible or intangible, organic or inorganic, it is undergoing a constant process of change. This is the essence of impermanence – reality is never stagnant but is dynamic throughout.

In the traditional Buddhist scripture Digha Nikay ("Collection of Long Discourses"), Buddha (c. 563– 480 BCE) is quoted as saying:

> Impermanent are all component things,
> They arise and cease, that is their nature:
> They come into being and pass away,
> Release from them is bliss supreme.[3]

This can be translated for the LEGO aficionado as:

> Impermanent are all aspects of LEGO,
> They assemble and are dismantled, that is their nature:
> The creative things you build come into being and are put away,
> What we gain from LEGO is bliss supreme.

If we cling to something (the current state of a relationship, a time in our life, a particularly impressive LEGO configuration), we will feel anxiety when it changes. However, when we avoid clinging, there is no anxiety. We are quicker to accept the change, thereby experiencing a painless adjustment (allowing relationships to evolve, aging gracefully, discovering new LEGO configurations with which to shock and amaze).

People who tightly cling to ideas feel stress when they are wrong or when the idea becomes outdated. They typically come up with reasons and excuses to rationalize their decisions, holding onto behavior patterns or to a self-image even when it no longer benefits them. We all experience this to some degree; it can be difficult to change once we've found something that works. Buddhist philosophy, however, teaches that clinging is always unfavorable, even when the thing to which we cling has a positive effect. In his book *Positive Addiction*, famed psychiatrist William Glasser argues that compulsive habits such as jogging and transcendental meditation "strengthen us and make our lives more satisfying."[4] Yet, while these activities enhance health, creativity, and feelings of self-efficacy, Buddhist teachings warn against becoming dependent.

If you cling to daily meditation or exercise, you will feel anxiety on the days you break your routine – whether you have skipped a session or did not perform at your best, there's a sense of shame. To avoid this counterproductive stress, impermanence helps us eliminate our attachments. By removing them, we remove the delusions and trappings of false security, thus equipping ourselves for life's barrage of rapid-fire change and getting us closer to the Buddhist idea of Nirvana.

When we look at LEGO bricks, their impermanence is evident. For instance, the materials that make up a LEGO brick changed from Cellulose Acetate to Acrylonitrile Butadiene Styrene (ABS) in the 1960s. Some bricks have thinner walls with different shaped tubes when compared to their 1980s predecessors. Instructions are much more complex than they were 20 years ago, with some booklets containing hundreds of pages separated into multiple books. Even the LEGO logo has gone through multiple variations over the years – 12 at last count.

The process of change can be slow and incremental, yet it is constant and inevitable in all aspects of existence. While much change takes place without our ever noticing, impermanence is verifiable through direct observation. It may require patience, but it is there. A LEGO piece left in direct sunlight will take months before you realize its color has faded, and even then you may need another LEGO brick to distinguish the difference. However, since LEGO utilizes aerospace-like industry standards to mold their bricks, it is improbable that they will undergo significant physical changes. More likely, your perception of these bricks will evolve long before the pieces themselves do.

Consider the way you perceive a particular LEGO piece. The 1 × 4 blue brick with bow that was once associated with the roof of the LEGO Cinderella's Dream Carriage (set #41053) is now unidentifiable in a Tupperware container of assorted sets. And the structure you once believed to be the Da Vinci of all LEGO works is a pale comparison to what you are able to create today. Skills evolve, experience accumulates, and every LEGO project raises the bar for your next endeavor.

Benefits of an Impermanent Mindset

Understanding impermanence is necessary if we are to lead fulfilling, productive lives. In our relationships, how often are friendships made in the LEGO aisle of a store? How often do alliances deteriorate because someone refuses to share their LEGO blueprints? How often does a boyfriend evolve from a Non-LEGO spouse (NLS) into a LEGO enthusiast? And how often does an adult fan of LEGO (AFOL) become the parent of LEGO-loving kids?

Our relations with others are entirely marked by impermanence. When we fight this, we tend to put others in a box. We get locked into who someone is without allowing them room to grow and change over time. Then, when the change becomes too noticeable to ignore, we call them a fraud because they no longer match the person we somehow decided they were always going to be. Their growth was always happening, yet we feel betrayed because we became fixated on their imagined permanent state. This is true when we write off our LEGO-building buddies for only wanting to spend half their free-time on LEGO-related activities, and when we do not accept a newbie to the LEGO life because they haven't enjoyed LEGO as long as we have. In both instances, we are not allowing change, thereby alienating ourselves from reality and more meaningful bonds. Here we can learn a lesson from Buddhism.

Even in death, Buddhist practices celebrate the ever-changing nature of the world. At funerals, flowers and lit oil lamps are ceremonially placed before the statue of Buddha. This is not intended to be a prayer to Buddha, but to acknowledge that as the flowers wilt and the flames subside, so does the state of all things. As the Buddha said:

> Life is like a floating cloud which appears.
> Death is like a floating cloud which disappears.
> The floating cloud itself originally does not exist.[5]

Funeral attendees are then asked to "remember death" for this will discourage excessive desire and remind us of our own ultimate impermanence. From the moment of birth, we move inexorably toward death. It is easy (and understandable) to view this as bleak, but Buddhist philosophy does not emphasize death to depress us. Instead, the certainness of death is intended to motivate us to make the most of our time by not getting fixated on petty, unimportant items. LEGO is no different.

From the moment a new LEGO set goes on sale, it is one step closer to being discontinued. The set may still exist on eBay, but the opportunity to buy a new set will never be available again. Once you purchase it, the LEGO set progresses inescapably toward the land of misfit toys. You can do everything possible to preserve them, but the unventilated attic will not allow your LEGO to remain in "good as new" condition. Even if the LEGO bricks manage to retain their freshness, the pieces will quickly decay once you pass your LEGO collection on to your children.

Finally, impermanence is key to understanding the ultimate nature of life. With all things being perishable, we begin to see their lack of substantial existence. This is true for ourselves and for the world around us. In a sense, impermanence is the property of "not-self." To explain, self is a convenient term for a collection of your physical and mental personal experiences. It is no different than using the name "LEGO Star Wars Death Star" for a collection of LEGO pieces that when assembled, creates the iconic Star Wars structure. The gray, rectangular plates are not the LEGO Star Wars Death Star (set # 10188). Neither is the hallway structure, the elevator pulley, or the Darth Vader figure.

The LEGO Star Wars Death Star illustrates the basis for the Buddhist rejection of the self. To disagree is to believe in the existence of something that does not exist, an independent, permanent entity. There is no core of personal experience apart from the ever-shifting, inter-reliant, transitory elements of our beliefs, and behaviors, and judgments, just as there is no LEGO Star Wars Death Star without its 3803 pieces.

By denying self, we begin to recognize that personal experience is like our aforementioned LEGO Star Wars Death Star. When we dismantle it brick by brick, systematically examining each piece, we find that the self, like the Death Star, lacks any substantial permanent essence, that it is bereft of the sum of self. Then, once we remove the delusion of seeing things as permanent, wisdom occurs. Wisdom is truth – seeing the world as it really is, understanding our strengths and weakness without ego, appreciating others for who they really are. And when this wisdom is embraced, personal experiences can then be fully experienced. So let's dismantle our personal experiences.

Aggregates of Impermanence

We are all made up of a collection of our personal experiences. This assortment of experiences makes up the five aggregates of Buddhism. As per Buddha's teaching in the Samyutta Nikaya, "When you understand that form, sensation, perception, formations, and consciousness are impermanent then you understand right view." The aggregates – form, sensation, perception, formations, and consciousness – serve as the impermanent elements that work together to produce the mind–body entity of a person. One is not more important than another and, like the various pieces needed to construct a LEGO creation, all play a part in the various ways we experience life.

The aggregate of form serves as the initial way we observe the world. This encompasses the ways our five senses enable us to experience material objects. Form is how we *see* the studs on a LEGO brick, how we *hear* two pieces snap together, how we *smell* a bowl of LEGO figures melting in the microwave (this was a childhood experiment that I would not recommend), how pieces *taste* when dipped in pudding (another inadvisable experiment), and the way a stud *feels* when you step on it with bare feet. Each experience is a momentary observation with no judgment or interpretation. That comes with the next few aggregates.

With any personal experience, the aggregate of sensation dictates that it can take on one of three emotional tones – pleasure, pain, or indifference. Ever try to interlock four dozen LEGO pieces into your hair to create a multi-colored mohawk? No, just me? The cool sensation of the plastic on my scalp was pleasant; taking it out, however, was unpleasant. I write this not to brag about my LEGO hairstyling skills, but to demonstrate that the same object can lend itself to different sensations, which further exhibits its impermanence.

Just as sensation produces an emotional reaction, the aggregate of perception is based around recognition. Perception helps us formulate an idea about an object of experience and attach a name to it. It is like seeing your son's latest LEGO composition and not being able to figure out what it is – it could be a car, or a plane. Then, once he tells you that it is an elephant, your perception is formed and you are able to turn your indefinite perceptual experience into an established idea.

After an established idea has been formed, the aggregate of mental formation determines our response. This involves opinions, prejudices, and compulsions as learned from previous experiences. Unlike the emotional or identifying responses, mental formations take on a moral dimension – wholesome, unwholesome, or neutral. If you have a positive experience building the intricately detailed LEGO Eiffel Tower (set #10181), you will consider this experience wholesome and respond by intentionally challenging yourself to build another complex LEGO set. Conversely, if the experience was frustrating, you will consider this experience unwholesome and your mental formation may direct you to attempt a simpler LEGO project or leave you screaming at the site of the catastrophe.

The last of the five aggregates is indispensable in its influence on experience. Consciousness is our awareness of an object. It occurs by utilizing perception and mental formation to establish a holistic, meaningful impression of the entity. Consciousness enables you to envision a potential LEGO configuration without having to rely on the cover of the box. It allows you to compare your imagination-based blueprints with the available LEGO pieces, adjust your schematics, and work at a speed that takes into account how quickly your "friend" is using the pieces you need.

The five aggregates of impermanence help us discern the rapidly changing interconnected acts of cognition. Together, they produce personal experiences and reinforce the ephemeral nature of existence. For instance, let's say you walk into your daughter's room. As you enter, your eyes come into contact with a visible object. As your vision focuses, your consciousness becomes aware of the as-yet indeterminate object. Perception will identify that object as your limited-edition Taj Mahal LEGO set (# 10189) that, until today, was in new, unwrapped mint condition. You then respond with the sensation of displeasure. Finally, mental formation leads you to react by crying or, if you can regain your composure, perhaps helping your daughter with the finishing details.

The physical and mental factors of our personal experience, the objects all around us, our minds and ideas are continually changing. They are processes, not enduring things. You were trying to keep the vintage LEGO set in a permanent state, but it was aging regardless of whether your daughter tore open the box. Even your perception of the Taj Mahal set was changing – what you once considered a "cool toy" transformed into "an investment that will one day pay for my daughter's college tuition" until you saw your daughter's enjoyment and perceived it as a "bonding activity." To gain a deeper understanding, let's move beyond a 10-year-old limited edition LEGO set and explore a much older art form.

The LEGOs of Impermanence

Thousands of years before the advent of LEGO, Tibetan Buddhist monks were mastering the MOC (My Own Creation). LEGO enthusiasts recognize the MOC as a LEGO creation that they designed and built (as opposed to using the provided instructions). The monks, however, were doing it with mandalas.

Mandalas are an ancient, sacred form of Buddhist art. Mandalas and LEGO are similar in that both are colorful, imaginative displays of creativity. Where they differ is in how the multicolored plastic pieces are replaced with multicolored sand.

The mandala is meant to represent impermanence. If imagining the creation and destruction of the universe sounds overwhelming, these elaborate exhibitions of artistic talent bring the abstract idea of temporariness into a more tangible, bite-size depiction. They also offer ways to further enhance our LEGO building experience.

Per the ancient Buddhist traditions that are still practiced today, the monks begin a mandala by determining its intention. The theme, which can focus on such topics as compassion or wisdom, is aligned with particular deities and geometric patterns to infuse the unique spiritual and sacred qualities that each mandala possesses. Once a theme is decided, the monks consecrate the site through music, meditation, and mantra recitation.

With a mental blueprint of the mandala, the monks then begin to draw the lines for the design on a table, which will serve as the base for the mandala. They measure out the architectural lines using a straight-edged ruler, a compass, and a white ink pen. Because every detail is deliberate from the design to the colors to the placement of symbols, this preparatory process can take days to complete.

Once the outline is complete, the team begins to gently place the sand granules along the drawing. Using small tubes, funnels, and scrapers, they create vibrations with the tools that cause the sand to slowly spill out, almost grain by grain, until the entire pattern is covered. Nothing holds the sand in place and there is no room for error; even a small sneeze would ruin it. The finished product is approximately the size of a queen-size bed, and will take days or weeks to complete based upon the precision of the work.

Unlike most art that is intended to last for the ages, after all the time and effort has been exerted to create the mandala, this stunning display of artistry is destroyed. In a Dissolution Ceremony the monks ritualistically dismantle the mandala, removing the colored sand. Some of the sand is distributed to the audience as a blessing for health and healing; what remains is collected and released back into nature.

How much of the mandala process sounds like your use of LEGO elements? Let's break it down. Both begin with a mental picture of what you want to create. Your LEGO build's theme may not be as altruistic as to embody world peace, but you don't begin building without some intention of what you would like to create. Plus, who's to say your LEGO Batman's Batboat Harbor Pursuit (set # 76032) is not as impactful or as life altering as the mandala that the Dalai Lama commissioned depicting the paradise of Avelokitshevara, the Buddha of Compassion?

Once you have an idea of what you will be making, it is time to prepare. We do not need to draw the sophisticated diagrams that the monks require, but that does not mean the planning stage should be overlooked. How much space do you have to work? How much time can you dedicate to it? And the question I rarely ask but always regret not asking, do I have the LEGO pieces needed to fulfill my expectations? You cannot make a mandala without a few pounds of sand just as you cannot build a life-size Kermit the Frog without a generous supply of green LEGO bricks.

Now that you have your schematics and have taken inventory of the needed materials, construction begins. As the monks scrutinize every grain of sand, you vigilantly choose each LEGO piece. A round brick cannot replace a cone just as pre-2003 light gray plates are not synonymous with their more bluish post-2003 "light bley" brethren. Minor details? Maybe, but art is intentional and purposeful.

With meticulous craftsmanship, your structure is finally complete. This is the perfect time to bask in the glory of your fine work. Rope off a viewing area so others can stop by to check it out. Take stock of what you've accomplished. Then, once you've received your share of accolades, it is time for your LEGO creation to follow in the ways of the mandala and begin its ceremonial demolition.

We all follow a different method for disassembling LEGO. Some take a set apart piece by piece so as to sort each bit into its respective plastic bags, thereby preserving newness and keeping it systematically organized for next time. Others take a more Godzilla-like approach where the structure is punched, swatted, kicked, and beaten into dismantled mess. Either way, the creation is no more.

Like my childhood obsession with supergluing LEGO bricks, some have tried to fight the mandala's temporariness. Back in 1992, Robert Jacobsen, the curator of Asian Art at the Minneapolis Institute of Arts, led an experiment where adhesive sand could harden into a "permanent" mandala capable of being hung on a wall. While technically a success, Jacobsen seems to miss the point – destruction of a mandala, like dismantling LEGO creations, demonstrates that beauty is only meant for this world for a short time.

By wittingly putting effort into a temporary piece of art, we reveal the fleeting nature of all material life. This is the very core of impermanence. It is a reminder that existence has a beginning, middle, and end. Then, once we've accepted the unremitting cyclical changes, it frees us to return to a mindset of infinite possibility where we no longer search for finality but rest in unbound awareness.

The creation of art, transitory or otherwise, involves skill acquired through practice and effort. An eye for detail separates a casual pastime from the creation of your chef d'oeuvre. If the particulars can be overlooked, at what point does your LEGO project become a mishmash of rainbow warrior-like chaos where you no longer attempt to coordinate colors?

Once your efforts become infused with lackluster motivation, it is a slippery slope to an inner monologue of, "Why bother starting a LEGO project if it is just going to be taken apart anyway?" This nihilistic reaction toward impermanence not only runs counter to Buddhist philosophy, but can only lead to a dissatisfied life. After all, with all things being momentary, a "Why Should I Care?" attitude would expand beyond LEGO, a mandala, or any other form of art you use to express yourself. You'd be left in a state of never bothering to do anything because it will inevitably come to a close.

Impermanence is not an occasion for sorrow, but rather recognition for the unavoidable realization that reality is in a perpetual state of change. It is a time to acknowledge that all things will end, appreciate the time spent doing it, and celebrate how it has enriched our life. This frees us from trying to "superglue" our worldview through failed attempts to keep everything as is or becoming overly fixated on any one goal or object. We can then adopt a renewed vigilance to remain open to new experiences, for as every LEGO project ends, another is soon to follow.

For pop culture resources and philosophical resources related to this chapter please visit the website for this book: https://introducingphilosophythroughpopculture.com.

Notes

1   Cotter, J. (2012). *Leading Change*. Cambridge, MA: Harvard Business Review Press).

2   Mann, T. (2015). *Secrets from the Eating Lab: The Science of Weight Loss, the Myth of Weight Loss, and Why You Should Never Diet Again*. New York: Harper Wave; Blame it on the Brain: The Latest Neuroscience Research Suggests Spreading Resolutions Out Over Time is the Best Approach. *The Wall Street Journal*. http://www.wsj.com/articles/SB10001424052748703478704574612052322122442 (December 26, 2009).

3   Wijesekara, O.H.deA. (1981). *The Three Signata, Anicca, Dukkha, Anatta*. Kandy, Sri Lanka: Buddhist Publication Society.

4   Glasser, W. (1976). *Positive Addiction*. New York: Harpercollins.

5   Sahn, S. (2013). *Only Don't Know: Selected Teaching Letters of Zen Master Seung Sahn* Boulder: Shambhala Publications.

41

Zen and the Art of Imagineering

Disney's Escapism Versus Buddhism's Liberation

Steve Bein

Summary

The Walt Disney Company is arguably the world's largest creator and distributor of escapism. Its films and characters are especially popular with children, and one reason for that is that many of its most iconic characters are child heroes who do strange and wonderful things once they escape adult supervision. A core philosophical principle underlying Disney's multimedia empire is, "Hey, kid, you can be a hero." In contrast, Buddhism promises not escape but liberation. It says escapism can only lead us to misery, and we will find peace only when we come to grips with the reality of our existence as fragile, temporary, dependent beings. Imagining the thirteenth-century Zen master Dōgen as the protagonist of a Disney film, this chapter highlights the difference between escape and liberation.

Syndrome, that self-styled nemesis of Mr. Incredible, has a retirement plan worthy of Walt Disney himself. Both he and Disney created products that just about everyone in the world wants to have. While Disney sold escapism and wonder, Syndrome wants to sell superpowers. As he famously quipped, "Everyone can be super. And when everyone's super, no one will be."

Strangely enough, Syndrome's decree lines up with a basic tenet of Zen Buddhism. Zen says all beings possess something called "buddha-nature," the intrinsic potential to become a buddha – that is, an enlightened being, a paragon of wisdom and compassion. Zen says enlightenment is latent in buddha-nature itself, so in effect everyone *is* super. The trick is just figuring out how that's true.

Obviously that's not what Syndrome had in mind. Originally his decree was probably just a commentary about the modern parenting ideal that every child is equally special. (*The Incredibles* itself is the extended commentary.) But the keen philosophical ear detects a deeper message, one that resonates in so many of Disney's most enduring films. It's the dream that any kid can be a hero. One trait many Disney heroes have in common is that they're children, and whether they're royalty or just ordinary schmoes, they don't

Introducing Philosophy Through Pop Culture: From Socrates to Star Wars *and Beyond*, Second Edition.
Edited by William Irwin and David Kyle Johnson.
© 2022 John Wiley & Sons Ltd. Published 2022 by John Wiley & Sons Ltd.

really get to be heroes until they escape the fetters of adult supervision. (Responsible parents don't allow their children to sail off alone to Te Fiti or shack up in the woods with seven short-statured strangers.) The characters resonate especially well with children because all of us dreamed – and some of us still do – of what epic adventures we'd have if only we weren't held back by all the adults.

This too bears a certain similarity to a fundamental teaching of Zen Buddhism. Zen advocates returning to a childlike state of mind, unburdened by the conceptual baggage that marks what we typically call "adult" and "mature" thinking – baggage that includes concepts of the self, of the future, and of hoarding worldly goods so your future self will live comfortably. Just as Mulan and Moana become heroes only after escaping the constraints placed on them by adults, so the childlike mind has its best chance to understand buddha-nature only after freeing itself of worldly assumptions.

Disney says, "Hey, kid, you can be a hero," while Zen says, "Hey, kid, you can be a buddha." But though they might not seem that way, those two maxims are actually direct opposites of one another. Escapism is the very opposite of liberation. To see how that's true – and to see why you might prefer one over the other – let's begin with a Zen master whose own life story is worthy of a Disney movie. His name is Dōgen Kigen.

When You Wish Upon a Bodhi Tree

Like Elsa, Ariel, and Tarzan, Dōgen was of noble birth. (The year was 1200, near Kyoto, Japan. His parents were aristocrats with links to the Imperial house.) Like Bambi, Cinderella, and Belle, he lost his mother at a young age. (That was c. 1208,[1] and legend has it he got his first inkling of the impermanence of all things while watching the smoke rise from the incense at her funeral.) Like Wall-E and Moana, he boarded a ship on an epic voyage that would ultimately reshape the history of his homeland. Unlike any of those characters, you can't buy pajamas with Dōgen's face on them, but like them, he did inspire some catchy tunes. (He was an accomplished poet, and various musicians have put his poems to music.)

If we wanted to tell the story of Dōgen as a Disney character, we'd start with his fateful choice at the tender age of 12 or 13: he had to decide whether to become the wealthy heir of his aristocratic uncle or to fulfill his mother's dying wish and become a monk. Then we'd take Dōgen through his formative years in the monastery, where he might break into a musical number about the people he saw violating their monastic vows. He'd sing about the monks who, after taking their vow of poverty, built secret cubbyholes in the walls to hide their riches. Then comes a verse about the vow of nonviolence, and the private armies that some of these monasteries mustered to defend their growing wealth. Then a verse about the vow of temperance, and about the debauchery and drunkenness and even orgies Dōgen saw in the temples. (On second thought, to keep our movie rated G, maybe we'll leave out the orgies.)

The musical number would end with a dramatic verse about wanting to seek out the Buddha's teachings as they were really meant to be. So after he sings his big solo, young Dōgen joins a Zen temple that emphasizes seated meditation, following the practice of the historical Buddha himself.[2] In this temple he meets the Raffiki of our movie, a wizened Zen master named Myōzen, who tells him he'll find what he seeks in China. Braving storms that would challenge even Moana and Maui, Dōgen and Myōzen, cross the sea together, and Dōgen ultimately comes to study at the feet of another great Zen master named Rujing. In our movie it will be Rujing who opens young Dōgen's eyes to what Buddhism is really all about.

Let's start with the basics. The Buddha said everything in existence has three qualities in common: it's *empty*, it's *impermanent*, and it's *frustrating*. These are the so-called Three Marks of Existence, and Mickey Mouse himself happens to be a perfect illustration of them.

Mickey became famous in *Steamboat Willie*, the first of Walt Disney's cartoons to feature synchronized sound. Mickey[3] spends most of his time making music. In the opening sequence he's whistling to himself, and by the end he and his girlfriend Minnie play music by tormenting various farm animals. (We might interpret this as the first instance of Disney's animal abuse, presaging the infamous incident with the lemmings.) But of course we know Mickey himself makes no sound at all. His whistling is just an illusion; the whistles come from a speaker, not the black-and-white figure on the screen. Even that figure is just an illusion. He looks like he's tapping his foot and whistling, but in fact he never moves at all. There isn't even a *he*; there's only a series of images, each one perfectly still, run through a projector so fast that there appears to be a mouse rocking out on a steamboat.

The Buddha says you're just like Mickey. What we think of as *you* is really just a bundle of mental and physical processes, not so different from still images running past a projector bulb, except that yours are a lot more complex and they change a lot faster than 24 frames per second.[4] Neither your molecules nor your thoughts are exactly the same as they were when you opened this book. Memories don't stay constant either – if they did, you'd never forget anything – and as for a soul or spirit that lives in the body and goes somewhere after death, the Buddha said he looked for one but couldn't find it. (He thinks this is good news; if you don't have one of these things, you don't have to worry about taking care of it.)

Now notice two important facts about you and Mickey, according to this view. First, you're *empty*. There's no self, no unchanging core that all of these ever-changing processes happen to; you yourself are nothing other than the processes all bundled together. Second, you're *impermanent*. In fact, you're so impermanent that the you who started reading this sentence is already gone by the time you finish it. A little while ago, there was a you who began reading this paragraph in what was then the present moment. That you is gone, just as that moment is gone; they exist now only as memories of the current you. Except – *whoops!* – now we've lost that you too. Dead and gone.[5]

Depressed yet? It gets worse. Because everything you love in this world is just as empty and impermanent as you are. And for that reason, everything is *frustrating*. (It's all *duḥkha*, to use the Sanskrit term, which is sometimes translated as *suffering*.) Our lives are frustrating through and through, because even the most supercalifragilisticexpialidocious parts still don't last. According to the Buddha, everything that exists is characterized by these three marks of existence – emptiness, impermanence, and frustration – and until we make peace with that fact, we're bound to be miserable.

Under the Sea or Part of Your World?

So how *do* you make peace with that? One really popular approach is to just pretend it isn't true. That's what the drunken bacchanals in the monasteries were for. If that's not your style, you could try . . . well, pretty much everything the Walt Disney Company sticks its label on. Movies, toys, theme parks, video games, entire TV channels, all perfectly calibrated for you to distract yourself from the here and now.

We can't single out Disney, of course. The fact is that day-to-day living in the modern world is mostly directed at seeking temporary distractions from the present moment. Disney is just one storefront in the distraction mega-mall. There's more to be said on this later, but for now let's just note that keeping yourself distracted from the here and now isn't just a twenty-first century pastime. Dōgen saw plenty of it in his day too.

He sailed to China to get away from it, and there, under Rujing's tutelage, he devoted himself day and night to seated meditation. This, he says, is the key to making peace with the empty, impermanent, frustrating nature of everything: you look right at it, you accept it for what it is, and you stop wanting it to be different. The problem isn't that you're impermanent, it's that you don't want to be. So you can either satisfy that want (by becoming immortal) or stop wanting it (which is a whole lot easier by comparison).

Ditto for those other two marks of existence, emptiness and frustration. It's perfectly natural to want an independent, blissful existence, just as it's natural to want that existence to endure indefinitely. But that's about as practical as wanting to become a mermaid. It's a pleasant fantasy, but by clinging to such fantasies you only set yourself up for disappointment. In Disney's version of *The Little Mermaid*, Ariel gets off light; in the original fairy tale from Hans Christian Andersen, her new human feet bleed terribly. She's doomed to feel like she's walking on knives for the rest of her life. She doesn't even get to marry her prince.

Dōgen would say Ariel ought to listen to her little crustacean buddy, Sebastian. Instead of wishing to be part of another world, accept the world you're in. It sounds paradoxical, but by embracing the idea that everything's frustrating, you're less likely to feel frustrated. (Maybe you've had this experience. If I go to the DMV expecting it'll take forever, I'm pleasantly surprised when it only takes 10 minutes. If I go expecting I'll get out lickety-split, 10 minutes feels like forever.) Similarly, by accepting that everything is impermanent, you're better able to make the most of every moment. And by accepting that nothing has independent existence, you're better at noticing the interdependence and interconnections between everything and everything else.

And that's pretty cool, because when you fully embrace these ideas you arrive at a new understanding of yourself. As a complex bundle of ever-changing processes, you realize that you're inextricably intertwined with the processes of others. For instance, you and I are bound up with each other right now. You've got my words bouncing around in your head, but as I'm choosing these words I've got you, my future reader, foremost in mind. Even Walt Disney and Hans Christian Andersen are bound up in us, as creators of the ideas we've just been thinking about. The upshot of all of this is that there's a meaningful sense in which I *am* you – or at least part of me is. The rest of me is bound up in all the other people, animals, objects, and ideas I interact with. I'm one with all of it, and so are you.

If that's how you think of yourself, then compassion should come pretty easily to you. You become like Tramp, whose immediate instinct when he sees Lady upset is to make her feel better. Or like Woody and Buzz and the rest of Andy's toys, who think nothing of self-sacrifice so long they can make their boy happy. In a moment like that, a moment of perfect selflessness, you may catch your first glimpse of your own buddha-nature. Hey kid, you can be a buddha.

Dōgen says that if you spend long enough in this mode of selfless awareness, a couple of things become clear. First, acquiring more stuff doesn't really make people happier.

Second, being attached to your *you* is just as toxic as being attached to your stuff. In fact, those two things are closely connected. It's a short leap from "you" to "yours" – that is, from *self* to *property* – and once we start thinking in terms of "mine" and "yours" we invite misery. On the smallest scale it's picking someone's pocket; on the largest scale it's conquering someone's country.

Dōgen said the best way to protect yourself from robbers is to simply not own anything, and the best way to protect yourself from murderers is to not mind being killed.[6] This is the ultimate liberation: to shed all sense of self and fully grasp your interconnected interdependence with all things. If you can do that, you realize your buddha-nature and *voilà*, you're a buddha. And if you can do *that*, then you can lead a life like one of Disney's most recent acquisitions: Yoda.

May the Cash Be with You

Yoda, shortest and coolest of all the Jedi Masters, was originally a Buddhist master. His home planet, Dagobah, is named for a type of Buddhist shrine called a pagoda, the Tibetan spelling for which is *dagoba*. (Yoda's creator, George Lucas, was on an Eastern philosophy kick while he was writing *The Empire Strikes Back*.) When we first encounter Yoda, he lives a life of peace and contentment on his planet-sized pagoda, as far from the materialistic life as he can possibly get. He's quite impish, even childish, for he's overthrown many of those "mature," "adult" assumptions that everyone else in the movie takes as bedrock. (He tries to pass the childlike mind on to Luke Skywalker: "Unlearn what you have learned.") Yoda has no interest in political power or material things, just as Dōgen himself claimed to have no interest in them; when he returned to Japan, Dōgen ultimately founded his temple deep in the mountains.[7] The great irony of Yoda's life is that he's quite literally the puppet of people who used him to make billions of dollars.

Lucas caught lightning in a bottle with *Star Wars*, but his real genius lay in merchandising. *Star Wars* films smashed one box office record after the next, but it's toys, not tickets, that created the world's most valuable movie franchise. Toy sales have roughly doubled ticket sales, and that's to say nothing of the other merch, everything from area rugs to zipper-lock bags. All told, for every dollar generated at the box office there's another $4 in sales of Star Wars loot.[8] To a company like Disney this ratio made a lot of sense – it too built an empire on its brand, not just its film studio – and so in 2012 it bought Lucasfilm for just over $4 billion. That drew a giant collective incredulous gasp at the time, but Disney had a plan: make *Star Wars* an annual event. No more three-year waits between films. Disney's ambition was to make one or two *Star Wars* movies every year. They've had to back off of that – after *Solo* bombed and *Episodes XIII* and *IX* fizzled, Disney tabled projects like the Obi-Wan and Boba Fett solo films – but even so, the financial gambit paid off. By 2017, the new *Star Wars* movies had already surpassed $4 billion in ticket sales alone.

This was no wish upon a star. Disney simply applied its time-tested formula: if it makes money, make a sequel. Almost all of Disney's animated films get a sequel or two. Some of these make it to the big screen, but there are dozens more that even many diehard Disney fans have never heard of. These aren't big-budget films but the direct-to-video efforts of Walt Disney Studios Home Entertainment. They're produced quickly and on the cheap, and audiences aren't fooled. They know the difference between a *Toy Story 3* and a *Cinderella III*. (Wait, there's a *Cinderella III*?) But the filmmakers aren't *try-*

ing to fool the audience. Everyone's in on the scheme: it's a cash grab, plain and simple, but if it keeps the audience entertained everyone's happy.

This, of course, is the opposite of everything a countercultural minimalist like Yoda stands for. He's more a Baloo sort of guy, seeking contentment in the bare necessities. Dōgen agrees with Yoda and Baloo. In fact, he said money is akin to poison, and he once praised a wealthy Chinese layman for throwing all his riches into the sea. When asked why he didn't give everything to the poor, the man said, "I threw it all away because I knew it was harmful. Why would I give something to another person if I knew it to be harmful?"[9]

Compare this attitude to the mission statement of the Walt Disney Company: "to be one of the world's leading producers and providers of entertainment and information." Dōgen would object to every part of that. Being a producer and provider of entertainment is already objectionable, if the primary function of such entertainment is to distract people from more important concerns. Being one of the world's *leading* producers is even worse; the goal should be detachment from self, not self-aggrandizement through victory in the marketplace. Put another way, the ideal goal is to be "at one with," not to be number one.

Now maybe all of this sounds high-minded to you. Maybe you're thinking Dōgen would have made a really bad capitalist. I'd agree with you on both counts. But as a counterpoint I'd ask what we the audience might think of a Disney character whose behavior was modeled on the marketplace behavior of the Walt Disney Company. Being the biggest wouldn't be enough; the character's central motivation would be to *keep getting bigger*. It wouldn't be content to grow by its own efforts; it would seek out other characters to gobble up. The character would do this over and over, no matter how big it grew.[10]

It's not hard to imagine such a character, but it's impossible to cast this character as the *hero*. More like the White Witch banishing spring, summer, and fall from Narnia, plunging all the realm into the Long Winter. Or perhaps this character isn't evil at all, but rather an amoral force, like Te Kā blighting one island after the next. He doesn't consume them because he's wicked; it's just in his nature. His heart's been stolen.

Even so, it's awfully hard to root for him.

Hakuna Matata, Bodhisattva

Perhaps you want to say that while Dōgen's idealism may be admirable, it's just not practical in the twenty-first century. Who has the luxury to sit around and meditate anymore? We have bills to pay. Bosses to please. Clients or customers to satisfy, or else risk their wrath in online reviews. Try telling your boss you have no intention to be the best because striving to outdo the competition just builds attachment to self. See if that gets you the promotion you were hoping for.

Such objections were just as relevant in Dōgen's day. Remember, he was faced with the same choice himself: become rich and powerful or become a monk. The life of luxury was just as glamorous back then as it is today. But I choose the word *glamorous* carefully: it derives from the root word *glamer*, a magical spell meant to deceive. Wealth and power promise happiness, but the promise is empty. If it weren't, then we wouldn't be able to find any examples of people who are wealthy or powerful and also unhappy. But of course the world is full of such examples, so Dōgen would have us ask why.

Here's a possible answer: if you return to the childlike mind, you understand wealth and power as mere distractions. Trying to enrich yourself or empower yourself is doomed to failure if you don't actually have a self. Remember, there's no *yours* without *you*, so if your *you* is really just a set of turbulent, ever-changing, interconnected processes, then so are any traits it could possess. Affluence and influence are just as frustrating as everything else.

The truth is, fantasizing about being better off is just another form of escapism, the kind Disney sells so expertly. And like all forms of escapism, the rewards are just imaginary. Sure, kid, you can be a hero, but the highest flights of heroic fantasy still come to an end. Emptiness, impermanence, and frustration will always be waiting for you when you come back down to the here and now.

Dōgen chose the monastic path because he wanted the opposite of escape: liberation. If the three marks of existence are the problem, the solution isn't to flee them. Rather, it's to make peace with them. If you can do that, maybe you can even reach a deeper level of insight: they were never the problem in the first place. They're just so. The only real problem is that we wish they weren't so. If you can stop wishing that, they don't bother you anymore. You're liberated. Hakuna matata for the rest of your days.

That's not to say the path of Zen is easy. Quite the contrary: it took the Dōgen *years* to get it right. But maybe we can forgive Timon and Pumbaa for making it sound too simple. After all, they were singing about excessive flatulence, not liberation writ large. But the heart of the path of Zen is in their song, if we're mindful enough to hear it. If you want no worries for the rest of your days, you've got two choices. First, you can turn your attention inward. Once you notice that worry is a subjective response, not an objective fact, then bit by bit you can recondition that response. By returning to the childlike mind you can come to terms with the Three Marks of Existence, thereby liberating yourself from them. Or option two, you can turn your attention outward. Try to escape the Three Marks of Existence, and with them you escape everything in life that might cause you to worry. I think I speak for Dōgen when I say good luck with that.[11]

For pop culture resources and philosophical resources related to this chapter please visit the website for this book: https://introducingphilosophythroughpopculture.com.

Notes

1 Scholars disagree on the exact dates in his life. We don't even know his name at birth; Dōgen Kigen is his monastic name, the name he took on when he first shaved his head and entered the monastery.
2 Siddhartha Gautama, whose biography is subject to much more debate than we can handle in a footnote. For our purposes I'll just note that traditionally he's said to have been an Indian prince whose dates are around 563–483 BCE, but modern scholars say all of that is almost certainly wrong. But historians agree that he was a real person, and Buddhist tradition has held from the beginning that he sat for 49 days under what's now called the Bodhi Tree, the Tree of Enlightenment.
3 Fun fact: Steamboat Willie is his nickname. The movie is a parody of Buster Keaton's *Steamboat Bill, Jr.*
4 In fact they're said to change thousands of times per second. If you want to read more about them – or anything else about the basics of Buddhism – see Rahula, W. (1959). *What the Buddha Taught*. New York: Grove Press.
5 For a connection between these ideas and LEGO, see Chapter 40 in this volume.
6 *Shōbōgenzō Zuimonki* 3.4, translated into English by Reihō Masunaga as *A Primer of Sōtō Zen* (Honolulu: University of Hawai'i Press, 1971).

7 I say "claimed" because there's reason to believe he didn't have much choice in the matter. He tried founding his temple in the capital city of Kyoto, and when that failed he chose instead to accept the mountainous land donated to him by a student.

8 This according to *Forbes* (Damodaran, A. Intergalactic Finance: Why the Star Wars Franchise is Worth Nearly $10 Billion To Disney [January 6, 2016]).

9 Dōgen recounts this story in *Shōbōgenzō Zuimonki* 3.11. The passage here is quoted from Bein, S. (2011). *Purifing Zen: Watsuji Tetsurō's* Shamon Dōgen, 80. Honolulu: University of Hawai'i Press.

10 The *Star Wars* acquisition was hardly a unique occurrence. Disney also bought Marvel Entertainment and most of 21st Century Fox. That means one company – Disney – now owns about one-third of the entire film industry. With Fox it also acquired a majority share of Hulu. It then pulled most of its content from all other online streaming services, rereleasing its family-friendly material on the new Disney+ streaming service and its edgier stuff (e.g. *Deadpool*) on Hulu. Cutthroat strategy it may be, but as Disney+'s cutthroat hero the Mandalorian would put it, "This is the way."

11 Thanks to Kalyn and Audrey Embry for their invaluable work as research assistants.

Part IX

The Afterlife and Meaning

Introduction

What is the meaning of life? This is the grandest of all philosophical questions. In fact, many other philosophical questions are asked solely in pursuit of shedding light on what the meaning of life is. Despite disagreements among philosophers, we can all agree that earthly existence is full of trials and tribulations. We might then wonder if it is all justified and made meaningful by an afterlife.

In Chapter 42, Jonathan Walls and Jerry Walls focus on *Deathly Hallows*, the final volume in the *Harry Potter* saga. Whereas the evil Voldemort tries to cheat death at all costs, the noble Harry Potter is willing to sacrifice his life for others. If this life is all there is, then perhaps Voldermort's plan would be understandable. But, as it turns out, death is not the end in Harry Potter's universe. The soul lives on. And, as the unmistakable Christian imagery of the resurrection suggests in *Deathly Hallows*, the God-given purpose of life is to love one another.

In Chapter 43, David Kyle Johnson considers *The Good Place* to argue that we could never really know if we were in the afterlife because it would always be more rational to believe that we were simply hallucinating. More importantly, though, we wouldn't want to spend eternity in heaven because, as the show suggests, it would eventually become intolerably boring. The meaning of life might be to become a good person, but we don't need forever to achieve that goal.

Introducing Philosophy Through Pop Culture: From Socrates to Star Wars *and Beyond*, Second Edition.
Edited by William Irwin and David Kyle Johnson.
© 2022 John Wiley & Sons Ltd. Published 2022 by John Wiley & Sons Ltd.

42

Beyond Godric's Hollow

Life After Death and the Search for Meaning (Harry Potter)

Jonathan L. Walls and Jerry L. Walls

Summary

The issue of death and whether there is an afterlife comes up early in the *Harry Potter* series, but it does not receive a clear answer until the last volume. This chapter examines thinkers ranging from the existentialist Martin Heidegger, who rejected life after death, to a number of diverse philosophers who affirmed it, including William James, John Locke, and Immanuel Kant. What one believes about life after death profoundly affects how one understands the meaning of this life, an insight as vividly demonstrated in the *Harry Potter* series.

After narrowly escaping death only because of his mother's sacrifice, Harry is an orphan, left on the doorstep of his aunt and uncle. Voldemort, we later discover, wishes above all things to avoid death and has performed the most treacherous actions to ensure it. Almost every book in the series results in the death of a significant character, perhaps none more so than Dumbledore in *Half-Blood Prince*. It's easy to hear the resounding echo of death all through the series, culminating in the near-death of Harry himself.

Death and Philosophy

Legend has it that there was a professional philosopher some years ago who decided to run for governor of his state. On the campaign trail, he was asked what the most important lesson was that we can teach our kids. He responded: "That they're going to die." He didn't win the election.

Philosophers deal in the great questions and ideas. Not surprisingly, therefore, many of them have been and are fascinated by death, the ultimate unknown. Since death is so unpleasant a prospect, however, some people try to avoid it, deny it, put it out of their

Introducing Philosophy Through Pop Culture: From Socrates to Star Wars *and Beyond*, Second Edition.
Edited by William Irwin and David Kyle Johnson.
© 2022 John Wiley & Sons Ltd. Published 2022 by John Wiley & Sons Ltd.

minds. Young people are particularly prone to feel invincible, as though death is some-thing that happens only to others. They often lack what the philosopher Martin Heidegger (1889–1976) calls *authenticity*, which comes from accepting death and reflecting deeply on our mortality.

Some philosophers, like the Epicureans in ancient Greece, have thought that we should be unconcerned about death, since when we die we cease to exist. Death doesn't exactly happen *to* us, it's merely the end of us. We're no longer around to experience it; the arrival of death corresponds with our departure, so why sweat it? Heidegger, in con-trast, thought authentic living requires a choice to face boldly what our death implies: that we will no longer be. As an atheist, he thought that at death we cease to exist, and living authentically is to live with a poignant recognition that death is ever close at hand. It's not simply a far-off event; it could happen any time, without warning or the chance to reflect about it, and its imminence should shape how we live and think right now. Our mortality confronts us with the task of defining ourselves, recognizing both our limita-tions and opportunities, and not wasting any of our short time living half-asleep.

Over 2000 years ago, Plato expressed similar thoughts. Indeed, he is famous for teach-ing that "true philosophers make dying their profession."[1] To pursue wisdom is to live in such a way that one is prepared to face death when it comes.

Harry was confronted with death right from the start, so it was from an unusually young age that he was aware of his mortality. While Harry leads an authentic life, Voldemort lives a highly inauthentic one. To see why, let's consider Harry's climactic death march and what follows in *Deathly Hallows*.

The Approaching Battle

The matured and battle-hardened Harry somberly marches toward the Forbidden Forest for what he honestly believes will be the last time. He's going there to meet his own doom with open eyes. He has just learned that the only way Voldemort can be finished off is for *Harry* to die, taking a piece of Voldemort's soul down with him. As Harry walks, each step bringing him closer to the end, his thoughts come sharply into focus. In the shadow of his impending death, his senses become sharper. A great appreciation wells up within him for all the things he has possessed (physical or otherwise), but failed to fully value. Yet he remains resolute in the task before him. Dumbledore had known that, if faced with this choice, Harry would follow through, even if it meant his death:

> And Dumbledore had known that Harry would not duck out, that he would keep going to the end, even though it was his [Harry's] end, because he had taken trouble to get to know him, hadn't he? Dumbledore knew, as Voldemort knew, that Harry would not let anyone else die for him now that he had discovered it was in his power to stop it.[2]

Harry had faced death before when he lost a number of loved ones. And despite Dumbledore's assurance that death could be the next great adventure and despite Nearly Headless Nick's wisdom on departed souls, Harry retained more than a few doubts about what death would bring. The fact that dead bodies decay and rot in the ground filled him with more than a little existential angst. Recall the scene in *Deathly Hallows* when Harry and Hermione finally reach the grave of Harry's parents in Godric's Hollow and Harry slowly reads the verse inscribed on the gravestone of his parents: "The last enemy that shall be destroyed is death."

At first, Harry worries that this is a Death Eater idea, more in line with Voldemort's quest to escape death than anything else, and he wonders why such an inscription is there. Hermione assures him: "It doesn't mean defeating death in the way the Death Eaters mean it, Harry . . . It means . . . you know . . . living beyond death. Living after death." But Harry's parents weren't living, Harry thought. "They were gone. The empty words could not disguise the fact that his parents' moldering remains lay beneath the snow and stone, indifferent, unknowing."[3] If this is what death involves, then talk of death's defeat seems a mockery, and death indeed means just this: moldering remains, decaying flesh, end of story.

This was the fate of Harry's parents, and Harry, in that dark hour, sensed it was the fate of everyone. Now, as Harry voluntarily marches to his own death, he realizes something: "And again Harry understood without having to think. It did not matter about bringing them (his departed loved ones) back, for he was about to join them. He was not really fetching them: they were fetching him."[4] He couldn't bring his parents back, but he could, and would, die, and thus join them.

Heidegger does not advise that we should morbidly reflect about death until we're depressed, but rather that we come to terms with death and the limitations it implies, so that we can move into our remaining future, however fleeting, boldly, taking advantage of what opportunities we have. Think not only of Harry in our scenario here, but also of Colin Creevey, the underage wizard who sneaks back into the Battle of Hogwarts to fight the good fight and loses his life. Harry and Colin's actions, regardless of their beliefs about life beyond death, are great examples of authentic Heidegerrian living: recognizing limitations, seizing opportunities, and accepting one's own mortality.

King's Cross Station

When Harry receives the apparent death blow from Voldemort, he awakens to find himself possessed of unexpected powers and in a place that resembles King's Cross station – a sort of ethereal realm, where time and space function differently. This scene is one of the strangest in the *Potter* books, but Rowling has made it clear that it is vitally important.

Waiting for Harry in this mysterious place is none other than Albus Dumbledore. This brings up another connection with Heidegger, who held that we should look into our past to uncover new possibilities for understanding life. One of his most important suggestions is that we need to choose our hero from the past, an exemplar we can use to guide us and help us make sense of our experiences. Heidegger proposes that we have a dialogue with this departed hero, thereby gaining insights that were won from his or her own experiences.

So who better for Harry to meet at this critical juncture than the beloved Dumbledore, who himself suffered death not long before and who'd devoted so much of his life to the fight against Voldemort? Not to mention that Dumbledore was, as Harry often says, the greatest wizard of all time.

Such a powerful wizard, one would assume, would be like a king in this place, but it is not so. He is simply kind, witty, patient Dumbledore. Dumbledore had once desired power and glory, until he realized, to his chagrin and shame, how dangerous these pursuits are, especially for himself. The Dumbledore we now see is the wise, gentle headmaster that we all know and love, who, by his own admission, is the better Dumbledore.

This mysterious way-station King's Cross evokes the image of Purgatory, the place of postmortem penitence, penal retribution, and spiritual growth in Catholic doctrine. As Dumbledore patiently catches Harry up on everything that was involved in Dumbledore's battle-plan against Voldemort, we see more than just answers to riddles; we see repentance and atonement. "For the first time since Harry had met Dumbledore, he looked less than an old man, much less. He looked fleetingly like a small boy caught in wrongdoing."[5] We also witness a full-fledged apology and confession from Dumbledore, tears and all. It is not that Dumbledore himself was wicked, nor that he is now being caught in some great lie or misdeed. But Dumbledore had been imperfect, and his mistakes, mainly those of his youth, had caused great harm. Now, in death, Dumbledore has come to terms with his past misdeeds, and has grown wiser and merrier as a result.

In stark contrast to Dumbledore in the King's Cross scene is the hideous Voldemort creature. One can only assume that the revolting, deformed atrocity present in the train station is the image of the vanquished bit of Voldemort's soul. It seems that the decisions made by Voldemort have rendered his soul quite beyond repair, as Dumbledore points out in the following exchange:

> Harry glanced over his shoulder to where the small, maimed creature trembled under the chair.
> "What is that, Professor?"
> "Something that is beyond either of our help," said Dumbledore.[6]

Dumbledore puts it into even plainer words as he and Harry discuss whether Harry will return to the living to finish his work or simply go on to the mysterious beyond:

> "I think," said Dumbledore, "that if you choose to return, there is a chance that he [Voldemort] may be finished for good. I cannot promise it. But I know this, Harry, that you have a lot less to fear from returning here than he does."[7]

It is Voldemort's misguided fear of death that has driven him to the unspeakable acts that have obliterated any trace of goodness within him, but ironically, it is *because* of these choices that Voldemort now *actually* has reason to fear death.

It's worth noting that J.R.R. Tolkien's *Lord of the Rings*, which ranks with *Harry Potter* as one of the most popular fantasy epics of all time, echoes this quest-for-immortality motif. As Tolkien notes in his *Letters*, the real theme of *The Lord of the Rings* is not power or heroic resistance to evil, but "Death and the desire for deathlessness."[8] Sauron, the Dark Lord, pours a good part of his life-force into the One Ring, tying his own incarnate existence irreversibly to the Ring. This ring is the catalyst for much evil, and eventually must be destroyed. Let's see what this motif represents and what insight it may have for our own lives.

Reap a Destiny

It's said that the great American psychologist and philosopher William James (1842–1910) once wrote in the margin of a copy of his *Psychology: Briefer Course* the following lines: "Sow a thought, reap an action; sow an action, reap a habit; sow a habit, reap a character; sow a character, reap a destiny." The idea is that it starts small and ends big; our thoughts lead to actions, which upon becoming habit yield a character and ultimately a destiny. Voldemort's destiny, as revealed in the King's Cross scene, is the result of a lifetime of choices that put him on a fatal trajectory to destruction.

This scene raises a possibility that would be quite foreign to Heidegger. After being raised a Catholic and seriously considering the priesthood, Heidegger embraced atheism, abandoning belief in the afterlife. He once described his philosophy as a "waiting for God," a phrase that inspired Samuel Beckett's famous play *Waiting for Godot*. But far from thinking that atheism empties life of meaning or significance, Heidegger thought that our mortality made choosing how we live this life all-important. As he saw it, death represents both the ultimate individuating event and the culmination of the process by which each of us forms our essence through our choices, since each of us must go through death's door alone.

Rowling's view is both similar and different. The Voldemort creature at the station is saddled with an unchanging destiny. It represents the culmination of his development of character, a process that is complete. Voldemort no longer merely did evil; he had become evil. He is, as Dumbledore says, beyond help. He's chosen his fate, and it's ugly. As William James would have put it, Voldemort's thoughts led to actions, then habits, then a character, and finally a destiny. Aristotle (384–322 BCE) notes how our actions put us on a trajectory, turning us gradually into particular kinds of people, each choice incrementally shaping our soul. Rowling's portrayal of Voldemort's terrifying fate represents the ultimate culmination of such a process, if, contrary to Heidegger's view, we don't cease to exist at death but instead must continue to live with the consequences of who we have become.

To put it another way, we might say that in death we will *fully* become who we were in the process of becoming, and now we must live with our chosen selves forever. Dumbledore was imperfect, but he showed remorse for his mistakes and was freed from their harmful effects. In a similar way, the ghostly images of Harry's loved ones who walk with him to the Forbidden Forest also reflect the good-natured, loving people they had been in life, something apparent in their appearance and conduct. Lily is nurturing; James and Lupin are reassuring; Sirius is casual and even a bit flippant, just as we remember him.

Voldemort, by contrast, obstinately refuses to turn from his self-imposed path to perdition, all the way to the very end. And it's not as if Voldemort didn't have his chances. Right down to the waning minutes of his life, Voldemort willfully rejects the one thing that can save him: remorse. Facing a terrible yet vulnerable Voldemort, Harry tries to offer a path of redemption still:

> But before you try to kill me, I'd advise you to think about what you've done . . . Think, and try for some remorse, Riddle . . . It's your one last chance . . . It's all you've got left . . . *I've seen what you'll be otherwise* . . . Be a man . . . try . . . Try for some remorse[9]

Of course, remorse is not something Voldemort can muster, and this is his undoing. He may have retained his freedom to show remorse even at that last stage, but undoubtedly the pattern of behavior that had recurred so often made it exponentially harder for him to do so. For if Aristotle is right, repeated wrong behavior makes us yet more likely to continue in it, and makes it harder for us to resist. Willful choices of evil in the end, then, detract from freedom, if Aristotle's philosophy and Rowling's fiction is right. If such a picture of the human condition and our moral development is accurate, our choices bring certain truths into being and forge our characters. William James was a firm believer that we are free, an assumption Heidegger made as well. James stressed that this freedom, this liberation from a deterministic universe, is the most intimate picture each of us has of "truth in the making":

> Our acts, our turning-places, where we seem to ourselves to make ourselves and grow, are the parts of the world to which we are closest, the parts of which our knowledge is the most intimate and complete. Why should we not take them at their face-value? Why may they not be the actual turning-places and growing-places which they seem to be, of the world – why not the workshop of being, where we catch fact in the making?[10]

Such freedom, if it exists, is truly one of life's great mysteries, for it would enable us to make decisions on the basis of reasons that aren't causes; we would be morally and metaphysically free agents whose decisions shape our destinies but whose choices aren't written in stone. Such a view of human freedom need not require a denial that all events are caused, but it demands that some events are caused not by other events, like the physical processes of our brains, but by us, by persons.

On this view, our actions don't merely reflect who we are, they shape who we are becoming. To the last, Voldemort retains the capacity, however diminished, to show remorse, but he refuses and thereby seals his fate and grows literally beyond redemption. Plato (428–248 BCE) said that evil is only done out of ignorance. But might some people actually prefer the darkness to light, because they've cultivated appetites that only vice can satisfy? Voldemort's fate raises just such a question.

How we live, and what the significance of death is, are importantly connected to questions of whether, as Heidegger believed, death is indeed the end or, as Rowling's fiction depicts, there's life after death. Both Rowling and Heidegger highlight the Jamesian point that our choices here shape our destiny: either our completed human essence at the time of our deaths in Heidegger's case, or the part of ourselves that we take to the next life if death isn't the final end. The philosopher John Locke (1632–1704) suggested that the things that give us our most real identity are our memories and character. Locke's view of personal identity as inextricably connected to our characters, together with the possibility that death may not be our end, ratchets up the importance of developing the right character to literally infinite significance. For this will be a character with which we might be stuck for more than three-score and ten, a character that is the result of our own contingent choices, rather than something inevitable or unavoidable.

In one of his most famous arguments, the German philosopher Immanuel Kant (1724–1804) claimed that, to ensure the ultimate harmony of virtue and happiness, we have to assume the existence of an afterlife. Before him, the French philosopher Blaise Pascal (1623–1662) was astonished at how many people draw up their ethics and carry on their lives indifferent to the question of whether there's an afterlife:

> The immortality of the soul is something of such vital importance to us, affecting us so deeply, that one must have lost all feeling not to care about knowing the facts of the matter. All our actions and thoughts must follow such different paths, according to whether there is hope of eternal blessing or not, that the only possible way of acting with sense and judgment is to decide our course in the light of this point, which ought to be our ultimate objective.[11]

Heidegger rightly sees that, if death is the end of us forever, that has implications for meaning and morality. The flip side of the same coin is that if death is *not* the end, but just the beginning, even bigger implications follow.

In the early volumes of her series, Rowling left it ambiguous whether death is the end or just the beginning in her fictional world. In *Sorcerer's Stone*, Dumbledore, in a trademark showcase of wisdom and foreknowledge, tells Harry that "to the well-organized mind, death is but the next great adventure."[12] But it remained unclear just what the great adventure consisted of and whether it included life beyond the grave. Now, however, the scope of the adventure has been brought more fully to light.

One of the most gripping aspects of Rowling's magical fiction is its compelling character development. Imperfect and morally flawed characters tangling with profound choices between what's good and what's easy provide insight into the "moral fiber" of characters we've come to care about. Adding to the drama and lending more potency to watching these characters progress or digress into what they will ultimately be is Rowling's sober recognition of human mortality. Even beyond that Heidegerrian focus, though, is this: if Rowling's fictional portrayal of the afterlife captures an aspect of reality, the choices we make in this life may be vastly more consequential than if death, the last enemy, were never destroyed.

For pop culture resources and philosophical resources related to this chapter please visit the website for this book: https://introducingphilosophythroughpopculture.com.

Notes

1 Plato, *Phaedo*, 67e (trans. G.M.A. Grube, 1977) Indianapolis: Hackett .

2 Rowling, J.K. (2007). *Harry Potter and the Deathly Hallows*, 693. New York: Arthur A. Levine Books.

3 Rowling, *Deathly Hallows*, 328.

4 Rowling, *Deathly Hallows*, 698.

5 Rowling, *Deathly Hallows*, 712–13.

6 Rowling, *Deathly Hallows*, 708.

7 Rowling, *Deathly Hallows*, 722.

8 Carpenter, H. (1980). *The Letters of J.R.R. Tolkien*, 262. Boston: Houghton Mifflin. Perhaps the clearest example of the quest for immortality in Tolkien's writings is the invasion of Aman, the Blessed Realm, by Ar-Pharazôn and the men of Númenor in Tolkien, J.R.R. (1977). *The Silmarillion*, 279. London: George Allen & Unwin. The Númernoreans sought to wrest immortality from the gods (the Valar) and were destroyed for their impiety. For an insightful discussion of this theme in Tolkien's writings, see Davis, B. (2003). Choosing to die: the gift of immortality in middle-earth. In: *The Lord of the Rings and Philosophy: One Book to Rule Them All* (ed. G. Bassham and E. Bronson), 123–136. Chicago: Open Court.

9 Rowling, *Deathly Hallows*, 741.

10 This is a quote from James's last lecture at Harvard, given on December 6, 1906. Quoted in Richardson, R.D. (2007). *William James in the Maelstrom of American Modernism*, 287. New York: Houghton Mifflin Company.

11 Pascal, B. (1966). *Pensées* (trans. A.J. Krailsheimer), 427. London: Penguin.

12 Rowling, J.K. (1998). *Harry Potter and the Sorcerer's Stone*, 297. New York: Arthur A. Levine Books.

43

Why it Wouldn't be Rational to Believe You're in The Good Place (and Why You Wouldn't Want to Be Anyway)

David Kyle Johnson

Summary

The Good Place is about four people, Eleanor, Chidi, Tahani, and Jason, discovering that the afterlife is not quite what they expected. The show raises numerous ethical questions, but also some hard nonethical ones: (i) Could you ever actually know you were in The Good Place?; and (ii) Would you even want to be in the first place? This chapter argues that the answers to these questions are "no" and "hell no," respectively. Regarding the first, it would always be more likely that you were the victim of some kind of hallucination. And regarding the second, while an eternity of paradise and pleasure seeking might seem desirable on its face, it would eventually turn into hell.

> *I'm a neuroscientist, so I get what's going on here.*
> – Simone, "A Girl from Arizona, Part 1"

The Good Place is a show about four people, Eleanor, Chidi, Tahani, and Jason, discovering that the afterlife is not quite what they expected. To help them reach "The Good Place," Chidi has to try to teach them ethics (that is, moral philosophy). Therefore, a lot of the show is about moral philosophy. But one reason everyone hates moral philosophers like Chidi (especially other philosophers) is that they think everything is about ethics. It's not. And the same is true for *The Good Place*. Indeed, it raises two very interesting nonmoral questions: (i) Could you ever actually know you were in The Good Place?; and (ii) Would you even want to be? As we'll see, the answer to these questions are "no" and "hell no," respectively.

Cartesian Skepticism About The Good Place

When I pose questions about whether you could ever know you were in The Good Place, you probably think back to season one and it's big reveal: everyone thought Eleanor, Chidi, Tahani, and Jason were in The Good Place, but they were actually in The Bad

Introducing Philosophy Through Pop Culture: From Socrates to Star Wars *and Beyond*, Second Edition.
Edited by William Irwin and David Kyle Johnson.
© 2022 John Wiley & Sons Ltd. Published 2022 by John Wiley & Sons Ltd.

Place. In an effort to torture them, the demon Michael had deceived them. So, one might wonder, even if The Good Place and The Bad Place were real, how could a person ever know that they actually were in The Good Place (instead of the victim of some elaborate demonic hoax)?

This question brings to mind the philosopher René Descartes (1596–1650). In his famous *Meditations on First Philosophy*, Descartes looked for an unshakable undoubtable belief upon which to ground his endeavor for scientific knowledge. An early candidate he considered was his belief that the physical world existed. But he soon realized that belief was not indubitable. After all, he'd had dreams where he was completely convinced that what he was experiencing was the physical world. How could he know for sure that he wasn't dreaming?

Now, contrary to common opinion, that didn't make Descartes doubt the existence of the physical world. After all, the ideas in his dreams came from his waking experience of the physical world – so, even if he was dreaming, the physical world would exist. But then Descartes considered another possibility. What if "some malicious, powerful, cunning demon has done all he can to deceive me [and] the sky, the air, the earth, colors, shapes, sounds, and all external things are merely dreams that the demon has contrived as traps for my judgment"?[1]

In other words, what if a demon (perhaps named Michael) had tricked Descartes into thinking that a physical world exists when it doesn't? Descartes didn't actually think he was being tricked, mind you. But he concluded that the fact that he couldn't prove that he wasn't being tricked entailed that he couldn't *know* that a physical world existed (even if it did). And so, in the same way, one might wonder: "Even if I did arrive in The Good Place, how could I ever know that a demon (named Michael) wasn't fooling me into thinking I was, when I wasn't?"

Now, the answer to that question might be similar to the solution that I think works for Descartes's problem. How can I know the world is real when I can't prove that it is? Because knowledge doesn't require proof. It doesn't require certainty. Since Plato (428–348), knowledge has been defined as "True belief with an account" – or, as philosophers put it today, "justified true belief." But a belief can be justified, even if it is not certain. To quote my favorite contemporary philosopher, Ted Schick:

> [K]nowledge doesn't require certainty, [it] doesn't require enough [justification] to put the claim beyond any possibility of doubt, but rather enough to put it beyond any reasonable doubt. [And a] proposition is beyond a reasonable doubt when it provides the best explanation of something.[2]

Although it's possible that a demon is deceiving me into thinking that a physical world exists when it doesn't, that is not the best explanation for my experience. That a physical world really exists is a much better explanation. And thus I can know that the physical world exists. In the same way, although I could never know for certain that Michael wasn't fooling me into thinking that I was in The Good Place when I wasn't, that I was in The Good Place could be the best explanation for what I was experiencing. For example if, unlike Eleanor, I had no reason to think I didn't deserve to be there, and there weren't things that bothered me – in other words, if the place I was in really was good – then "I am in The Good Place" would be the better explanation for the wonderful experiences I was having.

The Good Place as a Good Explanation

But now you are probably asking yourself:

> Wait a minute. What makes one explanation better than another? Why is (for example) "a physical world exists" a better explanation for my experiences than "I am being fooled by a demon"? Or why would "I am in The Good Place" be a better explanation than "I am in The Bad Place"?

This is a great question. Clearly you're paying attention.

For the answer, we can once again turn to Ted Schick. In the sixth chapter his book, *How To Think About Weird Things*, he lays out what explanations must be to, by definition, be good explanations. They must be:

> Testable: make novel observable predictions.
> Fruitful: get the predictions they make right.
> Wide Scoping: explain a vast number of phenomena, and not raise unanswerable questions.
> Simple: not unnecessarily invoke new entities or forces.
> Conservative: cohere with what we already have good reason to believe.[3]

These are called the "criteria of adequacy." A good explanation need not always meet all these criteria, but all things being equal, the explanation that is more adequate – that adheres to the most (when compared to other explanations) – is the one we should prefer.

When it comes to Descartes's concerns, we can see why "a physical world exists" is a better explanation than "a demon has created a dream world to fool me." First, unlike a physical world, the hypothesis that a deceitful demon exists is not testable (and thus also can't be fruitful). He's not observable, and he'd sabotage any test you performed to see if he existed. It's not wide scoping because it raises unanswerable questions (like, "How does the demon create this dream world?" and "Why is he intent on fooling me?").[4] And since the demon hypothesis also requires the existence of the demon, his dream world, and an elaborate deception, it's not as simple as the physical world hypothesis.[5]

When it comes to The Good Place versus The Bad Place hypothesis, the big give away is simplicity. The Good Place hypothesis doesn't require a grand deception and all the planning that would be necessary to keep it afloat. The Bad Place hypothesis does. In this respect, it's essentially a conspiracy theory; and one of the (many) reasons conspiracy theories are irrational is because of the grand assumptions one must make to believe that such grand deceptions exist.[6] And while both hypotheses raise unanswerable questions – we are dealing with an ethereal afterlife here, after all – The Bad Place hypothesis seems to raise more. Why would a demon create a place that truly seems good to torture me? How is that torture? Since The Good Place hypothesis is simpler and wider scoping than The Bad Place hypothesis, it would be the preferable explanation.

But this raises a different question. If you found yourself in a situation like the one Eleanor and Chidi found themselves, would "I am in The Good Place" and "I am in The Bad Place but being fooled" be the only two possible explanations? It seems not. Recall that, at the beginning of season four, Simone suspects that The Good Place is just a product of her imagination:

You know, clearly, I was in some kind of horrible accident. I'm on my deathbed, and this entire thing is just a hallucination constructed by my damaged brain as it slowly shuts down. It's not real, so I'm just gonna wander around until I wake up or die. See you later, figments of my imagination! ("A Girl from Arizona")

Since she's a neuroscientist, Simone is aware that this could be an explanation for what she is experiencing. But is it really the best explanation for what she is experiencing? This is the question I have in mind when I wonder whether one could ever know that they were in The Good Place.

Scientific Skepticism About The Good Place

Sadly, it seems, "I am hallucinating" would in fact be the best explanation for what a person was experiencing if they found themselves in The Good Place. Why?

Elsewhere, I have explained why justified belief in things like demons and miracles is impossible.[7] In order for such beliefs to be justified, "a demon did it" or "a miracle occurred" would have to be the best explanation for some event or experience. But such explanations are, by their very nature, not wide scoping, simple, or conservative. They raise unanswerable questions, invoke extra entities, and violate physical laws. And on the rare occasions when they are testable, they have always failed the test. Natural explanations will always be better, so thinking that there is one will always be more rational – even if you can't figure out what it is. Of course, it's logically possible that supernatural forces have violated physical laws. But it's also possible that you simply are not smart or observant enough to figure out what really happened. And that will always be the better explanation because it is simpler, wider scoping, and more conservative. The supernatural explanation invokes supernatural entities, raises unanswerable questions about how supernatural entities interact with the natural world, and conflicts with well-established causal closure principles. The natural "I missed it" explanation does none of these things, and aligns quite nicely with what we know about the powers and limits of human perception, memory, and intellect.[8] Indeed, although you may think what occurred defied the laws of physics, it's more likely that you are simply wrong about what the laws of physics allow.

And this line of reasoning is not a stubborn, pigheaded, irrational refusal to believe in the supernatural. Indeed, it employs exactly the same logic that one employs at magic shows – a logic that avoids what I have elsewhere labeled the "mystery therefore magic" fallacy.[9] When I see the magicians Penn & Teller do something I can't explain, I don't conclude that they have magic powers. I conclude that there's a natural explanation I'm not smart enough to detect. And this would be true, even if I were an expert at detecting such natural explanations. After all, Penn & Teller themselves (who are experts at figuring out magic tricks) have a show (*Fool Us*) where they are fooled by other magicians at least once an episode. But never, upon being fooled, have Penn & Teller said, "Well then, I guess you have magic powers." The fact that magical, miraculous, or demonic explanations are never justified is merely a consequence of the fact that they are, by definition, inadequate explanations. And this would be true, even if magic, miracles, and demons were real.

And so, even if The Good Place was real and we were in it, we could never be justified in believing that we were. That we were experiencing a hallucination caused by our brain as it slowly shuts down would be the better – simpler, wider scoping, and more conservative – explanation. The Good Place is an extra entity that raises unanswerable questions, and our being in The Good Place conflicts with facts that we have good reason to believe.

What kind of facts, you ask?

Well, for example, discoveries in neuroscience have shown that the functioning of my brain is necessary for the existence of my mentality. When certain parts of person's brain cease to function specific parts of their mentality disappear, and once a person's brain shuts down, that individual no longer experiences anything. In other words, our mentality is not housed in a separable entity, called a soul, that can float away from our body when we die.[10] So, the idea that our soul can float away to some afterlife, like The Good Place, conflicts with well-established science.

Of course one might argue that since, in The Good Place, one seems to have a body and brain, one could still have experiences. But consider the fact that if someone went looking for Eleanor's body on Earth, they would presumably find it lying in her coffin. At best, what's in The Good Place is a copy of Eleanor's earthly body. But if what's in The Good Place is a copy of your earthly body, then it's not really you; it's just someone who looks and acts like you. Indeed, contemporary philosopher Peter Unger has argued that in order for our personal identity – the fact that we are one and the same person – to be preserved, it must be the case that the physical continuity of our body (or, more specifically, our brain) is preserved over time.[11] Since, when you die, your brain ceases to function, your personal identity ends there.

Now, this particular difficulty could be overcome. To preserve your personal identity into the afterlife, Michael could just swoop in and steal and heal your body before you die (and replace it with an inanimate replica). Interestingly, this is what Christian philosopher Peter van Inwagen suggests that God *must* do if he is to fulfill his promise to propel faithful Christians into the afterlife: God must be a body snatcher.[12] But even if Michael did this to Simone (or Eleanor, or you), for all the reasons I have laid out, she would still be more justified in believing that she was the victim of a hallucination.

Sadly, not even all brain experts realize this. In his book, *Proof of Heaven*, neurosurgeon Eben Alexander claims he had an experience while in a coma induced by an e. coli infection that could only be explained by his soul floating away to heaven. But not only did later reports reveal that the coma was actually induced and maintained *medically* (not by his e. coli infection), his argument that his experiences couldn't have been the result of a hallucination is fallacious. He assumes his experiences happened when he was in the coma, but they would have actually occurred while he was being weaned off his anesthetics and in a "conscious but delirious" state.[13] Indeed, near death experiences can never provide evidence of an afterlife for much the same reason that "it's magic" could never be the best explanation for anything. For the reasons we have discussed, there will always be a better natural explanation. And for the same reason, "I'm hallucinating" would always be the better explanation for whatever you experienced in The Good Place.

Now, Simone did eventually come to believe that she was in The Good Place. One presumes that, since the experience lasted a long time, Simone eventually concluded that it couldn't be a hallucination. In reality, however, this line of reasoning is unsound. As anyone who has watched *Inception* knows, time passes in dreams (and hallucinations) differently. What's more, one might hallucinate the memories of a year's worth of experiences, or the feeling that years had passed when they hadn't. So, again, you really could never know that you were in The Good Place . . . even if you did spend millions of bearimies there.

But the prospect of spending millions of bearimies in The Good Place raises the prospect of spending an eternity there – and this raises the second question I want to address: Would you actually *want* to end up in The Good Place?

Cosmic Coachella

The prospect of spending an eternity in The Good Place might seem – well, *good*. But as Eleanor and company discovered when they finally got there, it probably wouldn't be. To begin to understand why, it's important to realize that merely existing is not an intrinsic good – a good, in and of itself. It's only instrumentally good as a means of attaining pleasurable experiences or alternatively as a means of achieving what philosophers call eudaimonia: a kind of life worth living. This fact is often cited in debates about euthanasia; if one is facing only a future of illness and pain, it can make sense to want to end one's life early.[14] But to establish that mere existence is not something to preserve for its own sake, one need look no further than The Bad Place. Everyone would prefer nonexistence to having their penis flattened forever.

But the biggest worry about an eternal life in something like The Good Place was made famous by the philosopher Bernard Williams (1929–2003): boredom.[15] If you really lived forever, no matter how great you had it, you would eventually become bored. You'd do everything you ever wanted to do – visit Greece and Paris, taste what fully understanding the meaning of *Twin Peaks* feels like, sniff the bedpan that Stone Cold used to beat up Vince McMahon . . . and then you'd do it again, and again . . . and again. Eventually, you would have done it all, so many times, that you'd be sick of it – all of it. And then there you'd be, with all of eternity to do . . . what? All the things you are now sick of doing? Drink milkshakes? Ask Janet for random objects? Nothing at all? As Patty (Hypatia of Alexandria [360–415 CE]) put it (in the show):

> On paper, this is paradise. All your desires and needs are met. But it's infinite. . . . [y]ou get here and you realize that anything's possible, and you do everything, and then you're done. But you still have infinity left. This place kills fun, and passion, and excitement, and love, till all you have left are milkshakes ("Patty").

Although it might take a while, The Good Place would eventually, and inevitably, turn into The Bad Place. Immortality would become torture.

As a way out of this problem, Williams considers the possibility of making boredom "unthinkable" by magically stripping you of the psychological ability of being bored. Or perhaps infinity just turns you into what Eleanor calls "a happiness zombie" that is just "too far gone to care" about the boredom. "[W]hen perfection goes on forever, you become this glassy-eyed mush person." Williams argues that this wouldn't solve the problem, however, because such an existence isn't really desirable. From an objective standpoint, no one would want to be this dumbed down. As, again, Patty put it:

> I used to be cool, man. I studied so much things. Art and music and the, um, the one with the number piles? Where I'd be like, "Two!" and you'd be like, ""Six!" [Math?] Yes! And then I came here where time stretched out forever, and every second of my existence was amazing, but my brain became this big dumb blob.

Even Jason is too complex of a person to not look past the problem. "Go-karting with monkeys got boring really fast." And no one wants to be exponentially dumber than Jason for eternity.

Alternately, maybe one could become so involved in some pursuit that one becomes oblivious to the boredom. Williams imagines a philosopher – much like Chidi – so bogged down in an eternal pursuit of knowledge that he never notices how bored he is. But again, Williams argues, this solution doesn't work. While knowledge is intrinsically valuable, intellectual pursuits seem to only fit into a life of variety in which they can be applied. No one would really want to live the eternal life of such a "bogged down" philosopher.

A second problem, with both of these suggestions, is that it's not clear that a person so dumbed down, or so lost in their work, would still be the same person. According to Williams, in order for some depiction of the afterlife to be desirable to me, two conditions must be met: (i) the life actually has to be attractive – the kind of life I would want to live; and (ii) the person living the life actually has to be me. And if you eternally strip me of the ability to be bored, either by dumbing me down or eternally distracting me, it's not clear that it really is me.

In an attempt to meet these conditions, Williams also imagines someone who lives a series of consecutive lives, one after the other, where there is no memory overlap. This is exactly like Michael's suggestion to fix The Good Place: "What if we do what I did to you in the original Neighborhood? Erase their memory every once in a while? That way, paradise would seem fresh and new" ("Patty"). But this wouldn't work either. First, as Chidi is quick to point out, "You were doing that to torture us. Actual paradise can't use the same playbook as hell." And second, as Williams points out, such a solution would violate the second condition. Even if each of these consecutive persons has the same body, they wouldn't all be the same person. The psychological break caused by the memory wipe would create a new person. Notice that, if I told the first person that the fifth one was going to be tortured in 100 years, the first person would feel no sense of dread. They wouldn't think that *they* were going to experience the torture.

All in all, given an eternal existence, it doesn't seem that you can meet both conditions at once. To make an eternal life desirable, you'd have to break the identity condition; but preserving the identity condition would make the life undesirable. And so it doesn't seem that you should want to be in The Good Place at all. Eternal life, even in a place as good as The Good Place, would eventually become torture.

Conclusion: The Meaning of Life

Now, of course, everything I laid out in the last section 43.4 is what motivates the crew to "fix" The Good Place by letting its inhabitants choose to leave:

> We're gonna set up a new kind of door . . . when you feel happy and satisfied and complete, and you want to leave The Good Place for good, you can just walk through it, and your time in the universe will end ("Patty").

But would setting up (what we might call) an "oblivion door" really work? Would that make (what we might call) Michael's "Better Place" a place you'd really want to end up after you die?

I think so. As Williams points out, even though (i) given what we've discussed, a desire for immorality is irrational, and (ii) as Epicurus (341–270 BCE) pointed out, the state of being dead is itself nothing to dread (because it doesn't *feel like anything* to not exist) – it's still perfectly rational to want to live a longer life rather than a shorter life. And this is what a Better Place would allow you to do.

Now, such a life might never present you with challenges. Janet could just do every-thing for you. And that could very easily strip existence of meaning. It doesn't seem that this problem would be unavoidable, though. Consider Michael who is trying to learn to play guitar in the last episode, "Whenever You're Ready." Janet offers him a "a magic guitar that plays all the notes for you. It's the number one request among men over 50 who have gotten in here." But he quickly replies, "the whole point is to learn how to do stuff without using afterlife magic." Notice that, in the same episode, Tahani *learns how* to do wood working (from Nick Offerman); she doesn't just ask Janet for the perfect chair. Worst case scenario, in Michael's "Better Place," people would just learn the hard way that they need to do things for themselves.

Another problem might be that no one would ever actually walk through the oblivion door; they would always be too afraid of nonexistence. But I don't think this would really be a problem. First, for the reasons stated earlier, boredom really could get that bad. Nonexistence would eventually be preferable. Second, everyone could easily come to embrace the aforementioned Epicurean truth that nonexistence really is nothing to fear because there is nothing *it is like* to not exist. As Epicurus put it in his Letter to Menoeceus:

> Death is nothing to us, for good and evil imply awareness, and death is the privation of all awareness; therefore a right understanding that death is nothing to us makes the mortality of life enjoyable, not by adding to life an unlimited time, but by taking away the yearning after immortality.[16]

And third, I think it makes sense that, given long enough, everyone would reach a sense of peace, just as they do in the show, where they are ready for it to end. And if they don't, they can just use Chidi's final speech to get them there:

> Picture a wave in the ocean. . . . you can see it, you know what it is . . . And then it crashes on the shore, and it's gone. But the water is still there. The wave was just a different way for the water to be for a little while. That's one conception of death for a Buddhist. The wave returns to the ocean, where it came from, and where it's supposed to be. ("Whenever You're Ready")

The only real danger, it seems to me, lies not in a Better Place – but in the hope that one exists. Don't get me wrong; it'd be nice if one existed. But if you *truly believed* that this life will be followed with a paradise that lasts as long as you want, your life would have no urgency. Why bother doing anything now? Why make the most of the time you have, if you think you'll have as long as you want in paradise to do it later? In a sense, really believing that a Better Place exists could turn people into the same kind of "glassy-eyed mush person" that being in The Good Place did. It could make you waste the one and only life that you likely have.

Yes, the concept of death might be scary. As Eleanor told Michael, "every human is a little bit sad all the time, because you know you're gonna die" ("Existential Crisis"). But it's that knowledge that "gives life meaning." That's why adding the oblivion door "restore[d] meaning to the people in the Good Place." Contemporary philosopher Julian

Baggini, author of *What's It All About?: Philosophy and The Meaning of Life*, would likely agree.[17] What's the point of a truly never-ending movie or, say, a never-ending basketball game? The conclusion of such things gives them meaning. In the same way, our lives have meaning only if they have a conclusion.

And so it is also, with books that introduce philosophy through popular culture.

For pop culture resources and philosophical resources related to this chapter please visit the website for this book: https://introducingphilosophythroughpopculture.com.

Notes

1   Descartes, R. (2013). *Meditations on First Philosophy* (ed. J. Cottingham), 19. New York: CambridgeUniversity Press

2   Schick, T. and Vaughn, L. (2019) *How to Think About Weird Things*, 8e, 76–77. New York: McGraw Hill.

3   Schick and Vaughn, 180–190.

4   The existence of the physical world is at least in principle explainable, and indeed has been largely explained by science. For more on this, see Johnson, D.K. (forthcoming). Does God exist? *Think*.

5   One might also think that the demon hypothesis doesn't cohere with the common belief that the physical world exists, making it seem conservative. But to invoke that when comparing it to "a physical world exists" explanation, begs the question – it assumes the truth of what you are trying to prove. For more on this kind of refutation of Cartesian Skepticism, see Vogel, J. (1990). Cartesian skepticism and inference to the best explanation. *Journal of Philosophy* 87: 658–666.

6   For more on why conspiracy theories are irrational, see Johnson, D.K. (2020). How fallacies fuel conspiracies. In: *Conspiracy Theories: Philosophers Connect the Dots* (ed. R. Greene and R. Robison-Greene), 59–70. Chicago: Open Court.

7   See Johnson, D.K. (2017). Justified belief in the existence of demons is impossible. In: *Philosophical Approaches to Demonology*, 175–191 (eds. McGraw, B.W. and Arp, R.). New York: Routledge; Johnson, D.K. (2015). Justified belief in miracles is impossible. *Science, Religion and Culture* 2: 61–74.

8   For more on such limits and powers, see Schick and Vaughn, chapter 5.

9   Johnson, D.K. (2018). Mystery therefore magic. In: *Bad Arguments:100 of the Most Important Fallacies in Western Philosophy* (eds. Arp, R., Robert, B., and Barbone, S.) 189–192. Hoboken: Wiley Blackwell.

10 For more on this, see Johnson, D.K. (2013). Do souls exist? *Think* 12: 61–75.

11 Unger, P. (1990). The physical view. In: *Identity, Consciousness and Value*, 192–211. New York: Oxford University Press.

12 van Inwagen, P. (1978). The possibility of resurrection. *International Journal for Philosophy of Religion* 9: 114–121.

13 Zuckerman, E. (2013). The "Proof of Heaven" Author Has Now Been Thoroughly Debunked by Science. *The Atlantic*, July 2. https://www.theatlantic.com/entertainment/archive/2013/07/proof-heaven-author-debunked/313681.

14 For more on this, see Johnson, D.K. (forthcoming). More on the relevance of personhood and mindedness: euthanasia, salvation, and the possibility of an afterlife. *SHERM*.

15 See Williams, B. (1973). The Makropulos case: reflections on the tedium of immortality. In: *Problems of the Self: Philosophical Papers 1956–1972*, 82–100. Cambridge: Cambridge University Press.

16 Epicurus, *Letter to Menoeceus*, trans. R.D. Hicks, available at http://classics.mit.edu/Epicurus/menoec.html.

17 Baggini, J. (2004). *What's It All About?: Philosophy and the Meaning of Life*, 28–31. Oxford: Oxford University Press.

Index

abortion 26
ad hominem fallacy 21–2
Adult Fans of LEGO (AFOL) 315
aesthetic Africanism 325
African art 325
Africanfuturism 322, 326–7
Afrofuturism 322, 326–7
afterlife
    Kant, Immanuel 382
    Rowling 381, 383
    soul 388
agent-specific rules 177
agnosticism 60
Alexander, Eben 388
Alexander, Michelle 324, 328n20
"All About Mormons" 38, 41
"All Lives Matter" 322
"all-or-nothing" approach 21
All-Star Superman series 225
alternate possibilities, principle of 116, 122n4
"alternative reality" 49
"Amazon" 239
American moral values 34n20
Americans with Disabilities Act 301
Anarchy, State and Utopia (Nozick) 292
Ancient One 83, 84, 87, 88
Anderson, Thomas 44
angiotensin 98
"animal spirits" 86
The Animatrix 53n5
anthropocentrism
    critique of 256
    shortsighted *vs.* enlightened 254
anti-Blackness 323, 326
The Antichrist (Nietzsche) 225n4
Anti-Life Equation 218, 225n4

Apollo 59
Apology 6, 10–12
Appiah, A. 319n6
Arendt, Hannah 9, 10, 345
    Eichmann in Jerusalem 7
argument
    bad 19
    claim 16
    cogent 19
    deductive 17–18
    from divine hiddenness 158–9
    evidence 16
    God's existence 150–1
    good 18
    inductive 18
    logic 15–17
    premise 15–1716
    sound 19
argument from inappropriate authority fallacy 21
Aristotle 120, 229, 381
    critical reflection 8
    friendship 199, 205–6
    morality 192–4
    Nicomachean Ethics 119, 199
    pleasure-based friendships 199–200
    true friendship 201–2
    utility-based friendships 201
Arnopp, J. 347n26
artificial intelligence (AI) 322
astral bodies 85
Atlas Shrugged (Rand) 15
Augustine 151
authenticity 325, 378
    existentialism 231–5
authoritarianism 184
Automatic Computing Engine (ACE) 123

Introducing Philosophy Through Pop Culture: From Socrates to Star Wars *and Beyond*, Second Edition.
Edited by William Irwin and David Kyle Johnson.
© 2022 John Wiley & Sons Ltd. Published 2022 by John Wiley & Sons Ltd.

Autonomous Drone Insects (ADIs) 338, 342
Avengers: Endgame 136–7
  disappointment, in end 140–3
  grandfather paradox 137
  time travel 137–40
awareness 209

bad argument 19
The Bad Place 385, 386, 389
Baier, Annette 250, 251
"Bastille Day" 59
Batman 317
  and Joker 175–6, 179–81
  trolley case 178–9
  utilitarianism 176–7
Battlestar Galactica 54–6
  belief-forming process 56
  democracy 59
  epistemology 56, 57
  faith 59, 60
  life-quest 60
  reliability of beliefs 56–7
  testimony 57, 58
Battlestar Galactica episodes
  "Bastille Day" 59
  "Crossroads, Part 2" 56, 57
  "Exodus, Part 2" 57
  "Flesh and Bone" 57
  "The Hand of God" 57
  "Home, Part 2" 56
  "Kobol's Last Gleaming, Part 1" 58
  "Kobol's Last Gleaming, Part 2" 56, 59
  "Lay Down Your Burdens" 57
  "Lay Down Your Burdens, Part 2" 60
  "Maelstrom" 57
  "Miniseries" 57
  "Resistance" 57
  "Torn" 56
  "Water" 56
Beauvoir, Simone de 237
  Wonder Woman 237–9
Beckett, Samuel 381
belief-forming process 56
beliefs 38–9
  Earth 58–61
  justification 55
  unsupported 42
  see also religious belief
Benjamin, Ruha 323, 324
Bentham, Jeremy 184
"The Bicameral Mind" 134
The Big Bang Theory 198–9
  complete friendship 202, 203
  friendship breakthrough 204
  pleasure-based friendships 199–200
  true friendship 201–2
  utility-based friendships 200–1
The Big Bang Theory episodes
  "The Bad Fish Paradigm" 203, 205
  "Celebration Reverberation" 202–3
  "The Confidence Erosion" 202–3
  "The Electronic Can Opener Fluctuation" 204
  "The Friendship Algorithm" 201
  "The Jerusalem Duality" 203
  "The Large Hadron Collision" 204

"The Proton Displacement" 204
"The Cornhusker Vortex" 200
"The Biggest Douche in the Universe" 41, 42
biological essentialist 313
Black Lives Matter 63, 322
Black Mirror episodes
  "Hated in the Nation" 338, 339, 343
  "Men Against Fire" 329, 330, 334, 335
Black Panther 62, 321, 322
  Black people, stereotypical resources of 65–7
  epistemic resource 63–5, 68–9
  imagination 64–5
  Mackie, Anthony 62
  Paradox of Fiction 63
  racism and sexism 68
Black people 321–2, 327
  racist stereotypes of 65–6
"bleeding-edge" experimental procedure 83
Blink (Gladwell) 29
Boaz, Franz 313
body 85–7
Boethius 111
"Booby Trap" 77
Book of Genesis 165
Bostrom, Nick 74–5
Bradley, L. 33n7
brain
  biochemistry of 98
  biology of 97
  ever-increasing knowledge of 118
  functionalism 98–9
Brooker, C. 347n26
Buber, Martin 257
Buddha 360
buddha-nature 367
Buddhism 73
Buddhist philosophy, of impermanence: *see*
  impermanence
Buolamwini, Joy 323

Calvin, John 149–50
Cantor, P.A. 310n17
capitalism 285–6, 306, 309n7
care ethics
  activities 249
  emotions 250
  engrossment 251
  feminism 245–7
  maternal work 249, 251
  morality 247, 248
  motivational displacement 250, 251
  proponents of 248
Carpenter, H. 383n8
Carson, Rachel 255
Cartesian dualism 84, 86, 89n7
Cartesian skepticism 384–5, 392n5
"Cartmanland" 40
categorical imperative rule 188
"cave allegory" (Plato) 73
Cawley, Stephanie 242
censorship 11–12
Chalmers, David 130, 135n4
chamalla-tripping oracle 57
Chewbacca defense 6, 14–15, 19–20, 22, 149
  argument 15–17

deductions and inductions 17–18
  good and bad argument 18–19
  slippery-slope fallacy 20–2
"Chinese room argument" 124–5
Christianity 162
Christine Blasey Ford 346n15
Christ-like savior 222
Christopher New 182n17
Chuck, E. 346n4
Churchland, Paul 95–7
  Matter and Consciousness 97
civil society 278
civil war 269
classless society 284
Clifford, William Kingdom 42
  "The Ethics of Belief" 37
Clifford, W.K. 58–60
Cloak of Levitation 85
Cloud City set 312
Cochran 19–20
Cochran, Johnny 6
cogent argument 19
Colbert, Stephen 23–4
  I Am America (And So Can You!) 26
  "My Truth" 25–6
  philosophy 32–3
  right to opinion 30–2
  truthiness 28–30
  Wikiality 26–8
  WORDs 28
Coleridge, Samuel Taylor 143
Collins, Phil 42
colonialism 259n2
color perceptions 52
communism 286–8
Communist Manifesto 290
compatibilism 119
complete friendship 202, 203
conclusion, defined 15–16
consciousness 80, 126–7, 128–9, 132–5, 363
consequentialism
  and deontology 183–4, 189–90
  ends/means 184
The Consolation of Philosophy (Boethius) 111
constructivist approach 314
contractualism 247
Cooper, Anderson 24
counterexample 120–1
Crimes Against Logic (Whyte) 31
"Crossroads, Part 2" 56, 57
cultural relativism 26–8
Cylon 56

Daodejing 351–4
  awesomeness 354–5, 357
  design 356
  sages, of ancient times 355, 356
  willingness 354
Daoism 351, 356
David, Peter 105
Davidman, Joy 157
Days of Future Past 102
death
  Harry Potter 377–9
  inescapable 233

nightmares and premonitions of 211
  remember 362
  see also afterlife
Death Star 167–9
#DeathTo hashtag 340, 342
deception
  intentional 47
  Matrix-type 48–50
deductive arguments 17–18
deep humanity
  anthropocentricism 254, 256
  authenticity 256
  conversion 255
  decolonial thinking 260n15
  ecocentrism 254
  ecological reflexivity 259n5
  inside-out moment 256–7
  morality 260n10
  relational reason 257
  value of discovering 258–9
  virtue of 255
deGrasse Tyson, N. 347n25
dehumanization
  immigration 336
  language of 330–1, 333–4
  rehumanizing 335
  violence of 331–2
democracy 59
Dent, S. 337n22
deontology
  consequentialism and 183–4, 189–90
  dichotomous thinking 187, 188
  as rationalization 187
  and utilitarianism 176–7
Descartes, René 49–50, 73–4, 385, 386, 392n1
  Cartesian dualism 84
  evil demon 47
  Meditations on First Philosophy 45
  mind-body dualism 92, 100n3
  soul 86
destiny 380–3
detailed division of labor 288
DiCaprio, Leonardo 39
dichotomous thinking 187, 188
Dick, Philip K. 180
difference principle 296, 297
In a Different Voice (Gilligan) 246
Discourse on the Origin of Inequality (Rousseau) 275
Disney corporation 161, 162
divine foreknowledge 108–10
divine hiddenness
  argument from 158–9
  experience of 156–8
  Hidden Mickeys and 161–2
Doctor Strange 82–3
  body and soul 85–7
  duality 87–8
  metaphysics 83, 86
  philosophy 88
  physicalism 83
  soul 83–5
  substance dualism 84–6
"double-movement" 167
"Double Slit" experiment 75
Downing, D.C. 163n3

Down's syndrome 323
Drake, M. 337n17
dualism, mind-body 91–2
Dubs, Kathleen 113n17

Earth 54–6
　beliefs 58–61
　faith 60
　testimony-based justifications 58
ecocentrism 254, 259n3
ecological reflexivity 259n5
Edward, John 40–2
Edwards, Jonathan 149–50, 154n5
egalitarianism 184
Eichmann, Adolf 7
Eichmann in Jerusalem (Arendt) 7
eliminative materialism 95–7
eliminativist approach 313
Emad, M.C. 243n3
emergent property 97–8
emphatic silence 156–8
Engels, Friedrich 286, 287, 289
engrossment 251
Enlightenment 58
Enterprise 79
enthusiastic technology 322
environmental ethics 254, 260n8
Epictetus 208, 209, 211
epistemic injustice 68–9
epistemic resource 63–5, 68
epistemology 30, 56
escapism 367, 373
Esquire 67
An Essay Concerning Human Understanding (Locke) 28
"the eternal recurrence" 225n7
ethics
　Arendt 9
　care 247–9
　duty 174
　environmental 254
　friendship 9
　of killing 176
　knowledge 195
　traditional 215
Ethics of Ambiguity (Beauvoir) 237
"The Ethics of Belief" (Clifford) 37
evidence 38–41
evidentialism 58–9
evil
　banality of 7
　consequences 345
　existence of God 148
　free will 151–2
　God 150–1
　and good 151
　natural 152, 155n9
　problem of 148
　risk of 151
　South Park 9–10, 147–8
　Stoicism 212–13
Evil and the God of Love (Hick) 152
existentialism 228
　authenticity 231–5
　bad faith 231

　being-in-question 230
　"existence precedes essence" 230
　leadership 229
　Nietzsche, Friedrich 232–4
"Exodus, Part 2" 57

faith 39–41
　in Earth's existence 54
　movement of 167
fallacy of hasty generalization 14
false dilemma fallacy 21
Federation's *economic* system
　capitalism 285–6
　communism 286–8
　democratic body 285
　Marx, Karl 286–8
　necessity to freedom 289
　principles 284
　profit-and-growth-based 290–1
　"realm of necessity" 284
　revolution 289–90
　self-enhancement 284
Feinberg, Joel 175
female circumcision 27
femininity 236
feminism 239, 242
　care ethic 245–7
　justice 246–9
　morality 247, 248
"Flesh and Bone" 57
folk psychology 95
force, bringing balance to 170–1
Force persuasion technique 212
Ford, Robert 124–6, 131, 132
forlornness 233
Fox and Friends 29
Frankfurt, Harry 119
　counterexamples 120–1
free will
　alternate possibilities, principle of 116
　Augustine 151
　compatibilism 119
　counterexample 120–1
　determinism 117
　good/evil 151–2
　indeterminism 122n15
　quantum mechanics 118
Freud, S. 10, 11, 118
Fricker, Miranda 68
friendship 199
　complete 202
　pleasure-based 199–200
　true 201–2
functionalism 98–100
fundamental attribution error 340

Game of Thrones 265
Gandhi, Mahatma 255
Gardinier, L. 347n22
Gebru, Timnit 323
generalization, hasty 14015
Gettier, Edmund 55, 56, 58
Gibbons, Dave 184–6, 188–90

Gideon 28
Gill, C. 214n1
Gilligan, Carol 246, 249
Gladwell, Malcolm 29
Glasser, William 360
globalized economy 259
God
    monster 166
    revelation 28
God's existence
    argument 150–1
    arguments 153
    demonstration 150
    Disney corporation 162
    divine hiddenness 156–9
    evil 148
    Job's story 148–9
    premises 159, 163
    South Park 147–8
Golden Age of Comics 221
good argument 18
The Good Place 191–7
    Cartesian skepticism 384–5
    eternity in 389–90
    explanations 386–7
    hypothesis 386
    meaning of life 390–2
    scientific skepticism 387–9
grandfather paradox 137, 139
A Grief Observed (Lewis) 157

Hackman, Gene 39
"The Hand of God" 57
Harry Potter
    death and philosophy 377–9
    destiny 380–3
    ethereal realm 379–80
hasty generalization 344, 14015
Hayek, Friedrich 302, 306
hedonism 184
Heidegger, Martin 378
heliocentric theory 16
Hick, John 152–3
Hidden Mickey 160–1
    and divine hiddenness 161–2
Hinduism 73, 77
Hitler, Adolf 219
Hobbes, Thomas 110, 274
    centralizing power 268
    civil war 269
    Leviathan 266, 267, 274
    lofty principles 272
    political theory 271
    rebellion 269–70
    selfishness 266–7
The Hobbit 107, 108, 110
Holmes, Sherlock 78
holodeck technology 73, 74
holographic hypothesis 74–8
holoprograms 78–9
"Home, Part 2" 56
homo superiors 102
host
    "analysis mode" 132

consciousness of 128–9, 132–5
    depiction 133
    experience 135
    freedom 134
    memories 130–1
    mental states 129
    perception 131
    philosophical zombies 130
    reflections 131
    self-consciousness 134–5
    testimony 132
hostile policies 334
House of M 101
How To Think About Weird Things (Schick) 386
Hulk 101
humanity 237–8
human nature 275–6
human psychology, oversimplification of 271
Hume, David 110, 274, 275
    testimony 57–8

I Am America (And So Can You!) (Colbert) 26
identity, personal 102
imagination 64–5
impermanence 360–1
    aggregates of 363–4
    benefits of 361–2
    LEGOs of 364–6
inception 115–16, 120–2, 122n1, 122n16
indigenous scholars 260n17
indirect duties view 259n3
individual relativism 25–6
inductive arguments 18
Infinite Crisis crossover 220
"infinite resignation" movement 167
Info Wars 24
initial public offering (IPO) market 310n13
innocence 275
intentional deception 47
intertheoretic reduction 95
intuitionism 28–30
Islam 162

James, William 60, 380–2
Jedi council 208
The Jedi Knights of Faith 164–71
Joker, Batman and 175–6, 179–81
Jones, A. 347n26
Judaism 79, 162
justice 246–9
    liberal egalitarianism 292
    libertarian conception of 294
    libertarianism 292
    Occupy Metropolis 296–7
    personal liberty 292–4
    power 345
    Rawls, John 294–5
    self-administered 339
    truth 294
    veil of ignorance 295–6
justification
    belief 55
    means/ends 187
    testimony-based 58

Kadyrov, Ramzan 334
Kanin, Eugene 347n17
Kant, Immanuel 73–4, 187–9, 190n16, 382
Keene Act 188
Kelly, L. 347n24
Kelman, Herbert 332
Kierkegaard, Soren 164–6, 169–71, 171n9
  "double-movement" 167
  ethical stage 168
Kim, J.Y. 337n15
Kipnis, Laura 347n19
knowledge 385
  justification 55
  nature of 56
"Kobol's Last Gleaming, Part 1" 58
"Kobol's Last Gleaming, Part 2" 56, 59
Kohlberg, Lawrence 194, 195
Kotter, John 359
Kryptonian physiology 220, 222–3

labor, detailed and social division of 288
Laplace, Pierre-Simon 117
Last Billboard project 322
lawbreaker 222
"Law of Attraction" 78
"Lay Down Your Burdens" 57
"Lay Down Your Burdens, Part 2" 60
Leading Change (Kotter) 359
"leap to faith" 165
Lebron, C. 328n4
The LEGO Movie 316–17, 359
Lepore, Jill 236
Lessing, Gotthold 165
Less Than Human (Smith) 330
Levinas, Emmanuel 335
Lewis, C.S. 157–8, 162, 163
Lewis, David 138–40
Lex Luthor: Man of Steel 224
libertarianism 300
  of Parker and Stone 303
  philosophy of 301–2
libertarian justice 294
Lisak, D. 347n22
Locke, John 102–3, 119, 122n6, 273, 275, 277
  civil society 278
  commonwealth 281
  enthusiastic people 28
  An Essay Concerning Human Understanding 28
  identity 382
  testimony 58
Loffman, M. 3376n14
log-and-truck arrangement 160, 161, 163n10
logic
  argument 15–17
  conclusion 16
  defined 15
The Lord of the Rings 108
Lost
  confidence 279–80
  Innocence 275, 282
  language barrier 278–9
  medical ethics 277–8
  medical supplies 280
  state of nature 273–5, 281–3

tit for tat 281–2
Trust No. 1 275, 276, 278, 279, 281, 282
Lost episodes
  "Confidence Man" 278
  "Pilot: Part 1" 278
  "Pilot: Part 2" 279
  "Tabula Rasa" 280
  "Walkabout" 280
  "White Rabbit" 276, 277, 280
Lovett, J. 347n24

Mackenzie, Catriona 64
Madrox, Jamie 105
Madrox miniseries 105
"Maelstrom" 57
Mann, T. 359, 366n2
marriage 59
Marshall, Samuel Lynman 329, 332
Marston, William 238–43, 244n7
Martin, George R.R. 267
Marvel Comics Presents 101, 104
Marx, Karl 284, 286–9
MASS implant 330
  consequences 331–2
  dehumanization language 330–5
  reset 335
materialism
  eliminative 95–7
  mind-body 92–4
  reductive 95
maternal work 249
The Matrix Reloaded 99
The Matrix trilogy 90–1
  "alternative reality" 49
  deception 47–50
  destruction 93
  mind-body dualism 91–2
  mind-body materialism 92–4
  mystery and miracles 91
  Oracle 44–5, 91
  skepticism 45–7, 50–2
  truth 48
Matrix-type deception 48–51
Matter and Consciousness (Churchland) 97
medical ethics 277–8
Meditations on First Philosophy (Descartes) 45, 385
memory 56, 76
  host 130–1
Men Against Fire: The Problem of Battle Command
  (Marshall) 329
mental state 94
  eliminative materialism 95–7
  reductive materialism 95
metaphysics 83
#MeToo hashtag 342–4
Middle-earth theologians 110
Milgram, Stanley 195–6
Mill, John Stuart 121, 122n17, 184, 186
mind-body relationship
  biology 97–8
  dualism 91–2
  functionalism 98–100
  materialism 92–4
  Matrix trilogy 90–1

mental state 94–7
  mystery and miracles 91
"Miniseries" 57
"The Minority Report" (Dick) 180
Minsky, Marvin 100
miracle hypothesis 100n2
miracles 91
Mises, Ludwig von 302
Misty Mountains 107
  goblin tunnels under 108
modern societies 325
Mohawk, J.C. 260n11
Moon, E. 347n18
Moore, Alan 184–6, 188–90
  V for Vendetta 189
moral character
  Aristotle's four levels of 193–4
  situationism 195–7
moral development, Kohlberg's Model of 194–5
moral growth, Aristotle 192–4
Morissette, Alanis 19
Morrison, Grant 217, 222
motivational displacement 250
Munsterberg, Hugo 244n20
My Own Creation (MOC) 364
mystery 91

Nagel, Thomas 129
naive realism 51, 52
narrative meaning-making practice 65
National Basketball Association (NBA) 312, 319n1,
  319n12
"Native Americans" 39
natural evil 152, 155n9
Neo: *see The Matrix* trilogy
"New Jim Code" 324
The New Jim Crow (Alexander) 324
"New Thought" 78
Newton-John, Olivia 83
"New Women" 239
Nicksa, S. 347n22
Nicomachean Ethics (Aristotle) 119
Nietzsche, Friedrich 217
  "beyond good and evil" 219, 223, 225
  on Christianity 218
  creativity 219–20
  existentialism 232–4
  on God 218
  nihilism 218, 219
  savior 221–2
  Superman 220–5
  will to power 219–20
nihilism 218, 219
nobility 224
Noddings, Nel 249, 251, 252
"non-player characters" (NPCs) 79
Norlock, K. 341, 346n8
Nova, Cassandra 102–3
Nozick, Robert 292, 293, 295, 298n1, 298n2
Nussbaum, Martha C. 260n13

O'Brien, P. 337n21
Occupy Metropolis 296–7
omni-temporalism 139

On the Genealogy of Morals (Nietzsche) 225n4
Origins of Totalitarianism (Arendt) 345

Palmer, George Herbert 239
Panama Canal 32
Paradox of Fiction 63
Parfit, Derek 105
Parke, Karin 338
Parker, Trey 301, 303, 307
Pascal, Blaise 40, 41, 157, 382
Pascal's Wager 40, 41, 154
Pauling, Linus 30
Peirlott, Matthew 29
perfect friendship 199, 201, 202
personal access display devices (PADDs) 321
personal identity 102
personal liberty 292–4
Persson, Ingmar 323
persuasion 212
The Phantom Menace 209
philosophical zombies 130
philosophy 32–3, 88
Pilkington, E. 346n2
Pinnock, Clark 109
pit of skepticism 46, 49
Plantinga, Alvin 58, 153
Plato 299, 353, 378
  Apology 6
  "cave allegory" 73
  critical reflection 8
  death 382
  knowledge 385
  libertarianism 300
  Phaedo 383n1
  Theaetetus 55
pleasure-based friendships 199–200
poetic faith 143
political climate, in United States 333
political correctness 301
political philosophy 273, 292, 352, 356
Positive Addiction (Glasser) 360
post-conventional moral development 195
power 208–10, 213
  centralizing 268
  justice 345
premise 15–1716
prepunishment 180
Pribram, Karl 76
primary goods 296
The Prince and the Pauper 102–3
"the principle of charity" 25
prisoners' dilemma 281, 283
problem of divine foreknowledge 109–10
problem of skepticism 45
"Process theologians" 109
profit-and-growth-based economic system 290–1
Proof of Heaven (Alexander) 388
prosthesis 327
proto-post scarcity economy 285, 291n1
Psychology: Briefer Course (James) 380
psychotropic drugs 93

quantum mechanics 118
  multiverse interpretations of 142

quantum physics 74, 75
"question reality" 44

race 311
    building bricks of 312–15
    The LEGO Movie 316–17
    postscript 317–19
    three-part conception of 313
racial constructivism 314
racism 68, 318
Rand, Ayn 15
Rawls, John 294–7, 341
Rawlsian justice 296
Rayworth, M. 328n5
reality 76–7
rebellion 269–70
red herring fallacy 20
reductive materialism 95
relational reason 257
relativism
    cultural 26–8
    individual 25–6
reliabilism 56–8
religious belief 40, 41
    Pascal's Wager 154
repression 10
"Resistance" 57
Resources Development Administration (RDA) 253
roaches 329, 330
Robbins, J. 327n2
Robert, G. 358n4
Rodin, Auguste 351, 352
Romanization transliteration system 358n3
Rothbard, Murray 302, 309n4
Rousseau, Jean-Jacques 273, 275
Rowling, J. K. 379, 381–3
Ruddick, Sara 249–50
rule utilitarianism 185

Samyutta Nikaya 363
Sartre, Jean-Paul 117, 230, 231–3, 238
savior 221–2
Savulescu, Julian 323
Schellenberg, J.L. 158, 160, 163
Schick, Ted 386
science-fiction neurology 100n7
scientific skepticism 387–9
"Scott Tenorman Must Die" 39
The Screwtape Letters (Lewis) 162
Searle, John 97–9, 123–5, 129, 130, 134
The Second Sex (Beauvoir) 237, 242
The Secret History of Wonder Woman (Lepore) 236
Seinfeld 301
self-administered justice 339
self-consciousness 134–5
self-empowerment 239
self-enhancement 284, 286
self-interest 39–41
selfless awareness 370–1
sensory perceptions 90
sexism 68
Shakespeare, William 249
shape perceptions 52
sight 56

Silent Spring (Carson) 255
The Silmarillion 110
Silver Age of Comics 222
situationism 195–7
skeptical theism 149
skepticism
    Descartes, René 45
    The Matrix trilogy 45–7, 50–2
    pit of 46, 49
slippery-slope fallacy 20–2
Smilansky, Saul 182n17
Smith, Adam 302, 304, 307
Smith, David Livingstone 330–2
Smith, Joseph 40, 41
social division of labor 288
social media
    benefits 341–4
    power, of justice 345–6
Socrates 30
    Apology 9–12
    defense of 6
A Song of Ice and Fire 265, 266
Sorcerer's Stone (Rowling) 383
soul 80, 83–7
"soul making" 153
sound argument 19
South Park
    adults in 8
    Big Gay Al 302
    capitalism 306
    critics of 299
    culture's tolerance 12
    "Danger" of 5–6
    "Death" 5, 15
    evil 9–10
    gadfly role 10
    libertarianism 301, 302
    philosophy 6
    slippery-slope fallacy 20–2
    Terrance and Phillip 5, 7, 11
    vs. Harbucks 304–6
    vulgarity 10–11, 300
    Wall-Mart 307–9
South Park episodes
    "All About Mormons" 38, 41
    "The Biggest Douche in the Universe" 41, 42
    "Cartmanland" 40, 147–54
    "Chef Aid" 19, 20, 148
    "Chef Goes Nanners" 21
    "Chickenlover" 15
    "Clubhouses" 21
    "The Entity" 15
    "Gnomes" 303–7
    "Here Comes the Neighborhood" 15
    "Ike's Wee" 16
    "Kenny Dies" 149
    "The Passion of the Jew" 16
    "Scott Tenorman Must Die" 18, 39
    "Super Best Friends" 42
    "Timmy 2000" 41–2
    "The Tooth Fairy Tats 2000" 17
    "Towelie" 18
    "Trapped in The Closet" 39
    "Weight Gain 4000" 20

Special Olympics 301
spirit of inquiry 42
Spohn, C. 347n20
Thus Spoke Zarathustra (Nietzsche) 225n3
Stanton, Gregory 332
Star Trek 284, 289
  holocharacters 80
  holodeck technology 73
  holographic hypothesis 74–7
  holoprograms 78–9
  "limit conditions" in nature 75
  players 79–80
  reality 76–7
  transcendence 81
Star Trek episodes
  "The Big Goodbye" 79
  "Elementary, Dear Data" 74, 78
  "Galaxy's Child" 79
  "Hide and Q" 77
  "Homeward" 79
  "A Matter of Perspective" 77
  "Our Man Bashir" 74
  "The Practical Joker" 74
  "Ship in a Bottle" 80
Star Trek: The Original Series 64
Star Wars trilogy 207, 213
state of nature 273–5, 281–3
Stein, L. 244n39
stereotypes 65–6
Stoic ethics 208
Stoic philosophy/Stoicism 208
  awareness 209
  evil 212–13
  Force 208–9
  Force persuasion technique 212
  power 208–10, 213
  principles 211–12
  strength of mind 208, 209
Stoic virtue 208
Stone, Matt 301–3, 307
string theory 75
substance dualism 84–6
"Super Best Friends" 42
Supergods (Morrison) 217
superheroes 184
Superman 220–5, 292, 297–8
Swinburne, Richard 151
Symposium 299, 300, 309n1
A System of Logic (Mill) 121

Taylor, Paul C. 325
technologized racism 324
Tellis, K. 347n20
temperance 193
Terence and Phillip Show 20
Teresa, Mother 157, 158
The Terrance and Phillip Show 5, 7, 11, 15, 300
testimony 57, 58
texture perceptions 52
Theaetetus (Plato) 55
A Theory of Justice (Rawls) 295, 341
Thomson, Garrett 87
Thomson, Judith Jarvis 177–8
thought experiment 265, 274

Thrasher, Steven 67
time travel, in *Avengers: Endgame* 137–40
"Timmy 2000" 41–2
Tolkien, J. R. R. 143
  Boethian solution 111–13
  freedom and music 110–11
  The Hobbit 107, 108, 110
  Letters 383n8
  The Lord of the Rings 108, 111, 380
  "Music of the Ainur" 111–12
  "Osanwe-kenta" 112
  problem of divine foreknowledge 110
  "The Quest for Erebor" 110
  The Silmarillion 110, 383n8
"Torn" 56
torture, debates on 180
Totality and Infinity (Levinas) 335
Tower Commission Report 189
traditional African artworks 325
tragedy of the commons 276–7
transcendence 81
transcendental hypothesis 100n2
transhumanism 323
"Trapped in The Closet" 39
"trial by mob" 339
trolley problem 177–9, 181n13
true friendship 201–2
true power 212
Truman, Harry 88
The Truman Show 126
Trump, Donald 63
  dehumanizing language 333
Trust No. 1 275, 276, 278, 279, 281, 282
truth
  justice 294
  The Matrix trilogy 48
  philosophy 8
  relativism 25–6
  universal 34n17
truthfulness 55
truthiness 28–30
Turing, Alan 123–5
Turing test 124
Twain, Mark 286
Twitter
  benefits 341–4
  dangers 339–41
  #DeathTo hashtag 338
"Typhon Pact" 291n17
Tyson, Neil deGrasse 344

Uncanny X-Men 103
  Days of Future Past 102
United Nations Education, Scientific, and Cultural
      Organization (UNESCO) 313
universal truth 34n17
unsupported beliefs 42
Unwanted Advances (Kipnis) 347n19
utilitarianism 176–7, 181n5
  Batman-Joker 176–7, 181n5
  and consequentialism 184, 185, 189
  happiness 186–7
  motivation 186
utility-based friendships 200–1

veil of ignorance 295–6
virtual reality 76
virtue ethics 260n7
virtue utilitarianism 185
vulgarity 300

Wade-Giles 358n3
Waid, Mark 224
Waiting for Godot (Beckett) 381
Wakanda, technological advancement in 325–7
Wall-Mart 307–9
Walt Disney Company 372
Washington, George 240
Watchmen
   consequentialism/deontology 183–4, 189–90
   Ozymandias 183–7, 190
   power 189
   Rorschach 183, 186–90
   watching the watchmen 189–90
"Water" 56
Watership Down 278
The Wealth of Nations (Smith) 304, 307
Weapon X stories 101
Wells, I. 346n5
Westworld 123
   Chinese room argument 124–5
   consciousness 126–7
   hosts and guests 125–6
   Turing *vs.* Searle 123–4
White C. 347n20
White House Correspondents Dinner 31
Whyte, Jamie 31
Wikiality 26–8
Wikipedia 26
Williams, Bernard 389
will to power 219 226n9

Wilstein, M. 33n4, 33n9
Wilt Chamberlain argument 293
Windsor-Smith, Barry 104
Wiseman, Richard 359
Wittgenstein, Ludwig 331
Wolverine 101
   brain damage 105–6
   Origin 103–4
Wonder Woman
   in *All-Star Comics* 236
   Beauvoir, Simone de 237–9
   exceptionalism and achievement 240
   feminism of 241–3
   identity 237
   philosophical quandary 240
   self-empowerment 239
   strength and endurance 241
   "woman of tomorrow" 237

Xavier, Charles 101–3
X-Factor 105
X-Men 105

Zagzebski, L. 114n23
Zen Buddhism 367
   emptiness, impermanence, and frustration 369, 370, 373
   escapism 367, 373
   fundamental teaching of 368
   interdependence 370, 371
   liberation 373
   selfless awareness 370–1
   three marks of existence 369
   wealth and power 372–3
"the Zero Point Field" 75
Zuckerman, E. 392n13

Printed and bound by CPI Group (UK) Ltd, Croydon, CR0 4YY

09/06/2025

14686000-0001